D0597291

ROBERT KENNEDY

BROTHER PROTECTOR

Airing

Robert Kennedy

BROTHER PROTECTOR

James W. Hilty

Temple University Press Philadelphia

Temple University Press, Philadelphia 19122

Published 1997
Printed in the United States of America

∞ The paper used in this publication meets the requirements of American National Standard for Information Sciences—Permanence of Paper for Printed Library Materials, ANSI Z39.48-1984

Text designer: Kate Nichols
Compositor: Peirce Graphic Services, Inc.
Printer/binder: Thomson-Shore, Inc.

This book was set in 11.3/14.4 Bembo text type with Copperplate and Engine type and a Type Embellishment Two ornament for display. The text was printed on 50# Glatfelter Supple Opaque, and the insert was printed on 70# Fortune Matte, with an initial print run of 5000.

Library of Congress Cataloging-in-Publication Data

Hilty, James W.

Robert Kennedy, brother protector / James W. Hilty.

p. cm.

Includes bibliographical references (p.) and index.

ISBN 1-56639-566-6 (alk. paper)

1. Kennedy, Robert F., 1925–1968. 2. Kennedy, John F. (John Fitzgerald), 1917–1963—Assassination. 3. Kennedy family. 4. Legislators—United States—Biography. 5. United States. Congress. Senate—Biography. 6. United States—Politics and government—1961–1963. 7. United States—Politics and government—1963–1969. I. Title.

E840.8.K4H55 1997
973.922′0922—dc21

[B] 97-16908

Dedicated to my mother,

Henrietta Isabel Hilty (1903–1978),

in whose quiet countenance reposed a profound faith,

an indomitable will,

and the boundless courage still to dare

Contents

Preface

ROBERT F. KENNEDY was a principal political enigma of the 1960s. We owe part of our puzzlement about him to his own bafflement over who and what he was or should be. Beset by many demons, he was a virtual bundle of contradictions. I have oscillated in Robert Kennedy's rainbow (to borrow from Melville) for the better part of eight years but cannot catalogue all of those demons or sort out all of those contradictions.

What has become clear, however, is that a personal understanding of Robert Kennedy begins with the realization that most of his life was dictated by his place within the Kennedy family, his obeisance to its rules and rituals, and his resolute loyalty to John Kennedy. His life literally became a trial by existence—a series of experiences, one bound to the other, based solely on his being the third of Joseph Kennedy's four sons.

This book carries Robert Kennedy through his brother's assassination to the end of the first act of his life and to the precipice of despair from which he stepped off into a political life of his own. Mostly about what Robert and John Kennedy did in tandem, it hardly resolves all doubts.

History, of course, is never a closed book. Beneath the glitter of

Camelot lie many unanswered questions about the Kennedys' reach for power, their possible involvements in unsavory and dangerous events, their true commitment to social justice, their personal conduct, and their leadership abilities. These questions have led some historians and investigative journalists to deny substance to the Kennedy legacy, attributing to the partnership only high-blown rhetoric at best and scandal and duplicity at worst. Those views, now firmly implanted in the public memory, often in competition with elements of the Kennedy legacy, cannot be ignored. But readers hoping for mythoclastic revelations will be disappointed here.

This book cannot offer a complete and detailed account of Robert Kennedy's personal life, for, among other reasons, tens of thousands of personal papers and records pertaining to his life remain closed. What it does offer is a reinterpretation based on my examination of the literature, buttressed by research into archival sources, and enriched by many memoirs, personal accounts, and interviews of Kennedy associates. Still, the Kennedys may perhaps best be examined from a safe distance, for their tantalizing allure, like that of a Venus's-flytrap, can be fatally encapsulating.

Broadly speaking, the Kennedy literature falls into two competing nomothetic universes, prompting the construction of myths and countermyths about the family. Although some of the literature admittedly resembles folklore more than history, critics contemptuously label the defenders of the Kennedy legacy court historians and imply that any favorable assessment of the family must necessarily be biased either by the authors' personal proximity to the Kennedys, their reliance on selectively released historical materials, or both. The fairness of such charges depends on the author and the circumstances. The rush to revise insiders' accounts and to demythologize (even to demonize) the Kennedys threatens to become excessive, leaving room at this juncture, one hopes, for more measured assessments.

That the book was completed at all owes much to the kindness of strangers (apologies to Tennessee Williams), coupled with the encouragement of old friends. Thanks, first of all, to Sid Feders, Merle Rubine, Jamie Paksima, Cathy Porter, Tom Brokaw, and other members of NBC-News for the unique perspective on RFK gained through the

1993 production of "Robert F. Kennedy: The Man and the Memories." Serving as historical consultant for the documentary not only allowed me to benefit from many interviews of RFK and JFK intimates (over 150 in all) but also brought me to a fuller appreciation of the varied and complex dimensions of the Kennedy brothers' partnership.

Archivists, of course, are historians' lifelines. Without them we aimlessly drift. For their gracious support I particularly thank Maura Porter and Donna Cotterall (John F. Kennedy Library), Pamela Austin (Temple University Urban Archives), and Steve Tilley (John F. Kennedy Assassination Records Collection, National Archives at College Park, Maryland).

An even greater delight for me, as the work on this book dragged on seemingly without end, was beholding (some might say testing) the patience and tolerance of students, colleagues, friends, and family. I am grateful now for all the times they tenaciously (and sometimes unknowingly at their peril) inquired, "How's *Bobby Kennedy* coming?" Only because they kept asking has it finally appeared. My special thanks to the undergraduate history students at Temple's Ambler Campus; their infectious enthusiasm and unfettered excitement for the study of contemporary U.S. history rekindled my own fervor at a propitious moment.

Singular thanks are due my mentor and friend, Herbert J. Bass. For his guidance and constructive criticisms, I shall always be indebted. I owe a special debt of gratitude to Waldo Heinrichs for persuading me to return to the classroom and to historical research. Thanks, also, to Gary Fink, William H. Chafe, and Rodney Olsen, who read portions or all of the manuscript and provided useful comments and suggestions. Several historians offered assistance and encouragement along the way, including Lee Benson, James M. Burns, John C. Burnham, John Milton Cooper, Jr., Marc Galicchio, James Giglio, Ira Harkavy, George Kellner, Richard S. Kirkendall, William Kuhn, and Terry Parssinen. I benefitted greatly from conversations with several people who knew Robert Kennedy at one point or another in his life, and I wish to thank John Bates, Ira Cooperman, Edwin Guthman, Wayne Hardin, Fred Lindquist, Arthur M. Schlesinger, Jr., Donald Stone, Kevin Tucker, Harris Wofford, and Adam Yarmolinsky.

For courtesies large and small I thank my colleagues at Temple University, particularly Allen Davis, Herbert Ershkowitz, Mark Haller, Richard Immerman, Kenneth Kusmer, Margaret Marsh, John Raines, David Rosenberg, Dennis Rubini, Morris Vogel, and Russell Weigley. Helpful in diverse ways were Christopher Preble, George Shore, Harold Gullan, Nancy Banks, Katie Parkin, Kathy Pfizenmayer, Andrew Harrison, Randy Wenhold, Alice George, Sean Morley, and Gang Loa. For friendly nudges and favors along the way, I thank Bob Bush, Dick Cervone, Ray and Judy Coughlin, Norton Freedman, Bob and Jan Frisch, Carolann Hilty, George Ingram, Anne Jones, Lynn Knetlar, Neal and Emily Kresheck, Gladys MacCartney, Vince Maggio, Rob Marland, Nancy and Ted Quedenfeld, Chuck Schalch, Jack and Norma Silcott, Bob Smith, and Patricia Williams.

I gratefully acknowledge the support of Temple University and the Faculty Senate for a grant-in-aid of research and a one-semester study leave, and Dean Lois Cronholm for a brief respite from duties as department chair. To David Bartlett and Janet M. Francendese of Temple Press, my sincere gratitude for their personal encouragement, gracious advice, and earnest endeavors on behalf of this project. Thanks, also, to Roberta L. Needham for her patience, care, and insights in copyediting the book.

Providence has taken Bill MacCartney, my brother protector, and Dan Cook, as close as a brother, and bound my brother, Robert, in sweet, perpetual innocence. Yet, somehow, I know they share in this moment of completion.

My greatest appreciation and deepest affection go to my wife, Kathleen, and my children, Carolyn, Robert, and Maura, for whose forbearance and devotion I will remain eternally grateful.

ROBERT KENNEDY

BROTHER PROTECTOR

INTRODUCTION

Am I My Brother's Keeper?

Robert Francis Kennedy, brother of John F. Kennedy, thirty-fifth president of the United States, was a complex man, a sheaf of incongruities bound around one certainty—his love of family. That love spawned his unconditional dedication to his brother John's political success, fed his obsession with preserving the historical and public memories of Camelot, and compelled him as the final deed in a lifetime filled with feats of family sacrifice to pick up the fallen standard and seek the presidency himself.

Robert Kennedy's life played out in two acts. Act 1 (the subject of this book) finds him struggling for acceptance and recognition from the Kennedy males, proving himself as a dauntless investigator of America's enemies within, then absorbing himself totally in making John Kennedy president, shielding him from destructive forces (including JFK's own compulsions), and overseeing his presidency. That unique partnership in U.S. politics and Act 1 of Robert Kennedy's life ended abruptly with President Kennedy's assassination in November 1963. Act 2 (which I intend to explore in a later work) reveals Robert Kennedy the survivor, beleaguered by the ghostly image of his slain brother and determined to make it on his own; this act too ends abruptly, when Robert Kennedy is struck down by an assassin in June 1968.

Today, most Americans, even those not yet born when John and Robert Kennedy served in office, know the brothers simply by their initials—JFK and RFK—so pervasive is the Kennedy mystique and its influence on the latter four decades of the twentieth century. Americans find the Kennedy family singularly fascinating, according its members a blend of the treatments usually reserved for royalty and for film or sports stars. If anything, the Kennedys' celebrity status has been magnified in the years since their deaths; they have become not only political icons but fixtures in U.S. popular culture.[1]

Regardless of how one feels about the policies and politics of the Kennedy years, the tale of the Kennedy family's ascension to the pinnacle of American power, of the young president's tragic death, followed in less than five years by the murder of his brother and partner in power, has embedded itself firmly in the nation's collective psyche. The story retains an intimate and familiar quality, freshened by periodic bursts of media attention to the fate of the survivors and to the controversies of the assassinations, kept before us because of its timeless captivating essence and because of what we are able to read into it for ourselves.

Resonating from the extraordinary circumstances that carried the two Kennedy men to power and cut them down in their prime is more than a collective national sorrow or a pervasive melancholy. What lingers—what has almost taken on a life of its own—is variously referred to as the Kennedy mystique or the Kennedy legacy, actually two distinct aspects of how America remembers John and Robert Kennedy. On the one hand, recollections of the Kennedys' physical attractiveness, charismatic style, competitive drive, chauvinistic verve, intense devotion to each other and their families, and the manner and circumstances of their deaths have blended to create a tantalizing mystique—the president's widow wanted it called Camelot—that has transformed the Kennedys into near-mythical figures transcending written history. To understand the places of John and Robert Kennedy in U.S. history requires some appreciation for the complex set of images and symbols comprising the mystique. The Kennedy legacy, on the other hand, comprises their lasting contributions to U.S. politics, to the tenets of U.S. liberalism, and to U.S. political culture.

It is difficult to thoroughly chart and assay either the mystique or the legacy, for at bottom they are blends of crafted images and scandalous realities, high expectations and unfulfilled promise. We remember John and Robert Kennedy less for what they did than for what they might have done, more for their personal magnetism and popular appeal than for their impact on the politics and policies of their time. Like the mythic Camelot to which it is often compared, John Kennedy's presidency represented a brief shining moment to many, an enigmatic interlude to others.

That we speak at all of a Kennedy legacy, rather than of simply a Kennedy presidency, is because of Robert Kennedy. Many of the most enduring ideals associated with the Kennedy legacy, especially those involving an empathy for the young, the poor, and minorities, derived in large part from Robert's efforts after JFK's murder. Both Kennedys spoke of sacrifice and service, compassion and understanding, discipline and self-help, moral obligations and responsibilities. Robert, however, conveyed a greater, more genuine sense of indignation and moral outrage over America's social problems while his brother was still alive, and he later broke new ground for the Kennedys by directly advocating the causes of the disadvantaged and underrepresented; ultimately he was hailed as the "people's tribune."[2]

In both life and death the Kennedys often got credit for more than they achieved. John and Robert Kennedy lived in changing times and stood at the epicenter of the tumultous sixties, but they were reactors to, rather than initiators of, change. Splendid opportunists, they carefully gauged events to leverage positions, maximize advantages, and minimize weakness. Their principal objective was political power and prestige; their often soaring eloquence raised expectations and promised greatness for their country and themselves.

Lest we forget, the Kennedys were, above all else, politicians. (In spite of their high regard for the profession, they preferred to call its practitioners "public servants.") Acclaimed in death as statesmen, their profession was also their passion; they were absorbed with pursuing, holding, and wielding political power. Unlike that of most politicians, the Kennedys' power emanated from political organizations built on their own personalities, not based on their leadership of political or social movements or their advocacy of specific ideologies. Like classic charismatic leaders, they relied on qualities of personal magnetism and influence.[3] Not only were they their own political party, they became, in effect, their own political movement. They adopted highly personalized forms of decision making, delegated little, avoided traditional lines of authority, and demanded and received intense loyalty from their associates, who understood that power depended on personal access and proximity to the Kennedys. And at the core of the Kennedy Party lay the Kennedy family. To Robert, it was his *raison d'etre*.

Political labels, therefore, do not attach easily to either of the Kennedy brothers, especially Robert. While serving as chief counsel of the Senate Rackets Committee in the late 1950s, he was criticized by liberals for his apparently blatant manipulation of Senate investigatory powers and for his conservative zeal in prosecuting persons whom he considered domestic enemies. In the early sixties, liberals and New Leftists scored his seeming insensitivity toward personal liberties, his fixation on the means and goals of counterinsurgency, and his involvement in expanding the U.S. military role in Vietnam. Likewise, many conservatives and those on the far political Right opposed (some even despised) Robert Kennedy's facilitating role in the civil rights movement, his later opposition to the Vietnam War, and his courting of minorities and the poor to the apparent exclusion of the business community and the white middle class.

Robert Kennedy's complex personality and political views defy simple explanation. A man "not just complex," reporter Jack Newfield said, "but contradictory," he struck novelist Philip Roth as a "vital, imperfect, high-strung, egotistical, rivalous, talented brother, who could be just as nasty as he was decent." Roth described him as "nakedly ambitious and virile," with a smile "as distinctive as Franklin Roosevelt's and weighted with a similar bravado." Richard Goodwin, advisor to Presidents Kennedy and Johnson, found Robert Kennedy a "constellation of contradictions," a "battleground where exuberance and the hunger for experience warred with melancholy touched with despair."[4]

Perhaps, as cartoonist Jules Feiffer once suggested, there were two

Robert Kennedys, a ruthless and unyielding "Bad Bobby" and a "Good Bobby," who emerged from JFK's assassination a more tolerant and flexible person. Victor Lasky, author of critical books on both John and Robert Kennedy, defined the Bad Bobby as "the Bobby who refused to match his eloquent speeches with deeds."[5]

Clearly, we cannot hope to understand Robert Kennedy by looking at only his behavioral excesses and personality extremes. Rather, we must look at the totality of his character and, as Feiffer intimated, at its dual essence. His ruthlessness (or, as his wife preferred to call it, his "singlemindedness") reflected one side. On the other side we find his compassion for underdogs. He could be vexedly absurd yet coldly deliberate, wildly irrational yet profoundly logical, extremes that the public nature of his political education only magnified.

Throughout his early life Robert found himself relegated by his father to the family wings, attended only by his mother and older brother, Joe Junior. As a young man he was brought on stage in a prominent but decidedly supportive role in the Kennedy repertory. As John Kennedy ran for and won the presidency, Robert took on another part—again, at his father's insistence—vizier and brother protector. In time, he shared billing with his brother, as the administration's actions became attributed collectively to "the Kennedys," an entity driven by a singular partnership in governing.

"No one can appreciate what he became," Harris Wofford once observed of Robert Kennedy after his brother's death, "without remembering what he had been."[6] To hone that appreciation this book focuses on what Robert Kennedy had been, on what he had done, and on what he was becoming before John Kennedy's assassination—and on the Kennedy brothers' partnership from Robert's perspective.

The two acts of Robert Kennedy's life unfolded in four phases or scenes. The three scenes of Act 1, covered in this book, included a formative period (1925 to 1946), dominated by his struggle for family recognition; a transitional period (1946 to 1952), marked by the male Kennedy rites of passage; and a self-discovery period (1952 to 1963), bracketed by his entry into politics and the gunshots in Dallas and pervaded by his conspicuous commitment to and personal sacrifice for John Kennedy. Act 2, a time of self-actualization (1964 to 1968), marked his assumption of family leadership and his development as a prominent national figure in his own right.

Extended bouts of brooding, confusion, and disorientation, often lasting several months, marked the transitions from one phase or scene to another. At these points Robert Kennedy tended to be combative, morose, and introverted. He often broke out of these moods with fearsome demonstrations of physical rage or reckless challenges to real or imagined antagonists. Indeed, throughout his life he struggled to harness inner conflicts and to guide his passions in useful directions. Dedicated early to a life of serving his family, he struggled to meet his parents' competing (often contradictory) standards and high expectations, while trying in vain to match the records of his older, more talented brothers. Born in another time and another place, he might well have dedicated himself to his church and perhaps become, as he once mused, a "revolutionary priest."

Robert's energetic and accomplished family often overlooked, ignored, or took for granted the son described as "the least poised, the least articulate, and the least extroverted of the Kennedy brothers."[7] The gentlest, shyest, best behaved, and most religious of the Kennedy boys, he revised his identity, according to his close friend and biographer, Arthur Schlesinger, Jr., "first to please his father and then, later, to serve his brother."[8]

As he matured, Robert loosened the psychological bonds to his father and forged new ones to his brother John. He survived the male Kennedys' gauntlet and earned his father's and brothers' respect and admiration, mostly for his physical prowess and for his dutiful managing of John Kennedy's 1952 senatorial campaign. Overshadowed by his older brother and in awe of his father, Robert did not begin to develop a distinct persona until his stint from 1957 through 1959 as chief counsel of the McClellan committee investigating labor racketeering.

In the meantime, John Kennedy had created his own agenda, seeking to release himself from his father's dominance; in the process, he turned increasingly to Robert for assistance.[9] From the beginnings of John Kennedy's presidential bid in 1959 until November 1963, Robert Kennedy devoted himself to helping his brother realize his father's and his own ambitions for the presidency. As attorney general, he dedicated himself to shaping the policies and politics of his brother's administration and to protecting his brother's and his family's reputations. Widely regarded as the second most powerful man in Washington, he remained happily and productively absorbed during the thousand days of John Kennedy's presidency.

Robert Kennedy left a remarkably distinguished record as attorney general, especially considering the criticisms he and his brother endured over the appointment and the many other responsibilities he accepted. He nurtured a particularly talented group of subordinates and through them managed to redefine the scope of Justice Department operations, to humanize and modernize its mission. His direct involvement in advocating (reluctantly at first) the moral and legal dimensions of the civil rights movement molded the course of events in the 1960s. However, his achievements as attorney general were offset by his failure to constrain the excesses of FBI director J. Edgar Hoover and by his troubling indifference toward the protection of civil liberties.[10]

In an extraordinary departure from precedent, Robert Kennedy headed the Justice Department at the same time that he served as a top advisor on matters of national security, even taking operational control of a major clandestine operation. Indeed, events frequently pulled him away from his responsibilities at the Justice Department to attend with his brother to a series of crises. His duties in crisis managment combined with his unprecedented access to the president to yield a historically singular political partnership. His influence percolated through all departments of the executive branch. So accustomed was he to wielding power in his brother's name that he was more than the number two man, he was "number one and one-half."

Biography, to paraphrase William Faulkner, is but the outer cloth, the clothes and buttons, of a person. The full, true life story of any person cannot be written, for the first casualty in writing biography, as in war, is often the truth. And "truth," Lord Bolingbroke reminded us, "lies within a little and certain compass, but error is immense." The biographer's judgment in selecting and ignoring topics and questions is always prejudicial to one degree or another, and the truth seems inevitably bent in the process. The historian, however, must be mindful of alternative explanations and, as Cicero decreed two millennia ago, not only "never dare utter an untruth" but take care to "suppress nothing that is true." With those admonitions in mind, we turn now to examine Robert Kennedy, with particular emphasis on how his place within the family evolved into the extraordinary partnership that marked the Kennedy administration and forged the Kennedy legacy.

CHAPTER 1

The Seventh Kennedy

ROBERT FRANCIS KENNEDY, the seventh of nine children born to Joseph Patrick Kennedy and Rose Fitzgerald Kennedy, was bound to his family with a force of extraordinary magnitude. His birth order in this tight-knit family would shape his character, mold his private and public personalities, and determine his family and public roles—in short, his place in the family would determine his place in history.

No family in U.S. history has produced holders of high political office in such proximate abundance.[1] Multiple members of the Adams, Lodge, Taft, Roosevelt, and LaFollette families achieved high office, but usually decades apart. Comparisons with the Adams family come most readily to mind. Massachusetts, as a member of Congress once noted, has given the nation many great families, but in the case of the Adamses "these blessings were staggered over the centuries"—the Kennedys arrived "in one big batch!"[2] In 1963 Joseph Kennedy's oldest living son, John, was president of the United States; his next oldest, Robert, was attorney general; and his youngest, Edward, was a U.S. senator from Massachusetts. "One Kennedy is a triumph, two Kennedys at the same time are a miracle," *New York Times* columnist James Reston observed, "but three could easily be regarded by many voters as an invasion."[3]

The Kennedy brothers' arrival on the political scene represented the realization of family ambitions and was the product of long, deliberate, and exhaustive family efforts, especially of its patriarch Joseph P. Kennedy. The enormous increase in government power during the Depression had convinced him that "in the next generation the people who run the government will be the biggest people in America."[4] He determined then that at least one, perhaps all, of his sons would be among their number.

The Kennedys and the Fitzgeralds

The Kennedys' political aspirations reflected their Irish American heritage. "The search for power," according to historian and former U.S. ambassador to Ireland William Shannon, "has been the main motif of Irish history in the country." In the Boston of the late nineteenth and early twentieth centuries, politics offered Irish immigrants and their offspring the best chance at access to that power.[5]

Robert and John Kennedy descended from famine-generation Irish Catholics who shaped Irish American culture in the eastern cities of the United States. The potato blight drove their great-grandfather, Patrick Kennedy, to emigrate in 1849 from Dunganstown in County Wexford to Boston. There he worked as a barrel maker, married Bridget Murphy, and died of cholera in 1858. Patrick's son, Patrick Joseph "P. J." Kennedy, worked as a dockhand, saved his money, and bought a saloon, then another and another. Before he was thirty P.J. opened a liquor import business and branched out into banking and politics.[6]

In 1887 P. J. Kennedy married Mary Augusta Hickey, the quick-witted, capricious daughter of a successful Boston businessman. P. J. Kennedy's income afforded his family a comfortable life that included a four-story house in East Boston overlooking the harbor, servants, and vacations in Maine and Palm Beach, Florida. Not rich by Boston Brahmin standards, nor members of the upper echelons of "lace curtain" Irish society, the Kennedys rose far above the poverty of "shanty Irish" immigrants.[7]

A large man with thick red hair, bushy eyebrows, and piercing blue eyes, P. J. Kennedy had about him an air of dignity and wisdom. East Boston saloon patrons respected this teetotaling, no-nonsense tavern keeper, and Kennedy's Haymarket Square saloon became a gathering place for local politicians. A local ward boss, P. J. served eight successive terms in the state legislature and earned a reputation for behind-the-scenes political brokering. By the early years of the new century, he had gained a seat on the powerful four-member Board of Strategy, which controlled Democratic party patronage in Boston, and for a time he figured prominently in Boston politics.

Mary Hickey Kennedy wanted her only son, Joseph Patrick, to "be somebody" in a way her husband was not, an ambition she knew he would have small chance of fulfilling in East Boston.[8] She pressed P. J. to enroll Joseph in the Boston Latin School, a select high school founded in 1635 whose alumni included Samuel Adams, Benjamin Franklin, John Hancock, five other signers of the Declaration of Independence, and Ralph Waldo Emerson. Then still thoroughly Protestant and Yankee, Boston Latin offered Mary Kennedy's son access to the edges of upper-echelon Yankee society. Joseph Kennedy later acted upon that same calculation in the education of his own sons.[9]

Tall, lean, and sandy haired, Joseph Kennedy excelled at baseball and politics at Boston Latin. Popular enough to win election as class president, he still failed to crack the barriers of social snobbery erected by the sons of proper Bostonian families. At Harvard University, he felt similarly rebuffed. Despite his determined cultivation of star athletes and popular classmates—a process "without scruple," a classmate recalled—and despite his admission into several upper-echelon clubs including Hasty Pudding, Kennedy never received an invitation to join Porcellian, Harvard's most exclusive club. Having conditioned himself to settle for no less than the best, he was embittered for life by the Porcellian rejection.[10]

Joseph Kennedy acquired many acquaintances at Harvard, but few close friends. Most classmates knew him to be a sharp financial operator who earned $10,000 in a tour bus venture and in Boston real estate while still an undergraduate. By then Kennedy was convinced that money, not politics, would prove his passport to acceptance, a conviction probably solidified by his father's surprise defeat in the 1908 primary race for Boston street commissioner. P. J. Kennedy's loss to a political unknown after twenty-five years of faithful party service shocked the still impressionable young Kennedy and ended any illusions he may have had concerning elective politics. Joseph Kennedy cynically concluded that partisan loyalty and political power could be bought. Certain that real power, lasting control, and personal independence emanated from wealth, he pursued money.[11]

By the time Joseph Kennedy graduated from Harvard in June 1912, he had won the love of Rose Elizabeth Fitzgerald, the attractive and vivacious daughter of his father's sometime rival, Boston mayor John Francis Fitzgerald. Fitzgerald's political career began in Boston's North End, where he built an ethnically diverse coalition held together by Irish machine politics. An indefatigable campaigner, the dapper and ebullient Fitzgerald served briefly alongside P. J. Kennedy in the state senate before winning election in 1894 to the first of three consecutive terms in Congress. Fitzgerald was denied renomination for a fourth term by the Board of Strategy, of which P. J. Kennedy was then a member, for reasons long since lost in the arcane world of Boston politics.[12]

Elected mayor of Boston in 1905, Fitzgerald failed in his bid for reelection two years later because of a major financial scandal. Denying his own fault, Fitzgerald implicated his closest political associate. Whether Fitzgerald's denials or his personal popularity convinced Boston voters, they put him back in the mayor's office in 1909. This campaign spawned the legend of Fitzgerald as Honey Fitz, the gregarious, back-slapping, quintessential Irish politician who knew every voter's name, attended every wake, and concluded each campaign appearance by leading the crowd of "Dearos," or political hangers-on, in "Sweet Adeline" or other popular Irish songs.[13]

During the investigations Fitzgerald had sent daughter Rose to a convent in Holland. She returned in time to celebrate her father's electoral vindication, then left for the Convent of the Sacred Heart in the Manhattanville section of New York City. Rose would have preferred to attend Wellesley, a private women's college outside Boston, but Archbishop O'Connell had told Fitzgerald it would be a poor example to Catholic girls in Boston if the mayor's daughter attended a Protestant college. "My greatest regret," Rose told an interviewer at age ninety, "is not having gone to Wellesley College. It is something I have felt a little sad about all my life."[14]

Denied her choice of colleges, Rose wanted for little else. Standing in for her publicity-shy mother, Rose accompanied her father on official trips and events and immersed herself in the social life, culture, travel, and privileged existence afforded by her father's status. Mayor Fitzgerald harbored grand aspirations for Rose and objected to her romance with P. J. Kennedy's son. Although the Kennedy and Fitzgerald families vacationed and socialized together, Fitzgerald felt socially superior to the Kennedys, having maneuvered his family through the torturous terrain of Boston politics to the pinnacle of Irish society. He believed himself within hailing distance of—or perhaps only a strategically arranged marriage away from—acceptance by the Yankee elite.

In 1913 James Michael Curley, a boisterous, unpredictable Irish rogue, challenged Fitzgerald for the mayoralty. Curley, later caricatured in Edwin O'Connor's novel *The Last Hurrah,* expected Fitzgerald to drop out of the race and run for the U.S. Senate. When he did not, Curley threatened to expose Fitzgerald's relationship with a twenty-three-year-old cigarette girl, Elizabeth "Toodles" Ryan. Under stress, Fitzgerald collapsed from exhaustion and withdrew from the race on advice of his physician. Honey Fitz ran several more times for public office, the last time in 1942, but, unable to recover the voters' confidence after Curley's humiliation, he never won again.[15]

Meantime, Joseph Kennedy started his business career as a clerk in the Columbia Trust Company, a small East Boston bank founded by his father and other Irish businessmen. Drawing on his father's connections, he then won a civil service appointment as a bank examiner and set about learning banking from the inside out. He resigned the examiner's job when a hostile takeover threatened the Columbia Trust. Moving quickly to arrange proxies, borrow money, and gain majority control, Kennedy succeeded in blocking the takeover and successfully maneuvered his own election as bank president. In January 1914, at age twenty-five, Joseph Kennedy won recognition as the "youngest bank president in the country."[16]

The Toodles episode deeply upset Rose. She adored her father and had given up Wellesley for him. She refused to give up Joseph Kennedy.

Willing to concede Kennedy's success and chastened by the Toodles fiasco, John Fitzgerald agreed to the marriage. On 7 October 1914, Rose Fitzgerald and Joseph Kennedy exchanged vows in William Cardinal O'Connell's private chapel. They moved into a nine-room house at 83 Beals Street in the middle-class predominantly Protestant suburb of Brookline. Joseph Patrick Kennedy, Jr., was born in 1915, and John Fitzgerald Kennedy in 1917. Rose stayed home while Joe pursued his announced goal of making a million dollars by age thirty-five.[17]

In 1917, with the country at war, Kennedy resigned the presidency of Columbia Trust and accepted a position as assistant general manager of Bethlehem Steel's shipbuilding plant at Fore River Shipyard in Quincy. Like many Irish Americans, Joseph Kennedy was ambivalent toward the war, particularly after the brutal British suppression of the Easter Rising in Ireland in 1916. But Kennedy rejected patriotic war fervor less for ethnic than for economic reasons. He considered the war an enormous waste. He himself wanted no part in it and, through some adroit string pulling, secured a deferment from the draft.[18]

At war's end Kennedy joined the venerable investment firm of Hayden, Stone and Company. Given limited opportunities for advancement, he soon decided to strike out on his own, leaving Rose alone much of the time. She missed both her husband and the Boston social whirl. She also learned of Kennedy's deserved reputation as a ladies' man. Matters became intolerable in 1920. After a three-week separation and time alone at a religious retreat, Rose returned to Brookline vowing to eschew the role of martyred wife and to look upon child rearing as "a profession that was fully as interesting and challenging as any honorable profession in the world."[19]

Shortly after Rose returned home, John Kennedy nearly died from scarlet fever. The double shock of Rose's brief absence and his son's near death stirred Joseph Kennedy to attend with greater fervor to his family's needs. To preserve the marriage and the family, the couple developed a partnership built around the children. Loving respect for each other and mutual concern for the rearing of their children replaced their dissipated romance. The arrangement allowed them to pursue their separate interests without inflicting guilt on each other, but not without affecting their children, who gradually came to place more trust in each other than in their inaccessible parents.

In August 1920 the Kennedys moved into a larger house a few blocks away at the corner of Abbottsford and Naples Roads in Brookline. The fourteen rooms afforded space for more live-in help—a maid, a nurse, and a nanny—and, most importantly, a room for Rose to withdraw to read, think, sew, and be away from the children. A large front porch, divided into sections by folding gates, provided separate sitting areas for the adults and children's play areas for the growing family.[20]

Robert Francis Kennedy's arrival on 20 November 1925 followed the birth of four girls—Rosemary (1918), Kathleen (1920), Eunice (1921), and Patricia (1924). Another sister, Jean, arrived in 1928. "He's stuck by himself in a bunch of girls," Rose's mother worried, "he'll be a sissy." Family and friends feared Robert would harbor feelings of inferiority because of his place within the family and his small size. The shyest, gentlest, and least articulate of the boys, by all accounts Robert was an "extremely sweet child," generous with his possessions, and openly affectionate, especially with his mother, who protected and consoled her "own little pet."[21]

With the birth of Edward Moore "Teddy" Kennedy in 1932, Robert had two older brothers and one very much younger, "none of whom," Rose felt, were "much use to him as boyhood pals."

"My brother Joe took the greatest interest in us," Robert recalled. "He taught us to sail, to swim, to play football and baseball." Jack, the gregarious charmer, eight years older than Robert and full of fun and mischief, regaled him with stories of heroes and adventures gleaned from the many books he read during his numerous illnesses. As a small boy, Robert desperately sought the attention and approval of his older brothers, who generally ignored or overlooked him. "He was just a nice kid," long time family friend LeMoyne Billings said of Robert. "We barely noticed him in the early days, but that's because he didn't bother anybody."[22]

Their parents made significant, sometimes conflicting, demands on all the Kennedy children. None of the boys seemed so affected by those demands as Robert.[23]

Rose encouraged neatness, social grace, gentle behavior, self-improvement, proper grammar and diction, dutiful obedience, and Catholic piety. She insisted on a prescribed and regulated family life, believing a fixed routine would enable her children to resist the pressures of "moral and social drift."[24] The young Robert strove to be the most dutiful, religious, affectionate, and obedient. The more he met his mother's expectations, the greater grew his distance from his apparently omnipotent, usually impatient, and often absent father. Joseph Kennedy stressed discipline, self-control, hard work, competition, physical toughness, perseverance, resolve, punctuality, and, perhaps above all, winning. Kennedy told his children, "We don't want any losers around here. In this family we want winners." As Robert Kennedy recalled, "A Kennedy learns not to be a loser at the age of two."[25] Joe also warned against maudlin sentimentality and feeling sorry for oneself. "I don't want any sourpusses around here," he would say. Robert Kennedy translated this remark to mean that "Kennedys never cry."[26]

Considered together, the father's standards formed a code of manly conduct that threatened to consume Robert at various points during his youth and early manhood. Joseph Kennedy embellished the code with advice and directions on how to gain access to and succeed in a masculine world and how to establish independence from institutions and the control of other men. The elder Kennedy repeated these admonitions during dinner discussions, drove them home during family competitions, and spelled them out in detail in more than two hundred letters to his children. Not once, according to Doris Goodwin, the only historian to have read the letters, did Kennedy put forward ultimate moral principles for his children. The only general family value he emphasized was the importance of respecting their mother.[27]

What kind of a role model was Robert's father? Consumed by the task of building a financial empire, Joseph Kennedy spent relatively little time with his children. In 1923 he opened his own office, identified himself simply as "Joseph P. Kennedy, Banker," and involved himself in far-flung enterprises. Known for his lone-wolf talents at stock market manipulation, Kennedy used such then legal techniques as stock churning, pooling, and insider trading and made a fortune speculating in the bull market of the mid-1920s. Suspicious of the over valued market, he liquidated most of his assets well before the Crash of 1929, invested heavily in the motion picture industry, purchased a chain of movie theaters, and engineered a merger with David Sarnoff of RCA to form RKO Studios. He helped Gloria Swanson, the reigning movie sex goddess, establish her own production company, took personal charge of her financial operations, and was soon involved in a lengthy romantic affair with her.[28]

Away from home for weeks, sometimes months, at a time, with Swanson or his business and golfing cronies, Kennedy missed the births of daughters Patricia (1924) and Jean (1928) and even his father's funeral in 1929. In the summer of 1929, Joseph brought Gloria Swanson with him to the family vacation home in Hyannis Port. Robert, at four, was too young to grasp the significance of the episode, which evidently had a profound effect on his older brothers; the gamble Joseph Kennedy took with Swanson offered a role model that Joe Junior and John seemed not to mind.[29] "A very important and conscious part of the male Kennedy mystique is a pride in womanizing," historian Garry Wills observed. "Only Robert broke free of this —he had other demons."[30]

Swanson wondered whether Rose Kennedy, who said nothing, was a fool, a saint, or "just a better actress than I was."[31] But armed with her Catholic faith and increasingly reclusive, Rose by then simply refused to worry about other women. When her husband returned home from one of his escapades, she would take a trip of her own to seasonal locales and favored social spots; she usually spent a month or more away from home after the birth of each child. While Rose was away, Joseph arranged either to be home with the children or, more often, to have Eddie Moore—a faithful Kennedy associate, after whom their youngest son was named—and his wife stay at the house as surrogate parents.

During the children's formative years, Rose made seventeen trips abroad without her husband, including a trip to Paris on their twentieth wedding anniversary. The two maintained separate apartments in New York City. Rationalizing the arrangement in her later years, Rose described the marriage as having a "synergistic" quality. "We were individuals," she said in a detached manner, "with highly responsible roles in a partnership that yielded rewards which we shared."[32]

Rose "managed" the family, she said, placing herself in charge of "planning, organizing, and supervising." She regarded herself as an "executive," overseeing the live-in help who performed all household chores. She set the household rules, kept the children's medical records, organized and supervised daily excursions, hired sports and physical fitness instructors, tutored the children on the elements of grammar and speech, and served as family disciplinarian. In all of this she rationed her affections and withheld a part of herself from her children. Yet John Kennedy would later say that he considered his mother the "glue" holding the family together.[33]

Despite frequent absences, Joseph Kennedy created and maintained a tenacious hold on his children's lives. The more distant the father, the more idealized and powerful he became in the eyes of his children, especially Robert's. When at home, Kennedy disciplined the children with a stern disapproving look over the top of his glasses, a frozen stare through slightly squinted eyes the children called "Daddy's look." Family members said Joseph Kennedy inherited "Hickey eyes" from his mother's side of the family.[34] Robert Kennedy, who also inherited his grandmother's eyes, would later assume his father's "look" when disciplining his own children. When he was angry, Robert's eyes, like his father's, filled with light, transformed into eerie deep-blue orbs.

At home Robert's father presided over the now fabled dinner table seminars on current affairs and self-improvement, insisting the children examine and discuss the larger issues of the day, inculcating in them a sense of obligation to participate in public life, and prodding them to develop opinions of their own at the same time he subtly shaped them to think as he did. "My father," John Kennedy recalled during a White House interview, "wasn't around as much as some fathers, [but] he held up standards for us, and he was very tough when we failed to meet those standards."[35]

The Children's Inner World

With their parents away so often, it was left to the Kennedy children to define, even to invent, a Kennedy family. The children created their own inner world. When together, they focused intensely on each other. One visitor found them akin to an exotic tribe with its own folklore, customs, and codes.[36]

The children aimed barbed jokes at each other's shortcomings and addressed each other in affectionate diminutives. Joseph, Jr., was Little Joe or Joe Junior. John became Jack to school friends, with the more familiar Johnny reserved for family and the very closest friends. Joe Junior and Jack called each other Brother, perhaps to acknowledge their near equal status as pursuers of future supremacy. Edward became Teddy to family and friends, but the children teasingly called the pudgy boy fatstuff. Robert was Robby to his younger brother and Bobby to family, school chums, and, later, a mourning nation. To Robert's discomfort, John persisted in calling him Bobby as attorney general. Robert directed his Justice Department staff to call him Bob.[37]

A hierarchy developed among the children. At the top stood Joe Junior, the eldest and his father's favorite, "the model for all of us, except Jack," recalled Robert. The two older brothers fought incessantly. "I used to lie in my bed at night sometimes," Robert later confided, "and hear the sound of Joe banging Jack's head against the wall." The combination of his brothers' intense competition, his parents' high expectations, and the sheer size of the family made life at home for Robert a "struggle to survive." Later, Robert attributed his reputation for toughness and for being a fighter to the rivalries within his family, saying, "I think in any family where there are a lot of children, they're always fighting with one another, competing with one another. And the same situation existed in our family. We always competed with one another."[38]

The nine Kennedy children divided chronologically and socially into two groups. Joe Junior, John, and Kathleen became the "golden trio" of the family. Their parents and the youngest children, Patricia, Robert, Jean, and Edward, lavished attention and devotion on them. Eunice tended to her younger siblings and took a large share of responsibility for her older sister Rosemary, whose mental disability the family kept secret for many years.

Joe Junior excelled at nearly everything he attempted, whether athletics, academics, or social skills. Tall, handsome, and physically imposing, he was also an overbearing bully.

Kathleen, nicknamed Kick because of her high-spirited nature, was the physical embodiment of Rose as a young woman, lovely and dark-haired. She was popular, warm, easy to know and to like, but unexpectedly independent.

John was the children's Pied Piper, a playful, charming brother who won their love and affection. His sloppy, informal habits and his irreverence toward the Catholic church greatly concerned his mother. In turn, her frequent trips away by herself unsettled John, who became an autonomous youth, challenging his parents' standards, rebelling against the control of his older domineering brother, and defying his parents' attempts to pass judgment on him.[39] His loss of trust and respect for his mother left John more independent, doubting, and intellectually inquisitive than his siblings, but apparently at the cost of incapacitating him for true intimacy. Not surprisingly, he and Kathleen were the first to break free of their parents' tight bonds.

Robert reacted very differently to the competitive and emotional tensions within the family and his parents' contradictory messages and inconsistent affection. He became dependent and obsessively obedient, developed a precocious conscience, and emerged from childhood less self-reliant yet more loving, cooperative, and morally judgmental than his older brothers.

Struggling to find his place within the family, Robert strove to exceed his parents' expectations. To please his mother, he became a dutiful Catholic, attending mass regularly, serving as an altar boy, faithfully rehearsing the rituals of the Church, and practicing his Latin, all more intensely and more obviously than any of the other Kennedy children. In response to his father's demands for punctuality, he became, in his mother's words, "spectacularly prompt."[40]

Nothing came easily for Robert. Socially and physically clumsy, he stammered and was accident prone. When only four, he crashed head first into a heavy glass partition separating a passageway under a stairwell in his hurry to be on time for a meal. His sister Patricia remembered there "was blood all over the place, a horrendous scene." Yet what he lacked in self-assurance, social skills, and physical coordination, he made up for in strength of will and tenacity. Slow in learning to swim, Robert threw himself off a boat into Nantucket Sound, determined to swim or drown trying. Brother Joe pulled him from the water. "It showed either a lot of guts or no sense at all, depending on how you looked at it," John later remarked.[41]

Robert did not share his older brothers' worldly dispositions and outlooks. Quite the opposite, he willingly accepted moral imperatives, trusted his Catholic faith, and proved decidedly capable of true intimacy. He remained emotionally and psychologically bound to his parents longer than did his siblings, developing an idealized, romantic view of family life encouraged but not practiced by his parents.

For the Kennedys, constantly on the move, home became wherever they came together, and that was determined by the father. The most important of their many moves occurred in 1927, when Joe booked all the compartments in a Pullman railway car to transport his family (with chauffeur, cook, and nurse) to Riverdale, New York. Boston, he said, "was no place to bring up Irish Catholic children"—a curious remark less important for what it revealed about the condition of the Irish in Boston, where many thousands of Irish Catholic children grew up quite satisfactorily, than for what it expressed about Joseph Kennedy's social aspirations.[42]

On Being Irish

Most Irish Americans were content to build a society within the larger American society, an inclination that often left them behaviorally but not structurally assimilated.[43] The senior Kennedy rejected the rules of Irish American social mobility, which from his point of view mandated living equal to but separate from Yankee society. Kennedy yearned not only for assimilation but ultimately for full acceptance as a peer among Yankee aristocrats, opening the way for his children to achieve on their own merits.[44]

When Robert Kennedy asserted many years later that his father left Boston because of the signs reading "No Irish Need Apply," Michael Mooney, senior editor of the *Saturday Evening Post,* took him to task. Conceding to Kennedy the "distinct right of all the Irish to invent for themselves mythological backgrounds—little lies that amuse their audience and serve their tellers well in diplomacy and love and politics," Mooney drolly observed that surely it was not the signs, gone for many decades, that forced Joe Kennedy to flee in his own railway car. Robert admitted the signs were only "symbolic" of the lack of opportunity in

Boston, whether it was "the business establishment, the clubs, the golf course—at least that was what I was told at a very young age . . . both my parents felt very strongly about the discrimination."[45]

All the Kennedy males invented and reinvented their Irish heritage. It proved a convenient means of establishing audience rapport, expressing identification with the underdogs, or coalescing ethnic support in campaigns. But the Kennedys, at best, were semi-Irish who bore little resemblance to typical Irish Catholics in Boston.[46] They paid appropriate homage to their Irish ancestry, following Irish customs and cultural habits regarding patriarchy, fatalism, and clannish behavior. But Joseph Kennedy believed in the Americanization of Irish immigrants, and he particularly rejected the "stage-Irishman stereotype" of gregarious blarney practiced by his father-in-law. When a newspaperman once described him as an Irishman, Kennedy reacted sharply: "I was born here. My parents were born here. What the hell do I have to do to be called an American?"[47]

In a St. Patrick's Day speech in Boston in 1937 Kennedy asserted that too many Boston Irish suffered under the handicap of "not possessing family tradition adequate to win the respect and confidence of their Puritan neighbors." His implied endorsement of the Puritan ethic and the myth of Yankee superiority left him vulnerable to Irish critics. Indeed, Joseph Kennedy often found it necessary and convenient to step away from his Irish roots. Yet neither he nor his sons could escape them.

Despite his wealth, Joseph Kennedy found it difficult to gain the respect and confidence of his Yankee neighbors. In 1922 he was blackballed from the Cohasset Country Club, a private summer beach preserve of old Boston families. Rose, who like her husband craved unconditional social acceptance, plaintively asked, "When *will* the nice people of Boston accept us?" Feeling rejected by Boston society, the two became more determined than ever to make it on their own in New York, Washington, London, or all three. As reluctant and sad to leave Boston as Rose must have felt, she had little say in the decision. Joseph Kennedy's business required him to be near the money, and the money was in New York.[48]

In 1929, his movie empire and other businesses prospering, Kennedy moved the family again, this time into a twenty-room Georgian mansion set among six acres of manicured lawns, verdant gardens, and secluded woods on Pondfield Road in Bronxville in Westchester County, New York. For thirteen years Rose called Bronxville the Kennedy "base of operations."[49] The comment, as it implies, meant that the Kennedys had several houses, but not one they called home.

LeMoyne Billings, John's roommate at Choate, recalled that the Kennedy children "didn't have a real home with their own rooms where they had pictures on the walls or memorabilia on the shelves but would rather come home for holidays from their boarding schools and find whatever room was available." Joseph Kennedy had turned his children into "proud nomads," moving them—usually by chauffeur-driven cars—from the Bronxville embarkation point to train stations, boarding schools, vacation homes, and back again.[50]

To keep one foot in Massachusetts and probably to mollify Rose's concerns over leaving Boston, in 1926 Joseph Kennedy had leased, then purchased and extensively remodeled, a large summer home in Hyannis Port on Cape Cod. From then on, the family spent summer vacations together at Hyannis Port and wintered in the Florida sun. In 1933 Kennedy acquired his third estate, a sixteen-room stucco neo-Spanish ocean villa, with swimming pool and tennis court, on two acres of luxuriant grounds on North Ocean Boulevard in Palm Beach. Each December the family traveled to Florida by train, filling several drawing rooms. The household staff drove two or three automobiles to Florida, loaded with Christmas presents and extra luggage.[51]

The Kennedys passed the years of the Great Depression in privileged and luxurious isolation from the economic deprivation that left an estimated one in four families without an income in the 1930s. The Depression that shaped the politics, policies, and attitudes of the country's leaders for decades left almost no mark on Robert Kennedy. He recalled "a good deal of conversation and discussion about the fact that people had problems" during the 1930s, and he received constant reminders of the many "who were less fortunate." He heard little, however, of the drudgeries or hardships experienced by workers. Joseph Kennedy's notion of noblesse oblige did not encompass sympathy for working-class conditions, which perhaps explains the Kennedy brothers' subsequent lack of passion for the issue.[52]

Like his brothers and sisters, Robert rarely thought about money. Although not taboo, it was a subject seldom discussed because money, Robert's mother said, did not meet the criterion for "interesting" conversation. Each Kennedy child received a small allowance, starting at a dime a week and accompanied by a lecture on "the painful consequences of heedless extravagance." Robert attempted to gain a modicum of economic independence by taking on a paper route one summer, but he soon wearied of the task and talked the chauffeur into driving him. "There he was," Rose said, "riding around all over Hyannis Port—making his deliveries from a Rolls-Royce." Denied his transportation, Robert dropped the route and with it all further entrepreneurial initiatives.[53]

Robert's schooling began in a Bronxville nursery school. He attended a private school for first and second grades and then a Bronxville public school for the next three grades. A teacher recalled him as "a nice little freckle-faced kid, his hair some shade of brown, a regular boy. He needed no special handling. It seemed hard for him to finish his work sometimes. But he was only ten after all." Robert was withdrawn from the sixth grade at Riverdale Country School in the spring of 1938 to go to England with his family.[54]

Patricia Kennedy remembered the years in Bronxville as "very, very happy times," particularly on weekends and holidays when Joe Junior and John returned from school, usually with house guests. Touch football games and other organized activities filled their days. The residences in Hyannis Port and Bronxville had built-in movie theaters with different first-run films shown three or four times a week. Guests found the Kennedy household teeming with energy, vitality, and an almost militaristic regimentation. Visitors also noticed that Joe and Rose Kennedy seemed almost as distant from their children as from each other.[55]

Joseph Kennedy decided as early as 1930 that Franklin D. Roosevelt, governor of New York, was the smart-money choice for the 1932 Democratic presidential nomination. Kennedy gave twenty-five thousand dollars to Roosevelt's campaign, lent the Democratic party fifty thousand, and raised another hundred thousand from wealthy friends and acquaintances. He also played a significant role, but not the decisive one he later claimed, in convincing publisher William Randolph

Hearst to endorse Roosevelt's nomination. For his efforts Kennedy was welcomed by Roosevelt to join his personal entourage during the 1932 campaign, serving as the candidate's informal liaison to the business and Catholic communities.[56]

Although Kennedy told Roosevelt he did not want a position in the president's administration "unless it really meant some prestige to my family," he expected to be offered the job of secretary of the treasury. When Roosevelt passed him over for the position, Kennedy became vindictive, criticizing the president and pressing the Democratic National Committee for the return of his loans. Although offended by Kennedy's brusque and rude manner, Roosevelt relented and in July 1934 named him the first chair of the Securities Exchange Commission (SEC), placing the notorious speculator in charge of policing Wall Street. Kennedy "knows all the tricks of the trade," FDR explained to his cabinet.[57]

President Roosevelt's reluctance to bring Kennedy into his administration had its basis in Kennedy's headstrong style, impatient demeanor, and often biased and prejudiced opinions. Far from a team player, Kennedy reserved his interest for himself and his family. His choleric disposition, mercurial behavior, and uneven judgments became political liabilities for Roosevelt and, ultimately, for Kennedy's sons.[58]

Nevertheless, few faulted Joseph Kennedy's tenure as chair of the SEC. He left the position to return to business after fifteen months, having impressed Roosevelt with his prodigious efforts in establishing the agency as one of the New Deal's most successful.[59] Kennedy, with the help of *New York Times* columnist Arthur Krock, wrote a campaign tract, *I'm For Roosevelt,* which helped Roosevelt gain reelection in 1936.

Temperamental opposites, Kennedy and Roosevelt had a tenuous personal relationship. But FDR was generous and gracious toward Kennedy's children. At Joe's urging, the president wrote Robert to encourage his stamp collecting. The country's best-known philatelist even enclosed some new issues for Robert's collection. Robert also received a personal invitation to FDR's second inauguration. The diary the twelve year old kept of the event, which he attended with his family, already exhibits Robert's inclination to understand events subjectively.[60]

In the spring of 1937, FDR appointed Joseph Kennedy to chair the new Maritime Commission, a second-echelon position, but one he took willingly as his reentry to government service. In December of that year, FDR finally gave Joseph Kennedy the kind of prestigious appointment he had sought all along, the ambassadorship to Great Britain. From then until his death, Joseph P. Kennedy would be called "the ambassador."[61]

The honor and prestige of the appointment set the family aglow. Rose and the youngest children arrived in London in March 1938. The city's newspapers fawned over the photogenic family during its first year in England. Rose, ecstatic to be back in the social spotlight, hosted parties and hobnobbed with English royalty and socialites. She described these years as "by far the happiest years of my married life." The family traveled through Europe, vacationed in Cannes, shopped in Paris, and attended the coronation of Pope Pius XII as honored guests.[62]

For Irish Americans the Kennedys displayed an inordinate, even paradoxical, attraction to English society and customs.[63] In London Rose believed she and her husband had found the uncritical acceptance so long denied them in Boston. The older children all formed binding British attachments. Young Joe fell in love with an English divorcee. Kathleen married an Englishman and spent the last years of her life in England, where she was buried. Patricia Kennedy married an English-born actor, Peter Lawford. John had a special fondness for English history and politics; he particularly admired, even emulated, the casualness and masculine prerogatives of the English way of life. The wives of two of John's wartime chums, infuriated by his disdain for them as an individuals, would later describe his incessant prowling and sexist conduct as an "English attitude."[64]

Although thoroughly American in most respects, Rose and Joe adopted the life-styles and social behavior of English aristocrats. In England and at home, the Kennedys sometimes behaved less like lace-curtain Irish Americans than twentieth-century versions of English Whig aristocrats. Kennedy households resembled the nineteenth-century country houses of upper-class Whigs, which were said to convey a sense of wealth and power amid a "splendid naturalness," along with energy and animation centered about unceremonious outdoor activities.[65]

Joseph Kennedy also adopted a Whiggish approach to the education and training of his sons. As the governing class in England, Whig males spent much of their time learning to govern, serving the country abroad, and engaging in politics. Kennedy, much like an English lord, deliberately prepared his sons for public service and politics. Politics to Whig aristocrats meant "first of all, personalities and, secondly, general principles."[66] Impressed by the English aristocratic approach, Joseph Kennedy discouraged his sons from adhering to absolute political or philosophical beliefs, encouraged their public involvement on the national and international levels, and impressed on them the exceptional status they enjoyed as his sons.

Robert did not share his family's Anglophilia. Unlike his older brothers and sisters, he cultivated few English friendships and developed no attachments to English institutions. Perhaps it was a natural reaction for a boy in his early teens seeking his own identity. Whatever the reason, at that impressionable period of his life, almost as though he were reminding his family of their origins, Robert embraced his Catholic faith more firmly than at virtually any other time in his life and came to identify more deeply with his Irish roots. Years later, during his brother's presidency, Robert responded to a query from the British ambassador during a White House dinner: "Why are we, the Kennedys, here in America? Why are we here at all? It is because you, the British, drove us out of Ireland!"[67]

The London years—a rare interlude when the mother and father and most of the children lived in the same house—gave Robert a clearer view of his family. Troubled by the disparity between his parents' ideal standards of behavior and their tendency to tolerate, even reward, the conduct of his older siblings, he sought the safety of moral absolutes.

One companion Robert could count on in London was his brother Edward. Although seven years apart in age, they together attended Gibbs, a private day school, and spent many hours playing in the ambassador's official residence. The children's nanny, Luella Hennessey, recalled Edward as a cheerful, garrulous extrovert attached to his father, Robert as less outgoing, "a deep-thinking boy and very close to his mother."[68] Hennessey believed Robert would enter the priesthood. She recalled him at fourteen, walking home from school in London and insisting that they stop by a local church to "pay a visit to the Lord."

When Robert found that the priests there lacked sufficient firewood for their wood-burning stoves, he prevailed upon his father to donate a year's supply. Still, most who knew Robert well, while acknowledging his devotion to the Church, doubted that he ever seriously considered the priesthood.[69]

None disagree, however, with the effects of religious and filial piety on Robert's developing personality. As his reverence toward his Church intensified and his sense of duty and obligation to his family grew, he became less tolerant of the failures of others. His tendency to make moral judgments on others' behavior, especially that of his older brothers and sisters, increased. Driven by an unrelenting conscience, his attitudes and personality became more rigid.[70]

Robert made his first public speech in England at the laying of a cornerstone for a youth club in April 1939. His brief remarks, according to embassy and newspaper reports, were penciled in his own hand and delivered in a "calm and confident" manner. But a typescript of "suggested remarks" prepared by the embassy staff and other reports, including his mother's recollections of the event, belie the published assessments of Robert's early public-speaking abilities.[71] No matter that Robert likely did as well as could be expected of someone his age; his father had still felt the need to manipulate public reports of the event.

Joseph Kennedy used every opportunity to enhance and craft the Kennedy image. His belief that appearances counted most led him to take extraordinary care to ensure that his family and each of its members appeared in the most favorable light. Robert's father fastidiously cultivated reporters and leaders of the print media, including, among others, *New York Times* columnist Arthur Krock and publishers Colonel Robert McCormick of the *Chicago Tribune*, Henry Luce of *Time,* and William Randolph Hearst of the *San Francisco Examiner.* He wrote countless letters thanking reporters for favorable stories and lavished expensive gifts on dozens of journalists each Christmas. When flattery or bribery failed, he resorted to threats and intimidation to get his way with journalists. Using his own public relations office, Kennedy became adept at shaping media images. He succeeded, for example, in forcing *Fortune* and *Ladies' Home Journal* to rewrite articles or assign new reporters whose interpretations conformed to his expectations.[72] The father passed on to his sons a haughty view of the press as mere image makers, easily manipulated.

No amount of image manipulation, however, could prevent Joseph Kennedy's undoing as ambassador. His disastrous record comprised a long list of judgmental errors and diplomatic faux pas. Kennedy erred, for example, in publicly supporting Prime Minister Neville Chamberlain's 1938 Munich agreements while a national debate over those policies proceeded in England. Believing everything possible should be done to avoid war, he unwisely advocated coexistence with the dictators. He and Rose were friendly with Lady Astor and the Cliveden set, a high-society clique with suspected pro-Nazi sympathies. Even his attempts at positive proactive steps seemed always to have a negative hue. Kennedy's proposal for a massive resettlement of German Jews, for example, betrayed anti-Semitic leanings. Up to moments before the Nazi invasion of Poland, he advocated political and financial appeasement of Germany for the sake of a stable world order. And when England entered the war in September 1939 Kennedy bluntly asserted that England's weaknesses left the country little chance of winning.[73]

Kennedy's insensitive and impolitic statements provoked FDR at one point to say, "This young man needs his wrists slapped rather hard."[74] Unable to depend on his ambassador, FDR worked around Kennedy on important diplomatic matters, including the destroyers-for-bases deal and other elements leading to the formation of an Anglo-American alliance. Feeling isolated and increasingly annoyed, Kennedy spoke of resigning and returning home early in 1940—perhaps in time to make a bid for the Democratic presidential nomination. Roosevelt for his part was angry with his ambassador's performance and exercised over recurrent reports of Kennedy's presidential ambitions. The president decided that, for the time being, political wisdom dictated leaving his piqued ambassador in London.[75]

In October 1940, after the Royal Air Force's success in the Battle of Britain diminished the threat of a German invasion, Kennedy thought he could return to the States without public scorn. He pressured Roosevelt by threatening to release to the press his critical views and inside knowledge of negotiations between Roosevelt and Prime Minister Churchill, revelations of which would play into the hands of isolationist groups, such as the America First Committee, and give needed ammunition to Republican presidential candidate Wendell Willkie, who charged FDR with attempting to push America into the European war.

Determined on an unprecedented third term as president, FDR set out to neutralize Kennedy's influence among isolationists and Republicans and to use him to rekindle support with the business and Irish Catholic communities. Drawing on all of his political guile and personal charm, Roosevelt called Kennedy back to the United States, told him the State Department was responsible for all his woes, and persuaded him to make a nationwide radio broadcast to announce his endorsement of Roosevelt's reelection. Joseph Kennedy told friends he made the broadcast in return for FDR's promise of support for either Joe Junior's run for the governorship of Massachusetts in 1942 or his own pursuit of the presidential nomination in 1944.[76]

Shortly after FDR's reelection, Joseph Kennedy's impetuous nature effectively ended his political career. Unable to conceal his contempt for Roosevelt, Kennedy gave an interview to the Boston *Globe* that included insensitive remarks regarding Eleanor Roosevelt, the Queen of England, and FDR. He reiterated his belief that "democracy was finished in England." Kennedy's comments, furthermore, were peppered with a casual anti-Semitism. He claimed the briefing was off the record and tried to stop publication, issues he made moot three days later by repeating the substance of his remarks before a gathering in California. Summoned by FDR to Hyde Park to explain himself, Kennedy infuriated the president, who according to some accounts called his wife into the room and exclaimed, "I never want to see that man again as long as I live. Get him out of here!"[77]

Out of necessity, FDR met a final time with Joseph Kennedy in January 1941, just long enough to dissuade him from openly siding with the isolationists against the lend-lease bill authorizing U.S. shipments of munitions and supplies to countries the President deemed vital to the defense of the U.S. Isolationists felt betrayed by Kennedy's confusing testimony before Congress, in which he neither endorsed nor opposed the bill. Relieved to be finished with this "tempermental Irish boy," FDR privately described Kennedy as "terrifically spoiled at an early age by huge financial success; thoroughly patriotic, thoroughly selfish, and thoroughly obsessed with the idea that he must leave each of his nine children with a million dollars apiece when he dies (he has told me that often). . . . To him, the future of a small capitalistic class is safer under a Hitler than under a Churchill. This is sub-conscious on his part and he does not admit it. . . . Sometimes I think I am 200 years older than he is!"[78]

Joseph Kennedy's inglorious retreat from public view had one unforeseen benefit for Robert and his brothers: their father was now free to concentrate on the advancement of their careers.

CHAPTER 2

Farewells and Foreboding

A WATERSHED YEAR for the nation and one of portentous change for the Kennedys, 1941 proved a prologue to traumatic events and family tragedies. For Robert Kennedy, the year marked the beginning of the transition from adolescent to adult.

The Kennedys and the rest of the country watched as the widening European conflict threatened to engulf America. Hitler's thunderous early successes were muted by his failure to subdue Britain. The fall of France in May 1940 had led to a pronounced shift in U.S. public opinion. Thereafter, a growing majority of Americans believed a German victory would be the worst possible outcome of the European war. International realities gradually overwhelmed isolationist sentiment. FDR's determination to make the United States the "arsenal of democracy" led the country by 1941 to institute a draft, to support the Lend-Lease of war matériel to Britain, and to tolerate other actions just short of all-out involvement in the war.

Family Transitions

In the spring of 1941, with the older children beginning to disperse, the younger children away at boarding schools, and Rose traveling a great deal, Joseph Kennedy sold the estate in Bronxville. He preferred to maintain his summer and voting residence in Hyannis Port and to spend the rest of the year in Palm Beach. Robert's twelve years at the Bronxville residence would be the longest time he would live in one house. That the move would deprive him and the younger children of a fixed home during their school years received little consideration.[1]

The house at Hyannis Port became the center of family activities. There, in the summer of 1941, Rose and Joseph Kennedy gathered their brood, none suspecting it would be the last time they would all be together.

John, just returned from a tour of South America, basked in the afterglow of the success of his book, *Why England Slept.* Published the previous summer, the book expanded his hurriedly assembled Harvard senior thesis, which his professors had graded "cum laude" even though they called it "badly written" and "defective." Rewritten and edited by *New York Times* reporter Arthur Krock; edited further by Harvey Klemmer, Joseph Kennedy's assistant; and given an introduction by Henry Luce, the publisher of *Time,* the book sold 80,000 copies. Its fleeting best-seller status was boosted by his father's purchase of a huge number of copies, rumored to be in the thousands. "You would be surprised," Joseph Kennedy informed his sons, "how a book that really makes the grade with high-class people stands you in good stead for years to come."

Still, the main ideas in the book were John's. He dispassionately analyzes the reluctance of the English people to mobilize for war by examining the historical background and political pressures shaping the 1938 Munich agreements. When John Kennedy began the thesis he was, like his father and most Americans, a believer in U.S. isolationism. By the time of publication he had moved beyond his father's perspective to urge that the United States not follow England's poor example. Still not ready to argue for actual intervention, he advocated preparedness and an arms buildup. John Kennedy would carry the lessons of Munich and the failures attending appeasement (his father's views notwithstanding) into his presidency.[2]

Joe Junior could not conceal his envy over the recognition John received, commenting sourly that the book "seemed to represent a lot of work but didn't prove anything."[3] The eldest son, who faithfully adhered to his father's viewpoints on most matters, had entered Harvard Law School and served as an anti-Roosevelt, pro–James Farley delegate to the Democratic National Convention in 1940. Foreseeing the inevitability of U.S. involvement in the war, he dropped out of Harvard and joined the navy aviation program in May 1941. Not to be outdone, John spent the summer maneuvering to secure a commission himself, but his weak back and chronic health problems (brought on by the as yet undiagnosed presence of Addison's disease) left him physically unfit for the service. After some string-pulling, Joe Kennedy found a navy physician willing to overlook his son's myriad ailments and certify his fitness. At summer's end, three months before Pearl Harbor, both of Joseph Kennedy's oldest sons held navy commissions.[4]

That summer Rosemary's behavior became unbearable to Joseph Kennedy. To control her sexual urges and violent mood swings, he allowed surgeons to perform a prefrontal lobotomy on her. Unable to care for herself after the operation, she was placed in a private facility in Wisconsin. He tried at first to conceal Rosemary's whereabouts, telling those who inquired that she had withdrawn to a religious order.[5] Over time, as public awareness about mental disabilities and their stigma faded, the Kennedys openly acknowledged Rosemary's condition. Under Eunice Kennedy Shriver, who has always attended to Rosemary, the Joseph P. Kennedy, Jr., Foundation, began in 1957 to focus much of its attention on children with mental disabilities. About that time, too, Rose Kennedy attended symposia and provided personal comfort and encouragement to parents of the mentally disabled.[6]

It was typical of Joseph Kennedy to manipulate the facts regarding Rosemary's and John's physical problems. More concerned with appearance than reality and unwilling to trust the public to accept any flaws in his family, he began systematically to suppress and contain unflattering information about any family member, a process that embraced the ever-widening arc of John Kennedy's romantic adventures. One such adventure that began in 1941 menacingly reverberated for decades.

That October, when Ensign John Kennedy was assigned to Naval Intelligence in Washington, D.C., John's sister Kathleen introduced him to a stunning co-worker, Inga Arvad, then married to Paul Fejos.

The former Miss Denmark, who had socialized with leaders of the Third Reich, had been photographed with Adolph Hitler while on assignment for a Danish newspaper at the 1936 Berlin Olympics. Suspecting Arvad to be a German agent, the FBI and the Office of Naval Intelligence (ONI) placed her and the young intelligence officer under visual and electronic surveillance.

Although aware of Inga and her husband's extensive but nonconspiratorial connections with fascist regimes, John Kennedy could not resist her allure. He continued to see her even though, as he told a friend, "I found out that son-of-a-bitch Hoover had put a microphone under the mattress!" Once Hoover established that Arvad was not a spy, he nevertheless continued the surveillance, unwilling to ignore the ominous nature of her past or her husband's business connections to Nazi Germany. Kennedy was soon transferred out of intelligence. Rather than joining others of his background and breeding who dominated the clandestine world of espionage and intelligence in the wartime Office of Strategic Services (OSS), he ended up skippering a PT (Patrol Torpedo) boat.[7]

The day the Japanese attacked Pearl Harbor Joseph Kennedy sent FDR a telegram: "Name the battlefront. I'm yours to command." FDR ignored the request for eight weeks and then offered Kennedy a minor position expediting ship construction. Kennedy refused to be humbled or to work his way back into Roosevelt's good graces. By declining the position, he gave President Roosevelt license to put him off for the duration of the war.

The farther Kennedy drifted from Roosevelt, the closer he got to J. Edgar Hoover. Beginning in 1943 Kennedy volunteered to be a Special Service Contact on national defense matters for the FBI. Until 1961, he regularly offered the FBI director unsolicited advice and opinions on various matters, including possible Communist infiltration of the motion picture industry. Kennedy meticulously cultivated Hoover's friendship, flattering him with letters of oily praise, slathering on effusive thanks for small or imagined favors, sending expensive Christmas gifts, and inviting him to Hyannis Port and Palm Beach. Kennedy, in return, received small courtesies from the Bureau and a place on Hoover's Special Correspondents List, an honor the director accorded only to influential dignitaries, uncritical benefactors, and, according to at least one source, persons on whom he had some "dirt."[8] Although Hoover and Kennedy were politically like-minded, if Kennedy's motive for striking up the friendship was to protect his sons' political futures, or if more specifically he hoped that Hoover would destroy or suppress the files on Inga Arvad, he greatly misjudged his man.

Joseph Kennedy assuaged the frustrations in his own life by taking an extraordinary interest in his children's. Robert later acknowledged that by this point his father had "decided his aims could best be accomplished" through his sons, for whom he now began to develop specific plans. Joe Junior, he told a listener partly in jest, would be president of the United States, John a university president. "And then there's Bobby," Joe said, tapping his nose in a cunning manner, "he's the lawyer."[9] To Robert's disappointment, however, most of Joseph Kennedy's energies and expectations were focused on his two eldest sons.

Adolescent Agonies

Robert during this period underwent a fundamental transformation. His personality and behavior were shaped by his abiding sense of moral certainty, by his attempt to gain his father's approval, and by his struggle to accomplish something as significant as his brothers' colorful achievements. His earnest nature made him feel an outsider among his more fun-loving, less doctrinaire siblings.

Unsure of his place within the family and, like most American adolescents, concerned with how others perceived him, Robert developed an intense identification with his older brothers and his father. To Rose's regret, Joseph Kennedy gradually asserted greater control over her "little pet." Rarely defiant of her husband, Rose did challenge him in a quiet tug-of-war over Robert's prep school education, in fact over that of all their sons.

On this topic Joseph Kennedy employed the same reasoning his parents had, preferring to send his sons to Protestant boarding schools where they could gain a toehold in WASP society. But when Joseph was away or temporarily distracted, Rose countermanded her husband's wishes and introduced her sons to the spiritual qualities she treasured from her own Catholic education. Joseph intended John to follow Joe Junior to Choate, an utterly Protestant prep school. But when the time came for John to enroll, his father was in California making movies and entertaining Gloria Swanson. Rose seized the opportunity to send John instead to Canterbury, a Catholic school. When John grew miserable from a combination of the discipline, the catechism, and his own health problems, his father arranged his transfer to Choate.[10]

Upon his return from England in the fall of 1939, Robert was sent to St. Paul's, an Episcopal school in New Hampshire. When he had difficulty getting settled in his sixth school in nine years, Rose blamed the school. With her husband stranded in England, she transferred Robert to Portsmouth Priory on Narragansett Bay in Portsmouth, Rhode Island. Run by Benedictine monks, the Priory offered a liberal education from a thoroughly Catholic view. Robert, required to attend morning and evening prayers and go to mass four times a week, said all the praying made him "feel like a saint."[11]

At the Priory Robert began to take an active interest in sports. He managed the hockey team and, thanks to lessons from brother Joe and from a private sailing instructor, became vice-commodore of the yacht club. His consuming passion, however, was football, but he lacked the size and coordination to make the varsity team. In all, he was no happier at the Priory than he had been elsewhere. "What I remember most vividly about growing up," Robert Kennedy recalled, "was going to a lot of different schools always having to make new friends, and that I was very awkward. I dropped things and fell down. I was pretty quiet most of the time. And I didn't mind being alone."[12]

Restive with his mother's choice of the Priory, Robert had problems adjusting. When his grades failed to improve, he blamed himself, not the school: "I guess it was because I wasn't studying as hard as I should have that I got such bad marks." His mother's letters urged him to read more, to strengthen his vocabulary, and to "please get on your toes." Yet Robert was developing in other ways. John noticed that his brother's strength had increased "to such a degree that I seriously believe he will be bouncing me around plenty in two more years. He really is unusually strong and that school [the Priory] seems to have done him an awful lot of good as he has improved immensely as everyone has noticed—in every way."[13]

By Christmas of 1941 even his mother noticed a few changes. She was pleased that Robert could play a fair game of golf, shooting 95, and "astonished" by his skill at bridge; otherwise, she said, he "was just the same." Annoyed when Robert refused to mingle with young people at their club in Palm Beach, she complained he was "very unsociable." Family friends observed changes his parents missed. Chuck Spalding, one of John's friends, recalled how hard Robert worked "to toughen himself up and get rid of that vulnerability everyone had remarked on since he was a boy. . . . The drive was incessant, just fierce. He simply remade himself. He got so he could just go through a wall."[14]

Improvement came too slowly to suit Robert's father. In September 1942 the family chauffeur deposited Robert at Milton Academy, once described as a "consummate WASP school," just south of Boston, his eighth school in ten years. His weak entering examinations and low initial grades prompted the headmaster to suggest reducing Robert's class load, which would have delayed his graduation, a prospect that triggered a personal appearance by Joseph Kennedy—he visited his children's schools only to head off trouble. The headmaster blamed Robert's problems on his rootlessness, but Robert's weak performance also owed something to his father's relative indifference.[15] Joseph Kennedy may have inundated Joe Junior and John with advice and reprimands regarding their studies, but his letters to Robert, as Doris Goodwin observed, reveal a subtly different array of expectations. Less demanding and less involved in his third son's education, Joseph Kennedy gave Robert the impression that his education was less important. Without his father's prodding, Robert had little incentive to do better.[16]

When Robert entered Milton at the beginning of his junior year, the social cliques that had developed among the students found no room for him. The few classmates who recalled anything about him commented on his Catholic devotion, his almost paralyzing shyness, his sexual prudery, and his all-out efforts for sports. Some noted his developing concern for the problems of others and for the plight of the underdog. He took no role in student governance and drew no attention to himself. Unlike his brother John, who was nearly expelled from Choate for organizing an authority-defying group known as the "Muckers," Robert never challenged the Milton hierarchy. The headmaster said Robert was a "very intelligent boy, quiet and shy, but not outstanding, and he left no special mark on Milton."[17]

Yet Robert made two lifelong friends at the school, David Hackett and Samuel Adams. Hackett, the hero of Milton, a star football player and outstanding student, recalled that Robert was "neither a natural athlete nor a natural student nor a natural success with girls and had no natural gift for popularity. Nothing came easily for him."[18] Still, his identity as Hackett's best friend gave Kennedy status at Milton and much-needed self-assurance. With Hackett's encouragement Robert doggedly worked his way up to a second-team backfield position in football.

Sam Adams's clearest memory of Robert as a teenager concerned his profound devotion to his faith. Robert walked a mile and a half to the nearest Catholic church each Sunday and on special Mass days, Adams recalled, and offered him spiritual comfort when Adams's father died in an accident. Robert Kennedy's prudish attitudes toward sex and his intolerance of smutty jokes also left an impression: "He wouldn't laugh at them, wouldn't even listen."[19]

Robert started to date while at Milton; he took Mary Bailey to dances, where he refused to dance, and escorted her home from chapel, walking about "four feet behind, his head down, looking out from underneath his forelock." Robert "was moon-faced then," she said, with "no hint of the angular frame that eventually came out." He "mostly stood on one foot with the other toe resting on top his hands way down in his pockets." Robert would mumble to himself, "Who could be dippier than me?" He occasionally invited a girl to spend a weekend at Hyannis Port, but, according to researchers who have looked in vain for evidence to the contrary, unlike his older brothers, he restrained his sexual urges.[20]

His strongest apparent urge was to follow his older brothers into the navy. By the end of 1942, U.S. military fortunes had begun to improve; the nightmarish reversals of the first months of the war were halted, and the promise of American successes buoyed public spirits. Wanting desperately to get in on the action and prove himself to his father and brothers, Robert was torn between following Joe Junior into aviation or John into PT boats.

The two men competed for their younger brother's allegiance. Joe Junior invited Robert to visit him at Norfolk, smuggled him aboard his airplane on a training flight, and even allowed him to take the copilot's controls when they were over the ocean.[21] John Kennedy, perhaps out of his rivalry with Joe Junior or perhaps because of the large losses among Allied pilots, implored friends and family members to steer Robert away from aviation toward small naval craft, such as destroyers or PT boats. In letters home from the Pacific John tried to convince Robert not to make an early commitment to the military, writing that he was "too young to be out here for a while" and could be more "effective" after a year of college and officer's training. "To try to come steaming out here at eighteen is no good," John wrote to his father, "but I imagine you know all of the above and are doing something about it."[22]

John's good sense and maturity were tested in August 1943 when his *PT-109* was rammed by a Japanese destroyer and sunk. The episode began as a bizarre shipwreck, but Kennedy demonstrated genuine courage in saving the life of one man and in securing his crew's rescue. The *New York Times* declared him a hero just as Joe Junior was preparing to depart Hyannis Port for combat flying duty in England. One of his father's retainers, former Boston police commissioner Joe Timilty, recalled Joe Junior as enraged by the attention given to John and frustrated by the family's disregard for his own sacrifices. The eldest son left for England promising, "By God, I'll show them."[23]

When Joe arrived in England, Kathleen was already there, having left the United States in June 1943 to work for the Red Cross. In May 1944, against her parents' wishes, Kathleen married a Protestant nobleman, William John Robert Cavendish, the Marquess of Hartington, known as Billy Hartington. The shock of Kathleen's marriage outside the faith had hardly settled upon the family when word was received on 12 August 1944 of Joe Junior's death. Aching to exceed John's accomplishment, Joe had volunteered to fly a plane loaded with explosives on a mission against a German rocket site in France. At a certain point he would bail out, and the plane would be flown into the target by radio control. The plane exploded prematurely. Nothing of Joe was ever found. Two weeks later, a German sniper killed Kathleen's husband in Belguim. "Life is cruel," Kathleen wrote. "Luckily, I am a Kennedy."[24]

On the brilliant sunny day in Hyannis Port when two somber-faced priests delivered the news of Joe's death, Joseph Kennedy ordered his children to participate as planned in a sailing race scheduled for that afternoon. Robert obeyed without question. John refused.

Joseph Kennedy had spent the war years seeing after his children's affairs and planning Joe's political future. "All my plans for my own future were all tied up with young Joe and that has gone smash," he wrote to a friend. John wrote in his memorial tribute to Joe, "His wordly success was so assured and inevitable that his death seems to have cut into the natural order of things." Feeling the "best part of his life was over," Joseph Kennedy sank into a gloomy, vindictive mood and, for several months, emotionally withdrew from the family. John's memorial book, *As We Remember Joe,* did not impress a father who thought the Kennedys should conceal their emotions.[25]

Then and later, Rose offered the strongest example to the children in time of mourning. Finding solace in her Church, she grew more resolute (and at the same time more distant). She said that the best way to survive tragedy was "to turn some part of the loss to a positive, affirmative use for the benefit of other people." Two years later, the family dedicated the Joseph P. Kennedy, Jr., Foundation. Rose intended the foundation as a monument to their fallen son, but her husband used it initially to further John's political career, naming John its titular head and featuring him in all of its news releases.[26]

Joe Junior's death came at a time of personal struggle for Robert, deepening his feelings of uncertainty and inadequacy. Already frustrated at not matching his brothers' academic and social accomplishments, deprived of the chance to approach their records as war heroes, Robert was greatly distressed over his father's withdrawal. What was he to think when his father despaired so over the loss of Joe Junior? Was his brother so important and he so insignificant in the scope of things? Robert's anxiety was doubtless tinged with guilt over the removal of a rival for his father's affections. Just as later tragedies would, Joe Junior's death propelled Robert into an extended period of isolation and introspection.

During World War II teenaged boys faced an onslaught of media images—popular songs, radio programs, advertisements, and propaganda-laden motion pictures—romanticizing strident masculinity, volunteer enlistments, and war.[27] Youth was a trap Robert yearned to escape. For him, the only question was, When will I be allowed to enlist?

His son's preoccupation with military service and repeated threats to drop out of Milton and enlist worried Joseph Kennedy. To his relief, Robert waited dutifully until just after his seventeenth birthday, the earliest age at which one could enlist with parental consent. Then he donned his brother John's favorite checked London drape coat and posed with his father and a naval recruiting officer for Boston newspaper photographs of the induction of a third Kennedy son into the U.S. Navy.[28]

Reluctantly, Robert agreed to defer active duty until he had completed officer training and gotten some of his college education behind him. In January 1944 he graduated from Milton. Two months later, he entered Harvard University and the Naval Officers College Training Program, better known as the V-12 unit. Admission to Harvard, an important accomplishment, drew grudging praise and even some slight encouragement from his father, tempered by a discouraging assessment of his latest efforts. "I don't think any real strides had been made [at Milton]," Joseph Kennedy wrote Robert. In a closing that reflected his tepid confidence in Robert's abilities, the father admonished the Harvard freshman to "stick in there and work as hard as you possibly can."[29]

Now more than ever, Robert's survival depended on winning his father's respect and praise. Gradual improvement in his studies and a flood of letters began to attract his father's attention. Robert's main ambition was to achieve at least symbolic parity with his older brothers. "I wish Dad," he wrote to his father, "that you would write me a letter as you used to Joe and Jack about what you think about the different political events and the war as I'd like to understand what's going on better than I do now." Joseph Kennedy's reply, a two-page single-spaced letter summarizing his view of political conditions, was "just what I wanted," Robert wrote back. His father's increased influence had its downside, as an outwardly tough, combative attitude gradually overwhelmed Robert's former sweetness and defenselessness.[30] His persistent shyness, a sign really of Robert's lingering uncertainties, was often taken for sullen arrogance by those outside the family.

Robert made virtually no attempt to socialize with classmates and became a loner in the Harvard V-12 unit, whose members included some decorated veterans of naval campaigns. Neither they nor the more typical Harvard undergraduates just out of high school found Robert's behavior acceptable. For instance, rather than take his meals in the dormitory, Robert often ate at restaurants in Boston or Cambridge where, his classmates presumed, he could order a decent steak dinner. One classmate said Kennedy came across as a "spoiled rich kid" who was "arrogant and not a little stuck up." Robert had the toothiest smile in the yearbook; for his picture he wore his enlisted sailor's hat squared away in regulation manner, rather than at the jaunty angle preferred by most of his classmates.[31]

During these years of transition and internal turmoil, Robert found school "inconsequential." Writing to his Milton roommate, David Hackett, he described himself as "my usual moody self," adding, "If I don't get the hell out of here soon I'll die." Of his desire to get into the war immediately, he admitted that "the Kennedys have all about shot their bolt." He told Hackett, "I wish to hell . . . people would have let me alone to do as I wished, but I suppose I simply must be an officer."[32]

Only after the war was over and only because his father arranged it did Robert Kennedy fulfill his obsession for sea duty aboard a fighting vessel; he resigned from the officer's training program to enter active service. "Pappy has finally got some angle for getting me out of college . . . and put on Joe's ship," he wrote to John. Indeed, when the USS *Joseph P. Kennedy, Jr.* set out on its shakedown cruise on 1 February 1946, Robert Kennedy was aboard as a seaman apprentice, standing watches and chipping and painting the decks.

"There I was," he lamented years later, "on a ship named for my brother, sailing the placid waters, and watching beautiful sunsets. Jack had been a hero. Joe had died a hero. Okay, I didn't especially want to be a hero, but it was galling not to have seen any action at all." For a time he endured gentle ribbing from John and his friends about being "enlisted personnel" and an "ordinary seaman." (Although he seldom mentioned his service as an enlisted man, it must have opened his eyes regarding how others outside his stratum lived.) Shortly after the ship's return from its Caribbean cruise, on 30 May 1946, Robert's brief stint in the navy ended with an honorable discharge.[33]

Those who knew Robert or met him during and just after the war were struck by his straitlaced attitudes and his submissiveness to his father's dictates. One revealing incident occurred when John invited a group of PT boat buddies to Hyannis Port for Labor Day weekend 1944. Bridling under Joseph Kennedy's house rule of only one drink per guest before dinner, John's crew helped themselves to a few more. The wife of one guest remembered that Robert, a "scrawny little guy in a white sailor suit," was "very upset that we were sneaking booze in the kitchen. He was afraid his father might catch us and he knew his father's wrath. But Kathleen handled him. She told him to get lost."[34]

His brothers and sisters were sometimes contemptuous of Robert's penchant for making moralistic judgments on virtually every matter, including their personal behavior. He had been unable to disguise his confusion and disappointment when Joe Junior, John, and Kathleen each violated church dictum, not to mention their mother's wishes, by conducting romantic affairs outside the faith. His siblings viewed Robert as a moody, combative, pranksterish prude, not likely to amount to much despite his iron-willed determination. Even Eunice, the most tolerant and socially sensitive of the Kennedy children, harbored few expectations for Robert at that time. "Bobby?" she asked when responding to praise for her brothers Joe Junior and John, "Forget it. Let's talk about the other boys."[35]

Robert was the only Kennedy son to win (or want to win) their father's standing offer of two thousand dollars for not smoking or drinking before their twenty-first birthdays. LeMoyne Billings recalled that Robert drank only soft drinks when they visited bars during their summer 1946 tour together of Latin America. Similarly, when he returned to Harvard that fall, classmates noted his prim and proper posture, his disdain for those who traveled to Boston's red-light districts, and his general lack of interest in partying and having a good time.[36]

Political Baptism

A turning point in the lives of John and Robert Kennedy came with their involvement together in John's 1946 primary election campaign for the U.S. House of Representatives in Massachusetts's Eleventh Congressional district.

John Kennedy's entry into politics was not unexpected. Joseph Kennedy assuaged his grief over Joe Junior's death by immersing himself in backroom political maneuvering to create possibilities for John to win elected office in Massachusetts. Contrary to legend, John was not without ambition for public office, as his close friends well knew. "Nothing could have kept Jack out of politics . . . no matter what," said LeMoyne Billings. His health, however, presented a major obstacle. Discharged from the navy on 1 March 1945 because of a variety of medical problems—some diagnosed, some not—John was gaunt and morbidly thin. He spent several months at a spa in Arizona recuperating from a failed back operation and trying to regain some semblance of fitness. He looked forward, as he explained to his PT-109 buddy Red Fay, to working with his "Dad trying to parlay a lost PT boat and a bad back into a political advantage."[37]

The Eleventh District seat became available when the incumbent, the old family rival James Michael Curley, was elected mayor of Boston in November 1945, a victory, sources say, aided by a substantial contribution from Joseph Kennedy. The Democratic primary election to fill Curley's congressional seat attracted ten candidates. In the predominantly Democratic Eleventh District, with Republican opposition weak and disorganized, the June primary election effectively determined the winner. The early favorite was an entrenched Irish pol, Mike Neville, who even John Kennedy later admitted was "the better man for the district and deserved to win."[38]

John Kennedy had misgivings about his brother working in the campaign. "It's damn nice of Bobby wanting to help," John told Red Fay, "but I can't see that sober, silent face breathing new vigor into the ranks." When efforts to loosen him up failed, Robert was exiled to East Cambridge to work three Italian American wards controlled by Neville. "The kid can't do any harm there," one campaign worker said. Fay conceded that Robert campaigned "as if his life and Jack's depended on it." Lem Billings, who was in charge of Cambridge, remembered how young, aggressive, and territorial Robert seemed. During those initial labors on his brother's behalf, he walked door to door each morning in the poorest part of Cambridge, introducing himself to residents. In the afternoons he joined in pickup basketball and football games with local youths. John Kennedy did not carry East Cambridge in the primary, but perhaps because of Robert he lost it by less than expected.[39]

The 1946 congressional campaign served not just as John and Robert Kennedy's political baptism but as their indoctrination into Irish political practices. Massachusetts's Eleventh Congressional District included East Boston and the North End, Cambridge, Somerville, and Charlestown. What the brothers knew about the district's politics and mostly working-class people was limited to anecdotes and lore passed to them by their mother and grandfather Fitzgerald. Neither Kennedy brother had ever lived in Boston. John used a hotel as his voting address in 1946. Later, both established legal residence in a three-room apartment at 122 Bowdoin Street. Robert retained this apartment until 1964, when he ran for the U.S. Senate from New York.

Not surprisingly, the Kennedy brothers had little regard for either the Irish Democratic machine politics of Boston or the gregarious, often transparent, mannerisms and crude, patronage-based approach of the machine pols. But the two men, entering politics with no agenda, public philosophy, or moral commitment, quickly learned how to use the machine to their advantage. John Kennedy's approach harmonized with Irish political traditions that emphasized loyalty and personal leadership over abstract principles.[40]

At first merely skeptical, the Irish pols came to resent John Kennedy, who, they said, was a Democrat in name only, a "kid who had never run for anything in his life," the tool of his powerful father. Veteran political operators were appalled at John's absence the day his father announced his son's candidacy.[41]

The Kennedys' sentimental link to the political past was their eighty-two-year-old grandfather Fitzgerald. He made introductions, organized his pol friends, and tutored John on techniques for working the crowds and making a lasting personal impression. Robert, unmoved by such tricks, thought his grandfather's "effectiveness in some of those areas was not overwhelming." Disdaining the contributions of party regulars like his grandfather, Robert insisted that John's success rested on his appeal "to young people" and "to people who had not been involved in politics and to a lot of [returning] servicemen."[42]

The campaign's practical and tactical political decision making fell to Joe Kane, a first cousin of Joseph Kennedy and one of several professional politicians brought into the campaign by John's father. Kane was responsible for reining in Jack's PT buddies and the other enthusiastic volunteers who gave the campaign a false veneer of refreshing amateurishness. He came up with a campaign slogan to emphasize John Kennedy's youth and his record in the war: "The New Generation Offers a Leader."[43]

John gradually made his peace with the Irish politicians and Democratic regulars. Robert did not. His obvious distrust of the street-corner pols, his ill-concealed contempt for the "Dearos" who sat around campaign headquarters smoking cigars and kibitzing, and his seeming arrogance and uncompromising attitude would not be forgotten, nor would their effects be washed away by the normally cleansing tides of electoral victory.[44]

Future Kennedy campaigns would display the Kennedy trademarks worked out in the 1946 campaign. Their use of the Democratic political machine, combined with Joe Kennedy's money and the unique Kennedy campaign style, created a new force in U.S. politics. As Thomas P. "Tip" O'Neill, Jr., elected to John's vacated seat in 1952 and later Speaker of the House, noted firsthand, being a Kennedy "was more than family affiliation. It developed into an entire political party, with its own people, its own approach, and its own strategies."[45]

The public's first inkling of the Kennedy party approach came with the intense and extensive involvement of the Kennedy family in John's 1946 campaign. Rose and daughters Eunice and Patricia hosted "house parties" in constituents' homes. Typically at one of these affairs, John made a brief speech and then left one or more of the Kennedy women to talk about the family, while he went on to another party, sometimes attending six or seven in a single evening. Socially conscious Boston Irish came to these gatherings to see Rose and to touch and be touched by the Irish American aristocracy.[46]

Every campaign decision required the personal approval of Joseph Kennedy, the Kennedy party's master strategist. He met each day with the candidate to analyze events and plan the next steps. He approved staff appointments, examined public opinion polls, reviewed advertising copy. The father thought it necessary to manufacture an image for his son, "to sell Jack like soap flakes," as he put it. He paid for the printing and distribution of a hundred thousand reprints of a *Readers' Digest* article on the *PT-109* adventure and spent hours on the telephone with newspaper reporters, editors, and publishers. As a favor to Joseph Kennedy, William Randolph Hearst's *Boston American* did not print the name of Mike Neville, John's major opponent, or even accept an advertisement from him.[47]

Estimates vary, but some say Joseph Kennedy spent as much as $300,000 on John Kennedy's first campaign, six times the amount Kennedy's successor spent six years later. The actual amount spent for this or any of the Kennedy campaigns may never be known; the family maintains tight control over existing records. Besides, political insiders have indicated that most of the outlays were cash transactions—many handled by Joseph Kennedy himself—often made in restrooms, basements, or behind locked doors. Pols winked at the practice of disbursing money to pay poll watchers and to reimburse homeowners for the expenses of the Kennedy house parties, knowing they were just buying votes. None of the paid or volunteer staff knew for certain how much was spent. Neither evidently did either of Joseph Kennedy's sons. Their father kept that information to himself and refused to entrust a dime to anyone not his personal employee. He took few chances in assuring his son's success.[48]

The sad irony of the matter, as Nigel Hamilton pointed out in *JFK: Reckless Youth,* is that the father underestimated his son's qualities, not the least of which were his extraordinary charm and personal magnetism. In Robert's estimation his brother was elected to Congress on the basis of "his own personality, plus the fact that he had the Kennedy name." But Robert was hardly in position to be the best judge. He knew little of his father's doings or expenditures. Joe Kane, who was better positioned, said the father's money was secondary but exaggerated when he added that "Jack could have gone to Congress like everyone else for ten cents."[49] John Kennedy easily won the primary election in June.

Harvard and Virginia

Since John faced only token opposition in the general election, Robert returned to Harvard for the 1946 fall semester. For the next two years he centered his attentions on football, paying scant attention to his studies. He roomed with Kenneth O'Donnell, quarterback and team captain. "I can't think of anyone," O'Donnell recalled, "who had less right to make the varsity squad than Bobby." Too slow and at 155 pounds too small for major college football, Robert played "like a wild Indian," said one teammate. Don Stone, the starting center and himself an army veteran, recalled Kennedy's toughness and the way he "willed" himself onto the varsity. Even with several bigger and faster athletes at his position, Robert Kennedy started at left end when Harvard took the field for its 1947 season opener against Western Maryland. He caught a short touchdown pass from O'Donnell in the blowout victory, but then injured his leg in practice and did not play again until the Yale game, when a sympathetic coach briefly put him in the game to insure Robert's varsity letter. Winning the award was an enormous boost to his ego. Finally, he had accomplished something his two older brothers had not. Hailed by his mother and sisters as their conquering football "hero," Robert sported his letter sweater and struck macho poses for snapshots that went into the family album.[50]

At Harvard Robert associated with people far different from those he had known during his sheltered upbringing. He was particularly attracted to a group of older football players, many of whom had served in the war and seen combat; several were from working-class families of Greek, Italian, and Armenian descent. They ignored him at first, "just a rich kid who happened to be hanging around," but several became friendly. When John Kennedy met this group at Robert's wedding, he said he had never seen such an "outrageous, irreverent group of characters in his life."[51]

Robert prided himself on his new toughness. But the paradoxical blend of this and other emerging characteristics with the now submerged tender side of his personality led to impulsive, often puzzling, acts. Known, for instance, by his classmates for his unquestioning acceptance of the Church and its doctrines, Robert once surprised them by publicly confronting a Catholic priest. In an episode that also suggested an expanding tolerance and sensitivity toward others, he became infuriated with the railings of Father Leonard Feeney, who was notorious for his controversial views of Catholic doctrine and his intemperate commentaries on Jews. Feeney was lecturing to Harvard students at the St. Benedict Center when Robert engaged the fiery priest in a public argument. His mother was horrified. "But you know," she told a friend of Robert's years later, "Bobby was right. When the Vatican excommunicated Father Feeney [five years after the argument], I knew Bobby had been right."[52]

Maybe so, but his personality had taken on a rough, disagreeably moody edge. Even when he argued on the side of noble causes, his comments had a cutting quality. A classmate recalled Robert as an outspoken debater who held his own at dormitory bull sessions, where he could be "kind of a nasty, brutal, humorless little fellow when he got going." Even his friends demonstrated little warmth or affection for him. "Bobby and I were very close friends from the beginning," George Terrien, an ex-navy fighter pilot, recalled. Terrien, who later married one of Ethel Skakel Kennedy's sisters, said, "You couldn't live with him, but we got along. He was a royal pain in the ass. He was a bulldog about certain things, but I tolerated him."[53]

Kenneth O'Donnell remembered an incident in a Cambridge bar, however, when Robert's moodiness turned to surliness and his toughness to unprovoked aggression. Robert was buying beers for the house in celebration of his twenty-first birthday. Another birthday celebration, this one for a student named John Magnuson, was taking place in the bar at the same time. When the Magnuson group sang "Happy Birthday, John," Kennedy became incensed at their ingratitude and, according to O'Donnell, hit Magnuson over the head with a beer bottle. O'Donnell said he visited Magnuson in the hospital to apologize, because "it just wasn't his [Bobby's] nature to apologize."[54] The attack on Magnuson marked a nadir in Robert's personal journey through the Kennedys' masculine rites of passage. The aggressive inner fire continued to smolder and occasionally to flare, but thereafter he began to channel his energies to more cerebral pursuits.

Robert graduated from Harvard in March 1948. His father, as he had for John and Joe Junior during career interludes, arranged for him to go abroad as an accredited newspaper correspondent. His paid traveling companion was George Terrien. "Old Joe," as Terrien ungraciously phrased it later, "wanted me to go along to take care of Bobby."[55] They visited the major European cities, as well as Tel Aviv, Cairo, Beirut, and Jerusalem. The *Boston Post* published four of Robert's articles on the Middle East situation and the impact of the state of Israel's establishment in May 1948. Robert came away from a visit to an Israeli kibbutz admiring the "dignity and self-respect" of the Jews; he noted that the Israelis were an "immensely proud and determined people," "hardy and tough" and possessed of an "undying spirit" the Arabs could never match. Thanking the editor for accepting Robert's articles, Joseph Kennedy added, "I think he writes better than Joe or Jack, but as a third son, he has had a lot of trouble basking in the reflected glory of Joe and Jack."[56]

During the trip Robert was recovering from jaundice at the Grande Hotel in Rome when word arrived that Kathleen Kennedy had been killed in an airplane crash near Lyons, France, on 13 May. She was en route to Paris with her new love, Lord Peter Fitzwilliam, to meet her father and seek his consent for their marriage. Fitzwilliam, a wealthy English peer, was a married Protestant in the process of divorce. Joseph Kennedy manipulated newspaper accounts of his daughter's death to eliminate mention of the intended marriage. Rose Kennedy, who had warned Kathleen that she would be disowned and regarded as dead if she married Fitzwilliam, refused to attend her daughter's funeral. For appearance's sake, she entered a hospital for routine tests and kept the rest of the children, except Robert, near her at Hyannis Port. Grief-stricken, Joseph Kennedy gratefully accepted the offer of Billy Hartington's family, Kathleen's former in-laws, to make all of the funeral arrangements. After a memorial service in London, with the inconsolable father the only family member in attendance, Kathleen was buried in the Devonshire family plot at Chatsworth in the English countryside.[57]

Terrien remembered that "Bobby broke down like a little kid" over Kathleen's death. When well enough to travel he visited his sister's grave and talked with her London housekeeper about Kathleen's last years in England. As he left, the housekeeper recalled his saying, "We will not mention her again." Robert's love for his sister conflicted with his faith in his Church and its doctrines, but he named his first child Kathleen Hartington Kennedy, reportedly with the proviso that she never be called "Kick."[58]

Returning to the United States that fall, Robert entered the University of Virginia Law School. His mediocre Harvard grades made his admission conditional. With George Terrien, admitted at the same time, he moved into a five-room apartment in Charlottesville whose landlord remembered Kennedy's "arrogant rich-boy's attitude" toward furniture and the belongings of others. He blamed Kennedy, not Terrien, for taking little care to protect the furnishings, for neglecting to replace broken items, and for tramping through the apartment in football cleats. He could complain of no parties, women, or raucous behavior, however; if anything, Robert's views had become more prudish. He expressed disgust with the loose sexual behavior of law students at parties. Considered priggish by his classmates, he apparently made few new friends.[59]

Robert graduated in the middle of his class. One professor judged his work "competent," another believed Robert made it on "sheer persistence," and still others thought he had the native ability to excel but exerted only enough effort to get by. His singular, not insignificant, accomplishment was chairing the Student Legal Forum, the three-person committee that arranged for guest speakers. Relying on his father's connections, Robert brought in such prominent individuals as Supreme Court justice William O. Douglas, former president Herbert Hoover, Senator Joseph R. McCarthy, Representative John F. Kennedy, and, of course, Joseph P. Kennedy.

In the spring of 1951 Robert found himself the center of controversy when on behalf of the Student Legal Forum he extended an invitation to Dr. Ralph Bunche, undersecretary-general of the United Nations, mediator of the 1948 Arab-Israeli war, and winner the previous year of the Nobel Prize for Peace. Bunche, an African American, informed Kennedy that he would not speak before a segregated gathering. Robert then tried to push a resolution through the student council requiring racially integrated seating for the speech. The motion failed, because the council claimed to believe that a Virginia law banned such a meeting.

Robert labeled the student council's stance "morally indefensible" in a statement to the university president. Asked by his fellow students to compromise, Kennedy exploded. "You're all gutless," he yelled at a meeting. An observer remembered that "the madder he got, the worse he got at talking. Very little came out." Eventually, two of Robert's law professors, his law school dean, and the president of the university settled the matter by declaring that a recent Supreme Court ruling (*Sweatt v. Painter*) banning racial segregation in higher education applied in this instance. Bunche spoke as scheduled to an integrated audience.[60]

Ethel Skakel

Robert Kennedy's academic achievements paled next to his older brothers', and he lacked the social graces they demonstrated in their early and middle twenties. Yet in many ways he was more mature and responsible than either had been at the same age and better prepared to assume adult obligations.

The maturity came with his love and courtship of Ethel Skakel. "Bobby," Eunice Kennedy recalled, "was a lonely, very sensitive and unfulfilled youngster." Then "he met Ethel, and all the love and appreciation for which she seemed to have an infinite capacity came pouring down on him. How he blossomed."[61]

Ethel Skakel grew up in a family environment outwardly similar to Robert's. Born 11 April 1928 in Chicago, Ethel was the sixth of seven children of George and Ann Skakel. Irish-born Ann Brannack Skakel was a large, good-hearted woman, who Ethel's brothers and some family friends referred to as "Big Ann" because of her size and domineering mannerisms. A devout Catholic, she inculcated her faith in her children, proselytized for the Church, and organized her children's lives around religious obligations. When not filled with priests and nuns, the house was an entertainment center for the clients and partners of George Skakel's vast business interests. A Dutch Protestant who never embraced the Catholic church, George Skakel started work as an eight-dollar-a-week railroad clerk and eventually built a coal and coke business into a diversified privately owned enterprise, Great Lakes Carbon Corporation. By the time his daughter Ethel met Robert Kennedy, Skakel was a millionaire many times over, as rich or richer than Joseph Kennedy, yet virtually unknown. He liked it that way. He refused to give newspaper interviews, once noting, "You can't quote Silence."[62]

When Ethel was five years old, Skakel moved his family east, nearer his business interests. After brief stays in rented mansions in Monmouth Beach, New Jersey, and Larchmont and Rye, New York, the Skakels moved to a three-story, thirty-one-room English country manor house set on ten and one-half acres on Lake Avenue in Greenwich, Connecticut. The estate included a guest house, a tea house, two servants' houses, a seventy-five-foot swimming pool, a six-car garage, a small stable, and formal gardens that before the Depression had required the daily services of eighty-three gardeners—plenty of room for the Skakels and a menagerie of horses, dogs, cats, goats, and assorted fowl.

The Skakel children were athletic, boisterous, prankish, irreverent, competitive, and closely bound—much like the Kennedy clan. But the loosely disciplined Skakel family, which one of Ethel's young friends described as "a bit bizarre," was a potpourri of compulsive-addictive personalities. Starting with the parents, who showed little self-discipline themselves and who permitted their children almost free rein, the household lacked the reserve and order of the Kennedys'.[63]

Ethel received her early education from Dominican nuns and a private tutor. After the move to Connecticut, her mother, an upwardly striving woman eager to fit in with her Anglo-Saxon neighbors, decided to enroll Ethel at the Greenwich Academy, an Episcopal day school for girls reputed to be one of the finest in the Northeast. Although Ethel was only an average student, her mischief and ability to amuse the other girls made a lasting impression; she regularly taunted and tormented her teachers with spitballs and practical jokes. Ethel's two strongest passions were her religion and her horses. Like her mother a fervent believer and a faithful communicant, "from the time she was a little child," her tutor later observed, "Ethel helped Big Ann carry the cross." An accomplished rider by the time she was eight years old, Ethel soon filled her room with trophies and ribbons from show-ring victories, often chronicled in the *New York Times*.[64]

For Ethel's final two years of high school, Ann Skakel sent her to the Convent of the Sacred Heart, Maplehurst—probably to quell her daughter's pubescent energies but also for religious reasons. Two of Robert Kennedy's sisters, Patricia and Jean, had also attended the strict, spartan boarding school in the Bronx. In a place demanding piety, discipline, silence, and sacrifice, Ethel was easily the most brazen and spirited. The pranks and jokes continued unabated. She greeted everyone, friend and stranger, with "Hey, kid!" or "Hiya, babe!"[65]

In September 1945 Ethel entered Manhattanville College of the Sacred Heart in the center of Harlem. She and her roommate, Jean Kennedy, the shyest and most inhibited of Robert's four sisters, hit it off immediately. Jean invited Ethel home during vacations and on a skiing trip to Mont Tremblant, Canada, where Ethel and Robert first met. It was not love at first sight. Ethel had a teen crush on John Kennedy and volunteered to work for him during his 1946 congressional campaign, while Robert dated Ethel's sister Pat and was also apparently smitten by Joan Winmill, a beautiful English actress he met during the 1948 trip and may have seen again in 1949.[66]

Ethel and Robert had a long, intermittent courtship, during which Ethel had some second thoughts; for a time she considered becoming a nun. They were married on 17 June 1950 at St. Mary's Church in Greenwich, with John serving as best man. The lavish wedding, with nearly two thousand guests, received widespread coverage not only as one of the "prettiest" weddings of the year but because it united two fortunes. Between Robert's football buddies, who served as ushers, and Ethel's rough and tumble brothers, the wedding was a near debacle. The young men wrecked the banquet room at the bachelors' party and the morning of the wedding tossed the bridesmaids in the Skakel pool. Just before the ceremony began, Ethel's roguish brother, George, Jr., tricked LeMoyne Billings into bending over to pick up some coins in the aisle of the church and kicked him in the seat of the pants, sending him sprawling in front of the bride's processional.[67]

After a month-long honeymoon in Hawaii, Robert and Ethel set out to realize their mutual ideal: a large, coherent, happy Catholic family. As Jean Kennedy had suspected, Ethel not only complemented Robert but, in a sense, completed him. He tended to be an introvert; she was a full-blooded extrovert. To involve her reticent husband in conversations at social gatherings, Ethel would begin a story then say,

"Bobby, *you* tell it."[68] As well as anyone can discern, Robert and Ethel for their entire married life remained genuine friends as well as lovers.

Their shared interests encompassed all varieties of outdoor activity and athletic competition—including horseback riding, skiing, and boating—as well as an eagerness to extend their personal knowledge and intellectual reach. They also had the same moralistic outlook on life. Fiercely competitive and given to moral absolutes, Ethel divided the world into "goodies" and "baddies." She was easily shocked by dirty stories and disgusted by sexual innuendo. Some who knew her considered Ethel inflexibly prudish and somewhat naive.[69]

The animated Skakel household had prepared Ethel well for the give-and-take dynamism, constant kidding, and frenetic pace of the Kennedy family; she fit in immediately. An acquaintance once said Ethel was intent on being "more Kennedy than thou."[70] She endeared herself to Joseph Kennedy with her gritty determination to be Robert's helpmate. For his personal happiness, his role within the family, and his ambitions for public service, Robert had found the perfect wife.

His marriage to Ethel Skakel marked the most important turning point in Robert Kennedy's life so far. Although still maneuvering his way through the Kennedy masculine passage, Robert as husband and father managed to put behind him most of the tormenting moments of indecision, inadequacy, and uncertainty of his adolescence. Some ghosts lingered or reappeared during his adult struggles to keep pace with John's accomplishments and to meet his father's spiraling expectations, but Robert's successful marriage and growing family allowed him to find a personal niche, to assume gradually the roles of expediter of the Kennedy fates and keeper and defender of the Kennedy faith.

The first of Joseph Kennedy's sons to have a profession, the first to marry, the first to have children, the seventh Kennedy pressed forward into adulthood, eager to guide the next generation of Kennedys, a treasured trust. He welcomed those challenges and responsibilities as readily as John Kennedy declined or postponed them. But John's position as the eldest, combined with Joseph Kennedy's impatient desires for power and prestige, left little doubt about Robert's future role. Soon enough he found himself subordinating his personal ambitions and career goals to advance his brother's.

CHAPTER 3

"Yes, Dad. Yes, Dad."

ROBERT AND ETHEL were on their honeymoon when North Korean armies crossed the 38th parallel to invade South Korea. The Kennedys had long believed that a monolithic international Communist conspiracy directed from Moscow threatened the United States. Americans regarded the North Korean attack as indisputable proof that such a conspiracy existed. After all, North Korea and its dictator, Kim Il Sung, were, in the language of the times, "puppets" of the Soviet Communist regime.

Cold War Jitters

"We are not at war," President Harry Truman insisted.[1] Yet he moved quickly, without direct congressional approval, to commit the United States to a UN "police action" to defend South Korea. During the drawn-out stalemate, Truman anticipated Communist thrusts elsewhere by launching a massive rearmament plan, bolstering NATO defenses, arming West Germany, concluding a separate peace with Japan, and providing assistance to the French in Indochina (the last opened the door for later U.S. involvement in Vietnam).

Truman's successor, Dwight D. Eisenhower, endorsed and expanded on the underlying ideological assumptions of containment, which were still in place when John Kennedy entered the White House in 1961. He would not alter them substantively. When these assumptions were at last publicly challenged at the height of the Vietnam War protest, Robert Kennedy stood among the few of America's leadership elite who raised questions regarding the U.S. view of the monolithic nature of Communism. His own intellectual journey away from the rigidity of Cold War reasoning had taken twisting and sometimes painful paths. In retrospect, it reflected a larger, near cosmic transformation underway in U.S. political culture.

Such thoughts, however, were far from Robert Kennedy's mind in the fall of 1950. Engrossed in his law studies and preparing for a family, he did not ache to rush into combat in the Korean War as he had in World War II. This war was different. Accustomed to the unambiguous successes and unequivocal objectives of World War II, Robert, like many Americans, found the "limited" war in Korea frustrating. At least initially, he, like his father, questioned America's military involvement. Speaking before Robert's classmates in December 1950, Joseph Kennedy condemned the Truman Doctrine and containment policies as drains on limited U.S. resources and as probably ineffective anyway. An advocate of reducing U.S. global commitments, Robert's father described American intervention in Korea as "suicidal."

During his years as law student and political neophyte, Robert Kennedy rejected the internationalist perspective of most Democrats to embrace the conservative, neoisolationist view popular among Republicans. He also judged U.S. leadership in foreign affairs weak and indecisive. One could trace the faults in the country's postwar policies, he wrote in his seminar paper on international law and repeated in newspaper op-ed pieces, to mistakes made at the Yalta Conference in February 1945. He asserted that "the peace of the world was lost" at Yalta when President Roosevelt made far too many concessions to the Soviet Union in negotiating postwar alignments.[2]

John Kennedy expressed similar sentiments from the floor of the House of Representatives, blaming Roosevelt, Truman, and George C. Marshall for the "loss" of China in 1949, and charging that "what our young men saved [in World War II], our diplomats and our President [Truman] have frittered away."[3] Cold War policy conflicts and their ramifications for domestic policy were central elements in the Kennedy brothers' political lives. Centrist and conservative in their views, John and Robert Kennedy employed vituperative Cold War rhetoric not only to gain attention but also because they believed the United States was involved in a dire struggle with the Soviet Union in which conflict was probably unavoidable. Yet neither Kennedy was exceptionally enlightened on the subject of the Cold War; their reactions on foreign and domestic issues conformed to the patterned and predictable responses of a political culture conditioned by unrelenting tension between the United States and the Soviet Union.

In the late 1940s and early 1950s the country reeled from the cumulative effects of several surprising and frustrating external events: the Berlin blockade of 1948, the success of Mao Zedong's Communist Chinese revolution, the Soviet detonation of an atomic bomb in late 1949, the Korean War, and the threat of Communist expansion. Americans were jolted, too, by the startling revelations of the Alger Hiss case, the admissions of Klaus Fuchs, and the subsequent convictions and executions of Julius and Ethel Rosenberg for conspiracy to pass atomic secrets to the Soviets. Imbued with a belief in the exceptionalism of the American experiment, many Americans could attribute such reversals only to treachery from within, an explanation with particular appeal for Robert Kennedy.

The enemies within became an obsession for young Kennedy, absorbing him professionally, propelling him forward in national politics, and providing him for the first time a way to make a reputation of his own. His career was launched with the search for those who betrayed the American creed, that core of political values upon which the American consensus is built. Ethel Kennedy had a simple label for such people. Whether they were corrupt government officials, members of organized crime, crooked labor leaders, or Communists, they were "baddies." Robert would hardly have used the word, but like his wife he responded to the uncertainties of the postwar world with moral absolutes.

In an era of loyalty oaths, blacklists, censorship, and overt propaganda, the most popular instrument for protecting the American creed—and, not entirely incidentally, for whipping up and manipulating public hysteria—became the congressional investigating committee. Its proponents presumed it to be the righteous vehicle for routing Communists from government, universities, and defense industries or for exposing corruption and criminal conspiracies in labor, business, and government. Investigating committees provided platforms for partisan maneuvering and ideological jousting within the Congress. As the United States stepped into the television age in the early 1950s, congressional hearings also furnished a national stage for legislators and investigators with larger political ambitions. By the end of the decade, the youthful, photogenic faces and vigorous political styles of John and Robert Kennedy had become familiar to most American households.

More familiar, however, were other, far less attractive faces, who manipulated the ideological illusions of the Cold War to their personal advantage. The Cold War fueled truculent partisanship, suspicion, and hysteria, creating opportunities for political charlatans; it was, in novelist Lillian Hellman's apt phrase, "scoundrel time." Many stood out, but only one—Senator Joseph R. McCarthy—was so audacious, so disrespectful of fair play, and so flamboyant in his reckless, unsubstantiated accusations of Communist subterfuge as to have the phenomenon named after him.[4]

The age of suspicion, or the second "Red Scare," was well underway before McCarthy burst upon the national scene in February 1950, claiming in a now infamous speech in Wheeling, West Virginia, to have a list of 205 State Department employees "known to the Secretary of State as being members of the Communist Party." McCarthy had no direct knowledge of Communists in government. What little he knew came through tutorials from Richard Nixon and information gleaned from FBI files supplied to him by J. Edgar Hoover. "Review the files and get anything you can for him," Hoover directed, and agents complied.[5] Despite Hoover's help, in four years of bellowing and bullying McCarthy found not a single Communist in the U.S. government. Still, his accusations sent shock waves through Washington corridors and Main Street America. McCarthy became a malevolent specter in American politics, far too dangerous to ignore.

Long before Wheeling, Joe McCarthy had become a Kennedy

family friend. He visited Hyannis Port, dated Eunice and Patricia Kennedy, occasionally traveled the night club circuit with John, and received large campaign gifts and much unsolicited advice from Joe Kennedy. The Kennedys welcomed McCarthy as a political asset, a phenomenon to be cultivated and used for his influence in the Irish American communities, and, later, for his leadership of the anticommunist movement.[6] Robert and his father particularly admired McCarthy's competitive instincts and political directness.

Family political interests aside, Robert and Ethel genuinely liked Joseph McCarthy. Their close friendship was solidified in 1950 when the Wisconsin senator accepted Robert's invitation to speak at the Virginia Legal Forum. McCarthy responded amiably to their hospitality and enjoyed the company of the younger Kennedys, who marveled at his spunk and bravado. On a Cape Cod sailing excursion the Kennedys, in their typically playful exuberance, once tossed McCarthy overboard and pushed him back under the water each time he tried to climb back aboard. McCarthy gamely clung to the side of the boat, smiling each time he was allowed to surface for air. Only later did they discover that the former marine and ex-boxer had never learned to swim.[7] As a sign of their esteem, Robert and Ethel invited McCarthy to serve as godfather to their first child, Kathleen, born in July 1951, a month after Robert's graduation from law school.

During that final year in law school, Robert and Ethel lived in a small, three-bedroom house on Cameron Lane in Charlottesville. "This place could fit in the living room of one of our guest houses," Ethel said, but "it'll have to do until Bobby graduates."[8] Although Ethel tried to learn to cook, after a few gastronomic catastrophes she abandoned the effort, hired a cook, and, for the rest of their married lives, never cooked again except in emergencies. A maid handled other chores.

When household help was unavailable, the house was a clutter. Robert had little concern for keeping his own possessions in order, and Ethel was not a fastidious housekeeper. The untrained habits of the Kennedys' English bulldog, Toby Belch, shocked guests. As pets and children multiplied over the years, the family's homes became even more chaotic. Neither Robert nor Ethel seemed to mind. Some friends thought their casualness toward their belongings (and those of their landlords) unforgivably irresponsible. Others found it endearing. When a Washington group named Ethel "Homemaker of the Year" in 1958, Robert advised her to hurry down and pick up the award "before they change their minds."[9]

Apart from homemaking, Ethel Kennedy's conception of her wifely roles was old-fashioned, even by the standards of the 1950s. Actively interested in Robert's career, she had no plans for one of her own. Still, she was self-possessed, personally independent, and, occasionally, socially defiant. If anything set her apart from other women of her strata and circumstance, it was her competitive toughness and the exuberance with which she strained to prove herself to her in-laws. One of her biographers suggests that Ethel's "conversion to Kennedyism" came at the cost of almost complete alienation from her family. "I just gotta keep up with them [the Kennedys]," one of her Charlottesville acquaintances recalled Ethel telling her, "I have to be on top of *everything*."[10]

Politically, socially, and morally conservative, Robert and Ethel allowed no smoking in their house, disapproved of smutty stories, and rarely served or drank alcohol. Except for Robert's involvement in the Ralph Bunche episode, neither expressed deep concern or urgency to correct social and racial problems. They participated in no social reform movements or political action groups. They joined a country club in Charlottesville with no apparent regard for its racial restrictions.[11]

1951 World Trip

After Robert's graduation from law school, the young couple spent the summer at Hyannis Port in Joseph Kennedy's guest house. In September, Robert's father arranged for him to go to San Francisco to cover the signing of the peace treaty with Japan and to file reports for the *Boston Post*. Joseph Kennedy also convinced John Kennedy to allow Robert and sister Patricia to accompany him on a seven-week congressional junket to Israel, India, and the Far East that took them around the world.

Fretting beforehand that Robert would be "a pain in the ass" on the trip, John was pleasantly surprised. Congressman Kennedy appreciatively noted Robert's growing political awareness and analytical insights on international issues. Robert kept a diary of the trip and wrote regularly to his father. Writing from Israel, he commented on a Communist insurgency in the Arab world and its appeal for developing nations. In India, he was distressed when Prime Minister Jawaharlal Nehru slighted his brother and devoted most of his attention to Patricia.[12]

Arriving in Vietnam in October, Robert observed that the United States, by helping the French retain control of their former colony, was becoming involved in the war in Vietnam "to a point where we can't back out." Vietnam and other emerging nations, John Kennedy said in 1952 after returning home, blazed with the "fires of nationalism," which were inextinguishable by external military power. Two and one-half years later, as the French teetered on the brink of final defeat and the Eisenhower administration considered expanding the U.S. role in Vietnam, John Kennedy criticized the president and his administration for concealing the "truth" from the American people. No amount of military assistance in Indochina, he said, "can conquer an enemy that is everywhere and at the same time nowhere." A decade later when he was president, Kennedy forgot his own astute observation.[13]

En route to Korea, John Kennedy became critically ill. Robert rushed his brother to a U.S. military hospital on Okinawa where he witnessed firsthand his brother's struggle with Addison's disease. The press received the standard cover story: the congressman, they were informed, had suffered a recurrence of the malaria he had supposedly contracted during the *PT-109* venture. When John's temperature went to 106, Robert said, "Everybody just expected him to die."[14] John required several days of rest and seclusion to recover. Awed by his brother's suffering, Robert gained new respect for John. "At least one half of the days that he spent on this earth," Robert wrote after John's death, "were days of intense physical pain."[15]

Those recurrent physical problems also filled some of John Kennedy's days with a fatalistic foreboding, allayed only when he gambled successfully on a series of risky back operations in 1954 and 1955. Thanks also to cortisone injections, the Addison's disease was brought under control. The lethargy and diffidence that had colored his first years in Congress vanished, and John Kennedy began to make plans for the future.[16] In part because of the compatibility he and his brother discovered on their 1951 trip, that future would now include a more prominent role for Robert.

Robert's 1951 trips made up part of a regimen designed by Joseph Kennedy to educate his sons for public service. He sent them to foreign capitals in Europe, the Middle East, and Far East to meet national leaders and assay political conditions in the most power-sensitive regions of the world. By contrast, until the presidential campaign of 1960, neither Kennedy brother traveled extensively in the United States. Reared and educated in privileged seclusion, they understood little of their own country's social or economic problems, especially those of race, poverty, environment, and labor. They had no feel for the land-based culture, the dissent-laden populist democratic traditions, or the economic problems of America's heartland. Their father's education plan left them no opportunity to discover the land or the people of the American Midwest or Great Plains, that great expanse called Middle America. "No one," Walt Whitman once wrote, "begins to know the real geographic, democratic, indissoluble American Union in the present, or suspect it in the future, until he explores these Central States, and dwells awhile on their prairies or amid their busy towns."[17] All of that had to wait.

Campaigning for the Senate

Home from the world trip, Robert spent several months studying for the New York state bar exam. He, Ethel, and baby Kathleen, with no place of their own, shuttled between Greenwich and Hyannis Port. After passing the bar, Robert was appointed assistant U.S. attorney for eastern New York as a result of calls by his father and Senator McCarthy. Commuting from Greenwich to work out of the federal courthouse in Brooklyn, Robert investigated criminal income-tax evasion cases, one of which led to the indictment of the former commissioner of internal revenue, Joseph Nunan.[18] After only three months on the job, Robert reluctantly resigned to manage John Kennedy's campaign for the U.S. Senate against Henry Cabot Lodge, Jr.

Robert entered the campaign and, with it, active political life, largely because his father's overbearing manner and interfering practices had made life miserable for John Kennedy's campaign staff, particularly for attorney Mark Dalton, who had managed John's earlier campaigns. Quiet and intelligent, Dalton served out of friendship to John Kennedy, without compensation or title. He finally tired of Joe Kennedy's abusive treatment and walked out when John refused to come to his defense.[19]

Another staffer, Kenneth O'Donnell, Robert's Harvard roommate, later recalled that John was upset over his father's intrusions and "angrily" agreed to let O'Donnell ask Robert to take Dalton's place. O'Donnell and other campaign insiders needed someone between them and the candidate's interfering father. Outsiders lacked sufficient cachet and could not effectively comprehend the peculiar mannerisms of this close-knit family. With the campaign headed toward "absolute catastrophic disaster," in O'Donnell's view, he pleaded with Robert to take over; only he would do. "Don't drag me into it," Robert begged, "I'll screw it up . . . and I just don't want to come." However, within a few days, Robert met with his father, resigned from the Justice Department, and soon after arrived in Massachusetts. Rose Kennedy said Robert set aside his personal concerns "not happily, but willingly" to serve his brother.[20]

Ostensibly responsible for administrative organization, Robert in fact found his principal, though unspoken, tasks were to "handle the father" and to take care of dirty jobs. Some viewed Robert as simply an extension of the father. Journalist Charles Bartlett overheard the candidate's brother talking on the telephone with his father, repeating "Yes, Dad. Yes, Dad." Robert acted as a buffer between his brother and father and between his brother and the hard realities of Massachusetts politics. Still not in the best of health, according to biographer Herbert Parmet, John Kennedy was "usually in pain and feverish" throughout most of the campaign. The candidate needed his brother to reassure him things were being properly handled and, when necessary, to talk back to their father.[21]

In the 1952 campaign the Kennedys refined the methods of their earlier campaigns and set the pattern for subsequent races involving members of the family. For John's 1952 Senate campaign the Kennedys developed a statewide organization independent of the regular Democratic party apparatus. Driving this process was Lawrence F. O'Brien, a public relations man from Springfield, aided by O'Donnell and other members of what became known as the "Irish Mafia." They established 286 suprapartisan units of approximately 50,000 volunteers throughout the state, each unit headed by a "secretary" who tracked registered voters and coordinated local activities. The Kennedy apparatus emphasized the candidate rather than the Democratic party or the issues.[22]

John Kennedy skirted sensitive issues, fearing to alienate large segments of the usual Democratic majority within the state. He attempted to immunize himself from his father's conservative and controversial views and to refute allegations of an anti-Israel attitude, traceable to his father's anti-Semitism.[23]

The Kennedys wanted to avoid the salient issue of the 1952 campaign season, McCarthyism. Ignoring the urging of his liberal-academic advisors to speak out against McCarthy, John Kennedy moved cautiously.[24] To avert a head-on crash, Joseph Kennedy reportedly contributed generously to Senator McCarthy's own reelection campaign, allegedly in return for promises not to campaign in Massachusetts and not to endorse the Republican, Lodge. Some have claimed the Kennedys' objective was to put distance between John Kennedy and McCarthy, implying the Kennedys were, after all, embarrassed by the connection.[25] More likely, they feared the substantial impact of McCarthy's throwing his support to Lodge. Robert Kennedy admitted McCarthy was "a highly regarded figure" who could have made a marked difference in the election. Whether he knew of his father's alleged payoff to McCarthy or not, Robert unrealistically claimed that McCarthy stayed out of Massachusetts because the Wisconsin senator "just didn't like Henry Cabot Lodge."[26]

No substantial differences existed between Kennedy and Lodge on the issues. Both ran on their personalities and their family connections. Both were perceived as basically conservative. Both took strong anti-communist stands. Each insisted he was tougher on Communists than the other. Kennedy could not afford to appear to be "soft" on Communism. "Hell," he once commented, "half my voters in Massachusetts look on McCarthy as a hero." Historian Herbert Parmet generously described the Kennedy position as "a deft combination of anti-communism and social welfare issues."[27]

Robert's presence in the campaign allowed Joseph Kennedy to remain in the background, where he believed he could be more effective. Insiders knew the father was the real power behind the Kennedy party. Although he had lived in New York and Florida for several years, Joseph Kennedy maintained his interests in Massachusetts politics. Democratic candidates, according to Tip O'Neill, would "go down to see Joe," and he would always send them home "with a briefcase full of cash." The more he liked you, the more you got.[28] Massachusetts politicians, Kenneth O'Donnell observed, "did not like Bob or Jack, but they wanted Joe's money."[29] Politicians who also sought personal endorsements and organizational support from the glamorous Kennedy family found these two commodities rarely, if ever, shared.

Take the case of Massachusetts governor Paul Dever, a Democrat running for reelection, who proposed an alliance with the Kennedys. Most candidates would probably have welcomed the assistance of an incumbent governor, but the Kennedys were simply not inclined to enter political coalitions or partnerships. Robert was sent to meet Dever with instructions from John to say no "without getting me involved in it." Bluntly and tactlessly, the candidate's tweny-six-year-old brother told Governor Dever there would be no merger. Furious, Dever risked further damage by telling Joseph Kennedy, "Keep that fresh kid of yours out of sight from here on in!" Dever's blaming Robert allowed John to avoid an open confrontation with the Democratic governor, keep his independence, and maintain an uneasy peace, without diluting his powers.[30] Whether by chance or design, Robert's brashness and his inexperience as a political operative worked to the candidate's advantage. In the years ahead John Kennedy would involve Robert in variants of this good-cop, bad-cop stratagem, with and without Robert's conscious participation.

Robert Kennedy had become his brother's political point man, clearing the way through the swampy backlands of Massachusetts politics, allowing John to walk the high ground. In the process, Robert earned a reputation as a ruthless operator who asked for and gave no quarter. He ferociously defended his brother's interests, sometimes losing himself in his zeal. At one meeting Robert became so angry at a state legislator that he had to be restrained from punching him. Witnesses remember Robert provoking the near melee by shouting, "I don't want my brother to get mixed up with politicians!"[31] Boston pols considered Robert a "royal pain in the ass." Yet when it came to energy, perseverance, and sheer dedication, they conceded, he could not be outdone. Robert ruffled feathers with his brusque, often abrasive manner and his refusal to defer to those he considered political hacks. Striding into campaign headquarters one day, he confronted a man doing nothing, whom he had failed to recognize as the head of the Massachusetts AFL-CIO. "If you're not going to work," Robert told him, "don't hang around here."[32]

The candidate's brother drove the staff long and hard, accepting no excuses for missed assignments in a campaign that got underway before Labor Day. "People didn't like me. But it never bothered me," he said, "and I never cared. I mean, it wasn't at all important to me."[33] Some of the staff complained directly to the candidate. "Oh, bullshit," John Kennedy responded to one critic, "everybody bitches about Bobby, and I'm getting sick and Goddamn tired of it. He's the only one who doesn't stick knives in my back, the only one I can count on when it comes down to it."[34]

Robert handled the administrative details and left the strategizing to his brother, his father, and Larry O'Brien. Although he also steered clear of financial matters, his father's domain, he was evidently privy to some of his father's controversial dealings, including those with John Fox, the editor of the *Boston Post.* Initially a strong supporter of Lodge, the *Post* suddenly reversed itself to support John Kennedy after receiving a $500,000 loan from the candidate's father. Joseph Kennedy and John Fox both insisted the endorsement came first, but Robert reluctantly admitted "there was a connection" between the loan and the endorsement. Much less guarded, John Kennedy later confided to journalist Fletcher Knebel, "You know, we had to buy that fucking paper or I'd have been licked."[35]

Of all the activities associated with political campaigning, Robert Kennedy disliked most the requisite hand shaking and the obligatory schmoozing at cocktail parties and political gatherings. He never became adept at or comfortable with small talk or exchanging pleasantries while moving through a crowd of strangers. John, who also disliked this aspect of politics, nevertheless turned brief introductions into long-time memories with his charm, smooth mannerisms, and locked-in eye contact.[36] In time, Robert would gain confidence and be less ill at ease in such gatherings, but in 1952 he labored to avoid them.

Robert, who abhorred crowds, made few speeches. Awkward and uncomfortable as a public speaker, he stammered, fumbled for words, and had difficulty forming full sentences when speaking extemporaneously. Even with his mother's coaching, Robert could not progress beyond a few spoken lines on his own. Here, purportedly, is the complete text of his first political stump speech: "My brother Jack couldn't be here. My mother couldn't be here. My sister Eunice couldn't be here. My sister Pat couldn't be here. My sister Jean couldn't be here. But if my brother Jack were here, he'd tell you Lodge has a very bad voting record. Thank you."[37]

The rest of the family more than made up for Robert's social reticence. Kennedys flooded the state, turning out wherever the Kennedy name might raise a vote. Ethel campaigned vigorously until the final hours of her second pregnancy. On 24 September, she went from a speech in Fall River directly to the hospital in Brighton to give birth to Joseph P. Kennedy II, hailed in the national press as "Joe's first grandson."[38] Within three weeks Ethel had rejoined Robert's mother and sisters on the campaign trail.

Among the innovative and highly effective tactics in the Kennedy party campaign repertoire were the "teas" hosted around the state by the Kennedy women. Directed by cousin Polly Fitzgerald and a Boston schoolteacher volunteer, Helen Keyes, these tastefully and carefully orchestrated gatherings graced the "fanciest rooms in the nicest hotels." An estimated seventy-thousand women came to meet the Kennedy women. Robert was skeptical about the value of the teas. Polly and Helen were "heartbroken" when he told them they were wasting their time inviting so many Irish-Catholic women. When the election was won by a margin nearly equal to the number of women who attended the teas, Robert apologized: "Little old Irish ladies did vote and it did count."[39]

On a homemade slide rule in those precomputer days, Robert privately projected a narrow loss for John. By late in the evening of election day, most of Kennedy's supporters sensed a Lodge victory on Eisenhower's coattails and began leaving campaign headquarters. Robert remembered standing with his brother in the near-empty command center as an old pol, Patsy Mulkern, stood outside the window and yelled, "You're dead! You're finished! Give up! Give up!" Around five o'clock A.M. the trend started to go Kennedy's way. About two hours later, Robert spotted Lodge leaving his campaign headquarters across the street. Within a few minutes, Robert stood atop a desk reading Lodge's telegram of concession to a joyful but exhausted cadre of Kennedy workers.[40]

When the counting was over, Kennedy had vanquished Lodge, the scion of Massachusetts's most venerable Protestant Brahmin family, by 71,000 votes. General Eisenhower had carried Massachusetts by a 209,000-vote margin. Governor Dever lost his reelection bid by less than 15,000. It was a magnificent victory for the Kennedys. Rose especially savored the triumph, seeing in it vindication for her father, John Fitzgerald, who spent half a century competing in vain against the Lodge family. Most important, John Kennedy must now be reckoned an influential electoral force in national politics. "Jack Kennedy," Governor Dever declared afterward, "is the first Irish Brahmin. Bobby is the last Irish Puritan."[41]

Others had their explanations for John's victory, but Robert characteristically attributed the win to lots of hard work by the Kennedy forces and lack of diligence by Lodge, who he regarded as a "very, very lazy man." Lodge, for his part, claimed he "could have made it if it hadn't been for all those fancy tea parties the Kennedys sponsored all over the state."[42]

John Kennedy singled out his brother for special thanks for his contributions to his victory. Kenneth O'Donnell thought Robert was the vital difference in the campaign, claiming that "if Bobby had not arrived on the scene and taken charge when he did, Jack Kennedy most certainly would have lost the election." John Kennedy's close friend, LeMoyne Billings, believed the campaign forever changed the relationship between the two brothers. "Until then," he told an interviewer, "I don't think Jack had been aware that Bobby had all this tremendous organizing ability. But during the campaign Bobby had proved himself again and again, forging a blood partnership that would last until the two of them died."[43]

While heaping praise on Robert, the family only grudgingly and patronizingly recognized the contributions of a legion of volunteers, friends, relatives, and political professionals. Robert often received credit for the accomplishments of Lawrence O'Brien, whose fourteen years' experience, conceptual powers, and organizational skills made a difference in the close election. Tip O'Neill and others who stumped for Kennedy felt the Kennedys slighted their efforts. In spite of hurt feelings, the core of the Kennedy team that would win the White House in 1960 was now assembled.[44]

After the election, Robert joined his family at Hyannis Port to spend a few days with Ethel and their new son, Joseph. In the steady grind of fourteen- to eighteen-hour days, Kennedy estimated that he had "lost ten or twelve pounds." His successful efforts for the campaign finally earned a few words of praise from Joseph Kennedy, who described his son as "hard as nails" and "the most determined person" he had ever known. But, the ambassador demanded, "What are you going to do now?" He answered his own question. "You'd better go out and get a job."[45]

CHAPTER 4

Joe McCarthy and the Enemies Within

SOON AFTER HIS BROTHER'S ELECTION to the Senate, Robert Kennedy joined the staff of Senator Joseph R. McCarthy. He was recommended for the position by James McInerney, the assistant attorney general for whom Robert had briefly worked before joining his brother's campaign. But the determining factor in his landing the job was a telephone call to McCarthy from Joseph Kennedy.[1]

Working for McCarthy

After the November 1952 elections, Senator Joseph McCarthy's star was in the ascent. For two years he had hurled one unsubstantiated charge after another of Communist infiltration in the government, had withstood Senate inquiries into his indecent and repulsive conduct, and had retaliated successfully against his detractors. In January 1953, with Republicans back in control of the U.S. Senate, McCarthy became chair of the Permanent Subcommittee on Investigations of the U.S. Senate Committee on Government Operations, a minor committee with wide discretionary authority to investigate "the operations of Government activities at all levels." The public would now witness the unbridled power of the phenomenon called "McCarthyism."

Convinced of the righteousness of McCarthy's anticommunist campaign, Robert Kennedy aspired to be more than a member of the subcommittee staff—he wanted to be chief counsel. That position, however, went to Roy M. Cohn. Eighteen months younger than Kennedy, a law school graduate at twenty and an assistant U.S. attorney at twenty-one, Cohn had already gained national attention for his supporting roles in the government's high-profile cases against the accused atomic spies Julius and Ethel Rosenberg, and an alleged Communist conspirator, professor Owen J. Lattimore. McCarthy selected Cohn over Kennedy, according to a close observer, because "Roy out-aggressived Bobby Kennedy."[2] Settling for a position as an assistant to Francis "Frip" Flanagan, the subcommittee's general counsel, Kennedy reported for work in January 1953.

Several factors help explain Robert Kennedy's attraction to Joe McCarthy and the anticommunist crusade. His Catholic upbringing with its emphasis on unquestioning faith and respect for authority drew him toward the one man he thought was trying to cope with the Communist atheists dedicated to subverting the American way of life.[3] He was, moreover, personally fond of McCarthy. Among all of his father's and his older brother's political acquaintances, McCarthy alone had shown him respect and attention while Robert was still in law school. Further, the McCarthy committee promised to be the center-ring show of U.S. politics. What better place to get one's first taste of national politics?

Yet it is fair to ask, What was the brother (and campaign manager) of a Democratic senator doing on the staff of the McCarthy committee? In that era of Cold War excesses, politicians of both parties often touted the passage of stricter measures to thwart internal subversion, urged the administration to tighten employee loyalty review programs, and called for investigations of possible Communist infiltration. But Joseph McCarthy's investigations obliterated bipartisan agreements on the issue, as he reserved his most venomous attacks for Democrats. Most Democrats (but especially liberal Democrats) reviled the Wisconsin Republican and his ilk for associating the achievements of the New Deal with socialism and Communism and for charging Democratic administrations with "twenty years of treason" for failing to take tougher anticommunist stands.[4]

Robert's position on McCarthy's staff, then, would seem an obvious liability for Senator John Kennedy. But the senator neither openly objected nor approved. His ambivalence toward McCarthy is puzzling. Justice William O. Douglas believed that John was "too close" to McCarthy to be objective and that he treated McCarthy as "a screwball guy" who needed help.[5] Whatever John Kennedy's reasons, he and his father appeared oblivious to the potential damage to his chances for the Democratic nomination for the presidency presented by Robert's close association with the stalking horse for stalwart Republican rhetoric.

By the mid-1960s, with a new political climate and the revulsion toward McCarthy and his methods virtually universal, some Robert Kennedy supporters went to extremes to deny his association with McCarthy. Kenneth O'Donnell, for example, stubbornly asserted in 1968 that Robert Kennedy "didn't know Joe McCarthy from a cord of wood" and did not meet him until 1954.[6] Others, however, recall him aggressively defending McCarthy, apologizing for him, and offering explanations for his outrageous behavior.[7] In fact, Robert Kennedy never disavowed his belief in a Communist conspiracy and never dissociated himself personally from Joe McCarthy. As for the excesses associated with McCarthy and his subcommittee, Kennedy did not blame McCarthy. Instead, he blamed Roy Cohn.

Because McCarthy knew virtually nothing about finding Communists in government, he gave Cohn a free hand to run the subcommittee and conduct investigations. A haughty, argumentative, and insensitive man with drooping eyelids and a perpetual pout, Cohn ran roughshod over the establishment throughout 1953 and into early 1954. He directed ersatz "investigations" into "subversion and espionage" in the State Department, the Voice of America, the Government Printing Office, and several other government agencies, exhuming old charges long before fully investigated by the FBI and other security agencies. Cohn's inquiries resulted in seventeen public hearings, ostensibly for the purpose of "exposing Communists." In reality most of the hearings were held only to gain publicity for McCarthy and for the subcommittee.

During those hearings Cohn and McCarthy engaged in imprudent cross-examinations of witnesses, destroying reputations and careers with devastating insinuations and groundless accusations.

Cohn's "chief consultant" was G. David Schine, a twenty-six-year-old heir to a hotel fortune and a self-styled expert on Communism. An unpaid staff member, Schine became Cohn's constant companion. In April 1953 Cohn and Schine rampaged through State Department information libraries in Europe, yanking from the shelves books they claimed were written by "Communists, fellow-travelers, *et cetera.*" They also traveled extensively to government installations in the United States, leaving headlines and consternation in their wake. Riding in the back of the Schine family limousine, staying in the Schine family hotels, dining at the best restaurants, partying long and hard into the night, Cohn and Schine plotted their next public escapade as the nation's foremost exposers of Communists in government.[8]

The attention Cohn garnered as Joe McCarthy's chief counsel galled Robert Kennedy, and Cohn knew it. Reveling in his moment in the sun, Cohn flaunted his seniority by assigning Robert menial and demeaning tasks and treating him, as one observer recalled, "as a kid. A rich bitch kid."[9] Robert Kennedy never forgave Cohn's treatment.

Meanwhile, the fledgling staffer was always first in line to pick up his paycheck, committee staffers remember, a steady but unenthusiastic worker but proud to be earning a salary of $4,952 a year. As a token gesture toward living within his earned income, Kennedy instructed Ethel to rent a house in Washington for no more than $400 a month—just $12 less than his entire monthly pay, before taxes. When his salary increased to $7,342 in June 1953, it still represented far less than what he spent on living expenses.

Because the Kennedy family prohibits access to financial information, just how well he lived and how much he spent is uncertain. However, according to one source, Joseph Kennedy's children on their twenty-first birthdays each received a trust of one million dollars. At a modest 5 percent interest, a million-dollar trust would have returned $50,000 a year for Robert. Ethel's family provided some financial assistance as well. Nonetheless, Ethel agreed to follow her husband's wishes and searched until she found a four-bedroom house on S Street in

Georgetown whose owner she charmed into reducing the rent to $400. Robert enjoyed family life immensely, rushing out to join Ethel and the children promptly at quitting time, while the rest of the McCarthy staff routinely worked late.[10]

Kennedy's first and only assignment as a member of McCarthy's staff was to investigate allied shipping during the Korean War. Applying a strictly moral perspective to the complex problem of international trade, he commented indignantly in his May 1953 report to the subcommittee on the policy of "fighting the enemy on the one hand and trading with him on the other." After sifting through reams of shipping records and Naval Intelligence files, Kennedy had found that fourteen owners of eighty-two ships flying flags of U.S. allies were trading with Communist China. British-owned vessels, he erroneously reported, were transporting Chinese troops. McCarthy stole headlines by rashly denouncing this practice as "unbelievable" and "unheard of."[11] The White House interpreted Kennedy's report as a partisan attempt to embarrass President Eisenhower, a judgment as erroneous as the report itself. Vice-President Richard Nixon was delegated to convince McCarthy to drop the matter.[12] On 1 July 1953, McCarthy quietly accepted the report and consigned it to oblivion.

Kennedy was by now having difficulty continuing to straddle the divide separating the two parties on the issue of McCarthyism. He soon found himself intimately entangled in the events leading to the demise of Joe McCarthy, which began on 18 June 1953, the day McCarthy hired J. B. Matthews as subcommittee executive director. Matthews's assignment was to clean up the administrative mess created by Cohn and to replace Kennedy's boss, the phlegmatic Frip Flanagan, whom McCarthy eased out under pressure from J. Edgar Hoover. McCarthy committed two significant errors by appointing Matthews.

First, he triggered a partisan reaction within the subcommittee by failing to consult other senators before naming Matthews. A former Methodist minister and recanted leftist activist, Matthews was to be McCarthy's resident expert on Communism. But Matthews's selection outraged southern Democratic senators, especially John McClellan of Arkansas. In an article published just before he joined the subcommittee, Matthews had singled out the Protestant clergy as "the largest single group supporting the Communist apparatus in the United States today." Influential clerics moved quickly, exhorting senators to remove Matthews. The subcommittee Democrats, Stuart Symington (Missouri), Henry "Scoop" Jackson (Washington), along with McClellan, succeeded in forcing McCarthy to fire Matthews; then they all resigned from the subcommittee. Their actions represented the first organized Democratic protest against McCarthy's tyranny in the Senate.[13]

McCarthy's second, far greater mistake was failing to clear Matthews's appointment with J. Edgar Hoover. Since the Wheeling speech, the FBI director had clandestinely served as McCarthy's political consultant, providing him direct (and illegal) access to FBI files, counseling him on handling personal attacks, and exercising a virtual veto over staff appointments, including, presumably, Robert Kennedy's. Hoover distrusted Matthews, whom he considered an irresponsible publicity seeker.

Thinking to appease Hoover, McCarthy named an active FBI agent, Frank Carr, to fill Matthews's position—though again, astonishingly, without gaining Hoover's consent in advance. Director Hoover feared he would have to "lean over backwards" to avoid appearances that "Carr was a pipeline" into a Bureau at the beckon of Senator McCarthy. By this time Hoover had concluded that McCarthy's impudence threatened the FBI's reputation for impartiality, even as it raised questions about the senator's future. The savvy Bureau martinet quietly but decisively cut loose McCarthy's foundering vessel.[14] Without Hoover's information, guidance, and protection, its sinking was only a matter of time.

Resigning from the Subcommittee

How much Robert Kennedy knew of these developments is uncertain, but he resigned on 29 July, a date that corresponds with the Matthews controversy, the fall from grace of his sponsors McInerney and Flanagan (both of whom failed to demonstrate sufficient anticommunist zeal for Hoover), the FBI abandonment of McCarthy, and the Democratic counterattack.[15] Taken together, those events offered sensible justification for Kennedy's resignation. But his 1960 book, *The Enemy Within,* makes no mention of Matthews, Hoover's reaction, the tenuous positions of McInerney and Flanagan, or the pressures from the Democratic side of the aisle. Likely influenced by such subsequent events as the army-McCarthy hearings and the Senate censure of McCarthy, and out of personal loyalty to McCarthy, Kennedy in the book blamed Cohn and Schine for the disarray within the subcommittee.

Most of McCarthy's investigations, Kennedy asserted, "were instituted on the basis of some preconceived notion" or "pet theories" of the chief counsel. "Cohn and Schine," according to Kennedy, "claimed they knew from the outset what was wrong; and they were not going to allow the facts to interfere." "I thought McCarthy made a mistake in allowing the Committee to operate in such a fashion," Kennedy concluded, "told him so and resigned."[16] But the reality had not played out so simply.

Undeterred by the torrent of criticisms of McCarthy, Kennedy would have preferred to remain on the subcommittee, on condition that Cohn be fired. McCarthy naively hoped to retain both young firebrands. Indeed, FBI files indicate that McCarthy considered offering Kennedy the staff director's position to replace Matthews and that he sent his administrative assistant, Jean Kerr to discuss the matter with J. Edgar Hoover.

Young, attractive, and clever, Jean Kerr was much more than an office assistant. An effective political operative and (along with Cohn) the McCarthy Committee's liaison to the FBI, she was also romantically involved with McCarthy. They were married in September 1953. During their lengthy courtship, Kerr and McCarthy often socialized with Robert and Ethel Kennedy, traveling with them to Hyannis Port and frequently dining with them in Georgetown.[17] Friendship or no, the prospect of Kennedy as staff director alarmed Kerr, who expressed those misgivings to J. Edgar Hoover.

Two weeks before Robert Kennedy's resignation, Kerr went to Hoover to secure his personal recommendation and approval for a new staff director. Such meetings were evidently common, as Hoover appreciated her stabilizing influence on McCarthy and respected her judgment. He also accorded her special treatment, ordering FBI agents to provide her "every possible courtesy" when traveling, which included chauffeuring her around on a Hawaiian vacation in 1950, a courtesy that did not escape the attention of columnist Drew Pearson. Kerr and Hoover shared concerns over the general incompetence of the staff and the frequent personality clashes, which seemed to pivot around the Kennedy-Cohn differences.

Hoover revealed no special animus toward Kennedy, contrary to Cohn's later claims. But neither was he enthusiastic about working with him. The director told Kerr that he "did not know anything about Mr. Kennedy," which, of course, was not true, but Hoover's indifference and Kerr's opposition foreclosed any possibility that Kennedy would be promoted.[18]

Whether he meant to or not, Hoover did a favor for Robert Kennedy and his family by saving them from greater attachment to the imminent political disgrace of McCarthy. In fact, some have wondered if Hoover warned Joseph Kennedy of the FBI's intentions to abandon McCarthy, after which the father convinced his son to resign.[19] Robert's less than forthcoming explanation for his departure invites such speculation. Asked ten years later why he had anything to do with McCarthy, Robert replied, "I thought there was a serious internal security threat to the United States; I felt at that time that Joe McCarthy seemed to be the only one who was doing anything about it. I was wrong."[20]

In accepting Kennedy's resignation McCarthy said he hoped Robert would "consider coming back later on in the summer."[21] But had Robert Kennedy remained on the subcommittee after July 1953, the McCarthy association would have seriously jeopardized the Kennedys' standing in the Democratic party and John Kennedy's chances of winning the Democratic presidential nomination. Curiously, the Kennedys ignored or considered themselves immune to the partisan risks entailed in Robert's relationship with McCarthy. Senator Kennedy, however, expressed pleasure and great relief when his brother finally resigned.[22]

Whatever may be said about his later attitudes and behavior, Robert Kennedy departed McCarthy's staff still believing in the rightness of the anticommunist crusade, still on good terms with McCarthy, and still possessed of a conservative view of world affairs and domestic politics.

Although his liberal supporters would prefer to believe otherwise, Kennedy's resignation was not the result of some liberal conversion experience or great awakening to the evils of McCarthyism. Instead, it seems the combined product of professional pride over not receiving the staff director's position, political expediency to avoid being caught on the wrong side of an impending partisan conflict, and personal revulsion over the conduct of Roy Cohn.

Kennedy went to work in August 1953 for the Commission on the Reorganization of the Executive Branch, chaired by former president Herbert Hoover and commonly called the Hoover commission. Joseph Kennedy, a member of the commission, hired Robert as his executive assistant. Robert developed a personal liking and great respect for Hoover, but he grew bored by the details and slow pace of the commission and uncomfortable working for his father. He resigned after a few months.[23]

The period from July 1953 to January 1954 marked a professional and personal nadir, a time of anger, confusion, depression, and disorientation, for Robert Kennedy. Committed to government service as a career, he found himself without a decent position or promising prospects. When not morose and withdrawn, he was ill-tempered and combative. As in similar periods, he vented his frustrations through physical violence, this time in a bloody fistfight with a Georgetown University student during a touch football game that fall. Lem Billings described these months as the "bad doldrums" for Robert.[24] Virtually all who met him then came away with the same initial impression: Here was an arrogant, argumentive, quick-tempered, opinionated, self-righteous, and extremely unhappy young man.

The growing attention paid by his family and the public to his older brother heightened Robert's discomfort. Senator John Kennedy was treated like a movie star, his achievements and personal milestones magnified and celebrated in the media. Such an event was his September 1953 marriage to Jacqueline Bouvier, which Joseph Kennedy succeeded in postponing until after publication of an extremely flattering *Saturday Evening Post* article describing John Kennedy as America's most eligible bachelor. The media labeled the wedding in Newport the social event of the year, and the bride and groom the perfect couple. Robert, as best man, stumbled and sweated his way through a wedding toast. One guest remarked that the Kennedy brothers looked "too tan and handsome to be believed."[25]

Army-McCarthy and Kennedy-Cohn

Meanwhile, in late July 1953, an armistice had ended the Korean War, reducing the public's tolerance of McCarthy's Communist-hunting forays and strengthening the courage of the scoundrel's critics. Apparently unconcerned, McCarthy, Cohn, and Schine continued to antagonize and attack. That fall they investigated an imaginary Communist infiltration at the Army Signal Corps installation at Fort Monmouth, New Jersey. McCarthy's fabricated claims that Fort Monmouth was the hub of a massive espionage ring caused a stir in both the army and the White House. In October, when G. David Schine was drafted, Cohn and McCarthy attempted to coerce the army into giving him a commission. Cohn threaten to "wreck the army" unless Schine received special privileges. The army wanted McCarthy to back down on the Fort Monmouth investigation. Schine did not get a commission, but he did receive preferential treatment.[26]

By January 1954 McCarthy had shifted to the defensive. Fearing his Senate appropriation would be imperiled, and with it his further investigation of the army, McCarthy coaxed the Democrats into ending their boycott of the subcommittee on condition that a "code of rules" be drawn up and a minority counsel appointed for the Democrats. Robert Kennedy, the new counsel, happily took up his duties in February.[27]

The furor between the army and McCarthy revolved around a series of charges and countercharges. McCarthy charged that "certain individuals in the Army have been promoting, covering up, and honorably discharging known Communists." It all came down to the promotion and discharge of one army dentist, Major Irving Peress, who claimed Fifth Amendment protection in testimony before McCarthy's subcommittee rather than answer questions about his political beliefs before he entered the army. The army countered with charges that McCarthy and Cohn had exerted undue influence in trying to gain favors for Schine after he was drafted. On 16 March 1954 the Permanent Investigations Subcommittee voted to investigate the allegations of both sides. McCarthy, in effect, would be investigated by his own committee, with Robert Kennedy as counsel for the prosecution.

The army-McCarthy hearings began 22 April and concluded 17 June 1954. Final reports faulted both sides. Although significant constitutional issues lay at the heart of the dispute, legal outcomes proved of less consequence than the images projected via television from the stately Senate Caucus Room into American homes. Each day twenty million Americans watched the hearings on television, as McCarthy and Cohn and their arrogant misdeeds, disrespect of authority, and disregard for common decency came gradually into focus. Joseph N. Welch, the eloquent and crafty special counsel to the army, exposed with patient questioning and polite disdain the often illegal and usually unethical workings of the subcommittee under McCarthy and Cohn.[28]

As dramatic public spectacle and massive electronic civics lesson, the army-McCarthy hearings became the fashionable place to be in Washington that spring. Robert made sure a seat was reserved for Ethel, who attended all thirty-six overflow public sessions. One day, Kennedy arrived in the Caucus Room to find Pearl Mesta, former ambassador to Luxembourg and celebrated Washington hostess, ensconced in his customary chair right behind Senator McClellan. The young counsel's sheepish pleas had no effect on the matronly Mesta, who regarded her presence as more important than his. Ruth Watt, the chief clerk, exclaimed later, "Bob couldn't get her out of the seat!" Finally, Kennedy pulled up a metal folding chair and squeezed in between Mesta and McClellan.[29]

An important partisan objective hovered over the hearings' carnival atmosphere. The Democrats intended to make it clear that McCarthy was a "Republican problem." As Democratic counsel, Kennedy's foremost responsibility was to focus on the fact that a Republican senator was challenging the constitutional authority of the Republican president. Kennedy, however, had a personal, secondary objective: to humiliate Roy Cohn and drive him from the subcommittee.

At the first opportunity, Kennedy went to work on Cohn. On 23 February, the day Kennedy and the Democratic senators returned to the subcommittee hearings, Cohn subpoenaed an unsuspecting Pentagon teletype worker, Annie Lee Moss, and accused her of being a member of the Communist party. Kennedy relished revealing that Cohn had called the wrong Annie Lee Moss. Democratic senators pounced on Cohn's error. McCarthy and Cohn found themselves defenseless before the Democrats' indignation and their unrelenting criticisms of the sloppy staff work.[30]

The Annie Lee Moss incident marked Robert Kennedy's first direct contact with the FBI and J. Edgar Hoover. At Senator Jackson's direction, Kennedy went to the FBI to request the file on Moss. (Cohn said Kennedy "stormed" into the Bureau and demanded to see the file.) Forewarned by Cohn, Hoover denied Kennedy access to the file and cautioned his assistants on the need to show "absolute circumspection in any conversation with him." Hoover, according to Cohn, referred privately to Robert as "an arrogant whipper-snapper."[31] But Cohn had made an enemy for life of Robert Kennedy. He would need more than Hoover to deter the minority counsel.

Robert Kennedy did little to conceal his animosity toward Cohn. Just before the commencement of the army-McCarthy hearings, Robert sent word to McCarthy that he intended to go after Cohn. And, according to a newspaper reporter, Kennedy offered to supply details of Cohn's demands on the army for preferential treatment for Schine, on condition they not be attributed to him.[32]

Once the hearings started, Kennedy sat in the background, wearing dark horn-rimmed glasses and a studious, often glum, expression, passing notes and whispering advice to the Democratic senators, making himself useful and slowly gaining their confidence. Because of his prior service to McCarthy, he often functioned as a courier between the Wisconsin Republican and the Democrats on the subcommittee.

One such instance involved Stuart Symington, the tall, imposing, and articulate senator from Missouri who carried the brunt of the Democrats' burden for exposing McCarthy's character and methods to the American people. Symington's reserved demeanor sharply contrasted with McCarthy's absurd bellicosity. When McCarthy sensed Symington ("Sanctimonious Stu," as McCarthy derisively referred to him during the hearings) gaining the upper hand, he passed a message to Kennedy: "Tell Stu that unless he takes it easy I will put his criminal record on television." Symington's "criminal record" consisted of a teenage misdemeanor of no consequence. Kennedy was invited to breakfast at Symington's house to review the situation with two of Washington's most respected lawyers, Clark Clifford and Abe Fortas. When Kennedy returned with a message to McCarthy that effectively ended the matter, he had crossed a partisan and professional Rubicon.[33]

During the army-McCarthy hearings Kennedy assisted Democratic senators by suggesting ways to ridicule Roy Cohn. On 11 June, during an examination of G. David Schine's hare-brained schemes to rid the world of Communism, Kennedy passed a note to Scoop Jackson suggesting the senator probe Cohn's incredible claim that, without benefit of formal scientific training, he had investigated attempts by certain scientists to retard progress on the construction of the hydrogen bomb. Jackson's questions drew derisive laughter from senators, staff, and the audience. Cohn stonily observed the snickers shared by Kennedy and the Democratic senators.

When the hearings recessed, Cohn approached Kennedy. As loud and angry words flew, bystanders stepped between them before they began throwing punches. Witnesses who heard Cohn threaten to "get" Senator Jackson for his ridiculing remarks saw him brandish a file folder with Jackson's name on it. A United Press reporter remembered Cohn yelling, "You hate me!" and Kennedy replying, "If I hate or dislike anyone, it's justified." Reporters also heard Kennedy say, "Don't warn me. You won't get away with that, Cohn. You tried it with the Army, you tried it with the Democratic Senators. Now you are trying it with me. Don't try it, Cohn."[34]

"Do you want to fight now?" Cohn yelled. Onlookers had to restrain him. Meanwhile Kennedy made his deliberate way through the crowd, away from McCarthy's infuriated chief counsel. To compose himself, Kennedy went directly to the Senate cloakroom, where he sought out his brother for solace and advice.[35]

The next day newspapers headlined the "Kennedy-Cohn feud." Its origins lay in Robert's disappointment over not being named chief counsel, Cohn's degrading treatment of Kennedy on the staff, and Robert's belief that Cohn's mismanagement of the subcommittee led to McCarthy's downfall. But the intensity of Kennedy's hatred for Cohn, his near obsession with humiliating him, lay in Cohn's far greater sin: He had tried to smear another member of the Kennedy family. In an attempt to keep Robert Kennedy in line, Cohn had told reporter Jack Anderson that an FBI report linking Edward Kennedy to a group of "pinkos" had kept Robert's youngest brother out of army radio school at Fort Holabird, Maryland, in 1951.

Anxious to track the source of the baseless rumor and aware that the FBI selectively leaked materials to McCarthy and Cohn, on 11 May 1954 Joseph Kennedy telephoned Hoover's assistant, Louis B. Nichols, the man later identified as the "chief leaker" within the FBI.[36] Kennedy told Nichols he was not going to tolerate his son's being "victimized." He demanded to know what, if anything, was in the FBI report. Nichols told Kennedy the FBI had not investigated Edward Kennedy and that the matter was an instance of McCarthy's staff "throwing the name of the FBI around." The ex-ambassador declared himself "outraged" over the unscrupulous conduct of Cohn and Schine. Nichols authorized him to state that the FBI had never investigated his son. So armed, the father blocked Anderson's publication of the story.[37] The Robert Kennedy-Roy Cohn confrontation occurred just one month after Joseph Kennedy's call to the FBI.

One week after that confrontation, Kennedy got what he wanted. Cohn quietly resigned and slipped out of Washington. He returned to New York, where he went on to a lucrative, highly controversial legal career.

Cohn later tried to patch up their differences, but Kennedy refused even to speak to him. One evening years later, seated at a table adjacent to Cohn's in a New York restaurant, Kennedy insisted on moving to another table. Cohn blamed Kennedy for some of his later problems with federal authorities, alleging that Kennedy, as attorney general, had created a "get Roy" squad in the Justice Department. In truth, Cohn's many run-ins with the law after leaving the McCarthy committee interested Kennedy only marginally.[38]

As for McCarthy, "Joe is getting out of hand," Senator McClellan told Robert Kennedy, "and we have to do something to control him."[39] On 30 June, Republican senator Ralph Flanders of Vermont introduced a motion of censure against McCarthy. In December, the Senate voted

67 to 22 to "condemn" McCarthy's conduct. John Kennedy did not vote on the resolution. Recovering from a back operation the day of the vote, he had the option of announcing his position on the vote, as is customary when a senator cannot be present to vote. He chose to remain silent on the foremost issue of the day.[40]

Senator Kennedy later said he could not oppose McCarthy "when my own brother was working for him."[41] But Robert was not working for McCarthy during the army-McCarthy hearings or at the time of the censure vote. In fact, he directed the writing of the Democratic report on the hearings, which was highly critical of McCarthy. Robert Kennedy later intimated that, had he had a Senate seat in 1954, he would have felt compelled to vote for McCarthy's censure.[42] For some reason his brother did not.

Although embarrassed by McCarthy's censurable conduct, Robert remained a loyal friend as the once powerful figure slipped into a psychological and physical tailspin after the condemnation vote. At a dinner at which he was to receive a major award, Kennedy walked out on a speech by broadcast journalist Edward R. Murrow, whose television show was frequently credited with exposing McCarthy.[43] Robert visited McCarthy in the hospital, comforted his wife, and wept openly on 2 May 1957 when the man who first befriended him as a law student succumbed from the cumulative effects of alcoholism. McCarthy's death "was all very difficult for me as I felt that I had lost an important part of my life," said Kennedy. He accompanied the senator's body to Wisconsin for burial, standing quietly off to the side at the cemetery. He asked reporter Edwin R. Bayley, one of the few who noticed him, not to mention his presence.[44]

Although Robert Kennedy later made it clear that he no longer regarded internal Communist subversion as a major menace and although his views on public policies shifted perceptibly left, he remained suspect in many liberals' eyes because he never apologized for his friendship with McCarthy.

In the climate of political consensus dominating the country during the middle to late 1950s, the anticommunist hysteria subsided and political labels grew less important.[45] Like most Americans of this generation, Robert distrusted ideology, disliked being categorized, and, for the sake of his own interests and personal advancement, disagreed with those who drifted very far from mainstream thinking.

Robert's work on the McCarthy committee brought him his first national award, inclusion in January 1955 on a list of "Ten Outstanding Young Men of 1954" by the U.S. Junior Chamber of Commerce, specifically for "helping to halt trade between allies of the U.S. and Red China." The nomination, arranged by his father, came from the Greater Boston Chamber of Commerce, which praised Robert's service as president of the Joseph P. Kennedy, Jr., Foundation and gratefully acknowledged the foundation's $50,000 donation to Boston's Jimmy Fund, then went on to praise his management of John Kennedy's 1952 Senate campaign, which the chamber citation (emended by hyperbole supplied by Joseph Kennedy's pen) labeled "one of the best organized in the history of man."[46]

Kennedy's career received a hefty boost when the Democrats recaptured control of the U.S. Senate in the 1954 congressional elections. When the 84th Congress convened, Senator John McClellan became chair of the Permanent Investigations Subcommittee; on 20 January 1955 he appointed Robert chief counsel and staff director. Anticommunist issues carried over into the McClellan-Kennedy regime on the subcommittee, including such unfinished McCarthy-Cohn business as the Irving Peress matter, security at Fort Monmouth, and alleged Communist infiltration of defense plants. McClellan's and Kennedy's reports did not contain the vituperative and vindictive flavor of McCarthy and Cohn's, but they took an equally direct and hard-line approach that emphasized the "clear and present danger" of Communist infiltration.[47]

Kennedy soon attracted headlines with his investigation of various conflict-of-interest cases. Included among them was that of Harold Talbot, secretary of the air force, who journalist Charles Bartlett found had solicited government business for a firm in which Talbot held a half interest. Once on the scent, Kennedy "bird-dogged" Talbot, tenaciously pursuing leads despite lack of support from the committee's senators, who respected the secretary. The evidence, however, was conclusive. Talbot was forced to resign.[48]

At the conclusion of the Talbot hearings on 28 July 1955, Robert Kennedy joined Supreme Court justice William O. Douglas on a tour of five Central Asian republics in the Soviet Union. Neither traveler was happy about being thrown together with the other. Justice Douglas obligingly complied with Joe Kennedy's insistent requests to allow Robert to accompany him on the trip, perhaps because Douglas felt he owed his Supreme Court seat to Kennedy's intervention with President Roosevelt.[49] Robert's mother knew he was "loath" to go and "rather depressed." But his father thought his son's "ego needed boosting and he needed to feel he was interesting to other people."[50]

At first, Kennedy irritated the famous liberal jurist with his negative comments, hostile attitude, and paranoic behavior toward their Soviet hosts. But Douglas and Kennedy found accommodation in their mutual interests in hiking along mountain trails and exploring the diverse natural beauty of Russia, Central Asia, and Siberia. They came to enjoy each other's company and, later, would hike and camp together in the U.S. wilderness and national parks. Kennedy's 1960s positions on the environment were at least partly influenced by his associations with Douglas.[51]

The trip with Justice Douglas gave Robert new insights into the Soviet system and increased his sensitivity toward the Soviet peoples at the same time it hardened his attitude toward the Soviet government. Douglas hoped that the trip would be the "final un-doing of McCarthyism" for Robert. But when Kennedy became ill on the trip, he insisted at first that "no communist is going to doctor me." Thanks, however, to the kind attentions of a Russian doctor, he quickly recovered, although seventeen pounds lighter—mostly because he refused to eat local foods of suspicious origins. He felt well enough to meet Ethel and sister Jean in Leningrad as planned at the conclusion of the trip.[52]

Robert brought back several notebooks full of information and more than a thousand photographs and slides. He wrote an article about impressions gained from the trip, was interviewed by *U.S. News & World Report,* and assembled a set of illustrated public lectures, which he presented before various political groups and service organizations.

These lectures, which decried the "peculiarly harsh and intractable" nature of Soviet colonialism, usually concluded with a warning against making any concessions to the Soviets. Friends described Robert's first efforts at public speaking with expressions ranging from "dismal" to "the worst." His high-pitched nasal voice lacked resonance and projected poorly. He still slurred words and, like his brothers, was prone to stammer. Trembling hands betrayed his nervousness before crowds.[53]

Testing the Waters

In the summer of 1956 Robert took a break from his chief-counsel duties to assist in John Kennedy's run for the Democratic nomination for vice-president. Planning had begun months earlier, when Senator Kennedy had Ted Sorensen prepare a report touting the benefits of putting a Catholic on the Democratic ticket.[54] John Kennedy's goal was to boost his stature within the party by delivering Massachusetts to former Illinois governor Adlai Stevenson, the 1952 Democratic nominee and odds-on favorite for 1956. That done, he expected Stevenson would consider him for the second spot on the ticket. First, however, he had to brave the unfamiliar and hostile arena of local politics. "Leave it alone," a skeptical Joe Kennedy told his son. "Don't get into the gutter with those bums up there in Boston."[55]

John and Robert generally obeyed their father's admonitions regarding local politics, which Robert regarded as an "endless morass from which it is very difficult to extricate oneself" and "where you always make enemies." Far better and less risky, they were taught, to get involved in national and international issues. Politicians had a choice, Robert said: "You're either going to get into the problems of Algeria or you're going to get into the problems of Worcester." Local politics, according to the Kennedys, "sucked away all of your strength" and had to be avoided.[56]

Nonetheless, John Kennedy inserted himself into the struggle for control of the state committee, challenging the Democratic regulars and powerful Boston congressman John McCormack, who was later elected House Speaker. Using the apparatus set up in 1952, Ken O'Donnell and Larry O'Brien helped Kennedy successfully wrest control of the Massachusetts delegation away from "those bums" and deliver it to Stevenson. For the first time, as one Stevenson insider remarked, John Kennedy had "control over a political situation, knows it, and likes it."[57]

John Kennedy wanted Robert by his side at the convention. He pressed Congressman Tip O'Neill into giving up his seat in the Massachusetts delegation so Robert could attend. "Lightning may strike at that convention," John Kennedy told O'Neill, "and I could end up on the ticket with Stevenson. I'd really like to have my brother on the floor as a delegate so he could work for me."[58] For effect, John Kennedy told a skeptical O'Neill that his thirty-year-old brother was the "smartest politician I ever met in my life." O'Neill could not attend the convention anyway, because a fire had destroyed his home, but he was peeved when Robert expressed no gratitude for the favor. He told Joe Kennedy of his displeasure. "Tip, let me tell you something," O'Neill said Kennedy told him. "Never expect any appreciation from my boys. These kids have had so much done for them by other people that they just assume it's coming to them."[59]

Lightning nearly did strike at the Chicago convention. In a surprise move, Stevenson threw open to the convention the nomination for vice-president. Robert Kennedy said the final decision to go for the nomination was made late at night at the convention by "five or six of us" meeting in a hotel room.[60] John Kennedy's amateur shock troops included his sisters Eunice and Jean; their husbands, R. Sargent Shriver and Stephen Smith; younger brother Teddy; and Jacqueline Kennedy, whose symbolic presence was ill-advised, since she was eight months pregnant and experiencing some difficulties. John Kennedy depended on Ted Sorensen, Connecticut state chair John Bailey, Connecticut governor Abraham Ribicoff, and, of course, O'Brien and O'Donnell. Robert Kennedy and Torbert Macdonald, one of John's Harvard roommates, served as floor managers.

Robert's job, again, was to talk to the father. Joseph Kennedy took Robert's telephone call at his vacation home on the Riviera. "Tell him I'm going for it," John said from somewhere safely in the background. The ambassador argued passionately against John's making a run for the vice-presidency, warning that winning the nomination and going down to defeat with Stevenson would ruin John's chances of winning the presidency in 1960. Ken O'Donnell, who was present when Robert made the call, said "blue language flashed all over the room." Robert gingerly replaced the receiver and said, "Whew, is he mad!"[61]

Busy tracking delegates, roaming the hotel corridors, and stalking the convention floors, the senator's brother always carried a yellow pad on which he kept a running tally of delegate votes.[62] Clumsily organized and fatally crippled by poor communications, the Kennedys in their haste slighted some important Democratic leaders and tactlessly pressured others, including Senator Hubert H. Humphrey of Minnesota and New York City Tammany Hall boss Carmine DeSapio. "Bobby and I ran around like a couple of nuts," Kenneth O'Donnell said later. "It was a joke; we didn't know two people in the place. It was John Kennedy by himself."[63]

The Kennedys arranged to have buttons and banners printed overnight and hastily lined up nominating and seconding speeches. Senator George Smathers of Florida reluctantly gave one seconding speech, thinking to himself that "the guy hadn't done anything politically really." Kennedy's desire for the vice-presidency, Smathers thought, was "totally devoid of any purpose for the country. The object of winning was simply to win."[64] Running short of superlatives, Smathers felt relieved when Robert Kennedy approached the dais, literally pushing John McCormack toward the microphone to make a seconding speech described as "both tepid and unenthusiastic."[65]

On the second ballot, after a flurry of switches and much confusion, the convention selected Senator Estes Kefauver of Tennessee by an extremely close margin over Kennedy. Robert, who suspected something "fishy" had occurred, chafed at the thought that the nomination might have been stolen away via some complicated parliamentary maneuver. However, John Kennedy made an impressive showing; his magnanimous concession speech effectively launched his campaign for the presidency in 1960. When they left Chicago, Robert told his brother, "You're going to be the candidate the next time."[66]

After the convention, John Kennedy flew to Paris, went on to the Riviera, and reported to his father: "We did our best. I had fun and I didn't make a fool of myself."[67] He then departed on a private Mediterranean cruise with George Smathers and brother Teddy. On 23 August, Jacqueline Kennedy went into premature labor. Out of touch aboard the chartered yacht, John did not reach his wife's side until five days later.[68] By then, Robert Kennedy, as had become his wont in life, had tended to matters for his brother. He had driven through the night from Hyannis Port to Newport to be at Jacqueline's hospital bedside when she awoke and to tell her that her baby girl was stillborn. Later, she learned he had taken care of all arrangements, including the burial.[69] "You knew that, if you were in trouble," Jacqueline said, "he'd always be there."[70]

Robert had become the binding force for the Kennedys. The son once viewed by the father as the least likely to succeed was now singled out for the most responsible of the family tasks. In December 1955, for example, Joseph Kennedy changed his will, naming Robert executor of his estate. The ambassador now looked to Robert as the one to "keep the Kennedys together in the future."[71]

Robert assumed the lead in sustaining the family momentum and in building the foundation for the next generation of Kennedys. His solid marriage and growing family encouraged his brothers and sisters both to follow his example and to remain together as a family. When Robert purchased a large house next to his parents' at Hyannis Port, the other children followed suit. Soon, a "Kennedy compound" grew up, where the "world's most exclusive club," as Joseph Kennedy called the family, could gather in seclusion to vacation and celebrate, plan and strategize.[72] In a matter of a few years Robert had moved from being a large question mark to serving as the family's emotional stalwart.

The Kennedy club continued to grow. Adding a child nearly ever year, Robert and Ethel had developed a code for informing their younger children of a new addition. Saying grace, Robert would ask God's blessings on all of the children present at the dinner table "and whatever God sends," setting the children to shouting their preferences for a new brother or sister.[73]

By September 1956, with the birth of Robert and Ethel Kennedy's fifth child, Mary Courtney, their house in Georgetown had become cramped.[74] At the same time, John and Jacqueline Kennedy could no longer bear the thought of living in Hickory Hill, the large Virginia estate they had bought and decorated in anticipation of the child they had lost at birth. They decided to move to a smaller house in Georgetown. Telling his brother, "You look like the one who's going to have all the kids," John sold the stately 130-year-old Georgian mansion to Robert for what he had paid for it.[75]

Situated on six and one-half acres near McLean, Virginia, a half hour's drive from the Capitol, Hickory Hill had once housed General George B. McClellan's Civil War headquarters and later the family of Supreme Court justice Robert H. Jackson. Perfectly suited to Robert and Ethel Kennedy's animated life-style and large family, the house was expanded to nineteen rooms and altered many times during the next eleven years to accommodate five more children, various animals, and a corps of household staff. The Kennedys added a new living room, several bedrooms and baths, a barn, a second swimming pool (for beginners), and a combination bathhouse and movie theater.

Besides a dozen or so dogs and cats, the inventory of animals included horses and ponies, ducks and geese, lizards and iguanas, a large turtle, and several rare species of wild birds, reptiles, and cats. For a time, the Kennedys kept a sea lion named Sandy, whose distracting habits of nuzzling female guests and waddling away to visit a nearby shopping center finally proved too much even for the amateur zoologists in the family. Brumus, an enormous black Newfoundland, and Freckles, a black-and-white spaniel, had the run of the house. Maintaining Hickory Hill required a large staff, including two cooks, a laundress, a governess, a nurse for the babies, two or three maids, social and corresponding secretaries, horse trainers and stable boys, and, in the summer, a yard crew, a pool person, and a swimming instructor.

Visitors to Hickory Hill admired the expensive furniture, handwoven rugs, silk tapestries, French impressionist art, and precious statues. They also could not help noticing that some of those valuable pieces sported the stains, nicks, chips, and other telltale signs of a large and exuberant child-centered family. Far too exuberant, according to the owners of the Georgetown house that the Kennedys had vacated to move to Hickory Hill. When they insisted that Robert Kennedy pay for the extensive damage caused by his children, he refused. The owners threatened to sue. To represent him in the matter Robert retained James McInerney, his boss during his brief stint as a U.S. attorney, who had recommended him for the position on the McCarthy committee.[76]

Ever the protective father, Robert was deaf to criticisms of his children's high-spirited behavior. In fact, he encouraged it, chasing them around the house, tackling them, and falling into a "tickle-tumble," as the children called it, until all collapsed exhausted in laughter and tears. He joined their pillow fights and allowed them to jump on him, all in a totally uninhibited manner.[77]

Robert's household lacked the regimentation and formality of his parents'. He seems to have chosen the opposite of his own upbringing for his children, giving them more autonomy and fewer reasons to question his love. Hickory Hill moved at a frenetic, unfettered pace more akin to Ethel's home in Greenwich. "No doors were ever shut," one overnight guest reported, "and everybody wandered through every room all the time . . . it was quite unlike living in any other house I'd ever lived in before." Even the Kennedy children sometimes found it difficult to live there. Ethel confided that Robert Kennedy, Jr., as a small boy once asked for permission to attend boarding school "to get away from this confusing family."[78]

The master of Hickory Hill was away from home during much of the fall of 1956, traveling with Adlai Stevenson's presidential campaign, to which Joseph Kennedy had reportedly made a large contribution. In return, Robert was permitted to join the official entourage. The Kennedys probably could have rallied the Catholic vote for Stevenson, as Joe Kennedy had for Roosevelt in 1932. But Stevenson was divorced, and Robert Kennedy in particular did not want to sacrifice his credibility on a losing cause. His real purpose in being with Stevenson was to observe how a campaign should, or should not, be run. Without formal duties, Kennedy remained aloof but carefully observant to every detail regarding campaign mechanics.

Summing up his impressions of the Stevenson campaign for Kenneth O'Donnell one evening over a drink, Robert said, "This is the most disastrous operation you ever saw." Stevenson, according to Kennedy, spent too much time writing his own speeches and not enough time working on strategy with his advisors. The campaign lacked proportion; Stevenson would give "an elaborate speech on world affairs to a group of twenty-five coal miners standing on a railroad track in West Virginia." Indeed, Robert found enough faults in the Democratic campaign and its candidate to persuade him in November to vote for Eisenhower.[79]

"I did not like Bobby Kennedy," political correspondent Harrison

Salisbury later wrote of his first encounters with Robert during the 1956 campaign. "He was hard eyed, hard faced, hard minded, and thin lipped. He seemed casual but I did not think he wasted a gesture and I was certain his quick eyes did not miss a thing nor his ears a word." Several journalists covering Stevenson's campaign believed "Bobby had come along without the slightest intention of helping Stevenson." They recognized him for what he was, a "hard-nerved political operator" bent on serving only one master, his family's interests.[80]

Yet, late in 1956, for the first time in his life, Robert deliberately placed his family's interests second to his desire to make a significant contribution on his own.

CHAPTER 5

Investigating Racketeers

A PROTRACTED ARGUMENT between Robert Kennedy and his father—"the worst we ever witnessed," sister Jean remembered—marred Christmas of 1956. The argument grew out of Joseph Kennedy's angry reaction to Robert's announcement of a new project: the investigation of organized criminal influences in labor unions. The Kennedy patriarch loudly decried his son as frightfully naive about the physical and political risks of such an undertaking. Invoking familial bonds that he knew had greater effect on Robert than on his other sons, Joseph Kennedy warned him that an investigation would certainly harm his brother John's chances for the presidency, costing him the support of labor unions. Seeing his arguments had no effect, Kennedy asked Justice William O. Douglas, among others, to try to deter Robert from this risky venture.[1]

All efforts to dissuade him failed. Until now, his father had arranged all of his positions and virtually dictated his professional development. Not only was Robert determined at last to do something of consequence on his own, he believed that the proposed investigation would bring enormous political returns, more than worth alienating unsavory elements in the union movement.

The Rackets Committee

Labor unions in the mid-1950s were tempting targets. Public attitudes toward organized labor, generally sympathetic during the Depression, had gradually stiffened during and after World War II. A rise in the number of work stoppages and an increase in labor violence alienated many Americans. Labor's foes played upon its historic flirtations with socialism to raise suspicions and erode support for unions during the era of anti-Communist hysteria. Further, revelations of corruption and disclosures of connections between certain unions and criminal elements tarnished labor's image. Senator Estes Kefauver's 1951 investigations of organized crime uncovered ties between the underworld and a Detroit local of the International Brotherhood of Teamsters. In 1953 mobsters' control of the International Longshoremen's Association (ILA) and the New York waterfronts became public knowledge and the subject of a movie, *On the Waterfront.* By 1957, with union membership at its peak (27.1 percent of the civilian work force), public opinion favored ferreting out the undesirable elements within unions and instituting long-term structural reforms.[2]

A small group of journalists, chief among them Clark Mollenhoff of the *Des Moines Register-Tribune,* prodded Robert Kennedy to open a Senate inquiry into labor corruption. Mollenhoff, who amassed considerable data on the labor racketeering activities of Detroit Teamsters leader James R. Hoffa, intensified his efforts after the April 1956 attack on New York labor columnist Victor Riesel, who was blinded by acid in retaliation for his attacks on racketeering in New York labor unions. Disturbed by the viciousness of the attack on Riesel (whose views thereafter Robert regularly sought) and impressed by Mollenhoff's investigations, Kennedy began giving the matter serious thought.

The event that finally tipped the scales for Robert was his brother's defeat by Senator Estes Kefauver for the 1956 Democratic vice-presidential nomination. "Well, Goddamn it. Do you believe me now?" Mollenhoff said he told a disappointed Robert Kennedy on the convention floor. Kefauver, Mollenhoff emphasized, "did his investigations [of organized crime] five years ago and it got him enough clout to beat your brother's butt."[3]

Ready to proceed, Robert was uncertain if the Senate had jurisdiction to investigate unions. Also, he knew that the Teamsters had applied intense political pressure to force the abandonment of two previous investigations in the House of Representatives. Mollenhoff argued that the Teamsters' tax-exempt status was all the jurisdiction the Senate needed. As for the two prior investigations, both, he insisted, were "fixed."

Mollenhoff probably was correct on both counts. In 1953, Representative Clare E. Hoffman, a Michigan Republican, had convened a House Government Operations Subcommittee to investigate labor racketeering in Detroit. Soon after, Hoffman, a longtime antagonist of James Hoffa, was ousted from the chair and replaced by Kansas Republican Wint Smith. Smith promptly adjourned the hearings, acting, he said, on political pressure "from way up there." The investigation was reopened in January 1954 with Representative George Bender, an Ohio Republican, as chair. Bender dropped the investigation in return for Teamsters support for his run for Robert Taft's vacant Senate seat. The lessons of these failed efforts were not lost on the young chief counsel.[4] Before facing his father's wrath and jeopardizing his brother's candidacy, he had to be sure the evidence was strong enough to brace himself and his family against any political backlash and to guarantee success. Kennedys did not back lost causes.

That November, Kennedy and two assistants, Carmine Bellino and Jerome Alderman, quietly visited journalists in various cities where investigations of labor racketeering were underway. Traveling under an assumed name, "Mr. Rogers" met Edwin Guthman of the *Seattle Times,* who had investigated David Beck, president of the Teamsters. He also contacted Pierre Salinger of the *San Francisco Chronicle,* John Seigenthaler of the *Nashville Tennessean,* and William Lambert and Wallace Turner of the *Portland Oregonian.* The evidence of labor corruption uncovered by these reporters, Kennedy later wrote, "cried out for an investigation."[5] Robert's boss, Senator John L. McClellan, agreed.

Investigating labor corruption became a political bandwagon. Senators competed for the privilege of leading the investigations. To resolve a jurisdictional dispute between senators on the Labor and Public Welfare Committee and those on the Permanent Investigations Subcommittee of the Government Operations Committee, a separate bipartisan investigating body was chartered on 30 January 1957 as the Senate Select Committee on Improper Activities in the Labor or Management Field. Four Democrats and four Republicans were appointed to the select committee, with Senator McClellan, the ranking Democrat, as chair. A farm boy from Arkansas, John McClellan became a prosecuting attorney known for his independent and righteous actions. Elected to the Senate in 1942, this pillar of the Baptist church adopted a conservative position on social-economic policies, remaining an ardent states' rights supporter and an opponent of racial integration.

McClellan was joined by fellow Democrats Sam J. Ervin of North Carolina, Patrick McNamara of Michigan (a former trades-union member), and John F. Kennedy, whom Robert insisted be added to "balance" the committee. The Republican members were the moderate Irving M. Ives of New York and the conservatives Karl E. Mundt of South Dakota, Barry Goldwater of Arizona, and Joe McCarthy. Of the eight, only John Kennedy and Pat McNamara were considered sympathetic to organized labor.[6] McClellan, of course, appointed Robert Kennedy as chief counsel and staff director.

Over the next thirty months the McClellan committee, or the "Rackets Committee," as the press quickly dubbed it, received testimony from 1,525 sworn witnesses in more than five-hundred hearings that produced 46,150 pages of testimony. The committee's purpose, as Kennedy defined it, was "to learn more about a menacing enemy within our national economic framework—an enemy that is the shame of our nation."[7] Robert Kennedy's pursuit of these enemies within evolved in three phases, beginning with hearings on the theft of union funds by Teamsters leaders, moving to investigations of organized criminal ties to unions, and finally focusing on organized crime itself. The committee scrutinized at various times the Hod Carriers, Carpenters, Sheet Metal Workers, and United Auto Workers Unions, but its main target was the Teamsters.

For this work Robert Kennedy recruited and directed the largest staff assembled for a Senate committee to that time. The thiry-two-year old chief counsel was responsible for 104 lawyers, accountants, investigators, and clerical staff; 46 staffers were on the committee's Washington payroll. To accommodate them, a corridor had to be blocked off and a new suite of offices constructed in the Old Senate Office Building. Another 58 staff members, paid by the General Accounting Office, worked out of offices in Detroit, Chicago, New York, and Florida.[8]

Carmine Bellino, who began working with Kennedy in 1955, was Robert's chief assistant. Formerly chief of the FBI's accounting section, the indefatigable Bellino had a knack for unearthing incriminating entries and deciphering deceptive nuances in the Teamsters' accounting records. When the Rackets Committee's work ended, he remained effectively on retainer to the Kennedys for another ten years. Bellino's sister-in-law Angela "Angie" Novello became Robert Kennedy's personal secretary on the committee staff. She, too, remained with Kennedy until his death.[9] No one on the staff saw him more often, suffered more from his perplexing mercurial personality, or worked through more difficult and trying situations than Angie Novello. Like Carmine Bellino and many others on the staff, she became fiercely loyal to her dedicated and demanding boss.

Kennedy selected Kenneth O'Donnell for his administrative assistant, "borrowing" him without asking from his brother's Senate staff. Several investigative journalists were closely associated with the committee. Although Mollenhoff, Riesel, Guthman, and Seigenthaler, the catalysts for the hearings, did not join the staff, they provided committee investigators with significant leads and filed favorable reports on the hearings. The Teamsters tried to co-opt Pierre Salinger by offering him a position as director of public relations, but Kennedy convinced the rotund and gregarious cigar-chomping reporter to work for the committee instead. Salinger said his first assignment for Robert Kennedy was to serve a subpoena on the Teamsters.[10]

For investigative support Kennedy relied heavily on the Internal Revenue Service (IRS), the Federal Bureau of Narcotics (FBN), and, especially, the FBI. J. Edgar Hoover assigned Courtney Evans, a section chief in the FBI's Criminal Division, as liaison to the McClellan committee. Evans and Kennedy formed a close working relationship that carried over into Kennedy's years as attorney general.

Walter Sheridan, whom Robert Kennedy hired while running up a flight of stairs on the way to a hearing, became the committee's most effective investigator. A former FBI agent and an investigator for the National Security Agency (NSA), Sheridan possessed all of the characteristics that Kennedy valued, including a stoic tenacity, a respect for detail and hard work, and a gift for sifting through mountains of documentation and finding a unifying thread.[11] Finally, he was not filled with self-importance. Kennedy and Sheridan established an almost instant rapport, laughing when they realized they shared a birthday (20 November 1925), navy service, and a love of football. Sheridan later wrote the definitive insider accounts of the government's various cases against James Hoffa.[12]

Kennedy exercised extraordinary control over the committee proceedings, to the point that Republican senators Mundt and Goldwater complained of the chief counsel's usurpation of the committee's discretionary powers. McClellan ignored their pleas and permitted Kennedy to determine the main areas of investigation, schedule hearing dates, arrange the schedule of witnesses, set the order of questioning, take a lion's share of the direct and cross-examination of marquee witnesses, and arrange for John Kennedy to make selected appearances, calculated to maximize media exposure and minimize political risk.

Impressed with the results, John McClellan overlooked Robert Kennedy's brashness and did not object to his manipulation of the agenda, perhaps because the young man's actions lessened his own vulnerability to criticism. Besides, the two unlikely collaborators worked well together. Their contrasting styles and personalities advanced the committee's visibility and effectiveness. The normally subdued McClellan rarely exposed the emotional depths of his concern for eliminating the "human parasites on society," as he referred to criminals, remaining more composed when questioning witnesses than did his irrepressible chief counsel. McClellan's deep-voiced southern drawl, measured speech, and courtly bearing contrasted markedly with Kennedy's sometimes shrill Boston-accented tenor, machine-gun delivery, and aggressive demeanor. Their shared objectives bridged the social and cultural gulfs between the deacon and the altar boy: exposing corruption in America's unions and ridding the country of the criminal scourge.

The Rackets Committee was Robert's show, but the public perceived it as a Kennedy brothers production. The hearings began with John Kennedy preoccupied by his health, his bid for reelection in 1958, and his preparation for the 1960 presidential nomination. To compensate, Robert made sure his brother was present whenever the hearings were televised or whenever an opportunity arose to advance his candidacy for the presidency. Although he spent comparatively little time with the committee, John Kennedy had a large stake in the product of its work. Robert once told O'Donnell that the hearings simply had to succeed. Otherwise, he warned, "it will hurt Jack in 1958 and in 1960. . . . A lot of people think he's the Kennedy running the investigation, not me. As far as the public is concerned, one Kennedy is the same as another Kennedy."

The Kennedys did little to discourage this notion. A witness once addressed Robert as "Senator Kennedy" and told him that the committee counsel "looks exactly like you!"[13] One day, Robert invited brother Edward, then a law student at the University of Virginia, to sit with them at the committee table. At the press's request, the three Kennedys struck thoughtful poses together, as if to intimate that all three were involved in solving some problem facing the committee.[14]

Hoffa: Round One

The McClellan committee, like any investigating body, had to beware of trampling the legally protected rights of those under scrutiny—in this case organized labor—as it went about weeding out the corrupt and irresponsible. Rather than concern himself with protecting the constitutional rights of the accused, Robert Kennedy was absorbed with uncovering wrongdoing and bringing it to light.

In this quest he saw a moral dividing line between "good" unions and "bad" unions. Leaders of bad unions, he believed, inappropriately resorted to constitutional rights or arrogantly invoked fine points of law to cover their misdeeds. By this logic the Teamsters was a bad union because its leaders, Dave Beck and James R. Hoffa, were incorrigibly corrupt, influenced by racketeers; in Kennedy's estimation, they cared only for themselves, not the workers. The United Auto Workers (UAW), on the other hand, was a "good" union, presumably because its leader, Walter Reuther, steered clear of racketeers and, in Robert's view, seemed truly concerned for the plight of working persons.

The first union leader investigated by the Rackets Committee was David D. Beck. A grade-school dropout from an impoverished background, Beck began as a laundry truck driver and was elected president of his Seattle local in 1925, the year Kennedy was born. Recognized as a dedicated and experienced labor innovator, Beck consummated the first areawide trucking agreement on behalf of the Teamsters when he organized the Western Conference of Teamsters. By 1956 Dave Beck had risen to the presidency of the International Brotherhood of Teamsters (IBT). Well-connected in Republican party circles and honored for his civic services, Beck identified with business leaders and considered himself the equal of any CEO. He also developed expensive tastes in clothing and life-style. Genial and convivial around business and political leaders, he was cool and aloof, "an iceberg," according to Hoffa, toward rank-and-file union members. Beck was also ponderous and pretentious, coated with unctuous affectations that Robert Kennedy found personally repugnant.[15]

When Beck finally appeared before the committee after dodging its subpoena for two months, he was defenseless before Kennedy's intense questioning, resorting repeatedly to a claim of privilege against self-incrimination under the Fifth Amendment. Thanks to years of investigative work by Edwin Guthman and the team of Lambert and Turner, Kennedy and his staff demonstrated that Beck had diverted $370,000 from the Western Conference of Teamsters to personal purchases. "He was dead," Kennedy wrote, "although still standing." The statute of limitations had expired on most of the charges, but Beck was ultimately convicted and jailed for income tax evasion and for grand larceny, for taking $1,900 from the sale of a union-owned Cadillac.[16]

Kennedy turned next to the man who followed Beck to the presidency of the Teamsters—James Riddle Hoffa. Born on Valentine's Day 1913 in Brazil, Indiana, Jimmy Hoffa moved to Detroit in 1924 with his widowed mother, who found work in an automobile body plant. He dropped out of school before high school, worked as a stock boy, and then was hired by Kroger's to unload produce from railroad cars. A born organizer, the street-smart teenager started a union of 175 warehouse workers at Kroger's. Fired from his job because of his volatile temper, Hoffa became a full-time but unsalaried recruiter and organizer for the Teamsters. The nineteen-year-old Hoffa received a percentage of the dues of each new Teamster he recruited.[17]

During the Great Depression, Hoffa used his toughness and physical strength to survive and thrive in the coarse business of union organizing. A compact 180 pounds on a five foot, five and one-half inch frame, "the little guy," as his Teamster associates called him, endured many beatings by police and the strikebreaking thugs hired by businesses. "Your life was in your hands every day," he later wrote. He never backed away from a fight. "Guys who tried to break me up," Hoffa said, "got broken up." His many scrapes with the law included one twenty-four-hour period when he was jailed eighteen times during a strike, along with thirteen other arrests on various charges; he was convicted for assault and battery (1937), conspiracy (1940), and extortion (1946). Being arrested, he said, was just part of doing his job.[18]

Teamsters membership tripled during the 1930s, due in large part to the efforts of a talented organizer named Farrell Dobbs. Influenced by the theories of the Russian Communist Leon Trotsky, Dobbs was also the Socialist Workers Party presidential nominee in four elections. In 1937, Hoffa went to Minneapolis for a brief stint to work with Dobbs and observe his techniques. He regarded Dobbs as the "master" and "a hell of an organizer" but could not abide his politics. Hoffa thought Communists were "screwballs" and "nuts."[19]

As the Teamsters grew, gaining respectability and political clout under president Daniel J. Tobin, they sought to sever all connections with Communists. In 1941, Tobin asked Hoffa to return to Minneapolis and physically drive Farrell Dobbs from the union. Using "a hundred crack guys" willing to employ whatever force was necessary, Hoffa defeated Dobbs and took his mentor's position as vice-president of the Central State Drivers Council.

Hoffa eventually extended his control from Detroit and Minneapolis throughout the central and southern states, rising to the IBT vice-presidency in 1952. Respected by Teamsters members for his organizing energies, his efforts to diversify Teamster membership, his independence and integrity, and his sponsorship of centralized bargaining and uniform standards for the trucking industry, Hoffa cared nothing for what critics such as Robert Kennedy said about his methods or his associates.

Hoffa never denied his associations with organized crime figures. Some say he flaunted them. The connection dated to 1941, when, he said, he first called upon Detroit mobsters to "neutralize" his enemies. Hoffa claimed he was no different from bankers, businessmen, and politicians, who he believed also used the services of criminals. Hoffa considered any union leader who did not avail himself of underworld muscle simply a "fool."[20]

The hard-bitten Detroit cynic and the self-righteous Hyannis Port inquisitor were on a collision course. Their paths first intersected on 19 February 1957, when they were the only dinner guests of Edward T. Cheyfitz, a public relations man for the Teamsters and an associate in the law firm of Edward Bennett Williams. Cheyfitz's entree to Kennedy, Williams was making his mark as a highly successful criminal lawyer defending notorious clients, including Teamsters officials. He and Kennedy first met while attending early morning Mass at St. Matthew's Cathedral. They became friendly and occasionally breakfasted together before going to their Washington offices. Partly as a favor to Williams and partly out of curiosity, Kennedy accepted Cheyfitz's invitation for a private meeting with Hoffa.

Cheyfitz hoped to convince the Rackets Committee counsel that Hoffa, unlike Dave Beck, had the best interests of the Teamsters at heart and that despite some rough associates he was honestly interested in reforming the union. Once the two strong-willed physical fitness enthusiasts met and learned of their common interests, Cheyfitz thought, they would come to respect each other.

These two men of divergent backgrounds shared a surprising number of similarities. Both were competitive, driven, unyielding, and demanding. Both were devoted family men. Neither approved of off-color stories. Kennedy rarely drank alcohol. Hoffa was a teetotaler. Both were nonsmokers. Both violated sartorial canon by frequently wearing white sweat socks with expensive tailored suits. Their tastes tended toward the austere and the commonplace. They differed politically, but both hated Communists. Interestingly, both supported the Jewish state of Israel and admired the Israeli people and their spirit.

Both workaholics, the two approached their jobs with spectacular zeal, granting few concessions and tolerating no nonsense. Pierre Salinger recalled leaving the Rackets Committee office late one night with Kennedy and driving by the Teamsters' ornate Washington headquarters. When they saw the lights still on in Hoffa's office, Kennedy said, "If he's still at work, we ought to be." He turned the car around and returned to the Senate Office Building. When Hoffa heard the story he reportedly ordered the lights in his office kept on all night, just to bother and confuse Kennedy.[21]

The veneer of similarities covered profound differences. Hoffa was an amoral opportunist who believed everyone had a price; it was only a matter of finding and meeting that price. Kennedy, although sometimes mercilessly quick to take advantage of a situation, particularly if it helped his or his brothers' political fortunes, nonetheless held a moralist's view of the world. He saw himself as using the forces for good to identify and uproot the forces of evil. To Kennedy's mind, Jimmy Hoffa was the devil incarnate.

On that snowy February evening at Cheyfitz's house Hoffa and Kennedy stalked and tested each other, posturing and posing, verbally strutting their toughness, and issuing thinly disguised challenges. Accustomed to measuring other males by their physical prowess, they sized each other up as combatants in some imaginary physical arena. The former Harvard football player's reputation as an athlete failed to impress the Teamsters boss. In Hoffa's version of the meeting—recalled years later—he claimed to have beaten Kennedy in arm wrestling. Kennedy denied the wrestling story, and the available information sustains his account.

Whatever happened that evening, the men parted loathing each other. Hoffa found Kennedy condescending, a "damn spoiled jerk" who treated him "like the butler." Kennedy, for his part, thought Hoffa "worse than anybody said he was," an insecure "bully hiding behind a facade."[22] Hoffa's claim to have broken everyone who stood in his way led Kennedy to comment later, "It had always been my feeling that if a person was truly tough; if he actually had strength and power; if he really had the ability to excel, he need not brag and boast of it to prove it."[23]

Kennedy had good reason to be wary of Hoffa. Six days before the Cheyfitz dinner, John Cye Cheasty, a lawyer formerly with Naval Intelligence and the Secret Service, told Kennedy, "I have some information that will make your hair curl." Cheasty said Hoffa had offered him $24,000 to get a job on Kennedy's staff, keep Hoffa informed of progress on investigations of the Teamsters, and, among other things, find out why the Teamsters lawyer, Edward Bennett Williams, "was eating lunch twice a week with Bobby Kennedy."[24] Kennedy and McClellan immediately turned over what they knew to the FBI. But Kennedy did not tell the FBI (or McClellan, for that matter) about the Cheyfitz dinner invitation. Although his acceptance of it risked compromising the government's case against Hoffa, to decline, he reasoned, might have raised Hoffa's suspicions.[25]

With Cheasty's cooperation, J. Edgar Hoover set in motion a sting operation to prove Jimmy Hoffa guilty of bribery. On the evenings of 12 and 13 March 1957, FBI motion picture surveillance cameras rolled as Cheasty met Hoffa, handed him a packet of secret documents taken from the committee files, and received cash from Hoffa. When Hoover telephoned the Rackets counsel to tell him the FBI had arrested Hoffa and charged him with bribery and conspiracy, the entire Kennedy household celebrated.

Robert telephoned associates, while Ethel alerted the press. Fifty reporters met them at the courthouse at one o'clock in the morning. Edward Bennett Williams soon arrived to represent Hoffa. Surprised to see Ethel, Williams blurted, "Why aren't you home with the kids?" She did not answer. Despite being her husband's Mass partner and a frequent dinner guest in her home, as Jimmy Hoffa's lawyer Williams had now become one of the "baddies." Ethel did speak that morning to a society reporter, admitting that she had "never been to an arraignment before" and found this one "very exciting." Inside, Williams said he found his client engaged in a heated debate with Robert Kennedy over who could do more pushups.[26]

Hoffa's subsequent indictment yielded a flood of publicity for Kennedy. *Newsweek* hailed him as the Democrats' "bright new star" and as "a man with political ambition himself." Confident the government's case was airtight and "Jimmy Hoffa was finished," Kennedy told reporters he would "jump off the Capitol" if Hoffa were acquitted.[27]

At Hoffa's trial Edward Bennett Williams outmaneuvered government prosecutors at every turn. He manipulated the courtroom atmosphere, devastated Cheasty with an unseemly attack on his human frailties, and surprised the U.S. attorneys by putting Hoffa on the stand to testify in his own behalf. Hoffa swore he had hired Cheasty only as a lawyer, given him money as a retainer, and knew nothing of Cheasty's plans to work for Kennedy.[28]

Robert Kennedy took the stand toward the end of the trial. Even though Edward Bennett Williams had once invited Kennedy to be his law partner and insisted they were "very, very close friends," Hoffa's counsel attacked Kennedy's credibility in what one observer described as a "brutal" cross-examination. Outwardly composed, Kennedy was shaken as Williams repeatedly impeached his professional competence as chief counsel, forced him to concede that he routinely leaked information to the press, and brought out Kennedy's dining with the defendant at Cheyfitz's house only a few weeks earlier.[29]

After a brief deliberation, the jury acquitted Hoffa. The government, according to the jury foreperson, failed to prove a conspiracy, and the jury simply believed Hoffa's word over Cheasty's. The victorious Williams told the press, "I'm going to send Bobby Kennedy a parachute."[30]

The Cheasty case represented the opening shot in a battle between Hoffa and Kennedy that lasted eleven years. After the trial, Cheasty said that Kennedy told him, "We'll get the son of a bitch yet. Don't worry about it."[31]

Hoffa: Round Two

In the summer of 1957, as Hoffa prepared to replace Beck as Teamsters president, Kennedy and McClellan turned their heavy guns directly on Hoffa, calling him before the Rackets Committee. When Pierre Salinger handed Hoffa a subpoena, the Teamster exploded, "You can tell Bobby Kennedy for me that he's not going to make his brother President over Hoffa's dead body!"32

The Rackets Committee hearings entered their most dramatic phase that August—the public confrontations between Robert Kennedy and James Hoffa. From the outset, the young chief counsel kept the street-wise union boss on the defensive. Kennedy probed around the edges of several matters, accusing Hoffa of illegally receiving $120,000 in unsecured "loans" from union officials and businesspeople and insinuating the existence of direct mob ties to the Teamsters, evidenced by the purchase with union funds of an estate owned by a former Al Capone associate. Kennedy showed that Hoffa betrayed rank-and-file Teamsters by creating "sweetheart contracts," revealing Hoffa's part ownership (in his wife's maiden name) of the Test Fleet Corporation, a trucking company financed and managed by a Michigan trucking company. Test Fleet Corporation was guaranteed contracts for shipping Cadillacs. Kennedy charged that the contracts were actually payoffs to Hoffa to guarantee labor peace.[33]

The most sensational allegations arose when Kennedy questioned Hoffa regarding convicted labor extortionist and notorious New York racketeer John Ignazio Dioguardi, better known as Johnny Dio. Confronted with recordings of their wiretapped conversations, Hoffa nonetheless denied conspiring with Dio to organize thirty thousand New York taxicab drivers and to create a group of "paper locals" to control New York City Teamsters. Hoffa told Kennedy he could not recall any of the specifics of his dealings with Dio and did not remember meeting with Dio a few months earlier in a hotel room.

"Mr. Hoffa," Kennedy said sarcastically, "I bet anybody in this country can remember what conversation they had with Johnny Dio or whether Johnny Dio was in their room two months ago."[34] Hoffa insisted he could not.

Hoffa occasionally became tense and argumentive. More often, however, he appeared relaxed, reacting breezily to Kennedy's fusillade of questions and charges. To every Kennedy question Hoffa offered a response but seldom a direct answer. Unlike many labor leaders called to testify, Hoffa never resorted to the Fifth Amendment. In Senator Ives's words, however, Hoffa did "a marvelous job of crawling around it." Kennedy claimed Hoffa often took the Fifth "by proxy," telling the committee he could not recall the details of an answer, then offering the name of someone who could; that person then claimed protection under the Fifth Amendment.[35]

Hoffa bluffed his way through the tough spots, throwing the hearings into confusion with a ploy Robert Kennedy labeled "the use of stout denial," whereby Hoffa insisted that minor points others knew to be true were not true at all. Rather than delay the hearings to recheck the record, such Hoffa statements usually went unchallenged.[36]

Hoffa's impudence frustrated Kennedy. Generally deferential toward McClellan and the other senators, Hoffa addressed the chief counsel as "Bob" or "brother" to unnerve Kennedy. "I used to love to bug the little bastard," Hoffa told an interviewer in 1966. "Whenever Bobby would get tangled up in one of his involved questions, I would wink at him. That invariably got him." Kennedy considered Hoffa's winks a "peculiar thing," opining that "maybe a psychiatrist would recognize the symptoms."[37]

Their mutual hatred intensified. Kennedy remembered Hoffa glaring at him "with a deep, strange, penetrating expression of intense hatred." For perhaps five minutes at a time, the Teamster boss and the young attorney would lock eyes; neither would blink. "There were times," Kennedy wrote, "when his face seemed completely transfixed with this stare of absolute evilness."[38]

Kennedy saw Hoffa as the fabricator of an evil conspiracy against the American creed and one of its most sacred tenets, the belief in the rule of law. From Kennedy's point of view, it was "the United States versus corruption."[39] An enemy of the very system from which he so handsomely profited, Hoffa was a corrupt infiltrator, on a par with Communist saboteurs. Both corruption and Communism had to be eradicated to preserve the integrity and purity of the American experiment.

Hoffa often blamed Kennedy's personal "vendetta" for his many problems with the law, but the Rackets Committee chief counsel was hardly the author of all of Hoffa's woes. In 1957 a dozen grand juries scattered across the country received testimony on suspected Teamster wrongdoing. In September 1957, Hoffa was indicted by a federal grand jury for conspiracy to wiretap subordinates in Detroit Teamsters offices and for five counts of perjury for lying to the grand jury about the wiretaps. The day the indictments came down, the AFL-CIO Executive Committee declared "evidence shows that the Teamsters Union continues to be dominated, controlled, or substantially influenced by corrupt influences." In December the AFL-CIO expelled the Teamsters because of Hoffa's leadership and his criminal associations. IBT secretary-treasurer John F. English defended Hoffa and the IBT at the AFL-CIO convention. "Teamsters never forget their friends," he warned. "As far as our enemies are concerned, they can all go straight to hell."[40]

Hoffa's associates knew Kennedy was not their only worry, although the McClellan committee's aggressive actions certainly generated some of the problems one of his lawyers described at the time as "dropping like confetti at a country fair."[41] Two days before the Teamsters convention, in a blatant attempt to influence the voting for president, the committee issued thirty-four new charges, asserting Hoffa had misappropriated large sums of union funds. Unswayed, the delegates elected Hoffa IBT president by an overwhelming majority.

Citing alleged irregularities in the selection of delegates, a group of Teamsters dissidents, aided by Kennedy's staff, filed an injunction to prohibit Hoffa from taking office. Robert Kennedy exclaimed to the press, "I don't believe we have found one local that elected its delegates properly." In January 1958, however, the dissidents dropped their suit and agreed to a compromise in which a board of monitors was established to scrutinize the management of union affairs. Hoffa was given title of provisional president of the IBT. With the help of Edward Bennett Williams, Hoffa finagled his way around the ruling and enjoyed virtually unconditional control of the Teamsters.[42]

Hoffa's remarkable record with the courts continued to hold. Encountering him in a courthouse elevator while his wiretap trial was underway, Kennedy asked how the trial was going. Hoffa told him, "You never can tell with a jury . . . like shooting fish in a barrel." The trial ended with the jury deadlocked eleven to one for conviction.[43] Then followed a Supreme Court ruling banning the use of wiretaps as evidence in federal courts, which effectively negated the government's perjury case against Hoffa. Retried in New York in the spring of 1958 on the wiretapping charge, Hoffa was acquitted outright. Kennedy was conducting a hearing when word came of Hoffa's latest escape act. His ashen appearance told reporters all they needed to know about the verdict.[44]

Unable to rely on government prosecutors to make a case against the Teamsters president, Kennedy called Hoffa back for another round of hearings. In the committee room bright television lights and boiling tempers stoked Washington's sweltering August heat. Kennedy and McClellan hurled new accusations at Hoffa, but no serious charges stuck.

By September 1958 the strain of the hearings began to tell on Robert. "I am mentally fatigued," he confided to his journal. "We have to keep going, keep the pressure on or we'll go under."[45] His antagonist sensed Kennedy's tiring state. "Look at him, look at him!" Hoffa once snickered as Kennedy reacted wearily to the prospects of extending a session. "He's too tired. He just doesn't want to go on."[46] But Kennedy went on, continuing his barrage of questions, probing for weak points, trying to uncover a crucial piece of evidence to validate his suspicions.

Kennedy proved that Hoffa was associated with a long list of felons, including Frank Kierdorf of Detroit, Joey Glimco of Chicago, Glenn W. Smith of Tennessee, Bernard Adelstein of New York, and Frank Matula of California. He also proved that the Teamsters continued to pay Sam Goldstein, the leader of a New York Local, a salary plus twenty-five dollars a week for "expenses" while he was in prison. Kennedy pounded Hoffa with questions about his personal finances, implying that Hoffa was shamelessly corrupt. Still he could not land a knockout blow. Hoffa fought back, presenting himself as a beleaguered victim of the millionaire boy lawyer and his ambitious brother.

Even as the drama in the Senate committee room played itself out, Hoffa's control over the Teamsters continued to grow. As other unions found themselves declining, the Teamsters negotiated large wage increases, gained employer concessions for additional benefits, and increased and diversified their membership. Hoffa wanted more. He abandoned a proposed giant federation of transportation unions only under pressure from the AFL-CIO. He threatened to call a nationwide "primary strike" to thwart further congressional attempts to regulate unions. Kennedy called the Teamsters Union "the most powerful institution in this country—aside from the United States Government itself." He emphasized that in many parts of the country accessible only by road, the Teamsters controlled transportation and could, if they wished, deny people the staples of life. He warned Americans: "Quite literally your life—the life of every person in the United States—is in the hands of Hoffa and his Teamsters."[47]

In early 1959 Kennedy subpoenaed Hoffa to answer a fresh set of allegations. Asked by reporters to respond to the new charges, Hoffa shouted, "To hell with them."[48] He again told anyone who would listen that he was the persecuted underdog—the victim, as he once put it, of a "vicious bastard" who had developed a "psychotic mania" to "get Hoffa." One did not have to accept Hoffa's version to be uneasy about Robert Kennedy's inquisitorial methods.

Criticism came from many quarters. Kennedy's mentor and friend, William O. Douglas privately admitted he was "not too happy" with some of the "techniques" used in the investigative hearings. Douglas was appalled that the Rackets Committee appeared to presume the guilt of those who invoked their constitutional rights under the Fifth Amendment.[49] Other critics judged far more harshly. Yale Law professor Alexander Bickel said Kennedy embarked on "purely punitive expeditions" and engaged in the "relentless, vindictive battering" of witnesses. No one since Joe McCarthy, Bickel inveighed, "has done more than Mr. Kennedy to foster the impression that the plea of self-incrimination is tantamount to a confession of guilt."[50] A Teamsters lawyer made a telling, if biased, point by listing the various ways the McClellan committee determined guilt, including "guilt by association, guilt by marriage, guilt by eating in the same chop house, guilt by the general counsel's amazement, guilt by somebody else taking the Fifth Amendment." One political scientist, "sickened" by what he considered Kennedy's badgering of witnesses, thought perhaps Robert Kennedy would produce a "Profiles in Bullying".[51]

Others wondered if he had the maturity and stature to manage such an important task with appropriate demeanor and respect for the traditions of the Senate. Kennedy's "fumbling and stumbling," one observer charged, "frequently caused the proceedings to become a Pier 6 shouting contest, rather than an inquiry." And it was true that Senator McClellan at times had to cut short arguments between his excitable counsel and biased witnesses and to rephrase Kennedy's questions to make them less contentious. Yet another critic questioned Kennedy's ethics, decried his "contempt" for the truth and for legal processes, and suggested his "temperamental instability" and lack of legal background made him unfit for the position of chief counsel.[52]

Except for one outburst against a particularly venomous writer, Kennedy offered no comprehensive rebuttal to his critics.[53] A three-part newspaper series and his book *The Enemy Within* put a positive spin on the committee's efforts and ignored the personal criticisms. In his writings Kennedy defended the power of Congress to investigate and stressed the extensive precautions his staff had taken to protect the reputations of innocent persons. The Fifth Amendment, according to Kennedy, makes the work of law enforcement officers "more difficult, but it does not prevent them from accomplishing their objectives." To reassure his critics, he added, "I would not have it changed." Yet Kennedy believed the colleagues or the employers of anyone who invoked their Fifth Amendment rights before Congress "should begin an immediate investigation into his affairs to determine his fitness to hold his position." Constitutional considerations and the presumptive innocence of the accused notwithstanding, Robert Kennedy could not conceal his disgust for those who took the Fifth. "I know of none [of them] whom I should like to work for," he wrote, "or have work for me—or have anything at all to do with."[54]

Various tactical and strategic errors prevented Kennedy from ever producing evidence of an indictable offense on Hoffa's part. His major weakness, in the opinion of UAW counsel Joseph L. Rauh, lay in the awkward way he examined witnesses. "Questioning is an art," Rauh said, "and Bobby wasn't experienced at it." Curiously, Rauh thought Kennedy "didn't know how to go for the jugular."[55]

The larger problem, however, was that Kennedy's approach to the prosecution of Hoffa was strategically flawed. Rather than focus on specific breaches of the law, as he had with Dave Beck, Kennedy fired off a vast array of accusations aimed at proving Hoffa guilty of pervasive wrongdoing. Associating with convicted criminals and giving the chief counsel evil winks, however, were not indictable offenses.

Charges with substantive merit—the Test Fleet Corporation arrangement and Hoffa's misuse of pension funds—eventually were investigated and led to convictions, but the Eisenhower Justice Department refused to present Kennedy's unrefined charges against Hoffa in federal court. Kennedy made the matter a public issue in September 1958. When

Justice refused to prosecute twenty witnesses accused of perjury before the McClellan committee, Kennedy announced that he was sending no further cases to Attorney General William Rogers. Partisanship and political posturing had something to do with Kennedy's conflict with Rogers's Justice Department, but, as William G. Hundley, chief of the Justice Department Organized Crime Section, pointed out, most of Kennedy's cases were not solidly made. Hundley referred some of them to the FBI and the IRS, anyway. But no one, Hundley said, was "breaking their back trying to make cases for Bobby Kennedy."[56]

For the time being, Hoffa had bettered Kennedy. But Robert was determined that there would be another day. "It's been a hard grind all along—for the people who work on our committee and for myself," he told a *Newsweek* reporter in August 1959. "I am not going to lie down and see all that work go to waste."[57]

Meanwhile, Republicans on the McClellan committee, sensing an opportunity to damage Democratic prospects with organized labor, pressed for turning the committee's investigatory spotlight on alleged misdeeds of the United Auto Workers, a union with strong ties to the Democrats. Senator Barry Goldwater, the era's chief advocate for conservative views, claimed that all of Robert Kennedy's public noise about Hoffa and the Teamsters camouflaged the Kennedy brothers' reluctance to investigate the UAW for fear that if they found corruption they would lose crucial partisan support. Senators Goldwater and Mundt insinuated that the Kennedys refused repeated requests to investigate the UAW because they were covering up for Reuther.[58] At the same time, they tried to restrict Robert Kennedy's control over committee procedures. During executive sessions, Republicans vented their hostility toward "that little snotnose," as Senator Homer Capehart of Indiana referred to the chief counsel.[59]

Senator McClellan, though embarrassed by some of his chief counsel's behavior and unsettled by the chiding of colleagues for ceding control over the committee to Robert Kennedy, refused to give in to the Republican demands.[60] He and the chief counsel agreed, however, to appoint an investigator to look into a long bitter dispute between the UAW and the Kohler Company, Sheboygan, Wisconsin, manufacturers of plumbing fixtures.

On 3 January 1958 Kennedy flew to Sheboygan to observe the situation. It was his first exposure to industrial working conditions and to the problems of workers, whose employer in this case refused to grant even a twenty-minute lunch break. Attending Sunday Mass where the sermon was in Lithuanian, walking through the German and Slavic working class neighborhoods, and rubbing shoulders with people devastated by four years of bitter labor strife, Robert Kennedy found himself stirred by the plight of Kohler workers. He returned to Washington with sympathy for the UAW and disgust for the Kohler management.[61]

On 26 February 1958—the day before Robert's sixth child, Michael LeMoyne Kennedy, was born—the UAW-Kohler hearings started in Washington. After five weeks, no evidence of any corruption in the UAW had turned up. "You were right," Senator Goldwater admitted to Kennedy. "We never should have gotten into this matter." All that the hearings proved, Kennedy later wrote, was "that when a strike is long and violent, it will engender great antagonism. And, of course, everybody knew that before we started." A second UAW hearing, called in 1959, closed after only six days. Walter Reuther, whose quiet dignity contrasted sharply with Hoffa's belligerent and defiant demeanor, impressed Kennedy as "an honest union official who attempts to run an honest union."[62]

The first two years of the McClellan committee proceedings produced mixed results. Hoffa remained unscathed, but Kennedy had discredited Dave Beck, exposed corruption in the United Textile Workers Union, and forced the removal of James Cross from the Bakers union, William E. Maloney from the Operating Engineers union, and Max Block from the Butchers union.[63] If the hearings yielded only a modest number of convictions, they paid off politically for the Kennedys in pure gold.

The Brothers Kennedy

The sheer volume of approving newspaper and magazine articles that boosted the Kennedys' popularity had to please Robert. Since the early 1950s, the press had lavished attention on John Kennedy, featuring his struggle to recover from two near-fatal back operations, revisiting his heroic wartime adventure in the Solomon Islands, glamorizing his family and marriage, and praising his skills as a writer of history, as evidenced by the Pulitzer Prize for *Profiles in Courage.* Gradually, however, the print media began to focus on John and Robert Kennedy as a duo.

"The Rise of the Brothers Kennedy," an eight-page illustrated feature in *Look* magazine, appeared during the summer of 1957, when a motion picture based on Dostoevski's novel *The Brothers Karamazov* was enjoying box-office success. Like the fictional Russian brothers, the article intimated, the Kennedys had become part of their country's destiny. That September, the *Saturday Evening Post,* influenced by the wishes of Joseph Kennedy, eerily prophesied that admirers of the Kennedys confidently looked forward "to the day when Jack will be in the White House, Bobby will serve in the Cabinet as Attorney General, and Teddy will be the Senator from Massachusetts."[64]

Meanwhile, the personal ties between John and Robert Kennedy drew tighter, strengthened by their mutual respect, their close working relationship on the McClellan committee, their growing family responsibilities, and their unspoken agreement to accede to their father's wish to put John's career first. When in November 1957 Jacqueline Kennedy gave birth to Caroline, Robert was the parents' natural and immediate choice as godfather. During John's frequent periods of hospitalization, Robert represented his brother at important public functions.[65] To casual observers, perhaps one Kennedy *was* the same as another.

Robert Kennedy must have taken great satisfaction in knowing that his activities on the McClellan committee, contrary to his father's dire predictions, were having positive effects. Never able to distance himself from his sons' affairs, Joseph Kennedy occasionally attended the committee hearings to watch his two sons in action. Word of the appearance of the demanding and critical elder Kennedy sent anxious ripples through the committee staff. They noticed that his father's presence made their boss a "little keyed up, a little tense."[66]

Joseph L. Rauh, Jr., one of the founders of Americans for Democratic Action and counsel to the UAW, remembered how the two Kennedy brothers worked together on the committee. Every time the UAW came under heavy fire from Goldwater and Mundt, John

Kennedy would suddenly appear from out of nowhere. Taking cues from his brother, Senator Kennedy would quibble and fence with Goldwater, inject some humor, ask a few tempering questions to deflate conservative, or anti-UAW, momentum, then leave before matters became too intense. The uncanny timing of John Kennedy's appearances made Rauh wonder if Robert Kennedy used a "walkie-talkie" or extrasensory perception to contact his brother.[67]

Robert Kennedy at once moved to capitalize on the rapport with Walter Reuther and the UAW built during the Kohler hearings. He directly informed the UAW leadership that the Kennedys needed and wanted their support in John's run for the presidency, and he questioned them on the kinds of support they could provide. At a dinner with Jack Conway, Reuther's administrative assistant, Robert made clear his intentions. "We don't want you on the opposite side from us [in 1960]," he told Conway.[68] What considerations the Kennedys gave, if any, remain unknown, but thereafter, the Kennedys could count on UAW support. But in the alliance, born of political expediency, not ardor, neither side was truly comfortable.

Labor leaders tied to the liberal wing of the Democratic party looked to John Kennedy to derive some positive results from the McClellan committee hearings. Here, too, Senator Kennedy saw an opportunity to establish a reputation for legislative competence. For the first time in an undistinguished congressional career, John Kennedy decided to concentrate on a single legislative field and attempt to get his name on a significant piece of legislation. Without his brother's efforts, even this modest foray into lawmaking would not have been possible.

John Kennedy used his seat on the Senate Labor and Education Committee to conduct hearings and draft legislation to implement McClellan committee findings and recommendations for the reform of organized labor. In March 1958, he introduced a bill to curb improper, unethical, and undemocratic practices in labor unions. Mindful of the power of organized labor, Kennedy asked AFL-CIO president George Meany and AFL-CIO chief counsel Arthur Goldberg to review the proposed bill. He amended the bill to eliminate measures they considered punitive, such as a provision to require all union officials to file personal financial reports.

The Kennedy-Ives bill passed the Senate but faced strong opposition from the Eisenhower administration, National Association of Manufacturers, Chamber of Commerce, and Republican interests, all of whom insisted on more restrictions, including one to require labor leaders to sign an affidavit stating they were not Communists.[69] Detractors included James Hoffa, who insisted "the two rich Kennedy boys are trying to get a law passed that will destroy the entire American labor movement." Despite intense lobbying by both Kennedys, the Kennedy-Ives bill failed in the House. "Jimmy Hoffa can rejoice," John Kennedy said afterwards.[70]

The resulting compromise labor reform bill, regarded as a victory for the opponents of unions, contained several provisions drawn directly from the testimony at the McClellan hearings. It banned convicted felons from holding union office for five years after conviction, required union officers to file annual financial reports, and regulated union elections. The AFL-CIO and the UAW opposed the bill, which put the Kennedys in a bind.

Robert Kennedy wanted labor reform, but the compromise bill went too far. John Kennedy gained the liberals' attention with what Arthur Schlesinger described as a "heroic" effort to amend the bill and find a "tolerable compromise." But it was a lost cause. Preferring to sacrifice years of work rather than risk further alienating organized labor, John Kennedy quietly withdrew his name from the final legislation.

Thus, the one legislative outcome of the McClellan committee hearings, the Labor-Management Reporting and Disclosure Act of 1959 (better known as the Landrum-Griffin Act), was regarded as a setback for organized labor. Some union leaders held the Kennedys partially responsible. But, as one of their sternest critics conceded, the Kennedys demonstrated "absolute brilliance" in straddling the issue of labor regulation and sustaining support among both prolabor liberals and antilabor conservatives. Most of the latter represented the electorally pivotal southern states.[71]

Little, however, could slow John Kennedy's presidential bandwagon. In November 1958 he easily won reelection to the Senate, overwhelming Vincent Celeste by a record margin. Joseph Kennedy put himself back into the thick of the action, moving to Boston to oversee the estimated $1.5 million he spent on the campaign. Like Robert six years earlier, Edward Kennedy, twenty-six years old and fresh from law school, wore the title of campaign manager. But, again, the father made all of the major decisions.[72]

The Mafia: Round One

Robert took no active role in John's reelection campaign, partly because he was not needed and partly because the McClellan committee was moving into the third and arguably the most controversial phase of its operations, the investigation of organized crime.

The first several months of testimony before the committee had convinced Robert that labor-union corruption rested on a broad foundation of organized crime that extended across the United States and burrowed into many legitimate enterprises converted to fronts for various illegal activities. During his final year of the hearings, Kennedy focused much of the committee's attention on publicizing the extent to which organized crime had infiltrated the union movement and taken over enterprises such as the garbage removal business and the coin machine industry, including jukeboxes and cigarette machines.[73]

Back in 1951, Senator Kefauver's investigations had disclosed the existence of a "loose-knit national syndicate" dealing in various illegal enterprises and "operating throughout the Italian element."[74] It was known by various names: the Outfit, the Syndicate, the Mob, La Cosa Nostra, and, most commonly by the late 1950s, the Mafia. On 13 November 1957, Joseph Amato, a specialist with the Bureau of Narcotics, testified before the McClellan committee that a certain union member was also known to be a member of the Mafia. Robert Kennedy skeptically inquired if any organization such as the Mafia actually existed.

His answer came the next day. State police became suspicious of a large gathering of luxury cars and limousines with out-of-state licenses at the secluded estate of Joseph Barbara, Sr., located near the small town of Apalachin in the western part of New York. When the police approached, more than sixty very nervous "businessmen" bolted from the house and fled directly into a police roadblock. Another forty persons, including Momo Salvatore (Sam) Giancana and the entire delegation of gangsters from the Chicago Outfit, remained in the house but were subsequently identified through car rental and motel registrations. Giancana later complained to an associate over a tapped telephone line, "Well, I hope you're satisfied. Sixty-three of our top guys made by the cops."

The Commission, as the Apalachin group called themselves, consisted of top-level hoodlums representing every region of the country. Described in the newspapers as a "gangland convention," the Commission had been meeting regularly since 1931 without discovery.[75]

When Robert Kennedy immediately initiated inquiries about the Apalachin meeting, he was startled to discover the FBI "didn't know anything about organized crime." Preoccupied with rooting out Communists, obtaining compromising information on illicit activities of politicians, protecting his bureau from budget cutters, and safeguarding his and the FBI's reputation, J. Edgar Hoover had denied the existence of organized criminal activity for three decades. Hoover told the Kefauver committee in 1951 that organized crime, if it existed at all, was purely a local problem outside the FBI's jurisdiction.[76]

When Kennedy formally requested information on the one hundred persons attending the Apalachin meeting, the FBI, he said, had "not even the slightest piece of information" on forty of them and precious little other than newspaper clippings on most of the others. When he made the same request of Harry Anslinger, director of the Federal Bureau of Narcotics (now the Drug Enforcement Administration [DEA]), Kennedy was impressed to learn "they had something on every one of them."[77] Prior to this he considered the FBI—to use one of his favorite words—"helpful" to the McClellan committee. Now he wondered. He began to ponder the desirability of a national clearinghouse on crime data, a proposal supported by Los Angeles police chief William H. Parker but regarded by Hoover as a threat to his personal hegemony.[78]

Invigorated by the Apalachin disclosures and relying heavily on FBN resources, Robert Kennedy turned the spotlight on organized crime in February 1959 when the McClellan committee opened hearings on the jukebox industry. Over the course of several months, Kennedy interrogated the likes of Antonio "Tony Ducks" Corrallo, so named because of his ability to duck subpoenas; Vito Genovese of New York, who chief clerk Ruth Watt remembered had the "coldest eyes"; and Anthony "Tony Pro" Provenzano, who controlled Local 560 of the Teamsters in New Jersey and who would become a prime suspect in the 1975 disappearance of Jimmy Hoffa.

Several witnesses compelled to act out their tough-guy roles often found themselves countered or matched by the bravura of the chief counsel. For example, Joseph "Crazy Joey" Gallo, the alleged killer of Mafia boss Albert Anastasia, appeared in Kennedy's office attired totally in black, looking as though central casting had sent him over for a part in a B gangster film. To punctuate his presence, Gallo felt the rug ("It would be nice for a crap game"), deliberately knocked a water glass on the floor, and ordered his bodyguard to frisk another man in Kennedy's waiting room ("If Kennedy gets killed now everybody will say I did it"). When Gallo offered to use his "influence" in Brooklyn to help John Kennedy get elected, Robert said, "If you really want to help us, you can tell everybody that you are voting for Nixon." Joking aside, Kennedy found these gangsters loathsome. When Joey Gallo and his brother Lawrence were called to testify, Kennedy recalled, "their dress, their swagger, their foxlike faces, and their 'two-step shuffle' to the witness stand created a furor in the hearing room."[79]

Through all of this the chief counsel betrayed not the slightest concern for his own personal safety. With audacious belligerence he questioned some of the most notorious and reputedly dangerous men in America.[80] Kennedy chiseled a reputation for toughness into the annals of congressional investigations through his exchanges with such gangsters as Joey Glimco, Sam Giancana, and Carlos Marcello.

Glimco, president of a Chicago Teamsters local, responded to a Kennedy question, "I respectfully decline to answer because I honestly believe my answer might tend to incriminate me." To which the chief counsel dryly responded, "I would agree with you." Kennedy gave brashness a new meaning when he continued, "You haven't got the guts to [answer] have you, Mr. Glimco?" Senator McClellan, taking a cue from his young associate, dispatched Glimco neatly: "Morally you are kind of yellow inside, are you not?"[81]

Sam Giancana, the heir of Al Capone's outfit and reputedly one of the most dangerous mobsters in the country, refused to answer any of Kennedy's questions about organized crime in Chicago. As Giancana sat smirking in the witness chair, appearing to enjoy some private joke, the following exchange occurred:

Kennedy: "Would you tell us anything about any of your operations or will you just giggle every time I ask you a question?"

Giancana: "I decline to answer. . . . "

Kennedy: "I thought only little girls giggled, Mr. Giancana."[82]

No one laughed, least of all Robert Kennedy, when Carlos Marcello sat down to testify on 24 March 1959. Earlier, Kennedy had received a personal four-hour briefing from Aaron Kohn, director of the Metropolitan Crime Commission of New Orleans, detailing the extent of Marcello's criminal network and his manipulation of law enforcement and public officials in Jefferson Parish and New Orleans, Louisiana. To the FBI Marcello was a harmless seller of canned tomatoes, "just a stupid little man." Aaron Kohn had spent years proving otherwise.[83]

Kohn offered Kennedy specific evidence of Marcello's illegal slot machine operations and bribing of public officials, as well as circumstantial evidence of his involvement in several murders, drug trafficking, and various other crimes. Impressed by the report, Kennedy assured Kohn, "We will do something about Marcello. We cannot permit this kind of corruption to exist in the United States."[84]

Carlos Marcello, the man who the House Select Committee on Assassinations concluded in 1978 had the "motive, means, and opportunity" to assassinate President John Kennedy, was born in 1910 in Tunisia of Sicilian parents. His parents later became naturalized U.S. citizens, but Carlos never bothered to apply. In 1953, after two felony convictions and accusations by the Kefauver committee of two decades of criminal activity, Marcello was declared an undesirable alien and ordered deported.[85]

Kennedy and several Rackets Committee members questioned why Marcello's deportation order, nearly six years after its issuance, had not been executed. They were exasperated by Marcello's scowling defiance of the committee and by his repeated, and, in their view, undeserved, reliance on the protection of the Fifth Amendment. Senator Sam Ervin spoke for the majority when he said, "Those who have no claim to any right to remain in America, who come here and prey like leeches upon law-abiding people of the country, ought to be removed from this country."[86] Seething at Marcello's arrogant and contemptuous behavior before the committee, Robert Kennedy promised that, if ever the opportunity arose, he would do whatever was necessary to carry out the deportation order.

The organized crime phase of the McClellan committee hearings grabbed a lot of attention but produced little in the way of substantive criminal prosecutions.[87] McClellan and Kennedy mainly intended to inform Americans of the existence of organized crime through public exposure of known or suspected criminals and of their infiltration of legitimate businesses. Being hauled before the committee and publicly accused was sometimes punishment in itself.[88]

Kennedy became convinced of the need to fight fire with fire. Observing firsthand how criminals such as Gallo, Giancana, and Marcello took advantage of the limitations of government powers, he concluded that "if we do not on a national scale attack organized criminals with weapons and techniques as effective as their own, they will destroy us."[89] This belief probably explains Kennedy's willingness to depart from established legal procedures when pursuing criminal conspiracies as chief counsel and later as attorney general.

Jimmy Hoffa's resort to no-holds-barred tactics and his rash use of bugging devices fueled Kennedy's conviction that stopping people of Hoffa's ilk required extraordinary means. Hoffa, as we know, attempted to infiltrate the committee by bribing Cye Cheasty. Rackets Committee investigators found that Hoffa had also purchased huge quantities of small ultrasophisticated eavesdropping devices and hired wiretap expert Bernard Spindel to record conversations in the office of the Teamsters local in Detroit and even to intercept the FBI's transmissions of surveillance reports on Hoffa.[90]

Growing impatient with the meager results produced by conventional investigatory methods, Kennedy sought more innovative and effective approaches. For example, he expressed no qualms about eavesdropping on suspected criminals.[91] Nor did he evidence interest in the legal distinctions between the deployment of a telephone wiretap and an electronic bug or in the legal restrictions regarding the use of information obtained from such devices.[92] Kennedy used such methods to gather information, knowing the results could not be admitted in criminal prosecutions but expecting the public exposure to ruin wrong-doers.

When questioning Hoffa, for instance, Kennedy often tried to "refresh" Hoffa's memory by playing tape recordings of Hoffa's telephone conversations with known hoodlums. Because the origin of the recordings was not always publicly specified, they opened the door to later speculation regarding how the tapes were obtained and by whom. As far as can be determined, the tapes played in public sessions were legally obtained by local law enforcement officials, such as New York City district attorney Frank Hogan. How much wiretapping the Rackets Committee, at Kennedy's direction, engaged in on its own remains uncertain. According to the chief clerk, wiretaps were used early in the probe—"just for a little while because it was a novelty more than anything else"—but stopped when the courts declared the practice illegal.[93] In March 1959 the FBI identified one of the McClellan committee investigators, Edward M. Jones, as the committee "wiretapper." On at least one occasion Kennedy investigators said they concealed a "recording device"—more likely a small transmitter—on an informant to eavesdrop on conversations with suspects. Those tapes, played during committee hearings and for the benefit of journalists, were not used in court.[94]

Robert Kennedy may have privately commissioned the use of wiretapping and eavesdropping. Edward M. Jones, besides working for the Rackets Committee, was also privately employed by the Kennedys to scan rooms for bugs and to investigate suspected wiretaps on the Kennedys. The Kennedy family, with some cause, was protective of their privacy and hypersensitive about wiretaps and bugs. Jones's duties evidently included tapping the telephones of employees suspected of compromising confidential information about the family. Robert Kennedy's involvement in such matters is unclear.[95]

If Robert Kennedy rationalized some of his actions, so did Jimmy Hoffa—in the form of personal attacks on Joseph Kennedy. To justify his own conduct Hoffa said, "You take any industry, and look at the problems they ran into while they were building up—how they did it, who they associated with, how they cut corners. The best example is Kennedy's old man." On another occasion Hoffa said, "To hear Kennedy when he was grandstanding in front of the McClellan Committee, you might have thought I was making as much out of the pension fund as the Kennedys made out of selling whiskey."[96] Repeated and embellished upon by mobsters, Hoffa's charges have gained a certain currency in the popular culture and among organized-crime researchers. Indeed, authors refer offhandedly to Robert Kennedy's father as an "old bootlegger." One writer claims that "mobsters recognized him as one of their own."[97]

These charges deserve mention only because some writers have asserted that a Joseph Kennedy bitterness toward alleged bootlegging competitors instigated Robert Kennedy's initial involvement in the Rackets Committee investigations and his later campaign against organized crime. One of them, gangster Frank Costello, claimed that he "helped Kennedy get rich."[98] Despite repetitious tales to the contrary, Joseph Kennedy accumulated an unconscionably large profit from his liquor import business, with some questionable manipulation of the import licensing laws, in entirely legal ways, according to Doris Goodwin.[99]

Hearsay abounds, but Robert Blakey, professor of law, director of the Notre Dame Institute on Organized Crime, and chief counsel for the House Select Committee on Assassinations, thoroughly investigated the rumors and found "no evidence that Joseph Kennedy was connected with [Frank] Costello or with any other crime figure." Noting, however, that Kennedy "was widely regarded in the underworld in less-than-flattering terms," Blakey concluded that "little of certainty could be established."[100]

Still, if Joseph Kennedy had something to hide in the months and years prior to the start of Robert Kennedy's campaign against labor racketeering, the FBI and the Anti-Trust Division of the Justice Department failed to uncover it. Between October 1953 and April 1954 the Anti-Trust Division conducted an "extensive" investigation into Kennedy's importation of scotch whiskey and the involvement of the Roosevelt family in abetting Kennedy's operations. The probe turned up no information to substantiate suspicions of illegal activity or antitrust violations. Further, Joseph Kennedy underwent a complete FBI background check pursuant to his 1956 nomination by President Eisenhower to the Board of Consultants on Foreign Intelligence Activities. All references regarding his character, reputation, and associates were positive. A check of FBI files and local police files turned up no indications of criminal activity or associations.[101]

Clearly, Robert Kennedy became chief counsel of the McClellan committee not to satisfy some sinister agenda of his father's—Joseph Kennedy, after all, bitterly opposed the move—but to gain a sense of his own worth, to establish himself within his family, and to respond to a compulsion embedded since early childhood to do the right and the moral thing.

The years of the McClellan committee investigations proved difficult yet fulfilling ones for Robert Kennedy. Friends and family noticed the effects on his outlook and his general behavior. "For the first time in his life he was happy," LeMoyne Billings noted. "He'd been a very frustrated young man, awfully mad most of the time, having to hold everything in and work on Jack's career instead of his own. I think he found himself during the Hoffa investigation."[102] Robert Kennedy's dream of succeeding on his own had started to come true.

Success did little to soften his personality. Journalist Clayton Fritchey, who met Robert during the Rackets Committee hearings, noted that he was "not warm or open" and often "gave the impression of being tough, somewhat suspicious, skeptical—if not cynical; he tended to look at people in a way that was a little forbidding." Robert Kennedy first impressed lawyer and civil rights activist Harris Wofford as "an arrogant, narrow, rude young man," in a word, "insufferable." The chief counsel kept Wofford and other nonaugust visitors to his office waiting at the far end of the huge room while he finished his lunch, attended to telephone calls, or worked on papers. After a time, Kennedy would lift his eyes from his desk and greet the intruder with a sullen, sulking silence; into the silence he would murmur inconsequential remarks, interspersed with moralizing diatribes against Communists and organized criminal influences.[103]

Regardless, Robert Kennedy had become a prominent newsmaker on the Washington scene. He maintained amicable, often close, relations with several of the reporters covering the hearings, inviting them to dinner parties at Hickory Hill and impressing them with his candor and directness.[104] Kennedy may not yet have realized that when he said something it was news. In January 1958, for example, he told reporters the Rackets Committee was looking into reports that large corporations were using "call girls" to entertain clients.[105] The sensational claim produced a headline but no committee follow up.

Kennedy encountered a totally different reaction in March 1959, when the *Washington Post* quoted him as saying he had received "several" offers of support for his brother's 1960 campaign, if the Kennedy brothers would go easy on certain witnesses before the McClellan committee. Robert told reporters he simply "dismissed" such propositions. Republican senator Karl Mundt, eager to throttle the brash Democratic counsel, said he was "shocked" at Kennedy's comments and demanded he reveal the names of witnesses who asked for leniency in exchange for political support.

Perhaps thinking Kennedy had gone too far this time, Senator McClellan said he knew of no "bribes" and called the committee into executive session to deal with the matter. The committee concluded that reports of political threats and deals offered to Robert Kennedy did not merit all the public attention they had received. In the future, McClellan announced, the chief counsel should report such incidents directly to the committee.

The serious nature of Robert Kennedy's charges attracted the FBI; who learned from Kenneth O'Donnell that the press had "unduly enlarged" upon his boss's comments. O'Donnell admitted that no evidence existed to back up the assertions and said the "contacts" with Robert came in the form of "innuendoes," rather than overt bribes. Finding no grounds on which to pursue the matter, one of Hoover's assistants penned a note on the bottom of the FBI report: "Re: Robert Kennedy—this is what happens when the prodigal son gets too far away from home and papa."[106]

Indeed, the time had come for Kennedy to return home. Besides, the chief counsel's ill-concealed activities on behalf of his brother's presidential campaign were reducing his effectiveness and widening partisan differences on the Committee. In a letter to Senator McClellan dated 10 September 1959, Robert Kennedy permitted himself a small deception when he described the passage of the Landrum-Griffin Act as "the purpose to which we have pointed two years of effort." With the pace of the committee's work slowed, he wrote, now was a convenient time to resign.[107]

Robert's attentions had already moved elsewhere. By early 1959 Kennedy was spending many hours meeting with Lawrence O'Brien, Pierre Salinger, and Kenneth O'Donnell for purposes clear to chief clerk Ruth Watt: "They were running for president in our office after five o'clock in the evening."[108]

Before dedicating himself full-time to his brother's campaign, however, Robert needed to do one more thing for himself. He retreated to Hickory Hill to write *The Enemy Within,* a personal account of his experiences on the Rackets Committee. Insisting this would be his own work, Robert did not avail himself of what John Kennedy's biographer Herbert Parmet has labeled the Kennedy "literary apparatus," that team of researchers, writers, and editors who had produced *Profiles in Courage.* Aware of accusations that John Kennedy did not write *Profiles* and had not deserved the Pulitzer Prize, Robert carefully documented his intellectual property rights to *The Enemy Within.*[109] John Seigenthaler, a prize-winning crusading journalist who later joined Kennedy's staff in the Justice Department, agreed to edit Robert's drafts, written out in longhand on yellow legal pads.[110]

Excerpts went out from United Press International to various newspapers during August of 1959, the book itself was released by Harper's in February 1960. At Joseph Kennedy's urging, Arthur Krock (the only member of the Kennedy "literary apparatus" involved in the book) wrote an introduction in which he described the McClellan committee as a "model" congressional inquiry. From its title onward, an urgent and ominous tone permeated the book, as Kennedy warned that within ten years unchecked organized criminal activity could drastically alter the U.S. economy. A weakening of the nation's moral fiber, he insisted, had given gangsters a toehold in the first place.

"It seems to me imperative," Kennedy concluded, "that we reinstill in ourselves the toughness and idealism that guided the nation in the past."[111] The theme would resound throughout his brother's presidential campaign. Having achieved some success on his own, Robert's next task was to put John Kennedy in the White House.

CHAPTER 6

Winning Jack the Nomination

THE ELECTION OF 1960 marked a transition in U.S. history. All that would follow in that decade cannot, of course, be imputed to the Kennedys, but when first John, then Robert, Kennedy summoned America to consider its values and ideals anew, millions of Americans, especially the young, stepped forward. In its early stages, that reconsidering of the rich diversity of the American experiment helped elect a Catholic as president.

The Political Culture of 1960

The United States in 1960 had settled into a pattern of Cold War normalcy in a world polarized between the U.S. and Soviet blocs. U.S. politicians, bound by the metaphors of Winston Churchill, portrayed the world as divided between the "free" and "enslaved." The two major powers competed for the loyalties and resources of third-world countries, where nationalist aspirations and rising expectations collided with the competing ideologies of Communism and free-market economies. U.S. policy analysts viewed each development in those lands, whether Cuba, Laos, India, or Vietnam, in the context of its effects on the balance of power between the United States and the Soviet Union. Although their many trips abroad had sensitized the Kennedys to the complexities of international events, the nearer they got to the presidential campaign of 1960, the more they saw the world in Churchillian black and white.

Strategic Air Command bombers patrolled the skies, and weekly air raid drills reminded the children of the postwar baby boom that nuclear annihilation should be their greatest fear. Meantime, the growth of the country's economy, stimulated by the welfare-warfare state, brought unprecedented affluence for some and a better life for most. Corporate profits and national income had risen dramatically since 1945; the average worker's income increased by nearly 40 percent in the 1950s. Demand for consumer goods fueled much of the growth. By 1960 87 percent of U.S. households had televisions and refrigerators.

Always a mobile society, the United States in 1960 had more than 61 million automobiles, about one for every three Americans. Four-lane ribbons of concrete, built with national defense dollars, connected the cities and carried increasing numbers of Americans away from the Northeast to the burgeoning population centers of the Sun Belt states. Automobiles also contributed to the development of the suburbs, which grew by 48 percent during the 1950s, a landscape of single-family homes on grassy plots.

Perceived as a struggle between competing ways of life, the Cold War mandated an emphasis on the positive. The unequal distribution of wealth and the significant numbers of poor Americans went unmarked or overlooked by the white middle and upper classes. With the white flight to the suburbs, the cities became increasingly the provinces of ethnic minorities, especially of African Americans. The population of 180 million included 19 million African Americans who still faced various legal and extralegal forms of social, economic, and political segregation and discrimination. Despite efforts of civil rights activists to bring the issue to center stage, most white Americans either did not care about these inequities or anticipated their eventual removal. Few whites outside the South, the Kennedys included, felt intensely about the matter.

Americans in general were self-satisfied, materialistic, and conformist. As common cultural values began to emerge through the standardizing and leveling influences of the mass media, Americans became alarmingly susceptible to the manipulative techniques of mass marketing. To say, as Joseph Kennedy supposedly once did, that John Kennedy was sold to the American people like "soapflakes" oversimplifies a complex matter.[1] Yet clearly the Kennedy brothers' appeal rested in large part on their personal magnetism, good looks, and media presence—in short, on their marketability.

Although neither John Kennedy's 1960 campaign nor Robert Kennedy's 1968 campaign was totally free of the "old politics," that is, the weighty influence of local leaders and national Democratic power brokers, the Kennedys did more than glamorize the political scene, they posited a redistribution of political power. Bypassing the brokers of U.S. politics to appeal directly to the voters, they fostered the conditions that prompted an expanded presidential primary system and altered the way Americans selected presidential nominees.

The Kennedy strategy in 1960 evolved out of necessity. Despite fourteen years of congressional service, John Kennedy remained a political outsider. His colleagues in the Senate regarded him as a playboy dilettante who cared little for his duties and a lot for his personal image. Kennedy had won elections in Massachusetts by creating his own political party, defiantly independent of the regular party machinery and its leadership. He owed few, but few owed him. What would have proved liabilities for other candidates, however, became assets for the Kennedys. Their independence and wealth worked to their advantage in the fragmented world of U.S. politics, where the disjointed collection of state parties, local machines, and interest groups that constituted the Democratic party assembled only once every four years to select a presidential nominee.[2] Winning the nomination required the support of substantial blocs of convention delegates from the large states, often controlled by a single person—Governor David L. Lawrence of Pennsylvania, Mayor Richard J. Daley of Chicago, Jesse Unruh of California, John Bailey of Connecticut, Lyndon Johnson of Texas.

The Kennedy strategy, as set forth in a meeting of the brains trust at Robert's Hyannis Port house in October 1959, built on the conclusion that the only way to win the support of the political bosses was to demonstrate John Kennedy's electability in the primaries. Most of the sixteen primaries in 1960, however, were moot contests controlled by state leaders and favorite sons. The others did not offer enough delegate votes to win an outright majority prior to the convention. The Kennedys decided to focus on those primaries they could win impressively, at the same time working behind the scenes to convert enough of the Democratic leadership to win a first-ballot victory at the Los Angeles convention. If the nomination went into the convention's back rooms, John Kennedy stood no chance.[3]

The Kennedys' 1960 campaign began earlier, spent more, and was better organized than any previous Democratic campaign. In January 1959, a year before John Kennedy formally announced his candidacy, the family quietly set up a paid staff in a ten-room office suite a few blocks from Robert's senate offices. Although its compartmentalized operation would distinguish the campaign, it was first and foremost a family endeavor, aided by trusted loyalists and abetted by paid and volunteer expertise.

Rather than a hierarchical structure, the table of organization was circular, with John Kennedy at the center. The candidate's poise, appearance, and political acumen, and, perhaps most of all, his sound political instincts and independence of mind were the campaign's primary assets. Although he accepted advice on improving his public speaking and his appearance before television cameras, John Kennedy refused to be manipulated by advisors and declined personal counselors. Nor did he require "spin doctors" to "interpret" his off-the-cuff remarks to the press.[4] His most difficult task within the campaign was reconciling his superior judgment on political matters with his father's domineering manner and independent actions. Joseph Kennedy, as senior strategist, chief contributor, and unfettered deal maker, at first answered only to himself. As the campaign wore on, he deferred more and more to his capable sons.[5]

The family simply "understood" that Robert Kennedy would manage the campaign.[6] Emotionally and physically at the organizational hub, he shared in most but not all consequential decisions. John made the strategic decisions, drawing on advice from many of the insiders but leaning most heavily on his father, Sorensen, and O'Brien. Robert, as chief of operations, was responsible for getting things done.

Although distracted during early 1959 by his McClellan committee duties and his writing of *The Enemy Within,* Robert kept in close touch, regularly visiting the campaign headquarters and making key operational decisions for the campaign.

In charge of the Washington office was Jean Kennedy's thirty-one-year-old husband, Stephen Smith. Cut from the Kennedy bolt, Smith was energetic, good looking, and athletic. A graduate of Georgetown University, he had gained valuable executive experience at the New York transportation firm founded by his Irish immigrant grandfather, William Cleary. Smith had a keen business sense and knew how to handle money. Those qualities immediately endeared him to Joseph Kennedy, who selected him to run the family's business offices and trusted him to manage campaign disbursements and expenditures. A Kennedy loyalist once tabbed Smith the "inside brother-in-law."[7]

R. Sargent Shriver, Eunice Kennedy's husband, received less trust and respect. A Yale graduate and a lawyer, reared in a family of Maryland's old Catholic aristocracy, Shriver managed the Chicago Merchandise Mart for Joseph Kennedy. Well known for dedicating his energy and talents to liberal causes, Shriver became president of the Chicago Board of Education and in 1959 was touted as a strong contender for the Democratic nomination for governor of Illinois. Shriver's independent ambition and Catholic piety, placed alongside his admiration for Adlai Stevenson and outspoken opposition to Joe McCarthy, made John and Robert Kennedy slightly uncomfortable. They kiddingly referred to him as the "house Communist" or the "boy scout." Yet they prevailed upon Shriver to set aside everything else and work full time in the campaign.[8]

By the early spring of 1959, with the major players in place, Stephen Smith's office hummed with activity. Smith and Lawrence O'Brien were joined by Kenneth O'Donnell, Pierre Salinger, and Walter Sheridan, who split their time at the McClellan committee. Robert Kennedy convinced David Hackett, his Milton roommate, to take a leave from an editing job and join the campaign.[9] Richard Goodwin, a bright young Harvard Law grad and former clerk for Justice Felix Frankfurter, assisted Theodore Sorensen with speech writing. Sorensen and Goodwin worked out of the senator's office, while Robert Kennedy controlled the "larger campaign structure," as Goodwin called Smith's offices.[10]

On 1 April 1959, at the first organizational meeting of the campaign, held in Joseph Kennedy's dining room in Palm Beach, Robert took charge, assigning each of the inner circle a region of the country to work.[11] Even at this early date, he chided the candidate, "It's ridiculous that more work hasn't been done," reminding him that "a day lost now can't be picked up on the other end."[12] In a move reflecting the innovative nature of the Kennedy campaign and the family's need for mobility—as well as the father's financial shrewdness—Stephen Smith, acting for Joseph Kennedy, negotiated the purchase of a Convair airplane for $385,000, formed the Ken-Air Corporation, and leased the airplane (named the "Caroline") to the Kennedy campaign.[13]

In an important example of the old and the new politics converging, the Kennedys retained Louis Harris as their private, full-time pollster to take regular soundings of voter preferences at a cost ($300,000 for the primaries alone) prohibitive to any other Democratic candidate. As party professionals lost their grip on the nominating processes because of the increasing focus on the primaries and because of the attention given candidates by the national media, they were being replaced by a cadre of communications and media specialists such as Harris. Of inestimable value, Harris served as both a hired expert and a Kennedy loyalist and had as much influence as any of the politicos within the operation.[14] John Kennedy, though unschooled in the new techniques of voter surveying, intuitively grasped the nuances of the Harris polls and understood that interpretative subtleties could be translated into political action.

Far from the a packaged commodity of his father's "soapflakes" description, John Kennedy demonstrated remarkable political savvy and independence. "A prince who is without any wisdom himself," Machiavelli instructed, "cannot be well advised."[15] So it was with John Kennedy. On most political matters he trusted his own judgments over those of any of his advisors, including his father and brother.

Entering the crucial primary contests of the early spring of 1960, John Kennedy disagreed with his brother and father on two important strategic matters. First, contrary to Robert's advice, he entered the Wisconsin primary. Robert warned that a defeat or even a close contest in the neighboring state of their major challenger, Senator Hubert

Humphrey of Minnesota, could knock them out of the race. Second, John Kennedy refused to take a passive position on religion, against the advice of both his brother and father, who recommended that he refrain from mentioning it. Instead, he agreed with Louis Harris and Theodore Sorensen; they told him he could not safely avoid confronting either Humphrey or religion.[16]

Proving a Catholic Could Win

Religion played an important role in shaping the outcome of the 1960 election. In an era of growing secularity, fewer Americans than in previous decades expressed distinct religious preferences: about 23 percent indicated they were Catholic, 35 percent Protestant, and 3 percent Jewish. But many Protestant clergy believed that John Kennedy's religion, with its presumed subservience to the pope and to Church doctrine, disqualified him from the presidency.[17] Kennedy's presence in the campaign resurrected old ethnocultural prejudices, some dating to the 1928 campaign, when Al Smith, the first Roman Catholic presidential nominee, took a beating from Herbert Hoover. Conservative Protestant ministers, relying on the same arguments used against Al Smith, circulated printed messages claiming that Kennedy, as a Catholic, could not place his country above his church.

John Kennedy soon convinced Robert that they had to neutralize the religious issue among Protestants and other groups and at the same time win back the Catholic Democrats who voted for Eisenhower in 1952 and 1956. They succeeded on both counts, effectively removing the issue as a factor in Robert's and brother Edward's subsequent campaigns and opening the door for other candidates whose ethnicity or religion put them outside mainstream America. But it was not easy. With Theodore Sorensen's guidance, the Kennedys managed to convert the religious issue to their advantage, even to exploit it, through subtle rather than direct means.

In the drive for the vice-presidential nomination in 1956, the Kennedy campaign had touted a Catholic on the Democratic ticket as an asset, given the large proportion of Catholics concentrated in the electorally rich urban-industrial states. But every politician knew that a substantial residue of anti-Catholic sentiment survived in the United States, especially in rural areas and in the South. To offset the negatives, John Kennedy portrayed himself as a victim of bigotry and challenged Protestant voters to prove they were not bigots in the only way possible, by voting for him. At the same time, Sorensen inserted subtle messages into Kennedy's speeches appealing to Catholics and other religious and cultural minorities to support Kennedy in his fight against prejudice.

The first test of the Kennedy scheme came in the Wisconsin primary. To benefit from the substantial Catholic population in the state the Kennedys counted on Senator Humphrey, a liberal proud of his splendid record on civil liberties, not to make an issue of Kennedy's religion during the campaign. And he did not.[18] Partly as a consequence, Kennedy received 56 percent of the vote and defeated Humphrey. Although impressive, the victory did not decisively prove the Kennedy strategy's workability, because the Catholic population in Wisconsin was proportionally larger than in other states. Indeed, various ethnic-religious factors, as Kennedy expected, had worked in his favor. According to CBS-News, which relied for the first time on computer projections developed by IBM and the Columbia University Bureau of Applied Social Research, Kennedy would have lost in other states lacking large Catholic populations.

The evening of the election, in a televised interview, CBS-News anchor Walter Cronkite put John Kennedy on the spot by asking about the Catholic vote, a question the candidate had trouble finessing. Believing Cronkite had violated an "agreement" not to mention religion, Robert Kennedy stormed into the studio after the interview and threatened to deny Cronkite and CBS any further interviews with his brother.[19]

Robert Kennedy then telephoned Columbia University president Grayson Kirk and IBM president Thomas Watson, demanding they quash the ethnic-religious analysis. Because it undermined their hopes of quietly manipulating the religious issue to their advantage, the Kennedys wanted the data projecting ethnic-religious voting patterns kept under wraps. Early the next morning the Columbia professors were called before CBS and IBM officials to "justify" their methods and prove their analyses were not politically motivated. CBS found the data and the analysis credible, but under continued pressure from the candidate's manager abandoned plans to emphasize the findings on a national news program the following Sunday. The Columbia researchers resigned from the IBM-CBS project, shaken by the brutal exercise of raw power and embittered toward Robert Kennedy, who, in the estimation of one professor, behaved like a "tough little white collar gangster."[20]

Electable in West Virginia

As the primary venue shifted from Wisconsin to West Virginia, acrimony between the Humphrey and Kennedy camps ratcheted upward. The normally friendly and genial Humphrey blamed the "young, emotional, juvenile Bobby" for the hard feelings, claiming he "didn't play fair" in implying in speeches that James Hoffa's support for Humphrey grew out of his hostility toward the Kennedys. In West Virginia, Humphrey became irate when Franklin D. Roosevelt, Jr., at Robert's suggestion, deliberately distorted the facts concerning Humphrey's medical deferment during World War II and implied that Humphrey was a slacker or possibly a draft dodger.

The Minnesota senator also suspected Robert Kennedy of arranging some "dirty tricks" in the campaigns, such as sabotaging meetings and secretly distributing anti-Catholic literature, implying it came from the Humphrey campaign. Such activities, if they occurred, were likely the work of Paul Corbin, a former CIO organizer intensely devoted to Robert Kennedy. Corbin's roguish behavior and willingness to do anything Robert asked—and perhaps many things he would not dare to ask—proved both an asset and a liability. Although highly effective, Corbin's methods (those of a "natural-born con man," according to Arthur Schlesinger) precluded sending him into a district a second time. Some of the staff detested Corbin, but Robert liked him and never disparaged his questionable methods or his loyalty.[21]

The Wisconsin primary had blown the Kennedys' cover in terms of subtly exploiting religion. Harris polls of West Virginia voters indicated that the 70 percent to 30 percent margin Kennedy enjoyed earlier over

Humphrey had disappeared, apparently because voters discovered that Kennedy was Catholic. After his first encounter with West Virginia campaign workers, Robert again recommended taking a low profile on religion, suggesting instead that they stress the bread-and-butter issues that had carried the Democrats since the New Deal. "What are our problems?" Robert had asked the volunteers. A man stood up and shouted, "There's only one problem. He's a Catholic. That's our Goddamned problem!"[22]

But John Kennedy manipulated the religion issue into one of tolerance versus intolerance. In masterly speeches and carefully planned televised presentations, he persuasively conveyed his belief in the separation of church and state, punctuating his remarks with a simulated affirmation of the presidential oath of office; he would "preserve, protect, and defend" the Constitution, he promised audiences, "so help me God." His impressive performance and the positive reactions of the voters of West Virginia marked turning points in the campaign and in the national experience.[23]

On election night, with the outcome decided, Robert Kennedy walked from his Charleston offices down the street through a steady rain to Humphrey's headquarters. Trying to appear the gracious winner and consoling healer—alien roles for someone of his temperament and experience—Kennedy caused a stir in the enemy camp. While amiable toward John Kennedy, Hubert Humphrey, his wife, and his staff had not concealed their bitterness toward the "devil" brother; they resented his arrogance and believed he resorted the "gutter politics." As Kennedy walked slowly across the room toward the Humphreys, the senator's surprised and annoyed supporters backed away as if fearing some dreaded contamination from the uninvited intruder. Kennedy leaned to kiss the cheek of Muriel Humphrey, who, her husband recalled, "turned in silent hostility" and moved away "fighting tears and angry words." Later the same evening, John Kennedy flew in from Washington, made a gracious speech, and smoothed over differences with Humphrey. Humphrey, however, never forgave Robert's behavior.[24] Robert, angry himself with that "Goddamned Hubert Humphrey," admitted that a lot of nasty things got said by both sides. Still, he hoped to patch up their differences and bring the Minnesota senator, along with his strong following among organized labor, farmers, and liberals, into the Kennedy column.

Kennedy's 61 percent share of the West Viginia primary vote, in a state where less than 4 percent of the population was Catholic, proved his electability and eliminated a top competitor.

One great asset of the Kennedy campaign in West Virginia was its seemingly unending supply of money. Joseph Kennedy, with wealth variously estimated at between $300 and $400 million, put a large sum of money at the service of his son's campaign. How much he spent and to what extent he was personally involved in the campaign remain matters of much conjecture.

For most of the campaign, Joseph Kennedy remained at Hyannis Port and Palm Beach, fearing his appearance would hurt John's chances. He engaged in some behind-the-scenes dealing, probably much less than legend has it.[25] Rarely traveling, except to visit a particularly recalcitrant politico or union leader, the father spent his days dictating letters and making calls, maintaining daily contacts with John and Robert. A friend once asked Joseph Kennedy why he did not tell his sons what he was doing for them. "I don't want them to inherit my enemies," he responded. "It's tough enough they inherit my friends."[26]

Besides his own money, he also committed his children's fortunes to the campaign, directing Steve Smith to tithe each of the children's trust funds.[27] How much Kennedy money was spent and for what cannot be established with certainty.

Embroidered into the lore of U.S. politics, however, are charges that the Kennedys laid out exorbitant sums and even turned to organized crime to help them buy the West Virginia primary victory and, therefore, the Democratic nomination for the presidency. Both the Kennedy and Humphrey campaigns conformed to West Virginia's political customs; that is, both disbursed cash to local officials and poll watchers. Exactly how much each dispensed is not known. Kennedy outspent Humphrey by at least a four-to-one margin in publicly disclosed expenses. But observers suspected his campaign spent much more illegally.[28] "No one could prove it," Harrison Salisbury admitted, "but everyone knew" that the Kennedy campaign gave district leaders "stacks of cash" to spread around. Prominent Democratic leaders, such as Averell Harriman and former president Harry Truman, were certain the Kennedys "bought" the West Virginia primary election.[29]

Lawrence O'Brien later admitted making payments to county leaders but claimed that "neither Jack nor Bob Kennedy knew what agreements I made—that was my responsibility."[30] Congressman Tip O'Neill claimed he knew of arrangements made by Joseph Kennedy to distribute cash payments to local sheriffs. He was equally certain the ambassador's sons knew nothing of the payments. About all one may safely infer is that the Kennedy campaign distributed more than the combined amounts disbursed by Senator Humphrey's campaign and by the friends of Lyndon Johnson and Adlai Stevenson, all of whom also engaged in such payments. To stop Kennedy from locking up the nomination before the convention, Johnson and Stevenson campaigns each contributed unknown amounts to Humphrey's campaign. Humphrey's aides admitted that giving cash to political leaders for places on the ballot and for poll watchers was "common practice" in West Virginia. Their only regret was that their resources were "peanuts" compared to the Kennedys'. "At this degraded level," Theodore White concluded, "all were evenly matched."[31]

Rumors and scattered accusations of vote fraud and vote buying circulated immediately after the West Virginia primary. In early July, Jack Anderson wrote a column stating that the FBI was investigating the matter. On 5 July, Robert Kennedy called Courtney Evans at the FBI and asked if Anderson's report was accurate. Evans assured him that no investigation was underway or contemplated.[32]

But decades later, the accusations of Kennedy misconduct in West Virginia persist, complicated by charges that the Kennedys allegedly had help from organized crime. Judith Campbell, who conducted simultaneous affairs with John Kennedy and Sam Giancana, claims to have couriered money and messages between the two regarding the buying of votes in the West Virginia primary. Another allegation holds that Giancana sent Paul "Skinny" D'Amato, reportedly another of Campbell's bedmates, with "a suitcase full of money" ($50,000) into West Virginia and spent an additional $500,000, supposedly "skimmed" by James Hoffa from Teamsters' funds, as part of an absolutely implausible "agreement that Bobby will leave Hoffa and the Teamsters alone." In March 1960, an FBI informant claimed that Frank Sinatra's uncle, Joe "Fish" Fischetti, and "other unidentified hoodlums" were financially supporting Kennedy's nomination.[33] No incontrovertible or unbiased evidence exists to verify the accuracy of these hearsay accusations and gangster braggadocio.

Claims of the Kennedys' direct participation in soliciting Mafia involvement are questionable on their face because of their origins among unsavory underworld figures. FBI wiretaps of Sam Giancana and John Roselli allude to "the donation that was made" to the Kennedy campaign (allegedly through Frank Sinatra). But no credible evidence suggests that the Kennedys solicited money from organized crime figures or that they asked Sinatra to do it for them.[34] One must also be skeptical of claims (such as Judith Campbell's) that the candidate himself handled large sums of cash, behavior irreconcilable with the way the Kennedy family did business. Cash transactions were made by the father and Stephen Smith. John and Robert Kennedy rarely handled or even carried cash. "Listening to the Kennedy brothers talk about money," their friend Charles Spalding once said, "was like listening to nuns talk about sex. It was awkward."[35]

Kennedy money doubtless contributed to the victories in West Virginia and elsewhere, but the sums could not have been as large as opponents imagined. Further, unless one is so jaundiced as to believe that the votes of the vast majority of West Virginians were for sale to the highest bidder, money alone could not have delivered such a lopsided victory.

Revisionist thinking notwithstanding, John Kennedy, after all, proved more than a handsome face, more than a manufactured image. He and his skilled group of political advisors knew how to make the most of their resources. And his father—the frugal fount of campaign funds—insisted on nothing less. Senator Kennedy liked to disarm his and his father's critics with a piece of humor containing more than a germ of truth. "I got a wire from my father," the candidate would begin. "It reads: 'Dear Jack: don't buy one vote more than necessary. I'll be damned if I'll pay for a landslide.'" The Kennedys, as Richard Whalen concluded in his biography of Joseph Kennedy, "were not only the richest family ever to make politics their business; they also were by far the most sophisticated. They were able to demand full value for every dollar spent."[36]

A positive imprint left on the Kennedy image by the West Virginia primary of 1960 was the vaunted first contact of the Kennedy brothers with poverty. The hardships of rural poverty in Appalachia seemed to particularly affect Senator Kennedy. Many among his staff and the reporters accompanying the candidate sensed an emotional change brought about by a genuine concern for what he saw.[37] Neither brother, however, sought immediately to convert his feelings or impressions into specific policy proposals.

Of more immediate concern for Robert were his campaign tasks, which he approached with dedication and fervor. Over the course of the campaign, he became more involved in campaigning itself, rising before dawn to shake hands with West Virginia coal miners before they descended to their jobs, dutifully litanizing, "My name is Bob Kennedy. My brother is running for President. I want your help." Unlike 1952, he made a few stump speeches during the primaries and began to gain confidence on the platform.[38]

To keep the campaign on track, Robert's responsibility, he placed demands on the volunteers and even on his own family as insistent as those he made of the paid staff. He impatiently exacted total commitments.[39] He telephoned the Boston superintendent of schools to release Helen Keyes from teaching duties so that she could help Polly Fitzgerald organize the teas and receptions for the Kennedy women. He spent ten minutes issuing detailed instructions on where and how to deploy sisters Patricia, Eunice, and Jean, scheduled to host as many as nine house parties a day in Wisconsin. Joining them, Rose Kennedy cheerfully agreed to appear wherever asked, unbothered by the rigorous itineraries and unaware they were designed by her seventh child.[40]

Robert willingly immersed himself in the campaign, giving up a portion of his identity in the process. He received some media exposure of his own, including several appearances on national television to promote his book, and on Father's Day 1960 he was named "Father of the Year." As the father of seven children, Robert was hailed by the National Father's Day Committee for his "investigation of rackets and because he is looked up to by all America as the young Lochinvar whose achievements bespeak the spirit of the young fathers who are beginning the second half of the century with the accent on youth."[41]

The responsibilities of running the campaign had a noticeable effect.

"All life took on a new meaning for Bobby," Justice William O. Douglas observed. Ethel Kennedy recalled that her husband spent "every waking minute" working on the campaign.[42] He radiated enthusiasm. Many of the people Robert recruited to the 1960 campaign, such as advance man Jerry Bruno and political operative Paul Corbin, became permanent converts, staying with him until his death in 1968.

Robert Kennedy was the indispensable man in his brother's campaign for the nomination. Every campaign, John Kennedy said, needed a tough-minded task master, a "son-of-a-bitch." In his campaign, that man was Robert.[43] John at times even turned the negative reactions of others toward Robert to his advantage. Equally mindful of Congressman Tip O'Neill's value to his campaign and of O'Neill's dislike of Robert's brashness, John Kennedy engaged in a small deceit to gain O'Neill's help in organizing the big-city politicians. "Bobby will be running the campaign," he told O'Neill, "but don't pay any attention to what he tells you. Here's what I want you to do."[44]

A string of primary victories gave rise to the impression that the Kennedy campaign was an efficient, tightly organized, monolithic operation.[45] John Kennedy, always one to put things in perspective, once told Arthur Schlesinger, "If you win, your campaign is always regarded as brilliantly designed; if you lose, it's always regarded as incompetent." Schlesinger acknowledged the myth of the "well-oiled Kennedy machine" as a misconception. Neither Kennedy, he conceded, was highly organized or a systematic planner, but both were "brilliant improvisers." Harris Wofford aptly described the result as "creative chaos."[46] Robert Kennedy's genius, according to Schlesinger, "lay in his capacity to address a specific situation, to assemble an able staff, to inspire and flog them into exceptional deeds, to prevail through sheer force of momentum."[47]

Counting Delegates in Los Angeles

All the same, as the Los Angeles convention drew nearer, many Democratic regulars remained unpersuaded. Looming in the wings, the one remaining serious challenger, Senator Lyndon B. Johnson, planned a major effort at the convention, as did the die-hard supporters of Adlai Stevenson, the failed candidate of 1952 and 1956. Stevenson realistically stood no chance. But just a few days before the convention, Johnson's chances improved as a result of indirect support from an unexpected source.

In a news conference in early July, former president Harry Truman, addressing himself directly to John F. Kennedy, said, "Senator, are you certain that you are quite ready for the country, or that the country is ready for you?" Truman urged the forty-three year old to be patient and implied that he should step aside for a more experienced person. Asked later if Kennedy's religion was a factor, Truman replied, "It's not the pope I'm afraid of, it's the pop." Truman then announced he would not attend the Los Angeles convention because he believed it was "rigged" in Kennedy's favor.[48]

John Kennedy answered Truman in a televised news conference. Reading from a statement written by Sorensen, Kennedy pointed out that his fourteen years in Congress represented more experience in elective office than that of Woodrow Wilson, Franklin Roosevelt, and Truman before they became presidents. Many influential statespersons, Kennedy emphasized, had assumed office at forty-three or younger, including Theodore Roosevelt, William Pitt, Napoleon, and Alexander the Great. At age forty-four, he added, Washington commanded the Continental Army, Jefferson wrote the Declaration of Independence, and Columbus discovered America.[49] Youth, in other words, was a virtue, not a drawback. The rebuttal to Truman, though pure Kennedy hubris, proved effective and would be reprised in various forms during the campaigns of Robert and Edward Kennedy.

John Kennedy's rejoinder to Truman received network television coverage because of yet another angry confrontation between Robert Kennedy and television executives. Because NBC had telecast Truman's critical comments live, Robert Kennedy, at his father's behest, telephoned NBC executive Robert Kintner and insisted that NBC "owed the Kennedys free time" to respond. "We don't owe you a thing," Kintner told Kennedy, advising him to read the Federal Communications Commission regulations. Unable to bully NBC as he had CBS, Kennedy convinced the network at least to cover his brother's press conference. Favorable shifts in public opinion polls and the positive reaction of party professionals showed John Kennedy had passed this second test with high marks. The Kennedys, moreover, had used television, that medium so ripe for exploitation by the right political candidate, to change the balance of political power heading into the convention.[50]

Democratic delegates arriving in Los Angeles in July 1960 received Frank Sinatra recordings of the campaign theme songs, "High Hopes" and "All the Way," and settled in to enjoy the traditional convention hoopla. Robert Kennedy, however, remained all business.

Those meeting Robert for the first time in Los Angeles were struck by this incisive thirty-four year old, clearly the man in charge. He read the riot act to a campaign worker who had the temerity to take time out to visit Disneyland. Without raising his voice, an aide noted, Kennedy made subordinates feel smaller and more guilty than the occasion demanded.[51] Robert told a volunteer who complained of working twenty hours straight, "Look, nobody asked you here. You're not getting paid anything. If this is too tough for you, let us know and we'll get somebody else."[52]

Robert Kennedy impressed other Kennedy delegates, according to Arthur Schlesinger, a Kennedy delegate himself, with his humor and charm. Harvard economist John Kenneth Galbraith and Connecticut governor Abraham Ribicoff were struck by the politeness and unfailing deference of the young man who called them "sir." Others came away with far different impressions. "Whenever you see Bobby Kennedy in public with his brother," columnist Murray Kempton said, "he looks as though he showed up for a rumble." Another observer noted that Robert Kennedy carried himself like "the hit man in a prep-school gang."[53] Adlai Stevenson privately referred to Senator Kennedy's brother as the "Black Prince."[54]

Robert Kennedy's combative nature permeated the management of his brother's nomination. He established operational centers in a suite of rooms at the Biltmore Hotel and in a small house (left over from a model home show) inside the Los Angeles Sports Arena. The Kennedy command post, however, was wherever the candidate's brother happened to be; often, according to most recollections, this was standing on top of a chair hoarsely shouting instructions to workers. He frequently huddled with party bosses, gesturing or shaking hands emphatically to signal opponents' scouts or wavering delegates. He knew he was being watched, and he kept an eye on the competition. Kennedy deployed his floor troops at strategic points around the Sports Arena, assigning one staff member to each delegation, where they monitored activity and collected intelligence.

Robert Kennedy left nothing to chance. The communications snafu that bedeviled them during the 1956 convention led the Kennedys to take extra precautions with their elaborate telephone system, stationing well-muscled labor leaders near some telephones to make sure they remained accessible.[55] To prevent deceitful rostrum maneuvers of the kind Robert believed occurred in 1956, he assigned two Colorado lawyers, Joseph Dolan and Byron "Whizzer" White, the former All-American football player and future Supreme Court justice, to review the convention rules and scrutinize all parliamentary procedures.[56]

The Kennedys' great fear was a deadlocked convention. They went to Los Angeles with 600 of the 761 delegate votes needed to win the nomination, which meant some backroom maneuvering still to do. Joseph Kennedy invited several party and labor leaders to visit with him during the convention and succeeded in winning over pivotal delegates from New York and New Jersey.[57] Tip O'Neill helped sort out divisions within the Pennsylvania delegation and gained support of other city machines.[58] Although a majority was not assured as the balloting approached, newscasters and reporters confidently predicted a Kennedy victory.

Yet Robert fretted. Various "Stop Kennedy" coalitions formed amidst talk of the risks of nominating a Catholic. Others raised questions of Senator Kennedy's health and his commitment to Democratic policies. Robert was livid when John Connally of Texas, pulling out all stops on behalf of Lyndon Johnson, told a news conference that John Kennedy had Addison's disease and was physically unfit for the presidency.

Robert, however, reserved most of his fury for Lyndon Johnson himself, whose transgressions he viewed as even greater. Robert never forgave Johnson for describing John Kennedy at caucuses of various state delegations as a "little scrawny fellow with rickets" and referring to Joseph Kennedy as a "Chamberlain-umbrella policy man" who thought "Hitler was right," and who wanted his son to be president so he could "run the country."[59] "I've seen Bobby mad," Kenneth O'Donnell told interviewers years later, "but never as mad as the day he heard what Johnson had said about his father." Robert Kennedy lashed out at Lyndon Johnson's aide and protege, Bobby Baker. "You've got your nerve," he told Baker. "You Johnson people are running a stinking damned campaign, and you're going to get yours when the time comes."[60]

For now, all of Robert Kennedy's passion and energies had to remain focused on the delegate count. Robert drove himself and others mercilessly to nail down uncommitted delegates and to negotiate the winning margin. Every morning at seven he went through a roll call of the states to get the latest tabulations. "Bob never wanted good news," Galbraith recalled; he wanted precision and accuracy.[61] "I don't want generalities or guesses," he told the staff. Throughout the day and into the small hours of the next morning he met delegates and caucused with the Democratic brokers, such as Carmine DeSapio of New York's Tammany Hall, Governor G. Mennen Williams of Michigan, Mike Pendergast of Kansas City, John Bailey of Connecticut, and Matthew McCloskey of Philadelphia.[62]

Neither Kennedy had done much to inspire confidence in liberals and civil rights advocates, but now Robert called in Harris Wofford, the campaign's civil rights coordinator, admitting the campaign was "in trouble with Negroes" and would have "to start from scratch." Wofford, an experienced activist and an advisor to Martin Luther King, Jr., bluntly informed his new boss that civil rights leaders placed John Kennedy "very far down the list" of the people they would support. Kennedy instructed Wofford to "do everything you need to do to deliver every Negro delegate going to the convention." Wofford built a solid corps of advisors, anchored by Louis Martin, a no-nonsense African American publisher and media specialist, whose salty manner at first irritated but later endeared him to Robert Kennedy.[63]

The 4,500 convention delegates included only 250 African Americans, and, according to Wofford, Robert Kennedy was a "question mark" for all of them. He surprised everyone, however, with his support of the liberals' "maximum" position on civil rights drafted by Wofford and Chester Bowles. In fact, Kennedy stunned Wofford by taking the draft containing all that the party liberals and civil rights supporters wanted, barely glancing at it, stepping up on the back of chair and inveighing, "All the way with the Bowles platform."[64] Arthur Schlesinger remembered Kennedy telling the staff, "Don't fuzz it up." Southerners would support John Kennedy for other reasons, said Robert, but "don't let there be doubt anywhere as to how the Kennedy people stand on this." Robert pledged that the Wofford-Bowles plank, which subsequent events made appear tepid, would not be "watered down."[65]

Organized labor, another important element in the coalition, remained skeptical but ready to lend backing. The enthusiastic support of the UAW and the Steelworkers Union helped paper over deeper concerns arising from the Kennedys' roles during the McClellan committee hearings and their ambiguous involvement with the Landrum-Griffith Act. Earlier, Arthur Goldberg, counsel to the AFL-CIO, had written Robert Kennedy thanking him for a copy of *The Enemy Within* and congratulating him for his "outstanding work" on the McClellan committee. Goldberg circumspectly told Kennedy he was "aware of no instance where any legitimate, honest labor leader or labor organization had any cause for complaint because of your conduct as counsel." The Teamsters, of course, had cause for complaint, but the leaders of other unions made an uneasy alliance with the Kennedys.[66]

Just before the balloting began, Robert's delegate tally revealed that they were still twenty-one short of a first-ballot victory. "If we don't win tonight," he warned the staff, "we're dead."[67] Residual doubts among Americans for Democratic Action (ADA) liberals and former Stevenson supporters, such as Senator Joseph S. Clark of Pennsylvania, threatened the fragile Kennedy coalition. Under pressure from liberals Clark publicly announced his intention to reconsider his position if Kennedy did not win on the first ballot.[68] Although visibly upset and angered by such manipulations, Robert Kennedy refused to cut eleventh-hour deals. He calculated that a strong showing early in the roll call would create a surge effect and pull along uncommitted delegates wanting to be on the winning side. As predicted, small shifts occurred early in the roll call and the Wyoming delegation, cajoled by brother Edward, put John Kennedy over the top.[69]

At the moment of triumph, just before his entry into the Sports Arena to acknowledge the delegates' vote, John Kennedy motioned to his campaign manager. Robert leaned in close to the Democratic presidential nominee, his head bowed as usual when in conversation with his older brother. "The only show of emotion," a reporter noted, was Robert "hitting the open palm of his left hand with the fist of his right hand repeatedly and a kind of smile on Jack Kennedy's face: the ultimate satisfaction."[70]

CHAPTER 7

Electing Jack President

TO WIN THE PRESIDENCY John Kennedy needed a running mate who would help sustain the traditional elements of the Democratic electoral coalition, including the South. Winning in the South presented a particularly formidable problem for a Catholic nominee with a Boston-Harvard accent. Only his chief rival for the nomination fit the bill, Kennedy concluded. After John announced Lyndon Baines Johnson as his choice; Joseph Kennedy told him that putting the Texan on the ticket would in time be seen as "the smartest thing you ever did," an assessment ratified many times over.[1]

The VP Debacle

A close look at the episode raises questions about the accuracy of Robert Kennedy's later claim that "just my brother Jack and myself" made the decision to take Johnson, for if the choice proved spectacularly logical in hindsight, initially it seemed a blunder to most Kennedy insiders, especially Robert. After the eighteen or so hours of missteps and contradictions, the offer of the nomination for the second highest office in the land, Theodore White concluded, was made "without dignity, without honor"; the residue of bitter feelings between Johnson and Robert Kennedy affected their relationship to the end of Robert's life.[2]

Viewed even in the light most favorable to Robert, the decision-making process shows two brothers not always in sync. Viewed in the worst light, it reveals John Kennedy manipulating his brother's emotions and using him as a pawn in the political maneuvering necessary to win support for his own decision.

Robert Kennedy said he and his brother "promised each other that we'd never tell what happened." But Robert broke that promise in 1965 when he offered his version in an oral history interview for the Kennedy Library. He spoke with one eye on his brother's place in history and the other on Lyndon Johnson, by then his chief political antagonist.[3] Johnson had given his side of the story in early 1964, asserting that, contrary to the advice of Kennedy insiders, John Kennedy had wanted him on the ticket all along. Robert ignored the story when it first appeared. "I just decided the thing was past and we should get on to something else," he said. A year later, however, he branded Johnson's account "wrong" and "false," describing his brother's successor as "incapable of telling the truth," a man who "lies all the time" about "everything."[4]

Robert Kennedy's rendering was incorporated into Theodore White's *The Making of the President 1960* and *The Making of the President 1964,* as well as Arthur M. Schlesinger, Jr.'s *A Thousand Days,* best-sellers that shaped the public's perceptions of the decision. Both authors, attentive to Robert Kennedy's views on the matter, invited him to comment on draft narratives. When Theodore White gave Robert the opportunity to review and change the first draft of *The Making of the President 1964,* he admitted to Kennedy that he was "still toying with the phrase that will cover the truth and yet protect you at the same time." "If you feel I've hurt, or drawn blood, or violated confidence in any way, just tell me and we'll fix it," White promised.[5]

In his first draft, White wrote, "Bobby, that day had been caught in a snarl of contradictory signals and instructions." Although a frank and fair assessment of Robert's predicament, the statement cast doubt on the image of the two brothers as inseparable partners. Robert "straightened out" the matter, as he noted in the margin of White's letter, with a telephone call to White in which he dictated a revision, presumably as it appeared in print.[6]

Central to Robert's version is his contention that neither he nor his brother had time to give much thought to a vice-presidential nominee before John had won the nomination on the evening of 13 July. "You know," he said, "there were just about thirty-two balls up in the air." The next morning, Robert recalled, he and John conferred briefly before the candidate went to meet with Johnson. Robert said that his brother visited Johnson's suite at 10:58 A.M. solely as a gesture to party unity and in deference to Johnson's seniority and his second-place finish in the convention balloting. His brother, he said, intended to offer Johnson the second spot on the ticket as a strictly pro forma matter and "never dreamt that there was a chance in the world that he would accept it." When John returned from the meeting, he told Robert, "He wants it."

"Oh, my God!" Robert remembered gasping.

"Now what do we do?" his brother asked.[7]

Several hours of confusion followed. "The most indecisive time we ever had," said Robert. He was certain "this wouldn't have happened except that we were all too tired last night."[8] Edward Kennedy remembered that his brothers huddled privately in the Biltmore suite and "talked and talked and talked."[9] According to Robert, "We changed our minds eight times" over the next few hours, with most of that time spent trying to figure out "how could we get out of it."[10] Robert wanted others to believe that he and his brother "came upon this idea of trying to get rid of him, and it didn't work." Ultimately, in Robert Kennedy's telling, his brother had no choice but to live up to his offer and to invite Johnson to be his vice-president. Johnson's presence on the ticket, Robert insinuated, resulted from a political misunderstanding that the power-hungry Texan craftily maneuvered to his advantage. A more honorable man, he implied, would have responded differently to John Kennedy's offer.

The truth about the events leading to the selection of Lyndon Johnson may never come clear. John F. Kennedy, the one person who knew the whole story, decided that "it's just as well it never be told."[11] Almost surely, however, the entire truth is not to be found in Robert Kennedy's recollections.

Contrary to Robert's avowals, John Kennedy had given the question of a running mate more than passing attention before his nomination. Several weeks before the convention Senator Kennedy's principal aide, Theodore Sorensen, had prepared a list of possible candidates, presumably at the senator's direction. By the time the Democrats convened in Los Angeles the list had been pared to four: Governors G. Mennen Williams of Michigan and Orville Freeman of Minnesota, and Senators Stuart Symington of Missouri and Lyndon Johnson. Robert personally favored Washington senator Henry "Scoop" Jackson, with whom he had worked during the army-McCarthy hearings, but his brother evidently never gave serious consideration to Jackson. During the primaries, in an unguarded moment with two reporters, John Kennedy mentioned Symington and Johnson as the only two viable candidates. At about the same time, he told Chester Bowles that Johnson would be the "wisest" choice but admitted to *Washington Post* reporters in an off-the-record interview that he felt sure Johnson would not accept it.[12] We have no record of other remarks by John Kennedy regarding his preferences before his nomination, but it is difficult to believe that he (indeed, that any candidate) would have given the matter no further thought until the morning after his nomination.

Besides Sorensen, John Kennedy also discussed the vice-presidency with Philip L. Graham and columnist Joseph Alsop. Graham, the mercurial son-in-law of the owner of the *Washington Post* had unmatched access to political figures. Although friendly with both Kennedy and Johnson, Graham went to the convention committed to Johnson. After the Pennsylvania delegation announced that the majority of its votes would go to Kennedy, thus dimming Johnson's chances and putting Kennedy closer to the nomination, Graham and Alsop, a close friend of John Kennedy, asked for and received a private meeting with the senator. They beseiged him not to name Stuart Symington vice-president, as rumor had it he intended to do. Johnson, they argued, was both the most logical and astute choice. Kennedy surprised them by immediately agreeing.[13]

A day later, Graham's *Post* ran an article claiming that Kennedy was giving serious consideration to selecting Johnson. ADA, labor, and African American delegates expressed immediate disapproval. African American delegates resented the prospect of a southerner on the ticket, but the Kennedys neither consulted them nor attempted to reassure them.[14] Joseph Rauh of the ADA went to Robert Kennedy, apparently still unaware of his brother's meeting with Graham and Alsop, and gained his personal guarantee that Johnson was not their choice. "He meant it," Rauh said later; he really "believed it."[15]

Persisting on Johnson's behalf, Graham the next day finagled a ride in Senator Kennedy's limousine to suggest that the senator defuse the building opposition to Johnson by asking Adlai Stevenson to call for delegates to draft Johnson for the second spot on the ticket. Such a move, Graham said, would unite the convention behind Kennedy. He offered to prepare a draft message summarizing why Johnson should be on the ticket and said he would give it to Sorenson or to Robert Kennedy. "Leave it with me only," Kennedy instructed.[16]

On the morning following his brother's nomination, Robert confidently told Edwin Guthman, "It's between Symington and Scoop [Jackson]."[17] If Guthman's recollection is accurate, then John Kennedy had failed to take his brother into his confidence at this point, for several sources agree that the nominee had by then narrowed his choices to Symington and Johnson after privately sounding out, then dropping Governor Williams, never indicating to anyone other than Robert that he was considering Senator Jackson for the position.

The day before, Kennedy had asked Clark Clifford, former strategist for Harry Truman, to "find out if [fellow Missourian] Stuart [Symington] will accept and let me know right away." Taking this to be an "unequivocal proposal," Clifford convinced Symington to accept. He was surprised, then, when Senator Kennedy called sometime the next morning (14 July) and apologetically reneged. The vice-presidential selection process, he told Clifford, had caused a "family ruckus," and Kennedy was now "persuaded that I cannot win without Lyndon on the ticket."[18] Since the only two family members likely to have been consulted were Robert, who was opposed to Johnson, and his father, who believed the choice of Johnson a wise one, there is little room for doubt about the loudest voice in the family ruckus.

Further, Robert Kennedy's version that his brother's tender of the nomination to Johnson was a pro forma offer of "first refusal" does not jibe with historical precedent. Nothing in Democratic party or U.S. political traditions bound a nominee to offer the vice-presidency to his chief rival. Indeed, this had never been done, although a presidential nominee often picked a running mate from his chief rival's camp. To make the offer to Johnson, then, was an anomalous leap, clearly a move that John Kennedy had thought through. At least two weeks before the convention, he had consulted with Theodore Sorensen, who assured him of the logic of offering the number two spot to his closest competitor. In a 1964 interview Sorensen denied that Kennedy had made the decision, which he called "a logical and happy choice both for the campaign and the country," hastily or under pressure.[19]

Both Kennedys, moreover, had ample warning that Johnson was willing to take the second spot if offered. "Bob, don't do it," Jack Conway of the UAW admonished Robert Kennedy when he heard reports that Johnson was being considered. "If you offer it to him," Conway said, "he'll take it. And if he takes it, it'll ruin everything that we've done."[20] Sargent Shriver had it on good authority that Johnson would accept the post if offered, and he so informed John Kennedy two hours before Kennedy's visit to Johnson's suite. In their meeting with Kennedy, Joseph Alsop and Philip Graham had also cautioned him not to count on Johnson to turn down the vice-presidency.[21]

Then there was Tip O'Neill, who recalled in his memoirs that on the evening of the presidential balloting (13 July) he had waited forty-five minutes outside a Los Angeles restaurant to tell John Kennedy that he had talked with one of Johnson's closest advisors—his mentor and fellow Texan, the redoubtable Speaker of the House "Mr. Sam" Rayburn—who after first opposing the idea of Johnson going on the ticket was now in favor. Kennedy, according to O'Neill, had said, "Of course I want Lyndon. But I'd never want to offer it and have him turn me down." O'Neill evidently facilitated a meeting between the speaker and John Kennedy, which occurred sometime early the next morning (probably in a stairwell of the Biltmore Hotel). Whether as a result of the meeting or not, by the morning of 14 July Rayburn was convinced that Johnson should accept and that he should help persuade him to do so.[22] Thus, later that morning, when John Kennedy entered Lyndon Johnson's room with his offer of the vice-presidency, he must have known that Johnson was prepared to accept.

To whom, exactly, did John Kennedy plan to turn when Johnson refused the offer? This was, after all, the very day on which the convention would ballot on the nominee. Robert Kennedy never said, nor did he put forward any evidence that John Kennedy had settled on anyone else in his own mind.

Other than Johnson's, the only name on John Kennedy's short list still viable as late as 14 July was Senator Stuart Symington's. A few days earlier, Phil Graham and Joseph Alsop, arguing the case for Johnson, had pleaded with Kennedy not to "risk leaving this country to Stu Symington." Kennedy assured them, "You know damn well I would never do that."[23] But Kennedy reneged on his proposal to Symington in the call to Clifford, only hours before the afternoon announcement of his selection of Johnson. Having eliminated his second choice either just before or after going to meet with Johnson, John Kennedy's intentions were clear.

Lyndon Johnson's published recollections of his meeting that morning with John Kennedy appeared a decade later, long after Robert Kennedy's unflattering account of the episode had become the standard one. Directly rebutting Kennedy, Johnson wrote, "I asked him [John Kennedy] to be candid with me." Senator Kennedy assured him that the offer was genuine and, according to Johnson, not just a courtesy because he needed Johnson on the ticket in order to win. Johnson said he then asked for time to consider the matter and to consult with his wife, Sam Rayburn, and other advisors, a request apparently made for show. Rayburn was now convinced that his fellow Texan should accept the nomination, Johnson's staff knew that he wanted it, and Lyndon Johnson knew the political hazards of refusing. If Kennedy lost the election, Johnson would bear the blame for not helping the party; if Kennedy won, he would be relegated to a secondary role in the new administration.[24] A man of enormous pride, Johnson wanted to be courted before finally accepting. Instead, the new partnership would sour almost from its first hour.

For the remainder of the morning and into the early afternoon, John

Kennedy set about the task of pulling the party together behind his choice. To his hotel suite he called various groups, including northern and southern governors, labor leaders, and urban politicos, for their opinions on Johnson as the vice-presidential nominee. Governor Michael V. DiSalle of Ohio, present at two of the meetings, recalled the "consensus was that if Jack Kennedy wanted him that the rest of us would support him."[25] A few of those briefed that morning, such as Governor David L. Lawrence of Pennsylvania, insisted they had known "for days" that "it's all set" for Johnson. "We've all known it, and I'm for it," Lawrence told a reporter that morning.[26] The nominee also spent time assuaging the misgivings of many of his own staff, fuming over the idea of having Johnson on the ticket. Kennedy testily told them he wanted Johnson in the vice-president's office where he could control him, rather than in the Senate where he could do little to restrain him. A few party liberals, such as Joseph Rauh, felt they were part of something "disreputable," but in short order Rauh and other dissidents fell into line.[27]

All the while, Robert was working at cross-purposes with his brother. He made two, perhaps three, trips to Johnson's suite and stirred a hornet's nest each time. The first trip, he said, was "just to sort of feel him out," to determine how "strongly he was in favor of it." Disgusted, Sam Rayburn dismissed Robert's awkward attempt to dissuade Johnson. "Aw, shit, sonny," he said, steering Robert from the room.[28]

As the day drew on and John Kennedy delayed a formal announcement, Johnson's anxious rage fell on the "little shitass, Bobby." When the nominee's brother appeared at his door the second time, Johnson turned wearily despondent. During this visit, which Robert later insisted he made with his brother's explicit knowledge, Robert tried to convince Johnson to drop off the ticket and accept the chair of the Democratic National Committee. Struck by Robert's seeming independence, John Connally, a Johnson advisor, asked, "Who's the candidate, you or your brother?"[29]

Apparently unmoved, Robert perhaps took inward pleasure at Johnson's maudlin reaction. "You know," he said later, "he can turn that on. I thought he'd burst into tears. I don't know whether it was just an act or anything. But he just shook, and tears came into his eyes, and he said, 'I want to be Vice President.'" Robert said he responded, "Well, then, that's fine. He wants you to be Vice President if you want to be Vice President, we want you to know."[30] Why would Robert have said that when he did not want Johnson as John's running mate? Given the recollections of others present at the time—even though all were from the Johnson camp—Robert Kennedy's purported gesture of reconciliation looks like an invention after the fact.

At around 4:00 P.M., just a few hours before the delegates were scheduled to begin the vice-presidential nominations, Robert was in Johnson's suite, either back for a third time or still on his second visit. Rayburn and Connally kept him safely distanced from the infuriated majority leader. John Kennedy, without consulting with his brother, but very likely prompted by a call from his father, decided to proceed with the announcement of Johnson's nomination. He telephoned Philip Graham and asked him to relay the decision to Johnson.[31]

Of all the participants in the discussions that day, Graham was the only one who made a contemporaneous written record.[32] According to Graham's account, when he returned to Johnson's room with the good news of John Kennedy's choice for the vice-presidency, Robert Kennedy had been telling Rayburn and Johnson that "there was much opposition and that Lyndon should withdraw for the sake of the party." With Johnson "about to jump out of his skin," Rayburn asked Graham to call Senator Kennedy and tell him what his brother was doing.

"Oh, that's all right," the nominee calmly told Graham. "Bobby's been out of touch and doesn't know what's been happening." Graham handed the receiver to Johnson and listened while Kennedy smoothed Johnson's feathers with some supportive words. Johnson handed the phone back to Graham just as Robert Kennedy walked into the room. Seeing that Robert looked "sullen and dead tired," Graham told the senator, "You'd better speak to Bobby." Robert listened for a few moments in icy silence, then said, "Well, it's too late now," and slammed down the receiver.[33]

Later in the day, when the candidate and his campaign manager went to meet their father, John's friend Charles Bartlett noted that "Jack was in a low state of mind; Bobby was in near despair." Although it was on this occasion that Joseph Kennedy assured John that the selection of

Johnson would soon be seen as "the smartest thing you ever did," there was no consoling Robert. "Yesterday," he said, "was the best day of my life; today is the worst day."[34]

The question is not whether John Kennedy deceived his brother and other advisors regarding his preferences for a vice-president, but why. And why willingly absorb criticism for allowing the decision to get out of hand? Perhaps the nominee was manipulating events himself. Perhaps John Kennedy deliberately allowed his brother's and other supporters' frustrations and deep antagonisms against Johnson to surface and exhaust themselves before he announced the necessary choice—and before he assumed the roles of party conciliator, peacemaker, and coalition builder.

John Kennedy's charming veneer obscured his calculating interior. Aloof and detached, the candidate emotionally distanced himself from the fiery center of events, seeming to peer in on conflagrations of his own making. In this instance he found his brother's emotional reaction useful for testing the heat, but not very helpful for making the final decision. John used Robert to probe the situation, counting on his combative instincts and defensive inclinations to stir the political cauldron.

Not outwardly angered, Robert later took pains to dispute and correct accounts that implied that his brother had used him as a pea in some political shell game. For all of his protests, Kennedy never clarified exactly what he and his brother were thinking that day. As a conversation a few years later with Graham's widow revealed, his abstruseness begged further questions. When Katherine Graham, a prominent figure in her own right as publisher of the *Washington Post,* mentioned that President Johnson now refused to speak to her, Kennedy said, "What do you mean, he's not speaking to you, when Phil made him president?" Incredulous, she asked Kennedy why, then, did he persist in dismissing her husband's memo as inaccurate. With a promise someday to explain, Kennedy enigmatically replied, "Because of what Phil didn't know, his role was more important, not less." The crucial point, he maintained—evidence to the contrary withstanding—was that "My brother and I were never apart."[35]

Still, he had to have been personally mortified and professionally embarrassed by his brother's selection of the man who had defamed their father and threatened to expose guarded family secrets. The episode not only cast doubt on his presumed status as his brother's closest political confident, it also damaged his credibility when his personal guarantees to the liberal wing of the party proved worthless. Most hurtful of all, he had suffered the humiliation of his brother's rebuke in the presence of his adversaries in the Johnson camp.

In the span of twenty-four hours a magnificent triumph had soured. As with so much else that befell him as Joseph Kennedy's third son, Robert bore the brunt of the criticism for his brother's political expediency.

"You Can Rest in November"

After the convention, the Kennedys repaired to Hyannis Port to vacation and to plan the campaign, where the media blitz during the next weeks recorded the informal and relaxed Kennedy style. Typical were photographs of CIA director Allen W. Dulles, Averell Harriman, and State Department officials arriving at Hyannis Port in business suits and hats for their briefing of John Kennedy, with Robert Kennedy greeting them at the airport attired in cotton polo shirt, shorts, and sneakers with no socks, and accompanied by several of his children in full beach regalia.[36]

When it came to running the general campaign, however, Robert's style was anything but casual. Setting to work immediately, he told his staff, "You can rest in November." His basic approach was to "run and fight and scramble" all the way. Within minutes of John Kennedy's victory in Los Angeles, his Washington staff had set up shop in the offices of the Democratic National Committee. Robert Kennedy and Lawrence O'Brien quickly reorganized Democratic party machinery to give the Kennedy party leverage across the nation.[37] An expanded campaign staff embraced operatives from the staffs of the losing Democratic candidates, experts of various kinds, and squads of friends, school chums, and Kennedy pals from the *PT-109* adventure. A loose-knit organization was built around semi-autonomous sections devoted to such important issues as civil rights, urban affairs, agriculture, business, religion, voter registration, and elderly citizens.[38]

Over the whole, Robert Kennedy kept a tight control. When Clark Clifford, the seasoned presidential advisor and architect of Harry Truman's 1948 election, suggested a small group be formed to assess the campaign and to act as a kind of strategic planning council, Robert rebuffed the suggestion as an attempt to dilute his authority. Thereafter, Clifford said, his relationship with Robert Kennedy was "clouded with tensions and disagreements."[39]

Similarly, many of the Democratic party regulars grew uncomfortable with Robert's forceful and intrusive management of the state-level organizations. His approach was simple: If an existing state organization strongly supported his brother, Robert Kennedy worked with it. If not, Byron White arrived to form a Citizens for Kennedy committee, similar to the organizations built in John Kennedy's Massachusetts campaigns. Nothing but the Kennedy party mattered to Robert Kennedy. One experienced politician marveled that Robert "didn't mind telling a mayor of a city or governor or anyone else what he thought if he stepped out of line."[40] He once told two feuding politicians, "Gentlemen, I don't give a damn if the state and county organizations survive after November, and I don't give a damn if *you* survive. I want to elect John F. Kennedy."[41]

Robert's blunt manner offended many, including some of John Kennedy's strongest supporters. Southerners, said Senator George Smathers of Florida, particularly resented Robert's interference in the campaign. A personal friend of John Kennedy's with an exalted estimation of his value and proximity to the campaign and to the candidate, Smathers once said, "We had a lot of trouble with Bobby," because he "wanted to run the campaign himself." He described a blowup that occurred during a meeting in Atlanta, when Robert tried to change plans for Lyndon Johnson's campaign train through the South. "We told Bobby to shut up and get the hell out of the way," Smathers said. When he refused, Smathers said he called John Kennedy, who "told Bobby to back off, get out of there, and leave it to us. He was an arrogant guy, Bobby was. He didn't have respect for anyone's views but his own. He was just like the old man."[42]

Such comparisons must have pleased Joseph Kennedy, who once complained to Tip O'Neill that John was "too soft." "You can trample all over him," he told O'Neill, "and the next day he's there for you with loving arms. But Bobby's my boy. When Bobby hates you, you stay hated." In another version of the same sentiment, the father once said, "He's a great kid. He hates the same way I do."[43]

Talk of Robert's ruthlessness and stories of his hard-driving, unforgiving nature and omnipresent management style circulated throughout the campaign, prompting staffers to whisper, "Little Brother is watching." John Kennedy heard the stories but was careful not to criticize his brother in front of others. Once greatly annoyed that Adlai Stevenson would introduce him before a speech in Los Angeles, he angrily demanded to know who made the decision. Told by Jesse Unruh that it was his brother's idea, Kennedy replied at once, "He must have had a good reason."[44]

Robert's job was to push and prod the staff and keep the campaign headed in the right direction. "I'm not running a popularity contest," he told a *Time* correspondent. "It doesn't matter if they like me or not. Jack can be nice to them."[45]

While Robert attended to the scut work, his brother wooed supporters from among the doubtful and the undecided. John visited Eleanor Roosevelt, paying homage to the godmother of American liberalism at Val-Kill cottage in Hyde Park. With memories of Senator Kennedy's fainthearted performance on McCarthyism still fresh in her mind, Roosevelt bestowed her tepid blessing on the nominee of her husband's party. A few days later Kennedy received the unenthusiastic endorsement of the ADA leaders, who were prepared to vote for Kennedy only because they considered Vice-President Richard Nixon, nominated by the Republicans in Chicago on 28 July, a worse alternative.[46]

With neither John Kennedy nor Richard Nixon drifting far from the security of the political center, the campaign of 1960 turned less on political ideology or policy positions than on three influential factors—religion, race, and television.

"Let's not con ourselves," Joseph Kennedy said, "the only issue is whether a Catholic can be elected President."[47] The father who dreamed of seeing all three of his surviving sons win national offices feared the inevitable Protestant backlash. Religion was one issue he could not control. Soon enough the backlash manifested itself in an intense and persistent campaign against the "forces and beliefs" that Protestant fundamentalists said controlled all Catholics. No Catholic could take the oath of office, they held, unless he renounced his faith. The leading lights of the Protestant clergy, such as Norman Vincent Peale and Daniel A. Poling, organized their campaign under the banner of the National Council of Citizens for Religious Freedom.[48] Their religious freedom, it seemed, depended on denying the White House to a Catholic.

As he had in the primaries, John Kennedy confronted the issue directly. On 12 September 1960, he appeared in Texas before the Greater Houston Ministerial Association and described, "what kind of America I believe in." He emphasized his absolute belief in the separation of church and state, "where no Catholic prelate would tell the President (should he be a Catholic) how to act." Religious views, he insisted, are a private matter even for the president. "I am not the Catholic candidate for President. I am the Democratic Party's candidate for President," he explained, "who happens also to be a Catholic." The most aired ad in the 1960 general election contained clips of Kennedy's skillful and patient disarming of critics in the Protestant ministry in Houston.[49] What came through clearly and impressed many voters, as one observer noted, was John Kennedy's ecumenical spirit and his antithetical approach to parochialism in human affairs.[50]

Robert Kennedy, on the other hand, was hypersensitive about religion and unable to treat it with detachment. Only once during the campaign did he publicly mention it. At a rally in Cincinnati he posed a rhetorical question, "Did they ask my brother Joe whether he was a Catholic before he was shot down?" His eyes filling with tears, he was unable to continue.[51] A minor incident in a large campaign, to be sure, but a poignant illustration of how Robert differed from his brother. John had challenged the ministers in Houston with similar questions, in a cool analytical manner, largely devoid of emotion. Robert, despite his tough exterior, could not place politics ahead of family and religion, for in his mind they were intertwined.

Although the candidate and his brother rarely raised the religious issue, others in the Kennedy campaign subtly implied that a vote against

Kennedy was a vote for religious intolerance. Republican strategists advised Richard Nixon to denounce this suggestion as "reverse bigotry." Instead, he ordered that religion not be mentioned. According to biographer Stephen Ambrose, Nixon "was entirely free of anti-Catholic prejudice and wished that others would put it out of their minds."[52] Nixon, of course, could not dictate the actions of Protestant fundamentalist clergy. Indeed, they doggedly continued their campaign even after the election, launching a last-ditch letter-writing campaign to dissuade presidential electors in the states carried by Kennedy from voting for a Catholic.[53] Ironically, the 1960 election broke along religious lines that tended to favor Kennedy, as a substantial majority of Catholics and sympathetic ethnic groups helped him carry several of the electoral-rich urban-industrial states.[54]

Robert Kennedy played a more prominent role influencing the perception of his brother by African American voters. Before 1960 the Kennedys were, in Arthur Schlesinger's charitable words, "only intermittently sensitive to racial injustice."[55] Robert said his parents had instilled a "social responsibility" toward the economic problems faced by African Americans and the poor of all races, but the matter of equality between the races, he admitted, "was not a particular issue in our house."[56]

Civil rights leaders remained ambivalent toward John Kennedy for various reasons. He had voted in favor of the 1957 Civil Rights Act but against an amendment providing a jury trial (and thus white control over southern courts) when civil rights cases involved criminal contempt. Further, he was generally ignorant of the major directions of the civil rights movement and knew few of its leaders. Speaking for those leaders, Martin Luther King, Jr., said he had "very little enthusiasm for Mr. Kennedy," who struck the young Baptist minister as someone who "would compromise basic principles to become President."[57]

The Kennedys' quest to win African American votes in the pivotal urban-industrial centers was tempered by their fear of alienating white southerners, which precluded not only an overt alliance with the civil rights movement but even a close public identification with African American politicians. They decided to treat African American voters as they did other groups in the broader Democratic party urban-industrial coalition, that is, as machine voters who could be reached through the political bosses.[58] Robert Kennedy was convinced that the black vote could be delivered by just three or four people, "And you never had to say you were going to do anything on civil rights. You never had to say you were going to do anything on housing. It was mostly just recognition of them [the three or four leaders]."[59]

Robert Kennedy disliked machine politicians who raised corruption and double talk to an art form. Whatever their color, Robert said he simply could not "sit around and bullshit with those guys." Of those politicos who could deliver blocs of African American voters, Kennedy particularly disapproved of Congressmen William L. Dawson, the leading black politician in Chicago and committeeman for the notoriously corrupt Second Ward, and Adam Clayton Powell, the rogue Democrat from Harlem. Yet recognize them he must. On the recommendation of Mayor Richard Daley, Robert reluctantly appointed Dawson to chair (in name only) the civil rights division in the Kennedy campaign.

Possessing neither the stomach nor the streetwise panache to bargain with the African American politicos, Robert left that task to the big-city mayors and to one of his staff, Louis Martin. A former insurance executive and newspaper editor, Martin was recruited by Harris Wofford as a media consultant in the campaign's civil rights division. Martin immediately impressed Robert Kennedy by devising a safe means for diverting cash into the African American community by purchasing advertising in black-owned newspapers and magazines.[60] Besides his can-do attitude, Martin's tough outspoken demeanor also fit the Kennedy style. After Robert Kennedy once chastised Wofford, Martin, and the entire civil rights division for "not doing enough," Martin disgustedly fired back, "You don't know anything!" To make something happen, Martin retorted, the Kennedys would have to "do business" with Dawson and Powell. Of the meeting Kennedy had Martin arrange with Dawson, Dawson "wouldn't say what happened," Martin later recalled, "but he didn't like it." Thereafter the Kennedys channeled "business" with Dawson through Mayor Richard Daley, with whom they had a more cordial understanding.[61]

Robert had slightly better success in dealing with Adam Clayton Powell, although he was personally repulsed by the flamboyant minister and international playboy, a nominal Democrat who had endorsed Eisenhower in 1956. Powell, he said, always "exacts a price, a monetary price, for his support" and bids "one party off against another."[62] True to form, Powell sent word from his yacht that he was ready to negotiate. The Kennedys sent Louis Martin to represent them. When Powell reportedly demanded $300,000 in cash in return for his support of Kennedy, Martin convinced Powell's emissary to accept $50,000, or $5,000 for each of ten Powell speeches on Kennedy's behalf. Because of the distrust between Powell and the Kennedys, the payments were disbursed through New York mayor Robert Wagner.[63]

Early polls showed the African American vote evenly divided. Those leaning toward Vice-President Nixon included Martin Luther King, Jr., and Ralph Abernathy, leaders of the Southern Christian Leadership Conference, the keystone organization of the civil rights movement. King had known Nixon for several years, was flattered by his regular calls for advice, and once described Nixon as "magnetic," with a "genius for convincing one that he is sincere." By early fall, Nixon had gained a small advantage with African American voters in the polls, helped by endorsements from baseball legend Jackie Robinson and Reverend Martin Luther "Daddy" King, Sr., who joined other leading Baptist ministers in a full-page newspaper advertisement supporting Nixon.[64]

Although John Kennedy's first two meetings with Martin Luther King, Jr., (a hurried one during late June 1960 and another in mid-September) were inconsequential, King advised Kennedy at the close of the second that "something dramatic must be done to convince Negroes that you are committed on civil rights."[65]

Two Telephone Calls

Two telephone calls from the Kennedy brothers changed the outcome of the 1960 election.

On 19 October 1960, Martin Luther King, Jr., was arrested during a sit-in protesting segregated services at an Atlanta department store. Harris Wofford, King's longtime friend and colleague, called Morris

Abram, a prominent Atlanta attorney, who talked to Mayor William B. Hartsfield about releasing King. Hartsfield, looking for a way to end demonstrations in his city, told a press conference that "in response to Senator Kennedy's personal intervention" he reached an agreement on the release of King and the other sit-in prisoners. Although Wofford had made the call to Abram on his own, not on behalf of the candidate, Georgia Democrats demanded to know why Kennedy was involved. This, of course, was just the kind of thing to send shock waves through the skittish Kennedy staff. Kenneth O'Donnell and Pierre Salinger issued a neutral comment, averring only that the senator, through an aide, had made an "inquiry" into King's constitutional rights. They were relieved when the press gave little attention to the matter.[66]

Before King could be released, Judge Oscar Mitchell of neighboring De Kalb County issued a bench warrant to detain him on an unrelated charge. In September, King had received a suspended sentence for a conviction on a charge of driving a car with expired license plates and for neglecting to get a Georgia driver's license within three months of moving into the state from Alabama. After a quick hearing, Judge Mitchell revoked King's probation on the misdemeanor and ordered him to serve four months at hard labor on a state road gang, an outrageously harsh sentence and clearly racially motivated.[67]

When Coretta King, six months pregnant, expressed her fears for her husband's safety to Harris Wofford—"I know they are going to kill him"—Wofford suggested to Shriver that John Kennedy place a private call to King's wife. "All he's got to do is to show a little heart," Wofford pleaded. "The trouble with your beautiful, passionate Kennedys is that they never show their passion." Shriver waited until O'Donnell, Sorensen, and Salinger had left the room, then told Kennedy, "Negroes don't expect everything will change tomorrow, no matter who's elected, but they do want to know whether you care." Shriver continued, "If you telephone Mrs. King, they will know you support a pregnant woman who is afraid her husband will be killed." The candidate then made the ten-minute call that changed history. Afterward, Mrs. King told Wofford she was "very moved and grateful" for Kennedy's concern.[68]

When word of his brother's call to Coretta King reached him,

Robert knew immediately whom to blame. Wofford received a call from John Seigenthaler: "Bob wants to see you bomb-throwers right away." When Wofford, Shriver, and Louis Martin entered Kennedy's office, they met a livid campaign manager. "With fists tight, his blue eyes cold, he turned on us," Wofford remembered. Kennedy was convinced his brother would be the first Democrat in one hundred years to lose the South. "Do you know that this election may be razor close and you have probably lost it for us?" he demanded. Kennedy ordered the civil rights division to issue no further press releases or engage in anything controversial for the remainder of the campaign. The scolding he gave brother-in-law Sargent Shriver in front of those from outside the family opened an irreparable rift.[69]

Within a matter of hours Robert Kennedy made an astonishing turnabout, contradicting all he had said to Wofford, Martin, and Shriver. While on a flight to New York, Kennedy stewed about the harsh treatment of King. "I thought about it and I kept thinking it was so outrageous. When I got off the airplane," he would tell Seigenthaler a day later, "I'd made up my mind that somebody had to talk to that judge." Fuming, he went directly to a pay telephone and called Judge Mitchell, because, as he later told Wofford, "it made me so damned angry to think of that bastard sentencing a citizen to four months of hard labor for a minor traffic offense and screwing up my brother's campaign and making our country look ridiculous before the world." Kennedy demanded of the judge, "Are you an American? Do you know what it means to be an American? You get King out of jail!"[70]

Judge Mitchell thereupon issued a statement saying the brother of the Democratic nominee had called him and rudely criticized him for arbitrary use of judicial power. When NBC-News coanchor David Brinkley asked Harris Wofford to confirm the call, he responded, "I just can't believe it." Among other reasons for this disbelief, Wofford questioned whether Kennedy, as a lawyer, would violate an ethical legal canon by attempting to influence a sitting judge on a case.[71] Richard Nixon, who earlier refused to comment on the King case, told an associate, "It would be completely improper for me or any other lawyer to call the judge. And Robert Kennedy should have known better than to do so."[72]

At Kennedy campaign headquarters, Seigenthaler found the reports of Kennedy's call to Mitchell simply incredible and, without waiting to check their validity, issued a denial. Then his boss telephoned and sheepishly admitted he had, indeed, made the call. Perhaps the most surprised person of all was Louis Martin, who received a call at three in the morning. "This is Bob Kennedy. Louis, I wanted you especially to know that I called that judge in Georgia today, to try to get Dr. King out." A jubilant Martin proclaimed, "You are now an honorary brother!" Thereafter Kennedy used the title in dealing with Martin, identifying himself on calls and cards as Louis Martin's "honorary brother."[73]

Robert Kennedy's call to Judge Mitchell, some thought, marked the awakening of his social conscience. Others viewed it as a characteristic display of his impetuous bullying streak. Four years later, perhaps because his service as attorney general had heightened his sensitivity to the ethical questions involved in the episode, Robert Kennedy emended his original account to Seigenthaler and Wofford. Kennedy now claimed he had made the call at the request of Georgia governor Ernest Vandiver, who thought a long jail sentence for King would hurt John Kennedy's chances of carrying Georgia. Robert claimed he did nothing more than innocently inquire, "Will he [King] get out on bail?" To which the judge responded, "Bob, it's nice to talk to you. I don't have any objection about doing that." "Whatever I said," Kennedy concluded, "he got him out."[74]

Southern Democrats reacted angrily to news of the Kennedys' involvement in King's release, exaggerating the impact of the two telephone calls and predicting a costly white southern reaction.[75] Of greater importance to Kennedy's election, however, was the reaction to the calls in the African American community. On his release Martin Luther King, Jr., said, "I am deeply indebted to Senator Kennedy, who served as a great force in making my release possible. For him to be that courageous shows that he is really acting upon principle and not expediency." King stopped short of endorsing Kennedy's election, asserting that his special role required him to remain nonpartisan, but his father, Martin Luther King, Sr., felt no such constraint. He had "expected to vote against Senator Kennedy because of his religion," said the senior King, but the telephone calls had changed his mind. "I'll take a Catholic or the Devil himself if he'll wipe the tears from my daughter-in-law's eyes," King vowed. "I've got all my votes and I've got a suitcase and I'm going to take them up there and dump them in his lap." Ralph Abernathy told an approving crowd it was time to "take off your Nixon buttons."[76]

To exploit this change and minimize white backlash, Wofford, Martin, and Shriver, in defiance of Robert Kennedy's gag order and without either Kennedy brother knowing, ordered the printing of two million pamphlets quoting various civil rights leaders' favorable reactions to Senator Kennedy's call to Coretta King. Called the "blue bomb" by Wofford for its cheap blue paper, the pamphlet, entitled *"No Comment" Nixon Versus a Candidate with a Heart, Senator Kennedy,* circulated exclusively in black communities in northern cities, with a special distribution in front of black churches on the Sunday before election day. Five hundred thousand pamphlets went to Chicago alone. Although little noted by the white media, the pamphlets, along with the phone calls on behalf of Reverend King, muted anti-Catholic antagonism among blacks, particularly black Baptists, and helped win many black voters over to Kennedy.[77]

Television, a third factor—with religion and race—that helped elect John Kennedy president, has continued to shape the way Americans perceive the Kennedys. Television lodged the Kennedy brothers in the public's collective conscious, playing and replaying their telegenic good looks, intimate personae, and the saga of their lives (and deaths). The 1960 election was the beginning. The medium most Americans depended on for news developments was about to transform U.S. politics.[78]

Robert Kennedy recognized television's effect on Americans, especially children, as it challenged home, church, and school for their attention. Unlike Adlai Stevenson, who Robert believed had vastly underestimated the impact of television in the 1956 campaign, he would use the medium to his brother's full advantage. Although unfamiliar with the technical aspects of television production, as campaign manager Robert oversaw several innovations in television campaigning and advertising, among them the use of a mobile videotape unit. The first of its kind deployed in a national campaign, the unit sped same-day coverage of the campaign to television stations and filmed commercials on location, not only showing the candidate and voters in natural poses and coloring the campaign with a spontaneous quality, but allowing them customized appeals to specific groups and regions. Perhaps because he lacked the knowledge, Robert did not assert control over the technical communications side of the campaign, which was plagued by poor coordination, with the authority for producing film and videotape advertisements split between two persons and two production companies.[79]

John Kennedy's mastery of television as an intimate communications instrument more than made up for his brother's small appreciation of its technical complexities. Using television, John Kennedy became a "new type of politician," a candidate able to distill for the small screen the high drama of political theater, its rallies, parades, music, and torchlight processions.[80]

Four televised Kennedy-Nixon debates during the 1960 campaign changed the contours of U.S. politics, legitimizing television, in David Halberstam's estimation, "as the main instrument of political discourse." As for substance, the debates featured heavy-handed attempts by both candidates to prove their commitment to sustaining U.S. autonomy and promises to take tough decisive stands on all international issues. Kennedy alleged the existence of a "missile gap" between the United States and the Soviet Union, argued for the necessity of increasing U.S. prestige abroad, and stressed the need "to get this country moving again." Nixon assailed Kennedy's attacks as unpatriotic, warned against tampering with America's leadership, and questioned Kennedy's youth and experience. The candidates appeared to say that the single measure of their fitness for the office ought to be their relative toughness on Communism. Kennedy called for U.S. assistance to Cuban exiles to overthrow Fidel Castro, unaware, he said later, of the Eisenhower administration's progress on such a plan. The presence of the Cuban dictatorship just ninety miles from U.S. shores, said Kennedy, was one example of the drift and decline that occurred during Republican years. Radio listeners, presumably focused on the substance of the candidates' comments, thought Nixon won.[81]

But content mattered less than image—the way the candidates

looked and managed themselves before the cameras. In that regard Robert Kennedy played a small but significant role. Early in the campaign he hired William Wilson as a television advisor, gave him free rein to plan the details of John Kennedy's television appearances, and warned him, "You better not fuck up." Before the crucial first debate, Wilson talked John Kennedy into allowing him to apply a light coat of makeup that lent him a healthy natural appearance. Nixon's heavier makeup failed dramatically; he perspired profusely under the hot studio lights, revealing the gray pallor of his nervous and tired face. In body language and confidence, Kennedy won the battle of appearances, and his campaign received an enormous boost.[82]

In the merging of old and new political methods in the 1960 election, Robert Kennedy took advantage of both. His activities, which required him to deal simultaneously with the political machines and the intruding eye of television, personified the transition. To hold together the Democratic coalition, for example, he was obliged to confer with Mayor Robert Wagner at Gracie Mansion in New York City and to act as peacemaker between feuding factions in the city and state. One day he would be meeting with New Jersey Democratic leaders and the next rallying the United Steelworkers in Philadelphia. Nearly every day included a stop at a television studio.

The thirty-four-year-old campaign manager's casual well-mannered demeanor and good looks projected well on television, where he seemed less nervous than when speaking before formal gatherings. Relaxed and in good humor, he acquitted himself well as a guest on Jack Paar's late-night show and began to garner notice as a celebrity in his own right. An appearance on *Meet the Press* with his counterpart in Nixon's campaign, the balding and earnest Leonard Hall, exaggerated Robert's youth and relative inexperience. His boyish smile and self-confident deportment, however, carried him over rough spots then and in other media appearances.

Robert found other obstacles along the campaign trail more difficult to overcome. Besides the ordinary calamities, such as the candidate becoming hoarse from shouting and the delays due to weather or poor advance work, the campaign faced its share of unexpected problems. Their innovative methods of political advertising fell prey to technical glitches, their mobile videotape unit burned to the ground, and, astonishingly, they ran short on money.

The popular myth of "Old Joe" Kennedy buying the 1960 election notwithstanding, Robert Kennedy did not have unlimited funds to operate his brother's campaign. Even the Kennedys did not have bottomless pockets. Advanced communications services, public opinion polling, and political advertising were expensive. Some bills were paid late or not at all. When funds ran short, the campaign had to cut down on signs and bumper stickers, long distance phone calls, and television time. Disputes arose over obligations incurred by the Democratic National Committee, and some of those bills went unpaid. Not surprisingly for anyone familiar with the manner in which the family patriarch managed his assets, the Kennedys did not rush to plug funding shortfalls with their own money.

Normally outspent in presidential elections, the Democrats in 1960 reported spending approximately the same as the Republicans, or about $13 million. The Kennedy campaign ended with a reported deficit of $3,820,000, while the Republicans were left with a $993,000 debt. During his first year in office, the richest man ever elected to the presidency recommended federal financing for presidential campaigns.[83]

As the campaign entered its final days, public opinion polls showed Nixon leading Kennedy by less than a single percentage point, with 7 percent undecided. On election day, 8 November 1960, Robert's Hyannis Port home became election central for the Kennedys. Clerks worked on the sunporch tabulating returns. Upstairs, pollster Louis Harris analyzed incoming data. Robert, an observer noted, appeared "in total command of the situation," but his mother measured the anxiety of the moment in her son's obvious tension.[84] The continual calls to check returns reportedly ran up Robert's telephone bill for that day to more than $10,000.

Early in the evening John Kennedy leaped to a two-million-vote lead, prompting one television network to project him the eventual winner. The margin steadily declined as returns from the West and Midwest offset the early gains in the East and Northeast. By midnight in Hyannis Port, it was too close to call. Results in several states with a large number of electoral votes remained uncertain into the dawning hours of the next day in what would become closest election in the twentieth century.

By 3:00 A.M. Kennedy needed a win in either California, Michigan, Illinois, or Minnesota for a majority. The *New York Times* late (3:18 A.M.) city final declared "Kennedy Elected," but then stopped the presses at 4:47 A.M. By then, Robert Kennedy sat alone at the command post, his tie long ago discarded, shirt sleeves rolled up his forearms, waiting for something to break. At 5:30 A.M. Michigan went to John Kennedy. By 7:00 A.M., when the Secret Service took up their places around the Kennedy compound, Robert permitted himself a short nap, removing only his shoes and falling into bed next to Ethel. At 7:17 A.M. the *New York Times* declared, "Kennedy Is Apparent Victor."[85]

Considering the election irregularities that abounded in 1960, the headline was apt. "The night of the gnomes," Theodore White called that evening. "No one will ever know precisely who carried the majority of 1960," he has asserted, "for on that night political thieves and vote-stealers were counterfeiting results all across the nation. The three o'clock-in-the-morning contest rested on whether the Democratic crooks or the Republican crooks were more skillful." Vote fraud appeared to center on Illinois and Texas, but Republicans cried foul in nine other states, too.[86]

The implications of that supposedly massive vote fraud in Chicago reverberate decades later. The telling and retelling of the city's voting irregularities has yielded a rich lode of folklore featuring the exaggerated powers of city bosses and Mafia dons, conjecture about Kennedy ties to organized crime, and speculation of purported double crosses leading to one, perhaps both, Kennedy assassinations. Chicago gangsters, eager to promote their own legends, have claimed dubious credit for delivering the Chicago vote and, therefore, Illinois's twenty-seven electoral votes to Kennedy. Sam Giancana, the Mafia don whose corrupt tentacles purportedly reached virtually everywhere, bragged that he was responsible for electing John Kennedy. Giancana and other gangsters, according to the theory, expected favors in return, felt betrayed by Robert Kennedy's war on organized crime, and ordered one or both of the Kennedys assassinated.[87]

The tale of Mafia double cross meshed well with conspiracy theories during the 1970s and even gained credence with investigators of the House Select Committee on Assassinations (HSCA). In 1978 HSCA counsel Robert Blakey reported that the Chicago syndicate controlled the West Side Bloc, a handful of legislators and ward politicians who, in turn, controlled working-class ethnic and black wards on the West Side and may, therefore, be "justified in taking some credit for Kennedy's election." The Kennedys, Blakey writes, "apparently neither sought nor rejected" the group's support.[88]

All of this might be historically riveting, except that the Kennedys did not need Illinois's electoral votes to win the election. By the time Mayor Daley belatedly reported out the vote totals for Chicago, the Illinois votes only added to Kennedy's winning margin. Moreover, no credible evidence has been unearthed of Kennedy involvement in the voting irregularities. Official recounts of Cook County ballots and several legal probes (including investigations by a grand jury and a special prosecutor) found no irregularities sufficient to support the contention that Chicago Democrats had wrongfully deprived Nixon of Illinois's electoral votes. Whatever Nixon lost in Cook County he very likely made up in vote-counting fraud downstate.[89] A final irony emerges from a detailed analysis of the patterns of voting irregularities, which unequivocally demonstrate that Chicago Democrats considered the presidential race of secondary importance to the heated race for state's attorney, where evidence of systematic vote fraud abounded.[90]

Despite all the mythologizing about fixes and fixers, most certainly it was not West Side hooligans but the huge African American vote that spelled the crucial difference in Kennedy's 8,858-vote victory in Illinois. The Illinois vote included an estimated 250,000 African American votes, and Kennedy carried Chicago's predominantly black wards by an 80 to 20 percent margin over Nixon.[91] If Kennedy had received the proportion of the African American vote that went to Adlai Stevenson in 1956, he would have lost not only Illinois but probably Michigan, New Jersey, and Pennsylvania.[92] President Eisenhower complained that Nixon had lost because of "a couple of phone calls."[93]

Official returns gave Kennedy a margin of 112,881 votes out of more than 68.8 million cast, a plurality so small that a switch of only

12,000 votes in five states would have shifted forty-five electoral votes and given the election to Nixon. John Kennedy maintained his customary detachment regarding the narrowness of his victory and saw the folly of taking too much credit. When a reporter referred to one of the campaign staff as "coruscatingly brilliant," Kennedy responded, "Sometimes these guys forget that fifty thousand votes the other way and they'd all be coruscatingly stupid."[94]

A transition in U.S. politics, midway between the old and new, the 1960 election exposed both the shallowness of boss-dominated politics and the fragility of a nascent politics built on electronic images and driven by pride and personal ambition. On the other hand, the huge voter turnout (64.5 percent of the eligible electorate) evoked hope. No election since has created the same invigorating spark and the same high expectations.

On Wednesday morning the president-elect and his family made their way to the armory in Hyannis. An exhausted Robert Kennedy stood unnoticed at the end of the platform, hands jammed into his pockets, staring vacantly into the crowd. His brother, aware of the consequences of the moment, held his text in trembling hands and addressed the nation. "The margin is thin," he said, "but the responsibility is clear."[95]

CHAPTER 8

Justice in the New Frontier

THE KENNEDY PRESIDENCY, in many important respects, functioned as an extension of the Kennedy family political organization and shared its objective: securing and maintaining power. All else was subordinate to that goal. Weighed first in terms of its probable impact on the reelection chances of John Kennedy, every matter of importance gravitated to the center, filtered through the finely meshed sieve of Kennedy politics.[1]

President Kennedy's egocentric management style and personal attachment to each decision mandated absolute loyalty from his staff. None of his assistants or members of his cabinet was more loyal and trusted than his brother. None had more at stake. *Primus inter pares,* Robert was the one person on whom the president could always rely. Intimately involved in virtually every aspect of his brother's presidency, Robert served as the junior, often not-so-silent, partner in the limited partnership called the Kennedy presidency.

The Best and Brightest

Together, the two handpicked the other members of the team. John Kennedy's selections tended to be thinkers, his brother's to be doers. To join the New Frontier Robert recruited several old friends, including a few football buddies from Milton and Harvard such as David Hackett (executive director of the President's Commission on Juvenile Delinquency), Kenneth O'Donnell (White House appointments secretary), Nicholas Rodis (State Department), and Dean Markham (executive director of the President's Advisory Commission on Narcotic and Drug Abuse). From the McClellan committee staff Pierre Salinger became the president's press secretary, and Walter Sheridan and Lavern Duffy moved into the Justice Department. Robert found room at the Democratic National Committee for Charles Roche, Louis Martin, and Paul Corbin.[2]

The Kennedy men—no women held top positions—were younger, more aggressive, more pragmatic, more personally devoted, and fewer in number than their immediate predecessors and successors. Many came from the upper strata of business, the professions, and academe. Robert told *Newsweek* in November 1960 that they intended to "bring a new spirit to the government. Not necessarily young men, but new men, who believe in a cause, who believe their jobs go on forever, not just from 9 to 5; who believe they have a responsibility to the United States; not just to an Administration, and who can really get things done." Crisp, dynamic and goal oriented, the "brightest and the best," as John Kennedy called them, prided themselves on their toughness of mind and competitive successes.[3]

Irrespective of academic pedigrees or rank within the government, the Kennedys exacted a high degree of personal fealty from this coterie of dedicated and energetic assistants. Robert evaluated aides according to their "helpfulness" to his brother's presidency, reserving his harshest condemnation for the "unhelpful."

The talent search, headed by Sargent Shriver with assistance from Harris Wofford, Lawrence O'Brien, and Adam Yarmolinsky, received unregulated input from all the Kennedy faithful and, according to Yarmolinsky, became "terribly unsystematized."[4] Robert loomed over the entire process, intruding more or less at will. He screened selected candidates before they received an audience with the president-elect. Together, the Kennedys interviewed most prospective cabinet members at either Joseph Kennedy's Palm Beach estate or the senator's N Street house in Georgetown. "Bobby did most of the talking," postmaster-designate J. Edward Day remembered of his interview. There he learned that all applicants for top appointive positions in his department, the largest patronage plum in government, were to be cleared through the president's brother.[5] When candidates insisted on private discussions, Robert obligingly withdrew into a side room, sat quietly, and at John's direction eavesdropped on the conversations.[6]

Robert McNamara, the brilliant, Harvard-trained, forty-four-year-old president of the Ford Motor Company, epitomized the targets of the Kennedys' search for the best qualified candidates and their desire to connect with the managerial revolution in U.S. business. A registered Republican, the renowned "whiz kid" had no prior contacts with the Kennedys. When Robert called to offer him the choice of either secretary of defense or secretary of the treasury, McNamara asked his secretary, "Who's Bobby Kennedy?" Initially reluctant, McNamara met with the Kennedys and was greatly impressed by Senator Kennedy's charm and obvious intellect. He accepted the Defense post, on condition that he have final approval on all appointments in his department. McNamara detailed his conditions in a letter, which John Kennedy glanced at and handed to his brother. "Looks okay," Robert said, with admiration for McNamara's take-charge attitude. "It's a deal," the president-elect confirmed.[7]

Adlai Stevenson expected to be named secretary of state, but neither Kennedy respected him; Robert likened him to an "old woman." They also knew that Stevenson's national constituency could, if provoked, cause the Kennedys difficulties. Robert said his brother hated the thought of having Stevenson near him in Washington and thus appointed him ambassador to the United Nations in New York, away from the seat of power. When Stevenson blithely publicized their negotiations over the appointment, Robert remembered, his brother became "absolutely furious." Stevenson apparently never grasped the depth of the Kennedys' contempt. Once in office they puckishly conspired to make him uncomfortable but never to the point of driving him away, for fear of liberal defections if he resigned in protest. Robert later conceded that Stevenson performed well in the UN job but, predictably, said he "was not really much help."[8]

Robert later recalled that he and John engaged in "a rather strong argument" regarding his brother's first choice for secretary of state, J. William Fulbright, the erudite and highly visible chair of the Senate Foreign Relations Committee. Because the Arkansas senator had publicly disapproved of the Supreme Court's 1954 school desegregation decision, Robert thought he would weaken the Kennedys' credibility with African Americans and emerging nations. "I really stopped Fulbright," Robert said later. Instead of Fulbright, John Kennedy named Dean Rusk, president of the Rockefeller Foundation, an experienced State Department hand, and the personal choice of former secretary of state Dean Acheson. The Rusk appointment, a compromise decision made in haste, Robert Kennedy would repent at leisure.[9]

Robert later had reason to regret also the reappointments of FBI Director J. Edgar Hoover and CIA Director Allen Dulles, which his brother made the day after the election, following hurried consultations with their father, himself, and Clark Clifford. At the time, however, retaining Hoover and Dulles was not a publicly contentious matter. Given the thinness of the electoral margin, the need to maintain continuity in the face of Cold War tensions, and the public's naive perception of the CIA and FBI as above politics, the president-elect would have invited a political crisis—an "internal disruption," in Robert Kennedy's words—had he not reappointed them.[10] Besides, the Kennedys had a generally high regard for both the CIA and the FBI and their directors. Dulles, of course, shared John Kennedy's determination to put an end to Castro's rule of Cuba.

The Kennedy brothers had gained Hoover's grudging respect during their McClellan committee days. In addition, Joseph Kennedy had a long and apparently cordial relationship with the director. In any case, like most other politicians of this era who fashioned themselves as "tough" on Communism, the Kennedys dared not offend Hoover, the living embodiment of America's will to resist Communist infiltration. Further, John Kennedy knew the director held at least one piece of embarrassing information, the surveillance reports on Inga Arvad Fejos, and perhaps more.

Naming Bobby Attorney General

On the appointment of the attorney general, Joseph Kennedy had the first and last words. Driven by family pride and the desire to protect his personal investments in all of his sons, the father had publicly ordained

Robert for the office in the 1956 *Saturday Evening Post* article. The family had humorously bandied the idea about for several years. Eunice Kennedy Shriver once playfully suggested that Robert be made attorney general "so he can throw all the people Dad doesn't like in jail. That means we'll have to build more jails."[11] John knew his father was "absolutely determined" that Robert be named to the post, yet he joked about making the announcement by opening the front door at three in the morning, checking to make sure no one was nearby, and whispering, "It's Bobby." The father found the appointment no laughing matter, insisting that John "needs all the good men he can get around him," and "there's none better than Bobby."[12]

John Kennedy wanted his brother near him in Washington but worried that appointing Robert attorney general would cost him credibility and weaken his already thin mandate to govern. Aware of his brother's dilemma, Robert told John shortly after the election that he did not want to be attorney general, because, among other things, the inevitable involvement of the Justice Department in civil rights cases ultimately would hurt the president's popularity. Uncertain about his own future, Robert once mentioned returning to Massachusetts to run for governor in 1962.[13]

If he were to work in his brother's administration, it could only be under certain conditions. "I wasn't going to work in the White House," he said later. Whatever position he took, it had to give him "equality of responsibility and prestige" with any of the other advisors. He could not, he said, take "direct orders from anybody" except the president. "I would be resented," he reasoned, "and rightfully so, by anybody for whom I would be working or anybody else who had a higher position."[14]

All the same, John considered putting Robert in the number-two post in the Defense Department, intending initially to ask Paul Gates, Eisenhower's secretary of defense, to remain on until Robert gained enough experience to take over. Unwilling to confront his father directly, John coaxed his carousing buddy Senator George Smathers into testing Joseph Kennedy's reaction to the idea of putting Robert in the Defense Department. One afternoon while sitting around the pool at the Palm Beach house, Smathers casually broached the question. For his efforts Smathers received a disdainful "down his nose" stare from the ambassador, who without acknowledging Smathers said to John, "I want Bobby to be Attorney General. He is your blood brother. Nobody has sacrificed more of his time and energy in your behalf than your brother Bobby, and I don't want to hear any further thing about it."[15]

Notwithstanding, a few days later, John asked the same favor of Clark Clifford, who was acting as Kennedy's transition liaison to the Eisenhower administration. "Bobby says he does not want the job, and he thinks it will hurt me," Clifford recalled John Kennedy telling him. In a "grave, low, intense voice," the president-elect explained the situation: "I have told my father that Bobby would create a real problem as Attorney General," but "my father said, 'That doesn't make any difference . . . [only] he can protect you.'"

"Only the Kennedys!" an amazed Clifford later observed. Still, he presented the father a careful legal and political briefing, emphasizing that the attorney general, the top law enforcement officer, must be free of partisan and personal biases. Joseph Kennedy, according to Clifford, did not mince words. *"Bobby is going to be Attorney General.* All of us have worked our tails off for Jack, and now that we have succeeded I am going to see to it that Bobby gets the same chance that we gave to Jack."[16] In any event, the president-elect had to drop the idea of putting Robert in the Defense Department when McNamara opted for secretary of defense and demanded and received a free hand to run the department.[17]

The president-elect's quandary became apparent in the vacillating signals he sent to his transition staff. Early in November he instructed Shriver to prepare a list of candidates for attorney general because "Bobby's not going to take it." When Shriver handed him four names a few weeks later, Kennedy told him not to bother with the matter further because "Bobby's going to be Attorney General." A week after that, leading Democrats voiced opposition to Robert, among them House Speaker Sam Rayburn, he again asked Shriver for a list.[18]

Around mid-November, John Kennedy defied his father and offered the post of attorney general to Connecticut governor Abraham A. Ribicoff, who declined because, according to Robert Kennedy, "he said he didn't want a Jew putting Negroes in Protestant schools in the South." Ribicoff wanted a seat someday on the Supreme Court and thought the attorney general post would undermine his confirmation chances. He agreed, instead, to be secretary for health, education, and welfare. "So actually," Robert Kennedy said later, "I was second choice."[19]

Once John Kennedy yielded to his father's demand, he still found it difficult to win Robert over. "I had been chasing bad men for three years," Robert said, "and I didn't want to spend my life doing that." Ethel Kennedy is certain: "He did not want to do it." Convincing her husband, she recalled, required "every ounce of Jack's charm and persuasion." By the same token, she added, "I thought he had worked every living minute for his brother, day and night, and whatever Jack gave him was deserved." Before deciding, Robert consulted Justice William O. Douglas, Senator John McClellan, and FBI director J. Edgar Hoover. None was enthusiastic, although Hoover advised him to accept the position and wished him well. "I didn't like to tell him that," Hoover admitted to his assistant William Sullivan, "but what could I say?" Later, Hoover claimed it was "the worst damn advice" he ever gave.[20]

Favorable and unfavorable, there was no shortage of advice. Columnist Drew Pearson, never one of Robert Kennedy's admirers, urged him not to take the job. With patronizing fatuity, Pearson wrote of his concern that Robert would do "such a good job" and "handle so many controversial questions with such vigor" that John Kennedy "would be in hot water all the time." To protect President Kennedy from being blamed for his brother's "forthrightness," Pearson and others suggested that Robert remain in the background as an "unofficial but very important personal advisor."[21] Like many pundits, Pearson misunderstood the relationship between the Kennedy brothers. The good Kennedy, bad Kennedy routine had served them well thus far. The question was, what title would Robert take as they played out the next act in their conjoined life scenarios?

Robert put off serious discussion of John's offer until the second week of December. Then he told his brother he could not accept the nomination to be attorney general because the newspaper critics and Republican opposition would "kick our balls off." The next day, at a breakfast meeting at Senator Kennedy's Georgetown townhouse, with

John Seigenthaler at his side Robert asked his brother to discuss some alternative appointment.[22] "Johnny, let's talk about me," Robert pleaded. There was nothing to discuss, John replied, "I need someone I know to talk to in this government." Robert would be attorney general, and "that's the way we'll do it," the older brother said. Robert appealed for Seigenthaler's help in making his case for a position other than attorney general, but John Kennedy had left no openings. Outside, reporters waited impatiently for an announcement. "That's it, General," Senator Kennedy told his brother. "Let's grab our balls and go." Reaching for the door, the president-elect said to the attorney general–designate, "All right, Bobby we're ready. Comb your hair before we go out."[23]

The wave of negative reaction to naming his brother attorney general did not surprise John Kennedy. Besides the obvious charge of nepotism, the host of concerns aired included Robert's age, lack of legal experience, and dubious record on civil liberties. The Democratic National Committee reportedly was inundated with letters of protest. *New York Times* reporter Harrison Salisbury's view typified the reaction: "Where his brother was concerned, I did not think he had a scruple." Senator Richard Russell of Georgia thought the appointment a disgrace. Harris Wofford regarded it as "indefensible."[24] Alexander Bickel in The *New Republic* asserted that Robert Kennedy was "not fit for the office," and The *New York Times* declared the selection "most disappointing."[25]

Robert had a ready retort for most critics. When reporter Charles Bartlett, John Kennedy's longtime friend, registered disapproval because "he was not a diplomat in any sense," had "so little instinct for politics," and was "so direct in his approach," Robert told him the appointment was his father's idea and invited Bartlett to call his father and report his misgivings directly.[26] To those who questioned his commitment to legal ethics, Robert responded that ethics were mostly a matter of morality, and he learned everything he needed to know about morality when he was six years old. Morality and the law, he reminded attorneys, were not always compatible, as Abraham Lincoln once said: "Some things legally right are not morally right."[27] To complete the syllogism for Robert, some things morally right, as he had discovered with his call to Martin Luther King's judge during the campaign of 1960, may violate legal ethics.

Organized labor had reason to object to Robert's appointment, but AFL-CIO general counsel Arthur Goldberg again intervened. Appointed secretary of labor in the Kennedy administration, Goldberg said he spoke for Walter Reuther (UAW president), David Dubinsky (Garment Workers' Union president) and "many others" when he asserted that Robert Kennedy was "eminently suited" for the office of attorney general. The "real spokesmen for the honest unions," Goldberg averred, were "almost without exception" enthusiastic about the appointment.[28]

During his confirmation hearings, several senators questioned but did not pursue the fact that Robert, less than a decade out of law school, had never tried a case in court. Otherwise, the hearings went routinely. Lyndon Johnson, still a titan in the Senate, convinced a few reluctant southern senators to hold their tongues and go along. Richard Nixon tried to goad Republican senators into asking embarrassing questions that would force Kennedy to divulge the extent of the family financial empire; when Republicans failed to probe deeply, Nixon said the Senate had done a "lousy job." With only one dissenting vote, Kennedy was easily confirmed.[29] The rest of the Kennedy nominees fared as well. The New Frontier began, as advisor Fred Dutton noted, with "nine strangers and a brother for a Cabinet."[30]

The sixty-fourth attorney general of the United States, at thirty-five years and two months the third youngest, Robert Kennedy took the oath of office on 21 January 1961 in the family quarters on the second floor of the White House.[31] Rather than take the elevator to the East Room reception, he descended to the first floor by sliding down the bannister of the great curved staircase, followed by ten-year-old Kathleen, four-year-old Michael, and assorted other Kennedy children, to the mortification of their nanny, Ena Bernard, who exclaimed, "Mr. Kennedy, you'll never grow up"—just moments before Senator Hubert Humphrey happened upon the scene.[32]

The new head of the Justice Department did not present an imposing figure. Muscular and fit, his weight fluctuating between 155 and 165 pounds, Robert Kennedy possessed an exceptionally strong upper torso and thick forearms more characteristic of a professional athlete than a politician. His light brown hair already showed traces of gray. A prominent nose and sharp cheekbones highlighted an angular face, its youthful roundness gone. Deepening lines in his brow and at the corners of his eyes betrayed the cumulative effects of a month-long sleep deficit at the end of the campaign. Kennedy's body language conveyed a deceptive fragility. A perpetual stoop made him appear shorter than his five feet, ten and one-half inches. In casual conversations his inherently shy mannerisms and defensive postures made him appear smaller and somehow subordinate to those around him. Up close, however, no one could mistake the intensity of his deep blue, almost violet, eyes.

Robert at first found the formal trappings and official protocol of office restricting. He tried to dress the part. With the expensively tailored blue worsted business suits he ordered in lots of four or five from fashionable haberdashers in Washington and New York, he wore silk rep ties and custom-fitted cotton shirts, which he changed several times a day.[33] Yet stepping from the chauffeured Cadillac limousine and entering the Justice Department, Kennedy customarily loosened his tie, opened the top shirt button, removed his suit coat, rolled up his shirt sleeves, and strode to his office.

Kennedy's work habits and office mannerisms reflected his personality. His handwriting, a tight, barely legible scrawl revealing purpose and control, sometimes wandered across the pages of his personal notes, rising and falling with his emotions.[34] His compulsive doodles of complex geometric diagrams within fixed boundaries suggested a need for order and hinted at the restrictive roles his lot in life cast for him. Even when seated, Kennedy was a restless, constant fidgeter. At his desk, characteristically with telephone in one hand and a pencil in the other, he impatiently pushed back a forelock or jabbed in annoyance at an unruly cowlick. A wing-tip-shod foot propped on an open side drawer drew visitors' eyes to his drooping socks; his wife had at least broken him of the habit of wearing white wool athletic socks with business suits. Benjamin Bradlee once remarked that Robert Kennedy dressed like a "Brooks Brothers beatnik."[35] Indeed, the Milton product projected an air of studied casualness, a rehearsed nonchalance that, prior to the sixties' revolution in manners and dress, was the preserve of young, wellborn New Englanders but rarely observed among Washington's governing elite.

The new regime's informality and the traditional formalism of

Washington officialdom collided head on in the attorney general's baronial office, a converted conference room of nearly eleven hundred square feet. On any given day the stately office might be a frenetic communications center for a civil rights crisis, a command post for coordinating CIA sabotage operations against Cuba, the setting for formal staff meetings, a romper room for Kennedy's children, or the scene of an after-hours beer and pretzel bull session with young attorneys. On its expensive walnut-paneled walls hung his youngsters' latest works of art, a trophy sailfish, a dart board (with holes in the paneling from errant tosses), and assorted Kennedy family memorabilia. No one entering the office could fail to detect the special relationship with the president. On the credenza behind the desk, next to a football, rested a leather-bound copy of *The Enemy Within.* Jacqueline Kennedy's inscription read, "To Bobby, who made the impossible possible and changed all our lives. Jackie," and below it, "To Bobby, the brother within, who made the easy difficult. Jack, Christmas 1960."[36]

Work days often began with briefings at the White House, State Department, or Pentagon. During the frequent foreign crises, Kennedy seldom arrived at the Justice Department before noon. Once there, the attorney general might prowl the corridors in his shirtsleeves, introducing himself to the staff, "I'm Bob Kennedy. What's your name? What are you working on?"[37] Finding someone momentarily idle, he might thrust at them a copy of his book *The Enemy Within* and advise them to read something worthwhile, rather than waste time. Kennedy's management style, in sum, was "anti-bureaucratic, informal, impulsive, chaotic, spontaneous and personal."[38] It swept through the department, winning converts and transforming old habits everywhere except in the FBI. Rather than finding themselves "stuck with the kid brother" as they had feared, professionals were delighted when their young boss invigorated the department of 31,700 career employees with a lively sense of mission.[39]

Robert Kennedy did not consciously adhere to a prescribed managerial theory. More flexible than one might expect, given his rigid views on other matters, he adapted to changing circumstances and often responded with creative improvisations. He emphasized action and results and valued self-reliance and initiative, often assigning difficult, time-consuming tasks without detailed written or spoken instructions. Kennedy might ask an aide "to look into a situation" and "see what it was all about," a practice one assistant described as "like being dropped into an ice-cold lake." Although accessible, Kennedy avoided micro-managing and did not demand regular detailed activity reports when brief follow-up conversations sufficed. Kennedy's special assistant, John E. Nolan, Jr., said his boss "certainly never *explained* to anybody how he wanted this process to work." But it did. Most who worked for Kennedy found it an exhilarating challenge.[40] Yet while his style and methods gave his staff a personal stake in the enterprise at Justice, all understood that the overriding aim of the attorney general was the advancement of the Kennedy presidency.

Little of the formerly staid routine at Justice was left untouched. When his senior staff were denied access to the FBI's basement gymnasium, Kennedy ordered a new exercise room constructed on the roof.[41] To liven the environment for employees, Ethel arranged for music to be piped into an outdoor courtyard and dining area.[42] In January 1962 Kennedy hosted a "picnic" in his office for 125 children of cabinet members, cooking hot dogs and hamburgers in the huge fireplace. Some days, Kennedy children rummaged through their father's papers, climbed over and under desks, playfully invaded administrative sanctuaries (including J. Edgar Hoover's), imposed on secretaries, and gleefully shared telephone calls with the attorney general and his subordinates.

Presiding over this congenial mayhem was Angie Novello. Those initially deceived by the petite frame and apparently demur demeanor of Robert's gatekeeper soon learned to contact her for access to the attorney general. She handled personal correspondence, deciphered her boss's cryptic notes scribbled in the margins of incoming letters, drafted bread-and-butter responses, and took the initiative, as she said, to "unruffle the feathers" of people who experienced real or imaginary slights. She was particularly attentive to needs of the female volunteer staffers, called the "boiler-room girls."[43]

For all of his abilities at organizing others, Robert Kennedy was not well organized personally. He annoyed his staff by habitually forgetting or losing important papers, sloppily cramming items into his briefcase, and frequently ignoring or misplacing letters and then blaming the staff for delays in responding.[44] His desk diaries and message sheets bristle with reminders, chiding comments, and prods like this one from Angie Novello regarding his tendency to misplace things and to blame others for it: "I hear you're looking for a white shirt with JFK on it, and your gold cuff links. You were wearing the cuff links one day last week (they were in your top desk drawer); the shirt was in your little suitcase in the study—now it isn't there. YOU took it, I'm sure!"[45]

One feature of the office that particularly annoyed hidebound purists was the frequent presence of Kennedy's dog, Brumus. Because the free-spirited black Newfoundland howled inconsolably whenever his master left Hickory Hill, Robert often took him along in the limousine. Although secretaries escorted Brumus on well-photographed walks to the curb, he often soiled the expensive office rugs. These antics prompted indignant columns in The *New York Times* and brought anonymous complaints to the FBI from upset and sometimes outraged taxpayers. This "damnably undignified conduct" led Hoover to convene a futile day-long meeting of assistant directors specifically to consider launching a formal investigation against Kennedy for destroying federal property (the rugs Brumus peed on and the paneling Kennedy hit with the darts) and for violating federal regulations prohibiting dogs in public buildings.[46]

Into this environment Kennedy attracted an exceptional group of highly skilled professionals with three things in common: mental toughness, nonideological temperaments, and loyalty to the Kennedys and, ultimately, to each other. Deputy Attorney General Byron "Whizzer" White, later to be a Supreme Court justice, administered the department and took charge when Kennedy was out of the office. John Seigenthaler served as Kennedy's administrative assistant for two years before becoming editor of the *Nashville Tennessean.* He was succeeded by James Symington, son of the Missouri senator, later a member of Congress himself. Edwin Guthman, the socially conscious Pulitzer Prize–winning journalist who had been on the edges of the Rackets Committee investigations, became Kennedy's public affairs officer. Nicholas de B. Katzenbach left a professorship at the University of Chicago Law School to head the Office of Legal Counsel. Archibald Cox, lured away from Harvard, served as solicitor general and achieved greater fame when President Nixon fired him as independent prosecutor during the Watergate scandal. Ramsey Clark, son of former attorney general and Supreme Court justice Tom Clark, headed the Lands Division. (Clark and Katzenbach would later hold the office of attorney general themselves.) The team was rounded out by the other division heads—Burke Marshall (Civil Rights), Herbert J. Miller (Criminal), Louis Oberdorfer (Tax), and William Orrick (Anti-Trust).[47]

Kennedy set high expectations for his staff. Although seldom effusive in praise of their work, he convinced them he cared about them. He "doesn't just stand up for you," James McShane, head of the U.S. Marshals, later commented, "he goes to the wall for you."[48] Kennedy proved especially supportive during times of personal tragedy, when his deep moral reserve and Catholic piety overflowed. He waxed pontifical when consoling New Frontier friends over deaths in their families, his condolence letters echoing priestly homilies and Catholic rituals. To a colleague whose mother died, Robert Kennedy wrote, "She is now raised above all earthly problems" and "the everlasting joys and light of heaven are hers," for she is in a "very high place in paradise."[49] A camaraderie of almost religious intensity bound this band of brothers, as Kennedy's staff later styled themselves.[50]

Robert Kennedy's most lasting and least conventional contribution to the Justice Department was his impact on its humdrum routine. Many observers noted the improved quality of day-to-day law business, the possible result, at least in part, of Kennedy's decision to give his staff their heads without imposing his legal views on them. "He never questioned anybody's legal judgment," Nicholas Katzenbach told Arthur Schlesinger, Jr. When reviewing a legal problem, Kennedy would say, "Everybody here knows more law about this than I do, but I'm the Attorney General and it's my responsibility, so you've got to make it clear to me so that I can make a decision." According to Solicitor General Archibald Cox, Kennedy possessed other qualities that compensated for his lack of legal expertise. Cox, widely admired and respected for his judgment and integrity, attributed the Justice Department's success largely to Kennedy's incisive analytical abilities, his willingness to make decisions, his skills at delegating, and, perhaps most important, his unwavering support and trust of his staff. These attributes, in Cox's estimation, made Robert Kennedy "a first-rate Attorney General."[51]

The Mafia: Round Two

Kennedy intended to remake the Justice Department. While on the Rackets Committee he had maintained a running critique of the department, castigating it for its handling of cases and accusing it of incompetence and blundering delays. Now, within two weeks of taking office, he declared a "war on crime," which, he said, had "outgrown the authorities"; "the rackets have become too widespread, too well organized and too rich."[52] Only a coordinated federal effort could control this menace, Kennedy believed. He threw the federal system into the fray from the beginning to the end, investigating and prosecuting organized crime in defiance of previous conventions regarding the separation of federal, state, and local authority. He wanted to be remembered as the man who broke the Mafia, he announced, and he took personal charge of changing the Justice Department's approach to fighting crime in a war that held first place in the Kennedy administration's domestic priorities from early 1961 through the spring of 1963, when it gave way to civil rights.[53]

Kennedy's offensive against organized crime unfolded along five strategic fronts. First, he instituted a campaign to educate people about the threat of organized crime, mobilizing them with speeches and publicity and drawing upon government data, criminal informers, and his own book, *The Enemy Within,* as resources. Second, he leveraged his brother's position to influence other departments and to gain the cooperation of competing bureaus and agencies, while minimizing the foot-dragging of Hoover's FBI. Third, he allocated significant funds and manpower to the Organized Crime Section, which spearheaded the effort. Fourth, he assigned a team of centrally coordinated prosecutors to investigate, indict, and prosecute cases against key racketeers. Fifth, he lobbied for passage of a series of bills defining interstate racketeering and expanding federal prosecutorial powers and, unsuccessfully, for laws to authorize court-ordered wiretapping in limited instances.

Among the less useful means of educating the public about organized crime was *The Enemy Within.* Published in 1960 and a moderate best-seller in 1961 when Kennedy took office, the book failed to arouse the public's passion. Kennedy's heated and imprecise prose, generously lifted from his sometimes meandering accusations delivered before the Rackets Committee, had led to distracting controversy, and provoked several lawsuits before and after he became attorney general. During television appearances to promote the book in 1959 and 1960, he oversold his thesis and more than once appeared to cross the line between crusading prosecutor and public defamer. When Robert accused James Hoffa of all manner of theft, extortion, and criminal wrongdoing, *Meet the Press* moderator Lawrence Spivak and NBC talk-show host Jack Paar cautioned him about the laws of libel. "Inside Jimmy Hoffa," an NBC Television special roughly based on Kennedy's book, aired in 1963 and elicited a $2.5 million libel suit from Hoffa.[54]

Because he felt "wronged" by statements in the book, Roy Fruehauf of Fruehauf Trailers Company, one of the nation's largest trucking companies, hired renowned attorney Louis Nizer to deal with Kennedy's implied accusation in *The Enemy Within* that a $200,000 transaction between Fruehauf and Dave Beck was a bribe. Fruehauf insisted it was a "loan." *Readers' Digest,* which published a condensed version of the book, felt obliged, without consulting Kennedy, to issue a mollifying statement on the Fruehauf matter. Kennedy refused to apologize, but John Seigenthaler supplied *Readers' Digest* with revised wording regarding the Fruehauf-Beck relationship.[55]

All the while he was actively promoting the book, Kennedy peevishly complained of being "shortchanged" by his publisher's (Harper and Brothers) advertising efforts.[56] Soon after he took office as attorney general, his father's lawyers completed negotiations on the film rights for *The Enemy Within* with producer Jerry Wald. Budd Schulberg, who wrote the screenplay for *On the Waterfront,* an Academy Award winner on corruption in the Longshoremen's union, adapted Kennedy's book. Paul Newman was proposed for the role of Robert Kennedy. Perhaps because he hoped to prove himself in a medium in which his father had gained success and possibly because he saw it as a way to compete with *PT-109,* the successful Hollywood production of his brother's wartime exploits, Robert was more absorbed with the project than one might expect, given his other duties. He spoke regularly on the telephone with Wald, Schulberg, and Lester Linsk, a producer at 20th Century Fox, and met with them at his home, in his office in the Justice Department, and in Los Angeles.

The Enemy Within, however, posed significant problems for Hollywood. Notwithstanding the critical success of *On the Waterfront* (or perhaps because of it), no sane producer, reporters opined, would attempt an antiunion film when approximately seventy unions and guilds were involved in the making of motion pictures. "We have no desire to criticize unionism," Wald told the press, "so this won't be a documentary." But when Wald died suddenly in July 1963, the head of 20th Century Fox dropped the project, reportedly the Teamsters had threatened not to deliver the prints to theaters. Budd Schulberg tried to revive the project at Columbia, but the Teamsters pressured that company too into abandoning the idea.[57]

Meanwhile, Kennedy's campaign to educate the public about organized crime received an important boost from an unexpected source—the first public defection within the Italian Mafia. Joseph Valachi, marked for death by New York crime boss Vito Genovese and facing a laundry list of federal charges, violated the code of *omertà* (silence) and admitted to Harry Anslinger's Federal Bureau of Narcotics (FBN) his thirty-year involvement in organized crime and his participation in thirty-three gangland murders. The attorney general seized upon Valachi's testimony to broaden his public relations crusade. "Before you knew it," said the annoyed FBN agent in charge, "Bobby Kennedy, because of his hatred for the mob, had completely taken charge of Valachi."[58]

In June 1962, in return for protection from Kennedy's Justice Department and a life sentence, Valachi named names and described the innermost workings of the Italian organized crime network he called *la Cosa Nostra* (our thing). He identified the regional families, mapped their influence, and labeled their members—the *capo* (boss), *consigliere* (legal counsel), *sottocapo* (underboss), and *caporegime* (lieutenant). The regional families, he confirmed, were directed by a national commission. Regarded as the most important intelligence findings since the Apalachin conclave, Valachi's revelations startled the American people, particularly as the FBI director had repeatedly assured them that organized criminal activity did not exist.[59]

When Senator McClellan's Rackets Committee convened hearings to receive Joseph Valachi's testimony in September 1963, Robert Kennedy was the leadoff witness. Before his old committee, Kennedy reported to a national television audience that the information supplied by Valachi allowed the Justice Department "to prove conclusively" the existence of the nationwide crime organization known as the Mafia. "Our principal problem," Kennedy emphasized, "is insulation. The kingpins of the rackets would become inoperative if stripped of the protective layers of complex secret organizations" of the type described by Valachi.[60]

As Kennedy turned the media spotlight on organized crime, he simultaneously moved to coordinate the government's scattered and diverse efforts and to disseminate information throughout the federal establishment. "Our first and most urgent need," he stated in *The Enemy Within,* "is for a national crime commission" to serve as a central clearinghouse for information on criminal activities. The idea was widely credited to Los Angeles police chief William H. Parker, a personal favorite of the Kennedys and a longtime Hoover antagonist. Hoover regarded the proposed commission as an affront to his authority and reportedly threatened to retire immediately if Kennedy pursued it.[61] To work around Hoover, rather than a national commission Kennedy created an informal information exchange system to coordinate activities across twenty-seven agencies, some of which were notoriously independent—most notably the FBI.[62]

Young Justice Department attorneys such as G. Robert Blakey, later to become a leading authority on organized crime, marveled at the charismatic authority with which Kennedy cut through the otherwise impenetrable levels of the federal bureaucracy. Most bureaucrats, Kennedy realized, "hated the idea" of cooperating with him. He knew his relationship with the president was the deciding factor in bringing together these diverse units. "They wouldn't have paid any attention to me otherwise," he said.[63] (Indeed, they went along only for as long as his brother was alive.)

Kennedy found an unlikely ally in C. Douglas Dillon, who chaired a prestigious Wall Street financial house and served in the Eisenhower State Department before becoming secretary of the treasury in the

Kennedy administration. Robert Kennedy and Dillon agreed on nearly all of the larger issues, enjoyed each other's company, and struck a lasting personal friendship.[64] The alliance would prove fortunate for Kennedy, who regarded the cooperation of the Internal Revenue Service (IRS) and Anslinger's FBN, both situated within the Treasury Department, as critical to the success of his anticrime program. On 16 February 1961, Dillon hosted Kennedy and Hoover at a luncheon where the main lines of agreement between the two departments were set forth.

Central to the plan was an aggressive use of the IRS. Earlier, Dillon had acceded to the appointment of Robert's former law school professor, Mortimer M. Caplin, as IRS commissioner, with the understanding that the IRS would vigorously enforce the tax laws against criminals. Caplin delivered with a nine-fold increase in the number of IRS workdays devoted to criminal investigations; between 1961 and 1965, 60 percent of the organized crime prosecutions originated in tax investigations.[65]

At the administrative hub of the war on crime stood the Justice Department's Criminal Division, headed by Herbert J. "Jack" Miller, a strict constructionist Republican lawyer who discreetly served the Kennedys for decades thereafter. Reporting to him was the Organized Crime and Racketeering Section born during Eisenhower's administration. To direct that section Kennedy initially appointed Edwyn Silberling, an experienced prosecutor and an expert on wiretap evidence who had worked with New York District Attorney Frank Hogan, the country's most effective prosecutor of organized crime. When Silberling proved indifferent to the political consequences of prosecutions and "difficult to get along with," Kennedy replaced him with William Hundley, a holdover from the Eisenhower era whom Kennedy had once berated but later came to appreciate for his bureaucratic tenacity.[66] Hundley's group, for its many successes, did not enjoy good relations with the FBI. Suspicious of Hundley and his connections, Hoover was certain "the hoodlums of Las Vegas had a direct line" into his section. This was not literally true, of course, but Hundley was a close friend of famed attorney Edward Bennett Williams, who apparently was not beneath using his friendships with Hundley and with Robert Kennedy to probe for information about government cases against clients such as the notorious gangsters Sam Giancana and Frank Costello.[67]

Confident that Hundley and the Organized Crime Section could make a difference, Kennedy expanded its numbers from seventeen to sixty attorneys. Field units appeared in Chicago, New York, Los Angeles, and Miami. Based on prosecutorial activity alone, the Kennedy crime campaign set impressive new standards. The year before Robert Kennedy came into office, only forty-nine indictments against organized crime figures were brought. In 1961, Kennedy's first year, the number jumped to 121, then 350 in 1962, and 615 in 1963. Acknowledging that "this is going to be a long-range struggle which must be continued over the next several years," Kennedy was pleased when convictions steadily rose each year, from 45 in 1960, to 73, 138, and 288, for 1961 through 1963. Where Justice Department attorneys under Attorney General William Rogers spent 283 days in court in 1960, in 1962, under Kennedy, they were in court 809 days. Investigative work in the field increased more than 300 percent. In all, the Kennedy Justice Department produced 116 indictments against members or associates of the Commission that gathered at Apalachin.[68]

The department achieved conspicuous successes in the face of a host of difficulties, some of which threatened to compromise Robert Kennedy's program all together. The FBI, in some ways the young attorney general's biggest problem, was arguably also one of his most valuable resources in the fight against crime. The Bureau over the years had taken on its director's characteristics, becoming fearful, static, unimaginative, and averse to risk, operating like a secret society embedded in the government. Robert Kennedy alternately flattered and cajoled Hoover, acting as if he assumed the FBI was already doing what he requested. He never succeeded, however, in gaining Hoover's trust and cooperation or in bringing the FBI under control.[69]

Hoover not only disapproved of Kennedy's high-profile approach to the war on crime, he doubted the extent and significance of organized crime itself. Caught short by what the Apalachin confab revealed, Hoover set in motion the Top Hoodlum Program, an extensive surveillance and illegal eavesdropping campaign against leaders of organized crime intended primarily to gather information, not to prosecute.

He learned enough by the fall of 1958 to admit to his FBI associates, "The Mafia does exist in the United States." But he suppressed a potentially humiliating internal report indicating that organized crime had flourished during the years Hoover had denied its existence. Gradually, one agent in the field recalled, Hoover "seemed to lose interest" in organized crime. Kennedy later said that when he arrived at Justice, Hoover had assigned four hundred agents to work on Communism in New York and only ten on organized crime. Determined to shake Hoover out of his lethargy and change his priorities, Kennedy said, "I asked them to go into it like they went into the Communist Party."[70]

Hoover's lack of enthusiasm for Kennedy's war on crime derived from several factors, the first and most persuasive being his own and other law enforcement officials' genuine skepticism toward Kennedy's claims regarding the size and extent of organized crime.[71] Second, Hoover was compulsively committed to eliminating the presumed internal threat of Communist subversion, which he, unlike Kennedy, regarded as the foremost danger to U.S. security. Third, he resisted reassigning large numbers of agents in labor-intensive, high-risk investigations of difficult-to-prove criminal conspiracies yielding low public relations and risky political returns. Fourth, Hoover feared corrupting his beloved agency. Fighting crime, Ramsey Clark once said, is "dirty, and sometimes the dirt rubs off." Hoover, according to Clark, "wanted clean work, easy work. He wanted to be a winner."[72] And, finally, Hoover disliked being ordered to do anything by the boy attorney general.

Rumors of other, more sinister reasons for Hoover's comparatively passive tack toward organized crime abound. Among those speculative and largely unsubstantiated accusations are that Hoover covered up the criminal involvement of rich and influential friends and benefactors, that he secretly associated with gangster Frank Costello, and that he was blackmailed by criminals who manipulated his ten dollar racetrack bets and possessed photographic evidence of Hoover's alleged homosexuality.[73]

In truth, both Kennedy and Hoover vigorously attacked the mob—one publicly, the other in a clandestine operation, the scope of which will probably never come to light. Hoover's massive eavesdropping operation, according to one informed estimate, may have placed "in excess of a thousand bugs in operation at any one time." Hoover cleverly disguised the purchase of equipment and his staff reportedly destroyed records of its deployment.[74] Where Kennedy prosecuted organized crime figures, Hoover secretly collected information on them and their political associations that he could use to extend his and the FBI's bureaucratic lifeline.

Behind the FBI's success over the years lay Hoover's ability to shape the Bureau's popular image through shrewd and callous manipulation of news reports and clever public relations. Attorney generals had given Hoover free rein in dealing with the press for more than three decades, that is, until Robert Kennedy arrived with entrepreneurial instincts and bureaucratic survival skills of his own. Moving quickly to cut Hoover short, Kennedy ordered that all of Hoover's press releases and publications be cleared through Edwin Guthman's office. Accustomed to having FBI agents or friendly journalists ghostwrite articles and books for his byline, Hoover directed the writing of an article in 1962 intended for publication in *Readers' Digest,* where he planned to preempt public credit for the Valachi revelations and the rash of new prosecutions and to imply he knew all along of the existence of organized crime. Kennedy ordered the article held until the inaccurate, self-aggrandizing comments were stricken. Hoover withdrew the article.[75] The New Frontier showdown against organized crime had room for only one top gun.

Kennedy's war on crime faced another problem in the CIA, elements of which had gone out of control. In the last months of the Eisenhower administration the CIA recruited several top Mafia leaders to assassinate Cuban premier Fidel Castro, a move that would later prompt some gangsters to expect favorable treatment and force unwanted compromises on the attorney general.

Finally, Robert's efforts also ran up against persistent rumors of Kennedy family connections to organized crime, the president's involvement with a Mafia party girl, and singer Frank Sinatra's resolute attempts to gain favors for unsavory friends, all of which imperiled the legitimacy and credibility of Kennedy's anticrime program. Although the conjunction of these impediments clearly annoyed and frustrated the attorney general, none weakened his resolve.

To focus his efforts, Kennedy turned once again to Harry Anslinger, director of the FBN. Nearing retirement after thirty years' service and delighted to make one final contribution, Anslinger brought Kennedy a thick black book with data on eight hundred hoodlums. Handing the book to his Organized Crime unit, Kennedy instructed, "Don't tell me what I can't do. Tell me what I can do."[76] In short order, Kennedy designated forty organized crime figures as priority targets, a number later expanded to twenty-five hundred. Kennedy's campaigns against three of the target figures—Carlos Marcello, Sam Giancana, and James Hoffa—illustrate both the effectiveness and the frustrations of his war on crime.

Described by Kennedy as "head of the underworld in the southeastern part of the United States," Carlos Marcello by 1961 had served six years in prison for two felony convictions, evaded prosecution under a dozen or so indictments, acquired interests in at least forty businesses, intruded into Louisiana politics, and sidestepped a 1953 deportation order with a forged Guatemalan birth record. Kennedy moved immediately to do what he had promised before the McClellan committee. On 4 April 1961, when Marcello went to the New Orleans office of the Immigration and Naturalization Service for his required quarterly report, INS and Justice Department attorneys arrested and handcuffed him and, without allowing Marcello to telephone his family or a lawyer, placed him on a Border Patrol airplane and deported him to Guatemala.[77]

Unaware and unconcerned about the exact methods used by the INS and Border Patrol, Kennedy accepted praise from public officials for taking prompt action. The grateful mayor of Bossier City, Louisiana, described Marcello as the "moving force" in organizing gambling, prostitution, and narcotics traffic in the region. The attorney general assured him, "We are well rid of Mr. Marcello."[78]

It was not that easy. Passed along by Guatemalan authorities to El Salvador, Marcello eventually found himself stranded by soldiers in Honduras. Trudging through the jungle, propelled by his hatred for Kennedy, the bullnecked semiliterate racketeer supposedly told a companion, "If I don't make it, tell my brothers, when you get back, about what dat kid Bobby done to us. Tell 'em to do what dey have to do."

Several days later, Marcello reached a coastal town and finally made his way back to New Orleans. In June 1961 he was indicted for illegal entry and for faking his Guatemalan birth record. In addition, he faced a $835,396 tax lien. Robert Kennedy never gained a conviction on those or a half-dozen other criminal charges. Tried in federal court on the fraud charge, Marcello was acquitted in New Orleans the afternoon of 22 November 1963.[79]

Consumed with hate, the man the FBI once regarded as a harmless seller of tomatoes reportedly told Edward Becker, a criminal associate turned FBI informer, "Don't worry about that little Bobby son of a bitch. He's going to be taken care of!" Becker testified that Marcello spoke of getting Robert Kennedy off his back by finding some "nut" to kill the president. He reasoned, according to Becker, that "if you want to kill a dog, you don't cut off the tail, you cut off the head." Those remarks, among other things, led the House Select Committee on Assassinations to name Marcello as a prime suspect in a "probable" conspiracy to murder John Kennedy. Called before the HSCA in January 1978, Marcello emphatically denied ever making such statements.[80] When the committee asked him to detail his deportation to Guatemala, chief counsel Robert Blakey remembered Marcello's resentful voice and the fire in his eyes. Seventeen years later, Marcello still hated Robert Kennedy.[81]

Even more tangled is the story of Robert Kennedy's relentless pursuit of Salvatore "Sam" Giancana. Born in the United States in 1908 of Sicilian immigrant parents, Giancana progressed from a teen gang leader through the felony matrix from mayhem to murder, eventually controlling large parts of the Chicago criminal organization once headed by Al Capone. An army psychologist labeled the draft-dodging Giancana a "constitutional psychopath" with "an inadequate personality" and limited intelligence. Although described as having "the face of a gargoyle and the disposition of a viper," Giancana beguiled several show business personages, impressing them with his control over selected night clubs and gaming casinos through extortion or by skimming the profits. Asked what he did for a living, Giancana replied, "I own Chicago. I own Miami. I own Las Vegas."[82]

A target of the FBI's Top Hoodlum Program since 1958, Giancana and his activities were under intense scrutiny, some of it illegal electronic surveillance. In 1961, in response to Robert Kennedy's criticisms of the quality of Hoover's intelligence operations, the FBI accelerated its use of telephone wiretaps (Elsur) and concealed microphones (Misur). Listening in on Sam Giancana's conversations via microphones hidden in a Chicago tailor shop and in the Armory Lounge in the Chicago suburb of Forest Park, the FBI discovered the Mafia *capo*'s close relationship to show business luminary Frank Sinatra, who was also a friend of the president's. Suspecting the close surveillance, one of Giancana's *caporegimes* told the FBI, "If Bobby Kennedy wants to talk to Sam, he knows who to go through."[83]

By then Giancana did not care who knew of his friendship with Sinatra. Besides, Giancana and his Las Vegas associate, Johnny Roselli, were disgusted with Sinatra's inability to influence the Kennedys on their behalf. Reportedly in return for cash donations that Sinatra solicited for the Kennedy campaign, the hoodlums expected the Kennedys to intercede on behalf of Giancana, Marcello, and deported New York gangster Joe Adonis. Sinatra had worked his way into the Kennedy circle through his friendship with Peter Lawford and Patricia Kennedy Lawford. Although never a favorite of Robert's, Sinatra had coordinated entertainment for John Kennedy's inaugural celebration and was widely acknowledged as part of the Kennedy retinue. After the inauguration Sinatra claimed he spoke to Joseph Kennedy three times on the telephone, trying unsuccessfully to get him to call off the heat on Giancana. Roselli once told Giancana during an FBI-recorded telephone conversation that Sinatra had said to him: "I took Sam's name [Giancana], and wrote it down, and told Bobby Kennedy, 'This is my buddy, this is what I want you to know, Bob.'" Giancana laughed at the remark, mocking Sinatra's claim that he had clout with the Kennedys, especially Robert.[84]

Prodded by Justice Department attorney complaints that the president's associations with Sinatra undermined their investigations of Giancana and other organized crime figures, the attorney general in early 1962 ordered a series of investigations into Sinatra's close contacts with Giancana. Informed that Giancana frequently stayed at the singer's home in Palm Springs, where the president was scheduled to visit in March 1962, Robert insisted that his brother make other arrangements.

In a last-ditch effort to save his connection to the First Family, Sinatra tried to reach Robert Kennedy through Peter Lawford, heavily obligated to the singer for what remained of his show business career. Lawford told Robert that Sinatra was shattered by the cancellation and pleaded with his brother-in-law to change his mind. Robert refused. At Sinatra's command, Lawford then went to the president, who told him, "I can't stay there . . . while Bobby's handling [the Giancana] investigation."[85] When John Kennedy went to Palm Springs, he stayed at Bing Crosby's house. Two weeks later, armed with an FBI report that found a "possible community of interest" involving Sinatra with Giancana and nine other racketeers, the attorney general convinced the president to sever all contacts with Sinatra.[86]

Word of Sinatra's banishment by the Kennedys provoked a frenzy of contempt among gangsters, who derisively labeled Robert Kennedy's war on crime hypocritical and deceitful. The FBI heard mobster Vinnie Teresa say, "They [the Kennedys] used him [Sinatra] to help them raise money. Then they turn around and say they're great fighters against corruption. They criticize other people for being with mob guys. They're hypocrites."[87] The assertion that the Kennedys courted the Mafia through Sinatra and then refused to deliver on some unspoken bargain lacks substantive merit. But the underworld's belief in it may have been more important than the facts. From the mobsters' point of view, John Kennedy had already crossed the line; he had compromised himself by accepting the sexual favors of a woman made available to him by Sinatra.[88]

When the FBI uncovered Sinatra's connections to Giancana, they also discovered John Kennedy's two-year affair with Judith Campbell. On 27 February, Hoover informed Robert Kennedy and presidential assistant Kenneth O'Donnell that an investigation of Las Vegas gangster and card cheat Johnny Roselli connected him to Giancana, Sinatra, and Campbell. White House telephone logs, moreover, showed Campbell had placed seventy telephone calls over a two-year period to the Oval Office. At the same time, the FBI noted, Campbell was seeing Roselli, Giancana, Paul "Skinny" D'Amato, and Sinatra. One can only imagine Robert's anguish and chagrin, particularly since Hoover delivered the news. What Robert said to his brother regarding the FBI reports is unknown, but apparently they decided to let the director take his best shot and to deal with the consequences.

On 22 March 1962, Hoover went to the White House to discuss the Campbell calls and other matters over lunch with the president. John Kennedy emerged from the meeting angry and visibly annoyed. That afternoon he placed his last call to Campbell from the White House.

The existence of the affair seems beyond question, confirmed by Campbell's 1975 testimony before the Church committee. In the years since, however, she has embellished upon the relationship, claiming she acted as a courier between Kennedy and Giancana, who, she says, worked together on various illegal projects.[89] One has to wonder about Campbell's motives. Did the Mafia commission her to defame John Kennedy and his political heirs? FBI files reveal some evidence of the Mafia's intentions in that regard. A "confidential source" once informed the FBI of "a plot among the Italian hoodlum element" to work with associates of Frank Sinatra to "arrange for their women to be placed in compromising situations" with Robert and Edward Kennedy and Peter Lawford.[90]

The investigation of Giancana produced other revelations. By the time of the president's March meeting with Hoover, the FBI had stumbled across information linking Giancana to a CIA plot to assassinate Cuban premier Fidel Castro. Within a few weeks, Robert Kennedy learned that in the waning days of the Eisenhower administration, the CIA had paid Giancana, Roselli, and Santo Trafficante, Jr., $150,000 and supplied them with poison pills and other means to kill Castro. Sometime after December 1959, when Castro first announced he was a Marxist-Leninist and established a socialist state in Cuba, CIA Director Allen Dulles and Richard Bissell, deputy director of plans, approved a suggestion by Colonel J. C. King (CIA Western Hemisphere Division) to initiate an effort to assassinate Castro. In August 1960, Colonel Sheffield Edwards, who was placed in charge of the operation, hired Robert Maheu, a former FBI agent and private detective with Mafia connections, to recruit Roselli, Giancana, and Trafficante. The Mafia wanted Castro removed so Cuba could be reopened to gambling and organized crime. Trafficante, who lived in Tampa, once held significant interests in Havana casinos and various illegal enterprises before Castro had him arrested and then driven out.[91]

The FBI first got wind of a CIA-Mafia tie in September 1960, when Maheu, then in Giancana's employ, was arrested while attempting to install a wiretap in a Las Vegas apartment where Giancana suspected his girlfriend, singer Phyllis McGuire, was conducting an affair. Maheu, a slippery fellow who later became chief of staff for billionaire recluse Howard Hughes, told the FBI that the wiretap was connected to the CIA. In April 1961, Colonel Edwards informed the FBI that prosecuting Maheu and Giancana would expose sensitive information related to the aborted Bay of Pigs invasion. Although he made no mention of the assassination plots, Edwards made it clear that Maheu and Giancana were working with the CIA. On 22 May, Hoover sent the attorney general a memo informing him of what he had learned from Edwards. Deeply distressed to learn the CIA depended on such people, Kennedy instructed Hoover to follow up "vigorously" on the matter.[92]

Prosecution of the Maheu-Giancana case was temporarily halted in September 1961, but Justice Department attorneys, anxious to get something on Giancana, repeatedly pressed the matter with the FBI. Each time, Colonel Edwards objected and warned the FBI that prosecution would result in a "most damaging embarrassment" to the U.S. government. Hoover summarized Edwards's objections in a memo to Herbert J. Miller, head of the Criminal Division, who then advised the attorney general that national interest ruled out prosecution of the Las Vegas wiretappers. On 24 April, Kennedy reluctantly concurred.[93]

Two weeks later, the president and the attorney general received separate briefings on CIA activities in Cuba. According to the CIA briefing officers, even then they did not tell the president of the CIA-Mafia assassination plot. The attorney general, however, insisted upon and received a fuller report from Colonel Edwards and from CIA general counsel Lawrence Houston, who informed him of the operations involving underworld figures and falsely assured him that they had been terminated.[94] Houston described the attorney general's reaction: "If you have seen Mr. Kennedy's eyes get steely and his jaw set and his voice get low and precise, you get a definite feeling of unhappiness." Kennedy "was mad as hell," Houston said, not about the assassination plot, "but about our involvement with the Mafia" and its effects on the prosecution of Giancana. Houston recalled Kennedy's parting words: "I trust that if you ever try to do business with organized crime again—with gangsters—you will let the Attorney General know."[95]

Kennedy elaborated on his displeasure in a meeting with Hoover on 9 May. The CIA, he complained, had placed the Justice Department in a position where "it could not afford to have any action taken against Giancana or Maheu." Further, he knew that "gutter gossip" was circulating to the effect that the reason nothing had been done against Giancana lay in Giancana's close relationship with Sinatra. Kennedy, however, had no choice but to drop the case.[96] Because he could make no public explanation for his decision, the mob knew only that Giancana had avoided prosecution because the attorney general had intervened. For the moment, at least, they had reason to believe their influence extended into the Kennedy administration.[97]

They were wrong. Not in the least intimidated, Kennedy kept up the pressure on Giancana, placing him under "lockstep," or constant FBI surveillance. Frustrated and angry, Giancana exploded when the FBI detained his girlfriend, Phyllis McGuire, for interrogation at the Chicago airport and swore he would get "your boss's boss," that is, Attorney General Robert Kennedy.[98] With no place to turn, Giancana filed suit in federal court, alleging the FBI was harassing him by following him everywhere, even onto golf courses. To protect the Justice Department from what he believed would be an unconstitutional regulation by the judiciary, Kennedy instructed FBI agents not to answer the judge's questions. When an injunction was granted, the Justice Department immediately won a permanent stay and continued shadowing Giancana. This was precisely what Robert Kennedy had meant when he spoke of stripping away the Mafia's protective insulation.

The close surveillance and the publicity generated by his complaint against Kennedy's Justice Department eventually ruined Giancana. Other mobsters, afraid of being implicated or perhaps suspecting Giancana had violated the code of silence, stopped associating with him. Isolated and ineffective, Giancana joined the chorus of blustering gangsters bleating their hatred of Kennedy into FBI microphones; he even suggested putting a bomb in Robert's golf bag. Imprisoned for a year for refusing to answer questions under immunity before a federal grand jury, Giancana fled to Mexico in 1967 after his release. Deported back to the United States in July 1974, he returned to Chicago a broken man, claiming to be "retired." A year later, as Senate investigators prepared to take his testimony on the CIA-Mafia plots, Giancana was murdered in his home, shot seven times in the mouth and neck by an unknown assailant.[99]

Hoffa: Round Three

The whole time he pursued Marcello, Giancana, and other leading hoodlums, Kennedy never let up on his number one target, James R. Hoffa. Picking up where he left off with the McClellan committee investigations, Attorney General Kennedy created a subdivision of the Organized Crime Section on Labor and Racketeering, twenty lawyers and thirty FBI agents known in the Justice Department as the Hoffa Squad. Walter Sheridan, the Rackets Committee stalwart whom Kennedy trusted implicitly and admired greatly for his perseverance, energy, and nerve, headed the squad. Victor Navasky, who has given us the most insightful and comprehensive study of Kennedy's Justice Department, writes that Sheridan's group "did what the Attorney General of the United States would have done himself had he had the time."[100] Kennedy gave Sheridan a free hand in selecting staff and developing prosecution tactics for the labor racketeering cases. Occasionally, Sheridan resorted to irregular means, "creative counter-guerilla" tactics that included using reporters and the press as prosecutorial arms and drawing on Kennedy family money to pay informers. Sheridan's group, in Navasky's words, had about it a "permissive aura." Its methods pressed against the boundaries of prosecutorial ethics.[101]

Detractors allege that when Kennedy became attorney general, satisfying his grudge against personal enemies such as Hoffa became U.S. public policy.[102] The press, in fact, associated Kennedy with each step in the Hoffa prosecution. Personal vendetta stories, after all, sold newspapers. And Kennedy even admitted, "I spent a lot of time on it," but he rarely injected himself directly into these cases.[103] When he did, his awkward and ineffective manner often fueled criticism.

"In an ideal situation," Ramsey Clark later reflected, "an Attorney General would not have become so closely identified with one criminal investigation as Bobby was." Kennedy's Justice Department, according to Clark, filed more than thirty thousand criminal indictments a year. In his estimation, to emphasize one defendant or one group of cases created a certain "inequality" and perhaps biased the judgment of some U.S. attorneys anxious to make names for themselves. For all of that, Clark saw no evidence of a "naked use of power" to pursue Hoffa.[104]

Surely and effectively, Kennedy's Labor and Racketeering squad exposed and prosecuted corruption within the IBT. Working with fifteen grand juries across the country, Sheridan's group by 1963 had won convictions against several of Hoffa's closest associates, including William Presser (Ohio) for contempt of Congress, Anthony Provenzano (New Jersey) for extortion, Barney Baker (Chicago) for taking money from an employer in violation of the Taft-Hartley law, and Frank Collins (Detroit) for perjury.[105]

Hoffa tried to bully his way out of trouble, all the while taunting his tormentor. "Kennedy," he told television commentator David Brinkley, "is just a spoiled young millionaire." In Philadelphia in April 1961 Hoffa railed against the "pride and ego of those individuals that would convince the public they are different from the Teamsters—that they are holy." He complained of the "increasing pressure from cabinet officers like Bobby Kennedy." "Persecution, not prosecution," Hoffa charged. But, as his biographer Arthur A. Sloane has shown, Hoffa had developed paranoic fantasies and a Kennedy phobia, claiming, for example, that Kennedy had 150 FBI agents "bugging" him and following him everywhere. He warned fellow Teamsters that the FBI was using women agents as prostitutes to entrap them. He believed agents had sprinkled on his clothes an invisible powder that electronic listening devices could target from a mile away.[106]

All the same, Hoffa convinced the rank and file of the 1.7 million–member International Brotherhood of Teamsters (IBT) that Kennedy was a fanatical power-grubbing politician bent on destroying their leader. At their July 1961 convention the membership reelected Hoffa by acclamation and voted to exonerate him and all other Teamsters on every charge brought against them by Congress and the courts. Even IBT general counsel Edward Bennett Williams acknowledged the ineluctable odor of corruption within the IBT and privately admitted to Kennedy that his clients were "gangsters and crooks."[107]

Hoffa's luck held for a time. In December 1960, just before the Kennedys took office, Hoffa's lawyers won an indefinite delay on a Florida indictment on mail fraud and misuse of union pension funds. Drew Pearson charged that Vice-President Nixon, who felt indebted to Hoffa for his support during the 1960 election, had persuaded Attorney General William Rogers not to indict Hoffa.[108] Robert Kennedy did not comment on Nixon's possible involvement but he did call the judge who granted the delay "a very, very weak man." Without a strong judge, Kennedy said, "we could never have any hope of winning the case."[109]

As the Sheridan team searched for a venue where they could win in a court of law, Robert Kennedy tried to convict Hoffa in the court of popular opinion. In March 1961 he called to his office Hank Suydum, Washington editor of *Life* magazine, and introduced him to Samuel Baron, an official in the Teamsters ready to make a public break with Hoffa and to announce it with an article in *Life*. Baron, a mild-mannered Teamsters field director with a lengthy and varied career in trade unionism, had joined the Teamsters in 1953. Disillusioned with Hoffa and the corruption within the Teamsters, he began passing information to Kennedy in 1959. Unable to use Baron's inside slant as direct testimony in any specific case, Kennedy wanted to use the situation to discredit Hoffa generally and to encourage other Teamsters to come forward. To maximize the story's impact, Kennedy suggested that Suydum use a ghostwriter to assist Baron and "to help explain his disgust with Hoffa." *Life* agreed.[110] Then Baron got cold feet. In June, Walter Sheridan asked Kennedy to delay a final agreement with *Life*, because Baron "still doesn't want to do it." Although Sheridan then persuaded Baron to cooperate, Baron asked *Life* to hold his story as protection; he feared for his life.[111]

Hoffa had suspected for some time that Baron was talking to Sheridan and Kennedy. On 17 May 1962 in the president's office of the Teamsters' Washington headquarters, with a half-dozen other Teamsters officials looking on, Hoffa suddenly attacked Baron, repeatedly striking him in the face with his fists, knocking him to the floor. Hoffa was charged with assault, and a jury trial set for June. When Hoffa's IBT cronies pointed incredulous authorities to the diminutive, fifty-nine-year-old Baron as the aggressor, the government dropped the case.[112] To protect himself from further assault, Baron allowed *Life* to run his story. "I Was Near the Top of Jimmy's Drop-Dead List" appeared on 20 July 1962, sixteen months after Kennedy first proposed it.[113] Even disregarding the questionable ethics of arranging publication of prejudicial information with Hoffa under indictment, Kennedy's involvement in the Baron affair smacked of a prosecutor desperate to make his case but short on hard evidence.

Eager to make something stick, Kennedy was persuaded by Sheridan to prosecute Hoffa on a misdemeanor violation of the Taft-Hartley Act for accepting more than a million dollars in illegal payments from trucking companies through the Test Fleet Corporation, a leasing firm chartered in Tennessee under the maiden names of the wives of Hoffa and an associate. Sheridan supervised the case from a Nashville hotel room and telephoned Kennedy daily.[114]

On the opening day of Hoffa's trial, 22 October 1962, several prospective jurors received anonymous telephone calls from someone representing himself as a reporter for the *Nashville Banner.* Concerned that publication of the illegal contacts with the jury might lead to a mistrial, Robert Kennedy took time the next day between meetings on the Cuban Missile Crisis to call the *Banner* publisher and try to "work something out" to stop the story. He failed. The defiant *Banner* publisher, who later published a transcript of Kennedy's telephone conversation, refused, he said, to sacrifice his paper for "Jimmy Hoffa, the Federal Government or anybody else." The jury deadlocked, and on 23 December the judge called a mistrial. Hoffa's attorney, William E. Buffalino, told reporters, "Santa Claus has simply refused to put Jimmy Hoffa in Bobby Kennedy's stocking." Beginning with the Cheasty bribery trial of March 1957, Hoffa had beaten a federal rap for the fourth time in five years. To rub salt in Kennedy's wounds and further damage his credibility in the liberal community, a gloating Hoffa accused him of trying to "pressure" the *Banner* about what it "should or should not print."[115]

As it happened, Hoffa and his associates had, indeed, used bribery and intimidation to deadlock the Test Fleet case jury. Playing right into Kennedy's hands, Hoffa had turned a misdemeanor charge into a felony indictment for jury tampering, which was handed down on 9 May 1963. These "phony charges," Hoffa declared, were brought by a "spoiled brat," a "smart alec," a "nitwitted . . . moron." Hoffa then turned on Robert's brother, telling reporters that John Kennedy was "a fraud on the American people" and "not a fit person to be President."[116]

People accused Hoffa of many things, but not insincerity. He sincerely hated the Kennedys. In September 1962, Edward Grady Partin, a Louisiana Teamster-turned-informant for Sheridan's squad, stated that on several occasions Hoffa talked to him about assassinating Robert Kennedy. Partin recalled Hoffa saying, "I've got to do something about that son of a bitch Bobby Kennedy. He's got to go." According to Partin, Hoffa then described how Kennedy had no guards at Hickory Hill, swam alone in his pool, and drove alone in an open convertible. Partin told the FBI that Hoffa suggested killing Kennedy with a plastic bomb thrown in the car or the house. After Partin agreed to take a lie-detector test, Sheridan informed Robert Kennedy of his claims. "What do we do if that fellow passes the test?" Kennedy asked wryly. "I don't know, but I think he might," Sheridan replied. Kennedy simply shrugged and climbed into his car, recalled Sheridan.[117] Partin convinced the FBI of his veracity after he passed a polygraph test and after they listened in on a telephone conversation in which Hoffa elaborated on a plan to set up a lone gunman with no known connections to the Teamsters who would shoot the attorney general with a high-powered rifle while he was riding in an open car somewhere in the South.[118]

When he heard the news of John Kennedy's assassination, Hoffa reportedly said, "I hope the worms eat his eyes out." He became enraged at an IBT underling who, to honor the slain president, lowered the flag on union headquarters to half staff. He refused to authorize a statement of condolence—"I'm no hypocrite"—and demanded to know why a secretary was crying instead of "rejoicing." His most widely quoted remark: "Bobby Kennedy is just another lawyer now."[119]

Hoffa did not have much time to enjoy the "good news," as he described the events in Dallas. On 4 March 1964 in Chattanooga, after an explosive trial in which Hoffa accused Robert Kennedy and J. Edgar Hoover of official misconduct and the Justice Department produced the Partin testimony as evidence of a conspiracy by Hoffa to assassinate the attorney general, Hoffa and three codefendants were convicted of jury tampering in the Test Fleet case. "We made it!" a jubilant Sheridan rushed to report to Kennedy, distracted and unable to focus on department business since his brother's assassination. His spirits lifted by this long-awaited victory, "Nice work!" he told Sheridan. Robert then telephoned congratulations to the team of U.S. attorneys headed by James Neal and sent letters of commendation to the FBI agents who worked on the case. Congratulations poured into the office. He quickly arranged a victory party for eighty guests at Hickory Hill, although publicly he played down the government's success, telling the press, "It was in the hands of the jury, and the jury has given its decision."[120]

Hoffa said he was railroaded. Judge Frank W. Wilson sentenced him to eight years in prison, stating that he had trouble imagining a "more willful violation of the law." In a rebuke that echoed the thesis of *The Enemy Within,* Judge Wilson told Hoffa he stood convicted of seeking to "corrupt the administration of justice itself" and of tampering "with the very soul of this nation." Hoffa refused to back down, charging that Kennedy's prosecutions were politically motivated. Several Republicans in response to election-year pressures seized upon Hoffa's rancorous characterizations of Kennedy and, further evidence of Hoffa's criminal conduct notwithstanding, closed ranks with the IBT. That summer at the Republican National Convention the Teamsters made an empty boast, claiming that twenty-one members of the House Judiciary Committee stood ready to investigate the attorney general's handling of the Hoffa cases.[121]

Meantime, in Chicago on 26 July 1964, Hoffa was convicted and sentenced to five years in prison for conspiracy and mail and wire fraud in the process of obtaining $20 million in loans for himself and others from the Teamsters Pension Fund. Pending Hoffa's appeals, Kennedy and Sheridan briefly considered filing additional charges against the IBT president. Still grieving his brother's assassination and busy pondering his own political future, Robert was too distracted to pursue it. Moreover, he had by then directed Justice Department resources away from the war on crime toward civil rights cases. Thus, in May 1964 Walter Sheridan and his "terrible twenty" squad were dispatched to Mississippi to pick up the slack for the FBI and, according to Sheridan, "to get something going on the Klan." The Hoffa Squad had served its purpose. By the time it was disbanded and Kennedy departed, the Justice Department had won more than one hundred convictions against Teamsters leaders and their associates.[122]

Summarizing the most important contributions of his anticrime program, Kennedy listed his role in educating Americans about organized crime, his insistence that the FBI—who "made a helluva difference"—devote more resources to the effort, his negotiation of an agreement with other agencies to coordinate and disseminate information through the Organized Crime Section, and his success in gaining rapid enactment of a package of anticrime bills that expanded federal powers to prosecute interstate gambling and racketeering. At the time, however, Robert Kennedy was proudest of his conviction record. Including the Teamsters cases, he boasted a 700 percent increase in convictions of la Cosa Nostra figures.[123]

To his list we can add the contributions made later by the "band of brothers." G. Robert Blakey followed in Kennedy's steps as chief counsel of the McClellan committee and went on to author the RICO (Racketeer-Influenced and Corrupt Organizations) statute, the part of the Organized Crime Control Act of 1970 that permitted federal prosecutors to go after patterns of corruption such as those within Hoffa's Teamsters Union. David Hackett continued to probe for the root causes of crime by investigating the sources of juvenile delinquency and its linkages to poverty. Edwin Guthman, Clark Mollenhoff, and Walter Sheridan published books that kept alive the sense of urgency and the spirit of excellence that characterized Kennedy justice.[124]

Concentrating so much government power in the pursuit of one class of criminals raised reasonable concerns over the possible abuse of such powers and the potential endangerment of civil liberties. Such risks, however, gave Kennedy little pause. He saw himself as dedicated solely to the public interest, devoid, as he put it, of "narrow self interests," and therefore worthy of the public's trust and deserving of the right to exercise power in their name. Power was good, if exercised for moral purposes. Just because Hoffa sought power "merely for the sake of power" and used power, according to Kennedy, for "pure self-indulgence," Americans should not conclude that "all power is evil and that no human can be so entrusted." The "problem," as he saw it, was "how to get men of power to live *for* the public rather than *off* the public." Kennedy believed that men and women of moral standing working for the public good could be relied on to exercise power without abusing it, and he was confident that the U.S. system of checks and balances would restrain officials who might abuse their power. "It rests with all of us," Kennedy concluded, "to take care that all who do rise to power are men and women who hold no interest higher than that of maintaining the system itself."[125]

Robert Kennedy surely had few, if any, doubts about the legitimacy of his position or his claim to authority, which some thought he exercised as though it were a divine right. One can easily see why he remained, in Schlesinger's words, "baffled and dismayed" by the criticisms he received over the Hoffa prosecutions and other organized crime cases.[126] Kennedy saw no ethical dilemma. The Teamsters held a vice-like grip on the country's economic lifeline, and so Hoffa's involvement in criminal conspiracies—no matter how compelling his rationalizations of these actions as practical responses to circumstances in the combative labor negotiations arena—constituted, in Kennedy's view, "a threat to every decent person as well as to the very foundations of our democracy."[127]

Long ago persuaded by his father that he was entitled, even obligated, to gain and exercise governing powers, Robert was convinced that he served only the public good. His confidence in the Kennedy variant of noblesse oblige, buttressed by his Catholic beliefs in moral absolutes, tinged his official actions with self-righteousness. He transferred a self-conscious notion of his own importance to his government duties, which he construed in idealistic terms as ultimately based on moral obligations to his family and church. Harboring no self-doubts regarding the powers and authority of his office, Robert Kennedy consequently never hesitated to use those powers to prosecute Hoffa and all others who threatened the system he was so intent on defending.

When the law proved inadequate and prosecutions were thwarted,

Kennedy stepped beyond the normal limits of his office to create a climate "in which Hoffa's effectiveness diminished, in which his lieutenants would be willing to testify against him, in which his union members might vote to throw him out of office, in which the public would recognize him for the evil influence that he was."[128] Kennedy aimed to strip away the protective insulation, including, if necessary, some constitutional guarantees with which Hoffa and other criminals covered their illegal activities and protected themselves from prosecution. He never fathomed why civil libertarians with whom he shared the common tasks of pursuing justice and defending the rule of law should criticize his attempts to destroy evil conspiracies. He later confided that he was troubled by the conflicting needs to protect privacy and individual freedoms on the one hand and to control organized crime on the other.[129] But he offered no apologies or extended explanations of his tolerance of excesses in the prosecution of America's domestic enemies. He saw such actions as necessary for preserving stability and order.

Robert Kennedy's active involvement in the campaign against organized crime ended abruptly Friday afternoon 22 November 1963. Meeting that day with members of his Organized Crime Section to discuss, among other things, the status of the department's cases against Sam Giancana, Kennedy invited Robert Morgenthau, U.S. attorney for the Southern District of New York, to join him for lunch at Hickory Hill. After J. Edgar Hoover's telephone call matter-of-factly notified him of his brother's assassination, for reasons unclear but ripe for speculation Robert Kennedy never again convened the Organized Crime group. Nor did he ever again make a significant pronouncement against organized crime. The Justice Department program of stepped-up prosecutions, including the Hoffa cases, continued throughout 1964, but Kennedy's thoughts remained elsewhere. Before Dallas he gave ten speeches or formal testimony on organized crime. After Dallas, in the remaining ten months of his tenure, Kennedy gave only one speech related to the subject, a talk before the ABA Criminal Law Section on bail rights and criminal law reform.[130] In the years ahead, his interest would turn not to crime's organized elements, but rather to its social causes and its relation to the pathologies of poverty and urban decay.

After nearly a decade of "chasing bad men," as he so often described his work, Robert Kennedy had succeeded in dramatizing the issue and mobilizing the media; Americans had grown acutely aware of the pernicious nature of organized criminal activities and their pervasive influence on American life. Ironically, his revelations of networks of illegal cabals may have fed media appetites for sensationalist exposés and contributed to the cultural conditions that convinced so many to buy into the conspiracy theories surrounding his brother's and his own assassination.[131]

As for Hoffa, his phalanx of high-powered lawyers carried appeals to the Supreme Court before finally exhausting the process in December 1966. Perhaps the ultimate indicator of the fairness of the Kennedy Justice Department's vigorous prosecution of Hoffa, as Adam Yarmolinsky pointed out at the time, lay in the Supreme Court's support of both convictions.[132] In a letter to Edward Bennett Williams, a satisfied Kennedy scrawled a revealing postscript: "I noticed Hoffa lost his appeal. I guess I can climb back on the Capitol which I jumped off of about ten years ago. Just maybe this time Hoover will push me off."[133]

By then, J. Edgar Hoover had replaced Hoffa as Kennedy's public rival. All the while Robert Kennedy was gaining ground on Hoffa and winning tactical engagements in his war on crime, he was losing a protracted rear-guard action brought by Hoover, his chief lieutenant in law enforcement, for when Kennedy's service as attorney general ended, the FBI director's powers stood enlarged, but not his accountability.[134]

CHAPTER 9

Hoover and Bawdy Tales

Robert Kennedy ranked among the top three men on J. Edgar Hoover's hate list.[1] Ignited during the McCarthy era, Hoover's contempt for Kennedy flared intermittently during the McClellan committee days, reached a steady state of malevolence when Kennedy was attorney general, and exploded between late 1966 and early 1968 in a spate of public accusations. Not even Robert Kennedy's assassination quieted the director's scorn. Until his own death in 1972, Hoover maligned Kennedy's conduct as attorney general and accused him of undermining the credibility of the FBI, stealing credit for important accomplishments, and lying about his role in authorizing illegal microphone surveillance.

The Terrier Vs. the Bulldog

Born 1 January 1895 in Washington, D.C., Hoover was sixty-six years old in 1961 when Robert Kennedy was sworn into office. FBI-trained guides informed Justice Department tourists that Hoover took the director's post the year before the attorney general was born. Different generational perspectives told only a small part of the story. "There was something in Robert Kennedy that threatened Hoover, and threatened the values he stood for," one of Hoover's early biographers concluded.[2] Indeed, Kennedy was the first attorney general who imperiled Hoover's position as the preeminent law enforcement official in the land.

Disconcertingly alike in several respects, Hoover was frequently likened to a bulldog and Kennedy to a terrier. Their eyes and the set of their jaws warned of their tenacity. Both had short tempers and tended to break down complex issues into moral dichotomies or ad hominem arguments. Both projected prudish public images. Both had law degrees, but neither practiced law. Both began their careers fighting subversion and made their reputations chasing hoodlums. Both assumed positions of high responsibility at an early age. Neither brooked interference with control over his domain. "They were too much alike," said Special Agent Courtney Evans, whom Hoover assigned as Kennedy's FBI liaison. "When I looked at Bob Kennedy operating in 1961, I figured that's the way Hoover had operated in 1924 . . . same kind of temperament, impatient with inefficiency, demanding as to detail, a system of logical reasoning for a position, and pretty much of a hard taskmaster." Ramsey Clark put it more simply: "They did not get along."[3]

"I knew that he didn't like me much," Kennedy said later. Yet he insisted that his relationship with Hoover "was not difficult. I mean," he said, "it wasn't an impossible relationship." Kennedy frequently assured insiders, however, that Hoover would not be continued during a second Kennedy administration or at least not far beyond January 1965 and the mandatory retirement age of seventy. Learning of these intentions, Hoover became increasingly ill-disposed toward both Kennedys. Dismissing all speculation as to a successor, he overreacted to both real and implied criticisms of his bureau.[4]

Before Kennedy arrived, Hoover had steadily increased his control over the FBI and freed himself from virtually all external controls. In 1940 President Franklin Roosevelt had granted the FBI unrestricted discretion to investigate "espionage, counter-espionage, subversive activities and violations of the neutrality laws," permitting Hoover thereafter to combine intelligence activities with his already significant investigative powers. After the war, Hoover's ardent pursuit of Communists and left-wing dissidents went unchecked by a succession of intimidated attorney generals who dared not appear "soft" on Communism.[5]

Hoover's finely honed bureaucratic skills, his masterly manipulation of public relations, and his deft maneuvering inside the government all contributed to his tenure and his personal power. He had few concerns regarding appropriations. Potential congressional critics were kept in check with threats to publicize the contents of the "summary memoranda" the FBI prepared on all members of Congress, amalgams of derogatory information about their alleged "subversive activities" and their own and their families' "immoral conduct."[6] Congress, the president, and attorney generals were also held hostage by the general fear of political subversion and the threat of foreign attack bred by Cold War hysteria, some of it conjured up by Hoover himself. Accordingly, as the national security state was enlarged throughout the first decades of the Cold War, so also was Hoover's FBI.[7]

Hoover reached the apex of his power during the Eisenhower years, directing the bureau as he pleased, unfettered by either executive or legislative control and minimally constrained by the judiciary. He and his defenders justified such autonomy by the FBI's responsibility for combatting "subversive activities," a nebulous term defined at Hoover's discretion. Freed from critical scrutiny, Hoover made a "mockery of the American Constitution and its systems of checks and balances."[8] Under Attorney General Robert Kennedy, that state of affairs began to change, but it did not end.

The minor Hoover–Robert Kennedy rift of the McCarthy era, smoothed over by Joseph Kennedy's fawning intercessions, widened into a chasm when the new attorney general made it clear that he disagreed with Hoover that domestic Communism represented the greatest menace facing America (followed closely, to Hoover's mind, by organizations on the liberal-leftist side of the political spectrum). Hoover extolled the causes of conservative right-wing organizations that espoused anticommunism and, like them, saw Communist threats everywhere, particularly inside labor unions. He even warned Kennedy of James Hoffa's implausible "Commie ties."[9]

Robert Kennedy believed that Hoover greatly exaggerated the extent of Communist influence on domestic affairs in general and labor unions in particular. The negligible effect of Communists inside the union movement became evident to Kennedy as a result of his years of investigating labor racketeering, his success in working with labor leaders during the 1960 campaign, and his regular contacts with the likes of Victor Riesel, Clark Mollenhoff, and journalists such as Guthman, Seigenthaler, and Salinger who covered the labor beat.[10]

As for right-wing organizations, Robert Kennedy had little tolerance for them (or for any extremist group), even less after groups such as the John Birch Society attacked his brother's administration for not taking radical steps against Communism. Founded in 1958 by ultraconservative millionaire Robert Welch, Jr., the John Birchers had flourished under Hoover's open patronage. Far from helping the country, Robert Kennedy believed, the Birchers and other self-styled patriotic groups subverted the established order. At a November 1961 press conference in Dallas he averred that the Birchers meant to "undermine confidence in our government." Impatient with leftist defeatists "who would rather be 'Red than dead,'" he said, neither "do I have any sympathy with those, who in the name of fighting communism sow the seeds of suspicion and distrust by making false or irresponsible charges, not only against their neighbors but against courageous teachers and public officials and against the foundations of our government—Congress, the Supreme Court, and even the presidency." In a joking parting shot Kennedy told reporters, "The only Communist the John Birchers have uncovered is President Eisenhower."[11]

To be sure, Hoover and Kennedy agreed on the peril of international Communism, particularly the threat of espionage by foreign agents and the likelihood that Moscow controlled some domestic Communists. Kennedy's undiminished anticommunist ardor showed especially in his support of counterinsurgency efforts in foreign lands and his alarm over FBI reports of Moscow-controlled agents penetrating the civil rights movement.[12]

Robert Kennedy considered it utter nonsense "to waste time" infiltrating and contesting the legitimacy of the home-grown variety of communism in the form of the Communist party (CPUSA). "It couldn't be more feeble and less of a threat," he said, "and besides its membership consists largely of FBI agents."[13] To document the wasted resources dedicated to surveilling and infiltrating the CPUSA, the attorney general asked the FBI to prepare a "white paper" on the CPUSA's minuscule threat of subversion. Hoover's assistant, Cartha "Deke" DeLoach, blunted the effort, arguing that such a report would compromise FBI informants.[14] The FBI, however, could not thwart Robert Kennedy's decision to commute the sentence of Junius Scales, imprisoned under the provisions of the 1940 Smith Act that effectively made CPUSA membership illegal. Already pained by the decision to release Scales, Hoover became incensed when, contrary to prior practice, Kennedy did not require Scales to "name names" of other Communists as a condition for his release.[15]

In spite of Kennedy, Hoover functioned much as he had before. In 1956, acting on his own authority, he had instituted a series of secret counterintelligence programs, known as COINTELPRO, to "harass, disrupt and discredit" various dissident organizations that Hoover identified as "subversive." To "destabilize" or "neutralize" operations of targeted domestic groups, Hoover used agents provocateur, subterfuge, false information, mail intercepts, break-ins ("black-bag jobs"), and illegal microphone surveillance. Between 1956 and the mid-1960s the FBI targeted the CPUSA, Socialist Workers Party, Ku Klux Klan, various black nationalist groups, Malcolm X, Martin Luther King, Jr., and the Southern Christian Leadership Conference, as well as various New Left and anti–Vietnam War groups.[16] Except for a vague allusion to the COINTELPRO against the CPUSA deliberately buried in a dense January 1961 memo that he was sure Kennedy would never read, Hoover made no serious attempt to apprise the new attorney general of such activities.[17] Throughout his tenure as attorney general, Robert Kennedy remained ignorant (perhaps deliberately) of many FBI abuses. Like his predecessors, he admired the FBI's results and preferred not to know about their methods.[18]

Unlike attorney generals before him, Kennedy made it clear that the FBI was one bureau among others within the Justice Department and that the FBI director reported to him. Within a year's time he redirected the major thrust of the FBI's efforts and subjected Hoover to a series of constricting new administrative procedures that changed attitudes within the Justice Department and led to more stringent controls after

Kennedy left office. These changes also guaranteed Hoover's lasting enmity.

Determined to set the agenda for the entire department, Kennedy made unannounced visits to FBI field offices, telephoned agents, and directly accessed FBI case files without first informing Hoover. To make clear the reporting relationship, Kennedy ordered all FBI press releases cleared by Edwin Guthman and required each to mention the Justice Department and the attorney general in its first sentence.[19] He also directed that FBI contacts with the president come through the attorney general's office, denying Hoover direct access to the White House, a privilege he had enjoyed since Franklin Roosevelt's days. To keep Hoover "happy," the attorney general said, he arranged for the president to call the director "every two or three months" and to lunch alone with him at the White House. The only exception to this rule occurred when the president or appointments secretary Kenneth O'Donnell made a specific request of the FBI to investigate sources of leaked classified information to the press.[20]

Hoover insolently complied with the attorney general's directives, while constantly testing Kennedy's resolve and quietly defying him and his representatives. When Kennedy's brother-in-law, Peace Corps director R. Sargent Shriver, asked the FBI to do background investigations of Peace Corps volunteers, he was informed that the FBI was "too busy" for such work. The Peace Corps was one of the president's favorite programs, and so the attorney general was obliged to work out an accommodation.[21]

On one occasion Hoover followed directions only to embarrass Robert Kennedy. In April 1962 the Kennedys reacted angrily to announcements that steel companies intended to increase their prices in violation of government wage-price guidelines. Suspecting collusion among steel companies to fix prices in violation of antitrust laws, Robert Kennedy ordered the FBI to question three reporters who had taken notes during a critical meeting of the directors of the Bethlehem Steel Company when prices were discussed. Told time was of the essence, FBI agents awakened the reporters during the predawn hours to interview them. When criticism for these Gestapolike tactics rained down on the administration, the attorney general accepted "full responsibility" for them. Asked about the FBI's actions, Hoover replied, "I have to do what Bobby Kennedy tells me to do."[22]

Kennedy infuriated Hoover by pressuring him "a half dozen times," by the director's count, to balance the FBI racially by hiring more African American agents. In 1961 fewer than 50 of the 13,500 FBI employees and only 4 or 5 of the Bureau's 5,900 special agents were African Americans, among them three chauffeurs and an office assistant who served as valet and washroom attendant for visitors. With only 8 agents of Spanish American descent and 1 American Indian, the FBI may well have ranked as the most discriminatory agency in the federal government in 1961. Hoover indirectly defied the White House by refusing to cooperate with the Subcabinet Group on Civil Rights charged with coordinating President Kennedy's affirmative action agenda and with monitoring federal agencies' recruitment of minorities. Hoover claimed that minority hires would jeopardize the FBI's high standards and proven effectiveness. By the end of the decade the FBI still had only 51 black agents out of more than 7,600 agents.[23]

Even Robert Kennedy's admiration for the FBI caused friction between himself and Hoover. Kennedy over and over called the FBI "a helluva good investigative agency." On entering office he eagerly anticipated working closely with the Bureau, drawing upon its vaunted resources and receiving regular advice from Hoover himself, to which end he ordered a direct telephone line to the director's desk. Hoover moved the telephone to the desk of his assistant, Helen Gandy. The first time she answered the hotline she said a fuming attorney general told her, "When I pick up this 'phone, . . . there's only one man I want to talk to—get the 'phone on the Director's desk." Hoover's humiliation over being summoned by a buzzer probably was matched only by Kennedy's casually walking down the fifth-floor corridor in his shirt sleeves, sauntering into the director's office without being announced, and interrupting Hoover's daily two-hour nap.[24] The attorney general's disillusionment grew when he learned that the vaunted FBI intelligence system depended extensively on newspaper reports and that Hoover himself often heard about breaking events thirty minutes or an hour behind the national news services' wire reports.

More like a secret society than an agency of the federal government,

Hoover's FBI was built on a cumbersome method of hierarchical reporting. Everything passed secretly through the compartmentalized organization until it reached the "Seat of Government," Hoover's audacious label for his office. The FBI, then, proved a far less effective source of immediate information and advice than Kennedy hoped, partly because he never challenged the base assumptions of secrecy and compartmentalization upon which the Bureau operated and because he never managed to control its director.[25]

A close reading of the relationship between the FBI and Kennedy's Justice Department, such as Victor Navasky's *Kennedy Justice,* reveals a Robert Kennedy reluctant to impose more than symbolic administrative controls, to challenge the FBI's way of thinking, and to bend Hoover to his will. Despite insisting on stricter controls than his immediate predecessors, Kennedy had only limited success in changing the FBI's composition and in altering its operating procedures. In some instances he could not avoid being co-opted into accepting Hoover's methods and practices. Rarely did Kennedy question the bureau's own definitions of its legal boundaries and jurisdictions, its availability for certain duties, or its declared right to collect and maintain certain secrets. Navasky concludes that we should not belittle or diminish Kennedy's shrewdly conceived stratagems for containing Hoover, but understand that by "indulging in the illusion that they possessed power over the FBI" the Kennedy Justice Department undermined the possibility of achieving it. A few "random victories" do not "bespeak the power relationship one expects between Cabinet officer and one of his subordinates."[26]

Reluctant to confront Hoover and thereby embarrass the president, the attorney general said he "made a real effort" to reach out—"I really deferred to him." Besides, Robert added, the Kennedys found Hoover personally "helpful." "He had some very good ideas" about reorganizing the CIA and "the White House operation, and the whole business of checking people," Kennedy said without elaboration or qualification. Attorney General Kennedy also tried to quiet opposition to Hoover inside the department, cautioning his staff against leaping to conclusions and refusing to comment himself when criticisms were brought against the Bureau, as when agent William Turner sued the FBI in 1962 for violating his rights of free speech.[27] Kennedy even organized a small party in May 1962 to mark Hoover's thirty-eighth year as director. Typically, Hoover in a snit made it known that he wanted no party, especially one hosted by his young boss.[28] Kennedy also attended several dinners and luncheons in Hoover's honor, participated in FBI ceremonies, convinced the president to speak at graduation exercises at the FBI academy, and generally made himself available whenever the director requested.

Hoover did not reciprocate, conspicuously absenting himself from department social gatherings, declining invitations to Hickory Hill, and sending emissaries to department functions. James Bennett, director of the Bureau of Prisons (ostensibly a parallel position to the FBI director in the Justice Department hierarchy) did not recall Hoover attending a single staff luncheon throughout Robert Kennedy's tour of office at Justice.[29]

As long as President Kennedy was alive, the two men masked their feelings behind a screen of protocol charades. Publicly, each expressed his admiration for the other's dedication as a public servant. But on the few occasions they appear in photographs together, their body language and their lack of eye contact betray their mutual hostility. Communicating mostly through lieutenants, Hoover maintained a stiff and formal manner in contacts with Kennedy. He initialed bureaucratically correct memoranda with a flourish and, when political etiquette mandated, sent carefully worded "Dear Bob" letters signed "Edgar." Kennedy adopted a stylized, seemingly rehearsed informality toward the director, self-consciously addressing him as "Edgar" in staff meetings. Curiously, he sometimes crossed out "Edgar" in the salutations on letters and replaced it with the formal "Mr. Hoover" and signed "R. F. Kennedy." Not until his last months at Justice did he regularly use the familiar form of address in correspondence.[30]

Privately though, Kennedy was often less discreet in his comments about Hoover, joking with his personal staff about Hoover's diminished mental state, his "good days" and "bad days"—"He was out of it today, wasn't he?"—and commenting on the director's relationship with Clyde Tolson, Hoover's constant companion and second in charge. When Tolson was hospitalized for an operation, Kennedy reportedly cracked, "What was it, a hysterectomy?"[31]

Such comments often got back to Hoover. Kennedy later stated that he knew of no instances when his private conversations were repeated elsewhere, and he gave no indication that he suspected his telephone conversations or those of other officials were tapped or that his conversations were secretly recorded by hidden microphones planted by the FBI.[32] During those years Hoover often ordered the FBI's Washington field office, usually for counterintelligence purposes, to employ telephone wiretaps, microphone surveillance, and break-ins to obtain information from the offices of high-level officials. Some reporters strongly suspected that Hoover bugged offices. A few officials—even the president himself—sought safe areas for confidential interviews. Only hearsay evidence survives to suggest that Hoover tapped Robert Kennedy's telephones or bugged his offices. Relying on unattributed allegations, Curt Gentry in his critical biography *J. Edgar Hoover* asserted, "It was common knowledge within the Bureau that Hoover had bugged the entire Justice Department," including the attorney general's private elevator.[33]

Electronic Surveillance

Illegal electronic surveillance, or more precisely the FBI's deployment of wiretaps and bugs and the attorney general's knowledge or lack of it, sparked the discord between Hoover and Kennedy that eventually flared into a public confrontation. Part of the conflict stemmed from Kennedy's apparent ignorance of crucial distinctions between the FBI's use of telephone wiretaps and of hidden microphone surveillance. Grateful for the results, he did not probe the FBI's methods, a failure that stands as a reminder of the frailty of his liberal convictions as well as the limits of his personal power.

Wiretapping, or the interception and divulgence of telephone conversations, became illegal in 1934. In 1937, the Supreme Court (*Nardone v. U.S.* 302 U.S. 379) ruled that the ban applied to federal agents, but Hoover's FBI continued to tap telephone lines to gather intelligence, even though the information could not be used in court. A secret directive signed by President Roosevelt in 1940, continued in force by Attorney General Tom Clark and President Truman in 1947, and reaffirmed by President Eisenhower's attorney general, Herbert Brownell, in 1954, permitted the FBI to use wiretaps in connection with national security matters when specifically authorized by the attorney general. Attorney General Kennedy, although not fully versed on those procedures, generally followed them.

Robert Kennedy said that wiretapping, a valuable tool in law enforcement, required the "most scrupulous use." He often expressed his discomfort with the exclusive powers given to him as attorney general—"there's no check on what I do whatsoever"—when it came to wiretapping. Accordingly, in 1962 and again in 1963 he presented legislative proposals to legalize wiretapping in limited areas where serious offenses were involved and to require a federal bench warrant for all wiretaps, regardless of locality and jurisdiction. Worried, he said, about "indiscriminate" wiretapping, Kennedy testified in Senate hearings that the existing situation, in which federal authorities could listen in on but not divulge calls, was "chaotic" and "unsatisfactory to almost everyone." Kennedy's bills died in Congress under opposition from the American Civil Liberties Union, Joseph Rauh and the ADA, and other groups who adamantly opposed the legalization of wiretaps under any circumstances.[34]

Robert Kennedy's recommendations for legislative safeguards on wiretapping contrasted sharply with his actual management of FBI eavesdropping practices. Although acknowledging that eavesdropping "may present serious threats to privacy," the attorney general expressed no qualms about the FBI's wiretaps. To the contrary, on occasion he seemed to encourage their use. At a June 1961 staff meeting on organized crime, one of Kennedy's division heads, William Orrick, called tapping inherently wrong. "Do you mean to tell me," Kennedy asked, "that if your little girl were kidnapped and a tap might help her get home safely you still wouldn't approve?" Orrick said, "Hard cases make bad law" and hoped the matter would end there.[35]

Between 1961 and 1964 Attorney General Kennedy reportedly authorized more than six hundred FBI telephone wiretaps, most under the expansive rubric of "national security" cases. Usually taps were on alien nationals, but the telephones of some U.S. citizens were tapped, including those of Martin Luther King, Jr., and two associates, as well as

Malcolm X, an Alabama Klan leader, an ex-FBI agent, and two journalists suspected of publishing national security information.[36]

Kennedy handled department wiretap practices, according to Schlesinger, "with surprising casualness and inattention." He approved nearly all of Hoover's requests without hesitation, the one for tapping Martin Luther King, Jr.'s calls excepted. Of those taps he authorized he kept no records, set no time limits, established no system to evaluate their effectiveness; only once, in July 1961, did he ask to see the FBI's list of those he had approved. He examined the list and, without any comment for the record, returned it to the FBI files for safekeeping.[37]

Even more troubling, Kennedy failed to assert control over the FBI microphone surveillance (Misur) programs, which involved trespass on private property to plant bugs. The Communications Act of 1934, written before the technology was available, did not specifically ban bugging. Trespass, of course, was illegal everywhere. Acting on his own authority, J. Edgar Hoover first engaged in trespass surveillance in 1938 and, in the absence of clear directives and active monitoring by the Justice Department, continued without restrictions until 1965. In 1952 Attorney General J. Howard McGrath informed Hoover that the "use of microphone surveillance which does not involve trespass would seem to be permissible." Trespassing on property to install microphones was not permissible, wrote McGrath, because it violated the Fourth Amendment protection against unreasonable searches and seizure.[38] Hoover ignored McGrath's restrictions.

After the 1954 Supreme Court case (*Irvine v. California,* 347 U.S. 128) in which justices expressed outrage at the indecency of installing a microphone in a home, Attorney General Herbert Brownell reviewed the McGrath guidelines. Brownell authorized the FBI to use microphones in instances of "national security" with "discretion and intelligent restraint," but he required that cases involving trespass be reviewed by the department. Like McGrath before him and William P. Rogers after him, Brownell did not monitor the FBI's compliance with existing directives.[39] Allowed to define the limits of his agents' actions, Hoover, as noted earlier, unilaterally authorized trespass surveillance in the Top Hoodlum Program. Many of those bugs were in place when the Kennedys entered office in 1961.

Advances in the miniaturization of electronic components and refinements in the processes of transmitting and recording radio signals made electronic eavesdropping a more widely used method of criminal investigation, and a more controversial one. It was an issue about which an attorney general ought to be reasonably well informed. Yet, despite his background as an investigator, Kennedy apparently entered office with little understanding of the basic policy issues, let alone the technical nuances of electronic eavesdropping.

Some of Kennedy's staff found his ignorance about technical matters endearingly human. One aide said that Robert "couldn't tell a spark plug from a generator."[40] At a 1961 staff meeting on organized crime Kennedy ingenuously wondered aloud about deploying electronic devices against organized crime. The remarks alarmed his FBI liaison, Courtney Evans, who reported to Hoover that "there is a serious question as to whether he [Kennedy] has any comprehension as to the difference between a technical surveillance [a telephone wiretap] and microphone surveillance [a bug]."[41]

Such confusion could not have lasted for long. Hoover directed Evans to meet with Kennedy immediately and explain the differences. Evans failed to disclose enough technical information at their July meeting to satisfy the attorney general, for a few days later, Evans left a telephone message informing Kennedy that he had further information on the "technical surveillance methods you inquired about."[42] During his 1966 trip to South Africa, Kennedy visited privately with Ian Robertson, a student critic of South African apartheid, and revealed more than a rudimentary knowledge of the limitations of such devices. Told that the meeting room was bugged, Kennedy jumped in the air and landed with a resounding thud on the wooden floor. He explained that the noise and vibration would jar any listening devices for ten or fifteen minutes. Asked how he knew, Kennedy replied, "I was once attorney general."[43]

When news of the FBI's widespread secret surveillance began to circulate, Kennedy announced on 11 December 1966 that, while possibly "inconceivable" to Hoover, it was "nonetheless true" that "I was not aware of the 'bugging' practices of the FBI during my term as Attorney General." By limiting his public denial to "bugging," rather than wiretapping, Kennedy was splitting hairs to cover himself politically. His denials, however, had a hollow ring, especially to those in the Justice Department who believed he must have known about the bugging operations. Courtney Evans felt certain that Kennedy knew that "some coverage" was used in criminal cases because of the nature of the information supplied to him by the FBI. Edward Silberling, one-time head of the Organized Crime Section, remarking on the many intelligence reports Hoover sent to the attorney general, said, "You'd have to be pretty thick not to conclude that some came from overheard conversations." William Hundley, who succeeded Silberling, knew of the bugging but assumed that it was a matter "so delicate that it must be something that was just between the AG and the Director."[44]

Even if he could not infer the existence of the FBI's Misur program from intelligence reports, Robert Kennedy had ample opportunity to learn about it from other sources. In May 1961 Byron White asked Hoover for comments, suggestions, and background information on microphone surveillance in preparation for congressional testimony. Hoover supplied a distorted summary of Brownell's 1954 directive, falsely declaring that it granted the FBI "unrestricted use" of microphone surveillance "with or without trespass" in cases involving "internal security and the national safety." Then he audaciously volunteered that, although national security was not involved, the Bureau was using microphone surveillance in "investigations of the clandestine activities of top hoodlums and organized crime . . . even though trespass is necessary."[45] No one in the Justice Department challenged this sweeping claim to the FBI's right of trespass. Kennedy probably never saw the document. Ten years later Byron White could not recall seeing it. Hoover probably never meant it to be carefully read. Since the memo called for no response, he could take silence as acquiescence in his practices.[46] It is estimated that Hoover installed 738 bugs during the span of Robert Kennedy's service as attorney general.[47]

Further, once in New York and again in Chicago, Kennedy listened to illegally obtained surveillance tapes. Edwin Guthman, who was present on both occasions, insists the FBI agents gave them the clear impression that the recordings came from local law enforcement sources. It is worth noting, however, that while Kennedy the crime fighter listened raptly, Kennedy the quintessential interrogator did not raise a question about the circumstances under which the tapes were obtained or by whom. Nor did he comment on the legal implications of their very existence.[48]

No records exist of Robert Kennedy ever explicitly authorizing an illegal microphone surveillance, but evidence is sufficient to infer that he must have known or at least strongly suspected the FBI of engaging in such practices. Yet Kennedy never inquired about the FBI's authority for such operations. With the means to bring illegal bugging under control, he apparently lacked the will and the motivation to do it. One means of control was administrative oversight. Kennedy's Justice Department, however, never disputed or, for that matter, even scrutinized Hoover's claims of broad powers to engage in trespass surveillance. Neither of two Kennedy assistants responsible for polices and practices relating to eavesdropping—Deputy Attorney General Byron White, who was in charge of administration, and Jack Miller, who headed the Criminal Division—attempted to regulate Hoover's practices, nor did they formulate their own guidelines for microphone surveillance.[49]

Another means of control, of course, was to pass a law. Although Kennedy endorsed several proposals to amend the Communications Act, all related only to wiretapping, with the regulation of microphone eavesdropping through trespassing deliberately excluded. When Jack Miller testified during 1961 Senate hearings on the wiretap bill, he was asked whether the department would also support legislation on bugging. The "considered opinion" of the Justice Department, he replied, was that bugging should not be included in legislation at that time. Miller claimed that the Justice Department was "studying the problem of eavesdropping" and "all its ramifications." Earlier, Robert Kennedy told Peter Maas in an interview for *Look* magazine, "We are studying this question [of electronic eavesdropping] carefully."[50] But Kennedy's Justice Department never made such a study, leaving the matter in Hoover's hands.

Why? Robert Kennedy was intrigued with the possibilities that this new technique offered in the fight against organized crime. His obvious enthusiasm caused Courtney Evans to warn Hoover in July 1961 to expect a rush of "unwarranted requests" for technical equipment.

Arthur Schlesinger, Jr., admits that Kennedy did "not pursue the question as he should have" and perhaps, too, "he did not want to know." Kennedy, for his part, later acknowledged that "the bugging intensified under me," but he sought pardon, because "it didn't begin under me."[51] Still, his position obligated him to do something about it.

Kennedy's silence on bugging while he was attorney general likely was deliberate, a variant of the doctrine of plausible deniability used by executive branch officers to disclaim knowledge of covert operations in the foreign intelligence sector. He probably refused to commit to writing what he intended later to deny. His silence, then, appears induced by a naivete born of the presumption that Hoover, like the CIA director, would keep his peace when secret operations were divulged and would accept the consequences for his unit's actions. But Hoover was no Allen Dulles, nor was he bound by the same statutory and political limitations. When it came to bugging, Hoover made his own rules, and Kennedy chose silence over defiance.

Hoover schemed to ensure that any untoward consequences of his freewheeling use of microphone surveillance would be borne by the attorney general, not himself. To deflect blame and to enmesh Kennedy in the FBI's illegal surveillance operations, he secured what looked like a blanket Justice Department authorization for the Misur program. On 17 August 1961 he maneuvered Kennedy into signing what Evans described as a "routine" authorization for the lease of special telephone lines in New York. The request specifically mentions microphone surveillance, not telephone wiretaps. If Kennedy remained confused about the differences between them, he still should have known that by inserting small microphones in telephone receivers the FBI could eavesdrop on everything said in a room. Not questioning Evans's claim that the New York Telephone Company required a letter "on each occasion" that the FBI leased special lines, Kennedy gave the FBI a "specimen copy" that Hoover could duplicate. The telephone company, Victor Navasky later discovered, would have accepted the signature of one of Kennedy's assistants or of Hoover himself. The real purpose for the letter was to get Kennedy's participation on record.[52]

The FBI also carefully documented those instances where the attorney general had passively listened to tapes or reflexively voiced his approval of the results of microphone surveillance, lumping them into a post hoc authorization of the Misur program. For example, Hoover later supplied the Johnson White House and selected members of the press with excerpts of Courtney Evans's memoranda to Hoover quoting Kennedy as saying that he was "pleased" they had been using microphone surveillance and stating that he had advised Kennedy that the FBI was using bugs "in all instances" where it "was technically feasible and where valuable information might be expected."[53] Arthur Schlesinger, Jr., dismissed those reports, proposing that the entire controversy was a "misunderstanding" between Kennedy and Hoover brought on by Evans's well-meaning attempts to serve two masters at once. Schlesinger suggests that Evans may have told Hoover what he thought Hoover wanted to hear, knowing that Kennedy preferred not to be informed about such things.[54]

Evans's reports to Hoover tell only part of the story. In summary, the controversy's elements are these: Hoover willfully violated federal laws and engaged in treachery and deceit to cover his actions. Kennedy never authorized illegal microphone surveillance operations, questioned the FBI's claims to the tacit authority to use trespass surveillance, or insisted on procedural safeguards to protect the individual rights and privacy of the FBI's subjects. Indeed, Kennedy communicated only unambiguous approval for the results of the FBI bugging programs. Kennedy's faults were errors of omission, failures to ask the right questions and to take proactive steps to prevent abuses by a bureau within his department.

Before his death, Robert Kennedy sought to make amends for his diffidence toward wiretapping and bugging while attorney general. In January 1967 he announced his support of legislation to "reform completely our approach to wiretapping and eavesdropping." In a speech to the Law School Forum at Columbia University he reiterated his call to use "modern technology" in the fight against crime. Implicitly conceding earlier mistakes, he said, "We must act to assure that the new technology . . . does not invade the privacy of the individual."[55] A proposal similar to Kennedy's, requiring a bench warrant for each bug or tap, was enacted under Title III of the Omnibus Crime Control and Safe Streets Act of 1968.

Hoover's Secret Files

Another point of contention between Robert Kennedy and J. Edgar Hoover concerned the highly derogatory and politically explosive contents of the director's secret files. One set, Hoover's Personal and Confidential File, was destroyed immediately after his death in 1972. Of a second group of file folders, Hoover's Official and Confidential (O&C) File containing derogatory reports on leading political figures, heavily censored and sanitized portions are now available.[56]

Robert Kennedy knew about Hoover's secret files. Hoover regularly reminded him of some of their contents. "I suppose every month or so," Kennedy recalled, "he'd send somebody around [Louis Nichols or Courtney Evans] to give information on somebody I knew or a member of my family or allegations in connection with myself. So that it would be clear —whether it was right or wrong—that he was on top of all of these things and received this information. He would do this also, I think, to find out what my reaction to it would be."[57]

Hoover's curiosity about the Kennedys, which "bordered on the obsessive," began long before the Kennedys came to power when Hoover started collecting information on Joseph and John Kennedy. After July 1960, he paid greater attention to reports of questionable associations in John Kennedy's personal life.[58] More titillating than that held on most politicians, such information also proved far more voluminous. Apparently nothing comparable to the extensive FBI files on John Kennedy was kept on other presidents.[59] Hoover's clumsy pantomime in confronting Robert Kennedy with some of this information has convinced several scholars of his intention to blackmail.[60] Robert Kennedy, however, was certain the director did not engage in "wide scale blackmail." Hoover's methods were subtler.

So, too, were the Kennedys'. Confident they could handle the "old man," as they called him, neither Kennedy betrayed any sense of forced obligation to Hoover. Although Robert acknowledged Hoover as "dangerous," he felt "it was a danger that we could control, that we were on top of, that we could deal with at the appropriate time. That's the way we looked at it." Perhaps he meant they could hold Hoover in check by the threat of humiliating dismissal and eventual prosecution, should he dare attempt to blackmail the president. Robert Kennedy remained certain that "there wasn't anything that he [Hoover] could do. . . . And there wasn't anybody he could go to or anything he could do with the information or the material. So it was fine. He served our interests." With disdain, Robert dismissed Hoover as "really of no particular importance" to President Kennedy.[61]

In January 1961 Hoover started a file on Robert Kennedy that grew eventually to more than three thousand items detailing his public appearances, private contacts, physical movements, and rumors alleging sexual misconduct.[62] Judging from the file's contents, Hoover mostly wanted to know the attorney general's whereabouts and his opinions of the Bureau. Hoover assigned FBI agents to meet Kennedy at airports and to escort him during visits to other cities, not for his protection or convenience but to apprise the director about Kennedy's contacts and conversations, especially those with other law enforcement officials.

FBI agents escorting Robert Kennedy were told to inform Hoover of any discussions of "topics of interest to the Bureau."[63] Hoover also read Bureau summaries of books and articles by and about Kennedy, as well as all of his speeches and press conferences. Into such reports he often inserted sharply worded marginalia to signal his feelings and reactions to his subordinates. When Kennedy in a press conference called the FBI "the greatest investigative body in the world," the skeptical Hoover noted, "If correctly quoted, he certainly must have changed his mind."[64]

Hoover allowed his dislike of his young superior to impair his professional judgment, perhaps to the point of failing to protect the attorney general's life. The FBI's lapses before and after President Kennedy's assassination are documented in a score of studies and reports. Generally overlooked, however, are the threats against the attorney general and his family. They received a massive amount of hate mail and several death threats, some of which the FBI learned about through their Misur program and some through informants and infiltrators inside organized crime, the KKK, white supremacy groups, and the Teamsters. Informants within the KKK made the FBI aware of the intense hatred Kennedy faced from armed white supremacists whenever he entered the South. Each time, however, the FBI mechanically noted the threats and did little else.

Except for the period immediately after President Kennedy's assassination, when the FBI worked with the Secret Service and the U.S. marshals to protect Robert Kennedy, Hoover took no special precautions to secure the safety of the attorney general and his family. To the contrary, the FBI criticized spending taxpayers' money to protect Kennedy. Hoover expressed annoyance when the Border Patrol, U.S. Marshal's Office, U.S. Coast Guard, Interior Department, and other federal agencies provided communications services and security for the attorney general when he traveled and vacationed.[65]

While it does not appear that Hoover believed the attorney general had violated any laws or was involved in any misuse of his office, the FBI treated Kennedy as a subject under surveillance, a potential, if not a real, threat to their bureaucratic hegemony. They used informers to fill in gaps in their intelligence regarding the attorney general's intentions toward the FBI; when Kennedy made a "very secret trip" (so far as the FBI was concerned) to Los Angeles in October 1963, a "source" informed Hoover that he went to assure Los Angeles police chief William H. Parker that he would be replacing Hoover as FBI director.[66]

Rumors of Hoover's firing or retirement sprang up frequently during the Kennedy years, and Chief Parker was often mentioned as the likely successor. Perhaps tipping her husband's hand, Ethel Kennedy let others, including Hoover, know that she favored Parker.[67] Whenever a rumor surfaced, Robert Kennedy reaffirmed his admiration for Hoover, saying he "hoped Mr. Hoover would remain FBI Director for many years to come."[68] Hoover may have started some of the rumors himself, perhaps to salve his tender ego, such as those originating in newspapers friendly to the FBI (among them, the Hearst chain) and generally accompanied by a counterthreat or a counterrumor against the Kennedys.[69]

The possibility that Attorney General Kennedy would have fired Hoover is remote. Robert once told *New York Times* reporter Anthony Lewis that Hoover was insubordinate, "nasty and tricky," lamenting, "Isn't it terrible that I can't do anything about it?" Firing Hoover would have implicated his brother, raised questions of motive, and caused a tremendous political ruckus that would have directly threatened the Kennedy presidency. The Kennedys could handle Hoover as the intractable, irascible FBI director more easily than Hoover thrust back into private life, where he might claim to be a victim of Democratic political spoils, portray himself as a martyr of the Kennedys' purported lack of commitment to the fight against Communism, and become a force for right-wing politics—all the while in possession of secrets that could politically cripple if not destroy the president. Besides, as John Kennedy explained, "you can't fire God."[70] So they learned to live with him.

Marilyn Monroe

Hoover did his best to make life uncomfortable for Robert Kennedy. On 20 August 1962, for example, Evans informed the attorney general that a "highly confidential source" (a hidden microphone) overheard racketeer Meyer Lansky say that Robert Kennedy was having an affair with a woman in El Paso, Texas. Kennedy told Evans he had never been to El Paso and "there is no basis in fact whatsoever for the allegation." Blaming the report on "gossip mongers," Kennedy said he knew of rumors connecting him with Marilyn Monroe. He told Evans that he had "at least met Monroe since she was a friend of his sister."[71]

Kennedy's mention of Monroe just two weeks after her death marked the first time her name was linked with his in the FBI files. One of the enduring tales of contemporary folklore, however, is that Robert and John Kennedy both had affairs with Monroe;[72] that Robert's was more intense; that her death—ruled a probable suicide by acute barbiturate poisoning—was actually a murder, with Robert present either as co-conspirator or as a victim of a frame-up by Marilyn's killers; that brother-in-law Peter Lawford helped the attorney general flee the scene, destroyed some incriminating evidence, and hired an expert to sweep the house for bugs and wiretaps allegedly placed there by order of James Hoffa, who some claim knew of the affair all along; and that the FBI, or "Bobby's personal gestapo," as one writer inconceivably labels Hoover's Bureau, assisted in the coverup by destroying telephone records and confiscating other evidence.

The story has undergone several permutations since its first telling in 1964, when a man described by the FBI as a "right-wing zealot" called Monroe's death part of a Communist conspiracy that Robert Kennedy—incredibly branded by the writer as a known "communist sympathizer"—cleverly covered up.[73] Gossip columnists repeated the story before Norman Mailer recast it in 1973, adding menacing embellishments.[74] Taken up as a personal crusade by a man who claims (but cannot prove) he was once married to Monroe,[75] the story was enhanced in the 1980s and adapted to implicate Hoffa and the Mafia.[76] Anthony Summers then cultivated and skillfully refined the story in the argot of conspiracy theory.[77] Now it is repeated uncritically in some biographies of the Kennedys and Monroe, on tabloid television shows, and in smarmy made-for-television movies. It has thoroughly penetrated the public awareness.[78]

Perhaps the Marilyn-Bobby story has gained undeserved credibility in the popular culture because in today's intellectual and cultural climate, sophists regard knowledge as socially or culturally constructed, values and truth are subjective, and history has multiple meanings, none definitive. Perhaps its credibility springs from the popular attraction to conspiracy theories fed by tabloid journalism, where shocking allegations and personal opinion carry more weight than the thoughful evaluation of historical sources. And some people simply will insist on their right to their opinion that the story was so. No amount of exculpatory evidence, correction of historical error, or logic will dissuade them, as long as others with a stake in perpetuating the story loudly and persistently assure them it was so. Finally, any historian who criticizes the Marilyn-Bobby story risks being labeled an adjunct of the "Camelot School" or, as one Kennedy critic charged, of being "obsessed with protecting the Kennedy image."[79]

Just the same, critical evaluation of Marilyn-Bobby story sources supports the painstaking research of Donald Spoto, a biographer of Monroe, who concluded that the accounts of a sexual affair are "unfounded and scurrilous." Spoto labeled the tale itself a "great deception." He found that the two principal witnesses-cum-promulgators of the story simply were not credible.[80] Further, a comparison of the Kennedy and Monroe travel itineraries and their known whereabouts during 1961 and 1962 demonstrates they were rarely in the same city at the same time.[81] They very likely met on no more than four occasions and then apparently always in the company of others.[82]

Evidence adduced to support the Marilyn-Bobby tale rests largely on the unverifiable statements and hearsay comments of witnesses of questionable veracity and on a less than rigorous analysis of a few FBI documents.[83] One such FBI memorandum reports an anonymous source informing the FBI that he held information linking John and Robert Kennedy, Peter Lawford, Marilyn Monroe, and a censored list of others to "sex parties" at the Carlyle Hotel in New York City. Two allegations repeated by the same source debase his credibility: first, that Robert Kennedy had ties to the Communist party and, second, that Kennedy had proposed an "accommodation" with Fidel Castro.[84]

The accusers' reliability did not matter to Hoover, who voyeuristically collected and filed all manner of rumors about the Kennedys and other famous people. Perhaps in ironic retribution, Hoover has been reduced to a taffeta puddle, the man responsible for destroying so many others' reputations, vilified by allegations that he was a homosexual and in league with organized crime.[85]

The vilest accusation against Robert Kennedy is that he ordered or participated in Marilyn Monroe's alleged murder.[86] At the time of her death, however, the attorney general, Ethel, and four of their children were 350 miles away at the ranch of John B. Bates in Gilroy, California. Kennedy's presence at the Bates ranch the weekend of Monroe's death is established by FBI agents who met him and his family at San Francisco airport on Friday afternoon 3 August 1962, gathered up their luggage, and followed them to the Bates ranch eighty miles away in the Santa Cruz mountains, managing to get lost along the way. What they did after depositing the Kennedys at the Bates ranch is unknown, but FBI agents reported to director Hoover that Robert Kennedy spent the entire weekend there.[87]

Could Kennedy have left the ranch on Saturday and helicoptered or drove to Los Angeles to spend the afternoon and evening dealing with Monroe? "No way," John Bates answered. Bates, his wife, and his ranch foreman were certain that Robert Kennedy remained with his family from the time they arrived on Friday afternoon until their departure for the return trip to San Francisco on Sunday afternoon.[88]

All said, the Marilyn-Bobby story not only fails the standard tests of historical verification but defies logic. Granted, history is full of illogical events, and lustful emotions can drive people to impulsive and irrational acts. But why would Robert Kennedy fall into an affair with a woman, particularly one as well known and as emotionally unstable as Marilyn Monroe, at almost precisely the moment J. Edgar Hoover informed him of the existence of the president's relationship with Judith Campbell? Such an involvement would rightly have been "reckless in the extreme," as one historian asserted.[89] It also would have played right into Hoover's hands.

Nor does it logically follow that Kennedy would solicit his brother-in-law Peter Lawford to help cover up the affair. Lawford was notoriously unreliable. An abuser of drugs and alcohol, he mistreated Robert's sister, Patricia. And if Robert had any reason to be grateful to Lawford after August 1962, he never showed it. In 1965, according to sources close to Lawford, Kennedy personally set harsh terms for a separation agreement and advised Lawford to stay away from his sister.[90]

Even more difficult to swallow are assertions that the FBI covered up for the attorney general and supposedly confiscated crucial evidence.[91] Such claims ignore all that is known of Hoover's modus operandi.[92] If he had proof of Kennedy's involvement with Monroe or if Kennedy had asked for his assistance in covering up such an involvement, the director surely would have made a complete record of the matter for his files. Whenever Kennedy asked the FBI for even the smallest of favors—such as assistance with his wife's luggage when she was pregnant or verification of a purported signature of John Kennedy's— Hoover recorded it.[93] In 1966 Hoover's deputies stated in closed session with a Senate subcommittee that Robert Kennedy "had not had the nerve" to use the FBI for political or personal purposes, lest Hoover immediately resign.[94] If Kennedy had asked for assistance, Hoover would have used it against him at any one of several contentious flashpoints between 1964 and 1968.

Similarly, if James Hoffa possessed a compromising tape recording of either John or Robert Kennedy together with Monroe, such as Anthony Summers contends once existed, that, too, would surely have surfaced.[95] Facing thirteen years in prison and loss of control over the Teamsters, Hoffa resorted to desperate tactics, including the fabrication of evidence to disgrace his adversaries. Hoffa found prostitutes who obligingly provided affidavits stating they had sex with witnesses and jurors from both of the trials at which he was convicted. A streetwalker produced a tape alleging that Judge Wilson made obscene telephone calls to her. Hoffa surely would have brought forth Kennedy-Monroe tapes, if they existed.[96]

To be sure, Kennedy and Monroe knew each other. Each was fascinated by the other's personality and celebrity status. By mid-1962 Monroe had evidently fallen into a pathetic tailspin, propelled by paranoia, depression, and alcohol and drug abuse. Kennedy, according to Schlesinger, reached out to her, as he did to others, to offer a friendly ear to someone frequently distraught. His secretary, Angie Novello, has said that Robert "was such a sympathetic kind of person; he never turned away from anyone who needed help, and I'm sure he was well aware of her [Monroe's] problems. He was a good listener and that, I think, is what she needed more than anything."[97] Remnants of Monroe's telephone records indicate eight calls from her home to Robert Kennedy's office in the summer of 1962. Although Monroe's calls do not appear on Kennedy's telephone logs and desk diaries, Novello told Anthony Summers that she remembered taking them; most, she said, lasted less than a minute. Patricia Newcomb, Monroe's personal press representative, telephoned Kennedy's office twice, probably about dinner party invitations. Calls from show business people and their representatives were not uncommon. Other female movie stars, including Judy Garland, Kim Novak (once a houseguest at Hickory Hill), and Zsa Zsa Gabor, telephoned, sent notes, or paid casual visits to the office.[98]

Friends of Robert Kennedy, pointing to his ingrained sense of puritanic moral conduct and his love of and allegiance to Ethel, are resolute: The relationship with Monroe never went beyond casual friendship. An affair with anyone, they contend, would have been ridiculously out of character for him. Kenneth O'Donnell, who had known Kennedy since their days at Harvard, said Kennedy joked about the story and was flattered that anyone thought a prude like himself was "that good." "I know for a fact," O'Donnell said before he died, "that this Marilyn Monroe story was absolute horseshit."[99] Edwin Guthman, who traveled extensively with the attorney general and was present on at least two occasions when Kennedy met Monroe, is equally adamant: "I *know* there was no affair."[100]

Commenting on the strength of the bond between Robert and Ethel Kennedy, John Seigenthaler once remarked on how she teased her husband about dancing with Monroe several times at a dinner party at the Lawfords. He teased her back about her fondness for Byron "Whizzer" White. She also kidded him about a birthday kiss he gave Maya Plisetskaya, prima ballerina of the Bolshoi Ballet. When Robert traveled alone to Brazil in December 1962 on a special diplomatic mission for the president, she advised her husband in a telegram: "Kindly remove the mistletoe from over the top of your heads. Madame Goulart [the attractive wife of Brazilian President Joao Goulart] does not understand I or you. Yankee come home."[101] As Ethel's biographer Lester David noted, it simply is not likely that a prim woman, uneasy with liaisons between unmarried persons and holding a dim view of divorce, would have kidded her husband about Monroe or any other woman, if she believed for a moment that he actually was having affairs.[102]

Other than the fabricated rumors about Monroe, no gossip linked Robert Kennedy and other women during his lifetime and none have come forward since his death. In 1985, in an effort to prove "Robert Kennedy was, after all, human," Anthony Summers and ABC and BBC television producers claimed to have found evidence of extramarital affairs with three unnamed women besides Monroe. Summers has speculated that one of the women was Marilyn Monroe's publicist, Patricia Newcomb.[103]

Newcomb, after Monroe's death, worked in Washington for the USIA Motion Picture Service and socialized with the Kennedys. The daughter of a judge, with connections of her own and a lifelong interest in politics and social reform, Newcomb easily fit in with the regulars at Hickory Hill parties. The carefree notes she exchanged with both Ethel and Robert were too silly to suggest that they were anything but friends. For example, Kennedy once invited Newcomb horseback riding, then sent her a note jokingly asking her to pay a $1.50 fee and signing the request "Charlie Generous." She made out a check to "Charlie Generous," signed "Bertha Bronco." On another occasion, signing herself as "Sadie Southpaw" after breaking her arm in a riding accident at Hickory Hill, she invited the Kennedys to join her on a USIA-sponsored bus tour of New York City and quipped that Ethel might be known at the "Hotel Dixie."[104]

Robert Kennedy, who admired and befriended many women, made no effort to conceal his appreciation for female beauty. "Bobby was human," Arthur Schlesinger allowed. Women were drawn to his boyish, unrefined sensuality, but he was awkward and uncomfortable with women at first meeting.[105] Temptations were everywhere, with sex a form of political currency that some Washington lobbyists dispensed with impunity.[106] Kennedy's office staffs, moreover, included young, attractive women (and men, for that matter), and his celebrity status and frequent travels brought him into contact with many others.

Brother Protector

Assignations and affairs would not only have been wildly out of character for Robert Kennedy, they would have been wholly inconsistent with the roles thrust upon him by his place in the family and would have further complicated his already difficult task as his brother's protector. By 1962, with Joseph Kennedy paralyzed by a stroke (discussed in next chapter), the reproving little brother had become the substitute for the father, responsible for tending the family's political investments and for guarding the moral image of his brother's presidency. Those like General Maxwell Taylor who worked closely with both Kennedys noted Robert's "rather protective attitude" toward the president. "One had the feeling," Taylor said, "that he was looking after his older brother. . . . He seemed to look at every aspect of a given situation, asking himself, 'Now, how can this affect Jack? How can it hurt Jack?'"[107]

Among other responsibilities, Robert assumed the task begun by his father of concealing his brother's medical problems. That task was further complicated by John Kennedy's increased reliance on amphetamines and the risk of harmful interactions and possible mood alterations associated with the corticosteroid Kennedy took to control the Addison's disease. In 1960, John and Jacqueline Kennedy started receiving treatments from Dr. Max Jacobson, a New York physician known as "Dr. Feelgood" for his energy-inducing injections—a concoction of vitamins, steroids, and other substances, but mostly amphetamines. Robert became alarmed when he learned about the injections and demanded they be analyzed. "I don't care if it's horse piss," John reportedly told his brother. "It works." One uncorroborated source claims Robert had the FBI laboratories analyze Jacobson's concoctions. Although he could not have approved of the injections, he likely was pleased to see his brother's constant pain relieved and his spirits lifted with no obvious side effects, after years of ineffectual treatments by noted physicians. Jacobson continued the treatments, traveling to the White House and West Palm Beach, and even accompanying the president on his state visit to France.[108]

The risks of exposure of President Kennedy's frequent extramarital liaisons proved more troubling and more difficult to contain. John Kennedy was convinced these would not be revealed by the press, hobbled by contemporary rules of decent conduct that forbade reporting tales of infidelity and heterosexual lust involving political leaders.[109] Most reporters, as James Reston of the *New York Times* put it, had no interest in Kennedy's "monkey business." Ben Bradlee "heard stories," but Kennedy's philandering was "never Topic A" among reporters. Believing himself free from exposure by the press, John Kennedy once said, "They can't touch me while I'm alive. And after I'm dead, who cares?"[110]

He was mistaken on both counts. His indiscretions left him highly vulnerable throughout his presidency, and they have scarred and distorted popular and historical conceptions of the man and his presidency since they came to light in the mid-1970s. The perspective of more than three decades—one that includes the Nixon Watergate disgrace, the destroyed presidential aspirations of Gary Hart, and a cloud of doubt hanging over Bill Clinton—reveals that a personal misstep or the suspicion of a presidential scandal can ruin a political career. John Kennedy was fortunate, indeed, to have both a congenial relationship with the press and a brother protector for attorney general.

How much time and energy Robert Kennedy devoted to investigating and defusing such crises cannot be established conclusively. Hoover warned him about accusations of immoral conduct by the president on at least a half-dozen occasions, but the FBI apparently learned of only a fraction of the president's indiscretions.[111]

Thanks largely to Robert's efforts, John Kennedy escaped being drawn into the Profumo affair, a sex scandal in Britain that crippled the Conservative party government of Prime Minister Harold Macmillan and contributed at least indirectly to its fall. The scandal began when John D. Profumo, Macmillan's secretary of state for war and a member of Parliament, was discovered to have had a relationship with a nineteen-year-old party girl named Christine Keeler. Profumo met Keeler in 1961 through Stephen Ward, an osteopath with connections to English high society and a part-time procurer of a better class of prostitutes. Suspected of being a Communist agent and of using prostitutes to gain government information for the Soviets, Ward committed suicide at the peak of the scandal. Keeler told authorities that Ward asked her to get Profumo to divulge certain national security information and to pass it to the deputy naval attaché at the Soviet Embassy in London, Captain Yevgeny M. Ivanov, with whom she was simultaneously involved. Cast against a backdrop of several other cases of sex and spying, the British government's very unpleasant relations with its press, and the public's rising indignation, these indiscretions forced Profumo to resign his offices in June 1963.[112]

A few days after Profumo's resignation, the *New York Journal-American,* part of the Hearst newspaper conglomerate and an ardent opponent of Kennedy administration policies, alleged that an unnamed man holding "very high" elective office had, during the 1960 presidential campaign, used the services of prostitutes linked to Stephen Ward and Christine Keeler. The story appeared in only one edition of the newspaper.[113]

Forty-eight hours later, on 1 July 1963, a Saturday afternoon when Robert was scheduled to be at Hyannis Port on a holiday weekend with his family, he met in his office with Dom Frasca and James Horan, the two reporters who filed the story. Although the reporters had requested a private meeting, the attorney general insisted on Courtney Evans's presence. Frasca and Horan claimed they had information that linked John Kennedy prior to the election with some women connected to the Profumo affair. Refusing to be intimidated, the attorney general demanded that their information be "formally received" by the Justice Department; that is, if they had any hard evidence, he wanted it put on the record. The reporters then played a tape recording of an accusatory call they had received from a British newspaperman. In the background, a woman's voice—later identified as that of Mariella (Marie) Novotny, a prostitute of Anglo-Czech parentage linked to the Profumo affair and to an alleged Soviet vice ring at the United Nations—was heard providing details. Kennedy asked if the reporters had further corroboration, put them through some hostile questioning, and then cooly dismissed them.[114] Although far from disproving the allegations, Kennedy had put the *Journal-American* on notice: He would not tolerate the further publication of such accusations and, by insisting that all "information" be turned over to the Justice Department, he would invoke the powers of his office to deal with them.

Hoover already knew of the accusations and may have had a part in getting the story to the *Journal-American.* To protect FBI sources and to maintain the fiction that his agents did not investigate accusations of this ilk, Hoover withheld information until after Kennedy met with the reporters and until Evans's memorandum of the meeting formally requested the FBI's assistance. Three weeks later, Evans reported to Kennedy that Suzy Chang, a high-class prostitute who split her time between New York and the Ward-Keeler-Profumo circle in London, had alleged that John Kennedy had been a regular "client" during the 1960 campaign. She told the FBI that Marie Novotny had taken her place one night with Kennedy. However, an FBI check of immigration records showed that Novotny did not enter the United States until after the election.[115]

Robert Kennedy dismissed the remainder of Chang's allegations, labeling her story "preposterous" because his brother traveled with "scores of newspapermen" during the campaign and was too closely watched to have conducted such an affair. Kennedy told Evans that he was "grateful" to the FBI for bringing the matter to him personally. He proposed that they pursue this and "similar stories" "vigorously," instructing the FBI to keep him continually advised "on a personal basis, as he could better defend the family if he knew what was being said."[116] The FBI did nothing further with the Chang-Novotny allegations. As John Kennedy's biographer Herbert Parmet observed, "Once again Bobby handled a presidential lapse, or if not an actual lapse, vulnerability that came directly from both his behavior and reputation."[117]

Robert was pressed into service often enough to protect his brother's reputation that he needed a damage-control team to assist him in dealing with highly sensitive matters. Joseph Kennedy had first put the group together, which before 1960 worked exclusively for him. Gradually, however, Robert was entrusted with more sensitive tasks, such as quashing the breach-of-promise suit of Alicia Darr Purdom, the wife of actor Edmund Purdom, who claimed her involvement with John Kennedy had left her pregnant. Robert, according to FBI files, was pulled away during the 1960 campaign to handle a half-million dollar cash settlement to her.[118]

After his father's stroke in December 1961, Robert assumed the major responsibility for fixing his brother's mistakes. He retained many of the same men who had earlier worked for his father. For investigative work he hired James N. McInerney, the former U.S. attorney who had helped Robert get his first job on the McCarthy committee, and two McClellan committee stalwarts, Carmine Bellino and Lavern Duffy.[119] For legal matters he turned to Jack Miller, who served the family through and beyond Edward Kennedy's actions in August 1969 at Chappaquiddick Island. For financial and other kinds of assistance Robert relied, as always, on the resources of the family enterprises, coordinated by brother-in-law Stephen Smith. Not much is known about how this group functioned, but the results of their work were usually obvious. With help, Robert blunted, debunked, or deflated many of the accusations of immoral conduct brought against his brother the president.

Some were of less than blockbusting proportions. The charges of Florence Mary Kater, who claimed "personal knowledge and proof" that John Kennedy had an illicit sexual relationship with her neighbor Pamela Turnure, plagued Robert for years. Kater first made the charge in 1959 when she sent Hoover a photograph purportedly showing John Kennedy leaving Turnure's residence early one morning. Kater claimed that Robert Kennedy, whom she called an "arm twister" and an "enforcer," sent James McInerney to her home on seven occasions to intimidate her into silence. She expected Robert to put an end to his brother's "tomcatting" and complained bitterly to him of the president's cynicism in using the press to cover up his misdeeds. When Turnure became Jacqueline Kennedy's personal secretary, Kater revived her crusade. In 1963 she sent letters and copies of her picture of John Kennedy to every major newspaper, carried a sign in front of the White House, and confronted the president in public places. Her credibility suffered because of her eccentricities and because her cause was taken up by the *Thunderbolt,* a publication for the racist National States Rights party, one of hundreds of hate groups circulating vicious gossip about the Kennedys.[120]

President Kennedy did not rely exclusively on his brother to contain damaging allegations. When rumors surfaced that the first Catholic president once had been secretly married to a twice-divorced woman named Durie (Kerr) Malcolm, the president hired attorney Clark Clifford, reputedly the best "fixer" in all of Washington, to look into the matter. He also drew upon his friendships with Ben Bradlee and Phil Graham to debunk the story in the press. Even in this matter, however, it fell to Robert to deal with Hoover's attempts to use scandal as a lever to secure a free hand from the administration. When the FBI "alerted" the attorney general to the rumor—long after it had gained wide circulation—a confident Kennedy, backed by Clifford's legal opinions, explained to an incredulous Hoover that if a newspaper dared print the story then "we" could retire for life on what "we" collected.[121]

Robert's mettle, however, met a true test in the Rometsch case. East German–born Ellen Fimmel Rometsch had belonged to two Communist party organizations before defecting to the West, marrying a sergeant in the West German Air Force, and accompanying him to a duty station in Washington. There the beautiful twenty-seven-year-old Rometsch became a hostess and reputedly a two-hundred-dollar-a-night call girl at the Quorum Club, a private suite in the Carroll Arms Hotel patronized by many congressmen and operated by Bobby Baker, secretary to the Senate majority leader and a protege of Lyndon Johnson.

In late July 1963, the FBI informed the attorney general that Rometsch had named the president among the government officials who had called on her services. Baker also later claimed that he introduced John Kennedy to Rometsch through the railroad lobbyist

William Thompson. Robert Kennedy told the FBI that no one at the White House was involved with Rometsch or the Quorum Club. The president indirectly denied the story, telling Ben Bradlee, "He [Baker] was always telling me he knew where he could get me the cutest little girls, but he never did."[122] Few were persuaded by the Kennedy denials. The Rometsch case had the potential to become America's Profumo affair, a sex-and-security scandal of the first magnitude.

Fearing that Rometsch was working for the Communists and gathering incriminating information on government officials, the FBI, with Robert Kennedy's approval, arranged with the German government to have her and her husband quietly sent home in August 1963. On Hoover's recommendation, the attorney general ordered that Rometsch be denied a visa if she attempted to reenter the United States. When she protested, threatening to name some of her "important friends," Robert Kennedy sent LaVern Duffy to West Germany to quiet her down and keep her away from the press. With the help of a large cash payment and some security improvised on the spot, Duffy succeeded. The Bonn government declared that "the whole thing seems harmless."[123] But was it?

As the Rometsch matter unfolded, a Senate probe of Bobby Baker's activities took political center stage. On 30 October 1963 Clark Mollenhoff printed a front-page story in the *Des Moines Register* detailing the Rometsch expulsion, linking Rometsch to Baker's Quorum Club, and raising "the possibility that her activity might be connected with espionage." Until then the Senate Rules Committee had intended only to look into Baker's financial dealings and possible influence peddling. Mollenhoff's article threatened to force the Senate to broaden its investigation into security matters, casting nets that could snag the president himself. To put the press off the scent, John Kennedy told Ben Bradlee, knowing it would get into print, that he thought the Baker investigation had already gone too far and that it was threatening to alienate Southern Democrats sympathetic to Baker and aligned with Lyndon Johnson.[124]

To prevent a security scandal that might well have taken down the Kennedy presidency, Robert had to keep the Senate investigation of Baker's influence peddling from spilling over into his use of party girls such as Rometsch. Kennedy personally examined the FBI files on

Rometsch and the other girls at Baker's Quorum Club, discovering that "large numbers" of congressmen of both parties had used their services. He asked Hoover to meet with the Senate leaders—Mike Mansfield of Montana, leader of the Democratic majority, and Everett Dirksen of Illinois, leader of the Republican minority—and "explain" to them that revealing the materials in the Rometsch file would embarrass many Republicans as well as Democrats. Hoover told the attorney general that he ought to do the briefing himself, since he had reviewed the files. He made Kennedy grovel before eventually agreeing—probably for a substantial price—to talk to Dirksen and Mansfield. A meeting was held in Mansfield's apartment and a follow-up session with the president took place in the White House. The Senate pursued their investigation of Baker, but without mention of his use of party girls. Baker resigned his Senate position shortly afterwards.

Within a few days Hoover was called to the White House to lunch alone with the president, the sixth and final meeting between the two men. Looking forward to the 1964 campaign, John Kennedy told advisors he had begun to think he should meet more often with Hoover, the man his brother later claimed was of "no real importance."

The Kennedys lost whatever control they had over Hoover when the Rometsch matter concluded. Quick to take advantage, Hoover pressed Robert Kennedy for assurances that he would continue as FBI director. No record shows that Kennedy gave such assurances in so many words, but at about this time he finally approved Hoover's persistent requests to tap Martin Luther King, Jr.'s telephones. No conclusive connection links the two events, but in the King matter and almost every other issue involving Hoover, the Kennedys now found themselves obligated to the director, dependent on his judgment, and like it or not, committed to him personally.[125]

Robert Kennedy worried that exposing the Rometsch episode "would just destroy the confidence that the people in the United States had in their government and really make us a laughingstock around the world." He might doggedly insist that "we had it under control," but, as events hurtled toward Dallas, the president was more, not less, vulnerable to sexual compromise and blackmail.[126]

CHAPTER 10

Kennedy Aura and Kennedy Promises

THE KENNEDYS' DISTINCTIVE MANNER of governing created an ambience that attracted as much attention as their policies. Pledging "to get America moving again," the Kennedy fondness for doing things with "vigah," as the president pronounced it, took hold in Washington and stirred expectations across the land. Historians since have probed the dividing line between substance and reality, Kennedy promises and Kennedy achievements. Led by a president whom the Washington correspondent for the *New York Times* called "irresistibly witty" and "recklessly handsome," the New Frontier cast a brilliant aura.[1] Kennedy panache preempted the attention of the media and captured the public's imagination. When the Kennedy tenure ended, at the beckoning of the widow of the slain president, America called it Camelot.

Through films, television, magazines, the Broadway stage, and nightclub routines, the Kennedy interests, tastes, and Boston-Harvard accents swept the country.[2] Media coverage of presidential news conferences and White House events placed the Kennedys at the center of public attention. Kennedy images (some carefully crafted) fell one upon another in a kaleidoscopic tumble: the young, dashing president, the speed-reading intellectual surrounded by Ivy League professors and Nobel laureates, the witty and informed master of press conferences, the idealist summoning America's youth to sacrifice and service, the doting father, the handsome husband of the chic First Lady, all amid ubiquitous reminders of his membership in a large, talented, and physically imposing brood of thoroughbreds.

All was not what it seemed. Take, for example, the image of John Kennedy the intellectual-cum-statesman being served by America's academic elite, whose presence inspired Theodore White to proclaim the emergence of "a new power system in American life," a "new priesthood of action-intellectuals." Kennedy did, indeed, surround himself with such men, but less for the value of their ideas than for their problem-solving skills. Summoning them as needed, he incorporated an imposing array of gifted thinkers into White House decision making, primarily as personal consultants on foreign affairs. Using intellectuals this way, Garry Wills has argued, was deceiving, a part of the conscious pursuit of style as if it were substance. A few felt resentful, such as poet Robert Lowell, who said an intellectual should be a window, "not window-dressing." Most, however, were enthralled, seeming not to care whether Kennedy expected true brilliance or only the appearance of brilliance to mask baser political maneuvering. "Camelot," Wills wrote, "was the opium of the intellectuals."[3]

Another case in point: the family's celebrated preoccupation with athletic contests, which sparked a physical fitness boom. Yet despite his youthful appearance, President Kennedy seldom participated in strenuous sports. The effects of Addison's disease and a myriad of maladies were compounded by chronic back problems that sometimes forced him onto crutches. He limited himself to sailing, an occasional round of golf, throwing out the ceremonial first pitch of the baseball season, and therapeutic swims in the White House pool.[4] His brothers, particularly Robert, carried the Kennedy athletic banner.

Coming into His Own

Robert Kennedy crammed his weekends and family vacations with physical activities, many photographed or filmed for public consumption. None needed staging, for with the cameras on him or not, Robert exercised virtually every day, engaging in a remarkable variety of athletics. During the week he rode horses with his children just after dawn, played tennis on his home courts at noon or after work, spent an hour at handball in the Justice Department gym, and, more rarely, stole afternoons for golf at private clubs (and away from reporters' eyes, lest they think the Kennedys spent as much time at the game as Eisenhower). On vacations he camped and hiked in national forests, kayaked and canoed in river rapids, and skied every winter in Vermont or Colorado. He and brother Edward organized the fabled Kennedy touch football games, sometimes importing professional players to bolster their chances and add to the games' cachet. Footballs stayed near at hand for tossing with Robert's children or with colleagues in his office. He squeezed and massaged a football like some people manipulate worry beads. Even when not exercising, he was thinking about it.

One physical test Robert Kennedy faced, truly unique for an attorney general, originated in John Kennedy's casual allusion to a sixty-year-old presidential order requiring U.S. Marines to march fifty miles in twenty hours. When marine commandant David M. Shoup ordered marines to duplicate the feat, many civilians followed suit and a hiking craze took hold. To uphold family pride, Robert allowed the president to goad him into accepting the challenge. With one day's preparation and inappropriate shoes, the attorney general led four members of his staff and his dog Brumus on a fifty-mile forced march along the snow-covered Chesapeake and Ohio Canal towpath from Washington to Camp David. One by one his associates dropped out, Edwin Guthman being the last at the thirty-five-mile mark. With a *Life* magazine photographer charting their progress from a helicopter, Robert and Brumus trudged on to the finish. Before leaving Guthman, the attorney general knelt beside him and whispered, "You're lucky your brother isn't President of the United States."[5]

The New Frontier's luminescent social life centered on the White House, but its most prominent satellite was Robert's home on Chain Bridge Road in McLean. The sign on the front lawn warning "Trespassers Will Be Eaten," the menagerie, and the toys scattered about made clear to whom this domain belonged, but in the evening the large estate turned into an adults' playground. Ethel's posh parties brought out the Washington elite to enjoy the best food and liquor and to be part of a scene sure to be reported in the following day's newspapers. One frequent guest, Marian Schlesinger, then married to Arthur Schlesinger, Jr., remembered that Ethel "created a certain atmosphere of fun and games as it were, and everything was done on a lavish scale. It was like a great big party all the time, extravagant and excessive, too much of everything."[6] After-dinner entertainment might include such diversions as dancing to high-society bands, foot races, touch football, push-up contests, or Robert's favorite party games (charades and sardine), or guests might gather to watch the host arm wrestle with Georgi N. Bolshakov, the Soviet editor, interpreter, and KGB agent whom some guests called "Bobby's Russian." President Kennedy, who rarely went to Hickory Hill, asked that the frivolity be toned down after uninvited journalists noted how often fully clothed members of his administration tumbled into the swimming pool.[7] Fixing the blame for these highjinks became an insider's game that received serious treatment by some writers, as though it mattered.

Household routines grew more complicated with the added responsibilities of the master's official position and as the family grew. Keeping straight the family finances and household expenses became a problem. At one point Robert moved Carmine Bellino into the house with instructions to audit accounts and "to find out who was stealing what."[8] Ethel found it difficult to retain help and, by one account, exhausted thirty household workers in less than five years. She admitted the place was a "madhouse." Much of it was her own doing. Impetuously driven to outlandish pranks to amuse her children, Ethel once freed a greased pig in the dining room of the stately mansion.[9]

Hickory Hill also played a part in Robert's ongoing effort at self-improvement. Unable to match brother John's glib demeanor and facile management of facts and ideas, Robert never outgrew his insecurity over his presumed intellectual shortcomings. Just as he had extended himself to make the Harvard varsity, he disciplined himself to broaden his interests and to enhance his cultural sensitivities. Concerned about losing valuable minutes from his day, he listened to recordings of Shakespearean plays while shaving and turned learning into a social event, asking Arthur Schlesinger, Jr., to arrange monthly gatherings to hear lectures from noted authorities in various fields and to engage in lively discussion. The meeting place rotated, but the meetings began at Robert's house—thus the name, Hickory Hill Seminars.[10]

Riveted by discussions of complicated social dilemmas, Robert Kennedy began to see ideas as problem-solving instruments. Gradually, his views of himself and of the world around him were changing.

His personal habits changed little. He now took a cocktail before and a glass of wine with dinner. He discovered the pleasure of a good cigar and at informal gatherings in the family quarters following White House functions he joined the president and New Frontier cigar aficionados in clandestinely savoring the aromas and tastes of Partagas, Montecristos, or other fine Havana cigars, all, of course, officially boycotted by the Kennedy administration. Robert regularly received orders from a New York supplier of Uppman Petits, non-Cuban cigars favored by the president and smoked in public. He briefly tried smoking a pipe, but he distracted others, fussing with its lighting and relighting. Admiral Arleigh Burke, chief of Naval operations and an inveterate pipe smoker himself, admitted it was a bad habit, but he sent the attorney general some "equipment" (pipe cleaners and a tamper) so if he persisted it would be with the least adverse effects.[11]

Public speaking still posed a challenge. Kennedy's jitters, even when addressing small groups, surprised new assistants. Speaking extemporaneously, Robert fell prone to the distinctive Kennedy stammer shared by his brothers John (to a much lesser degree) and Edward (even more noticeably). Awkward pauses, faulty syntax, and a tendency to speak in fragments rather than whole sentences also punctuated his speech, habits that particularly annoyed older, well-educated listeners, including his own mother. The "continuing use of the sound 'uh,' such as 'and-uh,' 'that-uh,' 'would-uh,'" one elderly critic wrote to the attorney general, "detracts from the euphony of your remarks and many get the impression you are groping for thoughts, words—or both." Agreeing "completely," Robert promised to improve.[12] Speech lessons and hours of practice slowed the cadence of his formal remarks. The tradeoff was a somewhat mechanical style that left some listeners with the impression that he was stiff and humorless.

True, he lacked brother John's wit and sense of comic timing, as well as brother Edward's natural joviality. But Robert's correspondence and private quips revealed a dry wit often tinged with sarcasm. A South Carolina politician once admitted in a letter to Robert that, despite the attorney general's many "faults," he displayed a picture of him in his office. Happy to learn he was so "popular," Robert invited the politician to visit his office, with one caveat: "We eat little children on Tuesdays but almost any other day would be fine." And when a lawyer from the Anti-Trust Division once described a business run downhill by an incompetent son, Kennedy interjected: "That's one mistake our father never made—taking us into the business with him." But even with lines supplied by professional writers, including Bob Hope's, and with help from Ted Sorensen, who wrote clever parodies and supplied the president with one-liners, Robert never perfected a smooth comic delivery.[13]

Robert Kennedy found little to joke about when it came to money. Although uninterested in how money was accumulated, he avoided the appearance of profligacy, the most unforgivable of vices for a scion. Like his brother John, he seldom carried cash. For simple purchases he often borrowed from friends and assistants, to their annoyance. Ethel's brothers and some of Robert's school chums thought him a cheapskate, because while in college and into his late twenties he drove his father's used cars, sometimes wore old, tattered clothing, and rarely picked up the tab for anything.

Justice Department staff considered their boss a pennypincher. Indeed, he monitored office expenses closely, insisting, for example, that travel be conducted during nonbusiness hours. And scattered throughout his desk notes are probing questions and disbelieving reactions regarding everything from the costs of operating his government car and putting on private receptions to the hotel and airlines bills for himself and his staff and the entertainment expenses at Hickory Hill. He was quite generous, however, to White House and Justice Department employees at Christmas, handing out gifts to elevator operators, chauffeurs, telephone operators, messengers, and clerks. Angie Novello and Carmine Bellino kept the gift list and purchased and delivered the gifts. At the annual staff parties Kennedy typically gave out cuff links, earrings, or scotch whiskey.[14]

Exactly how generously Robert spent his own money and how much of it he gave to charity cannot be established with certainty. He donated all his writing royalties, the only source of income over which he had complete control, to carefully selected charities, among them St. Cecilia's Academy in Nashville. John Seigenthaler, who worked side-by-side with him on the writing and editing of *The Enemy Within,* had two sisters who were nuns there. Robert also helped establish a scholarship fund at Harvard for African American students from Fairfax, Virginia, and made other, equally modest (for someone of his reputed wealth), contributions to Milton Academy, the University of Virginia, the United Indian Ministry, Indian Missions, and the Boys Club.[15]

The blind trust established for Robert by his father and managed by brother-in-law Stephen Smith was subject to automatic deductions of varying amounts that went to the Joseph P. Kennedy, Jr., Foundation and other charitable causes selected by his father. Robert accepted such decisions without complaint. His fater controlled his financial position, like so much else in the first thirty-six years of his life.[16]

Taking Over for the Father

On 19 December 1961, Joseph P. Kennedy, then seventy-three years old, suffered a massive stroke. "As usual," Rose Kennedy recalled, her seventh child took charge of notifications, calling John and the other children to gather in Florida at their father's side.[17] Standing vigil at the hospital, Robert knew that the man who was his father had slipped away, now imprisoned within an unresponsive body.

Joseph Kennedy lived on for another eight years, long enough to grieve the violent deaths of his second and third sons and the humiliation of his fourth. He remained partially paralyzed and unable to speak except to say no, his still sharp mind compounding his resentment at depending entirely on others. Once, when he tried to stand and walk, he flailed at Robert with his cane when his son grabbed him to keep him from falling. Ignoring the blows, the ambassador's seventh child continued assisting his father, calmly assuring him, "That's what I'm here for, Dad. Just to give you a hand when you need it. You've done that for me all my life, so why don't I do the same for you now?"[18] Robert attended to his father's care, consulted with physicians, and arranged treatments. Yet, after a time, he and his brothers had to be reminded by their mother and sisters to call or visit their father.

Even if he saw his father less often, Robert telephoned him regularly to apprise him of political developments and to chat about family matters. To amuse him—and perhaps to elevate himself in the eyes of the former movie mogul—Robert once telephoned from his sister Patricia's Santa Monica house, where a large party was in progress, to boast that he sat next to Marilyn Monroe and Kim Novak at dinner and to have Monroe give a cheering message to his father. At family gatherings at Palm Beach or Hyannis Port, Robert often joined in his father's water therapy in the family pool and spent hours with him in quiet, one-sided conversation.[19]

One of Joseph Kennedy's last acts before his stroke was to insist, contrary to the recommendations of the president's advisors, that Edward run for John's vacated U.S. Senate seat. It could have been Robert's, if he had wanted it. After the 1960 election, John asked him if he would accept an appointment to fill the seat. "Never! The only way I'll go to the Senate," he told his brother, "is to run for it." The president-elect instead persuaded Governor Foster Furcolo to appoint Benjamin Smith, one of John's Harvard chums, to serve on an interim basis until a special election in 1962. Torbert Macdonald, another of John's acquaintances since youth, had expected the Kennedy endorsement for the seat. Macdonald said later that he did not receive the Kennedys' nod because "there was a prince and there was a court, and I was not part of it, by choice."[20]

The choice, however, was the father's. "Now it's Ted's turn," he announced. "Whatever he wants, I'm going to see he gets it." "Just as I would never have been Attorney General if it hadn't been for him," Robert said of his father, "he just felt that Teddy had worked . . . and sacrificed himself for the older brother and we had our positions and so . . . he should have the right to run." Twenty days after his thirtieth birthday, Edward Kennedy entered the special election to fill John Kennedy's vacated Senate seat. During the campaign he survived exposure of the news of his dismissal from Harvard his freshman year for cheating on a Spanish exam. A youthful indiscretion, the family said. "What I did was wrong," Edward admitted. "I have regretted it ever since." He disarmed the mock outrage of "a few cynical old pros," as he told his father, with "some old Irish stories that Grampa [Fitzgerald] used to tell." What pulled him through, however, was the Kennedy party apparatus. Fresh from wins in 1958 and 1960 and driven by Stephen Smith's experienced hand, it coasted to victory in 1962.[21]

By the time Edward's campaign got underway, their father was permanently disabled, leaving John and Robert to share the duties of Kennedy party strategist. Constrained by his position from taking too active a role in the campaign, the president issued carefully worded statements and avoided appearing to interfere. But, as Edward's biographer James M. Burns noted, John Kennedy could not avoid being "directly involved"; he asked Tip O'Neill to work with Democratic pols and smooth some ruffled feathers and sent Sorensen and other aides to help in the campaign. Knowing the importance of the race to their own political credibility, John and Robert nervously fretted over their brother's performance.[22]

Robert managed Edward's political image, aggressively stepping in when one of Edward's assistants described the first draft of a *Redbook* magazine article as "politically damaging in the extreme." The author of "What Makes Teddy Run?" intended to describe Edward as a "wealthy personable lightweight" trying to lay claim to the "honeymoon glow which his brother as President currently enjoys." Having learned at his father's side that journalists' words were neither inviolable nor immutable, Robert demanded that the author and editor correct certain "errors" and insisted that the article's tone be altered to cast Edward in a more favorable light. His six-page memorandum demanding specific revisions included suggestions for changing or deleting unflattering quotes taken from interviews of family friends. Concerned, for example, about Edward's playboy reputation, Robert wanted this sentence struck: "Ted loves his family but there are times when he likes being away from them." For his brother's edification, he listed examples of how Edward could avoid appearing to brag about his wealth and could defend himself against slanted views.[23] Robert's handling of

Redbook revealed a cynical regard for the press as well as a deft way with political imagery, both of which seemed to come naturally to Joseph Kennedy's third son.

In the closely watched Democratic primary Edward Kennedy swamped Edward McCormack, the nephew of House majority leader John McCormack, and in the general election he soundly defeated George Lodge, son of Henry Cabot Lodge, Jr. The success of the Kennedy party organization, the Kennedy brothers' youth and obvious ambition, and Edward's campaign theme ("From a great American family") all prompted writers to posit a "Kennedy dynasty" and the likelihood that Robert and Edward would, in turn, succeed John as president.

Public reactions to the proposition of a Kennedy dynasty took a generally negative slant. Before the 1962 Massachusetts election one comedian cracked, "If Teddy wins, Laos won't be the only country with three princes." A *New York Times* editorial described Edward's candidacy as "demeaning to the dignity of the Senate and the democratic process." Robert, however, was the focus of the most serious misgivings about a Kennedy dynasty, particularly among those left of center politically, among them novelist and social satirist Gore Vidal, who admired the president but despised the attorney general. Vidal could not forgive Robert for his former association with Joe McCarthy, for his tough campaign style, or for his various personal slights, real and imagined. Robert Kennedy, Vidal wrote in *Esquire,* not only lacked his brother's ease and charity but was "dangerously authoritarian-minded" and possessed a "simple-mindedness about human motives which may yet bring him down."[24]

Vidal and other critics aside, the president publicly stated that anyone who spoke of a dynasty implicitly embraced a system of succession, betraying a "failure to comprehend the democratic process in our country." Yet, he confided to Ben Bradlee, he found the idea of a Kennedy dynasty "not only legitimate, but fascinating." He even gave some thought to the consequences for himself. Paul "Red" Fay, the president's friend since *PT-109* days, remembered President Kennedy musing about what he might do after serving two terms, when he would have been only fifty-one years old. According to Fay, John speculated about serving in Congress, as John Quincy Adams had after leaving the White House. "Of course," he added, "when Bobby or Teddy becomes President, then I'd probably be most useful as Secretary of State." He paused, Fay recalled, before saying, "I'm just not quite sure that I would ever get adjusted to addressing Bobby or Teddy as 'Mr. President.' Let's not dwell too long on the prospect of taking orders from Lovable Bob."[25]

The dynasty stories annoyed Robert. They misrepresented the relationships within the family and minimized the differences between the brothers. As the "inside" Kennedy, or, as his first biographers described him, *The Brother Within,* Robert concentrated on advancing John's political interests and making his presidency an unqualified success. Any thoughts beyond that he quickly suppressed. His brother's willing instrument, Robert allowed himself to be used without regard for future consequences. When anything went wrong, "I take the hit," he often told Edwin Guthman. "Let them blame me, I'm never going to run for anything."[26]

Rather than elected office, Robert seemed destined to assume his invalid father's burden for preserving and perpetuating Kennedy family political interests, a role for which neither John nor Edward was suited. Taken up with their own responsibilities, both, to put it gently, were more self-absorbed than Robert, and such duties could not be entrusted to anyone outside the immediate family. Those eager to write books and articles with an inside slant on the Kennedys found Robert asserting more and more control over access to the family and to its secrets. After John's assassination, he would contour the historical records and images of the Kennedy presidency, but the responsibility began with managing the news media.

Readers accustomed to journalists taking an adversarial stance toward politicians, as many today do, would be struck by the social proximity of the Kennedy brothers to the major news reporters and opinion shapers and by the dexterity with which they managed and sometimes manipulated journalists. The president's close associations with many leading journalists were well known.[27] Less known at the time was the frequency of his brother's contacts with members of the news media.

Asked how he spent his first four months in office, Robert answered,

"For the most part, seeing newspaper people." He met with and spoke more often to journalists than to any other group outside government. Often beginning with breakfast meetings at Hickory Hill, occupying lunches in his private dining room at the Justice Department, ending in after-hours sessions in his office, and covering many hours in between, discussions with and briefings of journalists took up a significant portion of Robert Kennedy's working days. His contacts extended more deeply into the working press and involved closer social ties than did the president's.[28] "If a bomb had ever gone off at Hickory Hill on a summer weekend," NBC-TV correspondent Douglas Kiker estimated, "three-fourths of the most powerful print and broadcast journalists in America would have had to be replaced." The relationships between reporters and politicians, Kiker admitted, often were "incestuous," but he thought "the situation at Hickory Hill between Ethel, Bobby, and the press was extreme."[29]

Many of the elite of U.S. print and television journalism regarded themselves as friends of the Robert Kennedys. Among the closest were David Brinkley, coanchor with Chet Huntley of NBC-TV's national evening newscast, and influential syndicated newspaper columnists Joseph Alsop and Rowland Evans. Others included Sander Vanocur (NBC), Roger Mudd (CBS), Anne Chamberlin (*Life*), Art Buchwald (syndicated columnist), and Warren Rogers (*Look*). Amid Washington's insulated social world the upper echelons of the fourth estate and the leaders of the ruling party mingled in elegant black-tie formality, informal backyard cookouts, and intimate dinner parties; they shared, as seldom before or since, in shaping the country's sense of itself and its future. To be sure, even before the Kennedys came to power, some in the press had come to regard themselves as the fourth branch of government. However, an uncommon trust bound the newsmakers in the Kennedy administration to those who reported it.[30]

The Kennedys, as Benjamin Bradlee once observed, expected "110 percent from their friends, especially their friends in the press," and felt "cheated" by anything less. From time to time, Bradlee fell out of favor with John Kennedy without knowing why, although he was certain that he owed one stretch in "exile" to a critical article on the Kennedys' relations with the press.[31] The Kennedys cultivated their favorites in the press and used them to plant subtle, occasionally contradictory, messages. The president cagily played off *Time* (Hugh Sidey) against *Newsweek* (Bradlee), shrewdly exerted influence to get his versions of stories printed and unfavorable ones suppressed, and all the while kept journalists in his debt through casual social flattery. I. F. Stone, an experienced newsperson toughened by years of scratching away at pretentious political veneers, likened the climate in Washington to that of a reigning monarch's court.

Few reporters complained—at least initially. James Reston said the president "either overwhelmed you with decimal points or disarmed you with a smile and a wisecrack." Some in the press resented his use of the Secret Service to evade them, and they did not like him bending or ignoring old rules governing White House access. A few said he tended to "whine" about the fairness of the press coverage. Indeed, the president and the attorney general became extremely vexed over small slights and sometimes berated reporters and publishers about their treatment of their family and their administration.

Highly sensitive about security leaks, the Kennedys twice ordered the FBI to tap the telephones of reporters suspected of gaining information from unauthorized sources. The president himself may have been the source of one of the leaks, perhaps unwittingly divulging classified information to Bradlee. Robert had misgivings about Bradlee and apparently suspected the journalist of using his brother's friendship for professional advantage.[32]

Not until early 1963, however, did complaints surface of the Kennedys' "news management," which Arthur Krock (now alienated from the Kennedys) claimed they enforced "more cynically and more boldly than . . . any other previous administration." Accused of deliberate misstatements, intentional distortions, suppressing information, and controlling news sources by leaking information to selected journalists, the administration endured a brief congressional inquiry during March 1963, but nothing of substance came of it.[33]

Robert Kennedy treated journalists with a mixture of charm, candor, and calculation. In the pre-Watergate era of U.S. journalism most reporters were grateful for access to political figures and, if necessary, compromised professional standards to preserve that access. This truckle-down theory of political journalism led some journalists to prostrate themselves before the Kennedys. Hugh Sidey, *Time*'s White House correspondent, apologized profusely for his "grievous human failure" when a confidential memorandum expressing his candid (and uncomplimentary) assessments of the Kennedy administration was shown to the attorney general. The correspondent confessed the "error in my own heart," admitted that what he had done was a "gross violation of taste and decency," and begged Robert Kennedy's forgiveness.[34]

Some journalists ached to enter the Kennedy orbit, a few preferred to keep a safe distance, and others found themselves enticed in by Robert Kennedy, who deliberately ingratiated himself with several media figures. A loyal clutch of journalists kept him informed of breaking news stories, sent him advance copies of print material and previews of television and motion picture productions about the administration and the Kennedy family, and offered unsolicited opinions on important matters. In return, Robert was engagingly candid, but never totally honest with them. He stroked his favorites, regularly reminded them of his gratitude for their support, and thanked them, too, for the things they did *not* publish. "As we both know," the attorney general wrote to Marguerite "Maggie" Higgins of the *Herald Tribune,* "there have been many, many items over a period of years that you have been aware of which out of confidence you have never published nor, to my knowledge, mentioned to anyone else. For this, all of us are very grateful."[35] His deference to Higgins, one of the best-connected journalists of her time and an astute observer of foreign affairs, was due partly to the valuable observations she readily (and discreetly) shared with Robert over a span of several years and partly in compensation for the president's near-compulsive obsession with her criticisms and her inside slant, which sometimes preempted administration positions. "Who the hell cares who told Maggie?" National Security Advisor McGeorge Bundy once pleadingly asked the president.[36] The Kennedys cared. As with so many other things, they worked the press as a team.

The Limits of Kennedy Liberalism

Over the months, independent-minded reporters began assaying the administration's accomplishments, weighing them against the New Frontier's uncertain goals, and raising questions of substance versus style. The

Kennedys' youthful confidence and competency generated a sense of expectancy. Analysts wondered what they intended to do and when. The "Kennedy promise," as British journalist Henry Fairlie afterward labeled the phenomenon, was never quite fulfilled.[37] Fate intervened. The fault, however, lay with the Kennedys themselves.

Built not on ideology or a clearcut sense of where they wanted to lead the country, the Kennedys's ambition for office was personal. Moreover, the skills that served them so well in gaining election did not always adapt to a governing system that emphasized the president's responsibility for the brokering of competing interests. Further, the Kennedys entered office with no definite accumulation of legislative initiatives that one could confidently label the Kennedy program. As David Burner observed, the Kennedys "seemed to make sheer motion a program on its own," a phenomenon especially true in the early months. "Those were the days," Robert said later, "when we thought we were succeeding because of all the stories on how hard everybody was working."[38]

Pragmatic centrists in search of programs and policies to aid their hold on the presidency without disturbing the political status quo, the Kennedys accepted and adopted as their own those proposals that served this purpose. Thus, the New Frontier's legislative agenda largely embellished on programs advocated by activist-liberal Democrats in Congress during the late 1950s, among them the Peace Corps (Senator Hubert Humphrey of Minnesota), area redevelopment (Senator Paul Lucas of Illinois), civil rights (Senator Joe Clark of Pennsylvania and Congressman Emmanuel Cellar of New York), and federal aid to education (Senator Wayne Morse of Oregon). The Kennedys preferred to remain aloof from congressional maneuvering, and they dreaded defeat, hence their obvious reluctance to put their full weight and influence behind these proposals and their only moderate success in gaining passage of the programs they adopted as their own.[39]

Even more than parliamentary infighting, the Kennedys despised political labels. They especially did not like being called liberals. Ironically, the Kennedys' ultimate contributions to the advancement of liberal politics and policies partly won them their prominent place in contemporary history. But they were liberals when they came to office only to the extent that the middle ground, or the broad consensus of U.S. politics, was liberal.

The meaning of modern political liberalism differs depending on the context and timing of its use. Twentieth-century liberalism—to distinguish it from the more rigid nineteenth-century variety rooted in the earlier writings of John Locke and Adam Smith—is a malleable political philosophy. Over time, proponents have differed in the intensity of their support for the use of the state to assure individual freedoms, moral reformation, social equality, and economic stability. In one variant or another, liberalism reshaped the American polity in the twentieth century, imposing sweeping reforms during the Progressive, New Deal, and sixties eras.[40] On entering office the Kennedys found themselves in the trough between the second and third waves of modern liberal reform.

By 1961 the controversies over the liberal economic reforms of the New Deal had largely abated, with the acquiescence of the Republican Eisenhower administration. For the next few years, broad agreement—a liberal consensus, as British writer Godfrey Hodgson labeled it—characterized American politics. The road to consensus was not easily traveled. The absence of a legitimately contending U.S. socialist movement opened liberal activists to charges of socialist leanings or, worse, Communist sympathies. Thus obliged to oppose communism, liberals of the post–World War II years were attracted to vital center liberalism, named for Arthur Schlesinger, Jr.'s influential 1949 tract that stressed improving society with moderateness and gradualism, along the lines begun by Franklin Roosevelt's New Deal, and predicated on the assumption that the U.S. and Soviet systems were inherently incompatible. By the early 1960s centrist liberalism had taken hold. The Kennedys, like most Americans, assumed that U.S. capitalism, evidenced by the expansive growth of the consumer economy, had effectively reduced serious social conflict on the domestic level, which left the threat of Communism abroad as America's most urgent problem. The U.S. system, basically conservative and largely intolerant of radicalism, could indulge little more.[41]

Conventional wisdom at the time posited that political ideology based on class consciousness was alien to the American experiment. The Kennedys joined those who celebrated an "end to ideology" (more specifically, the decline of leftist, class-oriented politics) and who believed in U.S. capitalism as a force for revolutionary change throughout the world and the engine of social progress at home. Therefore, the central role for government, as John Kennedy told Yale University graduates in 1962, was to insure growth and productivity, manage the complex economy, and provide "technical answers—not political answers" to the sophisticated questions involved in "keeping a great economic machinery moving ahead."[42]

The Kennedys were perfectly sculpted to the consensus-based political milieu of their times. Comfortable with New Deal liberalism, they did not hesitate to step forward on economic matters and on questions of technical adjustments to the New Deal formula—to update New Deal commitments to Social Security, extend minimum wage coverage, aid depressed areas, and upgrade the federal housing program—for none involved serious controversy or significant risk. Demurring early on from taking a stand on moralistic matters that threatened to cause social divisions, neither Kennedy wanted to be thought of as an impassioned liberal. They distrusted the zealotry of those Robert called the "professional" or the "doctrinaire liberals," and they disdained systems of thought or ideologies for governing social affairs. Robert once said, "What my father said about businessmen applies to liberals. . . . They're sons of bitches."

Unwilling to be confined by ideology that stressed all-or-nothing results, Robert denounced those liberals who willingly sacrificed the whole loaf rather than compromise to get half. "An awful lot of them," he thought, "were in love with death."[43] John Kennedy was confident when he entered office that there would be no further need for "the great sort of 'passionate movements' which have stirred this country so often in the past." Time and circumstance, of course, proved him wrong. "The arrogance of power," as Samuel Huntington wrote of the early 1960s, eventually "was superseded by the arrogance of morality."[44]

The Kennedys were drawn at first only to liberalism's utilitarian aspects, to its emphasis on the application of technical expertise, rational thought, and a reasoned, consensus-laden approach to change. Old-line liberals derogated this as technocratic liberalism. Emerging "New Left" intellectuals—alienated by the governing elite's conceited notion that the United States should control the destiny of the world, estranged by the value system spawned from affluence, and critical of the Kennedys' acceptance of the primacy of large-scale business—called it corporate liberalism.

Kennedy liberalism was more a political strategy than a set of beliefs, less a scheme for social and economic change than an approach to resolve conflict and to maintain economic and social stability. In spite of its conservative goals, its method and style resonated with a creative vibrance (what one writer calls a "critical and experimental intelligence") based on the morally neutral logic of problem solving.[45] Except when their personal authority or pride was challenged, as in the war on crime and the steel crisis, the Kennedys often posed as impartial arbiters in social disputes. In time, they found themselves drawn into the key moral issue of the day—civil rights—but only under intense pressure. More typically, they inclined toward using government for incremental improvements in the quality of U.S. life and to correct imperfections in the market economy.

One such imperfection was slow economic growth and its offshoot of persistent unemployment, which lingered at recession levels throughout the first two years of the Kennedy presidency. To revive the economy liberal economists urged the president to apply the principles of the British economist John Maynard Keynes, who posited controlling the business cycle by coordinating the government's spending, taxing, and monetary policies. No longer new, the Keynesian theories were a staple of the liberal consensus, but no president had as yet formally acknowledged and consciously applied them. Such was the objective of a cadre of the country's leading economists, including Paul Samuelson of MIT, John Kenneth Galbraith of Harvard, and Walter Heller of the University of Minnesota. Heller became chair of Kennedy's Council of Economic Advisors. All three peppered the president and the attorney general with memoranda and studies asserting that aggregate demand would increase and the economy would revive if the government temporarily spent more than it collected in taxes.

President Kennedy studied their recommendations, faithfully recited the Keynesian lessons as though part of a new catechism, and ultimately called for across-the-board reductions in personal and corporate income taxes to stimulate consumption. Before his conversion, the president had to overcome his own fiscal conservatism (bred from a lifetime of his father's sermons), the opposition of his political advisors to unbalanced budgets, and his brother's advocacy of contrary policies.

Rather than tax cuts, Robert Kennedy intuitively favored tax increases. The patient tutelage of the president's economic advisors notwithstanding, the attorney general perceived taxation not as an exercise in macroeconomic theory but largely as an exercise in political psychology. In July 1961, for example, when a crisis over Berlin threatened to escalate into war with the Soviet Union and the president asked for and received an emergency increase of $3.5 billion in defense spending, Robert forcefully argued for a 1 percent across-the-board surtax on personal incomes to help pay for the spending increase and to bring home to the American people the importance of the crisis, giving everyone, he said, a chance to "feel involved" through common sacrifice. The president found his argument persuasive until Heller and Samuelson convinced him that a tax increase would slow recovery and that a $3.5 billion military spending increase would by itself prime the pump of the deflated economy. Robert took the setback in stride, admitting later that, from a fiscal and economic perspective, a tax increase in 1961 would have been a "bad mistake."[46]

Despite his brother's highly public conversion in a landmark speech on the myths and realities of economics, delivered in June 1962 at the Yale University commencement, Robert Kennedy remained unimpressed with Keynesian theories. The Yale speech, as historian Allen Matusow noted, summed up the premise of postwar U.S. liberalism that government was responsible for finding the "technical answers" to economic problems through a "dialogue" between government and business and through "the practical management of a modern economy."[47] John was more committed to finding those technical answers than Robert, whose economic views remained fundamentally conservative and whose interests in fiscal and economic policy were less well developed. Differences between the brothers became evident again in January 1963 when Robert challenged a proposal to seek across-the-board reductions in individual and corporate income taxes.[48] "Everybody thought that we'd been so committed to a tax cut that we had to go for it," he later recalled. "I just raised the point that I didn't think we had been so committed that it made it essential. It should be decided on its merits."[49] Less inclined to accept abstract arguments and unwilling to commit to ideas unless convinced of their efficacy, Robert, more often than his brother, allowed political intuition and his own feelings to guide him.

As for congressional relations, the Kennedys hesitated to challenge the seniority system and its manipulation by an entrenched coalition of conservative Republicans and southern Democrats who blocked many of the liberal-activist initiatives the Kennedys had adopted as their own. Partly explained by John Kennedy's razor-thin margin of electoral victory, their reluctance also sprang from John Kennedy's meager influence inside Congress. In fourteen years he had paid scant attention to its processes and had avoided taking on leadership roles or becoming entangled in partisan disputes. Although he reached the presidency without accruing many political debts, few members of Congress owed him. Democrats, after all, had not benefitted from Kennedy's coattails, losing twenty-two seats in the House during the 1960 election and sustaining numerical majorities in Congress mostly because of the party's strength in the South.

At Speaker Sam Rayburn's urging, the president joined a risky effort to reduce conservative influence by adding three members to the House Rules Committee, one of the places where conservatives, led by chair Howard Smith, a Virginia Democrat, quashed activist initiatives. Rather than getting pulled into Rayburn's fight, the Kennedys would have preferred "working something out" with Smith, as Robert put it. Acting on behalf of the president, the attorney general tried to negotiate a commitment from Smith to report out the bills the president "was really interested in." When Smith refused to deal, the Kennedys had no choice but to join Rayburn. Robert called the Rules Committee confrontation "a bitter fight between two old men" (Rayburn and Smith), but added that "once we got into it, it was important that we win it."[50] Rayburn engineered a 217 to 212 victory that required 22 Republican votes and the full exertion of the president's influence. Further expectations were inhibited by Sam Rayburn's death in 1962.

Summing up their position, Robert Kennedy observed "that here we had Sam Rayburn [during the Rules fight] and, therefore, the Texas delegation, that we had the maximum strength—the Democrats—and yet we won it by only a couple of votes. And how would we do on something that was far more controversial [after Rayburn's death], where we didn't have a Sam Rayburn, couldn't bring along a lot of these southerners that he could in this kind of a fight?" The *New York Times* and others, he continued, who criticized his brother for not using the art of persuasion to get more bills through Congress did not realize how difficult it was, "when the odds were much higher against us!"[51]

Historians differ over John Kennedy's effectiveness as a leader on domestic issues. The prevalent view is that his skill lay not in securing legislative initiatives but in crisis management. That view corresponds with the Kennedys' perception of the presidency itself and its limited powers. Each president, they knew, added his own flesh and sinew to the bare bones of constitutional authority. Presidential power, as political scientist Richard Neustadt had advised John Kennedy before he assumed the presidency, emanates from each president's ability "to engage in skilled interpersonal activity."[52] The Kennedys understood as much, but rather than use interpersonal skills to sort out diverse tensions within the political culture, formulate a position, and then persuade others to follow it, they saw their task as leading and manipulating the political elites and managing the government to make effective executive decisions.

John Kennedy, while enjoying varying degrees of success in maneuvering the political elite on foreign policy matters, was less effective than most of his successors at getting his top priority domestic programs through Congress. This shortcoming of the Kennedy administration—it cannot be called a failure, because they won more than they lost—largely attaches to the president's reluctance to become fully engaged and to his lack of enthusiasm for political compromise. It also reflects an inherent flaw in the Kennedy political style. Neither Kennedy paid much attention to the dynamics of the policy-making process that they sought to control. Coalition building, intense bargaining, attention to individual concerns, and detailed follow up fell beyond the Kennedy pale. As a result, as Tip O'Neill concluded, "for all of the sparkle, and for all of Jack's tremendous personal popularity, he never had much success in getting his programs through Congress."[53]

Robert and John Kennedy lacked an appreciation for what political scientist Barbara Kellerman labeled the "politics of leadership," meaning that neither liked to curry favor and both were uncomfortable with the give-and-take process necessary to educate and persuade the undecided, punish or reward the faithful, and convert or ignore opponents. They tried, instead, to remain aloof from congressional politics and to deal with them from afar. John Kennedy once told Ben Bradlee that he had too many important things to worry about to interrupt his day to call a congressman over a "coffee parity" or some other inconsequential matter.[54]

For dealing with Congress the Kennedys established an elaborate, unprecedentedly large and complex mechanism, anchored by a congressional liaison office headed by Lawrence F. O'Brien. A neophyte with no experience on Capitol Hill, O'Brien "didn't know one Congressman from another," Robert conceded. By the time he began to find his way around, many saw O'Brien as an unnecessary buffer between Congress and the president. Tip O'Neill, then a vital member of the House Rules Committee, judged O'Brien, his assistant Richard Donahue, and presidential assistant Ken O'Donnell (the "Irish Mafia," some members of Congress called them) ineffective, not necessarily due to any failures on their part but because members of Congress wanted and expected personal contact with the president and felt "froze out" by the president's surrogates. Part of the blame, O'Neill said, fell on Robert Kennedy, who he strongly suspected (and very likely correctly) had given instructions to keep O'Neill and other "gruff, old-fashioned" politicos away from the White House.[55]

Robert's palpable contempt for congressional lobbying and political brokering likely contributed to the modesty of his brother's record of accomplishments with Congress. Resentful of compromises and inclined more toward making and executing decisions than toward forging agreements, Robert balked at assuming the roles (except perhaps those of the hard bargainer or the threatening heavy) that would help his brother gain significant congressional support. Perhaps in recognition of "lovable Bob"'s limitations and perhaps as a reflection of the relatively low priority he placed on his domestic agenda, President Kennedy rarely called on his attorney general to lobby for legislative initiatives.

Consider the fate of the Kennedy administration's top priority, federal aid to education, which the president repeatedly declared was his "most important" legislative initiative. On 20 February 1961, the president proposed a comprehensive aid to education package, that included grants to elementary schools through colleges except private and parochial schools. Although a similar bill, introduced by Senator Wayne Morse of Oregon, had passed the Senate the year before, Kennedy's bill and his handling of it generated widespread antagonism and stoked opposition from a variety of sources, including the Catholic church, Negro leaders, and the omnipresent congressional conservative coalition. On the positive side, the president succeeded in facing down the hierarchy of the Catholic church, thus liberating himself from the charges raised during the campaign by Protestant clergy that he would not (or could not) act independently of his church. At the same time he succeeded in holding the votes of most Catholic members of Congress. But Kennedy failed with others, most notably an important member of the House Rules Committee, James P. Delaney, who refused to vote to release Kennedy's bill because it did not include federal aid to parochial schools. Delaney sided with five Republicans and two conservative Democrats to block the bill and kill its chances of passage.

Other factors, including the president's awkward management of racial politics, contributed to the defeat of the education bill. To appease southern Democrats the administration opposed efforts to withhold funds from racially segregated schools. That stance, of course, provoked opposition from Negro leaders, including Adam Clayton Powell, whose House Education and Labor Committee conducted hearings on the bill. Basically supportive of the measure, Powell wanted to amend it to prohibit giving federal funds to schools that practiced racial discrimination. Unwilling to confront Powell on the issue of funding segregated schools and reluctant to allow him to broker the House impasse, President Kennedy tried to mollify him with personal favors, then sloughed him off on the attorney general.[56]

Powell's subsequent telephone conversation with the president's brother manifests the Kennedys' aloofness toward congressional lobbying and their reluctance in the summer of 1961 to challenge southern Democrats over segregated schools. Powell told Kennedy that he would bring the education bill to the House floor (and bypass the Rules Committee), if the Kennedy administration issued an executive order stopping funds from going to segregated schools. "Impossible," Robert answered. But he promised Powell that the administration, through the Department of Health, Education, and Welfare and the Justice Department, would act in a "quiet manner" to insure that "funds would not go to institutions which were practicing unconstitutional acts." According to Kennedy's notes of their call, Powell "finally said that even though it would hurt him badly with members of his race" he would try to get the bill through. That day, as agreed, the Harlem congressman introduced a motion on the House floor to consider compromise school aid legislation. The House defeated it without debate.[57]

The *New York Times* called it a "stunning defeat for President Kennedy." The president's problem, according to one student of presidential leadership, was that he "did not understand the need to wheel and deal with passion" or "to convey empathy for what his followers felt about their own positions. Finally, he did not seem to know either intuitively or intellectually that politics cannot be played from a distance, nor by proxy when the chips are down."[58]

President Kennedy deftly rationalized setbacks on education and other measures, quoting Thomas Jefferson's admonition that "great innovations should not be forced on slender majorities." Believing it wiser to risk nothing at all than to risk something and lose, the Kennedys set forth proposals cautiously and avoided attaching themselves to losing efforts. As Irving Bernstein has shown, they succeeded far more often than they failed.[59] By exercising patience and taking a gradualist's perspective the Kennedys thought they would win in the long run. In the interim, they had only to avoid losing. Of course, they thought they would have more time.

The Steel Crisis

Rather than legislation, the Kennedy administration preferred, where possible, to use executive actions to deal with domestic issues.[60] Consider, for example, the Kennedys' handling of the steel crisis.

Late on the afternoon of 10 April 1962, Roger Blough, president of United States Steel, went to the Oval Office to inform the president that his company intended to raise its prices six dollars per ton across the board in direct defiance of the administration's wage-price guideposts. "You have made a terrible mistake," the president told Blough, because "you have double-crossed me." Only a few days earlier, the United Steelworkers of America, in compliance with the administration's guideposts and at the personal urging of Secretary of Labor Arthur Goldberg, had agreed to a new contract containing modest wage increases. The president had put his reputation with labor on the line in getting that agreement and an earlier one with the United Auto Workers. President Kennedy believed the steel price increases—more than four times the costs of the Steelworkers' settlement—threatened the country's balance of payments position, wholesale prices in general, and the president's hopes for containing inflation.[61] More to the point, the increases were a personal affront to the president's authority.

"They fucked us," the president told Arthur Goldberg, after Blough left the Oval Office. "And we've got to try to fuck them." He reached for the telephone to call Robert. No one knew the meaning of the president's directive better than the attorney general, who instantly mobilized the Justice Department.

Suspecting price collusion among the steel companies and anticipating an antitrust prosecution, Robert Kennedy called for data on steel prices and directed the FBI to prevent the destruction of relevant records, a task that J. Edgar Hoover opted to carry out in the middle of the night. Next, Robert directed Nicholas Katzenbach to prepare a legal memorandum regarding the powers of the federal government to prevent steel companies from increasing prices. Existing powers, Katzenbach reported, "seem to be inadequate" to prevent price increases.[62] Robert knew that other means were available.

The Kennedys retaliated across a broad front. They sent Clark Clifford into the enemy camp to talk the talk of power and to make clear to the steel executives what they risked when they bucked the power of the president. Secretary of Defense Robert McNamara denied U.S. Steel a multibillion dollar defense contract, awarding it instead to Lukens Steel, a small company that had not yet announced price increases. Besides an antitrust suit, the attorney general threatened that the government would reevaluate steel industry tax benefits, relax the "Buy American" Act with respect to foreign steel, and reduce import duties on foreign steel unless steel companies rolled the prices back.

The president denounced the increase as "a wholly unjustifiable and irresponsible defiance of the public interest." According to widely circulated reports, the president said, "My father once told me that all steelmen were sons of bitches, and I did not realize until now how right he was." Later, Robert hemmed and hawed a guarded response to questions about the accuracy of those remarks. (The quote was accurate enough, according to Ben Bradlee, except that John Kennedy didn't say, "sons of bitches," he said "pricks.")[63]

Within seventy-two hours U.S. Steel and five other companies rescinded their increases. At a celebratory dinner party for family and a few close friends, John Kennedy toasted his brother's achievements and alluded to fictive complaints from steel executives of FBI wiretaps and IRS audits of their tax returns. Robert, in mock seriousness, explained, "They were mean to my brother. They can't do that to my brother."[64]

The Kennedys could kid, but the big business world perceived their actions as heavy-handed and afterwards regarded them with suspicion, if not outright mistrust. The administration's overall policy toward business, however, is best characterized as "mild appeasement" (Arthur Schlesinger's phrase); the steel-price dispute was an anomaly. The Justice Department gave antitrust matters low priority and most of the Kennedys' decisions on regulatory and tax matters favored business.[65] Still, after the steel-price imbroglio, Robert Kennedy received no better than a tepid reception whenever he appeared before a gathering of businesspeople.

Omens of Social Change

The Kennedys also preferred executive to legislative action for responding to a number of social storm warnings. Contrary to the expectations of the liberal consensus, economic growth by the early 1960s had not eliminated social conflict and social inequities. Everything was not okay in America.[66] But almost everyone not directly affected, the Kennedys included, overlooked or ignored those problems. John's and Robert's formal educations and their father's postgraduate tutelage had conditioned them to look to international politics as the stairways to power. Their perspective was also hindered by being at the eye of the storm, where they may have remained less aware than most that, as Bob Dylan sang in 1963, "there's a battle outside and its ragin'" and "the times they are a-changin.'"

Although Michael Harrington's *The Other America* in 1962 warned of the systemic effects of deprivation in the midst of affluence, most Americans remained ignorant of the persistent and pervasive extent of poverty in the United States. While the affluent benefitted from the unprecedented economic expansion of the 1950s and 1960s, the leveling medium of television stirred poor peoples' rising expectations and simultaneously started reporting on the seething conditions in America's cities.

Robert Kennedy approached poverty through his special affinity for children. "He could communicate with a child," his friend Edwin Guthman wrote, "with a look or a touch on the head."[67] Before he became attorney general he gave little indication of the depth and intensity of those feelings, but in one of his earliest acts in office, even before the appearance of Harrington's influential treatise, Kennedy made juvenile delinquency a priority. He appointed his Milton roommate David Hackett to coordinate the Justice Department effort. A proven organizer and an energetic manager, Hackett had no special qualifications for the task, but he possessed two essential qualities for membership in the Kennedy innercircle, eagerness to learn and absolute loyalty.

Hackett knew from his years with Robert at Milton that Kennedy comprehended best those things he could feel and see for himself. He arranged for the attorney general to meet quietly with members of three New York City street gangs on their turf in Harlem. Struck by the despair and alienation that gripped these young people, Kennedy asked them what the government could do to help. Provide jobs and recreation facilities, they answered.[68] Kennedy directed Hackett to begin formulating a plan of government action. Meantime, Robert further immersed himself in the problems of inner-city poverty and juvenile delinquency, dropping in on several Washington, D. C., schools unannounced to talk with children and to see for himself the beleaguered conditions. Stunned by the dropout rate and the dilapidated facilities, he organized volunteers to raise private funds to assist struggling students and to build new playgrounds, swimming pools, and recreation centers. What, he wondered, lay at the root of the problem?

From among several competing theories, Kennedy and Hackett accepted those originating with sociologists at the University of Chicago who viewed juvenile delinquency as a rational response to the slum environment and to poverty caused by the larger social flaws and inequities. Two leading practitioners of the Chicago School were Columbia University professors of social work Lloyd Ohlin and Richard Cloward. Their 1960 book, *Delinquency and Opportunity,* blamed delinquency and poverty on inequities in the overarching social structures, not on poor people themselves. To combat juvenile delinquency they advocated giving the poor opportunities to participate in the social, cultural, and political structures. To test their theories they established Mobilization for Youth at the Henry Street Settlement House in New York City.

Persuaded by the Ohlin and Cloward model, Robert Kennedy (with a significant boost from sister Eunice) prevailed on his brother to establish the President's Commission on Juvenile Delinquency, which Robert chaired and which Hackett served as executive director. They gained enactment of the Juvenile Delinquency and Youth Offenses Control Act of 1961, which allocated $30 million for pilot programs modeled on the opportunity theory and involving the poor in the planning and implementation of local measures.[69] The programs soon encountered opposition from local politicians and social service agencies, who refused to surrender programmatic control, and from congressional skeptics, who blocked further expenditures in 1963. From these tentative beginnings, however, came the impetus for the subsequent enactments of the Johnson administration's War on Poverty.

Robert was genuinely moved by his experiences in the urban slums and by the enormity of the problem. "It's basically poverty," he later said in summing up what the juvenile delinquency initiative was about. "I just thought that things needed to be done for Negroes in education and employment and housing. And particularly for young people."[70]

He was certain that his brother intended to do something about poverty in a second term. White House aide Theodore Sorensen wrote that the president "started us working" on a "comprehensive, coordinated attack on poverty" more than a month before Dallas. Arthur Schlesinger, Jr., mentioned the president's "musing" on a "national assault on the cause of poverty." Walter Heller, chair of the Council of Economic Advisors, said he received a "green light" from President Kennedy in October 1963 to move ahead with a set of proposals on poverty to be introduced in 1964. Robert Kennedy, eager to believe his brother would have acted aggressively on poverty had he lived, found President Kennedy's notes from his last White House meeting, with the word "poverty" doodled repeatedly in the margins. Robert framed the piece of paper and hung it on his office wall.[71]

The Kennedys remained blind to most nuances of the social and political insurgency rising all around them. The campaign for women's rights, for example, a transcendent public issue of the 1960s, had only begun to penetrate the public conscious when the Kennedys came to office. President Kennedy, who appointed fewer women to high office than any of his three predecessors, appeared indifferent, if not insensitive to women's issues. The attorney general, for his part, sensed the onset of a new feminist activism in the early 1960s, but his blinkered perspective allowed him to see it only in terms of its political opportunities, not its social significance. He agreed with Stewart E. McClure, chief clerk of the Senate Committee on Labor and Public Welfare, that "women today have no great cause to work for" and "they are waiting to be called upon, to be mobilized." McClure proposed that the administration create a national organization to mobilize women as advocates for various international causes. Robert endorsed McClure's proposal and forwarded it to the president, noting, "Jack—I think this letter contains a very good idea and well worthwhile pursuing. Bobby."[72]

Robert Kennedy misread the feminist currents. Activists for women's causes wanted to mobilize the considerable energies of American women to combat and correct generations of injustices and discrimination at home, not abroad. They certainly had no interest in organizing a Kennedy-directed program of national service. Closer to the mark was Esther Peterson, assistant secretary of labor and director of the Women's

Bureau. On her recommendation, President Kennedy established a Commission on the Status of Women to reassess women's place in the economy, the family, and the legal system. Chaired by Eleanor Roosevelt, the commission issued a report in October 1963 recommending equal pay for comparable work, paid maternity leave, child care facilities for working mothers, and a broadening of the minimum wage and maximum hours provisions to include industries employing many women.

The commission's report, labeled an "invitation to action," led directly to an executive order banning sexual discrimination in the civil service. Earlier, Peterson had succeeded in gaining passage of the Equal Pay Act of 1963, which prohibited wage differentials because of sex but contained significant concessions on the issue of comparable pay. By the summer of 1963, when Betty Friedan's *Feminine Mystique* appeared advocating meaningful work outside the home as women's solution for "the problem that has no name," the Kennedy administration had taken tentative steps to restrict discrimination against women by employers and had given the women's movement a political starting point.[73]

Similarly, the Kennedys called U.S. youth to national service as the seeds of a new activist idealism were germinating. While many young people answered John Kennedy's "ask not" call and signed up for the Peace Corps, others preferred to organize themselves for change through their own devices. The Kennedys failed to notice a burgeoning youth movement profoundly critical of official indifference toward racial injustice and dedicated to something called "participatory democracy." In June 1962, forty-five quiet, neatly dressed young people met at an old United Auto Workers summer camp at Port Huron, Michigan, and founded Students for a Democratic Society (SDS). They approved a manifesto drafted by Tom Hayden, a twenty-two-year-old University of Michigan undergraduate. The Port Huron Statement denounced violence as a mechanism or catalyst for change, refused to declare itself either procommunist or anticommunist (but was "anti-anticommunist"), and decreed, "We would replace power rooted in possession, privilege, or circumstances by power and uniqueness rooted in love, reflectiveness, reason and creativity."[74]

The SDS became the vanguard of the New Left of the 1960s, replacing the older socialist-labor left in U.S. politics. Inspired, in part, by John Kennedy's call to service, the SDS, according to Todd Gitlin, one of its founding members, was "symbiotically connected with the very Kennedy liberalism it aimed to transcend." To Gitlin and other SDS leaders, the Kennedy administration—"that incarnation of normal politics"—provided a situation "tantalizing with the promise of change." SDS credited the Kennedys for ultimately recognizing that the domestic situation required an active response but labeled their performance "timid" and their actions "aggressive tokenism." At their 1963 convention the SDS called the Kennedy administration's responses to international and domestic crises "mediating, rationalizing, and managerial."[75]

In sum, reaction and caution characterized the Kennedy presidency on domestic issues. After nearly three years in office, John Kennedy knew that his record of achievement in domestic affairs was marginal. To be successful, he told Theodore White, he had to assert leadership with Congress. His relationship with Congress, White said, "really bothered him." Perhaps the lack of a clear mandate stifled creativity and innovation, but the president worried, he said, about taking on the most difficult issues for fear of "dividing the country." In assessing the administration in January 1963, Walter Lippman acknowledged that although President Kennedy had "some legislative successes," his administration "has not yet been able to win for itself a general understanding of its purposes." While "very popular," the president, according to Lippman, "has not yet won over the minds of the people. This may be because he has not yet conquered their hearts by opening his own." Journalists James Reston and Tom Wicker and other observers noted the hesitancy and the conflict between what the president promised and what he delivered, the enormous difference between what the Kennedy people said in public and what they said in private.[76]

No one, of course, can know what might have been. Given more time, some historians have argued, the Kennedys would have seen through Congress the same consequential initiatives passed during Lyndon Johnson's presidency. President Kennedy, according to Arthur Schlesinger, Jr., expected that Congress "would begin to accustom itself to unfamiliar ideas" and eventually, after modification, would pass his bills. Schlesinger also noted that congressional leaders of both parties believed the tax-reduction and civil rights proposals would have been adopted under either president. Most agreed with the leading policy analyst who discerned "considerable progress" during the third year of the Kennedy presidency, which "suggests strongly that most of what happened would have happened—more slowly, perhaps, but ultimately—if Kennedy had lived." Historian James N. Giglio cautiously concedes that the tax cut and the civil rights bills "probably" would have passed had the president lived, but notes that major proposals such as Medicare and aid for education were in limbo, bottled up in committees.[77]

Bitter toward James Reston and other Washington reporters who criticized his brother's record with Congress, Robert Kennedy felt they never gave him enough credit for his successes and ignored or underplayed his popularity with the public.[78] President Kennedy, however, was far from satisfied with his own record. In November 1963 he confided to Theodore Sorensen his frustration and annoyance at newspapers' insistence on ballyhooing the prevalence of "stalemate" and "deadlock." At the same time, he admitted to Tip O'Neill, Richard Bolling, and other members of the House, "The train is off the track." "We can't get anything through Congress. What's going on here," he asked, "and how can we straighten things out?"[79]

A cross-over year for the women's rights movement, for SDS and the New Left, and for the civil rights movement, 1963 was a year of social turmoil in which the evidence of later trends and events appeared.[80] As the voices of outrage and moral fervor began to penetrate the White House, Robert Kennedy heard them first.

CHAPTER 11

The Cauldron of Civil Rights

ALL THE WHILE Robert Kennedy sought out the enemies within and campaigned for his brother's election, the ground beneath America's crusty racial strata was shifting. For decades the civil rights movement, led by the NAACP and its counsel, Thurgood Marshall, had concentrated on removing the legal barriers to segregation and reversing the doctrine of "separate but equal" in the Supreme Court's ruling in *Plessy v. Ferguson,* 163 U.S. 537 (1896), which had followed the federal government's abandonment of Reconstruction in 1877 and the Court's decision to allow the states to interpret the civil rights provisions of the Fourteenth Amendment. The *Plessy* ruling had permitted the South to establish a system of laws and practices, known collectively as Jim Crow, segregating "persons of color" from the "whites only" prerogatives in the South. Many southern jurisdictions restricted the personal conduct of blacks, setting curfews, making miscegenation a felony offense, arresting black males for looking at white women, requiring blacks to yield the sidewalks to whites. The impossibility that blacks were the equals of whites was a point often enforced by terrorism and mob rule.

The Supreme Court reversed *Plessy* in the momentous and unanimous 1954 decision in *Brown v. Board of Education Topeka,* 347 U.S. 483.

Southern segregationists promised "massive resistance" in defiance of the Court and any attempt at ending U.S. apartheid. Civil rights leaders countered by directly confronting Jim Crow and publicly disobeying the "white only" restrictions. Unless those restrictions were removed, civil rights leaders warned, African Americans might never escape second-class citizenship and gain equal rights. The question, of course, was whether the federal government would extend its authority into southern communities to defend equal rights.[1]

When they entered office in 1961 neither Kennedy could see beyond the civil rights movement's legal and political aspects to its moral implications and social manifestations. John Kennedy was determined to go down in history as a "great President," but, as he made clear in an early discussion with historian David Donald, it did not occur to him that greatness could be found in taking Lincolnesque steps to intervene in the area of civil rights.[2]

An emotional and cultural gulf separated John and Robert Kennedy from the civil rights struggle, as it separated them from other mass political movements. John Kennedy viewed racial discrimination as "nonsense" and "irrational," but he had no interest in discussing the issue or in setting long-term priorities. His inaugural address contained no mention of civil rights (and barely mentioned domestic issues at all). He invited none of the prominent civil rights leaders to the inaugural, nor did he ask them to make recommendations for the new administration. The president's goal, Harris Wofford observed, was to keep his "civil rights constituency" from becoming "too unhappy." Beyond that he had no clear-cut intentions.[3]

Secretary of Integration

As for Robert Kennedy, most of his life he had responded to individual instances of discrimination with "impetuous decency" (Arthur Schlesinger's apt phrase), but he admitted that he "had not stayed awake nights worrying about civil rights" before becoming attorney general.[4] Up to this point in their political partnership Robert had little to say or to worry about as far as substantive issues were concerned, having left position statements to his brother and selected advisors. Civil rights—the defining issue of the 1960s—became a different matter. Within a few months he realized that it was too important to be left to others and even too critical to be left entirely in his brother's cool, pragmatic hands.

Like most white Americans reared in the North, Robert Kennedy saw civil rights as primarily a southern problem. Even after living in Virginia for more than a decade, he confessed in 1961 to lacking "a sense of Southern history" and its racist structure.[5] His assistant John Seigenthaler, a Tennessee native who became intimately involved in the Justice Department's management of civil rights crises, felt certain that Kennedy knew at the time that "what went on was wrong," but the rage, frustration, and trauma of the black experience remained beyond his grasp.[6] "At that time," civil rights attorney Marian Wright Edelman observed, "Kennedy was not attuned to what was going on in the black community. He really did not have the sense of outrage that eventually he did learn to experience in going to Mississippi, in going to California, in going out to Indian reservations."[7]

The enormity of events and the sheer weight of his duties caused a remarkable transformation. By the spring of 1963 Robert Kennedy had become the staunchest advocate for civil rights among the president's close advisors, prodding his brother into declaiming the moral consequences of racial discrimination and into denouncing the inequities African Americans faced everywhere in the United States. This path of personal discovery was complicated by conflicts with the Kennedys' desires to guide the country gradually toward racial tolerance without disrupting the fragile political equilibrium that put them in power.

Americans born since 1961 often have difficulty comprehending how much has changed in the United States since Robert Kennedy first stepped into the office of attorney general. To understand the attitude of the U.S. establishment toward the issue of race at the beginning of the 1960s, "requires a real leap of imagination, a willed immersion in the mind of another time."[8]

The Kennedys resembled most white northern Democratic politicians of their era. In deference to their urban black constituents they publicly expressed their personal disdain for southern de jure racial practices, used personal, often symbolic, gestures to demonstrate that they were not themselves bigoted, but generally did little to combat de facto discrimination in the North. Civil rights leaders derided this practice as "tokenism." But at a time when many politicians outside the South refused to declare themselves on the matter of racial segregation, tokenism was a positive indicator of a person's leanings, a means by which the Kennedys and others could express their readiness to accept full racial equality. For example, the president refused to speak before segregated audiences, pressured Washington-area restaurants to serve black African diplomats (but not African Americans), and, with the attorney general, urged the integration of the Washington Redskins professional football team. Both Kennedys resigned from segregated clubs, the president from the Cosmos Club and the attorney general, after a six-month attempt to convince the board to admit blacks, from the Metropolitan Club. Forty important positions in the administration went to black appointees, including James Benton Parsons, the first black named a federal judge; Thurgood Marshall, appointed to the federal Court of Appeals; Louis Martin, tapped for the Democratic National Committee; and Robert Weaver, former president of the NAACP, chosen to head the Federal Housing and Home Finance Agency. Weaver, the Kennedys' designee for secretary of the stillborn Department of Urban Affairs, would have been the first African American to attain cabinet rank. Also, Robert Kennedy advocated Judge William H. Hastie for Supreme Court justice until dissuaded by Chief Justice Earl Warren, who described the African American as a "judicial conservative."[9]

Limited to token gestures, the Kennedys often seemed less noble in action than in intention. But even their good intentions were not widely known until public opinion on the civil rights movement became favorable and presidential biographers and Robert himself sought to put a more favorable spin on the Kennedy administration's record.

Robert's contacts with blacks were limited and formal. He was, however, particularly fond of Louis Martin, his honorary "brother," with whom he was able to joke and to talk candidly about political issues. His relationship with most other blacks, however, was much less cordial. On first meeting him most black politicians and civil rights leaders thought the president's brother arrogant, abrupt, and dismissive. By contrast, black leaders felt the president listened attentively to their requests for legislation and "absolutely charmed" them, said Roy Wilkins, as he turned them down.[10]

Unable to sense the moral urgency of civil rights and distracted by the calculus of political power, the Kennedys could not see beyond the South's prominent contributions to the win in 1960.[11] To gain reelection in 1964 they believed they had to sustain their hold on Texas and perhaps four or five other southern states. Inside Congress, moreover, southerners controlled most of the important committees and stood as imposing barriers to the few with temerity enough to suggest using federal legislation to challenge U.S. apartheid, at the same time posing the constant threat of retaliation against other, unrelated initiatives.

Over the years, moreover, both Kennedys had developed close ties with southern politicians. "All the southerners," Robert Kennedy exaggerated, "were very much in favor of my being Attorney General." Through his investigations of union corruption he developed particularly cordial relations with segregationist senators John McClellan of Arkansas, Sam Ervin of North Carolina, Olin Johnston of South Carolina, and James Eastland of Mississippi. Kennedy was especially respectful and deferential toward Eastland, the powerful chair of the Senate Judiciary Committee, who, he said, provided "very helpful" advice, always made it clear where he stood, and kept his word. "I found it much more pleasant to deal with him than many of the so-called liberals" in Congress, Kennedy later recalled.[12]

Finally, consider that during these times white advocacy of civil rights was confined to a relatively small group of clergy, labor leaders, students, and political liberals, from whom the Kennedys, attached to the realities of power politics and obsessed with toughness as a measure of political mettle, tended to be personally and politically estranged.

America's remembrance of the civil rights revolution, as memorialized in songs, films, texts, and the sometimes hazy recollections of participants, places the Kennedy brothers and Reverend Martin Luther King, Jr., at the nexus of change, joined by martyrdom to a common purpose. In reality they seldom agreed on the means, pace, or direction of change. In the years since, historians have tended either to defend the Kennedys by rationalizing those differences or to criticize them for their relatively detached performance, particularly when compared to King's compassionate leadership and moral devotion to the cause of equal rights.[13] Differing roles, perspectives, and moral intensities notwithstanding, the Kennedys and King were drawn inevitably into the same political-philosophical orbit, for they all respected the rule of law and they all wanted American life to conform more closely to its founders' ideals.

Martin Luther King, Jr., rose to national prominence at twenty-six, the minister of the Dexter Avenue Baptist Church in Montgomery, Alabama. His eloquent and inspiring rhetoric during the 1955 Montgomery Bus Boycott vaulted him into the cochairmanship of the Southern Christian Leadership Conference and into spiritual leadership of the direct-action phase of the civil rights movement. Of their efforts to change segregationist laws and policies across the South, King said, "If we are wrong, the Supreme Court of this nation is wrong. If we are wrong—God Almighty is wrong." The movement, he said, was prepared "to work and fight until justice runs down like water, and righteousness like a mighty stream!" They would accomplish all that, he told his followers, without violence, and "there will be nobody among us who will stand up and defy the Constitution of this nation," for "first and foremost, we are American citizens—and we are determined to apply our citizenship—to the fullness of its means."[14] On those grounds the Kennedys and King ultimately found common cause.

At first, however, King made the Kennedys wary. Worried that he was an unpredictable firebrand and a publicity hound, Robert Kennedy did not invite him to an introductory meeting with civil rights leaders in his office on 6 March 1961. Feeling snubbed, King requested a private meeting with John Kennedy, who declined, pleading a pressing schedule on foreign policy matters.[15] Before allowing King to meet his brother, Robert wanted to size him up. Louis Martin arranged a secret luncheon meeting in a private dining room at the Mayflower Hotel. King impressed Kennedy and Burke Marshall with his quiet, thoughtful, self-effacing manner and won them over when he endorsed the Justice Department's voting rights plan and said he understood the need to conceal the department's role in facilitating voter registration drives. Reassured, the Kennedy people took King by the White House, where by prior arrangement the president chanced to have a few free moments to greet him. Before parting that day Robert Kennedy wrote down two telephone numbers and handed them to King. "Any hour of the day or night," he said, "you call."[16]

As King's methods of nonviolent passive resistance gained acceptance and the civil rights movement gained momentum in early 1961, the Kennedys looked on with guarded optimism, hopeful for gradual change yet fearful of explosive confrontations. A year earlier the Student Non-Violent Coordinating Committee (SNCC, pronounced "Snick") began sit-ins at southern lunch counters and hundreds of other segregated facilities across the South. However, except for the Court's vanguard decisions and the largely symbolic gains of the Civil Rights Acts of 1957 and 1960, the civil rights movement had not yet penetrated the consciences of the leadership in the legislative and executive branches of the federal government.

With John Kennedy's election, King and other civil rights advocates had reason to believe that might soon change. During the campaign Kennedy had voiced support for the "maximum" civil rights plank in the Democratic platform, supported the use of federal action (but no troops) to speed school desegregation, comforted Coretta Scott King when her husband was summarily jailed, and pledged to integrate federally assisted housing with "a stroke of the presidential pen."[17] But during the campaign John Kennedy walked what one historian called a "slippery ledge," mollifying the white Democratic South by criticizing Eisenhower's use of federal troops in Little Rock in 1957 and taking moderate positions on civil rights issues, a choice Southern politicians interpreted as born only of political necessity.[18]

Nevertheless, King appealed to the president-elect in an open letter outlining a program for "Equality Now." Calling for "new thinking" in a "new era," he urged the Kennedys to use the power of the presidency to transform America by eliminating racial discrimination through legislative action, moral persuasion, and executive order. "A truly decisive President," King wrote, "would work passionately and unrelentingly to change these shameful conditions" by bringing the states into compliance with the Fourteenth Amendment and by insuring that citizens not be denied the right to vote because of race. He reminded Kennedy, too, that the president's "own personal conduct influences and educates" and that through "moral persuasion" he can set an example easily understood and followed. If he chose to—as Lincoln did with the Emancipation Proclamation—the president could use an executive order to "give segregation its death blow." History, King concluded, thrust upon this administration "an indescribably important destiny" to complete a "process of democratization which our nation has taken far too long to develop."[19]

To coordinate the federal response, King recommended the appointment of a "Secretary of Integration," someone "free from partisan political obligations" to accomplish the "rapid and complete solution to the problem of racial equality."[20] King probably had Harris Wofford in mind for the position. An attorney, law school professor, and advocate of Gandhian passive resistance and civil disobedience against Jim Crow laws, Wofford was friendly with King and respected by other leaders of the movement. The coordinator of civil rights in the 1960 Kennedy campaign and coauthor of the civil rights plank in the Democratic platform, Wofford was the man whom John Kennedy once commanded, "Now in five minutes tick off the ten things a President ought to do to clean up this Goddamn civil rights mess." In short, he was the most likely person to serve the administration as point man on civil rights as head of the Civil Rights Division in the Justice Department.[21] That he was not selected for the position testifies to the Kennedys' cautious, legalistic approach to civil rights and at the same time reflects their conception of themselves as stewards of a government that had to serve their interests first, not those of others.

Robert Kennedy said he was "reluctant" to appoint Wofford "because he was so committed on civil rights emotionally" and "was rather in some areas a slight madman." Instead, the Kennedys wanted a "tough lawyer" who could "look at things objectively" and be "neutral," rather than act as an "advocate." When assessing a person's qualification for political appointment, Robert Kennedy considered ideology and past associations as handicaps.[22] Besides, Wofford's acts of independence during the campaign were fresh in the minds of Kennedy and his first deputy, Byron White, a conservative on racial matters who did not personally approve of Wofford. Further, J. Edgar Hoover had given the Kennedys an inaccurate report insinuating that Wofford had Communist sympathies and connecting him to a New York lawyer named Stanley Levison, whom the FBI suspected of being a Communist.[23] Whatever else, Robert Kennedy did not want an activist in his department telling him what to do.

Kennedy "finally settled," he said, on Burke Marshall, a brilliant antitrust specialist and a colleague of Wofford's in the highly influential Washington law firm of Covington and Burling. Wofford and Byron White, who had known Marshall at Yale Law School, both recommended him. Marshall had no connections or friendships within the civil rights movement, hated small talk, and was given to caution, patience, and precision, all assets prized by the attorney general. Marshall soon earned Robert Kennedy's trust over civil rights matters as completely as had Walter Sheridan, with a similar taciturn and circumspect demeanor, on organized crime.[24]

Nearly all of the Justice Department's civil rights team had Ivy League educations or connections. Several were born in the South. Besides Marshall, the team included Ramsey Clark (Texas), Louis Oberdorfer (Alabama-born graduate of Yale Law), White (Yale Law), Nicholas Katzenbach (Princeton), Archibald Cox (Harvard Law professor), John Douglas (Yale grad and a Rhodes Scholar), William Orrick (Yale), John Seigenthaler (Tennessee and a Nieman Fellow at Harvard), and John Doar (Princeton and a Republican holdover whose courage and skill as an arbitrator garnered widespread respect). More important than birthplace or alma mater was their common preference, either shared with Robert Kennedy or derived from his leadership, for negotiation and settlement over litigation, complex alterations of existing laws and, above all, provocative confrontations. Reasonable men—gentlemen—could always work things out.[25]

This group—often supplemented by Robert Kennedy with like-minded friends appointed as consultants and special trouble-shooters—functioned as the Kennedy administration's civil rights crisis management team. Adept at neither policy formulation nor innovations for expanding racial equality, they spent comparatively little time on proactive strategies. Their energies went instead into reacting to situations created by others, conjuring clever solutions for containing trouble, negotiating compromises, and placating truculent actors on either side.

Called to action when racial confrontations threatened civil strife, they always tried first to stabilize the situation. With his reverence for order and his fear of alienating the white southern power structure, Robert Kennedy frequently reminded his staff that the use (or even the threat) of federal force had always to be the last resort.[26] Their long-term goal, in concert with President Kennedy's overarching concern for America's image abroad, was to preserve law and order.

The attorney general never became the "secretary of integration" in the sense that King hoped, but he did become the administration's top man on civil rights matters. In March 1961 White House assistant Richard Goodwin sensed an imminent move in that direction when the attorney general complained to him that "too many people are getting involved in this thing [civil rights]. We have to decide whether we are going to have an administration position and what it's going to be."[27] In fact, the administration did have a fairly coherent and remarkably effective (albeit virtually secret) policy position built around recommendations submitted by Harris Wofford. Robert Kennedy went along with that position for a brief time before substituting one of his own.

Wofford, at John Kennedy's request, had worked out a civil rights strategy for 1961 and submitted it in a lengthy memorandum on 30 December 1960. It went unanswered until the first week of February, when two members of the Civil Rights Commission, chair John Hannah and Father Theodore Hesburgh of Notre Dame, met with the president. Among other things, they recommended that Kennedy appoint a White House assistant on civil rights. They were stunned when the president said he had already selected Wofford for the job, for only minutes before meeting with the president, Wofford had told them he had not yet received an assignment. Summoned to the White House, Wofford was unceremoniously sworn in as special counsel to the president on civil rights and rapidly briefed by the president, who told him the strategy for 1961, taken straight from Wofford's memorandum: "minimum civil rights legislation" (which could not be passed anyway) and "maximum executive action." "You're the expert," the president told him. "Get going."[28]

Intent on kindling in the Kennedy administration a genuine

commitment on civil rights, Wofford poured forth recommendations and initiated actions that went well beyond those taken by previous administrations but still fell short of the expectations of civil rights leaders. One such initiative created a Subcabinet Group on Civil Rights, chaired at first by cabinet secretary Fred Dutton, then turned over to Wofford. Comprised of key deputies from the executive departments (Burke Marshall represented the attorney general), it proposed "to survey civil rights aspects of public programs" within the agencies and "coordinate them on a government wide basis." That included coordinating the desegregation of federal facilities, which led Secretary of Interior Morris Udall to quietly desegregate all national parks and Robert Kennedy to direct a "thorough integration" of all Justice Department offices.[29]

Wofford's subcabinet group was also instructed to increase minority hiring, an objective set by the president when he noticed an absence of black faces in the Coast Guard honor guard at his inaugural parade. The president directed each cabinet member to survey the racial balance in his department and charged the subcabinet group with monitoring results. Although blacks constituted 13 percent of federal employees, few held upper-level positions. Only 15 out of 3,674 foreign service officers in the State Department and only 10 out of 955 lawyers in the Justice Department were black. Thus in April 1961 Wofford's group launched the government's first affirmative action program, forging an agenda to counter racial discrimination and to employ minorities in federal agencies. "No one," the group advised, "should be employed just because he is a member of a minority group" and "all persons appointed must be well qualified," but agencies were urged "to compensate for academic deficiencies" among minorities. Each agency was required to appoint one full-time assistant on civil rights, to submit regular reports on the recruitment of blacks, to employ blacks in "front offices," to recognize department officers who took "effective affirmative action," and to report progress and information to the "Negro and minority group press."[30]

The last requirement is revealing. With public opinion running against the civil rights movement, the Kennedy administration did not trumpet its efforts before the mainstream (white) press. Indeed, when white reporters got wind of Wofford's subcabinet group, Pierre Salinger, the president's press secretary, who knew only enough about Wofford's activities to see disaster looming, steered them away. Required to explain himself, Wofford, knowing he had gone beyond the president's personal comfort zone on this issue, responded with a memorandum promising Salinger that he "would seek no publicity" for his work "until it had some results to show."[31] Wofford was literally forced to apologize to the other White House advisors, as Taylor Branch described it, for being involved in an area that was "too prosaic, too small and quirkishly human, for the president's attention."[32]

All the same, Robert Kennedy had an earnest interest in affirmative action and (with the notable exception of the FBI) obtained solid results within his own department. "Get me a study of how many Negroes are working here," he directed Seigenthaler soon after settling into office. Told there were only ten black lawyers in the department, Kennedy wrote to law school deans around the country requesting they recommend their best black graduates, but stressing that "ability is the primary consideration" for appointment. In two years he added ninety black attorneys to his staff. Still, the attorney general was reluctant to link his efforts to those of Wofford's, declining to address the subcabinet group, which, in effect, would place his imprimatur on their activities.[33]

Another of Wofford's recommendations stoked Robert Kennedy's still-seething resentment of Lyndon Johnson. On 6 March 1961 the president signed Executive Order 10925 establishing the President's Committee on Equal Employment Opportunities (PCEEO), naming Vice-President Johnson as chair and the attorney general as a member. Although on the surface Kennedy's PCEEO resembled a committee chaired by Richard Nixon during Eisenhower's presidency, the Kennedys in this and every instance were determined to go Eisenhower one better. Indeed, the Kennedys' most important yardstick on civil rights, at least for their first two years in office (and afterward for many Kennedy biographers), was to draw direct comparisons, whether appropriate or not, between their efforts and Eisenhower's.

The PCEEO had an ambitious and unattainable goal: "to permanently remove every trace of discrimination" from government employment and from work performed for the government by contractors. To abate discriminatory hiring (and to outdo Eisenhower), President

Kennedy directed that "federal money should not be spent in any way which encourages discrimination." As a first step the PCEEO surveyed government contractors and discovered that 25,000 of the 35,000 companies doing business with the government employed no blacks.[34] Although empowered to do so, Johnson's committee held no hearings, terminated no contracts, and imposed no penalties for giving false information. PCEEO's most publicized effort was Plans for Progress, conceived by Robert Troutman, Jr., a Georgian and a school chum of Joe Kennedy, Jr. Its goal was to gain voluntary pledges from private contractors to hire more blacks, but its press releases exaggerated statistical gains, and an NAACP official labeled the program "one of the great phonies." One report indicated that blacks made greater employment gains in companies not enrolled in the program. The president, according to Robert Kennedy; blamed Johnson for the errors and was so embarrassed that he "almost had a fit."[35]

Nearly everything about the PCEEO's performance irked Robert Kennedy. To begin, he found it "not very well run or operated," he said. Kennedy dismissed Hobart Taylor, the vice-president's handpicked executive vice-chair, as "ineffective."[36] A black Detroit lawyer born in Texas, Taylor helped draft the executive order establishing the PCEEO and claimed to have coined the phrase "affirmative action," used there for the first time in an official government directive.[37] Still, Robert Kennedy felt "contempt" for Taylor's passive approach and said he behaved like an "Uncle Tom." Lyndon Johnson came in for even greater criticism for failing to give the PCEEO direction and for using it as a public relations vehicle. Wofford described the attorney general at PCEEO meetings as "not very respectful" of the vice-president; sometimes he would be "quiet, sullen, and sulk."[38]

Other times Kennedy made a deliberate nuisance of himself at the meetings, engaging in what he called "sharp disputes" with Johnson over the minority recruitment records of various agencies, particularly the National Aeronautics and Space Administration, headed by another Johnson protege, James E. Webb, whom Kennedy dressed down in front of the committee. He had no compunctions about openly confronting the vice-president, for, as he said in 1964, "I was a very big shot during that period of time." To Robert it was a straightforward matter.

The president wanted more minorities hired. The chair of PCEEO, therefore, must see to it that every agency director complied. Those who did not comply could expect to be called on the carpet. Robert openly criticized Johnson, he said later, to convey a message from his brother, who once told him, "That man can't run this Committee. Can you think of anything more deplorable than him trying to run the United States? That's why he can't ever be President of the United States."[39]

Only a small number of employers voluntarily accepted desegregation in the workplace, but the PCEEO demonstrated that gains could be made and that education was possible.[40] Robert Kennedy's critical judgments of the committee must therefore be considered in light of his intense personal dislike of Johnson, his impatience with anyone in the administration who did not carry out his brother's directives with vigor and enthusiasm, and his determination to himself control the administration's civil rights policies.

Another of Wofford's recommendations called for an executive order desegregating federal housing, which John Kennedy had promised during the campaign could be done with "a stroke of the pen." One historian has labeled the administration's failure to deliver in a timely manner on this promise "the most specific contradiction between promise and performance" on the Kennedy civil rights record.[41] The Kennedy brothers' strategy on the housing order is summarized in two words, compromise and delay. President Kennedy frequently told critics that he had to wait for "a useful and appropriate time" before signing the order.[42] Unwilling to wait, civil rights advocates started an "Ink for Jack" campaign, sending the White House thousands of pens and bottles of ink, which the president ordered piled on the desk of the author of the "fatal phrase" (as Schlesinger called it), Wofford. Presidential advisors fretted over the consequences of signing the housing order and warned of falling into congressional traps and jeopardizing the president's high approval ratings in public opinion polls. The order was delayed through 1961, according to Arthur Schlesinger, because the Kennedys needed the votes of southern members of Congress for a new Department of Urban Affairs, which the House Rules Committee killed anyway.[43]

Perhaps the major reason for the delay was Robert Kennedy's ambivalence toward the housing order. He viewed it as part of someone else's agenda, which he saw no great urgency in enacting. He thought lengthy, detailed analysis of its pros and cons a waste of time, certainly less important than spending time with his family. During the Thanksgiving weekend at Hyannis Port in 1961, the attorney general played touch football with his children in a cold rain while inside the president mulled over options on the housing order with Burke Marshall and other advisors. When the president needed his attorney general, he called "Hey, Bobby," and his brother came in dripping wet in an old sweater, said his piece, then went back out to his children and the game.[44]

The Kennedys invented reasons for the delay. At one point the president promised Wofford and King that he would sign the housing order after the spring 1962 primary elections, when the South was "safe" for the Democrats.[45] Then Robert Kennedy and Burke Marshall concluded that using the president's constitutional authority to stop discrimination in housing loans might conflict with the powers of the Federal Deposit Insurance Corporation (FDIC). To be safe, Robert said, they first had to gain "control" over the FDIC by putting in their own appointees before proceeding with the housing order.[46]

"How about the housing order?" Louis Martin chided the attorney general in April 1962. Kennedy's response to "brother" Martin is unknown, but six weeks later in an appearance on ABC-TV's "Issues and Answers" Robert again told reporters that it was a question of "timing." The president, he explained, "has responsibilities in many other areas at the same time, so it is just a question of his making a judgment as to when would be the best time to sign such an executive order."[47]

The timing was still not right that summer. Walking together on the beach at Hyannis Port, the brothers decided that because of its "political implications," the housing order had to wait until after the November 1962 midterm elections. As the elections approached, Robert fixed the blame on "liberal congressmen" from Michigan and elsewhere, who told the Kennedys that the housing order would be "damaging" within their districts and might feed the growing racial tensions in northern communities. They would go slowly, Robert said, and not "try to force it in 1962."[48]

The Kennedys believed their strategy had paid off in the fall of 1962. In every midterm election in the twentieth century (except 1902 and 1934), the party of the incumbent president had incurred heavy losses. The Democrats in 1962 actually added four seats in the Senate and lost a net of only two seats in the House.[49] The outcome of the election likely was more influenced by the resolution of the Cuban missile crisis than by Kennedy caution on civil rights. The black vote, however, had a surprising impact, as Louis Martin demonstrated to Robert Kennedy, pointing out places where part of the surge could be attributed to the increased loyalty of black voters to Democratic candidates. He noted specifically the impact of black disaffections from Republican candidates in Pennsylvania and California—the latter contributing to Richard Nixon's defeat for the governorship. Martin tried to convince the Kennedys to consolidate and capitalize on their advantage by calling a national conference on civil rights after the election. Concerned about its potential effect on white voters, Robert Kennedy queried Burke Marshall: "I don't think this probably necessary. Do you?" Marshall agreed.[50]

With the election behind them, on 20 November 1962 (Robert's thirty-seventh birthday), the Kennedys finally issued Executive Order 11063, with no press in attendance and at what Wofford called the "lowest-key time possible," when the public was distracted by other presidential announcements and by the Thanksgiving weekend. Ostensibly banning racial discrimination in federally supported housing, Kennedy's housing order pertained to less than 3 percent of existing housing and only an estimated 20 percent of new construction. It forbade the Federal Housing Administration to insure mortgages for builders who refused to sell to minorities, but, pursuant to a Justice Department recommendation, the prohibition did not extend to private financial institutions. Wofford observed that "people sensed the President's heart was not in it."[51]

By then Wofford had left the White House and assumed duties with the Peace Corps in Africa, relieved by his own choice of the uncomfortable position of being a staff advisor and policy strategist in a highly personalized and centralized administration, where access to the president and control over operational machinery took precedence. Wofford's presence in the White House had only worsened the president's discomfiture with the civil rights issue. He and Wofford rarely met and seldom spoke, except in passing, when the president would ask, "Are your constituents happy?" When Wofford left, the president abolished the position of civil rights specialist, signaling his reluctance to forge a direct link to the civil rights leadership and recognizing the attorney general's bureaucratic victory on the issue. Loyal to the end, Wofford insisted that his relations with the president "were good." "The negative factor for me," he said, "was simply that the center of civil rights power and decision-making in civil rights was in the Department of Justice." Of that influence Wofford was at first skeptical—"I guess I didn't have full confidence" in Robert Kennedy until "several years later," he said—but it became "good, better and better, day by day."[52]

The president made all important decisions on civil rights, Wofford acknowledged, "alone with Bob Kennedy."[53] As in the war on crime, the attorney general gathered key powers and functions under his personal umbrella and curtailed or preempted the powers of competing individuals and agencies. Besides Wofford as White House liaison and Lyndon Johnson and the PCEEO, a third body "cluttering up the field," in Robert Kennedy's view, was the Civil Rights Commission.

Created by the Civil Rights Act of 1957, the commission was charged with gathering information on voting rights violations and economic reprisals against blacks. Its liberal members, such as Father Theodore Hesburgh, and the commission staff (led by Berl Bernhard, a young Yale Law graduate and Kennedy appointee) believed the law required them to independently investigate all denials of civil rights. Robert Kennedy disagreed. The commission, he said, was going over "old ground, and they were doing what we were really doing," that is, "investigating violations of civil rights in areas in which we were making investigations." He found the commission, in short, "not helpful," and the president, he said, "never liked anybody who was sort of in existence and not accomplishing something."[54] Robert had "no confidence" in the commission, because, like Wofford, its members were handicapped by their liberal biases and therefore did not conduct "objective investigations." They acted, he said, like a "runaway grand jury" and approached their work "almost like the House Un-American Activities Committee investigating Communism."[55]

From Robert Kennedy's perspective, directing complaints to both the commission and the Justice Department caused needless duplication of effort and served to "confuse the people." For example, when the commission proposed to sponsor conferences in southern cities to avoid confrontations before they occurred, the attorney general cooly dismissed the idea, noting, "Our own program serves same purpose."[56] And once the Justice Department became involved in a civil rights case, he wanted the commission to butt out.[57]

Kennedy confronted the commission in the spring of 1961 at what was described as a "very unpleasant meeting." Hesburgh and other liberals on the commission saw it as their duty to act as a "burr under the saddle of the administration," and they argued for an across-the-board attack on inequality through legislative as well as executive action. Robert Kennedy had little tolerance for the commission's criticisms. "I am the one who has to get the job done," he retorted. As for new legislation, "I can do it, and will do it," he told them, "in my way, and you're making it more difficult."[58]

The commission refused to bend. As the civil rights conflicts intensified between 1961 and 1963, so did the tensions between Kennedy and the commission. Worried lest the commission get out in front of Marshall's Civil Rights Division, embarrass the administration, and stir up white antagonism, the attorney general on at least three occasions forced the postponement of commission hearings regarding white violence against black southerners.[59]

On another occasion Kennedy telephoned Bernhard at 1:00 A.M. to demand he cancel ("I want it called off—now!") a hearing on discrimination against blacks voting in Louisiana scheduled for later that morning. "Do you know what you are doing?" he asked Bernhard. The hearings, explained Kennedy, would surely cause DeLesseps Morrison, a racial moderate and a supporter of the president, to lose an approaching election. Bernhard asked what excuse he should give the press. "If you're not smart enough to give a good reason," the attorney general told him, "I don't know why my brother nominated you. And remember, you never talked to me." When Bernhard hesitated, Kennedy called Dean Storey, former president of the American Bar Association, who was to chair the session. At 2:00 A.M. Storey called Bernhard and

1. "The first time I remember meeting Bobby," John Kennedy said, "was when he was three-and-a-half, one summer at the Cape." This photo, taken in 1929 or 1930, may mark that meeting. *Left to right:* Robert, John, dog Buddy, Eunice, Jean, Joseph P. and Rose Kennedy, Patricia, Kathleen, Joe Junior, and Rosemary.

2. "My little pet," Rose Kennedy called the shyest and smallest of her four sons. Robert, age ten, outside the summer home at Hyannis Port.

3. The Kennedys at home in Bronxville, 1936. *Left to right:* Joseph P. Kennedy, Patricia, John, Jean, and Eunice; Robert, Kathleen, Edward, Rosemary, Joseph Junior, and Rose Kennedy.

5. Joe Junior, John, and Robert with the ambassador. Robert, who so often had to compete for his father's notice, enjoys a brief moment of attention.

4. (FACING PAGE) Classmates offer a mock challenge to the U.S. Ambassador's sons Robert, 12, *far left,* and Teddy, 6, *next to Robert,* on their first day at London's Gibbs School in March 1938.

6. Wearing JFK's London drape coat, RFK is sworn in as a naval aviation cadet, October 1943. Joseph Kennedy, *left,* would arrange duty after the war for RFK aboard a destroyer named in memory of Joe Junior.

7. The first Kennedy brother to earn a Harvard letter, RFK was a starting end, *far right,* for the 1947 team. All-American quarterback Kenneth O'Donnell, number 22, was RFK's roommate.

8. Assistant counsel to Senator Joseph R. McCarthy's subcommittee, RFK testifies in May 1953 on British trade with Communist China during the Korean War. He resigned from McCarthy's staff two months later.

9. Returning to McCarthy's subcommittee in January 1954 as Democratic counsel, RFK is shown with McCarthy, *left,* and Senator Henry M. "Scoop" Jackson before a hearing on Communism.

10. Kennedy-Cohn "feud." Senator Karl Mundt places himself between Roy Cohn, *far left*, and RFK during a heated moment of the army-McCarthy hearings, 15 June 1954. Senator John McClellan is in foreground.

11. RFK toured the Soviet Union in September 1955 with Supreme Court justice William O. Douglas. They pose here in ceremonial robes. RFK became ill on the trip and at first refused to allow "Communist doctors" to treat him.

12. Senator and investigator—the brothers Kennedy in front of the Capitol, June 1957.

13. RFK, flanked by Senator McClellan and JFK, questioning a Rackets Committee witness.

14. James R. Hoffa has words for RFK outside the Rackets Committee hearings, August 1957. George Fitzgerald, Hoffa's lawyer, is behind Hoffa.

15. The candidate and campaign manager confer on the eve of the Democratic convention in Los Angeles, 10 July 1960.

16. RFK: His deep blue eyes were his most distinctive feature.

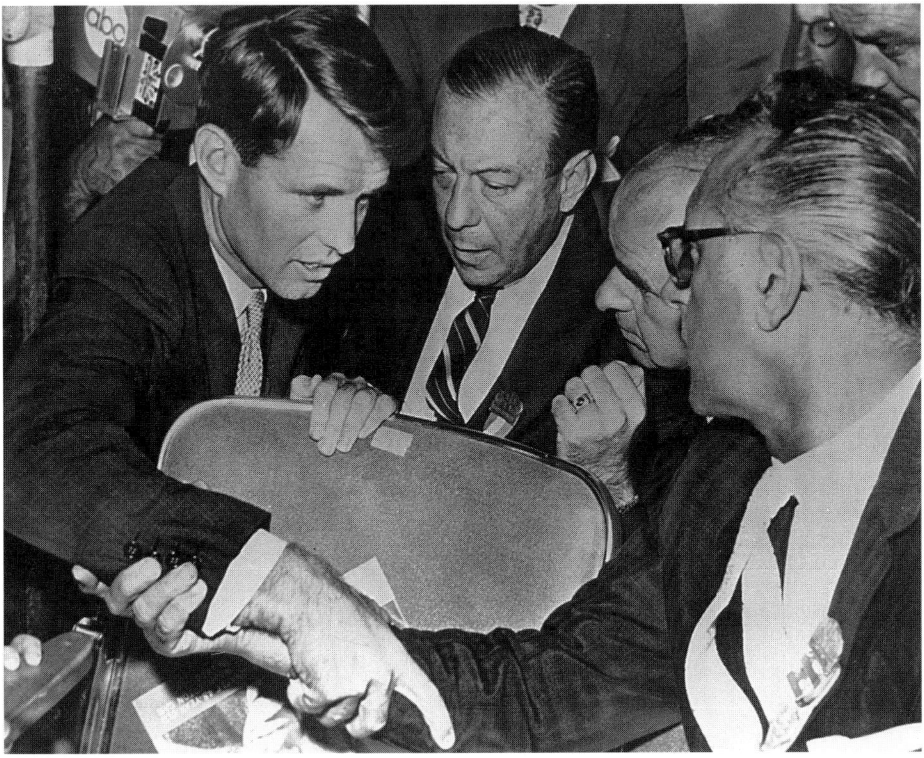

17. RFK gains support for JFK at the Democratic convention from key members of the New York delegation: *from left,* Mayor Robert F. Wagner, U.S. Representative Michael Prendergast, and Tammany Hall leader Carmine DeSapio (13 July 1960).

18. Averell Harriman and Washington dignitaries, arriving 22 July 1960 at the Hyannis Port airport to brief JFK, are greeted by RFK, as David, 5, scratches his back and Kathleen, 8, looks on.

19. Wasting few words, JFK and RFK spoke to each other in crisp, codelike phrases.

20. (FACING PAGE, TOP) RFK staff meeting. Much to J. Edgar Hoover's consternation, the ornate office incurred some damage from errant dart and football tosses, the exuberance of Kennedy children, and Brumus peeing on the carpet.

21. (FACING PAGE, BOTTOM) In the mix of politics and celebrity that marked the New Frontier, RFK met many glamorous Hollywood figures, including Elizabeth Taylor.

22. Addressing civil rights protesters in front of the Justice Department, 14 June 1963, RFK said, "I'm not going to go out and hire a Negro just because he is not white." One protestor, Jack Newfield, remembered RFK's "hard Irish face" and the "hostility radiating from his blue eyes."

23. An uncomfortable foursome on civil rights. Martin Luther King, Jr., SCLC; RFK; Roy Wilkens, NAACP; and Vice-President Lyndon B. Johnson outside the White House, July 1963.

24. Hickory Hill–style touch football featured RFK at quarterback, few conventional rules, and every child (and Brumus) participating.

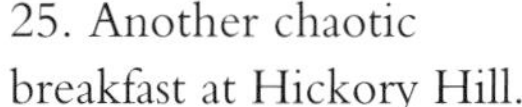

25. Another chaotic breakfast at Hickory Hill.

26. RFK in a "tickle tumble" with dog and child.

27. To the poised widow and the shattered brother fell the task of shaping JFK's mystique and legacy.

28. Stepping into the future. RFK's family in the late spring of 1964: Brumus, RFK, Ethel, Kathleen, 12, Joe, 11, Robert, 10, David, 9, Mary Courtney, 7, Michael, 6, Mary Kerry, 4, Christopher, 1.

said the meeting was called off. "We just can't ignore the request of the attorney general of the United States."[60]

Gradually it became apparent to all that the attorney general held exclusive strategic and operational responsibility over civil rights. When he acted, everyone understood that it was with the direct authority of the president. The Kennedys demanded they be in personal charge of the issue within the government. Astonishingly, they thought their control should extend beyond the government and into the movement itself, that their timing should dictate when the civil rights leadership should act. As historian Bruce Miroff emphasized in *Pragmatic Illusions,* the Kennedys "believed *they* should set the direction which the civil rights movement should take." The "Kennedy pragmatists," Victor Navasky similarly observed, "thought that *they* were the intellectual vanguard of the civil rights movement" and did not take seriously those they called the "knee-jerk liberals."[61]

The key to understanding their position, Miroff explained, lies in the conflict the Kennedys felt between mass politics and elite politics. They were comfortable with elite politics, uncomfortable with mass politics. They found mass movements and political confrontations difficult to comprehend or tolerate. The Kennedys, as political scientist James M. Burns put it, were "trapped by their own history," by the "notion that the give-and-take of brokerage politics would work amid the polarized politics of reaction and revolution."[62] Accustomed to operating as political insiders, not only did the Kennedys prefer to accomplish things by manipulating elite groups but their temperaments and ingrained attitudes toward politics left them indifferent toward, if not contemptuous of, pressure groups and confrontational politics.

Robert Kennedy, in particular, was action oriented. He preferred behind-the-scenes discussions and maneuvering with the principal actors or persons of influence who could do something more than posture, talk, or demonstrate.[63] Eventually, of course, the Kennedys were forced to deal with the mass nature of the civil rights movement and to address the concerns of the world outside of politics. Ironically, in the last days of his life Robert Kennedy himself became a player in the game of mass politics. But for now it was as alien to him as southern political culture.

A Federal Approach

On 6 May 1961, the new attorney general delivered his first major speech, the Law Day address at the University of Georgia. His was an unfamiliar presence among southerners—he was introduced as "Robert Fitzgerald Kennedy"—who politely received his direct message: "We are maintaining the orders of the courts," he told those who might have presumed otherwise. "We are doing nothing more nor less. And if any one of you were in my position, you would do likewise, for it would be required by your oath of office. You might not want to do it, you might not like to do it, but you would do it." In the audience that day was Charlene Hunter Gault, one of the first blacks then only recently admitted to the University of Georgia and later an Emmy Award–winning television producer. She felt that Kennedy spoke directly to her when he said, "Our position is clear. We are upholding the law. . . . In this case—in all cases—I say to you today that, if the orders of the court are circumvented, the Department of Justice will act. We will not stand by or be aloof. We will move."

Parts of his speech inspired blacks and white liberals, who anticipated active support of their goals. Other parts did not, for Kennedy stressed the importance of "facing this problem honorably," and he made it clear that the administration intended to give the South a chance to correct its problems through "amicable voluntary solutions." Above all, he said, it was imperative, as part of the battle against Communism, that Americans demonstrate to the world that they "are moving forward together—solving this problem—under the rule of law."[64]

Indeed, to Robert Kennedy the crucial element in resolving the civil rights issue, as he told the American Jewish Committee and the Anti-Defamation League of B'nai B'rith in Chicago six weeks later, was respect for law and order. These must be upheld "vigorously by the leaders of the community," for the law, he said, "stands as the bulwark of freedom." When "responsible officials do not stand for law and order," warned Kennedy, "then order begins to give way to violence."[65]

Taken together, Kennedy's speeches, comments, and interviews over the course of his first six months in office announced a "federal approach" to civil rights. Elaborated upon by Burke Marshall in department memoranda, letters to civil rights leaders, and a 1964 monograph, the Kennedys' federal approach held that the maintenance of civil order depended upon the states' exercise of their police powers. The federal government, they argued, could neither usurp nor replace that responsibility. The Justice Department, then, could not seek injunctions to protect civil rights activists because statutory authority rested within the states and locales where the violations occurred. Nor could they provide physical protection, as Marshall put it, "for everyone who is disliked because of the exercise of his constitutional rights." A person's civil rights within a federal system, Marshall declared, "are individual and personal, to be asserted by private citizens, as they choose, in court, speaking through their chosen counsel."

Civil rights attorneys argued that Kennedy's Justice Department, if it chose, could have prosecuted civil rights violations through the application of U.S. Code, Title 10, Section 333, which empowered the president to protect the constitutional rights of citizens and uphold the laws in any state where local authority refused or proved unable to do so. Robert Kennedy disagreed with that argument, which he believed presumed either creating a national police force or vesting police authority in the FBI, a step that would cause irreparable harm to the federal system and come back to "haunt you," he said. Federal intervention, he insisted, should occur only in extreme circumstances as a last resort.[66]

Proponents of civil rights who expected the federal government to act aggressively to end segregation and to protect the lives of those who challenged Jim Crow of course criticized the Kennedys' federal approach.[67] A SNCC worker once told the Kennedys, "If we are murdered in our attempts, our blood will be on your hands; you stand in the judgment of God and our people."[68] Sustaining the federal system, Kennedy knew, would exact a heavy price. "Mississippi is going to work itself out," he said later. "Maybe it's going to take a decade and maybe a lot of people are going to be killed in the meantime. . . . But in the long run I think it's for the health of the country and the stability of the system."[69]

The Kennedys' federal approach, Victor Navasky wrote, was built upon a "Burkean notion that the nation-state had some kind of organic reality over and above its parts and that to disrupt the fabric of the nation-state was a greater evil than not to protect the human rights that the federal system was supposed to guarantee in the first place." This approach, Navasky claimed, hardly went beyond "an enlightened apology for the existing social order."[70] So it must have seemed to those desperate to change the social order. But social change for the Kennedys came second to preserving political order. Ardent nationalists, the Kennedys believed that one should not accomplish social changes, however desirable, at the sacrifice of the state itself. Political order was the cornerstone of the nation's existence. Without political order, which flowed from the rule of law, there could be no human rights' guarantees and no social change.

Yet while Robert Kennedy knew that local authorities had first-level responsibility for maintaining law and order on civil rights matters, when it came to pursuing organized crime he frequently challenged the balance of power between the federal authorities and state and local jurisdictions, boldly construed federal powers to intrude in the criminal justice system, and aggressively stepped forward to fill the power vacuum when he thought it necessary. Viewed in that light, his federal approach on civil rights looks like a convenient rationalization for averting decisive action that could cause a white backlash and upset the political status quo.[71]

Are there other, more plausible, explanations for Kennedy's restrained position on civil rights? It is frequently asserted that Kennedy consistently misstated or underestimated his authority over civil rights largely because he did not want to antagonize Hoover's FBI.[72] There is evidence to support that view. Hoover's natural constituency and allies, after all, were white, southern, and conservative; they personally opposed the goals of the civil rights movement, disapproved of its leaders, suspected it was Communist-influenced, and behaved accordingly. Claiming that the FBI had investigatory powers only and could not intervene until a federal law was broken, Hoover's agents repeatedly observed white violence against blacks in the South but took no action. "Hoover's on the other side," Robert Kennedy was once heard to say.[73] When events escalated and local law enforcement agencies proved unreliable in containing the violence, Robert Kennedy did not call in the

FBI to restore order. He did, however, value the FBI's investigative skills and subtly maneuvered Hoover into focusing more of his efforts on civil rights cases.

Unable to force Hoover to send agents into the South, the attorney general sent in his own staffers first. They conducted preliminary investigations and gathered intelligence on violence, white supremacy groups, and local law enforcement personnel engaged in terrorist activities against blacks. To protect their own interests and to avoid being outshone, the FBI hastened to the scene and assisted in most instances. In 1961 the FBI had only 3 agents in Mississippi, by 1964 more than 150; by then Bureau agents (at Kennedy's request) had infiltrated the Ku Klux Klan almost as thoroughly as they had the Communist party.

Kennedy thus sacrificed control for cooperation. He did not press the FBI to make arrests, interfere with their cordial relationship with southern law enforcement officials, or challenge their policy of information hoarding. He judged the tradeoff worth it. "Any time I'd call and ask him [Hoover] to do something, which wasn't very frequent, where I'd have to put it on him directly," Kennedy said, "he was the most enthusiastic person you ever talked to." And "when they did things," he remembered later, "frequently they did them damned well. At least, before November [22, 1963]."[74] After his brother's assassination, Kennedy had less control but, in some respects, more maneuverability with the FBI. To make the FBI more responsive and cooperative, Kennedy resorted to what Navasky called "improvised countermeasures." Rather than send crafty memos or make polite telephone calls that Hoover likely would have ignored anyway, Kennedy and Marshall took a page from Hoover's book on bureaucratic end runs; for example, they successfully appealed in 1964 for a White House directive to the FBI to investigate the circumstances of three missing civil rights workers in Mississippi. However motivated, the FBI's field investigations significantly advanced the department's efforts to protect civil rights, according to John Doar and other attorneys.[75]

All things considered, the notion that the Kennedys constantly deferred to Hoover seems overworked, at least as far as civil rights was concerned. Hoover's insistence on limited authority over local cases, after all, conformed to the views that the Kennedys brought with them to office. From the outset, the attorney general and the FBI director agreed on the limits of federal authority over civil rights; both denied having the authority or manpower to provide protection for civil rights workers or to investigate allegations of police mistreatment in the South. Hoover did not force those views on Robert Kennedy. Indeed, in contrast to his actions in the war on organized crime, the attorney general's federal approach toward civil rights (except for the part about the rule of law) seemed more an ad hoc contrivance fitted to political exigencies than a sharply honed, cherished philosophy.

Further, Robert Kennedy frequently stepped beyond his own federal doctrine, particularly during crises. He quite aggressively applied federal power to extend civil rights when his department had unequivocal authority, as in the enforcement of court orders desegregating schools and in the protection of black voting rights. Those two initiatives, which he undertook upon entering office with no prompting by civil rights organizations, broke new ground in the area of federal-state guarantees of civil rights.

Progress toward school integration, despite the Supreme Court's order in the Brown case, moved slowly after 1954. By early 1961 token integration of colleges and universities had occurred in five former Confederate states (Georgia, Florida, Arkansas, Virginia, and North Carolina), but three (Alabama, Mississippi, and South Carolina) had refused integration of any kind. The Civil Rights Commission recommended in January 1961 that the federal government deny "subsidies," such as those under the Land Grant system, to racially segregated colleges.[76] Uninclined to pursue such sanctions, the Kennedys were equally unwilling to introduce comprehensive legislation to mandate desegregation. They chose a case-by-case approach, expanding federal participation in school desegregation by acting as amicus curiae in several court actions and by working behind the scenes to effect compromises.

In 1961 Kennedy worked with a federal judge to persuade Louisiana officials to desegregate schools in New Orleans. Without consulting the president directly, he decided that henceforth the Justice Department would assume full responsibility for enforcing school desegregation orders. He blamed the "failure" of Eisenhower's Justice Department "to recognize explicitly and give effect to this responsibility" for the kind of violence and law enforcement problems that occurred in Little Rock in 1957. Because Congress had refused to give the executive branch authority to initiate school-desegregation suits, Kennedy decided "to do whatever is necessary." This sometimes entailed legal actions, but more often it meant taking some personal action himself, such as telephoning state officials to warn them against trying to bypass court orders, or sending his personal emissaries to work out special arrangements.[77]

The Prince Edward County, Virginia case tested all of Kennedy's resources. After personal negotiations failed, the Justice Department in May 1961 joined other plaintiffs in a suit to force the county to open its public school system, which officials had closed two years earlier to avoid desegregation orders. White students attended schools financed in large part by public funds, while seventeen hundred black children had no schools. Burke Marshall's Civil Rights Division argued that the failure of Virginia to maintain public schools in Prince Edward County while doing so throughout the rest of the state denied blacks in the county equal protection of the laws guaranteed by the Fourteenth Amendment.[78] About this action Robert Kennedy said, "We have tried to work this out to permit Negro children to go to school. They are unable to. Court orders are being circumvented and nullified. Therefore, we have brought this action to protect the integrity of the judicial process of the United States." When the suit proceeded slowly through the courts, a third aspect of the Kennedy approach came into play. In February 1963 Robert asked William J. vanden Heuvel, a lawyer in Senator Jacob Javits's New York City law firm, to serve as his personal representative in working out a plan for a private free school association to reopen schools until the court made its ruling, which finally occurred in May 1964.[79]

"The long-range solution for Negroes," Robert Kennedy said, "is voting rights. I think all other rights for which they are fighting will flow from that. Political power comes from votes and rights come from political power."[80] "Nobody," he thought, "could really oppose voting." "You register those people [Mississippi blacks] to vote and Jim Eastland will change his mind," he told Martin Luther King, Jr. The Kennedys meant to appoint enough blacks and make enough token gestures to stay ahead of the Eisenhower-Nixon record and to placate the civil rights leadership, at the same time adding blacks to southern voting lists to put white southerners on notice and to counter some of the southern pressure in Congress. Taylor Branch labeled this a policy of "accretion." Someone else said the Kennedys intended to "appoint and appoint, elect and elect." The idea, of course, was to add to their electoral coalition without touching off a segregationist backlash.[81]

Robert Kennedy felt sure that candidates who delivered something to the black community would easily win the black vote. In the 1960 campaign he found that it did not require a great deal. He realized, however, that winning black support in 1964 required something more substantial than two telephone calls and some vague pledges. Therefore, Kennedy had Louis Martin research voting districts with 10 percent or more nonwhite populations, intending to target those districts for special consideration.[82] Kennedy knew that John Doar, while working for Eisenhower's Justice Department, had gone into Fayette County, Tennessee, and filed suits to protect black voters, who reciprocated by voting Republican in 1960. Not by coincidence, then, President Kennedy ordered the Agriculture Department to send surplus food to feed 14,000 evicted black tenant farmers in Fayette and Howard counties.[83] Also not surprisingly, Robert Kennedy invited Doar to join his staff.

"I want to move on voting," the attorney general told Doar in the first hours of the new administration.[84] In February 1961 Doar and Robert D. Owen presented Kennedy with a litigation plan intended to secure the right to vote for southern blacks.[85] Clear authority for the plan came from the Civil Rights Act of 1957, which empowered the Justice Department to file civil suits on behalf of persons deprived of their rights to vote or prohibited from registering to vote on account of race or color. The Civil Rights Act of 1960 required local officials to keep voting records and permitted federal inspection and investigation of those records.[86] Kennedy's Justice Department lost little time in getting started on the plan, filing eight suits in the first eight months.[87] Altogether they brought fifty-seven suits against violations of Negro voting rights in southern states. To gather information for the suits Kennedy dispatched John Doar and a group of assistants ("itinerant problem-solvers," Navasky called them) to travel the back roads of the South supervising litigation and directly involving themselves in local issues. For these missions Kennedy selected the most talented people available and delegated the maximum authority. Once there, they might be required to conduct criminal investigations, obtain court orders, face down local officials, contact corporate leaders—to do whatever was necessary. In the process they built credibility within the southern black communities and raised expectations among civil rights workers, at the cost of further alienating white southerners and stirring white-on-black violence in retribution.[88]

During the Kennedys' first months of office their actions lacked passion and often seemed cynical and apologetic, but the administration did, in fact, move more quickly and positively on civil rights than had Eisenhower's. Wofford approvingly noted the behind-the-scenes work of Robert Kennedy's key assistants, calling their approach to voting rights litigation "inventive and significant." All considered, he saw the administration as "prepared to go all out in breaking through the remaining obstacles in the right to vote."[89]

President Kennedy told the technical truth when he claimed to have "done more for civil rights than any President in American History." Missing, of course, was a moral commitment and any real attempt to educate and lead the nation. The civil rights issue, Theodore Hesburgh said, "really imposed itself upon" the Kennedys, "rather than they imposing themselves on civil rights." However, as Victor Navasky judiciously noted, they "cannot be blamed for not anticipating what few if any white liberals anticipated as the future of the civil rights movement, the future of integration. Neither should they automatically be credited with any particular vision."[90]

Freedom Rides

Events outstripped the Kennedys' good intentions, as civil rights activists forced them and the rest of the country to hear their demands. On 4 May 1961, two days before the attorney general spoke at the University of Georgia, a contingent of seven blacks and six whites left Washington, D.C., without fanfare on two regularly scheduled buses, a Greyhound and a Trailways, for New Orleans. Encouraged by James

Farmer, head of the Congress on Racial Equality (CORE), these Freedom Riders, as they called themselves, intended to challenge segregation in southern bus terminals, which persisted in defiance of the December 1960 Supreme Court ruling in *Boynton v. Virginia,* 364 U.S. 454, declaring segregation in interstate transportation facilities unconstitutional.

Reporter Simeon Booker, who forewarned Robert Kennedy about the rides, told Kennedy he was going to travel with the group and write an account for *Jet* magazine. Booker recalled the attorney general telling him to call if there was trouble. Absorbed with the failed Bay of Pigs operation and preparing for the University of Georgia speech, Kennedy did not register Booker's warning. He later insisted that "we never—at least, I never—knew they were traveling down there" until informed, along with the rest of the country, that Freedom Riders had been viciously assaulted.[91]

On Sunday, 14 May 1961, near Anniston, Alabama, a small city about halfway between Birmingham and Atlanta, Georgia, angry whites attacked the Greyhound bus carrying six Freedom Riders and five other passengers (including an undercover state investigator, E. L. Cowling). They slashed its tires, tossed a firebomb through smashed windows, then tried to barricade its occupants inside the burning bus. Cowling brandished his revolver, forced the mob to back away, pushed open the door, and freed himself and the other choking passengers, many of whom were then set upon by the attackers. State troopers arriving on the scene fired warning shots to turn away the mob and then drove injured passengers to the Anniston hospital.

At the Anniston terminal later the same day, eight burly Klansmen boarded the Trailways bus carrying the second group of Freedom Riders. As regular passengers looked on, the Klansmen beat two black youths who refused to move from their front seats and mauled two white Freedom Riders who tried to come to their aid. Following a high-speed ride to Birmingham to avoid the mob that had burned the Greyhound, the Freedom Riders limped off the bus into the Trailways terminal and right into a police-sanctioned Klan ambush. The white mob assaulted the Freedom Riders with clubs, fists, and lead pipes. Some of the seriously injured, including Jim Peck, who required fifty-three stitches to close six head wounds, had been beaten earlier in Anniston. The fury of the Birmingham mob soon turned on horrified bystanders and news reporters, including one radio reporter attacked and beaten in the middle of a live broadcast. The FBI, through a Klan informant named Gary Thomas Rowe (who actually participated in the beatings), had prior notice of the ambush and Police Commissioner Bull Connor's agreement to give the Klan fifteen minutes to do their dirty work. The FBI neither notified the attorney general nor took any action to stop the riot—Birmingham police arrived and dispersed the mob precisely on schedule—but agents filmed the beatings and later arrested four of the Klansmen.[92]

The country's insensitivity to civil rights issues made the Freedom Rides difficult for the administration to understand and to deal with. Arthur Schlesinger, Jr., described the Kennedys' first reaction as "one of dismay mingled with a certain exasperation." They viewed the actions as an "unnecessary burden" on them after the Bay of Pigs and just before a summit meeting with Khrushchev, according to Schlesinger, and thought the Riders' "undue militancy" "threatened the strategy of suasion."[93] The Freedom Riders, in other words, had brought this on themselves.

Aware of public opinion polls that showed 63 percent disapproved of what the Freedom Riders were doing, chagrined over the negative message the beatings conveyed around the world, and irritated that the civil rights leaders kept ignoring the Kennedys' programs and judgments, they tried to halt the rides. "Tell them to call if off!" John Kennedy implored Harris Wofford. "Stop them! Get your friends off those buses," the president shouted over the phone. But there was nothing Wofford could do to get the Freedom Riders off those buses.[94]

The common reaction at the Justice Department, Ramsey Clark remembered, was to ask, "Why are they doing this? Why are they making so much trouble for us? Why don't they stay home?" U.S. attorneys working the South worried about the effects of the Freedom Rides on southern blacks who had to live with the aftermath. They feared white southern animosity against "outside agitators" and anticipated a backlash against the violation of the "ultimate southern taboo," the presence of white females and Negro males together on the buses.[95]

Word soon got out that the Kennedys seemed more concerned for the sensibilities of southern whites than the violations of the civil rights of blacks. "You know," Martin Luther King, Jr., told friends, the Kennedys "don't understand the social revolution going on in the world, and therefore they don't understand what we're doing."[96]

The two attacks by the Klan left the Freedom Riders battered and frightened. Several had serious injuries, but local hospitals, fearing the wrath of the mob, provided only emergency treatment. The same mobs threatened the bus companies and drivers, if they allowed the integrated group to continue. Trapped in Birmingham, the Riders regrouped at the home of Reverend Fred Shuttlesworth, pastor of Bethel Baptist Church.[97] There, early Monday morning, the day after the attacks, they heard from the attorney general for the first time.

Alerted by Simeon Booker, Kennedy telephoned Shuttlesworth and spoke to some of the battered Freedom Riders. They were touched by his solicitous attitude, but the courtesies and deference he showed Shuttlesworth had even more impact. The backwoods-born minister who believed himself an equal of Martin Luther King gloried in the attention from the attorney general, who made the calls himself because Burke Marshall had the mumps. "Bob told me," Shuttlesworth boasted to his congregants at the Bethel Baptist Church, "'If you can't get me at my office, just call me at the White House.'"[98]

Robert Kennedy saw the Freedom Rides as a political booby trap, best left untouched by the president. As Ramsey Clark put it, the attorney general acted as "a lightning rod for the President" drawing away from him "a lot of the antipathy that comes from doing your duty." [99]

The best political cover for the president, then, was for the attorney general to do his duty. Converting his office into a crisis management center, he quickly gained assurances from Governor John Patterson and Commissioner Connor that the Freedom Riders would be permitted to leave Birmingham safely. Connor kept his promise, but Patterson was caught in a predicament. He could either use state powers to protect the interstate travelers (and therefore sacrifice the segregation laws) or admit he could not protect them (and thus invite the intervention of the hated federal government). Either meant political suicide. Thus, despite his personal friendship with both Kennedys—"He was our great pal in the South," Robert said—Patterson went back on his word, announced that he could not guarantee safe passage for the Riders, and refused calls from either the attorney general or the president.[100]

Wary of assurances from Alabama authorities and fearing further beatings or worse, the pummeled and shaken CORE group decided to abandon their Ride and fly to New Orleans to seek proper medical care. Some became hysterical when a series of bomb threats at the Birmingham airport stopped them from leaving. Concerned for their safety, Kennedy asked John Seigenthaler, "Do you think you can get down there and help them?" Kennedy said he wanted someone there "to hold their hand and let them know that we care." In a matter of hours, Seigenthaler arrived in Birmingham and, through no small amount of ingenuity, arranged the flight to New Orleans and safety.

In New Orleans, Seigenthaler learned from Burke Marshall that another group of Freedom Riders, a SNCC group out of Nashville headed by Diane Nash, intended to go to Birmingham, take up the cause for CORE, and ride from Birmingham to Montgomery. Marshall, at Kennedy's direction, asked Seigenthaler to contact his friends in Nashville and get them to stop Nash. "All hell is going to break loose. She's going to get those people killed," Seigenthaler told Nash's friends. Fred Shuttlesworth also tried to dissuade her. But Nash was insistent: "If they stop us with violence, the movement is dead. We're coming." When the first wave of Nashville students arrived in Birmingham, Connor put them in jail under "protective custody," then later drove them back to the Tennessee border.[101] That gave the Kennedys time to take stock of their position.

With Burke Marshall and Byron White at his side, Robert roused his brother from bed early the morning of 17 May. As he sat in his pajamas, his uneaten breakfast before him, the president listened intently as the attorney general began his explanation: "The situation is getting worse in Alabama." They faced a politically embarrassing, potentially humiliating stalemate in Birmingham. White told the president that if Governor Patterson refused to protect lawful travelers, the federal government would have no recourse but to act. But how?

As the president's toast grew sodden, White and Marshall explained the law and reviewed their options. Using troops was out of the question, and so was the FBI. A close reading of the U.S. Code, however, convinced Marshall and White that U.S. marshals could enforce federal law without invoking the president's name and without conflicting with states' rights. That morning it was agreed that Robert Kennedy's Justice Department would create a civilian force, an army of U.S. marshals; they were now engaged, like it or not, in a struggle with Alabama and other southern states over the power of the federal government to protect the civil rights of African Americans.[102]

The attorney general saw as his first obligation protecting the Freedom Riders whose constitutional rights were being assailed in Alabama. In practical terms this meant finding a way for them to resume the trip begun by the CORE group. He had promised them that he would get them out of Birmingham and out of Alabama. He hoped that could be the end of it. But with more Freedom Riders spilling into Birmingham from all parts of the country, the "festering sore," as Kennedy now viewed the problem, worsened on Friday, 19 May.[103] After a Pentagon briefing on guerilla warfare and the White House signing of a new bill expanding the number of federal judgeships, the attorney general returned to his office and called the Tutweiler Hotel in Birmingham. He spoke to John Seigenthaler, who, continuing on his personal mission for Kennedy, had registered there as "John Rogers" (the same code name they had used during the Teamsters investigations).[104] Seigenthaler told him that Greyhound refused to move the Freedom Riders without police protection and balked at assigning a driver to take the bus on to Montgomery. Circumstances had contrived a cruel test of Robert Kennedy's resolve. His and the administration's reputation, as Taylor Branch pointed out, "now hung on whether the Attorney General could empower a single bus to move out of the Birmingham station."[105] He could manage it only with the cooperation of local authorities.

Robert Kennedy finally got Governor Patterson to take his telephone call by threatening to issue a public ultimatum of federal intervention unless the governor spoke to him. Their conversation amounted to a long, rancorous argument. At one point the attorney general shouted at the governor, "You're making political speeches at me, John. You don't have to make political speeches at me over the telephone." Patterson, enraged, said he would speak no further unless face-to-face with a personal representative of the president. Robert consulted his brother, placed a call to "Mr Rogers," and Seigenthaler sped to Montgomery in a rented car as the personal emissary of the president of the United States.

Patterson greeted Seigenthaler by saying, "There's nobody in the whole country that's got the spine to stand up to the Goddamned niggers except me." He warned they would see "blood in the streets" if federal marshals entered Alabama. To avoid federal intervention, Patterson promised Seigenthaler that the state could "give full protection to everyone in Alabama, on the highways and elsewhere." In Patterson's presence, Seigenthaler repeated the assurance over the telephone to Robert Kennedy. "Does he mean it?" Kennedy asked. "I've given my word as governor of Alabama," Patterson shouted in reply. Working through the night, they framed an agreement to permit the Freedom Riders to go on from Birmingham to Montgomery.[106]

On Saturday morning Robert Kennedy intended to go horseback riding and play touch football with his children, and in the afternoon to participate in the annual FBI softball game. He awakened, however, to learn that at 6:05 A.M. the Greyhound driver assigned to the Birmingham to Montgomery route told reporters, "I only have one life to give and I'm not going to give it to CORE or the NAACP," and walked out of the terminal. Kennedy telephoned the Greyhound superintendent in Birmingham and demanded an explanation. Told all drivers refused to take the risk, he asked, "Do *you* know how to drive a bus?" "No," came the reply. "Well, surely somebody in the damn bus company can drive a bus, can't they?" Kennedy told the supervisor to get in touch "with Mr. Greyhound, or whoever Greyhound is, and somebody better give us an answer to this question. I am—the Government is—going to be very much upset if this group does not get to continue their trip." And in a sentence that Burke Marshall said was greatly misconstrued, Kennedy said, "We have gone to a lot of trouble to see that they get to this trip and I am most concerned to see that it is accomplished."

The conversation, recorded by the Greyhound superintendent and its transcript widely disseminated, seemed proof enough to many white southerners that Kennedy had put CORE up to the Freedom Rides in the first place.[107] "I never recovered from it," Kennedy said in his 1964 oral history. "That was damaging—just like waking the newspapermen up" [during the steel crisis].[108] The remarks to "Mr Greyhound," as Taylor Branch noted, eroded Robert Kennedy's political standing in the South, where the name "Bobby" became an epithet.[109]

Kennedy succeeded, however, in getting the Freedom Rides resumed. At 11:10 A.M., the driver, under orders from the head of his union and the Greyhound dispatcher, suddenly loaded the bus and left Birmingham. State police accompanied the bus as far as the Montgomery city limits, inside of which they were without jurisdiction. At the Montgomery terminal no local police were in sight. John Lewis, leader of the SNCC Freedom Riders (later elected to the U.S. Congress from Georgia), was answering his first question from reporters when a mob attacked. Savage and arbitrary, the mob beat not only the Freedom Riders but several local and out-of-state news reporters. Some Riders were able to flee. Others went down under five or six attackers brandishing fists, iron pipes, axe handles, and baseball bats. Women rioters used their pocketbooks and fists on women Riders, dragged them down, and stomped them.

John Doar, working on a voting rights case at the federal building across the street, saw it all from a window. He relayed the details by telephone to Robert Kennedy's office. "It's terrible! It's terrible!" he cried, "There's not a cop in sight." John Seigenthaler literally drove right into the melee. Looking for a parking place, he saw suitcases and bags flying through the air. Then he spotted a young white girl (Susan Wilbur) being attacked by a group of eight or ten. He tried to rescue her and her companion (Sue Hermann). "Mister," Wilbur shouted, "this is not your fight! Get away from here! You're gonna get killed!" Seigenthaler identified himself as a federal agent and was promptly struck on the head with a pipe, kicked under the car, and left there bleeding and unconscious for about thirty minutes.[110]

FBI agents, again forewarned of a Klan attack, watched and took notes on these violations of local law; they did not lift a finger to help Seigenthaler or any of the others injured in the melee. Jurisdiction mattered less to Floyd Mann, head of the Alabama State Police, who had helped negotiate the agreement the evening before. Acting alone, he stepped into the middle of the mob, drew his revolver, and ordered everyone, "Stand back!" Later, he wept in shame and disgust at the side of Seigenthaler's hospital bed.[111]

Robert Kennedy was "possessed by an enormous anger," said reporter Peter Maas, who saw him just a few minutes after Kennedy received the report on Seigenthaler. He looked, Maas said, as though he had "just been poleaxed *himself.*" Kennedy telephoned his assistant at the hospital and, with gallows humor typical of him during crises, thanked him for helping win the black vote. Seigenthaler responded in kind, suggesting that the attorney general rule out ever running for governor of Alabama. Seigenthaler's beating proved one of several turning points for Kennedy on civil rights.

Yet he remained equivocal about the civil rights movement as a whole. Generally speaking, Robert Kennedy sympathized with the Freedom Riders. He admired their courage and said they had "succeeded in moving the nation's conscience."[112] But they aroused his anger for, in his view, deliberately, almost joyously, causing political disruption by provoking white southerners to violence. Seigenthaler's ordeal, for Kennedy not only a personal affront but a revelation of the viciousness of the segregationists, tempered that anger. The true enemies, Kennedy ultimately decided, were the violent mobs and their compatriots in positions of authority in state and local governments who flaunted their power and taunted him and his brother so soon after the Bay of Pigs debacle. The effrontery of the humiliations of Anniston, Birmingham, and Montgomery and their embarrassing international repercussions sparked Robert Kennedy's enmity, for he saw them as stains on his brother's escutcheon.[113]

After the attacks in Montgomery the attorney general telephoned Patterson. Again, the governor was unavailable. Without local liaison and with no help in sight, Kennedy faced a decision. To justify federal intervention he sent John Doar to argue before federal judge Frank Johnson (the only sympathetic judge within fifty miles) that the federal government had authority to keep interstate commerce free of obstruction. Johnson agreed; in a decision that insured the further enmity of white segregationists, he issued a temporary restraining order against the Alabama Klan groups.[114] Kennedy then deployed four hundred U.S. marshals under Byron White's command to protect the Freedom Riders in Montgomery. Upon arriving in Alabama, White was summoned to the governor's office where Patterson berated him, calling his marshals unnecessary "interlopers," subject to arrest if they broke any Alabama laws. Patterson demanded that the federal authorities turn over the Freedom Riders, who, as the result of a state court injunction, were considered legally responsible for the rioting at the bus terminal. White refused, but Patterson's legal arguments gave him pause, and he left the meeting wondering if Robert Kennedy knew what he was doing. Bypassing the attorney general, White called the president directly and recommended that the marshals be withdrawn.[115] They were not.

Matters grew more complicated for Robert Kennedy when Martin Luther King decided to join the Riders in Montgomery. Kennedy and Marshall tried to talk him out of it, but King held firm. Given no choice, Kennedy sent staffers to Montgomery to organize protection for King.[116] He knew the move played right to the rumors circulating through the South that the Kennedys were in league with King and the Freedom Riders, but approximately fifty U.S. marshals stood by to protect King when he arrived in Montgomery.[117]

With the crisis deepening, the attorney general abandoned his regular weekend routine with his children, leaving Hickory Hill dressed for the softball game he had intended to play in or the touch-football game he had just left. He spent the remainder of the weekend until dawn Monday in his office command post closely following each breaking event, supervising tactical decisions, and consulting with his brother over an open telephone line to Glen Ora, the president's weekend retreat in Virginia.

Sunday evening, 21 May, fifteen hundred people crowded into Ralph Abernathy's First Baptist Church in Montgomery. Outside a white mob gathered. Growing bolder before a token force of U.S. marshals and with no police in sight, they firebombed a car and hurled Molotov cocktails and stench bombs at the church. The protocol-conscious ministers inside appointed their second-in-command, Reverend Wyatt Walker, to call the attorney general and inform him of the severity of the situation, leaving Martin Luther King to speak to the president.

"We are doing everything we can," Robert Kennedy told Walker.

He then asked to speak to King, making it clear that the attorney general, for that evening at least, was the man in charge. Help was on the way, he told King, meaning the remaining body of about four hundred U.S. marshals. In an attempt at humor, Robert added, "As long as you're in church, Reverend King, and our men are down there, you might as well say a prayer for us." King thought it a tasteless remark.[118]

Kennedy felt apprehensive about whether the marshals would get there on time and how they would react. Headed by James McShane, the president's former bodyguard, the "army" of U.S. marshals was, in reality, a makeshift group of federal prison guards, Border Patrol officers, and bureaucrats with no training in riot control. They were delayed in arriving because they had no transportation of their own and had to commandeer mail trucks. In case the marshals were overwhelmed, Kennedy kept Airborne troops on alert at Fort Benning. Several hours into the siege, Byron White decided the marshals could not hold back the mob and called the president to advise him to declare a state of public disorder and bring in the army. Before the Kennedys could act, Governor Patterson, listening in on all of White's calls through the switchboard at Maxwell Air Force Base, countered by ordering the Alabama National Guard to move in and place themselves between the mob and the church; this also brought the local police out of hiding. With local authorities in control, the marshals withdrew in their mail trucks.

When Patterson agreed to assume responsibility for restoring order, Robert Kennedy had gotten what he wanted. Relaxed, he granted an interview with *Time,* painted a story of federal-state cooperation for the *New York Times,* and allowed a UPI photographer to take a picture of him in a rather mussed state, wearing a polo shirt and baggy pants, with his feet propped on his desk and the phone wedged between his shoulder and ear. (The photos prompted a rash of mail criticizing his sloppy and undignified appearance.)

Kennedy had let his guard down too early. Once again, Patterson had deceived him. The guard refused to allow the people in Abernathy's church to leave.

King telephoned Kennedy and berated him for withdrawing the marshals. "Now, Reverend," Kennedy said, on the verge of losing his patience, "don't tell me that. You know just as well as I do that if it hadn't been for the United States Marshals you'd be as dead as Kelsey's nuts right now." Puzzled by the obscure Irish expression, which Kennedy had garbled anyway, King was too drained by the harrowing events to argue.[119]

Kennedy spoke next to Patterson, who baited him with sarcasm and blamed him for the violence. At some point in their raging argument, Patterson agreed to protect everyone in the church but King. At this, Kennedy demanded that the commander of the guard call him. "I want to hear a general of the United States Army say he can't protect Martin Luther King." Patterson told Kennedy that he had missed the point; protecting King was a matter of political perception, not military capability, and "you are destroying us politically." By then Patterson's political future meant little to Kennedy, but the president's political survival depended on him quelling the violence. "John," he said, "it's more important that these people in the church survive physically than for us to survive politically." Tired and distraught, the two friends-turned-antagonists wound down after forty-five minutes and allowed subordinates to handle the rest. The Montgomery siege ended quietly. William Orrick, a tax specialist who felt out of his element, was instructed by Kennedy simply to "do it," negotiate a truce with the guard. When just before dawn the people in the church were allowed to leave, some, ironically, were transported home by Alabama guardsmen.[120]

The Freedom Ride crisis was far from over. Returning home at 6:00 A.M. for a few hours' rest and a change of clothes, the attorney general met later that day with the president. They decided to withdraw the U.S. marshals from Montgomery and to return to their original strategy: Allow the Riders to test the local statutes and rely on the states to uphold law and order. Without consulting the Freedom Riders Robert Kennedy agreed, as he later admitted, to allowing them to be arrested if they continued their Rides.[121] On Monday and Tuesday Kennedy negotiated assurances from Alabama and Mississippi officials to protect the Freedom Riders on the next leg of their journey. During the complicated two-state negotiations Kennedy estimated that he spoke with Mississippi senator James Eastland perhaps sixty times. He also spoke at length with Governor Ross Barnett and with the mayor of

Jackson, Allen Thompson. Eastland gave Kennedy his personal guarantee that the bus could continue into Mississippi and no violence would occur.[122]

At 7:06 A.M. Wednesday, 24 May, the Freedom Rides resumed. Kennedy had FBI agents and U.S. attorneys staged along the way, with U.S. Border Patrol planes flying high-altitude reconnaissance over the forty-two-vehicle armed caravan. He continually reassessed the situation, ordering sudden changes in the itinerary when threats appeared. The trip, including the hand-off at the state lines, went without incident. When the bus arrived at Jackson, the Freedom Riders were promptly arrested for violating local Jim Crow laws. A second group of Riders, including James Farmer of CORE, boarded the 11:25 Greyhound from Montgomery, catching Kennedy off guard. The Alabama and Mississippi authorities, expecting only one busload, thought the attorney general had sandbagged them. Kennedy scrambled to extend the agreement with the now aggravated state officials to cover the second trip.

He chose that moment to issue his first formal statement on the Freedom Rides. Kennedy disavowed the second bus as having "nothing to do with the Freedom Riders." He complimented Alabama and Mississippi officials for maintaining order and warned others contemplating Freedom Rides that federal marshals would not be there to protect them. Kennedy then took a fateful misstep, as far as civil rights groups were concerned. Stressing the harmful effects of the Freedom Rides on his brother's upcoming meetings with French President Charles de Gaulle and Soviet premier Nikita Khrushchev, he cautioned against actions that would "discredit" our country at this crucial juncture, when "continuing international publicity about ugly race riots in the South would send the leader of the free world into European palaces with mud on his shoes."[123]

Kennedy's statement had hardly hit the news wires when he learned that yet another interracial group from the North, this one including Yale University chaplain William Sloan Coffin, Jr., had arrived in Montgomery. Fearing he might never see an end to the crisis and irritated by the presence of what he called "curiosity seekers, publicity seekers, and others who are seeking to serve their own causes,"

Kennedy issued a statement calling for a "cooling-off period" and for a "delay" in any further Freedom Rides. James Farmer, asked to respond upon arriving in Jackson, said, "Please tell the Attorney General that we have been cooling off for 350 years." A reporter in Montgomery asked Ralph Abernathy if he was not afraid of embarrassing the president. "Man," he answered, "we've been embarrassed all our lives."[124]

Even as the civil rights leadership tested Robert Kennedy's patience, he remained concerned about the twenty-seven Freedom Riders in the Jackson jail and directed attorneys to arrange bail. When all the Riders refused it, he called King that night to ask why. "It's a matter of conscience and morality," King said. "Our conscience tells us that the law is wrong and we must resist, but we have a moral obligation to accept the penalty." Thinking this a ploy, Kennedy became testy. "The fact that they stay in jail is not going to have the slightest effect on me." Perhaps, said King, the attorney general would be affected "if students came down here by the hundreds—by the hundreds of thousands."

"Do as you wish," Kennedy bristled, "but don't make statements that sound like a threat. That's not the way to deal with us." After an awkward pause, King pulled back. "I'm deeply appreciative of what the Administration is doing," he said, but "I feel the need of being free now!" Weary from lack of sleep, Robert Kennedy wanted closure. "If they want to get out," he told King, "we can get them out." Said King, "They'll stay."[125]

Tired and irritated from the tensions of around-the-clock negotiations, feeling that his efforts had gone unappreciated by King and his group, and looking forward to a family weekend at Hyannis Port, Robert let his guard slip again. "It took a lot of guts for the first group to go," he was quoted as saying, "but not much for the others." The decision of the Freedom Riders to stay in jail, he added, made "good propaganda for America's enemies." To Wofford he expressed doubts that the Freedom Riders had the best interests of the country at heart, saying he was shocked to learn that "one of them is against the atom bomb—yes, he even picketed against it in jail!"[126] The president shared those sentiments. "SNCC," he said, "has got an investment in violence. They're sons of bitches."[127] On 25 May in what was billed as his Second State of the Union Address of 1961, John Kennedy stated that he intended to promote the "freedom doctrine" around the globe but made no mention of Negro civil rights or the Freedom Rides, either then or during press conferences in the weeks following the crisis.[128]

The Kennedys' objective all along, Robert later admitted, was to focus "attention and resentment . . . on me rather than on the president."[129] The president remained in the background but in close touch with the attorney general. Everyone in the upper echelons knew that when Robert Kennedy spoke it was tantamount to the president himself speaking. But during the first few months of the Kennedy administration, the public at large, especially black and white southerners, associated the government's civil rights actions primarily with the attorney general. Both the blame and the credit seemed to fall on Robert. Asked to name the biggest problem in the country, a Mississippi woman said, "[President] Kennedy has too many brothers."[130] Most people in the civil rights movement appreciated the attorney general's combative involvement in the Freedom Rides. "We thank Jack, Bob, and God!" Fred Shuttlesworth exclaimed. At year's end, Reverend Wyatt Walker, King's associate in Atlanta, nominated the attorney general for "American of the Year in 1961."[131] Some remain grateful to this day for Robert Kennedy's actions. One Freedom Rider, recalling thirty years later a harrowing ride to reach New Orleans in the summer of 1961, said, "Bobby Kennedy saved my life."[132]

Despite his misgivings about their motives, Robert Kennedy made sure that the Freedom Riders' efforts were not in vain. He directed his staff on 29 May 1961 to gain a ruling from the Interstate Commerce Commission (ICC) to desegregate travel facilities. When Martin Luther King first made such a suggestion to Kennedy he had rejected it as naive. But Katzenbach's office did some furious digging and came up with the novel idea of petitioning the ICC. Kennedy signed the petition and forwarded it that same day, then hounded the nominally independent agency until on 22 September the ICC issued regulations ending segregation in interstate bus terminals, followed by similar orders for railroads and airline terminals.[133]

Freedom Rides continued throughout the summer of 1961, but they made few headlines, which pleased Kennedy. In effect, he had worked out a truce with the South. The new Freedom Riders, as Taylor

Branch has reported, were "funneled efficiently, almost protectively" into the southern prison systems. Soon, even Martin Luther King saw the futility of further Rides. When scores of SNCC activists descended on Jackson, bringing the number in jail to nearly 250, King recommended a "temporary lull," not a "cooling-off period."[134] On the question of what to do next, Robert Kennedy had one answer, Martin Luther King another.

At the height of the Freedom Rides crisis, Harris Wofford told the president, "What Eisenhower never did was to give clear moral expression to the issues involved. The only effective time for such moral leadership is during an occasion of moral crisis. This is the time when your words would mean most." Wofford advised the president that "Negro leaders feel sorely the absence of any such statement."[135] Martin Luther King wanted President Kennedy to take a moral stand by making a second Emancipation Proclamation. The Kennedys wanted King and the others to devote themselves to the federal voter registration projects, a political solution to the problem.

On 16 June Kennedy met with the Freedom Ride Coordinating Committee. They came to request additional government help, but Kennedy wanted the Freedom Rides ended. Voter registration, he told them, was a more effective alternative to direct-action protest. One member of the delegation, Reverend Charles Sherrod, considered that a presumptuous suggestion and lectured the attorney general on his duties. "It's your job," Sherrod shouted, "to protect us," not "to tell us how to honor our constitutional rights." Pacing the office in his stocking feet, Kennedy patiently replied that they could do something even larger than make headlines—they could change the politics of the South.[136]

Voter Registration

The voter registration strategy, of course, offered a way for the Kennedys to have their cake and eat it, too, a way to avoid further confrontations, minimize political backlash, and offer the black community something substantive (that might earn their support in 1964). Robert

Kennedy directed much of the resources of his office to the establishment of the Voter Education Project (VEP), a private, nonprofit umbrella organization to coordinate and fund a massive voter registration drive in the South. Kennedy sensed Martin Luther King's resentment over his attempts to dictate the movement's direction, "but I thought that's where they should go," he said, "and that's what they should do."[137] For a time at least, he deflected the direction of the mightiest social movement of the twentieth century.

Moving quickly and boldly, Kennedy sent Burke Marshall on missions to bring CORE, SNCC, SCLC, and the NAACP together under the Kennedy-sponsored umbrella of VEP. He asked Wofford to convince SNCC and CORE leaders to join, persuaded Harry Belafonte to use his influence with SNCC students, requested IRS commissioner Mortimer Caplan to issue a tax exemption for the VEP, helped secure $870,000 in funding from the Taconic, Stern, and Field Foundations, and generated a front-page story in the *New York Times* anticipating a political breakthrough in the South and announcing that King and other leaders had agreed (when they had not) that securing the vote was the key step toward equal rights.[138]

To win over young black activists, Kennedy's staff confidentially promised them draft exemptions and left them with the impression (well founded or not) that the federal government would protect them if trouble occurred. The issue of federal protection would prove of pivotal importance historically. "Bobby pledged marshals and what have you to help us out," one member of SNCC recalled. Another black person present at the same meetings said later, "I never heard anybody from the Justice Department say, 'Sure you fellows go out there and we'll give you all the protection you need.'" Yet they carried such an impression away from the meetings.[139]

In August 1961, Robert Kennedy persuaded SNCC to join VEP. CORE followed suit in September, and the Voter Education Project was formally launched in March 1962. Using information supplied by Louis Martin, VEP targeted southern districts, mostly in rural areas, where volunteers attempted to register blacks. In Amite County, Mississippi, for example, 85 percent of the people were black, and yet no black person had voted there since Reconstruction. At the same time,

Justice Department attorneys, headed by John Doar, instituted legal proceedings wherever they could demonstrate that blacks were systematically denied the right to vote. The VEP, however, was flawed at the outset by basic conceptual differences between Kennedy and the civil rights volunteers and by Kennedy's ignorance of southern history and culture. With little knowledge of or regard for the southern racial hatred that had seethed for generations, Kennedy allowed volunteers to enter the South laboring under the misapprehension that they were in a partnership with the federal government.

Violence was inevitable. The first attempts to register black voters in Mississippi resulted in the brutal beatings of volunteers John Hardy and Robert Moses; the murder of Herbert Lee, a local farmer with nine children; and uncounted perversions of justice. Doar tried to intervene in the Hardy case but was rebuffed by a Kennedy appointee, federal Judge Harold Cox. The murderer of Herbert Lee went unindicted because of FBI intransigence and ineptness, Burke Marshall's fear of sparking chaos, and the intimidation of three black witnesses by white locals.[140] Frustrated and feeling defenseless and betrayed, SNCC members and other activists cursed Robert Kennedy, Burke Marshall, and the FBI more than the southern sheriffs and rednecks who beat them.[141] SNCC chair Chuck McDew remembered Kennedy saying of the witnesses in the Lee murder, "They should testify. It's their duty as Americans." But when Kennedy said he could not protect them, "I remember cussing him out," said McDew. "We were very turned off by the Kennedy administration," he said, "because when we talked to Bobby or the president about federal protection, they would go into their song and dance: 'Well, the FBI is an investigative unit. They aren't there to protect you.' So the FBI would watch us being whipped and beaten, but do nothing about it."[142]

Robert Kennedy could not hold back the tide. Before the VEP began, SNCC organizers took protests to the streets of Albany, Georgia, a segregated city of 50,000 of whom 20,000 were blacks. The Albany movement attracted national attention after Martin Luther King was arrested for protesting Albany's Jim Crow laws. Robert Kennedy expressed his moral support for the movement but officially announced a "hands off" policy. Still clinging to his federal approach, Kennedy believed he could not intervene unless or until law and order broke down. "Real progress" in race relations, he told reporters, required that "local leaders talk it out." As tensions increased, he let it be known that he was in close contact with events, that Albany was "number one" on his agenda, and that he stood ready to give advice if requested by either side.[143] When an agreement was worked out to release protestors and restore order, Robert Kennedy telephoned congratulations to the mayor and police chief, but not the SNCC or SCLC leaders.[144]

As soon as the reporters left town, Albany officials broke the agreement. Black protest marches and SNCC's efforts to register voters met with violence. "Where was the Federal Government?" Charles Sherrod and other terrorized civil rights workers wanted to know. Kennedy's Justice Department refused to compel the desegregation of Albany's public facilities or to give the VEP workers the protection they believed had been promised. The Albany movement, along with many of the CORE and SNCC members working for VEP and experiencing the same situation elsewhere, turned against Robert Kennedy's grand scheme. A frustrated Robert Moses, working then on voter registration in Mississippi, tried to file a suit in federal court to force Robert Kennedy's Justice Department to protect the VEP workers.[145]

Activists accused the Kennedys of misleading them with rhetoric and promises. Outspoken blacks, such as historian Vincent Harding and SNCC activist Lonnie King, charged the Kennedys with trying to kill the movement by rechanneling its energies. They called the voter registration project a cynical plan to "get the niggers off the street."[146] James Forman of SNCC described the president as "quick-talking, double-dealing" and his VEP as preparation for his reelection in 1964. But, as Victor Navasky pointed out, SNCC had received no pledges; they acted on their assumption of tacit promises from the Kennedys.[147]

Looking back on 1961, Martin Luther King said, "This administration has reached out more creatively than its predecessors to blaze some new trails," and shown imagination and boldness, but in "melancholy fact," the Kennedys were "aggressively driving toward the limited goal of token integration." The country, King asserted, was ready for "bold leadership."[148]

CHAPTER 12

Toward a Moral Commitment on Civil Rights

IN BOTH THE CIVIL RIGHTS MOVEMENT and Robert Kennedy's education about its meaning, 1962 proved a transition year. "The more he saw," Burke Marshall said, and the more he learned about how Negroes were treated in the South, the "madder" he became, until Kennedy "was so mad about that kind of thing it overrode everything else."[1] Marshall exaggerated. Kennedy's indignation over the treatment of southern blacks deepened in 1962, to be sure, but few indications of anger and moral outrage appear before the early months of 1963. Until then, he frequently got as angry and frustrated with the black leadership as he was with hard-line segregationists, often condemning "extremists" on both sides.

Violence in the South escalated in the spring of 1962 with the fire-bombing of black churches, which John Kennedy labeled "cowardly" and "outrageous," but Robert Kennedy's Justice Department insisted it was powerless to provide "protection guarantees" for voter registration workers.[2] Black leaders could not understand why the Kennedys equivocated on protecting the very workers whose presence in the South they helped arrange.

An Alliance of Convenience

Snared in a moral and political dilemma, the Kennedys found partial relief by drawing closer to King, ultimately forming a tacit alliance with the man who came to embody the safe middle ground of U.S. race relations. In this alliance of convenience, each side, with reason, was wary of the other.

To begin, Robert Kennedy seriously wondered how long King could hold the reins of black leadership. Suspecting "a revolution within a revolution," Robert sensed a shift away from Martin Luther King toward "some of these younger people, who had no belief or confidence in the system of government that we have here."[3] The growing nationalistic mood of black Americans, he warned the cabinet in May 1963, meant that "you can't get a reasonable Negro leadership because . . . they're competing with one another."[4] Kennedy's views had a substantive foundation. Literally beaten down by southern racism, SNCC and CORE members questioned King's nonviolent and integrationist approaches and eventually proposed alternatives formulated around the rallying cry of Black Power.

Even as King found himself pulled to the political center and to a rendezvous with the Kennedys, he remained skeptical of their moral commitment and political motives. His hopes of convincing John Kennedy to invoke the moral power of the presidency in one impressive symbolic gesture were deflated when the president refused to sign a second Emancipation Proclamation and declined to attend the official ceremony honoring the hundredth anniversary of the original. In his place Kennedy sent a recorded message and his brother Robert, who made no speech. King, showing some pique in the attorney general's presence, used the occasion to criticize the administration's sluggish pace on civil rights.[5]

King found the Kennedys' fixation on voter registration misplaced. As uncomfortable with electoral politics as the Kennedys were with mass social movements, King could never truly appreciate the Kennedys' political dilemma. Nor could he understand their reluctance to make a full and genuine commitment to racial equality. Caught in political winds himself, King became the object of much political attention from white politicians but little affection. An exception was Governor Nelson Rockefeller of New York, who had a long history of advocating racial equality (and also had thoughts of running against John Kennedy in 1964). Rockefeller showered King with money and personal attention, delivering, as the Kennedys never would, on promises to disseminate his ideas and with funds to aid his ministry.[6]

Robert Kennedy would have pursued that strategy himself, if he, like Rockefeller, were a Republican. Kennedy—who often imagined how he would behave if he were in someone else's shoes—thought the smart, long-term approach for the Republicans was to take a moderate position on civil rights to distinguish themselves from the Democrats, shackled to the South and its antiblack biases. With that approach Republicans would "win all the elections," he said, "just because I think the Negro could be the swing vote."[7] In reality, of course, the Kennedys were loath to challenge southern Democratic leaders. And moderates like Rockefeller were a minority in a Republican party growing more conservative and less inclined to go after the black vote. That left the Kennedys some political wiggle room and allowed them to demand more of King.

Further impeding a Kennedy-King fusion, the Kennedys found it difficult to warm to King's intense, humorless moralizing and to deal with his methods, which in their view smacked of grandstanding. Strained from the beginning, the relationship between Robert Kennedy and Martin Luther King suffered a setback in October 1961 when King telegraphed Kennedy to protest the beatings of civil rights workers and the murder of Herbert Lee in Mississippi and released a copy of the wire to the press before Kennedy could receive it and respond.[8] Kennedy believed that King's intention, whether calculated or not, was to embarrass him. This kind of behavior incensed him. The following August, King again crossed Kennedy by announcing his intention to disobey a federal restraining order against further protests in Albany, Georgia. After a sharp and lengthy exchange in which King accused Kennedy of creating the problem himself by appointing segregationists to the federal courts, the SCLC leader reluctantly accepted the attorney general's reasoning that to disobey a court order, with southern governors looking for excuses to disobey federal desegregation orders, would destroy the credibility of King's movement and undermine the Kennedys' position as well.[9]

But by far King's greatest liability to the Kennedys was his persistent association with two persons the FBI identified as Communists. Nothing in the Cold War era could have damaged the Kennedys, King, and the struggle to end racial segregation more than proof (there were plenty of rumors and wild accusations) that the Soviet Union was directly influencing the civil rights movement. Enter J. Edgar Hoover. Until May 1961, the FBI paid scant attention to King. Then Hoover was made aware of King's published criticisms of the FBI. Told the FBI had not yet investigated King, Hoover asked, "Why not?"[10]

On 8 January 1962 Hoover reported to the attorney general that the FBI had identified Stanley D. Levison, King's friend, financial advisor, and ghost writer, as a "high official," a "member of the Executive Board," of the Communist party.[11] Robert Kennedy never divulged the background details (however much he knew of them) of these allegations. It is now known, however, that the FBI's sources were a pair of double agents, the brothers Jack and Morris Childs (code named Solo). Through them the FBI learned that between 1952 and 1955 Levison was closely involved in financial activities of the CPUSA. According to historian David Garrow, who disclosed the existence of Solo in 1981 and has thoroughly studied the FBI's surveillance of Martin Luther King, the reports of Levison's earlier activities "in all likelihood were quite accurate."[12]

Levison, according to the FBI, was active with the Communist party until 1955. When the FBI learned that Levison had broken with the party, agents ended their electronic surveillance of him and deleted his name from their list of "key figures" in the party.[13] Thus, when Levison met Martin Luther King (and Harris Wofford) in 1956, he was no longer active in the party. But to Hoover, once a Communist, always a Communist. Hoover informed Robert Kennedy in 1962 that Levison was a "secret member" of the party and a part of the Soviet espionage network. Kennedy did not know that Hoover's statements were based on sheer speculation and that beyond the dated Solo reports the FBI had no hard evidence to substantiate their allegations of Levison's on-going involvement with the party. Hoover said he could provide no explicit details out of fear of compromising Solo, the FBI's deepest, most effective penetration into CPUSA operations. Kennedy accepted the explanation. Matters became stickier on 14 February when the FBI reported that Levison had recommended the appointment to King's SCLC staff of Hunter Pitts "Jack" O'Dell, who, according to the FBI, had once been a member of the party's national committee.

This situation, Robert Kennedy later confided, explained why he and his brother were "so reserved" about King and "never wanted to get very close to him."[14] But because the public perceived the Kennedys and King as close allies, the attorney general had to act on the FBI information, lest the Kennedys be tainted. In February 1962 Robert Kennedy instructed John Seigenthaler to warn King that several persons close to him were Communists. Burke Marshall asked Harris Wofford to speak to King, also. When those efforts produced no immediate changes in King's behavior, the attorney general approved an FBI request for an authorization to tap Levison's office telephone. A month later, in April 1962, the Senate Internal Security Subcommittee, acting on a tip from Hoover, subpoenaed Levison. Under oath he denied ever being a member of the CPUSA, claimed to be a "loyal American," and took the Fifth Amendment in answer to most questions. Levison's evasive performance strengthened Hoover's speculative hypothesis and put Robert Kennedy even more on guard.[15]

"To protect ourselves," Robert Kennedy said, he then ordered the FBI to make an "extensive investigation" of King "to see who his companions were and also to see what other activities he was involved in."[16]

As they frequently did with potential allies of whom they were suspicious and even with some of their own staff members, the Kennedys tested King under pressure, putting him in a situation where they could assess his loyalty and reliability.[17] In these political set-ups each Kennedy knew his role. In King's case the attorney general had first warned King and then ordered wiretaps on Levison, while the president played the congenial and charming host to King at a private White House luncheon. Arriving for the luncheon, King was taken aside by Harris Wofford, who delivered a message from the president and the attorney general. Levison was a Communist, Wofford told King, and he must stop seeing him. Unbelieving, King asked for proof. Wofford, doubtful himself, said the FBI had classified the details to protect their sources.[18] But Wofford made one thing clear: The Kennedys' support was contingent on King's not mentioning their private meetings and on his ceasing to associate with Levison. King was then invited into the mansion's private quarters for a quiet luncheon with President and Mrs. Kennedy. No substantive discussions were held. When the event went unreported in the press, King had satisfied the Kennedys' first criterion.[19] Satisfying the second would prove more difficult.

Integrating Ole Miss

Meanwhile, other crises intervened. Robert Kennedy's most trying experience as attorney general, known to insiders as the "Oxford crisis," occurred in September and early October 1962.[20] In January 1961, James H. Meredith had applied for admission to the all-white University of Mississippi. "Nobody handpicked me," the twenty-eight-year-old Air Force veteran said, but he admitted being inspired to apply by John Kennedy's inaugural address. In June 1962 the NAACP obtained a federal court ruling ordering Meredith's admission. Mississippi governor Ross Barnett said he would go to jail before he would let "that boy" backed by the "Communist" NAACP get into Ole Miss. On 10 September Supreme Court justice Hugo Black issued an order enjoining interference with Meredith's admission.

At that point, according to Burke Marshall, Robert Kennedy attempted to take "control." Concerned about the international repercussions of another fractious civil rights confrontation (just as tensions were mounting toward what became the Cuban Missile Crisis), he tried but failed to stop a federal judge from citing Barnett for criminal contempt. Barnett responded to the contempt citation with inflammatory rhetoric. "We will not surrender to the evil and illegal forces of tyranny," he said, pledging to remain in contempt of the federal courts.[21] Now it was Robert Kennedy's duty, as he had promised at the University of Georgia, to enforce the court orders.

As with the Freedom Rides, Kennedy tried to avoid direct confrontations of federal and state authority through bargaining. He was less concerned with the enforcement of the court's contempt order against Barnett than with achieving the integration of the University of Mississippi without creating a "federal presence" in Mississippi. A large presence would surely cause embarrassment internationally and provoke southern whites' resentment over a matter that commentators were likening to the test of states' rights at Fort Sumter in 1861 that touched off the Civil War.

Amidst all the subsequent muddle, Barnett's basic position was manifest. He wanted Robert Kennedy either to back down all the way or to exert extraordinary force to accomplish Meredith's admission. Either way the governor would have done his duty in the eyes of the people of Mississippi. Any conciliation or compromise with the Kennedys would spell disaster for Barnett.[22]

So intent was Kennedy on avoiding a showdown confrontation that on three occasions he allowed Barnett and Lieutenant Governor Paul Johnson to block Meredith's attempts to register, permitting them to rebuff and upstage not only Meredith but his chief aides, John Doar and Chief U.S. Marshal James McShane, who accompanied Meredith. He tolerated Barnett's posturing as long as the governor remained reasonable in their private conversations and as long as a negotiated settlement seemed within reach. Kennedy and Barnett had twenty telephone conversations during the last two weeks of September alone. All the while, hundreds of angry segregationists flocked to Oxford from all parts of the South.

The attorney general and the governor of Mississippi, as Taylor Branch pointed out, shared the fraternal belief that politicians "weathered crises best by accommodating the interests of other politicians."[23] Realizing they stood near the edge of a political abyss, Kennedy and Barnett probed each other rather gently at first. Kennedy never threatened Barnett with prison or with military force. When Barnett broke the unspoken ground rules by suggesting that Meredith go to college elsewhere—a step that would have tossed the Kennedys into the abyss—Robert Kennedy could not resist tweaking the governor, answering, "But Meredith likes Ole Miss." Mostly, however, the two discussed possible scenarios for getting Meredith registered without violence and without destroying themselves politically. They even considered staging a mock scene where U.S. marshals would make a show of force before Barnett's state troopers, who would then withdraw. They threw out the notion when they disagreed over how many U.S. marshals would draw their guns. That scenario, as ludicrous as it seemed, contained a message apparently misread by Kennedy. Barnett had to yield at gunpoint or suffer political humiliation.

Kennedy underestimated Barnett's resolve, cloaked in a warm and cordial tone, a slow and formal manner of speaking, and country witticisms spun with a syrupy southern accent. Thinking at first that he was a "loony," Kennedy later described Barnett as a weak but "agreeable rogue," who gave assurances as easily as he withdrew them. Looking back, he thought Barnett behaved in "foolish ways" and "got himself into a bigger and bigger box." However, Kennedy lamented, "He eventually pulled me in with him."[24]

On Friday, 28 September, a federal court found Barnett and Johnson guilty of contempt and ordered them to purge themselves of contempt by obeying the court order and allowing Meredith to register within four days or face arrest and a fine of $10,000 a day. Barnett said he would rather spend the rest of his life in a penitentiary than admit Meredith to Ole Miss. Now at an impasse, Robert Kennedy ordered a contingent of U.S. marshals to begin assembling in Memphis. Having gained no ground with Barnett, Robert realized the time had come for his brother to try his own brand of personal persuasion.

That Saturday, for the first time in the course of the civil rights confrontations, John Kennedy became personally involved. Until then his brother's was the voice of government authority in civil rights negotiations. Before Oxford, Robert said later, "I wouldn't have to bother him with it [civil rights matters], nor would he have to think about it." Robert said he was in a better position than the president to evaluate the pros and cons and to make decisions, except when his actions might have adverse implications for the president. "Obviously, then we'd talk."[25] Oxford was the first such instance.

"Go get him, Johnny boy," said the attorney general as the president reached for the telephone to speak to Governor Barnett.[26] Deceived by Barnett's apparently deferential manner, John Kennedy hung up and told his brother, "You've been fighting a sofa pillow all week."

But the president had made no real headway with Barnett either. He had even agreed to give him "a few days" to think it over. The brothers consulted, and an hour later Robert called back to tell Barnett that, contrary to what the president had said, there was no reason for further delay.

Barnett disarmed the Kennedys by proposing that, rather than force a confrontation at the Oxford campus, they sneak Meredith onto the deserted Jackson campus and register him while students were away for the weekend. Barnett said he would announce that the government had surprised him, that Meredith was now registered, and that nothing more could be done. The governor also agreed to remain in Oxford and keep order there. The scheme appealed to the Kennedys because it avoided the use of troops. "We've got a deal with Barnett," a relieved Burke Marshall told the staff. But three hours later, Barnett backed out. Late Saturday evening, with no other recourse and the court-imposed deadline approaching, the president signed a proclamation ordering persons obstructing justice in Mississippi to desist and disperse. He then issued an executive order federalizing the Mississippi National Guard.

On Sunday morning, in a final negotiating ploy, Robert Kennedy overstepped the bounds of political courtesy. He called Barnett and told him that a federal force was on its way, that the president was going to go on television and say that Barnett, contrary to what the governor had told his constituents, had agreed the day before to register Meredith and then broken his word.[27] "We have it all down," Kennedy told Barnett, referring to tapes and transcripts of the telephone calls. An enraged Barnett decided that he would rather appear hoodwinked by a conniving attorney general than be exposed as a fraud for conspiring in a secret integrationist deal. "Why don't you fly him in this afternoon?" Barnett suggested. It would be safer, he said, because few students would be on the Oxford campus on a Sunday afternoon and everyone expected the showdown to occur on Monday or Tuesday, the deadline for Barnett's contempt citation. Barnett even agreed to provide an escort of state troopers for Meredith. Having gained the concessions through political blackmail, Robert Kennedy had reason to be apprehensive about Barnett's motives.

That evening James Meredith arrived at Ole Miss accompanied by sullen state troopers, protected by more than four hundred U.S. marshals, and escorted by the attorney general's crisis management team headed by Katzenbach, with Doar, Louis Oberdorfer, Joseph Dolan, and Ed Guthman playing key supporting roles. They took Meredith to his dorm room, and U.S. marshals were positioned around the Lyceum, the main administration building and an icon of the Old South. It was the "most offensive thing we could have done," Katzenbach later realized, "like surrounding the tomb of Robert E. Lee."[28]

Sensing a catastrophe in the making, Barnett moved to withdraw his state troopers. Robert Kennedy countered by threatening again to have the president, minutes away from a national television address, announce that Barnett had made a deal and then reneged. By then it was too late. Most of the troopers drifted away on their own. The gathering mob, hurling bottles and bricks, then surged into the line of marshals. Gunfire erupted just five minutes before President Kennedy went on television to inform the country of the integration of the University of Mississippi and to appeal to the pride of white Mississippians to preserve law and order. "Americans are free to disagree with the law," he told them, "but not to disobey it."[29] At that moment, unknown to the Kennedys, a full-scale riot was underway in Oxford. The president seemed so calm and confident on television that army troops on alert assumed he had matters under control and stood down.

Through the night the Kennedys maintained a grim vigil at the White House. In constant contact with the Justice Department team on two pay telephone lines kept open through the siege, they told Katzenbach that the marshals must not return fire "under any conditions" except to protect Meredith's life. Nearly overrun on several occasions, the marshals fended off the mob with tear gas and nightsticks. "It's getting like the Alamo," Guthman told the attorney general. "Well," Kennedy joked in the dark humor that filled the Cabinet Room that night, "you know what happened to those guys, don't you?"[30] At one point John Kennedy conceded that Barnett was right—the best thing to do was to remove Meredith from Oxford. "I *can't* get him out," Robert had to admit to his brother. Around midnight, with the marshals running out of tear gas, the Kennedys ordered the army into Oxford, but troops did not arrive until 5:00 A.M.

Those five hours were agony for Robert Kennedy. He had let his brother down. "I haven't had such an interesting time," John Kennedy said dryly in the only way that could hurt his brother, "since the Bay of Pigs." The comparison to the Bay of Pigs remained imprinted on Robert's mind. "The fact that I said that the troops would arrive and they didn't arrive was my fault," he said later. "We could just visualize another great disaster, like the Bay of Pigs."[31] The Kennedys could fault the CIA for the Bay of Pigs, but the debacle at Ole Miss was of Robert's making. Through the long night the attorney general, according to Taylor Branch's summary of White House tape recordings, "alternately joked, whimpered, seethed, and cursed."[32]

The fact that "people were being shot," Robert conceded, was "really my responsibility." The president, he said, was "torn between an Attorney General who had botched things up and the fact that the Attorney General was his brother."[33]

John Kennedy did not then or ever show displeasure with Robert in the presence of others. He turned his wrath instead on the army, whose planners had promised that in two hours they could move troops from Memphis to Oxford and bring "overwhelming force" to suppress any riot.[34] After repeated delays and several assurances that the army was "five minutes away," Robert said his brother had "one of the worst and harshest" conversations "I think I've ever heard" with Secretary of the Army Cyrus Vance.[35] The delay was nearly catastrophic. Before the army finally mustered in Oxford and restored order, 2 bystanders, including a foreign journalist, were killed and 375 others wounded, including 166 marshals, 28 of whom had been shot.[36]

One might ask whether the bloodshed in Oxford could have been prevented had Robert Kennedy not waited to call in the army, stubborn in his belief that he could persuade or manipulate Governor Barnett into maintaining order. But to call in the army before trouble started would have risked much politically and possibly provoked greater violence. One can more easily take him to task for misreading Barnett and miscalculating the resentment in Mississippi and the volatility of the situation in Oxford. To his credit, Robert Kennedy for the record in 1964 took responsibility for the failures to execute and the lapses in judgment that day. Less praiseworthy were his efforts to lay blame elsewhere: "The army botched it up," he said. "But we didn't have an exercise with the army in which they didn't screw up."[37]

Robert Kennedy did not take out his misery on Ross Barnett. Eager for the entire matter to fade from the public's conscious, Kennedy avoided prosecuting Barnett for contempt. In the margin of a memo concerning Barnett's case, Kennedy scratched, "Can't we remain silent on this unless asked by the court?" He was grateful when, after the passage of the Civil Rights Act of 1964, the courts dropped the case.[38]

Thanks to a favorable slant put on it by northern newspapers and to the overtaking pace of events, Ole Miss did not linger in the public mind long enough to register as the great imbroglio Robert Kennedy feared. In fact, the Kennedys' defense of law and order drew approval from racial moderates, the business community, and the center of the political spectrum in general. Pollster Lou Harris reported that the president's handling of the Ole Miss situation won him significant gains among northerners, especially Jewish voters, whose support jumped 12 percentage points in two days (to 73 percent), and Negroes (up from 65 to 84 percent positive).[39]

On the fringes, however, public perceptions of the Kennedys changed dramatically. After Ole Miss, the southern white invective that had focused almost exclusively on Robert Kennedy now targeted the president too. "Go to hell, JFK!" was one of the milder oaths Ole Miss students chanted that week. Radical right vigilantes and angry segregationists throughout the South proclaimed their hatred of the Kennedys, parroted Birchite-inspired accusations that the brothers colluded with the Communists, and were abetted to violence by former army major general Edwin A. Walker, who was arrested for insurrection in Oxford.[40]

Black leaders, for the most part, were not impressed with the Kennedys' showing at Ole Miss, which most thought clumsy and hesitant. Many said John Kennedy framed his Sunday evening television address around white interests and directed it specifically at white southerners. Martin Luther King complained that the Kennedys "made Negroes feel like pawns in a white man's political game."[41] He criticized the president's failures to praise Meredith's courage, to take a moral stand on the issue, and to educate the country on the meaning of the civil rights movement.[42] James Meredith, however, expressed his personal gratitude. "It seemed to me very clear that Bobby Kennedy was the main man in determining that these steps be taken. . . . His decisions," Meredith said, "kept me alive. I'm still here."[43]

A few weeks later, all Americans felt grateful to be "still here" following the Cuban missile crisis, which at least had the benefit, as far as the Kennedys were concerned, of diverting the public's attention and truncating their reactions to the Oxford crisis. Neither Kennedy now wanted to dwell on civil rights. But they were drawn back to it by liberals who pressured for legislation, by black leaders who denounced their timidity, by the stagnation of the VEP, and by veiled threats from within the NAACP that they might consider defecting to the Republicans, who, as promised in 1960, had introduced several civil rights bills in Congress and who had a legitimate champion in Nelson Rockefeller.

Experiencing what some saw as a crisis in conscience and what others saw as trying to get themselves out of a political corner, the Kennedys appeared to change their minds almost daily, as they sent a number of contradictory signals to civil rights and political leaders.[44] In late January, Robert Kennedy told NBC's *Today* viewers that civil rights is "not a field in which I think a great deal is going to be accomplished . . . by continuously introducing legislation which has no possibility of enactment." "The President," he said, "isn't interested in that."[45] Yet, three weeks later, after a Lincoln's Birthday reception to honor Negro leaders (at which the president refused to be photographed with the interracial show business couple of Sammy Davis, Jr., and Mae Britt), and after signs of disaffection had appeared among leading blacks, John Kennedy declared racial segregation "wrong" and asked Congress for a voting rights law.

Among the least comprehensive of the eighty-nine civil rights bills introduced in the House that session, Kennedy's bill contained no provisions for fair employment, school desegregation, public accommodations, or protection for civil rights workers. It disappointed King and the other civil rights leaders. Joseph Rauh called it "an inane package." One civil rights leader said, "We've gotten the best snow job in history. We've lost two years because we admired him [John Kennedy]." The Kennedys' tepid support of their own bill—the *Nation* called the president the "Reluctant Emancipator"—caused analysts to wonder if they had not introduced it just for show.

Robert Kennedy bristled at the suggestion that they were simply "going through the motions." The problem then, he recalled in 1964, was that "nobody was ready." He said that when he testified on behalf of the bill, "Nobody paid the slightest bit of attention to me." The bill was filibustered to death for lack of a "public outcry," Robert said, ignoring the president's own inaction on the bill, which left most observers believing him indifferent to its outcome.[46] The Civil Rights Commission, after all, had warned the White House that civil rights groups would greet the bill with "massive indifference or actual opposition."[47] Defending his brother's refusal to expend any real effort on the bill, Robert admitted that in early 1963, regardless of the intensity of his brother's commitment, "There wasn't anything he [John Kennedy] could do then."[48] If the president did nothing after sending up the legislation because nothing he could have done would have made a difference, then it seems hard to escape the conclusion that they sent up the bill for appearances' sake only.

Whatever the Kennedys' motives for presenting the voting bill, Robert now freely expressed his indignation over conditions in the South. On 3 March 1963 on CBS-TV's *Washington Report,* he spoke of the injustice of denying Negroes the vote one hundred years after the end of the Civil War and the emancipation of the slaves. He made a rambling, heartfelt effort to point out the contradictions between social realities and American ideals, claiming, "We hold to believe in certain principles, . . . we go around the world and tell everybody what a fine democracy we are . . . and yet . . . in many areas of the country we treat a portion of our population as inferiors—it doesn't seem to me it makes any sense." He closed with what was becoming his signature comment: "I don't think that is very satisfactory."[49]

Two weeks later in a speech in Kentucky, he said, "We must move ahead throughout the country in achieving, for all our citizens, access to public places and the freedom to live where they choose." Lincoln's Emancipation Proclamation, said Robert Kennedy, "must not be considered a purely American experience. It is a torch that men will pass from hand to hand into every dark place in the world where slavery, of one kind or another, exists."[50]

and the "timing" of the protests. As long as Negroes were refused equal rights and opportunities, he said, increasing turmoil was "inevitable," but the problem in Birmingham was "local" and should be resolved "in good faith negotiations, and not in the streets." Kennedy directed Burke Marshall to call King to request an immediate suspension of the demonstrations, then sent Marshall and Joe Dolan to Birmingham to mediate a settlement between SCLC and the city fathers.[56] Marshall and Dolan, as representatives of the federal government, had no status or authority in the Birmingham dispute, and neither side welcomed them with any warmth.[57]

That hardly mattered to the Kennedys, for they saw themselves as problem solvers and facilitators laboring to bring order out of chaos, to make sense of Martin Luther King's confused demands, and, in the process, to assert their superiority without exercising raw authority. As Robert Kennedy explained to the cabinet a few weeks later, King and "the Negro leadership didn't know what they were demonstrating about [in Birmingham] . . . and none of the white community knew what they were demonstrating about."[58] The Kennedys failed to realize that the SCLC leadership rejoiced in creating such befuddlement. Reverend Ralph Abernathy assured followers that he and King had the white folks on the run. They intended, he said, to fill the jails. If a problem arose, Abernathy said he would just call Burke Marshall. "And if he doesn't do anything about it, I'm gonna call *Bobby,* and if Bobby doesn't do anything about it," Abernathy shouted to the rising amusement of the gathered, "I'm gonna call *Jack.*"[59] But what exactly could Burke, Bobby, and Jack do?

At a four-hour White House meeting the Kennedys rejected martial law or any use of force that might involve George C. Wallace, the new governor of Alabama and an outspoken segregationist, who had his reactionary state troopers poised to intervene at the slightest justification. Again, Robert stressed, the strategy must be to seek "a solution through mediation."[60] Burke Marshall went to Birmingham, brought all sides together, and started them talking. Cabinet members received lists of business executives in Alabama to call and lobby in support of an integrationist agreement. Just when Marshall, nearing exhaustion, finally obtained a tentative agreement, King and Abernathy unexpectedly went back to jail, this time for refusing to post an appeal bond on their unlawful-parade convictions.

Sensing the situation was about to blow, Robert Kennedy telephoned Fred Shuttlesworth of the SCLC and convinced him not to react with further demonstrations, which would surely provide Bull Connor and George Wallace the pretext they sought to incite violence so as to declare martial law and destroy the tentative agreement. Kennedy arranged bond money for King, which he refused to accept while two thousand demonstrators remained locked up in Birmingham jails. Annoyed by King's obstinacy, Kennedy pressured SCLC leaders to bail King out of jail, more or less against his will. When freed, King refused to endorse any settlement until the remaining prisoners were released.

Holding most of the high trumps, King goaded Robert Kennedy. If the Kennedys could raise $60 million to free Cuban prisoners of the Bay of Pigs invasion (as Robert had done the prior December), then surely, King said, they could raise $250,000 to free the Birmingham protestors. King scolded the Kennedys for their aloofness, hinting that Governor Rockefeller might help if the Kennedys refused. He also took them to task publicly for not enforcing obvious violations of the constitutional rights of blacks in Birmingham. Following the tense exchange, King agreed to accept the tentative agreement if Kennedy found $160,000 to help cover bonds for the prisoners. To raise the cash Kennedy went immediately to union leaders. In a matter of hours, the United Auto Workers (Jack Conway, Walter Reuther, and Joseph Rauh), the AFL-CIO (George Meany), New York's transportation workers' union (Michael Quill), and the Steelworkers (David McDonald) produced a swirl of couriers carrying black satchels packed with $210,000 in cash from the very slush funds and secret accounts whose existence five years earlier had so revolted Kennedy.[61]

On May 10, as protestors streamed from jail, a settlement was announced whereby Birmingham's lunch counters, restrooms, fitting rooms, and drinking fountains were integrated and the city's businesses agreed to hire blacks. The next night the Klan and its ilk struck back, firebombing the house of King's brother and the motel where the SCLC leaders were staying. Told of the Ku Klux Klan's intentions to kill Martin Luther King with bombs, Connor said, "Let them blow him up. I ain't going to protect him." Violent street demonstrations erupted, as angry blacks threw rocks, battled with police, and set fires to shops. At 2:30 A.M. John Doar signalled the Justice Department that, as expected, Wallace's state troopers and Connor's police had moved in and brutally retaliated against every Negro they found on the streets.[62]

At an emergency White House meeting that Sunday morning, Robert Kennedy reviewed the administration's newest predicament. They could not, he said, send in federal troops to remove the state troopers, for that was tantamount to declaring war on the state of Alabama, and to send in troops to quell the Negroes would mean the end of the agreement. The latter prospect the president knew would leave the Negroes, in his word, "uncontrollable." "And I think not only in Birmingham," Burke Marshall added.[63] Understanding the import of the situation, King refrained from requesting federal troops. Instead, he went into Negro communities and pleaded with them to return to their homes and remain calm. To protect the Birmingham agreement, which the president proclaimed "a fair and just accord" that he would not permit to be sabotaged by a "few extremists on either side," the Kennedys deployed troops near to but not into Birmingham. Quiet soon prevailed and the agreement held.[64]

Black and White Confrontations

Much changed after Birmingham. With his credibility revived, King reemerged as the leading figure in the civil rights movement. Now tacitly allied, the Kennedys and King were denounced in the same breath. "The nigger King ought to be investigated," the former mayor of Birmingham told the press. As for Robert Kennedy, "I hope that every drop of blood that's spilled he tastes in his throat, and I hope he chokes on it."[65] Most black leaders welcomed the alliance. Andrew Young, a close associate of King's and later ambassador to the United Nations in the Carter administration, thought Robert Kennedy, Marshall, and Dolan "did some phenomenal things" behind the scenes, employing "a very creative and imaginative approach" to solving problems and easing tensions through "unofficial, personal reconciliation with both whites and blacks, which was very new."[66] But what, the black leaders wondered, would happen next?

Birmingham changed the rules of racial engagement. The passivity and nonviolence of U.S. blacks could never again be taken for granted. Many blacks now spoke of forsaking "gradualism" for immediacy.[67] It worried the attorney general.

Perplexed by the anger of the black masses and the inability of black leaders to dampen it, Robert Kennedy believed the next great battleground lay in the cities. In his search for guidance on strategies and policies for resolving racial problems, Kennedy spoke to comedian-activist-author Dick Gregory who recommended that he read James Baldwin's "Letter from a Region in My Mind," which appeared in the *New Yorker.* Moved by the piece's sensitivity and insights, Kennedy invited Baldwin to breakfast at Hickory Hill so he could pick his mind. Baldwin said of Kennedy, "I felt there was a way to talk to him, to reach him." When their meeting was cut short, Baldwin said that Kennedy suggested, "Why don't you get a couple of your friends together. I'm going to be in New York tomorrow, and maybe we could meet and talk."[68]

Baldwin arranged for thirteen other blacks to join him at the Kennedy family apartment on Central Park South. Among those present were Kenneth B. Clark, the social psychologist whose studies on the effects of segregated schooling on children were crucial in the *Brown* case; Edwin C. Berry of the Chicago Urban League; Clarence B. Jones, an attorney representing Martin Luther King; Lorraine Hansberry, author of *Raisin in the Sun;* Jerome Smith, a young CORE worker returned from the Freedom Rides; and singers Lena Horne and Harry Belafonte.[69]

Kennedy entered the meeting thinking he would be speaking to Negro experts on racial problems in the cities. He was always comfortable with problem solvers and policy mavens. Instead, he encountered a group of advocates "all worked up," Burke Marshall said, and eager to vent their passions. The attorney general became the object of what Kenneth Clark described as a series of "violent, emotional verbal assaults." "Nobody even cared about expressions of good will," Lena Horne recalled. For Kenneth Clark, it was the "most intense, traumatic meeting in which I've ever taken part . . . *the* most dramatic experience I have ever had."[70]

Jerome Smith began by saying he was nauseated at having to be in the same room as Kennedy, who instinctively turned away from Smith toward the others. That was a mistake, Lorraine Hansberry told him, because Smith was "the only man who should be listened to." Smith's nervous stammer made it difficult for Kennedy to understand his exact words, but the meaning was clear. When Kennedy tried to defend his brother's record on civil rights, Smith interjected, "I've seen what government can do to crush the spirit and lives of people in the South," referring to his experiences there with CORE. Smith said he was now ashamed of his country and unwilling to defend it militarily. "Bobby got redder and redder and redder," according to Clark, and virtually accused Smith of treason.

Then Hansberry spoke of giving guns to Negroes to kill white people. Kennedy warned against listening to dangerous extremists, such as the Black Muslims, who could cause real trouble. "You don't have no idea what trouble is," said Smith, who was recovering from injuries received in a beating in the South. "I'm close to the moment where I'm ready to take up a gun," he claimed.[71]

Kennedy said they must be patient and went on to speak of his Irish ancestry and the discrimination they had encountered without resort to violence. "Your family," Baldwin furiously retorted, "has been here for three generations. My family has been here far longer than that. Why is your brother at the top while we are still so far away?"

Baldwin's group then decried the FBI's failure to protect blacks in the South, jeered Kennedy when he spoke of how closely he had worked with Martin Luther King, and said the only way to convince all Americans of the Kennedys' sincerity was for the president to make a dramatic personal testament, such as taking the hand of a child and personally integrating a school. They chided the attorney general for not personally escorting James Meredith onto the Ole Miss campus. Unfortunately, Kennedy chuckled at the suggestion, which he regarded as politically naive; a month earlier he had felt the heat of segregationist hostility firsthand during a trip through the South that most Northerners regarded as an empty gesture and white southerners deeply resented. His dismissive chuckle angered the group even more. A "very tense" situation, Baldwin said, became "very ugly."

Kennedy grew defensive, then silent. Baldwin realized that "if we couldn't make the Attorney General of the United States, who was a fairly young and intelligent man, understand the urgency of the black situation, there wasn't any hope at all." The meeting ended, according to Baldwin, when Lorraine Hansberry said she understood all Jerome Smith was saying and she cursed "a civilization which produces that white cop standing on the Negro woman's neck in Birmingham." She stood, said, "Thank you, Mr. Attorney General," and walked out. The others followed.[72]

Kenneth Clark said Kennedy proved he was "among the best the white power structure has to offer," but he was still "an extraordinarily insensitive person." Respectful of Kennedy's complexity, Clark said he did not feel that he was "racist, by any means," but that he did lack empathy.[73] "Kennedy was not unimpressive," and "he didn't minimize or condescend. But he just didn't seem to get it," said Clark.[74]

Robert Kennedy rationalized the experience. Some of those present, he decided, had "complexes." The famous ones, he said, felt inadequate in the presence of Smith, who had sacrificed so much. Others, he implied, had sexual hangups, including Clarence Jones, who was married to a white woman, and Lorraine Hansberry, who Kennedy said spoke in "poetic terms" about the more virile Negro man's fear of being castrated by white males.[75] Worse, "they don't know anything," he told Arthur Schlesinger. "They don't know what the laws are—they don't know what the facts are—they don't know what we've been doing or what we're trying to do. You can't talk to them the way you can talk to Martin Luther King or Roy Wilkins. . . . It was all emotion, hysteria."[76]

James Baldwin informed the *New York Times* of the meeting, commenting in print on Kennedy's failure to influence Negroes at the "secret talks." When Clark and Baldwin appeared together on a television show to discuss the meeting and emphasized the Kennedys' unfulfilled promises, Robert Kennedy was convinced that Baldwin had not acted in good faith in setting up the meeting in the first place and had then used it to further his position in the Negro community. He never saw or spoke to Baldwin again.[77]

The FBI, at Kennedy's request, forwarded dossiers on all those present, a few of whom belonged to organizations suspected of being "subversive." That permitted Kennedy to minimize their criticisms even further. He forwarded the FBI reports to Burke Marshall with a note: "What nice friends you have.—Bob."[78]

Robert Kennedy felt betrayed. He admitted to Clarence Jones and Harry Belafonte that he was hurt when they failed to come to his defense. Belafonte told him, "I'd lose my position with these people if I spoke up and defended you." Jones made partial amends, declaring in a letter to the *New York Times* that Robert Kennedy and Burke Marshall "have been more vigorous in their prosecution of actions in behalf of civil rights than any previous Administration." Yet, he continued, they underestimated "the explosive ingredients inherent in the continued existence of racial discrimination." The real problem, Jones confided to Stanley Levison, lay in Robert Kennedy's arrogance. Levison agreed, noting that Kennedy and Marshall labored under the "mad illusion that they and not the Negroes won the Birmingham battle."[79]

Put in the perspective of the 1960s, the Baldwin meeting revealed to Kennedy the intense feelings permeating the black community as few white liberals and political moderates had yet seen them. It also demonstrated the futility of relying on a gradualist, paternalistic approach to civil rights. Indeed, the meeting was an early example of many heated sixties' confrontations between white authority figures and representatives of black frustration, in a process Tom Wolfe labeled "Mau Mauing the Flak Catchers"; in Kennedy's case the Mau Mau were the black radical chic.[80]

As for Robert Kennedy's personal education, the meeting at least forced him to reconsider the notion that the experience of Irish Americans or any white ethnic group could compare to that of African Americans. He had for the first time in his privileged and protected existence personally encountered the deeper, rawer emotions of racism—even if he did not understand their ramifications. Consequently he gained insight into the larger meaning of the civil rights movement itself.

Those close to Robert Kennedy described the Baldwin meeting as a "climactic point in his education," the "turnaround" experience on his journey to a full moral commitment to obtaining equal rights for African Americans.[81] Indeed, the meeting had a transcendental effect on

Robert Kennedy, simultaneously elevating his sense of reality and striking an intuitive chord. A few days later, Kennedy told Edwin Guthman that, if he had grown up a Negro, he would feel as strongly as the Baldwin group.[82] Far from a total conversion experience, however, the meeting left Kennedy still conflicted about the movement and personally confused and reticent about expressing newfound feelings.

Robert returned from New York intent on making sure that everyone in the administration heard him.[83] Now virtually obsessed with hiring more Negroes in government, he told the cabinet that Birmingham businessmen had commented repeatedly on the segregated federal workforce there and asked "Why should we hire Negroes? *You* don't hire Negroes." To make his point he brought the chair of the Civil Service Commission to a cabinet meeting to summarize the meager number of Negroes employed in federal facilities in the South. He issued tongue lashings to agency heads, ordering them to get busy. That mood grew even darker on 29 May—the day after the largest one-day drop in stock market prices since 1929, quickly labeled the "Kennedy Crash"—when the attorney general confronted James Webb of NASA before Lyndon Johnson's PCEEO and implicitly threatened to recommend that the president remove Webb from the position unless he began to show some results in hiring Negroes.[84]

All the same, every Kennedy step toward the civil rights movement during the spring and summer of 1963 seemed matched by a step away. Segregationists called them "nigger-lovers," while dedicated advocates for equal rights condemned them for not doing enough. Straddling the issue was wearing on Robert Kennedy. He detested being caught in the middle and complained to James Reston of the *New York Times* that the moderates were bailing out and placing the administration under pressure from extremists in both races. Much of this whipsawing, however, stemmed from the Kennedys' inability to abandon their strict constructionist views of federal powers, their reluctance to let go of southern electoral votes, and their less than full empathy for the civil rights movement.

After Birmingham, the Kennedys' dilemma narrowed. "There must be a dozen places where we're having major problems today," the attorney general reported to the cabinet. From anecdotal sources and from the offices of mayors and congressmembers across the country, Robert Kennedy was receiving warnings of a broad-scale Negro revolt. "The Negroes," Kennedy asserted in a statement betraying just how far he was from a full conversion, "are all mad for no reason at all." And, he added (probably with Jerome Smith's and Lorraine Hansberry's comments in mind), "they want to fight and they want to fight white people." Indeed, racial turmoil was brewing. Demonstrations had become a common occurrence. One estimate put the number of Americans participating in racial demonstrations in May 1963 alone at 75,000.[85] Most white Americans, the Kennedys included, viewed the demonstrations as a prelude to riots. Confused as to what exactly would satisfy Negro protestors but more concerned about the consequences of further delay, the Kennedys finally decided at the cabinet meetings of 20 and 21 May to proceed with civil rights legislation.

The Kennedys often said their civil rights bill should have been called "Bull Connor's Bill," because, Robert explained, of what the Birmingham commissioner "did down there, with the dogs and the hoses and the pictures with the Negroes." Those actions, in Robert's view, "created a feeling in the United States that more needed to be done. Until that time people were not worked up about it or concerned about it."[86] The situation, he said, would remain "unacceptable" until Congress passed legislation.[87]

President Kennedy did not feel the same urgency about civil rights as his brother, but the two had no dramatic confrontations. "We didn't make speeches to each other," said Robert. He and Burke Marschall made the decision to proceed with legislation, according to the attorney general, while on an airplane flight to North Carolina. The only rational solution, they concluded, was to remove the reasons for public protest with a law that integrated public accommodations, guaranteeing citizens equal access to hotels, restaurants, places of amusement, and retail establishments. Such a provision, Marshall suggested, should be based on the Commerce Clause, rather than the equal protection under the law provisions of the Fourteenth Amendment of the Constitution.[88]

Robert preferred the Commerce Clause approach because he opposed adding a provision similar to Title III, stricken from the original 1957 civil rights bill, that would have given the Justice Department broad powers to initiate suits for a variety of civil rights violations. He considered the latter approach "unhelpful . . . just awful," Kennedy told the cabinet, because it would tie up the Justice Department in endless suits to desegregate every swimming pool. Negroes, he said, would be "lining up outside. . . . Everybody would have a suit, and we'd be the ones who would be doing it."[89] When finally drafted, the Kennedys' bill strengthened the voting rights laws, empowered the attorney general to sue for school desegregation, granted the president authority to cut off federal funds to racially discriminatory state programs, and outlawed discrimination in places accommodating the public.[90] Although the bill met the most urgent needs, as Robert Kennedy perceived them, it left unsatisfied many other demands of the civil rights movement. But it was at least a start.

To launch the legislation Robert Kennedy recommended a series of White House meetings to take soundings from businesspeople, civil rights leaders, politicians, and other leading lights. The president agreed, with one condition: The meeting with Martin Luther King had to come late. "Otherwise, it will look like he got me to do it." "The trouble with King," John Kennedy said, "is that everybody thinks he's our boy, anyway. So everything he does, everybody says we stuck him in there. We ought to have him well surrounded . . . King is so hot these days that it's like Marx coming to the White House. I'd like to have some Southern governors, or mayors, or businessmen first. And my program should have gone up to the Hill first."[91]

At the same time, Martin Luther King stepped up the pressure on the Kennedys to make an uncompromising commitment to his cause. Fresh from the Birmingham triumph, the star attraction of a movement that each day gathered momentum and credibility, King told a Cleveland rally that yet another crisis loomed. Governor George Wallace, vowing "Segregation forever!" had pledged to defy a court order and block the integration of the University of Alabama. Taunting the Kennedys, King said, if the governor "will present his body by standing in the door to preserve an evil system, then President Kennedy ought to go to Tuscaloosa and personally escort the student into the university with *his* body."[92] A compelling demagogic device, King's challenge was legally and politically infeasible. Yet it raised expectations of further Kennedy involvement.

Actually, Robert Kennedy had put his body on the line a month earlier while traveling through the South to see for himself what conditions were like. (Memories of those experiences evoked the ill-timed involuntary chuckle that had angered the blacks at the Baldwin meeting.) At each stop along the way the FBI received reports from informants inside the Klan of threats against the attorney general and plans for demonstrations. During his visit to Columbia, South Carolina, seventeen demonstrators were arrested, including the editor of the *Thunderbolt,* the newspaper of the National States Rights party.[93] At Mobile, in the heart of Dixie, Robert Kennedy ignored threats and promised that law and order on racial matters would be upheld, "even if it cost the Democrats all fifty states in the next presidential election."[94]

Confronting George Wallace

He went on from there to Montgomery and a face-to-face meeting with George Corley Wallace. Just to arrange the meeting had required several months' effort on Kennedy's part. With a showdown over the integration of the University of Alabama fast approaching, he hoped a personal meeting with the volatile Wallace would lead to a rational accord. When Wallace refused even to take his telephone calls, Kennedy asked other, more racially moderate, Alabamians to try to calm the governor. "Inevitably," Kennedy said, those contacts reported that Wallace was "scared," "out of his mind," or "acting like a raving maniac."[95] Burke Marshall tried to approach Wallace through the state attorney general, Richmond Flowers, known for his progressive views on race relations. "Dammit," Wallace told Flowers, "send the Justice Department word, I ain't compromising with anybody, I'm gonna *make 'em* bring troops into this state." Wallace finally agreed to grant an "audience" to Kennedy for the sole purpose, he explained to reporters, of venting his displeasure over the central government's efforts "to destroy our cherished traditions."[96]

Arriving at the capitol, above which flew the stars and bars of the Confederacy but no U.S. flag, Kennedy, flanked by Marshall and Guthman, walked a gauntlet of jeering white segregationists waving placards with messages such as "Koon Kissin' Kennedy." When the attorney general tried to step to the side to greet a few well-wishers in the crowd, a burly state trooper, according to Kennedy, "took his stick and put it into my stomach . . . and belted me with the stick. . . . Not for laughs at all. They were most unfriendly." The president's brother, Marshall noted, was treated like a foreign dignitary and a "suspicious" one at that.[97]

Indeed, Robert Kennedy's confrontations with southern governors bore certain intriguing parallels to the foreign crises during the Kennedy administration. Each civil rights crisis, like the crises abroad, developed in reaction to events or circumstances initiated by others; each required the total attention of the attorney general and sometimes the president for extended periods, leaving little time for strategizing or pro-active planning; each was looked upon as a test of personal will; and, finally, each crisis brought recriminations and blame for poor intelligence and inadequate military planning, along with a determination to avoid repeating the same mistakes.

Military-diplomatic metaphors sprang up at every turn of the University of Alabama integration crisis. The attorney general, for example, said he hoped to avoid arresting Wallace, because "then we'd have to occupy Alabama."[98] To avoid repeating the mistakes made at Oxford—the most serious ones, in Kennedy's estimation, were the military's logistical and intelligence blunders—he requested the air force to conduct aerial reconnaissance of the Alabama campus. Governor Wallace learned of the reconnaissance flights when the Pentagon assigned the task to the Alabama Air National Guard. To foster the imagery of foreign surveillance, Wallace referred to them incorrectly as "U-2 flights," using them to his political advantage to color the Justice Department as outside agents and to treat Kennedy as a virtual invader of the sovereign state of Alabama.[99]

So the scene was set for the Kennedy-Wallace meeting of 25 April 1963, which rivaled the first Kennedy-Hoffa meeting in foreboding. This time, however, Robert Kennedy left the macho posturing to his adversary. Wallace, a five-foot-seven-inch former pugilist and self-styled tough guy whose mouth seemed fixed in a sneer, was spoiling for a fight. As Dan T. Carter has shown in his detailed examination of the governor's political career, Wallace wanted no private agreements or face-saving deals with Kennedy. Kennedy was forewarned of Wallace's intentions in a meeting the night before with Frank Johnson, the judge who had granted the injunction against the Klan during the Freedom Riders crisis. One of several southern moderates Kennedy sought out for advice on managing integration in the South, Johnson told Kennedy that Wallace intended to use the meeting as a political soapbox to advance his own political standing. Kennedy knew Johnson was right the moment he entered the governor's office and saw the tape recorder. Realizing that his responses to Wallace (like his telephone conversation with "Mr. Greyhound" during the Freedom Rides) would surely be broadcast throughout the South, Kennedy said he "couldn't let anything he'd say go by . . . unanswered."[100]

Probing for openings, they spoke at length of their differing views of the legal authority of a federal court over a state. Alluding to states rights interpretations of the Tenth and Eleventh Amendments, Wallace argued that integration had to be delayed indefinitely. "In fact," he said, "there is no time in my judgment when we would be ready for it in my lifetime." Rather than comment on the immorality of segregation, Kennedy repeated his mantra of responsibility for upholding orders of the federal court. "I don't think that the Union, or the country means anything," he said, "unless the orders of the land are enforced." Wallace, in turn, ridiculed the courts ("Nobody knows what the law is anymore"), called Kennedy an emissary for Martin Luther King ("a phony" and a "fraud"), and tried to make the attorney general admit that he intended to use troops to enforce a court order to integrate the University of Alabama. Twice Kennedy came close to losing his composure. They ended, however, by agreeing to disagree in separate press statements.[101]

At the press conference afterwards, a southern reporter stunned Kennedy by asking if he was a member of the Communist party. Alabama newspapers reported that Kennedy's "enemy foot" had trod the Capitol steps near the sacred spot where Jefferson Davis was sworn as president of the Confederate States of America. Summing up, one newspaper called Robert Kennedy the "worst enemy of the South since Thad Stevens."[102]

Not everyone in Alabama agreed with those sentiments or with Wallace. Kennedy's Justice Department worked clandestinely with the university president, Dr. Frank A. Rose, and its faculty and with the state attorney general, Richmond Flowers, to prepare the way for the admission of Vivian Malone and James A. Hood.[103] At the urging of Robert Kennedy, members of the cabinet telephoned prominent Alabama business leaders and encouraged them to accept integration. Burke Marshall personally contacted most of the leading newspaper publishers, ministers, and community leaders in the state. They, in turn, put pressure on Wallace. Actions of southern liberals and moderates, Robert Kennedy acknowledged, were critical in resolving the problem peacefully.[104]

However, much more than Kennedy was willing to concede depended on how the impulsive Wallace would react. Privately, Wallace hoped that integration, sure to reach Tuscaloosa, could be accomplished without violence and without loss of credibility among the voters of his state. He intended to make Kennedy resort to at least the appearance of overwhelming force, before which, as Dan T. Carter explained, Wallace "was determined to stand alone at center stage as the heroic defender of the rights of oppressed whites."[105] Wallace knew he had to yield. But first he intended to defy federal tyranny—at least symbolically.

As the confrontation drew near, then, Kennedy and Wallace had reached a fuzzy accord, an unspoken understanding of how each would play his role but with no precise script. Wallace assured *Meet the Press* viewers that he intended to "stand in the door," as he had promised in his campaign. He added, however, that "the confrontation will be handled peacefully and without violence." From this and other indirect sources Kennedy presumed that Wallace did not mean to provoke disorder. Still, he had no guarantees from the governor himself, who refused to yield anything to Kennedy or even to take his calls unless the attorney general was willing to discuss ways to withdraw the two black student applications.

On 8 June Kennedy telephoned the governor's office and was put through to an aide who refused to say what the governor intended to do, only that it was "a prerogative exclusively within the governor's mind." Kennedy scolded the aide, saying "I thought we were going to handle it as civilized people, but I can't get that obviously." The attorney general then coldly informed the governor's assistant that there was "nothing to be negotiated"; two black students were going to attend the University of Alabama.[106]

Kennedy remained uncertain even about his own actions. "Final plans," he later admitted, were "really not made until that morning," that is, regarding how the administration would respond if Wallace blocked the door. Kennedy and Marshall fully expected Wallace to refuse to move. Whether Katzenbach should try to use force himself (perhaps even push Wallace aside) was not decided until the last moment.

Other planning, however, was more advanced and detailed. To avoid the mistakes of Ole Miss, where Mississippians reacted bitterly to the presence of "Yankee" troops on southern soil, Kennedy approved plans to federalize the Alabama National Guard in the event Wallace refused to step aside. Because the guard commander and his troops were Alabamians, Kennedy believed it more likely that Wallace would peacefully capitulate.

The morning of Tuesday, 11 June 1963—the day the Kennedys bent history—began routinely at Hickory Hill, except for the presence of a documentary film crew. Cameras rolled as Robert's breakfast with his family was interrupted by several telephone calls, which he took while dodging the morning rush of children running out to school, servants cleaning up, and Ethel trying to maintain order and shouting last minute commands to the children. He paused to tousle one child's hair and to urge four-year-old Kerry to finish her milk by taking one gulp for each of her brothers and sisters and one for her grandmother Kennedy.

His office was, once again, the operations center of the administration. Nine telephones connected Robert Kennedy with the White House, Katzenbach and Doar in Alabama, the Pentagon, standby army units, and the rest of the world. As the attorney general bent over maps of the campus, a telephone cradled to his ear, three children sprinted across the office at full speed, stopping before their father. Kerry demanded to know who her father was speaking to on the telephone.

"Kerry wants to say hello," the attorney general told Nicholas Katzenbach. On the other end of the line in Tuscaloosa, Justice Department attorneys did a double take as Katzenbach became playful and patient "Uncle Nick." On film Kennedy and his deputy appear confident and unflappable—perhaps because of the presence of the cameras, but more likely because experience had made such crises somewhat routine. They had planned well and had anticipated contingencies. Besides, they had reached a tentative, if not definite, understanding with the flamboyant but shrewdly reasonable George Wallace.

Resuming their conversation, Katzenbach told Kennedy that the doorway to the administration building was only symbolic: "He [Wallace] can't block all the classroom doors." At about 10:15 A.M., while Kennedy and Katzenbach were still on the phone, Wallace arrived and took up a position behind a lectern blocking the front door of the building. As Wallace posed for the cameras, Kennedy and Katzenbach finalized a plan of action. Minutes earlier Kennedy had received word from the university president and a friendly trustee that Wallace was in an agitated state. Now convinced that he should not try to use force to push Wallace aside, Kennedy decided to "let Wallace have his show." Otherwise, Kennedy told Katzenbach, "God knows what could happen by way of violence." He instructed Katzenbach to approach Wallace alone, without the students, and to use a "tone of voice" that will "dismiss George Wallace as a sort of second-rate figure, . . . wasting your time, wasting the students' time, causing a great fuss down there." Otherwise, he said, "play it by ear."

As expected, Wallace blocked Katzenbach from entering the building and then made his statement to the nation, haranguing the "illegal usurpation of power by the Central Government." Wallace kept Katzenbach standing in the hot sun while he read his proclamation in the shade. After hearing Wallace "denounce and forbid" the integration of the state university, Katzenbach quietly withdrew. He telephoned the attorney general, who stood ready with the proclamation nationalizing the Alabama National Guard; its commander soon afterward faced Wallace in the doorway. The governor, by prior agreement with the commander and with the consent of Robert Kennedy, made another speech—this time decrying the "trend toward military dictatorship"—

then retreated. Alabama guardsmen escorted Vivian Malone and James Hood into the building and the university.[107]

When Wallace stepped aside, Robert Kennedy heaved a sigh of relief and lighted a cigar. It was a "pleasant moment," he recalled, because of his uncertainty that Wallace would, in fact, go peacefully. Robert telephoned his brother with the good news. "I think it'll be fine," he was heard to say. Only then, Robert later said, did he learn that the president had decided to go on television and address the nation on civil rights.[108]

John Kennedy's television address that evening marked the most dramatic presidential step in U.S. civil rights since Reconstruction. Persuaded by his brother that the time had come to clarify the administration's moral commitment to civil rights, President Kennedy decided to announce that evening his decision to introduce civil rights legislation. At White House meetings earlier in the day, Lawrence O'Brien and Kenneth O'Donnell recommended against a speech. But Robert Kennedy's was the "conclusive voice within the government," said Burke Marshall: "He urged it, he felt it, he understood it, and he prevailed. I don't think there was anybody in the Cabinet—except the President himself—who felt that way on these issues, and the President got it from his brother."[109]

Events in Alabama shaped the Kennedys' decision. Sending Katzenbach to face Wallace alone saved two students the humiliation of being turned away by the governor and spared Robert Kennedy from prosecuting a sitting governor for contempt of court, but it also gave Wallace a chance to express disdain for the federal government face-to-face with one of its senior representatives. Rebroadcasts of Wallace's speech on national television that day made him instantly viable as a spokesman and symbol for the conservative political impulse manifesting in the 1960s that would expand across three decades.[110] John Kennedy's exquisite political instincts moved him to counter Wallace's media thrust with one of his own.

Just before six that evening, the president decided to use the eight o'clock time slot television networks had reserved for him in the event of some dramatic development in Alabama. The attorney general and Burke Marshall rushed to join the president and Theodore Sorensen in the Cabinet Room. Robert recalled that they discussed ideas for the speech "for about twenty minutes" before Sorensen went to prepare a text, which they all knew he would not complete by eight. Robert told his brother not to worry, the speech would be better delivered extemporaneously. For another several minutes they brainstormed ideas. Adding a Lincolnesque touch, Robert recalled his brother busily "outlining and organizing," making notes "on the back of an envelope or something." At about five minutes before airtime, the president reworked Sorensen's partial draft, adding some suggestions from Louis Martin and a touch of fervor. The president's brother was the only one in the room not aghast at the realization that the president of the United States was about to ad lib large portions of this vital speech.[111]

John Kennedy's gifts for dramatic rhetoric reached apogee that evening, as he made his own righteous testament and stirred the passions of white Americans in support of equal rights for all Americans. "We are confronted primarily with a moral issue," he said in the peroration. "It is as old as the scriptures and is as clear as the American Constitution." Asking every American to "stop and examine his conscience," he reminded them that the country was "founded on the principle that all men are created equal, and that the rights of every man are diminished when the rights of one man are threatened." Every American, he said, "ought to have the right to be treated as he would wish to be treated, as one would wish his children to be treated." The pace of integration, Kennedy admitted, was "very slow," and the "fires of frustration and discord are burning in every city." He then pledged to send forward a public accommodations bill, to seek pledges from business leaders to end discrimination, and to authorize the federal government to "participate more fully" in lawsuits designed to end segregation in public education. Tying his appeal to the Cold War struggle, Kennedy said, "We preach freedom around the world, and we mean it, and we cherish our freedom here at home, but are we to say to the world, and much more important, to each other that this is a land of the free except for the Negroes; that we have no second-class citizens except Negroes?"[112]

Calling the speech eloquent and profound, Martin Luther King rushed his enthusiastic congratulations to the president. Roy Wilkins called it the "message I had been waiting to hear." Still, the fires of hatred continued to rage. That evening Medgar Evers, Mississippi field secretary for the NAACP, was assassinated outside his home. (Thirty years were required to bring his killer to justice.) At the time of his murder, Evers was attempting to gain authorities' concessions to speed integration in Jackson, Mississippi. Out of respect to Evers, the president and the attorney general used their influence to induce a settlement. Robert also attended Evers's funeral at Arlington National Cemetery. There he met Medgar's brother, Charles, and a lasting friendship resulted.[113]

Kennedy's speech and the continued racial violence in the South produced fallout at home and abroad. Worried about the "extremely negative reactions" overseas to America's civil rights crisis, the president directed Dean Rusk to mount a diplomatic effort to counter the reports. Domestically, the speech caused Kennedy to drop a few points, but his approval ratings remained high and never fell as low as he told civil rights leaders they had.[114] In Congress, the president suffered several legislative reversals probably attributable to his stand on civil rights, prompting Democratic majority leader Carl Albert to warn of defections among some of "the top men" in the House. Wearily, the president complained that "events are making our problems" and civil rights "has become everything." Robert said his brother feared that the speech may have been his "political swan song."[115]

President Kennedy then drew back, leaving center stage once again to the attorney general, who, though generally upbeat, also equivocated. Racial segregation, he told viewers of *Meet the Press,* was "unacceptable." He warned of problems in the future because "we have not met our responsibilities for a long period of time." "We are paying for it now," he added contritely. To deflect some of the heat away from the Kennedy administration, the attorney general said that government at all levels must now "rectify the situation."[116]

Despite Robert Kennedy's decisive role in persuading the president to make the famous speech and despite his obvious personal commitment to equal rights, many within the civil rights movement regarded him as an enigma, more a part of the problem than its solution. This view seemed justified on 14 June, when three thousand demonstrators gathered in front of the Justice Department. Taking a bullhorn to answer charges that his department discriminated by not hiring more Negroes, Kennedy did not handle the crowd or the criticisms well. Refusing to apologize for all his hard work and declining to be put on the defensive and thus appear politically weak, Kennedy projected proud defiance.

Jack Newfield, one of the protestors (and later the author of a penetrating personal portrait of Kennedy), recalled staring "with pure fury" at the attorney general's "hard Irish face," which he thought was "alert, but without much character." Newfield saw "the hostility radiating from his blue eyes become even more intense," when Kennedy told the crowd, "Individuals will be hired according to their ability, not their color" and "I'm not going to go out and hire a Negro just because he is not white." Such comments would have struck a responsive chord among conservatives thirty years later as debates over affirmative action flared anew, but to Newfield and the other protestors gathered that day "it was exactly the sort of impersonal, legalistic response, blind to the larger moral implications of our protest, that we felt made Kennedy such an inadequate Attorney General."[117]

Ten days later Kennedy amplified his sentiments on *Meet the Press.* He told viewers that he thought Negroes were entitled to special attention to try to "remedy the sins of the past," but

> I don't think that an individual should be hired just because he is a Negro, but, on the other hand, I think Negroes are not qualified for certain positions of skill because they have been discriminated against in the past, so I think we should make an extra effort to make sure that the problem has been remedied, that we do more for vocational training, that we do more for education, that we see they then are entitled to the same privileges that the white person is entitled to.[118]

Robert Kennedy was not yet prepared to allow his feelings of indignation over the treatment of blacks to overcome his practical devotion to the rule of law. That summer he finally involved the Justice Department in the still simmering disputes over integration in Albany,

Georgia, but not on the side of integrationists. He sent U.S. attorneys and FBI agents to investigate charges against blacks who picketed and boycotted a store owned by a white man who had served on a jury that refused to convict a white man of killing a black man. Ignoring deep divisions in his department, Kennedy proceeded with federal indictments against nine members of the Albany movement for violating the rights of the white store owner. At about the same time, he refused to intervene in an egregious case of police brutality in Americus, Georgia, and allowed local authorities to prosecute SNCC organizers under an arcane sedition statute. "I want to know," John Lewis of SNCC asked, in a question that summed up the attitude of the entire civil rights movement, "which side is the Federal Government on?"[119]

CHAPTER 13

The Kennedys and King

TO FORCE AN END to the Kennedys' equivocation and to move the federal government to their side, civil rights leaders decided to stage a massive, nonviolent protest march on Washington. During World War II, the mere threat of a march by A. Philip Randolph, head of the Brotherhood of Sleeping Car Porters, persuaded President Roosevelt to establish a Fair Employment Practices Committee to reduce discrimination against Negroes in defense industries. This time the civil rights leadership intended a march to take place.

The March on Washington

In mid-May Louis Martin suggested to Robert Kennedy several ways the administration could head off or at least parry mass protest.[1] Kennedy acted upon one recommendation, convincing the president to call a series of White House meetings to build support for the administration's civil rights bill and to dissuade the march organizers from making the president the target of the protest. Martin Luther King had, in fact, at one time considered "centering" the march on the Kennedys. King harbored "mixed emotions" about John Kennedy's intentions and even speculated aloud about his motives for introducing civil rights legislation. King wondered if the president presented the bill just to get himself "off the hook," perhaps intending to use it "politically by saying he *tried* to get it, knowing all the time it can't pass."

On Saturday, 22 June, three days after the civil rights bill went to Congress, the president met with civil rights leaders at the White House with several purposes in mind: he wanted to allay King's misgivings, to short-circuit Republican plans to exploit the march, and to preempt notions of turning the march against the Kennedys. As the leading figures of the civil rights movement preened for photographs and maneuvered for seats at the table with the president and vice-president, Robert Kennedy sat quietly on the perimeter of the Cabinet Room holding one of his daughters on his lap. John Kennedy spoke persuasively that morning of a partnership between his administration and the civil rights movement and described the "very serious fight" they faced in removing obstacles to passage of the bill. "A good many programs I care about may go down the drain as a result of this—We may all go down the drain . . . so we are putting a lot on the line," he told them. Joseph Rauh remembered the president declaring, "I may lose the next election because of this. I don't care."[2]

The president did care, however, about the message that a mass protest meeting would send, especially if it turned radical or violent.[3] Some moderates and conservatives, he told the civil rights leaders, "are looking for an excuse to be against us; and I don't want to give any of them a chance to say, 'Yes, I'm for the bill, but I am damned if I will vote for it at the point of a gun.'"[4] When someone asked if he supported the march, which earlier he had called ill-timed, the president replied, "We want success in the Congress, not a big show on the Capitol."

"Frankly," Martin Luther King interjected, "I have never engaged in any direct action movement which did not seem ill-timed. Some people thought Birmingham was ill-timed."

"Including the Attorney General," the president added with a smile.

"I liked the way he talked about what *we* are getting," said King afterwards. "It wasn't something that he was getting for you Negroes. You knew you had an ally."[5] Thus disarmed by the president's wit and confidence, the civil rights leaders decided not to target the administration but to focus instead on the anticipated southern filibuster in the Senate.[6]

The alliance between the Kennedys and King, however, had reached a critical juncture. For despite the Kennedys' many warnings—Burke Marshall gave King yet another one in January 1963—King had failed to break off with either O'Dell or Levison. King said his publicized dismissal of O'Dell in November 1962 (hastened by FBI leaks to southern newspapers) was pending "further inquiry and clarification." O'Dell said it was not a dismissal at all but a "temporary resignation." Robert Kennedy jotted a note to Burke Marshall in the margin of an FBI report of O'Dell's and Levison's continued presence in King's entourage: "Burke—this is not getting any better." And so on 20 November 1962 the attorney general authorized the FBI to expand its wiretapping operation on Levison to include his home telephone.[7]

The new tap revealed two things: Levison and O'Dell were still associating with King, and Levison was thoroughly alienated from the Communist party. Hoover reported the first but not the second finding to Robert Kennedy. On 22 June 1963, Marshall took King aside before the White House conference and told him that John Kennedy was about "to put his whole political life on the line" with the civil rights bill and simply could not make himself vulnerable to charges of Communist associations. Seeing that King remained unconvinced, Marshall asked the attorney general to speak to him. Five days earlier, Kennedy had asked for and received a full briefing from Hoover about how far he could go in warning King without compromising the FBI informants (Solo). He told King that it was now imperative that he break off ties with O'Dell and Levison immediately. King insisted that the FBI's allegations could not possibly be true. Irritated by King's combination of nonchalance and professed denseness over national security matters, Robert Kennedy decided the time had come for his brother to have a chat with King.

Later that afternoon President Kennedy invited King for a stroll through the White House Rose Garden, where, according to King, the president warned him against discussing significant matters over the telephone because he was under "very close surveillance." The president also told King that O'Dell was the "number five Communist in the United States" and that Levison's position was so highly classified he could not reveal it. "You've got to get rid of them," the president told King. Both men, Kennedy asserted, were "agents of a foreign power." Comparing the situation to the Profumo scandal in Britain, President Kennedy warned King, "If they shoot *you* down, they'll shoot us down, too—so we're asking you to be careful."[8] King shared this conversation with Andrew Young, who concluded that the Kennedys were "all scared to death of the Bureau."[9] Upon reflection, however, King realized that when "Burke Marshall, the Attorney General, *and* the President of the United States all come down on you in *one* day, you have to consider that. You have to give it some weight." A week later, as part of the price of Kennedy support, King made O'Dell's "temporary resignation" permanent.[10]

Still, King scoffed at the Kennedys' comparisons of Levison to Soviet spies and joked with his colleagues about their vague allusions to spies and code names for secret operatives. Levison, however, understood clearly the meaning of the Kennedys' warnings. He told King that the stakes were too high; they had to separate for the good of the movement, which, he said, "needed the Kennedys too much." King and Levison agreed to stay in touch through an intermediary, Clarence Jones, an attorney who had worked for King and also had been present at the Baldwin meeting. Jones made little effort to conceal his role, virtually admitting it in a mid-July meeting with Burke Marshall. Furthermore, Jones indicated that King had told others of his conversations with the president, including the warning about FBI surveillance, a breach not only of the implied contract between the Kennedys and King but also of national security.[11]

Taking into consideration all of the evidence before him, Robert Kennedy met with FBI liaison Courtney Evans on 16 July and admitted that he was considering placing both Martin Luther King and Clarence Jones under electronic surveillance. Seven days later, when Evans returned with documents requesting authorizations for wiretaps on King and Jones, Kennedy had changed his mind. A tap on King, he told Evans, would be "ill advised." Evans returned the FBI's memorandum requesting the authorization to Hoover with the notation, "A.G. said 'no.'"[12] Kennedy had changed his mind because earlier that day King had promised to break with Levison and O'Dell.[13] To make sure

King kept his promise, Kennedy approved the FBI request for a wiretap on Jones.

While these events unfolded, J. Edgar Hoover had been circulating rumors of Communist influence within the civil rights movement. To quell the spread of those rumors through the Congress, Robert Kennedy directed Burke Marshall to prepare a statement, released the next day in the form of a letter to Senator Michael Monroney of Oklahoma. "Based on all available information from the FBI and other sources," Kennedy stated, "we have no evidence that any of the top leaders of the major civil rights groups are Communists or Communist controlled." Kennedy and Marshall were making a fine distinction, for both believed that King, while not a Communist himself, was influenced by one.[14]

J. Edgar Hoover was deeply affronted by Kennedy's public defense of King, whom he despised. He already had begun plans to persecute the man who in 1964 he would publicly label the "most notorious liar" in America and "one of the lowest characters in the country." To counter the attorney general's statement, Hoover leaked to the press that Jack O'Dell, identified by the FBI as a "onetime Communist organizer," was working in the SCLC offices in New York City. (He was, in fact, only seen entering their offices.) Then, on 13 August, Hoover forwarded a two-page report, the first of several detailing Martin Luther King, Jr.'s drinking, cursing, and sexual activities. Robert Kennedy sent the report to his brother, noting only, "I thought you would be interested in the attached memorandum." The FBI, meantime, labored to document Hoover's hypothesis on King and Levison.

The result was an internal memorandum, "Martin Luther King, Jr.: Affiliation with the Communist Movement." Extremely displeased with the report itself, which cited no hard evidence, and with its timing (just before the March on Washington), Robert Kennedy ordered Hoover to retrieve all copies of the report, which Hoover in an audacious act of insubordination had distributed to government offices outside the Justice Department.

Kennedy's rebuke of Hoover may have sparked a minor and short-lived insurrection within the FBI. Assistant Director William C. Sullivan's domestic intelligence division prepared a second report heretically concluding that the CPUSA's tiny (4,453) membership had failed "dismally" in its attempts to influence Negroes in the civil rights movement and that fewer than two hundred Communists would take part in the March on Washington. Hoover quickly silenced the dissidents. Likening the report to those he had received when Castro took control of Cuba, Hoover's penned reply to Sullivan stated in part, "You contended then that Castro & his cohorts were not Communists & not influenced by Communists. Time alone has proved you wrong." Two days later, with no new evidence and only Hoover's scorn to motivate him, Sullivan reversed his field. "The Director is correct," wrote the repentant Sullivan, and "we were completely wrong." After King's "I have a dream" speech, Sullivan led the choir as the director's latest convert, stating, "We must mark [King] now, if we have not done so before, as the most dangerous Negro of the future in this Nation."[15]

Meanwhile, the brief era of black and white cooperation for racial justice, symbolized by expressions of goodwill between the Kennedys and King, reached its zenith on 28 August. The mass meeting and media event called the March on Washington attracted an estimated 300,000 people. Wearing twenty-five-cent buttons displaying a black hand clasping a white hand, the throng gathered at the Washington Monument and walked to the Lincoln Memorial.[16] With so much at stake, the Kennedys wanted the gathering to reflect unity and compromise, to be free of violence, major incident, or any semblance of radical—to say nothing of Communist—involvement.

Deciding that the March was "very, very badly organized," Robert Kennedy assigned assistant attorney general John Douglas to work full-time coordinating government services and managing logistics in cooperation with the nominal march organizers, Bayard Rustin and A. Philip Randolph. Burke Marshall said Rustin and Randolph got all the credit, while "the person who organized it, as a matter of fact, was the Attorney General." Concerned that it could turn into a general protest spawning violence and possibly even terrorist activities against the government, Kennedy directed Douglas to use the police and FBI to conduct "character" checks of the participants. Kennedy said later that the department "kept track" of the "many groups of Communists" (about two hundred individuals in all who tried to gain some role in the March) and made sure they were excluded.[17]

To make sure the march was interracial, Kennedy involved organized labor and white clergy; to direct the focus away from government and for better crowd control, he persuaded organizers to abandon the idea of a march on the Capitol in favor of a rally at the Lincoln Memorial, surrounded on three sides by water; to reduce the chances of violence, he negotiated for the closing of Washington's bars and liquor stores; to arrange seating, he brought in Jerry Bruno, the Kennedys' political advance man; and to minimize criticism of the administration, he scrutinized the speeches and reportedly had Bruno ready to "pull the plug" on the PA system if something went wrong. Indeed, the attorney general took such an active role in preparations that many of the participants spoke worriedly of being co-opted by the Kennedys. Malcolm X avoided the show, calling it the "Farce on Washington."[18] Robert took pride in pointing out later that despite "dire prophesies of angry crowds, of violence, and riot," the march became instead a "gentle flood."[19]

Throughout the sultry Washington afternoon speakers denounced conventional liberalism and the shortsightedness of Kennedy's legislative proposal. A few in the crowd were hostile toward the president. Reverend James Bevel, a Mississippi official of the SCLC, said, "Some punk who calls himself the President has the audacity to tell people to go slow. I'm not prepared to be humiliated by white trash the rest of my life, including Mr. Kennedy."[20]

Only one of the platform speakers, John Lewis—the chair of SNCC and a veteran of more than a score of civil rights confrontations, arrests, and beatings—got under the Kennedys' skin. After reading Lewis's prepared text, Robert Kennedy labeled it an inflammatory and radical attack on the country and the president. He demanded Lewis revise it. The text contained such pointed statements as, "This nation is still a place of cheap political leaders who build their careers on immoral compromises" and "The black masses are on the march for jobs and freedom, and we must say to the politicians that there won't be a 'cooling-off' period."[21] Those words sparked a chaotic backstage dispute. The archbishop of Washington refused to give the invocation until Lewis emended his "scorched earth" language. Burke Marshall, riding through Washington's jammed streets in the sidecar of a police motorcycle, reached the Lincoln Memorial with a new draft, edited by Marshall and Walter Reuther and cleared by both Kennedys. Lewis read the sanitized text and stirred the crowd with a compelling narrative of nonviolent protests and violent white southern reaction, ending each segment with the refrain, "What did the federal government *do*?" "The party of Kennedy," Lewis reminded the crowd, "is also the party of Eastland." By 1986, when Lewis was elected to Congress, he had to admit that it was his party, too.[22]

By far the most memorable speaker was Martin Luther King, Jr. "Boy," said Robert Kennedy, "he made a helluva speech."[23] King's formal bearing, clear diction, and resonant baritone magnified his oratorical brillance. Reaching toward the now familiar climax, the predictable and comforting cadences of the country preacher brought spontaneous shouts of encouragement. "Tell 'em about the dream, Martin," gospel singer Mahalia Jackson shouted. Departing from his prepared text, King said his dream was "a dream deeply rooted in the American dream." Carrying listeners on a philosophical excursion through the American creed, tolling freedom's bells from New Hampshire to California to Mississippi, he promised that, if Americans were faithful the country's dream, "we will be able to speed up that day when *all* God's children, black men and white men, Jews and Gentiles, Protestants and Catholics, will be able to join hands and sing in the words of the old Negro spiritual, 'Free at Last! Free at Last! Thank God Almighty, we are free at last!'" Standing in the shadow of the Emancipator, Martin Luther King, Jr., invoked the truths of the ages.[24]

After the speeches, Roy Wilkins, Bayard Rustin, A. Philip Randolph, Walter Reuther, and other march organizers visited the White House. President Kennedy greeted King, saying, "I have a dream."[25] Within the span of a few weeks they had each moved the nation with their appeals. The Kennedys and King seemed euphorically bound in common cause. Appearances, however, were deceiving.

Civil Rights Legislation

Reality intruded as the racial protests and the retribution for them spread. A dispute over school integration in Birmingham led again to Negro demonstrations and white counterdemonstrations, to street violence and, on 15 September, to a bomb that destroyed a church and killed four young girls. Revulsed, Robert Kennedy sent the FBI to investigate the bombings. Martin Luther King counted twenty-eight unsolved bombings in the city. However, the administration, with the president now the all-too-visible point man, proved ineffective in quelling the disturbances, leaving the city to solve its own problems.[26] In the eyes of the civil rights leadership, the Kennedys were right back where they had started during the Freedom Rides. Only now, said Robert with regret, the focus was "on both of us."

Robert worried about the effects of his civil rights actions on his brother's reelection chances. "The fact that I was Attorney General," he said later, "caused him many more problems [in the South] than if I hadn't been his brother." The press, Robert Kennedy noted, now talked about the "Kennedy Brothers—which he used to point out to me frequently. It was no longer Robert, the Attorney General, but now they were talking about the Kennedy brothers. In fact, it became so extensive that in [September or October] 1963, I discussed with him . . . getting out as Attorney General . . . , because I thought it was such a burden to carry in the 1964 election." His brother rejected the idea, Robert said, "because it would make it look as if we were running away from it." According to Robert, they decided to "watch it and see if there was something that we should do." They had made no definite decision by the time John Kennedy left for Dallas. But a few days before at an office party to celebrate his thirty-eighth birthday, Robert told his staff the struggle for civil rights must continue and hinted that he likely would not be there to lead it.[27]

By the fall of 1963 the Kennedys' strategy of moving forward gradually on civil rights while maintaining their ties with the white South had clearly failed. Yet alienating the extremes in both the black and white communities had done them no harm politically. Indeed, it may have helped. Pollster Louis Harris reported that, because of his civil rights stand, the president had lost the support of 6.5 million people who had voted for him in 1960, but he had gained the support of 11 million Nixon voters. Although incipient rumblings of discontent were heard in the white ethnic neighborhoods of the North, pollsters reported that 63 percent of the American people endorsed the Kennedys' civil rights bill, one percentage point higher than the president's overall approval rating as reported in Gallup polls in September 1963.[28] Those same polls showed that the president enjoyed an 89 percent approval rating among blacks. Among southern whites, 70 percent believed he was pushing integration too fast.[29]

Even then, the Kennedys apparently harbored illusions of capitalizing on a perceived Negro "swing vote" in a few southern states. "We thought that we could really do something [legislatively] which would obtain the registration of a large number of Negroes," Robert recalled. But with a year to go until the election, the Kennedys were ready to write off the South, except Florida, where George Smathers could be of help, and Texas, where they counted on Lyndon Johnson's continued presence on the ticket (which Robert later said was never in doubt) to strengthen their chances of winning.[30]

Much depended on the civil rights bill. They expected it to help offset southern losses by garnering enormous support from the masses of blacks who had migrated from the South (more than three million in the two prior decades) to the urban-industrial North. Too strong a civil rights bill, however, could finish them completely in Texas, as well as alienate border state voters and some northern moderates and white ethnic groups.

Texas and Lyndon Johnson loomed large. At Johnson's request, President Kennedy delayed sending his bill to Congress for eight days to allow time to alert key members of Congress and get them on board. Johnson, an expert legislative technician, knew from experience that the success of any bill depended on the president's giving advance notice and allowing Congress to accommodate itself to the proposition, trading benefits and favors with Congress members and leaving arm twisting until the very end.[31] Because so little had been done to prepare the way, Johnson confided his doubts about the bill's chances to its Justice Department authors, and he predicted its failure would be "disastrous" for other parts of the president's program.[32] At the meeting of civil rights leaders on 22 June, however, Johnson had appeared genuinely enthusiastic about the bill.[33]

Predictably, Robert Kennedy later gave contradictory assessments of Johnson's personal commitment to civil rights and his involvement in civil rights legislation. At one point during his 1964 oral history interview, Robert said the president "always felt that Johnson, on civil rights, wanted to get too far involved in it—personally—than was necessary." He said his brother wanted the vice-president to speak "no more than the president was speaking—when it was necessary to speak, and where it made a difference, and where it helped." In effect, as Anthony Lewis suggested during the interview, John Kennedy wanted Johnson to remain "a more acceptable southern figure" and fulfill his role of winning southern votes and carrying Texas.[34]

At another point in the same interview Robert paints a very different portrait of his brother's vice-president when he speaks directly to the historical record and tries to establish that the Civil Rights Act of 1964 owed its origins and ultimate passage more to his brother's memory, and perhaps also to his own perseverance and commitment, than to President Johnson's legislative skills. His brother, he said, requested Johnson's assistance "on virtually every occasion of a major bill, and it was exasperating to President Kennedy that Lyndon Johnson wouldn't do more or make more of an effort in connection with a lot of legislation."

Robert Kennedy conceded that Johnson had "helpful" ideas on how to proceed with the civil rights bill, but he said the vice-president refused to extend himself or to make "any personal effort" on the bill's behalf. Ever mindful of his brother's place in history, still stinging over criticisms that they had waited too long to introduce the bill, and defensive over intimations surfacing in 1964 that the civil rights bill might never have passed had his brother lived, Robert Kennedy implied that Johnson's suggestions served only to delay submission of the civil rights legislation to Congress and left scattered impressions throughout the interview of a vice-president lacking in both loyalty to his president and genuine concern for civil rights.[35]

Those 1964 remarks came soon after John Kennedy's death, when Robert was naturally contemptuous of anyone who had not supported his brother's programs and understandably bitter toward the man who had taken his brother's place. Unable or unwilling to make a realistic assessment of the legislative history of the 1964 Civil Rights Act, Robert Kennedy refused to believe that his and his brother's methods of proceeding on the civil rights bill, in contrast to those of Johnson and other presidents who were consistently successful in getting bills through Congress, almost certainly were not going to convert the opposition, win over the undecided, or even assure the votes of the staunchest liberals.

Throughout their careers, the Kennedys, and Robert in particular, had lacked a feel for coalitional politics and a willingness to bargain and compromise. It was highly improbable, then, at such a late date in their developments (the summer of 1963), that either Kennedy would suddenly gain an appreciation for such skills. Given the circumstances of congressional deadlock prevailing in U.S. politics in the early 1960s, however, no other approach could have succeeded. Thus, the Kennedys' civil rights bill, Robert's later protestations aside, faced a most difficult (some said an impossible) road to passage.

The largest share of the work required to move the Kennedy civil rights bill through Congress was borne by Burke Marshall and Nicholas Katzenbach. With an eye on history's judgments, Marshall later emphasized that it was Robert Kennedy who "took command."[36] Justice Department staff organized a series of meetings where the president, vice-president, and attorney general discussed the bill with groups of businesspeople, chain store owners, mayors, movie theater owners, clergy, college professors, women, lawyers, civil rights leaders, and others.[37] Historian Vincent Harding, who attended one of the meetings, recalled that "something got a little bit more beneath the surface where Bobby was concerned," and that the attorney general showed more "physical emotion" than the president. Eschewing legalisms and politics, Robert spoke at these meetings of the moral and social implications of segregation, often talking about how he felt he would respond to it were he a black person. The attorney general's sincerity impressed Harding, "even though," he said, "I thought that at certain levels it was really impossible for him to do more than *want* to feel that." Although John Lewis of SNCC called the bill "too little, too late," most of the blacks who attended the White House meetings did not criticize it. Harding, for one, knew the Kennedys did not invite them for "dialogue."[38]

Burke Marshall recalled that Robert Kennedy met with "virtually every Senator" and with most members of the House (except southerners).[39] On 1 July, testifying on the bill before the Senate Commerce Committee, Kennedy said, "The United States is dominated by white people, politically and economically. The question is whether we, in this position of dominance, are going to have not the charity but the wisdom to stop penalizing our fellow citizens whose only fault or sin is that they were born." Kennedy faced tough questioning by Senator Sam Ervin of North Carolina, a strict constructionist states rightist who believed the bill destroyed constitutional government. Unlike his exchanges with Governor Wallace back in April, Kennedy now talked about the moral aspects of racial discrimination and about the specific conditions Negroes faced in the South. His personal conversion seemed complete. "Civil rights," Arthur Schlesinger observed, "had displaced organized crime as the issue of law enforcement closest to his heart."[40]

Robert Kennedy's commitment to ending racial discrimination conflicted with his need to control the issue and with his contempt for the liberals who favored a stronger bill. Liberals such as Joseph Rauh of the ADA criticized the bill as the Kennedys' best estimate of what could be enacted, rather than a statement of what was needed.[41] The civil rights lobby wanted to add provisions to ban job discrimination, to give the attorney general authority to initiate suits to protect the constitutional rights of citizens (Title III), and to protect voting rights.[42] To Robert Kennedy, this was all obstructionist nonsense. The liberals, he said, preferred, "to have a cause than to have a course of action that's been successful."[43]

Appearing before the House Judiciary Committee, the attorney general grimaced when its liberal chair Emmanuel Celler of New York patronizingly labeled the administration's bill a "milder version." Celler offered a "tough" alternative version with nearly all of the civil rights lobby's demands, which a Judiciary subcommittee agreed to.[44] Robert Kennedy knew Celler's version would never get through the full House or Senate and feared they would lose the bill as a consequence. Calling Celler to his office for what Burke Marshall described as an "unpleasant" meeting, Kennedy admitted he "scolded" the aging Celler for his audacity in amending the administration's bill and for failing to demonstrate "leadership" on this crucial issue—by which Kennedy meant that

Celler should have rallied others to the Kennedy point of view rather than give in to the civil rights lobby.[45]

Admonishing congressional liberals failed to produce results. John Kennedy, improvising on a variation of the Kennedy brothers' standard theme, then stepped into the fray in the role of calm facilitator. He called the House leadership to the White House. With the attorney general notably absent, the president, according to Arthur Schlesinger, was "never more persuasive."[46] Perhaps so, but the president claimed astonishment when Indiana congressman and House minority leader Charles H. Halleck and Ohio congressman William M. McCulloch, the ranking Republican on the Judiciary Committee, agreed to endorse a compromise version of the bill, which contained the fair employment practices provisions (but not the other liberal add-ons) and was acceptable to the civil rights leaders. Robert Kennedy endorsed the compromise, although he, too, was surprised that the Republicans conceded so quickly. He had no idea why they would compromise at all.[47]

Halleck and McCulloch, as agreed, boosted the bipartisan measure over the Judiciary and the Rules Committee hurdles. By November the compromise version of the bill was positioned for full House approval sometime in early 1964. The next, most difficult, step would be to secure sixty-seven Senate votes, two-thirds, to invoke cloture—that is, to shut off an inevitable southern filibuster. Senate floor managers, however, could count on only about forty-two Democratic votes for cloture; they would have to get twenty-five Republican votes to pass the bill. When John Kennedy left for Dallas, he knew that upon his return he would have to woo Senator Everett M. Dirksen of Illinois, the Senate minority leader, without whose support the bill had no chance of passage.

Who received credit for the passage of the Civil Rights Act of 1964 meant a great deal to Robert Kennedy. His take on the situation—and one he hoped would work its way into the history books—was to portray his brother, on the eve of his trip to Dallas and martyrdom, as engaged in a heroic struggle against the forces of southern prejudice and blind partisanship, without help from the liberal "sons of bitches," organized labor, civil rights leaders, his vice-president, or anyone else—"just the President by himself, really," as Burke Marshall put it.[48] After his brother's assassination, then, Robert Kennedy carried on the cause, ultimately righting a terrible wrong and glorifying his brother's memory at the same instant with the passage of the act. Or so he hoped it would be written.

Lyndon Johnson seemed happy to oblige, telling Robert in January 1964 that he had complete authority for directing the civil rights bill's remaining course through Congress. Johnson, according to Kennedy, told him, "I'll do on the bill just what you think is best to do on the bill. . . . I'll do everything you want me to do in order to obtain the passage of the legislation." Johnson pledged not to water down the House compromise version negotiated by President Kennedy and remained steadfast throughout the congressional maneuvering. This was one of those times, like holding a big hand in a high-stakes poker game, where he felt obliged, he wrote in his memoirs, "to shove in all my stack."[49]

Kennedy wanted the bill passed, he said, "for personal reasons, you know, because I thought that it was so important for President Kennedy." But he was also suspicious of Johnson's motives. Kennedy said later that Johnson allowed him such extraordinary latitude because "he didn't think, number one, that we'd get the bill. I don't want to be unfair about it, but secondly, I think that if we were not going to obtain the passage of the bill, he didn't want to be the reason, to have the sole responsibility."[50] When the bill passed in June 1964, thanks in large measure to Lyndon Johnson's schmoozing of Everett Dirksen, Kennedy implied then and later that all the credit heaped on Johnson was undeserved because he was not nearly so committed to the cause of civil rights as were Robert and his brother.[51]

Robert Kennedy believed that he and President Kennedy would have succeeded in passing a civil rights bill.[52] Most historians find it difficult to disagree with that assessment, as far as it goes. John Kennedy seems certainly to have been able to build upon the scale-tipping agreement achieved with Halleck and McCulloch and to gain a similar agreement with Senate Republicans through Everett Dirksen. Less certain, however, is that the Kennedys could have stopped the Senate from stripping the compromise House version of some of its provisions, among others the fair employment section that Robert Kennedy thought of questionable viability in the first place, or that they could have gotten the bill passed as quickly.[53]

Passage of the Civil Rights Act of 1964—hailed by historian Allen J. Matusow as "the great liberal achievement of the decade"—proved a bittersweet, and, given Matusow's reading, an ironic moment for Robert Kennedy. He thought the final bill was attained in spite of the liberals, rather than because of them. "The only reason that the liberals came along," he said in 1964, was that President Kennedy had got Halleck and McCulloch to agree to the compromise version; otherwise he believed the deadlock would have continued interminably. Most analysts, however, recognize the determining contributions of liberal senators such as Hubert Humphrey of Minnesota and Mike Mansfield of Montana and note that, without the underlying compassion and idealism fostered by the Johnson White House, the 1964 act, like so many other of the Great Society programs, could not have passed.[54] Apparently what bothered Robert Kennedy most was Lyndon Johnson basking in the glow of achievement.

Still attorney general on 2 July 1964 when Johnson signed the bill into law, Robert appears in films of the signing ceremony standing somberly among an otherwise elated and animated group of Congress members and civil rights leaders. When Johnson calls Robert forward, with his head down and his face melancholy he brushes back a forelock and accepts several ceremonial signing pens from President Johnson, who orders him in a not very respectful tone of voice to be sure that John Doar, Nicholas Katzenbach, and Burke Marshall each receive one. No longer at the right hand of the man in power and with no reason to linger, Robert Kennedy steps unobtrusively aside as the lawmakers and celebrants jostle for a position of favor. He has the look of an outsider.

A reading of the history of the civil rights movement in the early 1960s leaves one a little bewildered over the strength and persistence of Robert Kennedy's conviction that he and President Kennedy went underappreciated for their achievements. After he left the Justice Department, he seems to have forgotten that most southern blacks and civil rights leaders tended to see him as the proconsul's adjutant, not as their partner in the struggle. There is no denying Robert Kennedy's indignation over racial discrimination or his building fervor for the equal rights struggle. Nor can it be denied that the Kennedys took political risks in declaring civil rights a moral issue and in supporting King in the spring of 1963. It is equally true that as attorney general Robert Kennedy did several things for the sake of political expediency and to protect his brother that harmed the cause, including his recommendations to appoint segregationist judges in the South who obstructed or overturned cases intended to broaden civil rights and his decisions to authorize the FBI to tap the telephones of Martin Luther King.

A large and important part of the attorney general's job is screening and recommending persons for lifetime appointments to the federal judiciary by the president, with the advice and consent of the Senate. In practice, Robert Kennedy said, "it's grown up as a senatorial appointment with the advice and consent of the President." Presidents and attorney generals have traditionally observed the practice of "senatorial courtesy" and not approved an appointment over the objection of a senator representing a state affected by the decision. Judicial selection, then, is the product of political bargaining. To give it an air of impartiality and to assist in evaluating the qualifications of prospective nominees, Robert Kennedy, like other attorney generals of the modern era, consulted with the American Bar Association (ABA) Standing Committee on the Federal Judiciary, chaired in those years by Bernard G. Segal of Philadelphia.[55]

The screening of judicial nominees was delegated to Byron White and, later, Joe Dolan. Each nomination involved substantial amounts of politicking and horse trading, evidenced by the huge bundle of telephone messages and notes in Robert Kennedy's files from advocates and foes of supplicants for the unprecedented numbers of vacant judgeships the Kennedys had to fill. The enactment in May 1961 of an omnibus judiciary act created more than seventy new federal judgeships. During his presidency John Kennedy sent forward 128 nominations for the federal bench. Most all of them were decent, honest, and competent. Ninety-one percent were Democrats, eight were considered "not qualified" by the ABA, and five could be classified as segregationists.[56]

After reviewing Robert Kennedy's recommendations on individual judgeships, Victor Navasky concluded that he occasionally was "soft on the proprieties of judicial selection." The sources of that behavior had their roots in his unique situation and his rather low estimation of the bench as a career choice. First, as both the president's campaign manager and his brother, he received a flood of requests from politicians to reward the faithful and anoint a scoundrel or two for what they did or did not do to elect the president. The ABA and department screenings for technical qualifications kept the spoils-and-patronage hounds at bay, but Robert Kennedy cannot be faulted for becoming slightly jaded by the raw politicking over the judgeships. Second, Kennedy lacked a "lawyerly view" of the bench (Navasky's phrase) and its activist possibilities for influencing the law. He thought of the bench as a sort of premature retirement place and could not fathom why a person active in politics would want to become a judge. When, for example, a vacancy occurred on the Supreme Court with the retirement of Justice Charles E. Whittaker in April 1962, Robert Kennedy was amazed when Byron White, who was involved in the initial screening of candidates, told Kennedy he wanted to be on the Supreme Court, rather than continue as the number two man at Justice.[57] For various reasons, then, Robert did not immerse himself in the details of the judicial selection process. As a result, he made some mistakes.

Arthur Schlesinger described some of the Kennedys' appointments as "disastrous." Segregationists who made it onto the federal bench in the South got there, according to Schlesinger, because of Kennedy's need as a Democratic president to propitiate southern senators, pressure from the legal establishment through the ABA, "worthless" FBI reports that miscast some of the nominees as impartial, and, in one instance, the misguided recommendation of a liberal judge. Robert Kennedy admitted some of the appointments were a mistake: "I must say," he wrote to Eleanor Roosevelt, "that we have had some disappointments." Convinced that Kennedy learned from his mistakes, Schlesinger found that appointments after 1962 did not repeat the earlier disasters and that the Kennedys' overall record of southern judicial appointments was "comparable" to the Eisenhower administration's.[58]

Eisenhower, however, avoided the mistake of appointing [William] Harold Cox of Jackson, Mississippi. Cox was the college roommate of Mississippi senator James Eastland, chair of the Senate Judiciary Committee, who proposed to Eisenhower's attorney general William Rogers that Cox be appointed a federal judge. Rogers literally laughed at the suggestion because of Cox's segregationist reputation; he did not even perform a background check. Eastland found the Kennedys more receptive. The Justice Department, Burke Marshall recalled, could find "nothing specific" in Cox's background that justified disqualifying him. The ABA rated Cox "extremely well qualified," but Bernard Segal warned of Cox's racial attitudes. Robert Kennedy obviously saw reason for concern, because he called Cox into his office—the only nominee for the federal judiciary that he personally interviewed—and asked him if he would "live up to the Constitution, and the laws, and the interpretation of the Constitution by the Supreme Court." Cox said that would not be a problem. "I was convinced he was honest with me," Kennedy said, "and he wasn't."[59]

The only reasonable explanation for Cox's appointment was that it accommodated Eastland, the chair of the Senate committee that reviewed all judicial nominations. If the Kennedys wanted their other nominations to go through (particularly that of NAACP attorney Thurgood Marshall to the U.S. Court of Appeals), they had to give Cox's name to Eastland.[60] After he was appointed, Cox revealed his true sentiments, once referring to black litigants in a voting rights case before his court as "a bunch of niggers . . . acting like a bunch of chimpanzees." All of his segregationist decisions were reversed on appeal.[61]

The Kennedys did not knowingly place racists on the federal bench in the South, but neither did they exercise great care to avoid it. In spite of their advocacy of change and their rhetoric in support of equal rights, they made no obvious attempt to dramatically reverse the situation in the South by appointing judicial activists and integrationists or, even more radically, by appointing blacks to the court. All ten of the blacks they appointed to federal courts served northern jurisdictions. Whatever their reasons, the Kennedys focused less on changing the South than on adapting to it.

Taking Robert Kennedy at his word, of all the policy issues of the day, civil rights clearly affected the Kennedys' judicial selections least. They were far more wary, for example, of crossing swords with Senator Robert Kerr of Oklahoma, the obdurate multimillionaire (owner of the Kerr-McGee Oil Co.) and a force on the Senate Finance Committee, whom Robert Kennedy described as the "one friend we had to obtain the passage of all bills dealing with finance and taxes." Kerr, he said, was "a real bandit" for holding up legislation until he got his man (Luther L. Bohanon) appointed a federal judge. "It sounds terrible," Kennedy admitted, but it came down to political expediency versus principle. "You stand fast on principle: Kerr doesn't get his judge and you don't get any tax legislation." Kerr and other senators, Kennedy said, played it "tough and mean." One Arkansas judgeship, according to Robert, involved tradeoffs affecting control of the House Interstate and Foreign Commerce Committee and the congressional investigations into spending on the tactical fighter experimental aircraft project.[62]

Had civil rights ranked higher among the Kennedys' priorities—as high, say, as taxation, commerce, and the Pentagon procurement system—they might have been more cautious in evaluating the racial attitudes of judges appointed to courts in the South.

Wiretaps on Martin Luther King, Jr.

Robert Kennedy's most controversial decision as attorney general, his approval of FBI requests for authorizations to tap the telephones of Martin Luther King and the SCLC, came after several FBI reports demonstrated that, contrary to his agreement with the Kennedys, King had contacted Stanley Levison (through Clarence Jones), allowed Jack O'Dell to enter the New York offices of the SCLC, and permitted Levison and O'Dell to ghostwrite materials for him. The Kennedys had also seen the FBI's initial surveillance reports on King's personal conduct. "If the country knew what we know about King's goings-on," Robert purportedly told a dinner companion the eve of the March on Washington, "he'd be finished."[63]

King's personal life, however, concerned the Kennedys less than his failure to keep his personal promises to them. Thus, on 10 October 1963 Robert Kennedy met with Courtney Evans and approved Hoover's request for authorization to tap King's telephone at the SCLC offices in Atlanta. Kennedy approved the tap on a "trial basis," to be continued if it yielded productive results. When Kennedy said he was "worried" about the "delicacy" of the tap and its security, Evans assured him it would not be discovered.[64] Evans noted that Kennedy was "still uncertain in his own mind about this coverage." But on 21 October he approved a second FBI request, this time for a tap on King's home phone, to be evaluated at the end of thirty days.[65] Ten days later, he approved a request to tap Bayard Rustin's phone.[66]

The wiretaps on King and the SCLC, which Attorney General Ramsey Clark ordered cut off in 1966 but which the FBI evidently illegally continued through 1968, yielded no evidence of Communist subversion.[67] That mattered not a whit to Hoover, whose real objective was to destroy King's reputation and influence. Hoover's antipathy toward blacks dated back to his coordination of the federal campaign begun in 1919 that broke Marcus Garvey and his black nationalist movement. He seems, however, to have wished to destroy not the entire black movement of the 1960s, but only those elements he considered "radical" and those persons he considered "subversive." Martin Luther King's name topped the list.[68]

The reason for Hoover's malevolence toward King has been widely debated. The Church committee, knowing that Hoover took any attack on the FBI as a personal attack on himself, concluded that Hoover was responding to King's public criticisms of the FBI. But the FBI's investigation of King predated those criticisms.[69] Another explanation, perhaps best labeled the "bureaucratic politics" hypothesis, assumes Hoover used his control over the investigative apparatus to manipulate government officials—possibly even Robert Kennedy—into doing his bidding. For example, in testimony before the Church committee William Sullivan said his flip-flop in August 1963, when he first stated that Communist influence in racial matters was virtually nonexistent and reversed himself, sprang from fear of Hoover's retribution.[70]

Whatever his motives, Hoover had intensified COINTELPRO operations on King and the SCLC even before Kennedy approved the wiretap authorizations. A month before Kennedy signed the authorizations Sullivan recommended the use of "all possible investigative techniques" and "aggressive tactics" to "neutralize or disrupt" suspected Communist involvement (broadly defined) in black groups.[71] On 23 December, with the wiretap approvals in hand and with Robert Kennedy distracted and still grieving over his brother's assassination, the FBI decided to "destabilize" King and to expose him "as an immoral opportunist who is not a sincere person but is exploiting the racial situation for personal gain."

Calling King a "tom cat" with "obsessive degenerate sexual urges," Hoover supplemented the wiretaps on King with illegal microphone surveillance. Without Kennedy's authorization or knowledge, Hoover's agents planted bugs in King's hotel rooms and elsewhere, collecting information for a campaign of character assassination. Afraid that Kennedy would discover the bugging operations and pull the plug, Hoover wrote at the bottom of an initial report, "No. A copy need *not* be given A.G."[72]

When in January 1964 Kennedy heard rumors of the FBI's Levison-King probe, he knew Hoover was spreading them. By then, however, Hoover had effectively circumvented him, sending his reports on King directly to the White House. Concerned that the FBI leaks would embarrass his dead brother's memory, Kennedy had Burke Marshall send the entire King file to the Johnson White House and advise them to read it. By bringing Lyndon Johnson into the picture, Kennedy hoped to reduce his own exposure, should King's contacts with Communists surface. Johnson's aides, Walter Jenkins and Bill Moyers, saw through the tactic, refused Marshall's request, and returned King's file with a reminder that, the contents of the file notwithstanding, the attorney general had publicly declared King neither a Communist nor Communist controlled. If King fell, Jenkins and Moyers wanted to be sure he did not fall on Johnson. If Robert Kennedy went down with King, so be it.[73]

Hoover now defied Kennedy to do anything about his campaign against King. He got Johnson to reissue the Sullivan report on King's alleged Communist connections and even sent Kennedy summaries of comments by King and his associates (obviously taken from illegal bugs) in which King told an explicit joke about the rumored sexual practices of President Kennedy, with references to Jacqueline Kennedy and the president's funeral.[74] Kennedy, according to Arthur Schlesinger, though "genuinely shocked" by the revelations about King, did not think they affected King's probity as a public leader.[75] What could Kennedy do? Now out of the loop of power, with Hoover and a new, unfriendly White House staff in control of very tender political information, he must have sat waiting for the other shoe to drop, which would not happen until December 1966.

With the nod from the White House and with Kennedy effectively neutralized, the FBI became bolder, stepping up the bugging operations on King, recruiting an informant from within the SCLC offices, and feeding the press a steady diet of invective and slander (most of which went unpublished). Hoover's fury erupted when *Time* named King "Man of the Year" in 1963 and again when he received the Nobel Peace Prize in 1964. In November 1964 Hoover denounced King as "the most notorious liar in the country." The campaign reached its low point when William Sullivan sent a composite tape of the FBI's recordings of King's indiscretions to King's SCLC office, along with an anonymous letter threatening to expose King unless he committed suicide, which King's wife inadvertently opened. King told one friend, "They are out to break me."[76]

How much Robert Kennedy knew of the FBI's harassment of King cannot be established with certainty. However, no record shows that King ever appealed to Kennedy for assistance, nor that Kennedy attempted to stop Hoover. For that matter, no evidence indicates that Kennedy took any further interest in the wiretaps—except, as mentioned, to try to shift part of the burden to Johnson. In his remaining nine months as attorney general, Kennedy never followed up to see if the King wiretaps had, indeed, been productive and never requested reports at the intervals specified in his initial authorizations. Writer Peter Maas said Kennedy "forgot" about the wiretaps while he was in the "tailspin" after his brother's assassination. Although Arthur Schlesinger found Kennedy's resort to wiretaps "understandable," he called his failure to terminate them "less excusable." Victor Navasky offered a harsher judgment, citing Robert Kennedy as "derelict" in not insisting on a regular examination of the FBI logs on King's wiretaps.[77] Perhaps he felt guilty about them, but all evidence suggests that Kennedy said or did nothing about the King wiretaps after he authorized them.

Why did Robert Kennedy authorize the wiretaps in the first place and thus present Hoover with such an important weapon in his campaign against King? Ideally, we would judge Kennedy's decision in the context in which it was made. As David Garrow pointed out, a full and accurate answer remains elusive, because many of the people near Robert Kennedy—mostly out of personal loyalty to him and in deference to his wish after his brother's assassination to be identified as a civil rights advocate—wanted to portray his feelings toward King as far more positive than they actually were. In truth, Kennedy had doubts about King and may have been closer to J. Edgar Hoover's point of view on civil rights than Kennedy's associates would allow themselves to say.

Various reasons have been suggested by Robert Kennedy's intimates for his authorizing the King wiretaps, among them, to save the civil rights bill, which faced an all-out attack by southern members of Congress eager to taint the whole civil rights movement with Communism; to protect King and prove to the FBI that he was not being influenced by Communists; and to cover his brother and himself with Hoover in case, as Arthur Schlesinger put it, anything "went wrong" later on.[78] All three explanations present problems, particularly the first two, which are no more than rationalizations for Kennedy's real intentions.

First, using a wiretap to protect the passage of civil rights legislation, Victor Navasky reproachfully submits, is "unconstitutional, illegal and outrageously improper."[79] To assume, moreover, that Kennedy used such an extraordinary means to "save" the bill presumes that he was prepared to throw the full weight of his office, regardless of marginal legalities, behind civil rights, which he was not. Further, nothing indicates that Kennedy ever employed surveillance and other investigatory techniques for other than prosecutorial purposes.

Second, the suggestion of a noble motive, that is, that he meant the wiretaps to protect King and prove him innocent of false FBI allegations, presumes that Kennedy caved in to Hoover and deliberately violated King's rights in order to protect them. Roger Wilkins, who served in Kennedy's Justice Department, said, "Mr. Hoover just kept pushing Bob, pushing him and pushing him. Finally, Bob said 'Okay, . . . just to prove to you that it's not true, I'll authorize the tap.' " As Navasky again argues, "It strains credulity (and is unforgivably patronizing) to suggest that it is permissible to invade the privacy of the spiritual leader of the civil rights revolution to protect him against himself."[80]

The most compelling explanation offered by Robert Kennedy's associates—one that explains at least part of Kennedy's motivations—was that by approving the wiretaps he hoped to protect his brother and himself from Hoover's zealous pressure. There would "be no living with the Bureau," acknowledged Navasky, if Robert Kennedy did not authorize the taps.[81] Burke Marshall thought Hoover "used" Courtney Evans to pressure and maneuver Kennedy into "a position of having approved, without knowing it, everything that the Bureau did."[82] Support for that idea comes from an unlikely source, William C. Sullivan, Hoover's deputy who headed the Intelligence Division in the FBI. In *The Bureau: My Thirty Years in Hoover's FBI,* Sullivan writes: "Bobby Kennedy resisted, resisted, and resisted tapping King. Finally, we twisted the arm of the Attorney General to the point where he had to go. I guess he feared we would let that stuff [the information on the King-Levison relationship] go in the press if he said no."[83]

The notion that Robert Kennedy allowed Hoover to manipulate and coerce him does not fit well with other impressions of the man. One can imagine him arranging quid pro quo with Hoover, as Taylor Branch implied, to approve a tap on Bayard Rustin's phone in return for Hoover's cooperation in convincing the Senate leadership to cut short the Bobby Baker investigation and divert attention from the Ellie Rometsch case. However, no incontrovertible evidence of such a deal exists—nor, for that matter, of any other deal with Hoover.[84]

In truth, the Kennedys found King's behavior naive and foolish. They believed it imperiled not only the civil rights cause, but the administration's credibility and the Kennedys' political fortunes. On the other horn of their dilemma perched Hoover, righteous and indignant, insisting that the Kennedys disavow King. Unable to control Hoover, Robert Kennedy worried that FBI leaks of sensitive information could hurt both King and the Kennedys. The excesses of the McCarthy era had abated, but the Cold War still raged, and Hoover knew that the Kennedys (or any other politician, for that matter) could not risk being labeled "soft" on Communism. Following each Kennedy endorsement of King a southern congressman appeared—(secretly briefed by Hoover, the Kennedys knew)—posing allegations of Communist control over King's organization. Hoover's behavior in these instances walked a line between insolence and insubordination.

Gaining Robert Kennedy's approval of his wiretap requests was only part of Hoover's agenda. In the interval between Kennedy's approval of the first and second King wiretaps, William Sullivan's Domestic Intelligence Division, still trying to get back in Hoover's good graces, completed "Communism and the Negro Movement—a Current Analysis," a report that described Levison as a "dedicated Communist" and King as "knowingly, willingly, and regularly taking guidance from communists." Acting on his own authority, Hoover distributed the report to the White House and secretaries of state and defense, the CIA, and the military service heads. Robert Kennedy learned of Sullivan's one-sided report and Hoover's wide dissemination of it four days *after* he signed the second wiretap authorization on King; the date is important because some have inferred that Kennedy signed the King wiretap requests to forestall the release of the damaging report to members of Congress who opposed the civil rights bill.[85] Sullivan's report (actually written by Charles D. Brennan) was based on inferences drawn from outdated reports and heavily fortified with speculation. Kennedy called it "very, very unfair" to King. After he met with Evans and had a heated telephone conversation with the director, Hoover recalled all copies of the report.[86]

Preventing Hoover from going off the deep end on King required Robert Kennedy's full attention and the weight of the White House. After Dallas, he could offer neither. In March 1964 Hoover told the House Appropriations Committee that "communist influence does exist in the Negro movement" and offered smear briefings on King to anyone who would listen. His attacks culminated at a press conference on 18 November 1964 when he called King a "notorious liar."[87]

Yet another reason for Kennedy's decision to approve the King wiretaps—one that deserves greater consideration—is that both the attorney general and the FBI director believed that Stanley Levison was an active Soviet agent and that Martin Luther King was trying to conceal something that only wiretaps would reveal.[88] Burke Marshall insisted from the beginning that "the Kennedys had no choice" except to tap King's telephone, which he said was justified on the grounds of national security.[89] The national security explanation fits within the context and timing of the decision. King had continued to contact Levison and O'Dell, despite repeated warnings from the top law enforcement officials and from the president of the United States himself and despite making a commitment not to contact them. King gave the attorney general no alternative except to investigate further. "I mean, if you accept the concept that there is a Soviet Communist apparatus," Marshall said, "and it is trying to interfere with things here—which you have to accept—and that's a national security issue and . . . taps are justified in that area."[90]

During a 1964 oral history interview, Robert Kennedy and Burke Marshall startled *New York Times* correspondent Anthony Lewis when they declared without qualification that Levison was a "high official," a member of the "Executive Committee" of the Communist party. Hoover had convinced them with reports from informants inside the party. When King kept "dismissing the whole idea," as Kennedy said, and refused to heed their advice and moved surreptitiously to contact Levison, the Kennedys had no choice but to investigate further.[91] Since the 1970s the common view holds that the international Communist conspiracy, like the infallibility of Hoover and the FBI, was a myth. In 1963, however, Robert Kennedy believed in an international Communist conspiracy, and he had firsthand proof from the FBI of the Soviet Union's internal spy apparatus. Just as Kennedy could not shirk making tough decisons to enforce federal law in southern towns, so with areas of national security.

As was often the case with things political, the Kennedys wanted it both ways. They needed King's support to get the civil rights bill passed and to hold the black vote, but they dared not risk the political fallout, both at home and abroad, that would occur over revelations of King's involvement with Communists. The Kennedys had committed themselves to King. Since King was committed to Levison, Levison became not just King's problem, but the Kennedys' as well.[92] Neither Kennedy thought King was a Communist, but they knew he was being influenced by one (perhaps two). Yet Robert was certain that Communist influences within the civil rights movement were never a "factor." "Negroes," Kennedy said, "didn't know exactly what they wanted," but he felt sure they did not want a Communist revolution.[93]

A way out of the quandary for Kennedy lay in King's indifferent attitude toward the entire matter, which ultimately convinced him that King was not what he appeared. "He's not a serious person," a dinner partner of Robert's recalled him casually asserting one evening. "He's just got some other side to him," Kennedy said in 1964. "He sort of laughs about a lot of these things [and] makes fun of it. . . ."[94] That other, unknown side of King struck Kennedy as ominous, especially when King tried to conceal his ongoing contacts with Levison and O'Dell. Beyond its national security implications, this kind of behavior was politically intolerable. Loath to tie themselves to political alliances of any stripe, the Kennedys had never given over control of the political variables affecting their destiny. It is unlikely that they made an exception for someone as unpredictable as King or that they would risk so much on someone as reportedly unstable as King without first being certain of what he was not. The Kennedys often protected themselves with the political equivalent of wearing both belt and suspenders. Wiretaps on King, Robert Kennedy reasoned, would clarify some of the uncertainty and, if the worst occurred, they would be protected from harmful repercussions, including an accusation from Hoover that they did nothing.

Anticipating Hoover's reactions became a routine part of most administrative decisions for Robert Kennedy. As the watchdog for the Right and the icon of stern patriotism, Hoover and his reactions were critical indicators of conservative sentiment. Contrary, however, to suggestions that Kennedy either forced Hoover's cooperation or entered into a Faustian bargain to get the FBI to involve itself in civil rights, evidence indicates a less adversarial relationship on civil rights.[95] "You know I've had a more difficult time with him personally," Kennedy told Anthony Lewis, "[but] I don't agree with this sort of general criticism that's been made that the FBI doesn't do anything in civil rights." Hoover was not always sympathetic, Burke Marshall added, because, among other things, "Communists are always hanging around" the civil rights leaders. Moreover, as David Garrow's detailed study revealed, the FBI's civil rights investigations drew far fewer complaints than is generally assumed. The notion of substantive conflict between the Justice Department hierarchy and the FBI leadership in the years 1961–1963 over the stance the federal government should take toward the civil rights movement, Garrow concluded, "is almost as much a myth as the beliefs about communism and the FBI's expertise that were held by the Kennedy Justice Department itself."[96]

Looking at the broad impact of Robert Kennedy's decision to wiretap King, Navasky concluded that Kennedy "inadvertently underwrote wholesale invasions of privacy" and "alienated the movement to which he was authentically drawn." Of the former there is little doubt, but, surprisingly, Kennedy's decision did not alienate everyone in the civil rights movement. Martin Luther King, Stanley Levison, and Andrew Young knew of the taps, but they still intended to support John Kennedy in 1964. Levison said he understood Robert Kennedy's position in light of the recent McCarthy period and the risk of what he admitted could have been "a terrible political scandal."[97]

Jack O'Dell, among others, was far less forgiving. Having grown up in the Detroit ghetto, O'Dell served in the Merchant Marine in World War II and worked on the 1960 Kennedy campaign in the Bronx. He also had a record of involvement with the CPUSA. Confronted by King with the information given him by the Kennedys, O'Dell remembers saying, "Now, I have Communist associates, and I'm not going to cross the street to keep from talking to them." To the allegation of his being a foreign agent, O'Dell replied, "It's ridiculous. It's ridiculous."[98] The Kennedys, O'Dell said later, caught by the "sickness and paranoia" left over from the McCarthy era, thought they had to impose standards of ideological "purity" on the black movement, which included pressuring King to fire O'Dell without any real evidence. "So you see," O'Dell said, "they ran a game on SCLC leadership."[99]

The Kennedys, O'Dell said in summing up their contributions, were "long on rhetoric about how they abhorred segregation" but acted only when "our movement embarrassed the president internationally" and then only with "token gestures." "Most of the books on this period," he wrote in 1989, "proceed from the premise that here was this nice administration up there in Washington that loved the Negroes." Other black leaders, such as Bayard Rustin, remained equally skeptical of the Kennedys. Rustin called John Kennedy "two-faced," because of his tendency to bow to the Dixiecrats and give them Southern racist judges.[100]

"I Believe He's Comin' Around"

Black leaders of the mid-1960s reacted ambivalently to the Kennedys' contradictory mixture of fervid rhetoric and tentative action, mixing their fault-finding with grudging acknowledgement of the Kennedys' substantive contributions and apparent good intentions. Robert Kennedy's judicial appointments distressed Marian Wright Edelman, the Mississippi lawyer and social activist (married to Peter Edelman, an assistant to Robert Kennedy), but she liked him personally and gave him credit for later on acknowledging that he had erred in some of them, especially Harold Cox's. Historian Vincent Harding described Robert Kennedy as "a good man . . . a white man whose basic commitment was to the destiny of white America" and to avoiding the "tearing of the fabric" of American society. "I don't buy the stories of how deeply he knew black people," said Harding. He thought Kennedy "brutally political" but "wise enough and sharp enough to see the ways black people had to be dealt with if the system was going to be carried on."[101]

For both better and worse, then, Robert Kennedy was responsible for the Kennedy administration's record on civil rights. Before leaving for the Peace Corps, Harris Wofford had advised civil rights leaders to "find some way to get to Bob Kennedy." By his return in 1965 he was "amazed" to discover that they had developed "enormous confidence" in him.[102] Feeling closer to the black leadership than to the black masses to which he was drawn in the last years of his life, Robert Kennedy empathized with their plight. Of the black leadership's struggle for equal rights, he said in a June 1963 interview, "It can't be done immediately, but if I were in their place, I'd be saying: 'We've been waiting a long time, we want to get it now,' and making that kind of an effort."[103] Roy Wilkins and Ralph Abernathy attributed the Kennedy administration's change in attitude on civil rights directly to the president's brother, who they thought "really did develop a very strong fire on this issue."

Martin Luther King, according to Wofford, while "fairly low on John Kennedy" in 1962, began to change his opinion because of Robert Kennedy. "King always felt that there was something genuine about Bobby," Andrew Young later recalled. "Bobby said all the right things; he had a way of coming through in a clutch." When asked about Robert Kennedy, King said, "Umm, I believe he's coming around. I believe he's comin' around."[104] As a group, the civil rights leaders questioned the Kennedys' record and wondered how much more could have been accomplished had the Kennedys, in their view, believed in and understood the meaning and consequences of the movement.

How, then, should we judge the Kennedys' record on civil rights? Early critical assessments sprang from the milieu of the late 1960s, when moralism and opposition to authority dominated U.S. politics and when outrage and protest were perceived as necessary catalysts for change. Ironically, much of the moral energy fueling the political passion of those years was unleashed by John Kennedy's assassination. Indeed, within the space of a single year a noticeable change occurred in the country's attitude and in Robert Kennedy's perception of the issue, as evidenced in his oral history interviews of December 1964, laced with activist jargon and criticism of those who had lagged behind the civil rights movement. Just one year after Dallas his tone is impatient, his standards of action higher, and his expectations much greater. In other words, had Robert Kennedy applied to his or his brother's record his own implicit criteria of success, he would have been one of his own harshest critics. In fairness, however, one must judge the Kennedys' record in the context of the early 1960s' more conservative political climate, before the surge in political activism.

The Kennedys at first held themselves above the protest, civil disobedience, and acts of conscience, for they were politicians of the political center, defenders of institutions, protectors and respecters of the politics of moderation.[105] John Kennedy, his attention usually diverted elsewhere, was less absorbed by the issue, and, as Martin Luther King put it, he was also lacking in "moral passion." The president, as Harris Wofford well knew, was "no hypocrite nor did he play politics as usual with civil rights." "Over time," Wofford wrote, "I concluded [John] Kennedy's coolness was because he was cool. Fortunately, the coolness in his soul was warmed by a comic spirit."[106]

Robert Kennedy, by contrast, seemed to be of two minds on civil rights. Historian David Burner describes him as by turns passionate and prudent in exercising a "strategy-tempered idealism." One side of him was passionately sympathetic to the basic rightness and morality of the activists' pleas. He lacked the eloquence of his brother and King, but he persuaded others of the genuineness of his commitment, which he seemed at times to communicate almost intuitively. "Bob Kennedy," Harris Wofford said in comparing him to President Kennedy, "comes with much more passionate Christianity, Catholicism, moral judgments." In the 1950s, Wofford thought Robert often exercised moral judgments without wisdom, but by the 1960s his wisdom seemed greatly improved.[107]

Robert's other side—the prudent political side he held in common with his brother—left him unable to understand why the civil rights leaders taxed the political system with unrealistic and impractical demands. He considered King, Wilkins, and other civil rights leaders political amateurs, unschooled in the intricate complexities of politics and unappreciative of his and his brother's valiant efforts on their behalf. Most civil rights leaders saw only the Kennedy brothers' prudent and politically realistic sides, leaving Martin Luther King, for one, amazed at the moral naivete and the "coldness" of their analysis, at how "unfeeling" they were at times, and how hesitant to move.[108]

Movement did occur. By the autumn of 1963 the Kennedys' conversion was nearly complete. Although the domestic achievements of Lyndon Johnson's presidency would overshadow their substantive contributions, they had opened the way for the beginnings of the end of Jim Crow and prepared the way for the country to pass through its Second Reconstruction.[109] In the process Robert Kennedy left a strong antisegregationist imprint on the Justice Department. "Alone—or at least first—among Attorneys General, so far as I can find," the distinguished legal and constitutional scholar Bernard A. Weisberger recently wrote, "he sent federal marshals into action to protect the civil rights of black Americans by force if necessary."[110]

Robert Kennedy's obvious commitment on civil rights caused reporters to wonder if something profound might be stirring within him. Harrison Salisbury, dean of U.S. political journalists, noted a change: "His lip still curled like that of a sulky child; he still gathered his team around him, his feet on his desk top, as though he was laying plans for a raid on the Yalies; but his acts were acts of manhood."[111]

CHAPTER 14

"Number One and One-Half"

ROBERT KENNEDY PLAYED a unique combination of roles—campaign director, attorney general, executive overseer, controller of patronage, chief advisor, and brother protector. No official in any earlier administration claimed the same level of direct access to the president or exercised executive power as unquestioningly as Robert Kennedy. This phenomenon did not go unnoticed by the general public or the press, which often spoke of what "the Kennedys" had done, as though the administration were a family enterprise. "When you had JFK," an anonymous African American woman recalled, "you had two Presidents: JFK and RFK."[1] A political cartoonist once depicted the president and attorney general returning home at the end the workday, with the caption: "You don't tell me how it went with you today and I won't tell you how it went with me."[2]

Few modern presidents have used their brothers as advisors and none have shared power with them. Indeed, the brothers of Presidents Johnson, Nixon, Carter, and Clinton were liabilities rather than assets. An exception was Dwight Eisenhower's brother, Milton, a confidant and highly effective advisor on Latin American affairs. But Milton refused to be a partisan advocate for his brother or to take a full-time position in his administration.[3] The Kennedy brothers' mingling of political skills and familial instincts, especially the intimate way in which they anticipated each other's thoughts, resembles the way a few recent presidents (Franklin Roosevelt, Lyndon Johnson, Jimmy Carter, Ronald Reagan, Bill Clinton) have relied on their wives for political advice and even occasionally for policy guidance. None of the presidents, however, has had both a formal and informal working association with members of their families to compare with the Kennedys'.

The only presidential advisor approximating Robert Kennedy's close affiliation was Harry Hopkins with President Franklin D. Roosevelt. Like Hopkins, whom Winston Churchill once called "Lord Root of the Matter," Robert Kennedy asked the tough, incisive questions and pressed an issue faster and farther than the president. Like Hopkins, Robert Kennedy did and said things the president could not, tested the water in places the president could not step, and served as his eyes and ears in councils where the president could not go. The FDR-Hopkins relationship, however, had its temperamental hiatuses and lacked the lasting intimacy of the Kennedys'.[4]

Perhaps the most striking feature of the Kennedy brothers' partnership was its complaisant durability. At times, of course, John Kennedy treated Robert as just one of many voices, and at times (the Bay of Pigs decision looms largest) the president did not consult with him at all. Often he shrewdly used him as a foil to do battle for him or as a messenger to test the loyalty of others. Now and then, largely for effect, he would derogate or minimize his contributions before others, sympathize with those who found it difficult or impossible to work with Robert, or even apologize for his aggressiveness. In times of dire need, however, President Kennedy invariably turned to his brother. He was always there.

Powerful, self-righteous, and demanding total loyalty to his brother's administration, Robert Kennedy saw it as his duty to accommodate and complement the president, not to second guess him. Although he held line authority over the Justice Department, Robert Kennedy was more than a cabinet member; his responsibilities overlapped every agency and department in the executive branch. More than a chief of staff—a position John Kennedy dispensed with largely because Eisenhower had relied on it so heavily—Robert did not manage (or care to manage) his brother's staff. Rather, he functioned in many respects like an executive vice-president in a modern corporation, as the chief trouble-shooter and the general overseer of his brother's administration. John Kennedy perceived the lines of power and authority as the spokes of a wheel, all coming to him and going from him.[5] Robert was both a spoke on that wheel and part of the hub.

No department within the executive branch escaped Robert Kennedy's scrutiny.[6] Likewise, no person in the government—from the vice-president down—escaped his often scathing criticisms or heated derision. He was just as likely to tell middle-aged government employees to work off their paunches as he was to chew out first secretaries at U.S. embassies for failing to respond promptly to his requests.

Called by some the "terror of the bureaucracy," Robert Kennedy earned a reputation for unflattering fits of temper. Known to storm into a meeting, express his displeasure in no uncertain terms (once slamming a chair on the floor of a State Department meeting), admonish bureaucrats in front of their superiors and subordinates, and then stalk out of the room, he seemed not to care whom he offended.[7] Many senior members of the administration felt the sting of his sharp tongue and resented it. He "tended to forget," U. Alexis Johnson said, "that he was not just Bobby Kennedy" and that junior officials were at an enormous disadvantage in dealing with him. One State Department official caught in an intense Kennedy ragging told a reporter, "If one of you guys writes one more time about his looking like a choirboy, I'll kill you. A choirboy is sweet, soft, cherubic. Take a look at that bony little face, those hard, opaque eyes, and then listen to him bawl somebody out. Some choirboy!"[8]

John Kennedy admitted that his brother could "be a pain in the ass sometimes," but he never expressed doubt as to Robert's enormous worth to his administration and to him personally. Asked which of his brother's attributes he valued the most, John Kennedy called Robert "the best organizer I've ever seen." "With Bobby," he once said, "I don't have to think about organization. I just show up." Actually, Robert's strength lay in his ability to organize others to help his brother. As McGeorge Bundy, president Kennedy's National Security Advisor, put it, Robert's function was "to go and prod and poke people into doing their best, and staying with the problem, and not giving up until we got a better answer. He was that kind of a terrier of a man."[9]

Others of President Kennedy's advisors had a different estimation of Robert Kennedy's value, role, and responsibilities. Averell Harriman, former governor of New York and undersecretary of state for political affairs during the Kennedy administration, said, Robert's "value was in his most extraordinary loyalty, his understanding of his brother's objectives, and his fierce instinct to protect him in every way he knew."[10] That often involved telling his brother things others could not and acting as an intermediary for others. "When we wanted to let Jack know about a problem too sensitive for one of us to mention to him," Kenneth O'Donnell said, speaking for other staff members, "Bobby would tell him about it and bring back an answer. When Jack was in one of his inaccessible moods," said O'Donnell, "Bobby could always reach him."[11]

Robert McNamara thought Robert Kennedy's role "really reflected his understanding of what the President needed, and his equal understanding of the lack of organization within the government to handle such an assignment." To remedy that deficiency, the president's brother frequently put aside his routine duties to concentrate on immediate problems, sifting and evaluating alternatives for handling the problem so that his brother could then make a decision. For instance, McNamara credits Robert Kennedy with setting up the Executive Committee (shortened to ExComm) of the National Security Council and for making sure that it placed in the forefront the interests of the president rather than those of a particular department or individual.[12]

In April 1963 the Associated Press formally hailed the attorney general as "Bobby—Washington's No. 2 Man," declaring he had "managed, on his own, to be the most hated, the most fiercely supported by co-workers, the most prolific (seven children going on eight), the most competitive and the most misunderstood of the extraordinary Kennedy boys." Once, partly in jest and partly out of pique over not getting his way with Maxwell Taylor and the Counterinsurgency Committee, Robert said, "Well, shit, the second most important man in the world just lost another one," and walked out of the meeting. The president sometimes kiddingly referred to his brother as "the second most powerful man" and once remarked (not so jokingly, according to Kenneth O'Donnell) that "even members of the Kennedy family thought that there were two number one men in the Kennedy administration."[13]

Those who worked with both Kennedys understood their uncommon relationship was closer than that of a number one and number two. "When Jack Kennedy wanted to be alone in a room with just one man," Democratic national chair John M. Bailey said, "that man was Bobby. He wasn't just the President's number two man. Bobby was number one and one-half."[14]

Vice-President Johnson could not conceal his resentment over Robert Kennedy's omnipresence in the White House. "Every time they have a conference," Johnson said, "don't kid anybody about who is the top advisor. It's not McNamara, the Chiefs of Staff, or anyone else like that. Bobby is first in, last out. And Bobby is the boy he listens to."[15]

The vice-president and the attorney general were the only two persons permitted unannounced and unseen access to the Oval Office, through the doors behind the president's desk leading from the Rose Garden. Both went on important diplomatic missions for the president and both were involved in nearly all of the high council meetings. Johnson, however, complained bitterly to the president about "that kid brother of yours." The vice-president felt slighted when one White House parking space went to him and his staff and three to the attorney general. Johnson's aides, denied White House credentials, saw the mansion only as tourists; the attorney general's key assistants were readily admitted.[16]

Generally speaking, Robert Kennedy behaved graciously toward Vice-President Johnson. There were, however, a few instances—enough to stir hard feelings—when he was deliberately and obviously rude or discourteous to Johnson.[17] But as he had done with regard to J. Edgar Hoover, Robert silenced aides who criticized Johnson in his presence. For his part, Johnson referred to the attorney general variously as "that snot-nosed brother," "that son of a bitch Bobby," "that little shit-ass," "little runt," "punk kid," or "little bastard."

How far the hard feelings between the two would extend gave rise to much speculation. Rumors circulated in 1962 and again in 1963 that Johnson might be dropped from the ticket in 1964. John Kennedy felt obliged to announce that Johnson would be his choice for vice-president, if he chose to run for a second term. Robert told interviewers after his brother's assassination that "there was never any intention of dropping him. There was never even any discussion about dropping him." He admitted, however, that he and his brother often discussed Johnson's "personality."[18]

The vice-president would have preferred otherwise, but the attorney general was the man in charge whenever the president left the room or left Washington. After April 1961, Robert was his brother's chief crisis manager for both foreign and domestic problems. Richard Reeves, a close student of the U.S. presidency, described Robert Kennedy as "a sort of surrogate President."[19] Connected to Robert by direct telephone lines and a squad of switchboard operators and communications specialists, the president had only to say, "Get Bobby" whenever a crisis arose.

Even while Robert Kennedy was managing the civil rights crises, he was becoming progressively more involved in foreign policy and national security matters. If his brother had lived and been reelected, Robert said he would have moved either to State or Defense, depending on Robert McNamara's preference. For various reasons, McNamara said later, he would have declined the State Department appointment, leaving the intriguing possibility that Robert Kennedy would have been secretary of state in a second Kennedy administration.[20] Based on the types of roles and missions given him by his brother and given what Robert said later about his brother's assessment of Dean Rusk's performance, that possibility is not as farfetched as it might seem.[21]

Robert Kennedy complained that Rusk "almost inevitably" came up with ideas that turned out to be "wrong" and that his administration of the State Department "really began to irritate the President."[22] Rusk, for his part, thought he had a solid relationship with John Kennedy. He knew, however, that the attorney general questioned his loyalty and the loyalty of some of his appointments and that he repeatedly criticized his effectiveness. Said Rusk, "I was never one of the 'Kennedy people' and never made an effort to become one." He disliked the president's brother, considered him "ruthless about people," and refused to cave in, he said, to demands that he stuff the State Department with "Kennedy people." The soft-spoken Georgian admitted he felt more comfortable with Lyndon Johnson than with either of the Kennedys.[23]

Robert Kennedy was never at ease with Rusk or the other "benevolent aristocrats" (Richard Barnet's term for the elite bipartisan group) selected to make and manage the national security apparatus. John Kennedy, on the other hand, moved easily within this circle of erudite, often well-born policy makers, who set the tone for U.S. foreign policy after World War II. Had he lived to enjoy the status of former president, he would surely have taken his place, as Barnet suggests, with the "Wise Men" and "emigrés in America" who knew little of the country itself but presumably knew more about the rest of the world than any other Americans.[24]

Despite being reared in the same circumstances and afforded similar opportunities to travel and to assay global conditions, Robert reacted skeptically toward those who behaved as if the truth had been revealed exclusively to them. The benevolent aristocrats, in turn, did not react well to him. General Lucius Clay, a Republican and close friend of Dwight Eisenhower, accepted appointment as John Kennedy's personal representative in Berlin, stating one condition: Never under any circumstances would he deal with Robert Kennedy. The president laughed and said, "I understand."[25]

Robert Kennedy's thinking and behavior on foreign policy was reminiscent in some respects of his father's independence and iconoclasm. Like his father, Robert took dead aim at the kind of arrogant presumptuousness and elitist thinking that had led his brother to accept the CIA's ill-fated plan for the Bay of Pigs. Once engaged in the foreign policy process, Robert Kennedy tested each subsequent recommendation to gauge its potential effects on the Kennedy presidency. Following his brother's assassination, Robert at first excused himself and was then purposely excluded by President Johnson from discussions on national security issues. Gradually he became more critical of Johnson's handling of foreign policy and Vietnam. By February 1968 (and the Vietnam Tet offensive) Kennedy had turned completely against Johnson and the inner circle (most of whom were the same people who had served his brother). His fascinating journey, from steadfast insider to a leading critic of establishment policy, extends across the most prominent terrain of U.S. national security and foreign policy in the 1960s, including crises in Cuba and Berlin, the opening debates over Vietnam, and various world trouble spots the attorney general visited as his brother's personal envoy.

The Kennedys in power accepted the liberal-interventionist foreign policy approaches of Woodrow Wilson, Franklin Roosevelt, and Harry Truman. Their goal was a stable world order, held in place by strategic security agreements, allowing the free expression of liberal democratic values and simultaneously, preserving U.S. security and self-interest. The Kennedys' thinking was influenced by pre–World War II international affairs and the unchecked aggression of totalitarian regimes in Germany and Japan. After World War II, they agreed, U.S. foreign policy objectives had to focus on the global containment of Communism. Containment to the Kennedys, however, was at best an intermediate objective along the way to their ultimate goal of ending the Cold War stalemate in victory for the United States.

The Soviets in the Kennedys' eyes were inherently aggressive. No amount of appeasement would satisfy their expansionist appetites. Any threat, therefore, to the balance of power mandated some expression of counterforce, an act of calculated toughness, especially if U.S. credibility and the personal reputation of the president were challenged. They believed in the "domino theory" and a monolithic international Communism and sought imaginative new approaches—with a disproportional reliance on the military as a political instrument—for blocking the fall of nations or for rebuilding those in the dominoes' path.[26]

Cuba Fixation

During the 1960 campaign John Kennedy criticized the Eisenhower administration for failing to remove the Communist presence in Cuba, only ninety miles from U.S. shores. He promised that, once in office, he would change the situation. "The forces fighting for freedom in exile and in the mountains of Cuba must," he said, "be sustained and assisted." In October 1960 the Castro regime expropriated approximately one billion dollars in American holdings without compensation and in

December openly aligned itself with the Soviet Union. Kennedy's first steps in office, then, were to embargo Cuban sugar and to endorse a CIA plan initiated a year earlier to recruit and train Cuban exiles for an invasion of the island. He told the CIA to plan a "quiet landing," one that could be plausibly denied and would under no circumstances commit U.S. military personnel. "I'm not going to risk an American Hungary," he told aides.[27]

Robert Kennedy did not participate in the decision to proceed with the Bay of Pigs, but he fully endorsed it. A week before the invasion he received a complete briefing from Richard Bissell, CIA deputy director of plans. Kennedy remembered Bissell telling him that the twelve-hundred-man landing force, even if initially defeated on the beaches, could stay in Cuba, melt into the countryside, and make a guerrilla war against Castro. "All the military people," Robert said, "were enthusiastic for it."[28] In fact, the military people had little confidence that the plan could succeed without U.S. military intervention. Admiral Arleigh Burke, chief of naval operations, estimated that without it the CIA's plan had less than a 50 percent chance of success. Burke did not inform the Kennedys of his skepticism or qualify his support for the plan. Victimized by the CIA's aura of invincibility and by the momentum of their own group-think processes, the president and practically all of the president's advisors (the attorney general included) thought the operation involved minimal risk.[29]

Once briefed, Robert enthusiastically defended his brother's decision and tolerated no dissent. For example, when Arthur Schlesinger, Jr., special assistant to the president on Latin American affairs, criticized the plan, Robert bluntly informed him that "everybody had made up their minds" and that Schlesinger was "performing a disservice to bring it back to the President."[30]

On 17 April Robert was in Williamsburg, Virginia delivering a speech. Within minutes of the landings at the Playa del Giron, he received a call from the president, who said grimly, "I don't think it's going as well as it should." Robert rushed to his brother's side and remained there for most of the next seventy-two hours, suffering with him over the lack of communications, flawed intelligence, and inaccurate situation reports.[31] Once, when the president was called from the room, Robert glared at his brother's advisors. "We've got to do something," he implored them. "All you bright fellows have gotten the President into this," he added sarcastically, "and if you don't do something now, my brother will be regarded as a paper tiger by the Russians."[32] Reflecting back, Robert said, "You know, we'd been through a lot of things together. And he was more upset this time than he was any other."[33]

When President Kennedy refused to authorize U.S. air strikes and thus broaden the engagement as the CIA planners had cynically presumed would occur, the Cuban Brigade was forced to surrender.[34]

In the immediate aftermath of the Bay of Pigs, a shaken and disillusioned John Kennedy drew his brother Robert into the formal decision-making processes on national security matters and assigned him oversight responsibilities for the CIA. "Up until that time," John Kennedy's close friend LeMoyne Billings recalled, "Jack more or less dismissed the reasons his father had given for wanting Bobby in the cabinet as more of that tribal Irish thing. But now he realized how right the old man had been. When the crunch came, family members *were* the only ones you could count on." Billings said that "Bobby *was* the only person he could rely on to be absolutely dedicated. Jack would never have admitted it, but from that moment on, the Kennedy Presidency became a sort of collaboration between them."[35]

Now admitting that it had been a "mistake" to put Robert in the Justice Department, President Kennedy asked his brother to consider replacing Allen Dulles as director of the CIA. "I said I didn't want to become head of the CIA. I thought it was a bad idea," Robert later explained, "because I was a Democrat and his brother." He agreed, however, that Dulles had to be fired (after a decent interval), and he accepted the assignment of keeping an eye on the CIA, beginning with the recruitment of a new director. To replace Dulles they selected John A. McCone, a wealthy Republican who held positions in both the Truman and Eisenhower administrations and was acceptable to the foreign policy establishment, to the Republican Right, and to both Kennedys.[36]

John Kennedy's calm and graceful public acknowledgement of his responsibility for the Bay of Pigs disaster masked his profound ire. Privately he said that he had been "set up" by the CIA and the Joint Chiefs.

"How could I have been so stupid?" he wondered aloud. Behind closed doors Robert Kennedy loosed enough pent-up fury for the two of them. At an NSC meeting shortly after the debacle, he came down squarely on Undersecretary of State Chester Bowles. Bad enough that Bowles had opposed the Bay of Pigs; he leaked word to the press of his opposition. In a testy confrontation Robert told Bowles that "as far as this administration was concerned, he should keep his mouth shut and remember that he was *for* the Bay of Pigs."[37]

Bowles, a darling of the liberal Stevenson wing of the party, had "irritated" both Kennedys for some time. John Kennedy disliked his wordy pretentiousness and his persistent failure to come to the point. Equally distressing was Bowles's post–Bay of Pigs white paper on Cuba, which, in Robert's eyes, second-guessed the president's judgment and offered nothing new. With the president calmly looking on, the attorney general tore into the undersecretary for several minutes in the presence of the National Security Council. Richard Goodwin, who was present at the meeting, remembered Robert Kennedy shouting that the white paper was a "disgrace," the "most meaningless, worthless thing I've ever heard. You people are so anxious to protect your own asses that you're afraid to do anything. All you want to do is dump the whole thing on the President. We'd be better off if you just quit and left foreign policy to someone else." As the tirade continued, Goodwin became certain, he later wrote, "that Bobby's harsh polemic reflected the president's own concealed emotions, privately communicated in some earlier, intimate conversation. I knew, even then, there was an inner hardness, often volatile anger beneath the outwardly amiable, thoughtful, carefully controlled demeanor of John Kennedy."[38]

The president's vizier let the word go forth from that time and place that in the future everyone was expected to fall in line once important decisions had been made. For emphasis, at a later meeting on Cuba, Robert grabbed Bowles by the coat collar and said, "I want you to know something. You're with us in this all the way, right?" With obvious relish, John Kennedy related the details of the encounter to Ben Bradlee.[39]

Criticisms of John Kennedy's handling of the Bay of Pigs came from every direction. Nikita Khrushchev had a field day in the international press. At their Vienna summit meeting in June, he chided Kennedy,

"Can six million people really be a threat to the mighty U.S.?" Richard Nixon led a tireless Republican attack, accusing Kennedy of deliberately deceiving the U.S. people before, during, and after the Bay of Pigs. In April 1962, CIA Director John McCone sent Robert Kennedy an advance copy of the critical excerpts from Nixon's memoir, *My Six Crises,* in which Nixon labeled John Kennedy "utterly irresponsible" for criticizing the Eisenhower administration for inaction against Cuba, claiming that CIA director Allen Dulles had briefed Kennedy on the covert plan in July 1960 (which Dulles denied). "I was not overwhelmed with the charges," the attorney general penned at the bottom of the note, adding, "As my father said to me, 'Don't put it in writing.'"[40]

The Kennedys refused to answer to the Soviets, the Republicans, or the public for the operational failures at the Bay of Pigs or for the amoral assumption that prompted the venture. Nevertheless, they learned from the experience. "I think," Robert Kennedy once said, "that the Bay of Pigs might have been the best thing that happened to the administration."[41]

Several things changed after the Bay of Pigs. John Kennedy centralized decision making in the White House, creating what Richard Reeves described as a "miniature and personal National Security Council apparatus" built around the people he could trust, starting with Robert Kennedy and including Theodore Sorensen, Robert McNamara, Maxwell Taylor, and McGeorge Bundy. He revived the National Security Council staff and put McGeorge Bundy in charge of the White House Situation Room. In place of the clumsy State Department bureaucracy President Kennedy ran foreign policy "by seminar" (as one analyst described it), relying on a young, highly intelligent, but largely inexperienced staff tied directly to the president. Rather than strategic planners, he drew around him a group of brilliant but like-minded crisis managers to analyze situations and advise how to react. Deceived once by the "experts," as they derisively labeled the CIA and the Joint Chiefs, Robert Kennedy said his brother was determined thereafter not to substitute "anybody else's judgment for his own."[42]

The first test of the new thinking came a few weeks later, when the president (this time with Robert's input) vetoed a Joint Chiefs proposal to put U.S. troops in Laos. Eisenhower had described Laos as the "cork in the bottle" of Southeast Asia. As Communist Pathet Lao forces threatened to overwhelm the U.S.-trained government army, President Kennedy was warned that the fall of Laos would lead to the fall of neighboring countries, including Vietnam. Robert said that the president "continuously prodded and probed" the military and found their plan to send troops to Laos ill-conceived and fraught with much the same odor of disaster that emanated from the Bay of Pigs. If it had not been for the Bay of Pigs, President Kennedy told Arthur Schlesinger, Jr., "I might have taken this advice [the Joint Chiefs'] seriously." Other factors, including the lack of congressional support, the depletion of the strategic military reserve, a personal warning to both Kennedys from Douglas MacArthur not to become involved, and the Joint Chiefs' refusal to "guarantee victory" unless they were given authorization to use nuclear weapons, also weighed heavily in the Kennedys' decision to seek a diplomatic rather than a military solution in Laos in the spring of 1961. In June 1962, thanks in large part to Averell Harriman's efforts, an agreement was reached in Geneva for a neutral Laos.[43] "I would say," Robert concluded, "that if it hadn't been for Cuba, we probably would have sent large numbers of troops into Laos and Vietnam [in 1961]."[44]

The "presence of Bob Kennedy," one White House aide recalled, was the most significant of all the changes occurring after the Bay of Pigs.[45] He began by devoting full attention to an investigation of why the Bay of Pigs invasion failed. With General Maxwell Taylor, Admiral Arleigh Burke, and Allen Dulles, Robert Kennedy spent six weeks studying the tactical aspects of the calamity, never once raising the question of the CIA's motives for planning the attack or questioning the morality of a decision to violate another nation's territorial sovereignty. The Cuba Study Group met twenty-one times and called fifty witnesses, all of whom the attorney general interrogated closely. During these weeks—some of which overlapped with the Freedom Ride crisis—Kennedy left the administration of the Justice Department to Byron White.

On 13 June the Cuba Study Group in its 154-page report concluded that the Bay of Pigs was Eisenhower's plan, that the president's decision not to call in additional air strikes did not doom the plan because such strikes were never a legitimate part of it, and that the CIA and the Joint Chiefs of Staff (JCS) shared the fault. The unstated purpose of the report was to explain why the first plan failed to overthrow Castro, presumably so that Robert Kennedy, Maxwell Taylor, and the CIA could find a way for the next one to succeed—a task Robert had given thought to even as the smoke of battle was drifting off the beaches of the Bay of Pigs.[46]

During the meetings of the Cuba Study Group, Robert became "terrifically taken," as he put it, by General Maxwell Taylor's intellect, judgment, and action-oriented approach. They became frequent tennis partners and close friends. Robert and Ethel named a child (Maxwell, born in January 1965) after Taylor. John Kennedy greatly admired the general's 1959 book, *The Uncertain Trumpet,* which departed from standard massive retaliation doctrine to posit the need for the "means to deter or to win the small wars."[47]

Taylor's visionary thinking shaped and refined the Kennedys' action-response inclinations, leading to the upgrade of conventional and special forces to deal with limited wars, providing a "flexible response" to international crises. Taylor's concepts amounted to a tactical plan for operationalizing John Kennedy's broader strategic objectives, which were to develop the capability to "meet all levels of aggressor pressure with whatever levels of force are required" and "to have a wider choice than humiliation or all-out nuclear action."[48] Other military strategists had raised these issues.[49] None, however, possessed Taylor's combination of personal chemistry and intellectual force that so appealed to the Kennedys. Taylor became the president's personal advisor on military affairs, and thereafter, "every decision that the President made on foreign policy," said Robert Kennedy, "was cleared through Maxwell Taylor." Ultimately, Robert said, Taylor was one of "the two people [Robert McNamara being the other] who . . . made the greatest difference" to his brother's administration. [50]

The humiliation of the Bay of Pigs partly influenced each of those decisions. Robert Kennedy could not put it out of his mind. In a position paper dated 19 April 1961, he warned against returning "to the status quo with our policy toward Cuba being one of waiting and hoping for good luck." The United States, in his estimation, had to *make* something happen, because in a few years, he predicted, "Castro will be even more bombastic, will be more and more closely tied to Communism, will be better armed." Cuba was central to U.S. "survival," he argued, so "our objective must be at the very least to prevent that island from becoming Mr. Khruschev's arsenal." "If we don't want Russia to set up missile bases in Cuba," he warned, "we had better decide now what we are willing to do to stop it." He outlined three options: (1) send American troops, (2) impose a "strict military blockade," or (3) embargo all arms to Cuba. Of the three, he preferred a military blockade.[51]

Many others besides Robert Kennedy saw Castro as the chief foreign policy peril. "We were hysterical about Castro," Robert McNamara admitted, "at the time of the Bay of Pigs and thereafter." A presidential task force headed by Assistant Secretary of Defense Paul Nitze concluded that Castro was "successfully defying the United States." His survival had "lowered the prestige of the United States." Walt W. Rostow, an economic historian and a White House aide in 1961, emphasized in a post–Bay of Pigs strategy paper that the Castro regime's continued presence represented a "moral and political offense to us."[52]

Even as the work of the Cuba Study Group wound down, Robert Kennedy warned that the "Cuba matter is being allowed to slide," because, he had to admit, "nobody really has the answer to Castro."[53] Until they found one, the Kennedys intended to avoid the making of another Castro. Thus, they pressed the development of an intense program in the use of counterinsurgency. Over the next several months Robert received special briefings and read extensively on its theories and methods. In May, President Kennedy asked Deputy Undersecretary of State U. Alexis Johnson to set up a five-week interdepartmental Seminar on Problems of Development and Internal Defense (Counter-Insurgency). Acknowledged inside the administration as the champion of the concept, Robert Kennedy addressed the seminar's first meeting.[54]

Counterinsurgency generally refers to actions taken to thwart guerrilla attempts to overthrow a friendly government. In the case of Cuba, however, the Kennedys sided with the insurgents and pressed the use of both guerrilla forces and covert operations to overthrow the Castro regime. How far they would go to eliminate Castro himself remains a question. Robert Kennedy was probably the only man who knew the full range of covert actions the president had approved, and through his oversight of the CIA, he possibly learned of some operations the president had *not* approved. Government records indicate CIA operations about which neither of them knew. As a participant in the 1992 Havana Conference on the Cuban Missile Crisis quipped, it may have been a case where "the right hand did not know what the far-right hand was doing."[55]

CIA covert operations against Castro and their use of Mafia figures in assassination plots, as we saw earlier, were hatched during the Eisenhower administration. Richard Bissell reactivated the plots in November 1961, after both Kennedys chewed him out, as he put it, for "sitting on his ass" and doing nothing to get rid of the Castro regime. In 1975 congressional investigators disclosed that Bissell and his successor Richard Helms (who replaced Bissell in February 1962) directed three different operations that led to at least eight ineffectual attempts to assassinate Castro. Among them were the CIA-Mafia plots supervised initially by Sheffield Edwards and after November 1961 by veteran CIA operative William K. Harvey. Harvey also set up an "Executive Action" training operation (for the assassination of foreign leaders) code named ZR/RIFLE. A third CIA operation, built around a Cuban double agent named Roland Cubela (code named AM/LASH), was run by Desmond Fitzgerald.[56]

Precisely how much Robert Kennedy knew of these plots is unclear. CIA general counsel Lawrence Houston testified under oath that he had informed Kennedy in May 1962 of the CIA's hiring of Roselli, Maheu, and Giancana to act as go-betweens with Cubans, presumably to overthrow Castro's regime. Richard Bissell also briefed Kennedy on some aspect of the same operation. Asked by the Church committee if that briefing indicated that the purpose of the operation was to kill Castro, Bissell replied, "I thought it signaled just exactly that to the attorney general, I'm sure."[57] Robert Kennedy, however, believed that he had terminated the CIA-Mafia plots. When rumors surfaced attaching Kennedy's name to attempts on Castro's life, he complained to Richard Goodwin, "I'm tired of all these Latins attacking me for going after Castro. The fact is that I'm the guy who saved his life."[57]

Beyond what the attorney general was told about the CIA-Mafia operations, there is, as Richard Bissell admitted, "awfully little evidence" of White House knowledge or complicity with these operations.[58] Moreover, it has never been established that Robert Kennedy was informed of CIA-Mafia operations that continued (contrary to his orders) into January 1963 or that he was ever informed of the existence of ZR/RIFLE or AM/LASH, both of which reportedly remained active into 1965.[59] CIA director McCone later testified that he did not know himself of the operations.[60] Apparently CIA officers drew upon an authorization from the Eisenhower years to use the Mafia in a Castro assassination scheme and expanded upon it during the Kennedy administration and into the Johnson administration without being accountable either to the director of the CIA or the White House.

Operation MONGOOSE

Yet the Kennedys sent no unequivocal signals to the CIA of their opposition to such operations, nor did they lack a scheme of their own to drive Castro from power. When we move from the CIA to the slightly less murky realm of the National Security Council (NSC), the Kennedys' plans for Castro are more evident, although still partially obscured.[61]

In the fall of 1961 President Kennedy took two decisive steps in the area of national security and covert operations. His brother had principal roles to play in both.

First, acting on a recommendation of Maxwell Taylor's contained in the Cuba Study Group report, the president established a subcommittee on counterinsurgency within the Special Group (the formal name of the NSC oversight committee). Designated as Special Group (CI), the subcommittee was charged with coordinating U.S. efforts in assisting foreign governments (Laos, South Vietnam, and Thailand) threatened by guerrilla insurrection. Its members included Taylor as chair, along with the director of the CIA (Dulles, later McCone), the chair of the JCS (Lyman Lemnitzer), the heads of USIA (Edward R. Murrow) and AID (David Bell), and deputies at State (U. Alexis Johnson) and Defense (Roswell Gilpatric), with Robert Kennedy as the group's goading minister without portfolio. Special Group (CI) was a belated response to Nikita Khrushchev's speech of 6 January 1961 on the inevitable spread of Marxism through wars of national liberation to overthrow noncommunist regimes around the world. It was also consistent with the Kennedys' concept of "flexible response," using groups such as the Army Special Forces (Green Berets) to counter threats short of all-out nuclear war. Special Group (CI)'s purpose, of course, was to prevent any more Castros from emerging and to figure out a way to prevent South Vietnam from falling to Ho Chi Minh.[62]

With conventional warfare doctrine well entrenched, winning the military over to counterinsurgency was difficult. Needing an advocate, Robert Kennedy appointed Marine Major General Victor H. Krulak as special assistant to JCS for counterinsurgency and as staff to the Special Group (CI). Krulak, nicknamed "Brute" because of his slight physical build and pugnacious attitude, had met Lieutenant (J.G.) John F. Kennedy in a brief but memorable encounter during combat in the Solomon Islands in World War II. The ambitious Krulak reminded the president of their first meeting, and they renewed their acquaintanceship in the Oval Office over a ceremonial drink of whiskey. When the Special Group (CI) billet opened in January 1962, John Kennedy told his brother to fill it with Krulak.

They hit it off immediately. Krulak ingratiated himself with the attorney general, working his way into a responsible if not indispensable position on Special Group (CI). Robert Kennedy admired the decorated marine's nerve and command presence, trusted him intuitively, and counted on him to be a forceful and energetic advocate for incorporating counterinsurgency training into standard infantry doctrine.[63]

In a second decisive step, President Kennedy authorized on 30 November 1961 a major new covert action program aimed at overthrowing the Cuban government. Code-named Operation MONGOOSE, it was placed under Robert Kennedy's guidance, with oversight by the NSC's Special Group (Augmented); that is, with the attorney general and Maxwell Taylor added to the Special Group overseeing the NSC. The next day, at the first meeting of MONGOOSE, Robert Kennedy stated that after discussions with "higher authority" (the president) it had been decided "that higher priority should be given to Cuba."[64]

The comparative importance of Cuba and Vietnam in the Kennedy scheme at this point was evident in Robert Kennedy's success in convincing the president to allow him to appoint as MONGOOSE's chief of operations Air Force brigadier general Edward G. Lansdale—the American guru of counterinsurgency, hero of *The Ugly American* (a 1958 novel by Eugene Burdick and William Lederer on America's clumsy efforts in Southeast Asia), and real-life architect of the suppression of guerrillas in the Philippines. Lansdale was surprised by the assignment. He had expected to return to an active role in Vietnam. But the president pulled Lansdale aside after a White House meeting to personally assign him to work with the attorney general on Cuba.[65]

With Lansdale's expertise, the Kennedys intended to build a new nation on the island of Cuba. To the MONGOOSE group Robert Kennedy emphasized "the necessity of coming to an agreement at some early date as to the future of Cuba after the Castro government is overthrown."[66]

MONGOOSE, according to insiders' reports, was the largest operation within the CIA, with a budget estimated between $50 million and $100 million. To support MONGOOSE the CIA established Task Force W (TFW), under the direction of William Harvey. TFW recruited and coordinated an estimated four-hundred operatives, most of them Cuban exiles, to restore intelligence assets inside Cuba and to build agent networks to overthrow Castro. Asked if MONGOOSE was legal, since it appeared to violate the Neutrality Act, CIA counsel Lawrence Houston responded, "If the President says it's okay, and if the Attorney General says it's okay, then it's okay."[67]

Robert Kennedy had become so enthralled by the possibilities of covert operations and counterintelligence sleuthing that, to the annoyance of sister Eunice, he invited Green Berets to Hyannis Port to give demonstrations on the lawn of the family compound.[68] His general oversight of the CIA included extensive briefing on intelligence and counterintelligence developments; he became intimately familiar with their details. He participated, for instance, in evaluating the credibility of Soviet KGB defector Major Anatoliy Golitsyn, meeting Golitsyn and listening impassively to his tale of a massive Soviet master plan to deceive the Americans, which he reported to the president. He knew, also, of CIA spying operations against the French and quite likely other nations as well.[69] In time, he became inured to the moral implications of such operations and the potential for retribution.

By the fall of 1961, then, Robert Kennedy had become caught up full-time in national security matters. His weekly meetings of the Special Group (CI) often spilled over into the meetings of the Special Group (Augmented) and then into the meetings of MONGOOSE, each involving the same core cast (Taylor, McCone, Kennedy) with different supporting players. These meetings often consumed six or seven hours of his day. Kennedy's desk diaries and telephone logs indicate huge chunks of time spent at the Pentagon, in Taylor's office at the White House, on the phone with McCone, or at the new CIA headquarters in Langley, Virginia. On many occasions the attorney general was the only civilian present at these meetings, where military and CIA officers predominated.

Robert Kennedy liked associating with men of action and sought out their companionship when the meetings ended. Besides Maxwell Taylor, Robert also drew close to John McCone during these years. McCone realized soon after his appointment that Robert Kennedy was the key to the administration. He cultivated the connection as the next best thing to intimacy with the president himself. McCone and Kennedy socialized after hours, attended church together (McCone was a late convert to Catholicism), shared family joys, and consoled each other during family tragedies, including the illness and death of McCone's wife. McCone (like Douglas Dillon, another Kennedy appointee who became a close friend of Robert's) was older, more conservative, and thoroughly Republican. With equanimity, he accepted Robert's oversight of the CIA, which sometimes came through good-natured kidding and sometimes through mild scolding.[70]

Fascinated by the CIA operations and intent on shaping them to meet the administration's most urgent needs, Robert Kennedy handled the CIA much as he handled the FBI. He routinely telephoned the CIA's upper- and midlevel officials or "invited" them to drop by his office to answer specific questions on operations. He once visited the operations station in Miami (codenamed JMWAVE) which dispatched MONGOOSE operatives to Cuba. CIA pros like William Harvey resented such intrusions and considered them meddling. Presidential staffers talked of how Robert Kennedy was "out-CIAing the CIA." He became, in Thomas Powers's words, a "haunting presence" over the CIA.[71]

Castro's haunting of the Kennedys was equally relentless. In December 1961 Castro avowed his commitment to Marxism-Leninism. A month later, in his Second Declaration of Havana, he labeled the United States an evil empire, the scourge of Latin America. Soon after, the United States succeeded in getting Cuba expelled from the Organization of American States. Humiliated by Castro's survival and frustrated by failed efforts to isolate his regime, Robert Kennedy told the members of the Special Group (Augmented) at a meeting in his office on 19 January that "no time, money, effort or manpower is to be spared" in promoting the overthrow of Castro's regime. He told them that just the previous day the president had said, "The final chapter [on Cuba] had not been written—it's got to be done and will be done." Thus did the president pressure his brother, who, in turn, leaned on McCone and the CIA at the Special Group (CI) and Special Group (Augmented) meetings. They passed it along to Lansdale and Helms, who then leaned on Harvey and Fitzgerald, the two men who gave the final instructions to field operatives. "My God," Richard Helms said, "these Kennedys keep the pressure on about Castro."[72]

On 20 February, Lansdale presented Robert Kennedy and the Special Group (Augmented) with an elaborate operations scenario and precise timetable for MONGOOSE, using guerrilla actions, paramilitary raids, sabotage, and "other means" projected to culminate in October 1962 with the overthrow of Castro.[73]

Did those other means include assassination? No written record shows either Kennedy ever authorizing or condoning it. Bits of evidence, however, leave room for doubt. President Kennedy actually mentioned the idea once. In November 1961 he asked *New York Times* reporter Tad Szulc, "What would you think if I ordered Castro to be assassinated?" Szulc said the United States should not be a party to murders. The president, Szulc remembered, quickly agreed. When Szulc had met with Robert Kennedy earlier the same day, Szulc said Robert made no mention of assassination.[74]

We know, of course, that Lawrence Houston informed Robert

Kennedy of the CIA-Mafia plots and requested that the Justice Department not prosecute Giancana and Maheu. Here Kennedy was only receiving a CIA report, not initiating discussion. Some reports (of dubious credibility) claim that Kennedy not only knew of the plans but directly facilitated them.[75]

However, Robert Kennedy may have once broached the question of killing Castro with General Lansdale. Whether he did or not cannot be firmly established or definitively refuted, partly because he and Lansdale communicated in a sort of code. Lansdale's handwritten notes attached to Kennedy's copies of MONGOOSE planning scenarios contained cryptic allusions to elements of the plan (some of which may not have been committed to paper), referring, for instance, to completing a "touchdown play," a phrase that apparently meant the overthrow of Castro by the Cubans themselves. Asked at the Church committee hearings in 1975 if he had ever discussed the assassination of Castro with Robert Kennedy, Lansdale answered, "No, not that I recall." Asked the same question about President Kennedy, he answered, "No," without qualification.[76]

Lansdale's qualified answer regarding discussions with Robert Kennedy may be because the assassination of Castro was, in fact, once raised at a meeting of the Special Group (Augmented). On 10 August 1962, after a long, inconclusive meeting, Robert McNamara commented, "The only thing to do is eliminate Castro." It was taken by those present as a hypothetical suggestion, made in frustration. Richard Goodwin, who was involved in many of the meetings on Cuba, said it was the only time he ever heard such a suggestion. Lansdale also heard the remark. Three days later he requested William Harvey to prepare a draft of various anti-Castro programs, "including liquidation of leaders." Harvey immediately informed Lansdale of the "inadmissibility and stupidity of putting this type of comment in writing." To cover himself Harvey reported the matter to McCone, who agreed. "It [the liquidation of leaders] is not proper for us to discuss," McCone stated, "and I intend to have it expunged from the record." Asked by the Church committee why he had made such a request of Harvey, especially after the Special Group (Augmented) had rejected it, Lansdale said he could not recall the reason.[77]

Lack of a paper trail does not necessarily prove that the Kennedys had no knowledge of or involvement in plots to kill Castro. Presidents have reportedly instituted covert activities with a nod of the head or with vague verbal instructions that later could be refuted under the doctrine of plausible deniability. Further, there is the possibility, albeit an unlikely one, that the CIA informed the Kennedys of the plots to kill Castro—beyond the CIA-Mafia plot that Robert Kennedy assumed he had terminated in May 1962—but in such an oblique or indirect manner that the Kennedys did not comprehend the CIA's meaning.[78]

We cannot disregard, however, the profane urgency of the Kennedys' wish to be rid of the Castro regime. Given the history of the concept of plausible deniability in the intelligence community and given the Kennedys' penchant to follow their father's admonition ("Don't put it in writing"), one might easily have construed their repetitive complaints about Castro as a command or as a verification of prior authorizations. CIA officers, according to a CIA inspector general's report of 1967, felt themselves subject to "severe pressure" from the Kennedys to do something about Castro. "It was the policy at the time to get rid of Castro," Richard Helms said later, and "there were no limitations put on the means."[79]

In 1964 Robert Kennedy unhesitatingly and emphatically denied authorizing or even knowing of assassination attempts on Castro; he insisted that he, in fact, had called off the CIA attacks.[80] Whether the Kennedys intended it or not, key persons in the CIA—excluding McCone, but from the deputy director of plans (Helms and Bissell) down—apparently all *thought* the Kennedys wanted Castro assassinated. The Church committee concluded that discussions in the NSC and Special Group(Augmented) "might well have contributed to the perception of some CIA officials that assassination was a permissible tool in the effort to overthrow the Castro regime."[81]

The written records do not directly confirm those perceptions, but, instead, dwell heavily on the Kennedys' desire to overthrow the Castro regime. Lansdale's operation plan for MONGOOSE, as rewritten by McCone and Taylor in late February 1962, placed highest priority on getting hard intelligence and ordered that covert operations inside Cuba remain inconspicuous, stopping short of creating a situation requiring

U.S. armed intervention.[82] Once Harvey's TFW commenced covert operations, Robert Kennedy followed its progress closely, taking particular note of efforts to disrupt the Cuban economy, demanding up-to-the-minute reports on operations such as the thrice-failed attacks on the Matahambre copper mines, and becoming more exercised and more demanding of success with every delay and failure.[83]

Robert Kennedy received the disapppointing results of the first phase of MONGOOSE from Lansdale in late July 1962. The attorney general blamed the failures on William Harvey's "half-assed" TFW operations, which Kennedy said were "just going in, blowing up a mine or blowing up a bridge. You know, some of them ended in disaster. People were captured, tried—and confessed. It wasn't very helpful."[84] At that point Robert Kennedy and the Special Group (Augmented) considered a larger move. Per their request, on 8 August they received and reviewed a JCS report on the prospects and consequences of U.S. military intervention in Cuba.[85] On 20 August, they reported to the president that they could see no likelihood of overthrowing the Castro regime short of direct U.S. military intervention. Three days later, with intelligence estimates confirming a Soviet military buildup in Cuba and with reports surfacing of possible Soviet missiles there, the president, through National Security Action Memorandum 181, directed that the next phase of MONGOOSE (moving beyond intelligence gathering and covert operations to ousting Castro without overt U.S. military support) be developed with "all possible speed."[86] Robert Kennedy was more satisfied with this phase (involving operations from August through October 1962) because it was "better organized" and "was having quite an effect. I mean, there were ten or twenty tons of sugar cane that were being burned every week through internal uprisings."[87]

In early October, in an extraordinary move indicative of Robert Kennedy's high position among national security advisors, he was appointed to chair the Special Group (Augmented) "for the time being," to replace Maxwell Taylor, appointed chair of the Joint Chiefs. As a first item of business Kennedy ordered "massive activity" in Cuba within the MONGOOSE framework, and instructed Lansdale to find "new and more dynamic approaches" with sabotage given priority attention. On 16 October—the day the CIA confirmed the presence of Soviet missile sites in Cuba—Kennedy convened a special meeting of the MONGOOSE group at which he expressed "the general dissatisfaction of the president" with the operation and said he intended to give it "more personal attention" by holding daily meetings.[88] However, Robert Kennedy was drawn closer to his brother's side as the crisis intensified.

With miliary intervention in Cuba a real possibility, the CIA stripped away MONGOOSE's action arm, reclaiming from Lansdale operational control over William Harvey's TFW. "The time has long since passed for MONGOOSE-type, Special Group–type consideration," asserted Lt. General Marshall S. Carter, deputy CIA director, on 25 October in a memorandum to McCone defending the action and explaining a "jurisdictional" dispute with General Lansdale. Intelligence gathering in support of an invasion, Carter argued, should be coordinated by the Joint Chiefs of Staff, not a "cumbersome" operation like MONGOOSE. Without the knowledge of General Lansdale or Robert Kennedy, but aided by the endorsement of General Carter and supported by the CIA and JCS, Harvey assembled six 10-man teams, composed mostly of Cuban exiles, and arranged to land them by submarine in Cuba to collect intelligence, as Carter confirmed, "in the event military operations took place."[89]

Kennedy said he became "furious" on learning of Harvey's sabotage operations, claiming "nobody knew what they were doing." The next afternoon, 26 October, McCone explained to the MONGOOSE group that Harvey's group had acted independently of Lansdale (and Kennedy) because the CIA was "obligated" by "long standing arrangements" to support the military in such instances. The group "reaffirmed" that Lansdale was in charge of "the MONGOOSE operations which cover all covert activities," but that the infiltration of agents was to be held in abeyance, "pending a determination by the Department of Defense as to just what military information is desired." In effect, MONGOOSE was ordered to stand down.[90]

Harvey's sabotage teams were not recalled until 30 October 1962, however, too late to prevent the bombing of a Cuban industrial facility on 8 November. The attack did not affect negotiations to end the missile crisis, but the CIA had made its point: Coordination of intelligence gathering and sabotage operations belonged in the CIA, not the NSC. By late January 1963 MONGOOSE was terminated; Edward Lansdale was in

Vietnam; William Harvey, chastised by Robert Kennedy at a Pentagon hearing for callously "dealing with people's lives," was reprimanded and sent to Rome; TFW under Desmond Fitzgeral continued covert operations against Castro during 1963; the Special Group (Augmented) was disbanded and replaced by the Special Group chaired by McGeorge Bundy; and Robert Kennedy's career in direct management of covert operations was over.[91]

MONGOOSE was an illusory enterprise. Arthur Schlesinger called it "marginal." Lansdale's reports of "wide-spread disaffection in Cuba" and rumors of "uprisings" notwithstanding, the realists inside the CIA knew MONGOOSE was fantasy. Lansdale admitted he had been "unable to surface the Cuban resistance potential to a point where we can measure it realistically." Without reliable assets inside Cuba, the CIA was forced to turn from resistance building to sabotage, paramilitary raids, and other disruptive actions that Robert Kennedy found "unhelpful."[92] Most damning, in light of subsequent events, was the ineptness of MONGOOSE, which allowed Cuban and Soviet intelligence to detect many signs of U.S. covert activity. That, in turn, caused Castro to be concerned, he said later, "about a direct invasion of Cuba by the United States" and about ways "to step up our country's ability to resist an attack," including the installation of Soviet missiles.[93]

Robert Kennedy's excitable and amateurish handling of MONGOOSE bore the marks of a neophyte adventurer. Newcomers to the field of foreign policy, Chester Bowles once commented (very likely with Robert Kennedy in mind), often turn to the military for solutions when they find themselves confronted by the nuances of international questions. In such instances, Bowles contended, the newcomer "becomes an easy target for the military-CIA-paramilitary-type answers which can be added, subtracted, multiplied or divided."[94] There is something to that view. Robert Kennedy was locked up for hours on end with military, CIA, counterinsurgency specialists, and national security strategists. After a time, his reactions became predictable.

The heady blend of drama, adventure, and power were a lot for anyone to handle, especially someone as burdened as the attorney general. "My friend Robert Kennedy, in one of his less uncritical moments," Arthur Schlesinger, Jr., explained in 1992, "let MONGOOSE get somewhat out of hand. He had a very busy year in 1962. . . so what attention he gave to Operation MONGOOSE was not very effective, and not very useful, since it was mostly devoted to telling them to do more."[95] Taking stock in 1964, Robert said, "I was involved in more things than I thought." Indeed, one must be impressed by his awesome display of energy, daring, and concentration while juggling so many important problems. In the final analysis, however, he was spread too thin to be able to effectively manage covert operations in Cuba. The assignment, however, reflects both the importance the president attached to Cuba and the depth of his confidence in his brother's abilities and judgment.

Berlin and Back Channels

Robert Kennedy was of greater value to his brother as an advisor and as surrogate president during crises, of which there were many during the thousand days. With dust hardly settled on the beaches of the Bay of Pigs, Rafael Trujillo, the corrupt dictator and pillager of the Dominican Republic, was assassinated on 30 May 1961. The strategic proximity to Cuba of the Dominican Republic and Haiti, which shared the island of Santo Domingo, had led the Kennedys to develop contingency plans for an invasion and occupation of the island. They saw Santo Domingo as the second in a row of dominos in the Caribbean upon which the first domino (Cuba) threatened to fall. "If [Castro] had the Dominican Republic," Robert Kennedy later explained, "it meant the whole part of the Caribbean would be hard to hold." No plans were in place for a successor to Trujillo's sadistic regime. Thus, when the president learned of the assassination while attending meetings with DeGaulle in Paris en route to the Vienna Summit, he directed, "Do whatever is necessary to prevent a Communist takeover."[96]

With the president and secretary of state out of the country, this was Robert Kennedy's first chance to manage a foreign policy crisis. Views differ as to how he handled it, or whether he handled it all.

According to Robert, upon word of Trujillo's assassination he telephoned his brother in Paris, set up a "command post" in the State Department, "sent the fleet" to the area as a show of force to back the anti-Trujillo forces, and "threw the Trujillos out" (the brother, José, and the son, Ramfis, who was actually in Paris at the time). "It was a question," he said, "about whether we'd move troops in, under what circumstances we'd move troops in, where they'd land, how far off the water they'd be."[97] Although Kennedy offered this description in 1964 with confident assurance, Dean Rusk and Chester Bowles have disputed it.

According to Rusk, President Kennedy had put his brother in charge, with certain reservations. "Let Bobby play around," John Kennedy reportedly told Rusk in Paris. "If he gets in your way, let me know." Robert definitely got in the way of Chester Bowles, acting secretary of state while Rusk was in Europe with the president, who was affronted when the attorney general strode into the State Department, took over the "Operations Center," and started giving orders. Supported by Robert McNamara, Kennedy talked of a limited U.S. intervention in the Dominican Republic, beginning with the movement of U.S. warships closer to shore. When Bowles expressed caution, Kennedy called him a "gutless bastard." Confused and frustrated, all three—McNamara, Bowles, and Robert Kennedy—called the president in Paris for clarification.

Bowles's account survives. When Bowles told the president that McNamara and Robert Kennedy "want to send in the Marines," the president, according to Bowles, said that was not what he wanted. "Well, I'm glad to hear it," said Bowles, "and in that case, would you clarify who's in charge here?" "You are," the president said. "Good," said Bowles. "Would you mind explaining that to your brother?" Bowles won the battle but lost the war. A few weeks later the man Robert Kennedy said "irritated me, and irritated everybody" was exiled from Washington to an amorphous post as roving ambassador, a victim of a quiet purge that marked Robert Kennedy's permanent ascendancy in the foreign policy hierarchy.[98]

Were the Kennedys aware of CIA involvement in the assassination of Trujillo? Trujillo, after all, was gunned down with U.S.-supplied weapons after more than a year of CIA-sponsored plotting against him. "The United States," Richard Goodwin recalled the president saying, "is not to get involved in any assassinations. I'd like to get rid of Trujillo, but not that way." In February 1961, President Kennedy stated as much to the CIA station in the Dominican Republic in a telegram laden with the heavily qualified language of plausible deniability. "We must not run risk of U.S. association with political assassination," Kennedy cabled, "since U.S. as a matter of general policy cannot condone assassination." But he added, "Continue to inform dissident elements of U.S. support for their position." Robert Kennedy was aware, he said, of "plans about the assassination . . . that various people [inside the CIA and the Dominican Republic] were meeting. But I never knew" of assassination plots. "To my knowledge," said Kennedy, the United States did not engineer the Trujillo assassination. Confident of his control over the CIA, he was certain, he said, that they "wouldn't have done it without telling me."[99]

More intrigued by technical intelligence matters than by the moral and strategic implications of U.S. policy toward the Dominican Republic, Robert Kennedy was chagrined by the CIA's confusion and their poor communications to the island during the crisis. At one point, he testily suggested that the CIA telephone a U.S. newspaper reporter there to find out what was happening. Afterwards, he recommended forming an NSC subcommittee to develop plans to avoid future foul-ups.[100]

To remove "cruel, inhuman governments" (such as Trujillo's) and to assure Communists did not replace them, Robert Kennedy recommended and the Special Group (CI) approved the use of U.S. police as counterinsurgent forces in Latin America. He personally arranged with Los Angeles police chief William H. Parker to send three officers from his department's "Mexican Squad" to restore order in Caracas, Venezuela. U.S. police also served in the Dominican Republic, and at one point, Ambassador John Bartlow Martin said, "Two cops held that country for us."[101]

Yet another crisis broke after the president's return from Europe, this time over Berlin. Khrushchev had run roughshod over John Kennedy at the Vienna meetings. "Worst thing in my life. He savaged me," said the president. Khrushchev's tirades were prompted in part by the opening Kennedy gave him with the Bay of Pigs and in part by the intolerable situation Khrushchev himself faced in Berlin, its western sector still occupied by U.S., French, and British forces sixteen years after the end of World War II. Unable to stanch the hemorhage of refugees flowing out of East Germany (an estimated twenty to thirty thousand a month by 1961), Khrushchev had threatened to conclude a separate peace treaty with Germany before the end of the year, to block passage out of East Germany, and to deny western access routes into Berlin. Germany and Western Europe were of central importance to U.S. visions of an "Atlantic Community" built upon the NATO Alliance and integral to John Kennedy's grand design for ultimate U.S. hegemony.[102]

Both sides said they would fight over Berlin. Neither believed the other.[103] The president charged Robert Kennedy with convincing the Soviets of U.S. resolve through face-to-face contacts with Georgi Bolshakov. A ranking officer in the Soviet intelligence apparatus using his editorship of a glossy Soviet news magazine as a cover, Bolshakov was well connected to Khrushchev through his friendship with the editor-in-chief of *Izvestia,* Aleksei Adzhubei, Khrushchev's son-in-law.[104] Two weeks before the Vienna summit, the attorney general met with Bolshakov and told him, "I know you're on intimate terms with Adzhubei and others. I think they wouldn't mind getting truthful first-hand information from you, and I presume they'll find a way of passing it on to Khrushchev." For four hours, the two men sat on a park bench across the street from the Justice Department while Kennedy tried to convince Bolshakov that Khrushchev would be mistaken to believe John Kennedy was weak and would tolerate being pushed around. Robert knew his brother's thinking: "I suppose if we get involved in a war in Europe," the president said, "we will have no choice but to use nuclear weapons."[105] The Kennedys feared a war might start as a result of miscalculation or misjudgment, and so Robert warned Bolshakov not to push too hard.[106] Still, Khrushchev persisted in proclaiming his intention of driving the Western powers out of Berlin.

Administration thinking in the summer of 1961 reverted to the brinkmanship and massive retaliation approaches of the Eisenhower administration. It was dominated by the hard-line attitudes of former secretary of state Dean Acheson, whose advice President Kennedy solicited during the Berlin crisis and regularly thereafter. John Kennedy's position led to massive military buildups and the escalation of nuclear bargaining. In what resembled an impetuous schoolyard shoving contest, the Soviets countered by resuming atmospheric testing of nuclear weapons. John Kennedy considered doing the same.

"I want to get off," Robert told his brother after one particularly gloomy NSC meeting. "Get off what?" the president asked. "Get off the planet," he answered. The chances of war that summer, Robert believed, were one in five.[107] "It was a harder period," he said, "I don't know how to describe it exactly. It was just a tougher, harder, meaner period than that which had gone before."[108]

In response to these meaner times the Kennedy administration took a "more realistic" view of thermonuclear war. Some called it thinking the unthinkable. "If we do not meet our commitments in Berlin," John Kennedy asked, "where will we later stand?" The military activated reservists, doubled draft calls, and expanded by two-hundred thousand as part of a request for a $3.5 billion increase in military spending.[109] A massive new civil defense effort included a fallout shelter program, directed by Assistant Secretary of Defense Adam Yarmolinsky. Fallout shelters seemed a logical step, given the growing risk of nuclear war and the infeasibility of evacuating cities. Even though the president endorsed the concept, Robert Kennedy opposed it, describing himself as "a minority of one." The gush of raw emotion triggered by the unseemly hurry to build individual fallout/bomb shelters and defend them, with firearms if necessary, appalled him.[110] The doomsday scenarists, "realist" thinkers, and war game strategists who calculated destructive yields and projected civilian casualties, questioning each other's figures but never the base assumptions, caused him personal discomfort. If the unthinkable occurred, he wondered, as his brother did also, would one not rather be among the dead?

Worried that a callous mistake might trigger war, the Kennedys saw the back-channel contacts with Georgi Bolshakov as a chance to personalize negotiations and reduce the possibilities of war through miscalculation. First, however, they had to convince Khrushchev that they were tough, but not "mean and tough" as Robert often described the Soviets. Toughness in the Kennedy argot meant not giving an inch—or at least not appearing to. Told that Khrushchev thought President

Kennedy did not have the guts for war over Berlin, Robert Kennedy told Bolshakov: "He does, I know. Tell Khrushchev that."[111]

The Soviets ran a gut check by building the Berlin Wall in August. "Go get my brother!" were reportedly the president's first words on learning about the Wall.[112] Robert was at his brother's side when word came that the Soviets had moved two divisions of troops in front of the Wall in September. President Kennedy countered by sending a battle group of fifteen hundred troops and his reluctant vice-president to provide a psychological lift for the West Berliners. Tension peaked on 27 October, when Soviet and U.S. tanks faced off at Checkpoint Charlie in Berlin. The president asked Robert to call Bolshakov and make a deal: If the Soviets pulled back their tanks, twenty minutes later the Americans would, too.

"Don't ask me what I think, Georgi," Robert recalled telling Bolshakov, "I just deliver the messages to my brother and he doesn't tell me what he does with them." Robert was sure that his message was clear: "I kept telling Georgi Bolshakov that we'd fight. He said he kept reporting it."[113] In his version of these events Robert, as usual, mentions no face-saving concessions or offers of U.S. flexibility on Berlin. Similarly, Nikita Khrushchev makes no mention of Bolshakov in his memoirs, but the Russian premier assured his Kremlin colleagues that "the Americans would pull back their tanks within twenty minutes [the time frame Robert Kennedy promised] after we had removed ours." For whatever reasons, Khrushchev withdrew the tanks, deciding, he said, "This is not worth war." President Kennedy escaped from the Berlin crisis, as James Reston pointed out, "not by military action, but by talking it to death."[114]

Robert Kennedy also served from time to time as his brother's personal envoy and international troubleshooter. In August 1961, he headed the U.S. delegation to the independence celebration of the Ivory Coast, where he developed a quick rapport with Felix Houphouet-Boigny, the country's Catholic president. Knowing little about Africa but eager to learn, Robert asked for Houphouet-Boigny's "counsel and guidance." As a former member of the French cabinet and an astute observer of politics, Houphouet-Boigny explained situations in political terms Kennedy easily understood. Realizing that his contacts and correspondence with a head of state posed protocol and diplomatic problems for the State Department, the attorney general asked their advice on responding on some matters. When they dallied in replying, Kennedy pleaded, "Does someone over there have a suggestion?"[115]

The State Department's uncertain posture on Africa merely reflected the Kennedy administration's own, although Kennedy's objective was easily stated: to contain Soviet influence among the dozens of newly independent nations, using the Peace Corps and economic assistance packages and avoiding military intervention. In short, it was "a defensive diplomacy that defined success as not losing."[116]

Influenced by Houphouet-Boigny's advice and by the pleas of civil rights leaders to take a more active interest in African affairs, Robert Kennedy openly disagreed with his brother's Cold War approach to Africa. Robert proposed that the United States spend its funds in Africa on "our friends," rather than on those, such as Ghana's mercurial leader Kwame Nkrumah, whom Robert described as "playing 'footsies' with the Soviet Union." In December 1961, President Kennedy told the NSC that he had decided to proceed with a $135 million loan package for construction of a power project on the Volta River in Ghana, noting, "The Attorney General has not yet spoken but I can feel the cold wind of his disapproval on the back of my neck."[117]

Such disagreements were rare. One memorable example of John Kennedy's trust in his brother came with his decision in January 1962 to send Robert on a highly publicized "goodwill" tour of the world. With Ethel at his side, he started the tour in Japan, where he said his mission was to "damp down" lingering anti-American feelings. First reports indicated that the presence of the "second Mr. Kennedy" in Japan only revived those feelings.[118] His appearance at Waseda University sparked a demonstration among student leftists, who heckled and jeered him and then cut off the main power source to the auditorium. Unfazed, Robert kept talking in the dark without a microphone until power was restored. Then he challenged the radical students to debate. By most accounts, he mollified the assemblage with some persuasive arguments, which one writer hailed as "forceful, elementary instruction in American capitalism."[119]

Robert Kennedy did his only substantive diplomatic work of the tour in Indonesia, where he met with President Achmed Sukarno, the revolutionary with a playboy's reputation who had combined Indonesian racial pride and mythology into a potent nationalism. Kennedy was instructed to evaluate and report back to the president on the dispute between Indonesia and the Netherlands over the future of West New Guinea, a vast wilderness area and former colonial possession of the Dutch, which Sukarno threatened to take by force. Robert succeeded in getting Sukarno to drop onerous preconditions before agreeing to talks with the Dutch. Later that summer in Middleburg, Virginia, an accord was reached in which the United Nations, in a face-saving move for the Dutch, took temporary administrative control of the territory before turning it over to Indonesia.[120]

The Virginia negotiations caused consternation among the Dutch and the Australians, who wanted nothing conceded to the Communist-courting Sukarno. Barry Battle, wife of William C. Battle, the U.S. ambassador to Australia, candidly informed Robert of a constant complaint she heard from the Dutch and Australians, namely that "the Netherlands has been sold down the drain by the United States and the man most responsible was Robert Kennedy." Kennedy justified his actions to Battle, claiming that "any alternative action on our part would have brought on a war in that part of the world which would have been no help to Australia or the U.S." The role of a mediator, the president reminded his brother, "was not a happy one."[121]

Robert Kennedy's diplomatic shortcomings surfaced during secret negotiations with Sukarno over the release of Allen L. Pope, a CIA agent captured during the Indonesian rebellion in 1958. Unaccustomed to compromising, Kennedy resented giving in to the imperious Sukarno, a man he described as possessing "few redeeming features" and who was also an "antiwhite" demagogue, "completely immoral," and "untrustworthy."[122] Sukarno wanted to use Pope as a bargaining chip on West New Guinea.

In the unfamiliar role of the leveraged party in a negotiation, Kennedy let Sukarno provoke him into an angry reaction, which led, Kennedy said, to "a rather bitter fight." Viewing Sukarno as "trying to string us along," Kennedy said, "I got up and walked out." U.S. ambassador Howard Jones talked the attorney general into returning to the table. Robert apologized, he explained, not "for what I said, because I thought that was correct," but for walking out on a head of state.[123]

As a diplomatic mission his goodwill tour offered no great successes. Nor did it cause great harm. Arranged by the president, it apparently was intended to introduce Robert to a select group of world leaders and to authenticate his foreign policy credentials. In some respects the journey formed part of Robert's continuing education, an expansion upon the kind of trips his father had arranged earlier. The tour, which consumed twenty-eight days and covered fourteen countries, paid princely political dividends, bringing Robert worldwide notice, important foreign service contacts, and stature and prestige among the world's ruling elites. Robert's and Ethel's personal demands and their whirlwind itinerary threw embassies and consulates into a frenzy, for at each stop they were welcomed with ceremonies and amenities usually reserved for heads of state. Robert Kennedy was hosted by some of the world's most venerable leaders, including France's Charles De Gaulle (whom he found "cold and tough and unfriendly") and West Germany's Konrad Adenauer (who Kennedy believed could never trust anyone as young as he). At a formal salute in Berlin, Ethel turned to her husband and said, "For a Seaman Second Class, you've come a long way."

During the tour, Robert committed a few gaffes and caused a slight tremor back in the United States with a garbled statement about the history of the United States war with Mexico. He managed, however, to avoid the "monumental blunder" predicted by the Republican National Committee and other critics who loudly questioned the motives and purposes of the trip. In an open letter to Secretary Rusk, New York Republican congressman John V. Lindsay decried "freewheeling" foreign missions by "highly placed amateurs." Rusk's transparent reply that Kennedy's trip was the State Department's idea disarmed few critics. Others were subdued when former vice-president Nixon surprisingly described Robert Kennedy's "tough-minded" intelligence and "tremendous will to win" as qualities that the State Department sorely needed.[124]

On his return, Robert had little of substance to report. His formal "briefing" of the president and vice-president on 28 February hardly went beyond a photo opportunity for the press. To capitalize on the trip and to build his credibility as a major player in the foreign policy arena, he wrote a book in the form of a personal report "to our people about the way other people see us." He dictated recollections during April. Then, during a frantic three-week period in May, John Seigenthaler, Angie Novello, and Evan Thomas (the team that produced *The Enemy Within*), put together the manuscript for *Just Friends and Brave Enemies,* with help from Brandon Grove in the State Department and from syndicated columnist Stewart Alsop. Robert sent out several hundred complimentary copies to members of the foreign service and to elected officials.[125]

Just Friends and Brave Enemies was no *Profiles in Courage.* Robert's book had none of the style, elegance, or historical detail of *Profiles,* perhaps, in part, because it was not produced by the same "literary apparatus" as *Profiles.*[126] Still, *The New York Times* hailed the book for its incisive wit and its concise overview of America's place in world affairs, thus bestowing on the author an authoritative cachet appropriate for one whose stature as a decision maker on U.S. foreign policy was steadily growing.[127]

CHAPTER 15

Missiles of October

ROBERT KENNEDY MADE only meager formal contributions to decision making in foreign policy and national security during the first eighteen months of the Kennedy presidency, but his brother more than made up for that, first, by using him extensively in secret, back-channel negotiating and then by making Robert his chief deputy and virtual surrogate in meetings of national security advisors during the crucial days of October 1962 known as the Cuban missile crisis.

"Most of the major matters dealing with the Soviet Union and the United States," Robert later claimed, "were discussed and arrangements were made between Georgi Bolshakov and myself." Besides Berlin, they passed information during the second Laos crisis in 1962 (which led to the agreement on a neutral Laos), and they exchanged ideas on the control of nuclear weapons (which contributed to the Limited Test Ban Treaty in the summer of 1963).[1]

Although it produced results, using Robert in back-channel communications was risky. The Soviets could easily disavow Bolshakov, but the words and actions of the president's brother were binding. The Kennedys took the risks so they could bypass the lethargic and cumbersome State Department and obtain their own slant on Khrushchev. In the summer and fall of 1962, as reports of a Soviet military buildup in Cuba began accumulating, they needed all the information they could gather.

The missiles of October, unlike the "missile gap" of 1960, were real. John Kennedy's campaign rhetoric aside, the United States had a vast superiority in nuclear weapons and a clear edge in intercontinental ballistic missiles (ICBMs).[2] The Soviet Union was in no position, as historian David Rosenberg concluded, "to successfully execute an intercontinental atomic rocket war." Or, as Robert McNamara told reporters at the president's request, "Our means of delivery and our nuclear power exceeds [sic] theirs—any place, at any time, in any way." Some within the Pentagon ached to take advantage of U.S. nuclear superiority with a preemptory first strike before the Soviets could build an adequate deterrent force—an idea President Kennedy and Secretary McNamara never entirely dismissed and which they allowed to linger dangerously.[3]

This was a transitional era in the history of the Cold War, when strategic theorists on each side contemplated general war presaged by thermonuclear exchanges and when the positioning of missiles was critical. Khrushchev wanted to put missiles into Cuba in part to counter U.S. Jupiter missiles poised threateningly in Turkey and Italy. U.S. nuclear superiority, therefore, made the placement of the Soviet missiles in Cuba (at least initially) more a political than a military threat. The key issue, as President Kennedy later noted, was that the missiles "appeared" to change the balance of power, "and appearances contribute to reality."[4]

An equally critical part of the explanation for the origins of the crisis known within the administration as "Cuba II" lay in the tensions between the United States and Cuba. Had there been no U.S.–supported invasion at the Bay of Pigs, no U.S. economic and political boycott, no U.S. covert operations—in short, no U.S. vendetta against the Castro regime—the placement of the Soviet missiles, as well as Cuba's enormous dependency on the Soviet economic lifeline, likely would have been avoided.[5] As it happened, American intimidation that was intended to drive Castro away from the Soviets actually provoked the action it was meant to avoid, namely, a deployment of Soviet military force, including missiles, in Cuba.[6]

Robert McNamara was "*absolutely positive* that President Kennedy never, at any time" between 20 January 1961 and 14 October 1962, "had any intention whatsoever to invade Cuba."[7] But Cuban fears of an invasion, activated by the unmistakable signs of U.S. sponsorship of Cuban-exile sabotage and paramilitary operations (Operation MONGOOSE), overrode all else. More than three decades later most of the surviving U.S. decision makers attending conferences in Moscow, Hawk's Cay, and Havana saw those concerns as reasonably founded.

Robert Kennedy remained at the center of the crisis throughout, playing several roles. His direction of MONGOOSE and his desire to wreak some measure of revenge for the Bay of Pigs had, in fact, contributed to precipitating the crisis. Surprisingly, once the crisis struck, his was a very persuasive voice for moderation. At critical points he also served the president as a personal emissary in the secret diplomatic negotiations with the Soviets largely responsible for resolving the crisis. And, finally, his posthumous memoir, *Thirteen Days,* edited by Theodore Sorensen, served for many years, before the declassification of NSC and CIA documents and the convening of international conferences, as a primary historic source for understanding U.S. motivations throughout the crisis.

Thirteen Days

In the summer of 1962 CIA reports and national intelligence estimates turned suspicions (increased shipping and troop buildups) into circumstantial evidence (surface-to-air missiles [SAM]) of possible Soviet offensive missiles and nuclear weapons in Cuba. Hard evidence was not secured until October. The Kennedys found themselves caught between Cuban charges that they were planning an invasion and congressional charges that they were "soft" on Communism and had better invade. On 31 August, Republican senator Kenneth Keating from New York, using information leaked to him by CIA sources ("those CIA bastards," President Kennedy called them), announced evidence of the massive Soviet troop buildup and attacked our "Do-Nothing President" for failing to stop it.[8]

Over the next few weeks the Kennedys denied Keating's charges, while maneuvering the Soviets into denying the obvious, laying a legal foundation for the impeachment of Soviet credibility. On the afternoon of 4 September, Robert Kennedy met with the Soviet ambassador to Washington, Anatoly Dobrynin. Dobrynin and his wife, along with Georgi Bolshakov, had been luncheon guests of the Kennedys at Hickory Hill back in May, and they had met a few times since, always cordially. This time Robert brought Dobrynin quickly to the point of the Soviet buildup. Dobrynin acknowledged it but said it was strictly defensive.

Next, the president and attorney general both met with Georgi Bolshakov. As usual, the president was tactful and statesmanlike—"Tell Khruschev I hope I'll be seeing him again in the near future"— while his brother got down to the nitty gritty, making it clear in a side-alley meeting with Bolshakov that the Kennedys would not tolerate an offensive buildup: "Goddamn it, Georgi, doesn't Premier Khrushchev realize the President's position? Doesn't the Premier know that the President has enemies as well as friends? . . . In a gust of blind hate, 'they' may go to any length." Bolshakov thought the president's brother meant the right-wing radicals.[9] Whomever it was they feared, the Kennedys again found themselves drawn into a critical situation not of their making over which they must struggle for control.

The president called on Tuesday morning, 16 October 1962, just as Robert prepared to attend the regular Special Group (Augmented) meeting: "We have some big trouble. I want you over here."[10] Robert entered McGeorge Bundy's office at 9:00 A.M. and met Ray S. Cline, deputy director of the CIA, who showed him U-2 reconnaissance photographs of a missile base under construction near San Cristobal, Cuba. Robert Kennedy's initial comment, according to Cline, "was one four-letter word, off the record."[11] For much of the next two hours the two Kennedys huddled in the Oval Office. Robert suggested that the crisis be handled by a select group of advisors to be known as ExComm, or the Executive Committee of the National Security Council. At 11:45 A.M. the president convened its first meeting. The majority came quickly to favor launching an immediate air strike against the missile sites before they could become operational. Robert passed a note to his brother: "I now know how Tojo felt when he was planning Pearl Harbor."[12]

Over the next twelve days, as the nation and the world teetered on the brink of nuclear catastrophe, ExComm deliberated, pored over intelligence reports, and met on nearly a continuous basis, either as a committee of the whole or in small working groups, where no one presided and rank was theoretically of no consequence. President Kennedy seldom attended, leaving the group to speak their minds freely. At all those meetings, as one participant put it, the "senior person" was the attorney general. McGeorge Bundy recalled that Robert Kennedy often did not even sit at the table in the Cabinet Room, preferring instead a smaller chair away from the table along the wall. "Wherever he sat was one of the most important places in the room," Bundy said, "and everybody knew that."[13]

Coming into this newest crisis so soon after the Ole Miss riots, tempered by the cumulative pressures of twenty months of near-perpetual crises, or perhaps simply stunned by the implications of these events, Robert Kennedy became, in Undersecretary of State George Ball's estimation, a "force for caution and good sense." That surprised Ball and others on the ExComm. "I had always had a feeling," Ball later recalled, "that Bobby had a much too simplistic and categorical position toward things—either you condemn something utterly or you accept it enthusiastically." Now he appeared as the thoughtful analyst, seeking alternatives for his brother, prodding and questioning the ExComm members, doing his best to avoid what he had frequently done himself in the past, that is, allowing positions to harden around a quick reactive response.[14]

Robert Kennedy adamantly opposed the Joint Chiefs' initial suggestion, launching a preemptory (or surprise) air attack on Cuba. "I could not accept the idea," he wrote in his journal, "that the United States would rain bombs on Cuba, killing thousands and thousands of civilians in a surprise attack. Maybe the alternatives were not very palatable, but I simply did not see how we could accept that course of action for our country." At one point he informed the group, "My brother is not going to be the Tojo of the 1960s!" According to Ball, Robert said, "My brother's got to be able to live with himself. If we did this [the air strike] I don't think America could, and I don't think my brother could."[15]

Such talk infuriated former secretary of state Dean Acheson, who with the other benevolent aristocrats called into service to advise on the crisis viewed Robert Kennedy as an inexperienced fool, present only because of his kinship to the president. Besides, in Acheson's view, Robert was obsessed with morality at a time when the country needed firmness and resolve, not idealism. Acheson was appalled when the president in a private meeting used the phrase, "Pearl Harbor in reverse." "I know where you got that," he said to John Kennedy. "It is unworthy of you to talk that way."[16]

On 17 October, with evidence of additional Medium Range Ballistic Missiles (MRBM) sites, the Kennedys decided, as they often did in tough situations, to hold their cards close and let the other side play theirs first. Robert met that day with Georgi Bolshakov, who told him that Khrushchev personally wanted to assure the Kennedys that under no circumstances would surface-to-surface missiles be sent to Cuba. Caught in a lie, Bolshakov's credibility was destroyed. Similarly, the president met with Soviet foreign minister Andrei Gromyko. He was astonished when Gromyko told him the missiles were nothing for Americans to fear.[17]

Rather than reacting angrily to the Soviet deceit, Robert argued persuasively before the ExComm for a full consideration of the moral implications of their next step. At least one member, Douglas Dillon, admitted that Robert's arguments persuaded him to drop his support of an air strike. "He spoke with an intense but quiet passion," Dillon recalled, and "as he spoke, I felt that I was at a real turning point in history." Dillon remembered the attorney general saying, "We've got to look at history over its length. We never want it said that the United States did the very same thing that we so resented when the Japanese did it to us in 1941. And it would be much worse since we are so much larger and stronger than Cuba."[18]

Just as "Pearl Harbor in reverse" was Robert's phrase, the latter comment on historical perspective was quintessential John Kennedy. At the outset of the crisis and at intervals throughout, as the brothers spent hours together privately considering options, their ideas and expressions gained greater hold on each other.

Between meetings Robert reported to his brother the results of Excomm's informal straw polls. By 22 October a majority of the ExComm was persuaded to put on hold the notion of an air strike and to support a naval blockade, or a "quarantine" of Cuba, which must have gratified Robert Kennedy, who had favored such an action as far back as April 1961. In his televised speech that evening the president called Soviet actions totally unprovoked (an "unjustified change in the status quo which cannot be accepted by this country"), announced a "strict quarantine on all offensive military equipment under shipment to Cuba," and declared that the United States would "regard any nuclear missile launched from Cuba against any nation in the Western Hemisphere as an attack by the Soviet Union on the United States, requiring a full retaliatory response upon the Soviet Union."

"It looks really mean, doesn't it?" John Kennedy said to his brother as they awaited the Soviet response. "I just don't think there was any choice," his brother tried to reassure him, "and not only that, if you hadn't acted, you'd have been impeached."[19] The political risks were great, but so were the risks of nuclear catastrophe.

Indeed, the possibilities of a nuclear war were greater than the Kennedys knew. Had Khrushchev challenged the quarantine and not agreed to withdraw the missiles, and had the United States then proceeded with air strikes and an invasion, as planned, a nuclear exchange would have followed. When Cuba was attacked, the Americans expected the Soviets to counter-strike in Berlin, which would likely have involved nuclear weapons. But unknown to the U.S. leadership, Soviet forces in Cuba were four times larger than estimated and they possessed nuclear warheads for the IRBMs, nuclear bombs for the IL-28 bombers being unloaded, and tactical nuclear warheads—an estimated 162 nuclear weapons in all—which in the event of U.S. attack Khrushchev had authorized the local Soviet commanders to deploy. A U.S. attack, Robert McNamara acknowledged in 1995, would have resulted in "utter disaster."[20] Thus, the Kennedys' efforts to resolve the crisis without U.S. military intervention takes on enormous historical consequence.

On 24 October, "the most trying, the most difficult, and the most filled with tension," Robert Kennedy wrote, the ExComm waited for news of U.S. Navy intercepts of incoming Soviet vessels. Standing "eyeball to eyeball," as Dean Rusk put it, they were greatly relieved when the other side "blinked" and the Soviet ships stopped short of the quarantine line. The problem of removing the missiles remained. Without telling the president, the military stepped up to Defcon 2 (Defense Condition 2, or one step short of combat) and over the next three days JCS continued to plan for massive air strikes and an invasion of Cuba. Feeling the mounting pressure from congressional critics and from the military establishment to make an even bolder move, Kennedy conceded on the morning of 26 October that "an invasion may be necessary"; full-scale planning for one was cranked up yet another notch.[21]

That afternoon the real "eye blink" in the crisis occurred when ABC-TV newscaster John Scali was approached by Aleksandr Fomin, chief of Soviet intelligence in the United States, and asked over lunch at the Occidental Restaurant to convey a message to the State Department of a possible solution to the situation. The Soviets would dismantle the bases under UN supervision and would agree to pledge not to place offensive weapons in Cuba, Fomin told Scali, in return for a U.S. pledge not to invade Cuba. The State Department initially regarded the Fomin contact as "nothing," but early the same evening a long letter from Khrushchev to John Kennedy arrived. Its rambling and emotional contents contained the outlines of the Fomin proposal. Based on their reading of several previous letters from Khrushchev, the Kennedys believed him genuinely committed to finding a solution.[22]

Late that night, Robert Kennedy met secretly with Anatoly Dobrynin at the Soviet embassy and, under secret instructions from the president, told Dobrynin that as part of a settlement the United States would consider withdrawing Jupiter missiles in Turkey (and possibly Italy, too).[23] Although the Kennedys refused to admit it for the record or to inform all of the ExComm members of their offer to withdraw Jupiter missiles, each side had given the other reason for hope.[24]

Early the next morning, perhaps as a direct result of Robert Kennedy's meeting with Dobrynin, Moscow broadcast a second message from Khrushchev; this one, much stronger in tone and not written by Khrushchev, called for the United States to dismantle its Jupiter missiles in Turkey in return for a withdrawal of Soviet missiles in Cuba. As the ExComm deliberated what to do, news arrived of the downing of a U-2 over Cuba. The Joint Chiefs urged immediate reprisals against

SAM sites in Cuba, but President Kennedy refused to give the order, insisting that ExComm (without the military present) focus, instead, on formulating a response to Khrushchev built around the idea of a "trade" of the Jupiters in Turkey. Late that afternoon, as the situation deteriorated and fatigue set in, Robert Kennedy summarized the prevailing view within ExComm: The core of an agreement, he said, was contained in the first Khrushchev letter and so, for the sake of maintaining the strength of NATO (and to keep the Kennedys' political heads on their shoulders), no mention of the missiles in Turkey (or Italy) should be contained in any final agreement on Cuba, which was a Western Hemisphere problem. Robert Kennedy and Ted Sorensen left the ExComm meeting for forty-five minutes to draft a letter accepting Khrushchev's first "offer" to remove the missiles in Cuba in return for the U.S. removing the quarantine and for assurances against an invasion of Cuba.[25]

Meeting again with Ambassador Dobrynin at the Justice Department that evening, Robert Kennedy vowed that the U-2 flights over Cuba would continue and warned that "if the Cubans or Soviets shot at these planes, then we would have to shoot back," which would, of course, inevitably escalate the conflict. He also issued an ultimatum—which Robert Kennedy insisted was not an ultimatum, but "a statement of fact"—namely, that if the United States did not receive a commitment from the Soviets "by at least tomorrow" to remove the missile bases, "we would remove them." In Kennedy's version of the meeting he cooly tells Dobrynin that the trade of the missiles in Turkey cannot be discussed, because "there could be no *quid pro quo* or any arrangement made under this kind of threat or pressure." Dobrynin, however, claimed that Kennedy again suggested that a deal could be struck for the missiles in Turkey.[26]

Dobrynin wired an account of the meeting to Moscow. When it was read to the Presidium of the Central Committee, Oleg Troyanovsky, Khrushchev's special assistant for international affairs, recalled that it created "a state of alarm" because of Robert Kennedy's twenty-four-hour ultimatum and because of Dobrynin's impression that the Kennedys might soon lose control of the situation to the "many hotheads" in Washington who wanted an invasion of Cuba.[27]

Indeed, Dobrynin's version portrays a man and an administration at wit's end. "Robert Kennedy looked exhausted," Dobrynin reported to Gromyko. "One could see from his eyes that he had not slept for days. He himself said that he had not been home for six days and nights." Dobrynin said Robert Kennedy told him that he and his brother were under severe pressure from the military and were gravely concerned that events might set off an "irreversible chain of events" that would lead to war. According to Dobrynin, Kennedy was near tears when he said, "I don't know how much longer we can hold out against our generals." Dobrynin's self-serving version, while accurately capturing Robert's deep distrust of the military (which he may have mentioned to Dobrynin), contains highly improbable elements, not the least of them the notion that Robert Kennedy would expose his inner fears or confess vulnerability to someone against whom he was maneuvering for advantage, particularly a Russian.[28] One could more easily imagine him pleading with Jimmy Hoffa for mercy and understanding.

Robert's recollections of his and the president's emotions that critical evening of 27 October—conceivably the eve of World War III—are melodramatic in places and incongruously understated in others. The president, he reported, felt "troubled" and "pained" by the "specter of the death of the children of this country and all the world." Yet he felt compelled to issue an ultimatum. "Time was running out," Robert realized.[29] But whether from exhaustion, pressure from the hawks, or sheer frustration, the Kennedys decided to let Khrushchev or the Joint Chiefs dictate the next move.

Khrushchev backed down. The next morning, Sunday, 28 October, attending a horse show with his daughters at the Washington Armory, Robert Kennedy received word that Khrushchev had signalled his intention to agree to terms, effectively ending the crisis. "This was not a time for gloating," John Kennedy cautioned, or for talk of "victory."[30]

Many problems remained. Denied their war, the Joint Chiefs complained, "We have been had." "We lost!" General Curtis LeMay exclaimed. "We ought to go in and make a strike on Monday anyway."[31] The smell of smoldering hawk feathers hung in the air as Robert Kennedy left his daughters to meet with Dobrynin. Over the next month the two men met several times each week to negotiate the final settlement, reached despite the intrusion of ominous forces set in motion during and before the conflict.

One potential glitch in reaching a final agreement came when Robert Kennedy refused to put in writing the U.S. promise to withdraw the Jupiters in Turkey. So intent were the Kennedys on keeping that part of the agreement secret that Robert threatened to leave the missiles in place if any mention of the deal was made public. "Take my word on this," he told Dobrynin, "that is sufficient." Dobrynin and Khrushchev accepted his word, and by 21 November the Soviets had provided sufficient assurances for the removal of offensive weapons from Cuba to permit lifting the U.S. quarantine. In January 1963, the United States began a quiet phase out of IRBMs in Turkey and Italy, and on 25 April the missiles in Turkey were removed with no public notice.[32]

Having made no visible concessions to the Soviets, the Kennedys emerged from the crisis looking like winners. "Looking back on it," British prime minister Harold Macmillan said, "the way that Bobby and his brother played this hand was absolutely masterly. . . . What they did that week convinced me that they were both great men." James Reston of The *New York Times* described President Kennedy's handling of the crisis as "masterful" and "the greatest achievement" of his administration. Arthur Schlesinger extolled the president's "combination of toughness and restraint, of will, nerve, and wisdom, so brilliantly controlled, so matchlessly calibrated." *Time* declared Kennedy had "won in his courageous confrontation," and *Newsweek* marked it as his "greatest political triumph." Such celebratory assessments more properly belong in the category of contemporary mythology.[33]

The Cuban missile crisis, as CIA historian Mary McAuliffe and others have pointed out, was neither a managed nor manageable crisis.[34] Kennedy truculence provoked it, with Kennedy brilliance reserved for extrication, rather than for avoiding the crisis in the first place. Kennedy toughness opened the door of miscalculation, which opened further with ExComm senses dulled by exhaustion and JCS appetites for war whetted by a taste for a first-strike success. Kennedy restraint prevailed, but barely.

The crisis was kept from spinning wildly out of control by John Kennedy's widening skepticism of military solutions, by Nikita Khrushchev's willingness, as he put it, "to look for a dignified way out of this conflict," by Robert Kennedy's conscience and his sense of morality in beating back the demands for air strikes—which we now know would have triggered a nuclear exchange—and by a great deal of good fortune. "We were in luck," Ambassador John Kenneth Galbraith observed, "but success in a lottery is no argument for lotteries."[35]

Most observers gave the Kennedys high marks for crisis management. A few, however, noted the lack of planning and the absence of real objectives in either foreign affairs or national security. Ralph McGill, publisher of the *Atlanta Constitution,* privately urged that Robert Kennedy, as the logical and perhaps only legitimate choice, provide broad oversight and "handle the long-range implications of the Cold War," suggesting that he form a committee and take over the "management of the Cold War." Eager for such an assignment, Robert replied that the State Department lacked a coherent plan and sensible controls and pledged to "try and see if we can get something started again."[36] McGill's proposal went nowhere.

Struck by the enormous role played by chance during those thirteen days and awed by the potential human losses, Nikita Khruschev and John Kennedy were persuaded to banish nuclear exchanges and general war between the superpowers to the realm of the unthinkable. They agreed to the installation of a "hotline" (teletype/telephone) between Moscow and Washington. And the following spring, in his finest hour, John Kennedy took the first U.S. steps toward arms reduction by initiating the Limited Test Ban Treaty, ratified in September 1963.

Relations between the United States and Cuba, however, only worsened. Some sketchy evidence suggests the Kennedys' willingness to consider a change. Robert Kennedy, for example, allowed journalist William Atwood to travel to Cuba in November 1963 for some preliminary discussions on normalizing relations with Cuba. Nothing, however, came of the effort.[37]

Freeing Cuban Exiles

A striking development in the immediate aftermath of the missile crisis was the successful negotiation for the release of the prisoners captured at the Bay of Pigs. The Kennedys' mistakes had caused the capture of the Cuban exiles, and so it became a matter of personal honor to effect their release.[38] Castro first proposed exchanging the Cuban prisoners for five hundred bulldozers or tractors. When that deal fell through, the prisoners were put on trial in April 1962 and sentenced to thirty years hard labor, which Castro said he would set aside if the United States paid fines of $62 million. Besieged by the Cuban emigré community to retrieve the prisoners, Robert Kennedy recommended sending James B. Donovan, a New York lawyer, to negotiate an exchange with Castro. Donovan had negotiated the exchange of the Soviet spy Colonel Rudolph Abel for Francis Gary Powers, the American U-2 pilot shot down over the USSR in 1960. Just a few days before missiles were discovered in Cuba, Donovan convinced Castro to "sell" the prisoners for $53 million in drugs, foodstuffs, and machinery. When the crisis was over, Donovan was able to hold Castro to the deal.[39]

"Bob has a project going," Assistant Attorney General Louis Oberdorfer told staffers. "We are going to try to get the Cuban prisoners out." For Kennedy's staff, by then conditioned to expect anything, Joseph Dolan's reaction was typical. He thought that perhaps "with Bob Kennedy we were going to get something going with some boats and we were going to get the prisoners out."[40] Rather than a clandestine military operation, the Cuban prisoner ransom involved a complex series of arrangements between the U.S. government, the Red Cross, shipping companies, unions, manufacturers, and Canadian intermediaries that succeeded because of Robert Kennedy's organizational skills and raw determination.

"We put them there," Kennedy told his assistants during the first week of December, "and we're going to get them out—by Christmas!" He operated best when improvising solutions and when the problem before him had a deadline and a specific goal. Above all, he valued action. Joseph Dolan, who was around Kennedy for many years in various capacities, said that Kennedy believed "the greatest sin is not doing something because you are afraid that you might not do it well." He could accept others' mistakes but did not want (or tolerate) explanations or excuses. "Bob had a lot of nerve" and was willing to fall on his face, said Dolan. Perhaps because of his experiences in political campaigns where everything is done on an ad hoc basis, Robert seldom paused to regroup and plan his next steps—he was already doing something.[41]

Audacity in this instance proved effective. Dolan remember a meeting on a Sunday afternoon when the attorney general called in the presidents of the largest U.S. manufacturers of baby foods to request their cooperation in getting the Cuban prisoners released. Robert's casual dress, indifference to protocol, and lack of specific details did not inspire confidence among the corporate lions, the youngest of whom was probably fifteen years older than the attorney general. Kennedy bluntly stated his expectations: To help correct a deal-breaking shortfall of $1.3 million in goods, he expected the baby food companies, which had set prices for some products at about three times the prevailing world prices, to make in-kind contributions of goods. When the executives flinched, Oberdorfer assured them that their donations would be tax deductible. Other businesses, such as drug companies and shipping firms, cooperated under similar persuasion.[42]

Oberdorfer and John Jones, an assistant in the Tax Division, worked more or less full-time on the Cuban ransom project, as did Katzenbach (the overall coordinator), John Nolan, and John Douglas. In this instance, Kennedy also needed outside assistance. The staff knew instinctively the kind of person he wanted for the team. "Our kind of guy," to the Kennedy people, was someone in whom the attorney general could place his personal confidence and trust, someone willing to do anything asked, and a pragmatic generalist—like a utility infielder in baseball, talented enough to play several positions.[43] Kennedy selected E. Barrett Prettyman, Jr., a former law school classmate to arrange transportation for a large portion of the medical supplies and foodstuffs to Castro. To allow Prettyman some room to maneuver through the bureaucracy, Kennedy made him a special assistant and backed him at every decision point.[44] The various tasks in this operation, like the way his brother managed the presidency, were spokes on a wheel that all led to the attorney general.

On Christmas eve 1962, with the materials delivered to Castro, the survivors of the Bay of Pigs were released and returned to Miami, where the President later addressed them at the Orange Bowl. Dolan and other members of the Justice Department team stood by as Katzenbach telephoned the attorney general to get his reaction. "Bob," Katzenbach said, "they are all in; it's over." "That's fine," came the reply. "All right you guys," he went on without a break, "what about Jimmy Hoffa?"[45]

To mark the end of another year of crises, Robert bought a commemorative gift for the president, an expensive gold cigar case from Tiffany's engraved with the names of the ExComm members. Concerned about costs, he prorated shares, assessing the "rich people" (Johnson, McCone, McNamara) and the "Republican" Dillon more than the others. Theodore Sorensen responded to Kennedy's request for fifty dollars with a parody of the president's remarks of 22 October: "It shall henceforth be my policy to regard any letter of assessment launched from the Department of Justice as a clear and present danger to the security of my budget."[46]

Cuba II, Oxford, and the midterm congressional elections all having gone their way, the Kennedys finished the year on a high note. After January 1963, with international tensions waning and with civil rights matters drawing more of his attention, Robert Kennedy broke off contact with Bolshakov and Dobrynin and, with the shutdown of MONGOOSE, ceased oversight of covert operations in Cuba. He continued attending the NSC and Special Group (CI) meetings, drifting in and out of discussions on national security, never more than a telephone call away.

CHAPTER 16

Lest Darkness Come upon You

> Yet a little while is the light with you. Walk while ye have the light, lest darkness come upon you.
>
> *JOHN* 12:35.

CUED BY THE CIVIL RIGHTS MOVEMENT, American democracy by 1963 was turning away from the relatively staid and predictable politics of the liberal consensus. Skepticism and anxiety were setting in motion new political energies manifested on the Left by the robust politics of mass movements and on the Right by a visceral populist rage. Slighting but not ignoring those incipient forces of change, the Kennedys persisted in the politics of the liberal consensus, for, like others in America's political aristocracy, they saw themselves as initiators of change, not reactors to it.

Simmering tensions between the elite-driven politics of the liberal consensus and the grass-roots politics of mass movements were stoked by the youth-oriented New Left, whose search to reify the spirit of the new activism ultimately settled on opposition to the Vietnam war. Although he showed few signs of it in 1963, Robert Kennedy gradually came to feel much in common with the young protestors, for the war in Vietnam—or more precisely the handling of the war by his brother's successor, Lyndon Johnson—became the fulcrum upon which his personal and political pasts and futures pivoted. During his brother's presidency Robert fervidly supported an American presence in Vietnam. By 1967, however, he was an unsparing critic of Lyndon Johnson's Vietnam policies and in 1968 he aligned himself with antiwar "doves" in the U.S. Senate. Out of his reexamination of a U.S. presence in Vietnam came an acceptance of political change and, eventually, an awareness of his own place in a political landscape stripped of the benchmarks that had guided him and his brother to power.

Events in his brother's administration did not map Robert Kennedy's remarkable political odyssey. Indeed, to appreciate just how far he would move in later years requires a look back at the Kennedy administration's policies toward Vietnam and consideration of two questions concerning the Kennedys and Vietnam that have lingered for decades: What responsibility did they have in escalating the war? And would President Kennedy (if he had lived) have withdrawn U.S. forces from Vietnam?

The Kennedy Buildup in Vietnam

Dating from their first visit in 1951 when the country was still a French colony, Robert and John Kennedy adopted identical stances on U.S. policy toward Vietnam. After the French defeat in 1954 and the partitioning of the country into North and South Vietnam, Senator John Kennedy urged the creation of an "independent, anti-Communist Vietnam," rather than endorse free elections, which Ho Chi Minh, the enigmatic leader of North Vietnam, likely would have won. Hailing South Vietnam as the "cornerstone of the Free World in Southeast Asia," John Kennedy declared its survival a "test of American responsibility and determination."[1]

The Kennedys (and most other U.S. analysts in the late 1950s and early 1960s) mistook Ho Chi Minh's ardent nationalism for Soviet- or Chinese-inspired Communist expansionism. They concurred, therefore, with Eisenhower's decision to prop up the South Vietnamese government with substantial economic and military aid and carried forward that policy into their administration. Only the metaphors—falling cornerstones and falling dominoes—differed.

Convinced that Vietnam was a vital location in a geopolitical power struggle, John Kennedy warned that its fall would open the "gates" and threaten Thailand, Cambodia, Burma, Indonesia, and the Philippines. Any sign of U.S. weakness in the face of Communist infiltration in Vietnam, he believed, would undermine the integrity and credibility of U.S. commitments everywhere.[2] In the 1960 campaign he promised victory over the Communists and resolved not to back down on Vietnam.[3]

During his second week in office President Kennedy received a full briefing on Vietnam and at once approved a State Department recommendation left over from the last days of the Eisenhower administration to provide $42 million in new aid to South Vietnam for a Basic Counterinsurgency Plan to combat an increase in Viet Cong terrorist activities. He made it clear that he wanted to see improvement within three months. Meantime, he intended to learn as much as he could about guerilla warfare.[4]

To Robert Kennedy, not a participant in those early briefings, Vietnam fell low on the list of important trouble spots around the world. In the spring of 1961, Stanley Karnow, a formidably informed correspondent (and later the author of an authoritative text on the Vietnam war), tried to convince him that Vietnam was the most serious problem in the Far East. "We've got twenty Vietnams a day to handle," the attorney general impatiently replied.[5] Although he did not say it in so many words, Robert Kennedy implied that Vietnam had to wait until they dealt with Cuba, gained the neutralization of Laos, and quieted the Berlin crisis. Each crisis, however, left them more vulnerable to Republican and hard-line conservative charges that they either were yielding ground before the Communists or were in a dangerously compromising frame of mind. The Kennedys remembered all too well the Republican gains from charges that Truman had "lost" China. Nothing like that, they vowed, would happen on their watch.

John Kennedy's commitment to a non-Communist South Vietnam deepened after the Bay of Pigs and intensified further as a consequence of Khrushchev's bullying at the June 1961 Vienna summit meetings. After the meetings, President Kennedy told an astonished James Reston, correspondent for the *New York Times,* that the place to demonstrate U.S. firmness and to stand up against the Soviet Bear was Vietnam. "We have to send more people there," said Kennedy. Soon after, Reston pointed out, the NSC declared that U.S. policy was "to prevent Communist domination of South Vietnam." Robert Kennedy later disputed Reston's linking of Khrushchev's tirades at Vienna to Vietnam and the NSC declaration. "But," Reston countered, "he didn't hear what his brother said to me in the Vienna embassy, and I did."[6]

Reston had a point. Robert Kennedy was only peripherally involved with Vietnam policy during the first eighteen months of his brother's presidency. John Kennedy apparently had said little to his brother about his intentions there. From other advisors, however, we learn that President Kennedy was preparing to draw the line on Vietnam. Arthur Schlesinger, Jr., recalled President Kennedy telling him after the Bay of Pigs that "we cannot accept a visible humiliation." Similarly, John Kenneth Galbraith, remembered the president saying, "We just can't have another defeat in Vietnam."[7]

A few advisors (not Robert) tried to steer President Kennedy away from involvement. Galbraith likened Vietnam to "a can of snakes."[8] Chester Bowles called it a "dead end street." General Douglas MacArthur counseled both Kennedys against a land war in Asia that could not be won. And in November 1961 when the Pentagon proposed sending 40,000 regular troops, Undersecretary of State George Ball blurted out that it was the "wrong war, at the wrong time, and for the wrong reasons." U.S. forces in such numbers, Ball warned, would commit the United States to an irreversible involvement that within five years might grow to 300,000 men in Vietnam. "George," John Kennedy told him, "you're just crazier than hell. I always thought you were one of the brightest guys in town, but you're crazy. That just isn't going to happen."[9]

Unlike Robert, who tended to focus relentlessly on one problem and one solution at a time, John Kennedy had the remarkable capacity to examine a number of problems and to embrace two or more contradictory possibilities at once. In the argot of the intelligence community, he habitually pursued "simulopts," or several options simultaneously. He also had an uncanny facility for manipulating situations, both political and personal, so that he could walk away at an optimal moment. He managed his private life and his foreign policies similarly, tracking several risky adventures at once, confident of his ability to handle them all. He was sanguine, then, that he could juggle the Vietnam hot potato.

Egged on by the "action intellectuals" led by McGeorge Bundy and Walt W. Rostow, and abetted by the benevolent aristocrats of the foreign affairs establishment, President Kennedy thought he had a formula for victory in Vietnam. Its main ingredient was Taylor's flexible response strategy, heavily laced with the tactics of counterinsurgency and covert operations and fortified by the presumably stiff backbone of the South Vietnamese Army (ARVN). Kennedy and his team exuded a euphoric sense of control. These "new mandarins," Noam Chomsky called them, were convinced they could do anything, even move a nation. Their thinking, as David Halberstam noted, exhibited a "remarkable hubris."[10]

Yet John Kennedy lacked a resolute sense of direction on Vietnam. Determined, above all, not to lose, he hesitated to take an unequivocal stand, preoccupied with retaining as many options as possible. Instead of sending regular troops in November 1961, he acceded to Maxwell Taylor's recommendation of substantial increases in economic and military aid to Vietnam, raising annual spending from $215 to $337 million, mostly to finance an increase of 50,000 ARVN. He agreed, also, to the creation of a Military Assistance Command Vietnam, increasing the number of U.S. advisors many times beyond the limit set by the Geneva agreement, bringing some of them into combat roles, and taking the first casualties. Intended or not, the Americanization of the war had begun.[11] No one around the Kennedys challenged the morality of their interfering in an "internal war," or an insurgency.

Vietnam, the Kennedys decided, would be the testing ground for counterinsurgency theories and practices. Both men were intimately identified with the effort. The president personally ordered the six-fold enlargement of the army's Special Forces, helped them select equipment, and directed them to wear green berets as a mark of distinction.[12] Within the government Robert Kennedy became known as "Mr. Counterinsurgency." He read Mao Zedong and Ernesto "Che" Guevara and insisted that his staff members do likewise. Unlike his brother, who viewed counterinsurgency mostly from a geopolitical perspective, Robert Kennedy took both a pragmatic and a romantic view of the threats of insurgency. Highly pragmatic about the necessity for counterinsurgency, he often reminded his staff that Mao once had said, "Guerrillas are like fish, and the people are the water in which the fish swim. If the temperature of the water is right, the fish will thrive and multiply." Kennedy also agreed with Mao's observation that the guerrilla campaigns were "a page of history that has no precedent." While Kennedy understood the potential of guerrilla warfare to disrupt the worldwide balance of power, he saw a few guerrilla leaders (such as Che Guevara) as revolutionary heroes and projected on the guerrillas some of the virtues of the noble warrior striving against the odds. He would sometimes show visitors to his office a captured Vietnamese guerrilla's handmade rifle with whittled stock and a length of pipe for a barrel.[13]

Despite his active involvement in counterinsurgency policy, Robert Kennedy made few on-the-record comments about U.S. policy toward Vietnam during this brother's presidency. He made an exception in 1962 when he stopped over in Saigon during a world goodwill tour, where he eagerly responded to reporters' questions about the war. "We are going to win," he vowed, and "we will remain here until we do win."[14] "The solution lies in our winning it. This is what the President intends to do." This is a new kind of war, he told reporters, "a war fought not by massive divisions but secretly by terror, assassination, ambush and infiltration." Asked if Americans understood the war, Kennedy said, "I think the American people understand and fully support this struggle. Americans have great affection for the people of Vietnam," he said. Working up to a modest Churchillian rouse, he concluded by saying, "I think the United States will do what is necessary to help a country that is trying to repel aggression with its own blood, tears, and sweat."[15]

In 1962 some ARVN victories rewarded the Kennedys' faith. After visiting Vietnam in May, Robert McNamara announced, "Every quantitative measurement we have shows us winning this war."[16] At the end of the year John Kennedy summed up accomplishments in Vietnam. The man who in April 1954 had criticized the Eisenhower administration for "two years of unrealistically optimistic predictions about the war" and for concealing "the truth from the American public" resorted to a metaphor heard frequently in the years ahead.[17] Victory, John

Kennedy said, was not imminent, but it was inevitable. "So we don't see the end of the tunnel," the President reported, "but I must say I don't think it is darker than it was a year ago and in some ways lighter."[18]

Kennedy's Vietnam plan, however, was defective from the outset. No matter how cleverly diagramed on Robert Kennedy's office walls or flawlessly demonstrated in showy Special Forces training exercises, the U.S. counterinsurgency schemes simply did not work in Vietnam. The execution of those schemes, after all, depended upon a corrupt South Vietnamese regime.[19]

South Vietnam was led by Prime Minister Ngo Dinh Diem, a Catholic aristocrat strongly influenced by his dissolute brother, Ngo Dinh Nhu, and his ruthless sister-in-law, Madame Nhu (called the "dragon lady" by some Americans). The repressive nature of the Diem regime was exposed in May 1963, when ARVN troops fired on a crowd of peaceful Buddhist marchers. Then, on 11 June—the same day John Kennedy urged all Americans to consider the moral implications of the civil rights struggle—Thich Quang Duc, a sixty-six-year-old Buddhist monk, burned himself to death to protest the persecution of Buddhists by the Catholic rulers of Vietnam. When others followed, Madame Nhu callously referred to the self-immolations as "monk barbecues."

Even though Diem professed his willingness to fight the Vietnam Communists, or Vietcong (VC), and to resist Ho Chi Minh's National Liberation Front (NLF), flagrant nepotism and rampant corruption poisoned the ARVN ranks. The ARVN lacked many things, including both the will and the ability to rapidly respond to tactical assaults by the lightly equipped, fast-moving VC guerrilla bands. This weakness became graphically apparent in January 1963 at the battle of Ap Bac, where ARVN forces supported by U.S. helicopters, planes, and artillery surrounded a VC battalion of about one-fourth its size but refused to close, allowing the VC to escape.[20]

In sum, the Kennedys' high regard for counterinsurgency notwithstanding, South Vietnam lacked the political and social reforms necessary to make it work. There was no systematic attempt to "win the hearts and minds" of the peasants by countering the social reforms promised by the VC and NLF. The Kennedys channeled funds through the Agency for International Development to train Vietnamese police in counterinsurgency tactics, but what General Victor Krulak called the "heart of the counterinsurgency strategy," was the ill-fated Strategic Hamlet Program. Modeled after a plan used by the British in Malaya to separate guerrillas from the peasants, the Strategic Hamlet Program forced peasants to relocate into secure areas, the functional equivalent of internment centers. That strategy, when sternly implemented by Diem's brother, only succeeded in alienating large numbers of South Vietnamese and in converting many peasants into VC sympathizers.[21] Neither John nor Robert Kennedy openly expressed concerns over the ramifications of this program. They appeared as uncertain about it as they were about most other things in Vietnam.

Confused by contradictory reports, the Kennedys fell into a quandary over whom they could trust. Robert said they were always looking for "more facts." They dispatched a procession of senior officials to Vietnam. Of those, Robert Kennedy placed the greatest trust in Victor "Brute" Krulak. After a year of working with Krulak on the Counterinsurgency Committee, the attorney general's store of confidence in the bantam marine remained undiminished. He even supported Krulak's unsuccessful bid to become commandant of the Marine Corps.[22] Krulak made three inspection tours of Vietnam between January and September 1963, each time returning with encouraging reports on the progress of the war and the likelihood of ultimate victory. Each time Robert Kennedy believed him.

Each time, however, Kennedy ignored the conventional military biases embedded within Krulak's reports, particularly the marine's inclination to protect senior military officers. The attorney general, moreover, apparently remained unaware that Krulak was suppressing contradictory views of the war, particularly the criticisms of Lieutenant Colonel John Paul Vann, a veteran advisor immersed in the tactics of U.S. military operations in Vietnam. As Neil Sheehan detailed in his book, *A Bright Shining Lie,* Vann tried unsuccessfully in July 1963 to brief the Joint Chiefs on the strategic flaws, missed opportunities, and misconceptions of guerrilla warfare held by the military command in Vietnam. Knowing that the Kennedys and JCS chair Maxwell Taylor prized tough, decisive analysis and unaware that he had himself been misled by "the bright shining lies" told visiting dignitaries by the U.S. military command in Saigon, Krulak coated his reports with vinegar rather than sugar. Victory was not assured, he reported, but it was a hopeful prospect. "The shooting part of the war," according to Krulak, "was moving to a climax."[23]

The subjectiveness of Krulak's views were exposed after his September 1963 toùr of the country. Joseph Mendenhall of the State Department, who was in Vietnam at the same time, presented a report directly contradicting Krulak's in every major aspect, prompting President Kennedy to ask, "You two did visit the same country, didn't you?"[24] Still, Robert Kennedy would take the word of his favorite marine over that of any other observer, particularly anyone from the State Department. Besides, Krulak's reports jibed with those of other senior officials and (equally as important to the Kennedys) with the reports of older, established journalists visiting Vietnam.

Surprisingly, one of those journalists was Maggie Higgins of the *New York Herald Tribune,* whose articles often second-guessed the Kennedys and whose newspaper always took a hard-line anticommunist stance. Higgins's scorched-earth style (McGeorge Bundy called her "firebug") was absent from her candid and confidential letter to Robert Kennedy of 20 September. Writing just after her own tour of the South Vietnamese countryside, Higgins eagerly reassured the attorney general (and the president, who was copied on the letter) that General Krulak's assessments were "more on target" than anyone else's, particularly those of Hilsman, Mendenhall, and others in the State Department. Krulak underestimated the ferocity of Diem's suppression of Buddhist dissent, Higgins wrote, but, based on all that she had seen, the marine was correct on the larger issue: Diem was, in fact, "beginning" to win the war.[25]

The Kennedys wanted to be told that the war was being won or, at the very least, that it was winnable, for John Kennedy had to win to avoid having his own words come back to haunt him. In his criticisms of Eisenhower's Indochina policy in 1954 Kennedy had said, "To pour money, material and men into the jungles of Indochina without at least a remote prospect of victory would be dangerously futile and self-destructive."[26]

Neither Kennedy, therefore, welcomed reports of U.S. and ARVN futility in Vietnam. John Kennedy became so angered by twenty-eight-year-old David Halberstam's *New York Times* reports on the venality of the government and the ineffectiveness of the ARVN that he went to the publisher and demanded Halberstam's reassignment.[27] The president even questioned the observations of Senate majority leader Mike Mansfield. A liberal and a Catholic, Mansfield, along with Supreme Court justice William O. Douglas, had originally encouraged Kennedy to support Diem. Then in late 1962 Mansfield returned from a fact-finding tour of Vietnam and recommended a careful reassessment of U.S. interests there. After spending $2 billion in seven years, Mansfield warned, the United States was being drawn in deeper, to the point where the United States might establish "some form of neocolonial rule in South Vietnam." Visibly annoyed, President Kennedy told Mansfield, "This isn't what my people are telling me."[28]

Over and over in 1963 President Kennedy asked his advisors, "Are we winning?" The answer usually was a qualified no. Not now, they told the president, but we will be later on. Each high-level mission sent to Vietnam that year reported variations on a common theme. "The country can be saved—if we move quickly and wisely," Vice-President Johnson's report typically observed. "The most important thing is imaginative, creative American management of our military aid team." Victory, all visitors agreed, would cost more than expected.[29] Each report led to an increase in U.S aid and military support, which in turn led to greater expectations that the war itself could, in Michael Forrestal's words, be made into a "conventional American enterprise."[30]

Matters came to a head that summer. On 21 August, American-trained Vietnamese Special Forces raided Buddhist pagodas and brutally suppressed dissent.[31] Those outrages were compounded when the administration learned that Diem, through his brother, Nhu had secretly contacted Hanoi, apparently with ideas of arranging a settlement of his own to neutralize the country.[32]

John and Robert Kennedy spent the weekend of 24 and 25 August at Hyannis Port in seclusion following the death of the president and Jacqueline Kennedy's infant son, Patrick Bouvier Kennedy. With Rusk, McNamara, Bundy, and McCone also away from Washington, the alarmists sought to take control. Convinced that the Diem government was about to topple, W. Averell Harriman and Roger Hilsman in the

State Department and Michael Forrestal of the NSC staff persuaded the president by telephone to authorize a telegram containing detailed emergency instructions for the newly arrived ambassador to Vietnam, Henry Cabot Lodge.[33] Lodge, whose appointment was intended to make the Republicans think twice before criticizing Kennedy on Vietnam, was one Republican internationalist appointee in his brother's administration that Robert Kennedy neither liked nor trusted. Within six months, he warned, Lodge would cause them "a lot of difficulty."[34]

Were he consulted, Robert Kennedy said later, he would not have agreed to the directions contained in the telegram to Lodge. Misled by Harriman into assuming that all of his top advisors had agreed, President Kennedy directed Lodge to tell Diem to rid himself of Nhu and his coterie. If Diem refused, then Lodge was instructed to tell dissident South Vietnamese generals that they had U.S. support for a coup.[35]

According to Robert Kennedy, his brother regarded the decision to approve the first Lodge telegram as a major mistake, precipitated by what Maxwell Taylor called the State Department's "egregious end run." Indeed, the following Monday during a heated NSC debate the president became unnerved when he learned the Harriman-Hilsman-Forrestal weekend machinations had bypassed Rusk, McNamara, McCone, Taylor, and, just as importantly, as later events demonstrated, Robert Kennedy. "This shit has got to stop!" shouted the president. He appeared more distressed by the extraordinary deviation from standard practice than by the contents of the cable itself, for when President Kennedy polled each advisor none wanted to retract the cable.[36]

Busy with arrangements for the next day's civil rights March on Washington, Robert Kennedy was absent from that Monday's NSC meeting. He was greatly disturbed, however, by the backstairs maneuvers and by the bickering in his brother's administration. From that day on—just as he had after the Bay of Pigs debacle—he inserted himself into the inner circle of Vietnam advisors. Those advisors, he said later, were "split in two . . . the only time really, in three years, the government was broken in two in a very disturbing way."[37] (Given the turmoil over civil rights, it is revealing that the Kennedys defined "the government" as the group of senior military and national security advisors debating the future of Vietnam.)

Once involved, Robert, as always, cut through to the root of the matter, posing questions that other advisors either could not or would not consider and playing the devil's advocate at each tortuous turn. Characteristically, he immediately declared in favor of getting "tough" with Diem. One way to bring him in line, he suggested, was to "grasp the nettle now" and threaten him with abandonment. At one point, Robert Kennedy even wondered aloud if Diem or any government could resist the insurgents. "If not," he said, "now was the time to get out of Vietnam entirely, rather than waiting."[38] Michael Forrestal—chastened after the President had upbraided him for his participation in the weekend intrigues—remembered that Robert Kennedy forced "people to take a hard look at what it was we were doing" in Vietnam.[39]

In contrast to his stance on the Cuban missile crisis, when Robert had compelling reasons for championing a position against the majority's grain, he felt less certain about the proper course in the Vietnam debates and reluctant to challenge the conventional wisdom of the senior military and national security advisors. With his probing questions he intended less to change minds than to make sure that the NSC had considered every contingency and, most importantly, that his brother was protected in each instance. During these few days of intense discussion, the idea of U.S. withdrawal, Arthur Schlesinger explained, "died away, a hopelessly alien thought in a field of unexamined assumptions and entrenched convictions."[40] Reflecting back after more than three decades, McNamara recalled Robert Kennedy's provocative comments as another of many missed opportunities to shape events in a positive manner during the crucial fall of 1963.[41]

Even with time to reflect and with the advantage of his brother's counsel, President Kennedy modified the instructions to Ambassador Lodge only slightly, guaranteeing support for a coup but reserving the prerogative to change course, pending the outcome of an ongoing review of the situation. "When we go," he wired Lodge, "we must go to win, but it will be better to change our minds than fail."[42] Two options were notably absent from the list of options President Kennedy maneuvered to retain. At no point, according to McNamara, had they thoroughly considered allowing Diem and Nhu to proceed with exploring the neutralization of Vietnam.[43] If a Laos-type neutralization was, indeed, John Kennedy's ultimate objective, as Arthur Schlesinger, Jr., later argued, then one has to wonder why it was never broached at this critical juncture.[44] A second option never considered was that of leaving the South Vietnamese people and their political system to their own devices. No senior advisor challenged the right of the United States to manipulate, even to overthrow, the government of an ally that failed to conform to U.S. expectations.[45]

Despite Robert Kennedy's pot stirring, a month of "agonizing reappraisal" passed during which President Kennedy failed to pull together his divided counselors. "Confronted with a choice among evils," Robert McNamara wrote in 1995, John Kennedy "remained indecisive far too long."[46]

The Kennedy administration's conflicted policy on Vietnam mirrored the personality of the president, looking in several directions at once, assaying options, analyzing facts, but drawing few conclusions. His indecision shows in September 1963 in two television interviews that in the decades since have been cited both by Kennedy apologists who insist he intended to withdraw and by critics who claim that he would have escalated the war. He tantalized CBS viewers (and later historians) with the prospect of disengagement when he told Walter Cronkite, "In the final analysis, it is the people and the Government [of South Vietnam] itself who has to win or lose this struggle. All we can do is help." In a direct message to Diem, Kennedy said that the government of South Vietnam "has gotten out of touch with the people." Still, a U.S. withdrawal, he warned, would be a "great mistake." A week later, speaking before NBC cameras, he endorsed the domino theory and emphatically rejected any notion of withdrawal. "We must be patient," he cautioned, "we must persist . . . I think we should stay."[47]

Holding on through September without a consensus among his advisors and well aware of dissident tensions mounting in South Vietnam, President Kennedy sent Taylor and McNamara on yet another inspection tour of the country. Their report of 2 October defended U.S. strategy and recommended using "selective pressures" to push Diem to get rid of the Nhus, end repression, and take bolder initiatives toward the insurgents. Adopting a position very close to Robert Kennedy's first take on the matter, they recommended reducing U.S. forces by recalling a thousand troops and by withholding some economic assistance "to impress upon Diem our disapproval of his political program." The Taylor-McNamara report projected that a withdrawal of most of the remaining 16,000 advisors could be considered by the end of 1965, or more than two years hence, provided the war in the countryside had been won.[48] The return of a thousand troops, then, was not the first step toward withdrawal, as some have suggested, but a means to pressure Diem to get the South Vietnamese to do more on their own. U.S. withdrawal in the Kennedy formulation was contingent upon military victory.

Thus, the final decision on the Diem coup was really a military one. Lodge complained that the "heart of the Army [ARVN] is *not* in the war." He blamed Diem. The Kennedys agreed. Victory under Diem's leadership, they now realized, was unlikely. Setting aside, for whatever reasons, their reservations about Lodge, the Kennedys delegated to him the power to manage U.S. policy in Vietnam and instructed him to tell Diem, in short, it had to be the American way or no way. John Kennedy told Lodge that the United States could not condone "any active covert encouragement of a coup," but he allowed Lodge to inform Diem's opponents that the United States "will not attempt to thwart" a coup. The White House then instructed Lodge that the coup must not end as an embarrassing failure and that the "effort must be totally secure and fully deniable." Those instructions were personally confirmed by John and Robert Kennedy at an Oval Office meeting with CIA director McCone, during which everyone carefully avoided using the word "assassination."[49]

Astonishingly, the Kennedys believed they could control the timing of the coup, turning it on and off at will. They changed their minds about the coup on 29 October, after General Paul Harkins, Commander of U.S. forces in Vietnam warned that Diem's overthrow meant a military calamity. Robert Kennedy said he was now convinced that a coup "risks too much."[50] The president also hedged, expressing his concerns over the CIA's tenuous links to the coup conspirators and worrying that "we could lose our entire position in Southeast Asia overnight."[51] They were trying at this point, Robert Kennedy said, "to throw some cold water" on the coup plans, to slow down events until they knew who would succeed Diem, and to avoid "a bloody riot out there."[52] In a futile attempt to prevent the murder of his fellow Catholic, Diem, John Kennedy sent Torbert Macdonald to advise Diem to take asylum in the U.S. embassy. Otherwise, Macdonald said he told Diem, "They're going to kill you."[53]

Events overtook the conflicted administration. Resigned to the necessity of Diem's removal, they reached a "decision by indecision," as historian Gary Hess put it.[54] At White House meetings where they talked about a coup, Robert Kennedy expressed three concerns: that a coup would place the government in the hands of persons "not now known to us"; that, if the coup failed, "Diem will throw us out"; and that Henry Cabot Lodge ultimately would overreach.[55] Predictably, as matters spun out of control, Robert reminded his brother of his warning that Lodge "would cause him a lot of difficulty in six months." To which John Kennedy sarcastically replied that he thought it was "terrific" that his brother could always remember when he was right.[56]

On 1 November, as the coup in South Vietnam unfolded, Robert Kennedy awaited developments in the Cabinet Room with other members of the president's crisis team. Robert McNamara remembered that when word came that Diem and his brother, Nhu, had been captured and summarily executed by a military junta, John Kennedy "literally blanched," then rushed from the room.[57] At the president's reaction, Maxwell Taylor asked, "What did he expect?" Other aides noticed that John Kennedy remained depressed and pensive for several days afterwards.[58]

No one remembered anything noteworthy in Robert Kennedy's reactions to the assassinations of the Vietnamese leaders.[59] Surely he felt some remorse and very likely vulnerability. The parallels between the Kennedys and the Ngo brothers, after all, could hardly have escaped him. Americans at the Saigon embassy even called Diem's brother "Bobby."[60] But perhaps after three years' involvement in national security matters he was becoming inured to the outcomes of that often grisly business, for he showed more concern with the consequences of the coup for his brother's presidency than with the moral implications of U.S. involvement.[61]

Characteristically, President Kennedy blamed the "bastards" in the

CIA for mismanaging the coup.[62] Robert, for his part, cast aspersions on Henry Cabot Lodge, charging that his brother's former political adversary went out of control and deliberately ignored instructions from Washington because, as Robert later insisted, he "wanted a coup."[63] In Robert Kennedy's totally biased view, his brother had not "authorized" the coup, it just suddenly "took place."[64] A few years later, when reporter Jack Newfield asked him if the U.S. government had a hand in overthrowing Diem, Kennedy hesitated. "Not in Washington," he lied.[65]

The deaths of Diem and Nhu brought no end to what McNamara called "the deep differences within the administration over Vietnam."[66] Lacking coherent direction and firm leadership, U.S. Vietnam policy, Robert Kennedy later conceded, had been "bobbled."[67] The VC and NLF made enormous gains after the coup. Hundreds of villages and outposts across Vietnam were overrun by insurgent forces armed with U.S. weapons channeled to them by the graft and corruption in Saigon. The United States responded, as usual, with various schemes to escalate action.

Victor Krulak came up with a daring and risky plan—one that very likely neither Kennedy ever saw—drafted to appeal to their preference for covert operations and their hope of containing the Pentagon hawks. Put together at a conference in Hawaii on 20 November 1963, Operation Plan 34A proposed a large-scale clandestine war in the form of a series of destructive raids against North Vietnam, intended to interdict the North's support of insurgents in the South. Four days after John Kennedy's death, the plan was formally incorporated within National Security Action Memorandum 273. Its implementation probably provoked the Tonkin Gulf incident of August 1964, which opened the door for a vast widening of the war under President Johnson.[68]

Whether John Kennedy would have walked through that door is uncertain. He probably would have accepted Operation Plan 34A and expanded covert operations; both Kennedys supported clandestine warfare doctrine and they personally liked Krulak and were wont to accept his recommendations on how to handle the war. Beyond that we are in doubt. The improvisational nature and the collegial style of Kennedy's national security advising, plus his willingness to tolerate the prolonged mulling of many options at once, invite speculation and open the way for inferences of all sorts.[69] At bottom, Hess noted, Kennedy and his advisors approached Vietnam as a series of problems, "without fully considering the reasons for the commitment to South Vietnam or the ramifications of the steps being taken."[70]

Exactly so. Asked in the spring of 1964 what his brother's administration would have done if South Vietnam appeared ready to go under, Robert Kennedy said, "We'd face that when we came to it."[71] We do, however, have one clear indicator of how Robert would have advised his brother in 1964 and thereafter: his undiminished support of counterinsurgency, which remained firm even after John Kennedy's death and even after the Senate passed the Gulf of Tonkin Resolution in August 1964. "We have made a beginning," he wrote in September 1964 upon the occasion of his leaving the attorney general's office, "but we have not mastered the art of counterinsurgency . . . we have not perfected the technique of training foreign nationals to defend themselves against Communist terrorism and guerrilla penetration. This kind of warfare can be long-drawn-out and costly, but if Communism is to be stopped, it is necessary. And we mean to see this job through to the finish."[72]

The Kennedy buildup in Vietnam, historian David Burner explains, "was a necessary but not a sufficient condition for the conflagration of the mid-sixties."[73] John Kennedy proclaimed South Vietnam a sovereign state, enveloping it in the prestige and protection of the United States. He fostered the notion that insurgency in South Vietnam was amenable only to an American solution. He authorized the use of toxic chemicals (such as Agent Orange) to defoliate the forests, encouraged the South Vietnamese to relocate peasants to Strategic Hamlets, authorized the use of napalm bombs, launched CIA commando raids against the North, and accepted the first U.S. casualties (109 dead, 486 wounded by the end of 1963).[74] President Johnson was responsible for the massive commitment of U.S. troops to Vietnam, but, in James Reston's words, "Kennedy started the slide."[75] According to Robert McNamara, who remained on as secretary of defense until 1968, "Johnson inherited a god-awful mess eminently more dangerous than the one Kennedy had inherited from Eisenhower."[76]

Likelihood of a Kennedy Withdrawal

Historians are far from agreed on what John Kennedy would have done had he lived. Herbert Parmet and James Giglio, have drawn reasonable conclusions, however, both observing that John Kennedy would not likely have withdrawn from Vietnam without a clear-cut settlement, meaning a military victory.[77] Some historians, however, feel that Kennedy, like Johnson, would almost certainly have continued to escalate the war, because withdrawal or deescalation, as David Burner argued, required the kind of political courage John Kennedy admired yet so rarely demonstrated.[78] Other analysts reason that unilateral withdrawal from Vietnam would have required the Kennedys to take the unthinkable step of admitting the failure of counterinsurgency, a strategy in which both Kennedys had deep investments.[79] Indeed, John Kennedy's public statements and policy decisions, up to the day of his death, emphasized a firm commitment to sustaining an anticommunist regime in South Vietnam.[80]

By the late 1960s, however, most Kennedy insiders held it on faith that John Kennedy had planned to reverse his course and withdraw all advisors soon after the 1964 election.[81] But if he planned a way out, he never mentioned it to his secretary of defense or his secretary of state or his attorney general or his national security advisor.[82] Arthur Schlesinger, Jr., interpreted John Kennedy's indecision on Vietnam as a positive sign that he was "looking for a way out." Building on a sophisticated set of speculative conditions and fallibilistic reasoning, Schlesinger argued that Kennedy would, eventually, have found a way out.[83] But the evidence of Kennedy's intent to withdraw comes largely from the intuitions of his former associates and selective recollections of the president's private comments, which were often extremely cryptic and laden with simulopt thinking. Robert McNamara, for example, concluded without citing any evidence that John Kennedy was too intelligent, too skeptical of the military, and too prudent in his use of military power to make the same mistakes as Johnson.[84]

No one, however, knew John Kennedy and his predilections better than Robert Kennedy, and in May 1964 he stated unequivocally that President Kennedy had no intention of withdrawing from Vietnam. He expressed that viewpoint so confidently and so explicitly that the editors of *Robert Kennedy in His Own Words,* the published 1988 version of his oral history interviews at the Kennedy Library, felt compelled to warn readers "that the Robert Kennedy who responded to . . . questions in 1964 was not the same Robert Kennedy who ran for the presidency in 1968."[85] Indeed, he was not.

In the spring of 1964, for instance, as he had throughout his brother's presidency, Robert Kennedy still stoutly defended the domino theory. Nothing had changed his mind on that score—not the failures to overthrow Castro, not the Diem and Nhu assassinations, not the changing situation in Vietnam, not even his brother's assassination. To underscore his commitment, Robert Kennedy wrote to President Johnson in June 1964 and volunteered to go to Vietnam as ambassador or to serve there in "any capacity."[86] President Kennedy, said Robert, "had a strong, overwhelming reason for being in Vietnam" and was convinced that "we should win the war in Vietnam." Asked the reason, he said, "I think everybody was quite clear that the rest of Southeast Asia would fall" and that would "have profound effects on our position throughout the world."

Asked if President Kennedy ever gave any consideration to pulling out, Robert Kennedy said, "No." Neither were they disposed, he added, toward all-out combat. General MacArthur, he recalled, had warned the Kennedys that a "land conflict between our troops—white troops and Asian—would only end in disaster," and so, Robert said, "we went in as advisers to try to get the Vietnamese to fight, themselves, because we couldn't win the war for them. They had to win the war for themselves."[87]

In sum, the weight of the evidence indicates that the Kennedys would surely have continued U.S. involvement in Vietnam through 1964 and 1965, with increased emphasis on paramilitary and covert operations, and that they would have resisted the introduction of large numbers of ground troops until, like Johnson, they reached a decision point they could neither ignore nor finesse.

Some of President Kennedy's aides, anxious to protect his reputation and to dissociate him from the Vietnam conflict when it became unpopular in the late 1960s, implicitly refuted Robert Kennedy's views.

One suspects that they also kept those views from being widely disseminated. Kenneth O'Donnell and David Powers were convinced, when the storm of protest over President Johnson's policies arose, that John Kennedy harbored a secret wish to withdraw, which could not be fulfilled until after the 1964 presidential election. O'Donnell said that President Kennedy once complained that he would be "damned everywhere as a Communist appeaser" if he pulled out of Vietnam before 1964. "I can do it after I'm reelected," Kennedy told O'Donnell. "So we had better make damn sure that I *am* reelected."[88]

Setting aside the authenticity of O'Donnell's recollection, its premise has no inherent logic. First, it presumes a John Kennedy held to an escalating Vietnam strategy by the powerful grip of the anticommunist lobby on the electorate, when vast amounts of evidence (not the least being his own public statements) indicate that he was deeply persuaded that U.S. interests were, indeed, at stake in Vietnam. Moreover, O'Donnell's presumption ignores the wealth of evidence showing that Kennedy was personally challenged (call it machismo) by Khruschev's 1961 pledge of support to national liberation movements in places like Vietnam. Further, O'Donnell implies that John Kennedy in a second, lame-duck term would have tolerated the label "Communist appeaser" and that he was prepared to take extraordinary risks (a state of mind for which there were no indications at all) to end U.S. involvement in Vietnam. Most important, however, O'Donnell's claim overlooks the effects on the other Kennedy brothers. It is unthinkable, given the immersion of the Kennedys in the political culture of the Cold War era and given the closeness of the male Kennedys, that John Kennedy would have encumbered his brothers (both of whom anticipated long political careers) with the label "Communist appeaser."

O'Donnell's argument contains one verity: Electoral politics intruded heavily during the brief Kennedy administration and the 1964 election was constantly on the Kennedys' minds. Indeed, John and Robert Kennedy peppered casual conversations and comments to advisors with references to the slimness of the 1960 election plurality, its inhibiting effects, the conditional prospects for reelection in 1964, and the anticipated impact of Kennedy's reelection on virtually every issue area, both foreign and domestic.

Still, the Kennedys had to use caution in partisan matters, especially Robert, who with circumspection balanced his role as his brother's campaign manager and his duties as attorney general. When speaking or writing for the record, Robert Kennedy told inquiring Democrats that he had "removed himself from political affairs since taking the oath of office" for attorney general. Off the record, he kept informed of all significant political developments, received regular updates and confidential assessments from operatives in important Democratic districts around the country, pored over poll results and vote breakdowns, recruited candidates (urging astronaut John Glenn, for instance, to run for the U.S. Senate as a Democrat), and used his influence to shape the direction of Democratic politics to his brother's advantage.[89] To make sure the Democratic National Committee (DNC) served his brother's interests, Robert Kennedy personally superintended its operations, approving registration campaigns, checking the payroll, clearing a campaign "Fact Book" for 1962, and influencing the choice of the 1964 national convention site.[90] Prohibited from actively campaigning during the 1962 midterm elections, he directed John M. Bailey, chair of the DNC, to target key congressional districts where "we have the greatest chance of being successful" and volunteered the services of the loyal Paul Corbin, "with some direction," and of Jerry Bruno, the president's personal advance man.[91]

Generally speaking, however, Kennedy succeeded to a praiseworthy degree in separating political interests from his duties as attorney general. Believing it necessary, like Caesar's wife, to avoid even the appearance of political partiality, he proceeded, in his words, with some very "unpleasant cases" potentially detrimental to his brother's political future and injurious to his family's interests. Those cases posed legal, political, and ethical dilemmas, from which he usually escaped through some sort of compromise. In the income-tax evasion case against old family friend James M. Landis—who for thirty years had given the family free legal services and who had helped Robert get through his law school exams—Kennedy initially recused himself, then later intervened to negotiate a more humane sentencing arrangement.[92]

Another case involved newspaper columnist Igor Cassini, whose brother Oleg designed Jacqueline Kennedy's fashions. The FBI suspected

Igor Cassini of using his acquaintance with Joseph Kennedy to lobby for favorable treatment for Dominican dictator Raphael Trujillo. Robert stopped the FBI investigation, "the only investigation I've called off since I've been Attorney General," he said in 1964 (forgetting the Giancana-Maheu prosecution), because Oleg Cassini "swore to me" that Igor was not involved. Journalist Peter Maas, however, presented evidence convincing Kennedy that Igor, not a disinterested party after all, was in fact paid by Trujillo for his services. "I felt really fooled," Kennedy admitted. Despite "an awful lot of pressure," he decided to prosecute Cassini. Cassini was convicted and fined $10,000 for failing to register as an agent for a foreign government.[93]

Similarly, Attorney General Kennedy had no alternative but to investigate and prosecute Judge J. Vincent Keogh, the brother of New York congressman Eugene Keogh, a major political benefactor and personal friend of John Kennedy. Eugene Keogh frequently called Robert Kennedy and sent him messages with unsubtle reminders of favors he had done for John Kennedy. Clearly annoyed by Congressman Keogh's guile, Robert did nothing to interfere when Judge Keogh was sentenced to two years in jail for bribery. Another case involved George Chacharis, the mayor of Gary, Indiana, who, despite delivering the Indiana delegation at the Los Angeles Convention, was convicted for accepting payoffs and for avoiding taxes. And journalist Charles Bartlett remembered that Robert insisted on indicting a man Bartlett thought had performed good service as an intermediary for the White House during the steel crisis. Bartlett called the president to plead the man's case. "You know," John Kennedy teased, "what this Administration needs more than anything is an Attorney General we can fix!"[94]

Although the Landis, Cassini, Keogh, and Chacharis cases tested Robert Kennedy's ethical constitution, it would be a stretch to portray him as the virtuous prosecutor motivated purely by high-minded ethics. He tried in various ways to ameliorate the outcome of each case and to reduce its effects on his brother's presidency. He could not, of course, cover up the evidence once it had been collected and analyzed. The attorney general, as one FBI agent put it, could not simply say, "Shshsh . . . and it will go away." But neither can Kennedy be denied the credit for bringing the cases. For in the end, as Victor Navasky's detailed study revealed, Robert Kennedy steadfastly refused to allow his office to be used for political purposes.[95]

The absence of political scandal during the Kennedy administration may be less a matter of Robert Kennedy's adherence to a strict moral and ethical code than his and his brother's refusal to make political deals that could trip them up later. Unlike their father, the Kennedy sons (particularly Robert) were reluctant to engage in the traditional quid pro quo of patronage-based politics. Indeed, the two obligations of the professional politician that bothered Robert Kennedy the most were making small talk at political gatherings and doing personal favors for other politicians, especially anyone who had criticized his brother.

That rule held even for former president Harry Truman. Truman, of course, had tried to block John Kennedy's candidacy before the Los Angeles convention and never confessed any particular fondness for either Kennedy. When asked what he thought of the attorney general, Truman said, "I just don't like that boy, and I never will." As his biographer David McCullough reminds us, the man from Independence was an old-school politician who performed many favors for others. He expected favors in return. He was more than mildly annoyed, then, when Robert Kennedy refused to approve his initial requests to pardon Matt Connelly, a former Truman associate convicted of income tax evasion. By the third letter Truman was furious. Demanding the pardon be granted immediately, Truman wrote, "So don't smile at me any more unless you want to do justice to Matt Connelly." When Connelly finally went free, Truman thanked the president and ignored the attorney general.[96]

By the fall of 1963 Robert found himself back in the role he had first played for his brother, that of campaign manager. As he began giving serious thought to his brother's reelection, Kennedy was encouraged by analyst Richard Scammon's confidential assessments and by the Gallup polls of October 1963, showing President Kennedy would carry 58 percent of the vote in a contest against Richard Nixon and 57 percent against Senator Barry Goldwater. Polls by Louis Harris gave Kennedy 54 percent against each. John Kennedy was well positioned in the electoral vote-rich urban-industrial states, where he was projected to win 84 percent of the Catholic vote, 91 percent of the Jewish vote, and 90 percent of the Negro vote.[97] After a thousand days in office the caution and tentativeness brought on by the paper-thin election margin of 1960 began to wane.

Plans for the 1964 campaign were formally launched at a three-hour meeting in the Cabinet Room on 13 November 1963. "As usual," the president informed his inner group, "the campaign will be run right from here," meaning by himself and his brother. The law, of course, prohibited Robert from serving as campaign manager while still attorney general, and so John Bailey and Steve Smith were directed to get the campaign organized. Two political tours were scheduled for later in the month, first to Florida and then to Texas.[98]

Early the afternoon of 22 November, Angie Novello sat motionless at her desk, mesmerized by the frayed UPI report ripped from the teletype moments earlier. She was startled when the FBI direct line rang. "This is J. Edgar Hoover. Have you heard the news?"

"Yes," said Angie, "but I'm not going to break it to him." Hoover understood. "I'll call him," he said.

Novello, Hoover, and several million Americans already knew what Robert Kennedy did not. Ethel picked up the phone by the pool of their Hickory Hill home, where her husband was having lunch with Robert Morgenthau, one of the U.S. attorneys involved in a daylong meeting of his organized crime unit. "The director is calling," said the White House operator. Ethel knew which director. "The attorney general is at lunch," she replied. "This is urgent," said the voice.[99]

Robert Kennedy reacted to Hoover's flat, impassively delivered message as though hit by a bullet himself. "Jack's been shot!" he gasped. Gagging and clamping a hand over his face, he said, "It may be fatal."[100]

His first instinct was to go to his brother. He called McNamara and requested a military jet to fly him to Dallas immediately. Meantime, on another phone, Ethel dialed several times before she managed to get through to Parkland Hospital in Dallas, finally reaching Clint Hill, a very shaken Secret Service agent. Taking the phone, Robert was assured by Hill that a priest had been called and that the doctors were doing all they could. Within a few minutes John McCone arrived at the house (only five minutes from CIA headquarters at Langley, Virginia) and found Robert pacing the floor of the upstairs library. When the White

House extension rang again, Captain Tazewell Shepard, the president's naval aide, confirmed the dreaded news. "Oh, he's dead!" Robert cried.[101]

Most of us never realize life's worst fears or attain life's fondest wishes. But Joseph P. Kennedy's oldest sons were not like most of us, either in the way they lived or in the way they died. The best and the worst were visited upon them with startling frequency, bringing many to puzzle over some possible greater meaning. "America wept tonight," James Reston wrote that evening, "not alone for its dead young president, but for itself. The grief was general, for somehow the worst in the nation had prevailed over the best."[102]

Even Kennedy critics grieved. Father Philip Berrigan, leader of a newly formed Catholic antiwar movement, had charged that Kennedy "appeased the Corporate/Pentagon martians with a doubled war budget, and with troop buildups." Yet he wept that evening. Berrigan, like most Americans, believed John Kennedy had given the country reason to be hopeful, simply because he was educable.[103]

For the moment at least, what others thought no longer mattered to Robert. His brother's death was first and foremost a family tragedy. His attention for the first hours, days, and weeks afterward focused on his family, not politics or power or his government duties. Lyndon Johnson and others apparently expected him to react otherwise. With his brother dead, however, being attorney general was no longer of consequence to Robert Kennedy.

Still, with the slain president and the new president en route to Washington and with the secretary of state and other members of the cabinet on a plane over the Pacific, the attorney general and the secretary of defense, as the ranking cabinet members in Washington, had to hold things together until President Lyndon Johnson arrived. McCone and many others in the administration had instinctively rushed to Hickory Hill. With its access to the White House switchboard (at times the only telephone line working in Washington that afternoon), Hickory Hill became a command post (albeit a passive one) for a government in transition.

Those who gathered at Robert Kennedy's home that afternoon saw no ugly recriminations or anger, no questioning of authority or frustrated accusations of possible coups. Through hours of anguish, John McCone observed, Robert Kennedy "never cracked." "Obviously he was seriously affected," said McCone, "but at no time did he lose his composure." McCone remembered Kennedy's grieving lament repeated often that day: "There's been so much hate."[104] As his children arrived home from school that afternoon Robert Kennedy pulled each of them to him, embracing as many at once as his arms could hold. He reached out to the rest of the family, telephoning his mother in Hyannis Port and discussing with Teddy the weight and timing of the effects of the news on individual family members.[105]

Robert Kennedy so internalized the tragedy of his brother's murder that, at least initially, he failed to respond to its political consequences. As he struggled with shock and grief the afternoon of the murder, Kennedy was first puzzled, then distracted, and ultimately annoyed by Lyndon Johnson's phone calls from Texas. Irritated by his absorption with legalities and impervious to the tone of alarm and uncertainty in the voice of the new president, Robert wondered how any of that could possibly matter.[106]

Robert Kennedy did not want a large gathering of officials at Andrews Air Force Base to meet Air Force One, but everyone in high office wanted to be there. "The last thing Jackie wants to see is a lot of people," he told Arthur Goldberg, who, speaking for himself, for members of Congress, and for other officials, urged him to relent. "If you want to go, go," said Kennedy. "I'm not going to get into an argument about it."[107] Leaving the house for a car ride to the Pentagon, the first thoughts of the future began to intrude. "People don't realize how conservative Lyndon really is," he told Ed Guthman. "There are going to be a lot of changes."[108]

At the Pentagon, Kennedy joined Maxwell Taylor and Robert McNamara for the helicopter ride to Andrews Air Force Base. No one spoke during the flight. At Andrews he avoided the press by hiding in the back of a pickup truck. As the plane came to a stop, he jumped from the truck and bounded up the front ramp.[109] "I want to see Jackie," he said, brushing past everyone, including the Johnsons. "I'm here," he said reaching her. How like Bobby this was, she thought. Always there when you needed him.[110]

Kennedy tried to persuade his brother's widow to go directly to the White House. "No, no, I just want to go to Bethesda," she answered. While in the air she had elected Bethesda Naval Hospital for the autopsy.[111] On the way there, riding in the ambulance next to the coffin, she told him the details about Texas. "I didn't think about whether I wanted to hear it or not," he later told William Manchester. "So she went through all that."[112]

From the tower suite at Bethesda, Robert Kennedy called Sargent Shriver and Ralph Dungan in the West Wing of the White House, conveying his sister-in-law's requests and helping accelerate and direct the flustered flurry of Washington motion required to pull off a state funeral in three days. Remaining abreast of developments in Dallas, he called to console the wives of slain Dallas policeman J. D. Tippit and wounded governor John Connally. He also tried to comfort friends and officials who felt obliged to be there, a group that one physician described as "the most disturbed and distressed people I have ever seen." Moving among them, Robert said over and over, "Don't be sad."[113] His calm demeanor and his apparent control over the situation impressed them all. That night, historian William Manchester later wrote, "the commanding figure in Bethesda Naval Hospital was Robert Kennedy."[114]

Out of concern for Jacqueline's comfort the attorney general asked the president's personal physician, Admiral George Burkley, to press the pathologists to expedite the autopsy and the preparation of the body for burial.[115] Thinking ahead, Kennedy also directed Burkley to recover all of the residual materials from the autopsy.[116] He may have decided that very evening to keep the autopsy X-rays and photographs safe from macabre displays by sensationalists. Later, when sensation seekers such as New Orleans District Attorney James Garrison tried to subpoena the materials, Robert gave Burke Marshall complete authority "to deal with them."[117]

Although Robert Kennedy seemed in total control, after the first round of duties were completed and JFK's remains lay in the East Room of the White House, he retired to the Lincoln bedroom for the few restless hours remaining until daylight. Friends and family heard him sobbing, "Why God?"[118]

The brother and the widow made most decisions jointly, but Robert had overall responsibility for the funeral. Jacqueline Kennedy insisted, among other touches, that her husband lie in state on the Lincoln catafalque (a replica was built); that the funeral mass be held at St. Matthews Cathedral, within walking distance of the White House, because she refused to ride to her husband's funeral "in a fat black Cadillac"; and that an eternal flame burn at the gravesite. Robert added a few touches of his own, such as the composition of the honor guard, which would include a representative of the Special Forces, and the playing of the "Navy Hymn" to honor both of his fallen brothers. On only one matter did they disagree. Jacqueline absolutely opposed an open casket. Robert thought tradition required it at a state funeral. However, after viewing the cosmetized waxen remains, he concurred and ordered the casket closed.[119]

Shriver, Dungan, Richard Goodwin, William Walton (Jacqueline's artist friend), and a battalion of aides attended to a mountain of minutiae, but Robert Kennedy was the court of last resort on major issues. Determining the burial place was made "rather difficult for me," he remembered, since the Irish Mafia (O'Donnell, O'Brien, and Powers) and Kennedy's sisters all thought burial outside of Massachusetts unthinkable. But that Saturday morning, after walking over the sodden terrain in a cold, pouring rain, Kennedy was persuaded by McNamara (who had Jacqueline's support all along) that Arlington National Cemetery was the most appropriate place. Jacqueline agreed with the brother's choice of a gravesite on the slope below the Custis-Lee Mansion, on an axis with the Lincoln Memorial across the river.[120]

The widow and the brother paid JFK a last, private visit just before the casket was removed from the White House to lie in state beneath the Capitol rotunda. Inside the coffin Robert placed an engraved silver rosary Ethel had given him at their wedding, his *PT-109* tie clasp, and a lock of his own hair.[121] Robert and brother Edward planned a formal graveside farewell, reading excerpts of JFK's speeches, but at the last moment decided to move directly to helping Jacqueline light the eternal flame.

Then the brother protector, appearing as the "strongest of the stricken"[122] and standing as erect as any marine present, took the hand of the president's widow and walked down the hill toward his life's second act.

EPILOGUE

There Has to Be a Morning After

It was the longest weekend of the American Century. The funeral of John F. Kennedy joined religious and military ritual to civic pageantry, transmuting tragedy into modern mythology, all compressed within the confines of television. Americans alive that November remember the clacking of a riderless horse's shod hooves, echoes of a caisson's tumbling wheels, and the throb of muted drums. Prominent among the memories are the images of the slain president's brother poised attentively at the elbow of the proud and graceful widow, striding beside her to church, lighting the eternal flame at the grave.

Robert Kennedy was a source of strength to his family and his brother's widow. "Bobby was the rock they clung to," LeMoyne Billings recalled, "the one who insisted that everything would be all right, the one who urged them to set a term to their mourning and get on with their lives."[1]

Yet when the funeral ended, the family saw that he was, in fact, shattered by his brother's death. "Bobby," his mother recalled, "at first acted as if he had been cut adrift." Then, she said, he went into a state of "almost insupportable emotional shock." Craving isolation after the funeral, he took Ethel and the children to Florida and did not join the family wake or attend the family Thanksgiving dinner at Hyannis Port.[2]

So deep was his anguish, Ethel remembered, that "you couldn't get to him." "His whole life," she said, "was wrapped up in the President . . . he was just another part of his brother—sort of an added arm. Bobby never thought about himself—or his own life. So when the President died—well, it was like part of Bobby died, too."[3]

LeMoyne Billings agreed. "He had tied up so much of his own self, his own career, to that of his brother. He had been totally involved, totally dedicated to helping and furthering the work of John Kennedy. Hitching himself so completely to Jack, he established no identity of his own and never wanted one."[4]

For weeks, Robert Kennedy seemed barely able to function. He failed to attend meetings, walking into Lyndon Johnson's first cabinet meeting only by chance; he left mail unanswered and never, in fact, responded to letters regarding the details of the assassination; he turned over Justice Department business to Nicholas Katzenbach. He thanked people for personal courtesies (Senator Yarborough for a box of candy, Burke Marshall's daughter Catie for cookies), and he hosted a Christmas party for poor children. Even then he seemed only to be going through the motions.[5]

"It was as though someone had turned off his switch," said David Hackett. Unable to sleep, he went for long rides in his convertible in the middle of the night, with the top down in freezing weather. The vibrancy and spirit visibly drained from him. Friends and family feared for his sanity.[6] "He would look at you," George Smathers said, "listen to you, but would not respond. You got the feeling he was there in body but he wasn't there at all."[7]

Robert Kennedy displayed many of the symptoms of clinical depression, including sleeplessness, lack of concentration, preoccupation with death, brooding, feelings of sadness, despair, and melancholy—except he also felt anger. As at previous turning points in his life, he vented his frustrations physically. In late December, while staying with family and friends at Douglas Dillon's home in Hobe Sound, Florida, he organized a very rough touch football game in which he played with reckless abandon. "Bobby was absolutely relentless," Pierre Salinger remembered. "He was getting his feelings out," Salinger noted, at the expense of others. "One guy broke a leg, and you couldn't count the bloody noses and contusions."[8]

He had, of course, always pursued fast and rough athletic action, perhaps, in part, to establish some superiority over his physically limited brother. But over the next few months and, indeed, for the remaining years of his life, Robert Kennedy was drawn to more life-endangering activities, such as kayaking, white-water rafting, and mountain climbing, and he pursued his favorite sports of skiing and sailing with break neck fervor. He took other physical risks, for example, refusing police protection when he emerged again in public life. Whether still anxious to prove himself—the young boy diving into the cold waters of Nantucket Sound—or in despair over the future, he seemed oblivious to fear.

Robert Kennedy could not physically excise the demons of his torment because their wellspring was the intense sibling rivalry among the three oldest Kennedy males. Just as Joe Junior was driven to a foolhardy and fatal action to match John's exploits in the Pacific, Robert had pushed the envelope in his own struggle to make a mark worthy of being John Kennedy's brother. He expected that he alone would pay the price for his assaults on the perceived forces of evil, according to the pattern of his relationship to JFK; a brother protector, after all, is there to take the hit.

Certainly, then, a large part of Robert Kennedy's agony stemmed from his fear that one of his campaigns—whether organized crime, union racketeers, Castro, or white supremacists, or right-wing forces within the government itself—had invited retaliation upon his brother. "I thought they would get one of us," he told Ed Guthman the afternoon of the assassination, "but Jack, after all he'd been through, never worried about it . . . I thought it would be me."[9]

Kennedy never told Guthman or anyone else who he suspected "they" were, but he behaved like a guilty survivor possessed of tragic knowledge. Unable to discuss the assassination or make anything more than an oblique reference to it, he ignored the Warren commission and other inquiries into his brother's death. He found the subject too painful to contemplate, dreading both what a truly exhaustive investigation would require of his family and what it might reveal about his and his brother's provocative actions.

Robert Kennedy showed no physical fear, although (based solely on what he told Guthman) no one could blame him if he had been terrified by the possibility of a broader conspiracy. So much had fallen on him at once, his own safety seemed of small consequence. Other worries plagued him, not the least being possible public exposure of MONGOOSE and the CIA-Mafia link to the anti-Castro plans, the plot against Diem, and JFK's amorous affairs, including one with a woman tied directly to the Mafia.

Robert, moreover, was apprehensive about facing a future stripped of the power he wielded as his brother's vizier. JFK's murder nullified Robert's leverage over Hoover's FBI, the CIA, and Lyndon Johnson. The immediate beneficiaries of the assassination, furthermore, were his nemeses—organized crime, Hoffa, and Castro. Robert Kennedy had become one of the most vulnerable men alive.

Yet he soon discovered that he was not wholly without power. The grief that followed John Kennedy's assassination soon transformed itself into a sentiment that elevated the slain president and his family to a unique level in American life and culture. He could convert the adoration of JFK, Robert came quickly to realize, into a power base sufficient to challenge Johnson and ultimately regain what he felt was rightfully his. So Robert Kennedy turned to the task of preserving JFK's memory and fashioning a JFK mystique and legacy, even if it meant making something of his brother in death that he was not in life.

Jacqueline Kennedy abetted Robert in this work. The week after Dallas, she told *Life* magazine's Theodore White that she had an "obsession," as she put it, for the lyric from the title song to the Broadway musical *Camelot:* "Don't let it be forgot / That once there was a spot, / For one brief shining moment / That was known as Camelot."[10] JFK's presidency, she insisted, was Camelot revealed, and "there'll never be another Camelot again." White wrote the story, even though he knew it was a misreading of history, and *Life* published it almost exactly as Jacqueline Kennedy wished.[11] Some of her husband's former associates considered it a fraud that would have repulsed JFK. The media in the years since have trivialized and caricatured the notion, and historians have generally regarded it as a perverse distortion of reality.[12]

Robert Kennedy indulged his sister-in-law's obsession—her "poignant conceit," one writer called it—knowing that Camelot would prove a transient metaphor at best.[13] He wanted a permanent legacy to incarnate JFK remembrances. His tacit aspiration was to see that legacy transmitted into the political culture, embraced by political survivors (beginning with himself), and kept alive for future progeny.

Unable to find the energy or the motivation to concentrate on other duties, Robert took up the task of cultivating the JFK legacy. He began in December, writing a foreword to a memorial edition of *Profiles in Courage* that was separately published by *Look* magazine as Robert Kennedy's "Tribute to JFK." With purpose and emotion, he set down his thoughts in his usual tight scrawl.

"Courage," he began, "is the virtue that President Kennedy most admired." Indeed, according to Robert, JFK had "modeled his life" upon the ideal of standing fast on principle. Like the heroes whose stories appeared in *Profiles in Courage*—all of whom demonstrated political courage and a deep-seated belief in the rightness of their cause—JFK, at great personal risk, Robert emphasized, had demonstrated "conviction, courage," and "a desire to help others who needed help." While expressing "hope and confidence for the future," he cautioned that "what happens to the country, to the world, depends on what we do with what others have left us."[14]

The legacy was the message. Never mind that the qualities and attributes Robert ascribed to JFK were overwrought and overdrawn. Such exaggeration was nothing new for the Kennedys. Joseph Kennedy had taught his sons to shield the family from critical eyes, to present them in only the most admirable light, and, if necessary, to manipulate the facts, their report, or both. The father regarded his own and his children's imperfections as "crises of explanation."[15] With the father a muted invalid, the obligations of taking care of the Kennedy family and of explaining JFK's legacy fell to the oldest surviving son.

Further, once Jacqueline Kennedy made her Camelot declaration, she willingly ceded to Robert responsibilities for handling all important matters involving the symbolic and historic preservation of JFK's presidency. Having depended on her husband's brother to help her through difficult times before, she gave him final authority over the design of the JFK gravesite at Arlington, made clear to all concerned that he had final approval on all decisions concerning the JFK presidential library, referred to him all requests to use JFK images on television, and asked him to review and clear all articles written about JFK, including her own piece that appeared in *Life* magazine in the summer of 1964.[16]

Adopting a proprietary attitude toward all information about JFK from the start, within minutes of the president's murder Robert Kennedy called McGeorge Bundy to establish his custody over his brother's personal papers. Bundy, after checking with the State Department, ordered the locks on the White House files changed before Lyndon Johnson could return from Texas.[17] Assured by brother-in-law Stephen Smith that he could "turn over only those papers that you care to," Kennedy denied the Johnson White House access to anything in JFK's papers he deemed personal. Two weeks after the funeral, in his capacity as attorney general, he ruled that "all correspondence [in JFK's papers] which deals with a personal medical matter should be regarded as a privileged communication, and should not go to Central Files."[18] Later, when arranging the deed of gift of JFK's papers to the United States, Kennedy insisted on retaining control over papers pertaining to the "personal, family and business affairs of the President."[19]

All historians still do not have full access to those papers or to Robert Kennedy's. Jacqueline and Robert Kennedy permitted "authorized" authors limited access to JFK's records and granted them exclusive interviews. They entrusted the task of telling the story of the Kennedy administration to Arthur M. Schlesinger, Jr., whose *A Thousand Days* appeared in 1965. They selected William Manchester to write an account of the events surrounding the assassination, which appeared as *The Death of a President* in 1967, after a Kennedy lawsuit and some testy, well-publicized negotiation. "Unauthorized" writers were refused cooperation. Some were personally discouraged by the president's widow, who would tell them she did "not think that another [book on JFK] would serve any useful purpose." To make herself clear, she closed such letters with, "I trust you will respect my feelings and proceed no further."[20]

Robert Kennedy emphatically discouraged members of the inner circle from writing memoirs. Those unable to resist had to clear their manuscripts with Kennedy in advance of publication. He asked Burke Marshall to handle legal matters in such cases and prevailed upon Harvard professor John Kenneth Galbraith, JFK's ambassador to India, to read manuscripts by Kennedy staffers, including those of JFK's secretary

Evelyn Lincoln and *PT-109* buddy Paul Fay. "I was nominated," Galbraith explained to Pierre Salinger, "as the only quasi-literate who wasn't writing a personal epic."[21] On Galbraith's recommendation, Robert and Jacqueline Kennedy personally excised portions of Fay's manuscript, initialing sections they demanded be deleted. Fay obliged, cutting more than two thousand words from his original draft of *The Pleasure of His Company*.[22]

Planning for the John F. Kennedy Presidential Library—where the JFK mystique and legacy were to be physically and symbolically joined—particularly interested Robert Kennedy. Insisting on family control over all sensitive matters and deflecting outside influences over policies and contents, Kennedy had the last word on appointing the board, selecting the architect, and directing the solicitation of funds. He appears to have gotten his way on every issue except the library's location. JFK had wanted the library built in Cambridge, Massachusetts, near Harvard University, but both the community and the university opposed the idea. Robert, of course, did not live to see the 1979 dedication of the impressive nine-story I. M. Pei design built on twelve acres of Columbia Point, an outcropping into Boston's Dorchester Bay.[23]

Offended by commercial use of JFK's photographs or information about him, Kennedy vetoed several proposals for television programs, including one by Pierre Salinger, Peter Lawford, and film star Jackie Cooper for a weekly series, *The 1000 Days of John F. Kennedy*. Refusing to elaborate, he told them, "I think it goes too far." Lawford persisted. Facing financial problems and eager to capitalize on his years in the Kennedy limelight, he tried to get Robert's backing for another series, *JFK: The Man*. Kennedy put Lawford off for five months, then sent a lengthy written opinion on the matter prepared by Burke Marshall. The programs were never produced or aired.[24]

In building the JFK legacy Robert Kennedy did not engage in wholesale revisionism, but he did frequently stoke his vanity, particularly when it came to defining his relationship with President Kennedy. To cast the best possible light on it and to conceal some deep disappointments, Robert modified history (such as the story of the vice-president's selection in 1960) and covered over or initially denied some administration actions, such as MONGOOSE, the tapping of Martin

Luther King's telephones, involvement in the Diem coup, and escalation of the Vietnam war. He consistently exaggerated their resolve, coherence, and success in confronting crises, among them the Freedom Rides, Oxford, Berlin, and Cuba I and II. Mostly, however, he amplified the importance and extent of his advisory roles.

Although unquestionably JFK's most important advisor, Robert Kennedy seemingly felt obliged to maximize his contributions and minimize those of others. Whether out of resentment or self-doubt, he found the truth sometimes too painful to admit, particularly when it implied his brother's calculated rejection of him or his advice. However, as historian James Giglio learned from his detailed study of the Kennedy presidency, JFK "never hesitated to reject his [Robert's] advice, nor did he always consult with him on important matters."[25]

Further, as Richard Reeves so skillfully demonstrated in his persuasive study, *President Kennedy: Profile of Power,* JFK was an egocentric who brandished his charm to manipulate people for his own ends. Reeves called him "an artist who painted with other people's lives. He squeezed people like tubes of paint, gently or brutally, and the people around him—family, writers, drivers, ladies-in-waiting—were the indentured inhabitants serving his needs and desires."[26]

Robert, of course, knew that his brother was practiced at exploring contradictory options simultaneously and that he was adept, too, at deceiving people. He sometimes joined JFK in such deceptions, as when they went into their good-Kennedy, bad-Kennedy routine or when Robert dealt with the FBI, newspaper reporters, or the courts over allegations of JFK's philandering. All the same, Robert convinced himself that his own role was distinctive, that he and JFK were part of a symbiotic process; they were different, in other words, but bound to a common objective.

Robert Kennedy willingly accepted his role as flak catcher and brother protector. As he once explained to *Look* magazine reporter Warren Rogers, "Any president bears so much responsibility that, when something goes wrong, somebody should move forward and take the blame or accept the heat if something unpopular must be done. People want the president kept as a higher authority to appeal to, and, if someone else attracts the anger and draws the fire, that's all to the good."[27]

Usually, JFK played his part with humor and without harming Robert. For example, when a southern member of Congress complained about the Kennedys' civil rights policy and threatened to attack the president in a speech, JFK laughed and said, "Why can't you just call Bobby a son of a bitch?[28]

At other times JFK made callous comments about Robert apparently to test their effects on listeners. (The Kennedys, as they put it, liked to "set up" people.) However, some of JFK's off-handed comments seemed intentionally hurtful and cruel, denigrating Robert as the number two person. Robert had to feel betrayed, for example, by JFK's dismissive comments (through Paul Fay) about his inconsequential role in the 1946 congressional campaign; by JFK assuring Tip O'Neill he could ignore Robert's criticisms because he was only nominally in charge of the 1960 campaign; or by JFK telling George Smathers and his fellow southerners that Robert's interference in Southern politics in 1960 was uninformed and meddlesome. Most scarring of all was JFK's wiggling out of a tight situation regarding Lyndon Johnson's vice-presidential selection by telling the Johnson people that Robert was "out of touch" with developments.

The more he learned of the secret side of JFK's life, the more Robert must have wondered where he fit in his brother's life, where he stood in his esteem and affection. He must have wondered, too, if he really knew his brother.

"No one ever knew John Kennedy, not all of him," said journalist and old school chum Charles Bartlett. Richard Reeves described him as "a compartmentalized man with much to hide, comfortable with secrets and lies."[29] Still, if anyone knew what was inside those compartments, it was Robert Kennedy.

One of the few to appreciate his brother's difficult physical struggles, Robert appeared to discern more of the complex facets of JFK's personality, to be aware of his insecurities and weaknesses, to know (and obviously forgive) his personal foibles, to understand him, in short, as a man. That knowledge, however, rather than drawing them closer, created an emotional buffer between them.

One reason for the emotional distance between the brothers was Robert's moralistic, often prudish attitude. As a youth, Robert had registered his disapproval of the private conduct of Joe Junior, Kathleen, and John. Later, he became the family's "sexual policeman," trying to keep John in line, and, when that failed, cleaning up the debris.[30]

Another reason lay in the Kennedy brothers' different personalities and interests. JFK was cool, self-disciplined, distrustful of passion. He was more wry and detached, less likely to make a personal commitment to causes or to people. JFK gained his autonomy at the cost of emotional distance. Preferring not to be known too well, he enjoyed concealing parts of himself from others.

Robert, on the other hand, trusted passion, allowed his emotions to show more often (some said too often), and was more successful at forging intimate relationships. Far less subtle than his brother, he believed in the direct approach. As political scientist Richard Neustadt once noted, Robert Kennedy was "terribly impatient with institutions." JFK, Neustadt said, accepted the limitations of "what human life was all about" as Robert probably never could.[31]

While JFK was the supreme pragmatist, Robert Kennedy was more a man of moral virtue and conscience. An inner struggle between the imperatives of correcting moral wrongs and advancing his family's interests marked most of Robert's adult life. Politics was the crucible for testing both. Whether over McCarthyism, labor racketeering, wiretapping, civil rights protests, CIA covert operations, or national liberation movements, he seemed perpetually conflicted. Most times he found his way to an ethical and principled resolution. On those other occasions—at least until JFK's assassination—he rationalized his actions as necessary to defeat the forces of evil or to protect his brother.

The Kennedy brothers' closeness, as LeMoyne Billings once observed, "really was based on their political work."[32] They intimately collaborated on running the family business (the Kennedy party apparatus), but John and Robert did not spend much free time together. As youths and as adults they traveled in different circles. Robert's "sober little face" was not one the urbane John Kennedy wanted to see after business hours, on vacations, or at small dinner parties. While Robert and Ethel saw John and Jacqueline frequently at family affairs and formal White House functions, they did not regularly socialize. When JFK wanted a quiet evening of dinner and conversation, he looked elsewhere—to the Bradlees, Alsops, Charles Bartlett, or others who could take his mind away from serious matters or touch them only lightly. "Lovable Bob" was too engrossed, too singleminded to suit his brother.

JFK liked people around him who boosted his ego, nonjudgmental people like LeMoyne Billings, Torbert Macdonald, and his personal factotum, Dave Powers. Billings was especially close, a regular companion for most of their adult lives. "He's been my houseguest since I was married," Jacqueline Kennedy once remarked. After JFK's murder Billings tried (but failed) to attach himself in the same way to Robert and, after Robert's murder, to Robert's children. He devoted his entire adult life to the Kennedy family. The evening before he died in his sleep, he asked, "Do you think I've wasted my life on the Kennedys?"[33]

Robert, by contrast, had more reciprocal friendships. Over the years his oldest friends, David Hackett, Sam Adams, and Ken O'Donnell, helped him and he helped them, often with personal and spiritual advice. His range of friendships was also broader, including nominal conservatives such as Douglas Dillon, John McCone, and Maxwell Taylor, African Americans such as Louis Martin and Charles Evers, and various members of the working press. Then, too, Robert formed uncommonly strong bonds with the men who worked for him in pursuing the enemies within. They called themselves a band of brothers. With his wife for a best friend and a house full of children, there was little room in Robert Kennedy's life for factotums or sycophants.

Finally, the Kennedy brothers' relationship, in large measure, was dictated by the simple matter of their chronological order in Joe and Rose Kennedy's family. Because the parents took much for granted, it was left to the second and third Kennedy sons, nine years apart in age, to find each other. Away at boarding schools for nine months of the year, with their parents traveling in their own separate orbits, the Kennedy children had to discover each other and define themselves as a family. "The first time I remember meeting Bobby," as JFK put it, "was when he was three-and-a-half, one summer at the Cape." In the insulated, regimented, and often widely dispersed Kennedy family, the two brothers did not spend much time together until their world trip in 1951. [34]

From that inauspicious start grew what remains a unique partnership in U.S. political history. Not everyone thought it was a healthy development for American democracy, and the so-called "Bobby Kennedy Law" blocks its recurrence. Signed into law by Lyndon Johnson in 1967 when both Robert and Edward Kennedy were members of the Senate, the little-known law prohibits the president from appointing a relative to a position in the executive branch.[35] Thus, even though their long-term impact on U.S. politics and policies remains modest, the brothers Kennedy left a mark by their very presence together in high office.

Looking back later in life, Robert Kennedy viewed the time he and his brother worked together as the most productive and satisfying of his life, perhaps because his dedication to his brother allowed him to channel or redirect some of his inner conflicts. Throughout these years Robert showed two distinct sides—a self-righteous, persecuting side that gave and expected little quarter and knew no scruples, particularly where his family was concerned, and a humanistic, tender side that cared greatly for children, the disadvantaged, and the underdog. His dual nature seemed perfectly fitted to his joint duties as attorney general and overseer of his brother's administration. At times during his brother's presidency his softer side emerged, but most remembered the tougher, uncompromising side.

When the darkness descended in November 1963, many were surprised when that tender side of Robert Kennedy became more pronounced. Compelled to see the uncertainty in life, he loosened his grip on the notion that the world was comprised only of good guys and bad guys. Robert Kennedy, as Richard Goodwin observed, "found ambiguities in once unquestioned truths" and his "frightening righteousness diluted by doubt."[36]

JFK's assassination also severely tested the code of manly conduct Robert had lived under since pulling himself into the male orbit of the Kennedy family. Kennedys, he had been taught, never panic, lose control, or cry. He conditioned his own sons in these lessons, sometimes by stopping abruptly in the midst of play and slapping their faces rather hard. Children, he explained to a startled onlooker, "have to get used to being hit" and "learn to take it and go on," so there is "no surprise, no shock they can't sustain." If his slap made them cry, he hugged them and softly told them Kennedys never cried.[37]

Robert Kennedy cried but never showed the tears. His "most tenaciously maintained secret," Richard Goodwin wrote, was "a tenderness so rawly exposed, so vulnerable to painful abrasion, that it could only be shielded by angry compassion to human misery, manifest itself in love and loyalty toward those close to him, or through a revelatory humor."[38]

Part of being manly meant accepting what fate had dealt you. To deal with the cruel intersection of fate and chance he read Albert Camus, the French existentialist author and Nobel laureate, who wrote of people helpless in life's grip. And at Jacqueline's suggestion he read the ancient Greeks, finding words of understanding in the works of Herodotus and Aeschylus. "Man is not made for safe havens," he concluded. "If it's going to happen, it's going to happen."[39]

Robert Kennedy appeared physically diminished by JFK's death. Before Dallas people thought of him as a small man who seemed larger in person. Afterwards people thought of him as a large man who seemed smaller in person.[40] Psychiatrist Robert Coles noted "a tentative quality about his body, about the way he moved and the way he talked, which bespeaks a man who has a lot to say but isn't quite sure how to say it; who has a lot stirring in him but doesn't know how to put it into words." Kennedy, Coles continued, had a "kind of groping quality . . . an urgent tension" that left him struggling to express things that he felt.[41]

Uncertain about his future, he considered several options, including teaching, writing, taking a university presidency, traveling abroad or perhaps living abroad, or running for office in Massachusetts. What lay ahead, of course, were nine more months as attorney general, during which he would finally gain a conviction against Jimmy Hoffa. Ahead, too, lay the widening of the rifts with Lyndon Johnson and J. Edgar Hoover, leading Kennedy to leave the administration and gain election in November 1964 as U.S. senator from New York.

In his recovery from the despair of JFK's assassination, Robert Kennedy learned that finding solutions to America's social problems, not expanding its power on the world stage, should be the most important goal of government. Toward that end, he learned the art of mass politics—to use rhetoric to afflict the comfortable while encouraging the better angels in people, to demand compassion and sacrifice while stressing duties and responsibilities even for the disadvantaged. By 1966, in an intriguing and revealing aspect of Robert Kennedy's personality, he began to move left, the year the country began moving to the right. Then came the inevitable challenge for the presidency, which carried him to his own denouement in Los Angeles in June 1968.

With the burial of JFK, Robert Kennedy's trial by existence had passed. Now he faced another trial, this time on his own. In his depression, however, he found within a spiritual intensity and a sense of invincibility that he could channel simultaneously toward achieving social change, preserving his brother's legacy, and seeking the presidential nomination. His fundamental instincts, basic temperament, and innate character remained the same. What changed were his public and family roles and his belief in his own political and historic destiny. JFK's death and his own intimate involvement in the civil rights revolution had deepened Robert Kennedy's concerns for social inequities, until finally he became champion of the outcasts, the Jeremiah of the sixties.

Notes

Abbreviations used in the notes:

AG	Attorney General's Papers (RFK)
AG-GC	Attorney General's Papers, General Correspondence Files
AG-PC	Attorney General's Papers, Personal Correspondence Files
CIA	Central Intelligence Agency
EMK	Edward M. "Teddy" Kennedy
JFK	John F. Kennedy
JFK-ARC	John Fitzgerald Kennedy Assassination Records Collection, National Archives (College Park, Maryland)
JFKL	John F. Kennedy Library (Boston, Massachusetts)
JPK	Joseph P. Kennedy
LBJL	Lyndon B. Johnson Library (Austin, Texas)
MACV	Military Advisory Command Vietnam
NSAM	National Security Action Memorandum
NSC	National Security Council
O&C	J. Edgar Hoover's Official & Confidential File
OH-JFK	John F. Kennedy Oral History Program, JFK Library
OH-RFK	Robert F. Kennedy Oral History Program, JFK Library
PAP-RFK	Pre-Administration Papers, RFK
PCP	Presidential Campaign Papers
RFK	Robert F. Kennedy
RFK-FBI	Robert F. Kennedy's FBI File
RFK-JFKL	Robert F. Kennedy Papers, JFK Library

SP	Robert F. Kennedy Senate Papers, JFK Library
SP-GC	Robert F. Kennedy Senate Papers, General Correspondence
SP-PC	Robert F. Kennedy Senate Papers, Personal Correspondence
WHCSF	White House Central Subject Files
WHSF	White House Staff Files

INTRODUCTION

1. For original expositions of the Kennedy legacy, see Theodore C. Sorensen, *The Kennedy Legacy: A Peaceful Revolution for the Seventies* (New York: Mentor, 1970); Arthur M. Schlesinger, Jr., *A Thousand Days: John F. Kennedy in the White House* (Boston: Houghton Mifflin, 1965), and *Robert Kennedy and His Times* (Boston: Houghton Mifflin, 1978); David Burner and Thomas R. West, *The Torch Is Passed: The Kennedy Brothers and American Liberalism* (St. James, N.Y.: Brandywine, 1984); and, more recently, Wilfred Sheed and Jacques Lowe, *The Kennedy Legacy: A Generation Later* (New York: Viking Penguin, 1988), and Hays Gorey and Bill Eppridge, *Robert Kennedy: The Last Campaign* (New York: Harcourt Brace, 1993). For critical analyses, see Henry Fairlie, *The Kennedy Promise* (New York: Dell, 1973); Garry Wills, *The Kennedy Imprisonment: A Meditation on Power* (Boston: Little, Brown, 1982); Bruce Miroff, *Pragmatic Illusions: The Presidential Politics of John F. Kennedy* (New York: McKay, 1976); Thomas Brown, *JFK: History of an Image* (Bloomington: Indiana U. Press, 1988); and David Burner, *John F. Kennedy and a New Generation* (Boston: Little, Brown, 1988).
2. Arthur M. Schlesinger, Jr., introduction to Robert Kennedy, *Robert Kennedy in His Own Words: The Unpublished Recollections of the Kennedy Years,* ed. Edwin O. Guthman and Jeffrey Shulman (New York: Bantam, 1988), xvii; Jack Newfield, *Robert Kennedy: A Memoir* (New York: New American Library, 1969), 9; Irwin Unger and Debi Unger, *America in the 1960s* (St. James, New York: Brandywine, 1993), 256–57.
3. On Max Weber's definitions of charisma and the transitory nature of the Kennedys' charismatic power, see Wills, *The Kennedy Imprisonment,* 170–74.
4. Newfield, *Robert Kennedy,* 32. Philip Roth, *The Facts: A Novelist's Autobiography* (New York: Farrar, Straus and Giroux, 1988), 147–48. Richard Goodwin, *Remembering America: A Voice from the Sixties* (Boston: Little, Brown, 1988), 443.
5. Lewis Chester, Godfrey Hodgson, and Bruce Page, *An American Melodrama: The Presidential Campaign of 1968* (New York: Viking, 1969), 116. Victor Lasky, *Robert F. Kennedy: The Myth and the Man* (New York: Trident, 1968), 396.
6. Harris Wofford, *Of Kennedys and Kings: Making Sense of the Sixties* (New York: Farrar, Straus and Giroux, 1980), 458, and Harris Wofford, interview by the author, 20 May 1989, in Philadelphia.
7. Newfield, *Robert Kennedy,* 42.
8. Schlesinger, introduction to *Robert Kennedy,* xiv, xv. Also see Doris Kearns Goodwin, *The Fitzgeralds and the Kennedys* (New York: St. Martin's, 1987), 424.
9. Goodwin, *Fitzgeralds and Kennedys,* 410–11; Peter Collier and David Horowitz,

The Kennedys: An American Drama (New York: Warner, 1984), 195; Herbert S. Parmet, *Jack: The Struggles of John F. Kennedy* (New York: Dial, 1980), 362–64.

10. For two disparate views, see Edwin Guthman, *We Band of Brothers* (New York: Harper and Row, 1971), and Victor S. Navasky, *Kennedy Justice* (New York: Atheneum, 1971).

CHAPTER 1

1. One might make a case for the four Washburn brothers. Born in Livermore, Maine, they represented four different states in Congress and held other high posts. Israel Washburn (1813–1883), a Whig, served in the House (1851–1861) and was Maine's governor (1861–1862); Cadwallader C. Washburn (1818–1882), a Wisconsin Republican, served in the House (1855–1861); William D. Washburn (1831–1912) was elected to the House (1879–1885) and the Senate (1889–1895) from Minnesota; and Elihu B. Washburne (he added the "e") (1816–1887), an Illinois Whig-Republican, served in the House (1853–1869) before President Grant appointed him Secretary of State (1869) and Minister to France (1869–1877). *Who Was Who in American Politics* by Dan and Inez Morris (New York: Hawthorn Books, 1974), 594–95.
2. Congressman Burr P. Harrison (D-Va.), "Introducing Bobby Kennedy," before the Virginia State Bar Association, Box 68, AG-GC. John Adams (1735–1826), the second president, was father of the sixth president, John Quincy Adams (1767–1848); grandfather of Charles Francis Adams, Sr. (1807–1886), ambassador to England; and great-grandfather of intellectuals Charles Francis Adams, Jr. (1835–1915), and Henry Adams (1838–1918). On the influence of a family's past on its children's destiny, see David F. Musto, "Continuity across Generations: The Adams Family Myth," in *Kin and Communities: Families in America,* ed. by Allan J. Lichtman and Joan R. Challinor (Washington, D.C.: Smithsonian, 1979), 77–94.
3. James Reston, *Deadline: A Memoir* (New York: Random House, 1991), 297. Two of Joseph Kennedy's daughters also achieved prominence as public servants: Eunice Kennedy Shriver became a foundation head and the founder of the Special Olympics; Jean Kennedy Smith was appointed ambassador to Ireland by President Clinton. At this writing, four of Joseph Kennedy's grandchildren hold public office: Joseph P. Kennedy II of Massachusetts and Patrick Kennedy of Rhode Island serve in Congress, Kathleen Kennedy Townsend is the lieutenant governor of Maryland, and Mark Kennedy Shriver is a member of the Maryland House of Delegates.
4. Quoted in Goodwin, *Fitzgeralds and Kennedys,* 496. "The boys might as well work for the government," Joe told his wife, "because politics will control the business of the country in the future." Arthur M. Schlesinger, Jr., *Robert Kennedy and His Times* (New York: Ballantine, 1978), 16.
5. William V. Shannon, *The American Irish: A Political and Social Portrait,* 2d ed.(Amherst: U. of Massachusetts Press, 1989), 393; Oscar Handlin, *Boston's Immigrants, 1790–1865* (New York: Atheneum, 1969), 176.

6. Peter Collier and David Horowitz, *The Kennedys: An American Drama* (New York: Warner, 1984), 10–17; Goodwin, *Fitzgeralds and Kennedys,* 264–271; John H. Davis, *The Kennedys: Dynasty and Disaster, 1848–1984* (New York: McGraw-Hill, 1984), 3–27. On the Irish in American cities, see Handlin, *Boston's Immigrants 1790–1865;* Dennis Clark, *The Irish in Philadelphia* (Philadelphia: Temple U. Press, 1973).
7. Collier and Horowitz, *The Kennedys,* 22; Herbert S. Parmet, *Jack: The Struggles of John F. Kennedy* (New York: Dial, 1980), 4–5.
8. Collier and Horowitz, *The Kennedys,* 21; Goodwin, *Fitzgeralds and Kennedys,* 265.
9. Until 1964, when entrance exams were instituted, and 1975, when an affirmative-action quota system was established, admission to Boston Latin was determined through an informal system linking a student's academic record and his parents' social or political prominence. *Philadelphia Inquirer,* 16 December 1996.
10. Classmate interview quoted in Collier and Horowitz, *The Kennedys,* 26. Also see Richard J. Whalen, *The Founding Father: Joseph P. Kennedy and the Family He Raised to Power* (New York: New American Library, 1964), 34–36; Ronald Kessler, *The Sins of the Father* (New York: Warner, 1996), 16–17, 20–23.
11. Goodwin, *Fitzgeralds and Kennedys,* 270–71; Nigel Hamilton, *JFK: Reckless Youth* (New York: Random House, 1992), 739.
12. Hamilton, *JFK,* 7–12; Goodwin, *Fitzgeralds and Kennedys,* 122.
13. "Though no charge of corruption was ever substantiated," Doris Goodwin concluded, "the gap between his legal income and his high level of spending would seem circumstantial evidence enough to suggest that something underhanded was going on." *Fitzgeralds and Kennedys,* 179; also see 184, 229.
14. Rose Fitzgerald Kennedy, *Times to Remember* (London: Pan, 1975), 33–49; Rose Kennedy, interview by Goodwin, *Fitzgeralds and Kennedys,* 167–68, 182.
15. Goodwin, *Fitzgeralds and Kennedys,* 294–96.
16. Whalen, *Founding Father,* 42–43, 46–47.
17. Ibid., 56.
18. Kessler, *Sins of the Father,* 32.
19. Goodwin, *Fitzgeralds and Kennedys,* 327, 351–59, 383; Whalen, *Founding Father,* 57–63, 68–71; Hamilton, *Reckless Youth,* 29, 34–37.
20. Rose Kennedy, *Times to Remember,* 89–90. The address of the house, originally 51 Abbottsford Road, later changed to 131 Naples Road. Kessler, *Sins of the Father,* 36.
21. Rose Kennedy, *Times to Remember,* 110; K. LeMoyne Billings, interview by Jean Stein and George Plimpton, eds. *American Journey: The Times of Robert Kennedy* (New York: Harcourt Brace Jovanovich, 1970), 38; Schlesinger, *Robert Kennedy,* 23; Goodwin, *Fitzgeralds and Kennedys,* 424 ("little pet" quote, 738).
22. Rose Kennedy, *Times to Remember,* 110; Robert E. Thompson and Hortense Meyers, *Robert F. Kennedy: The Brother Within* (New York: Macmillan, 1962), 64; Parmet, *Jack,* 23; Goodwin, *Fitzgeralds and Kennedys,* 424; K. LeMoyne Billings (John Kennedy's roommate at Choate School), interview by Lester

David and Irene David, *Bobby Kennedy: The Making of a Folk Hero* (New York: PaperJacks, 1988), 15.

23. Cf. Nancy Gager Clinch, *The Kennedy Neurosis* (New York: Grosset and Dunlap, 1973), 260–322, who concluded that all the Kennedy men suffered from "personality neurosis" due in large part to their family environment. She found Robert "torn by inner turmoil, indecisiveness, and self-defeatism," possessed of "profound self-doubt" since childhood (320–21).
24. Goodwin, *Fitzgeralds and Kennedys,* 366.
25. Michael Novak interview by Stein and Plimpton, *American Journey,* 235.
26. Schlesinger, *Robert Kennedy,* 15. Not all Kennedys pretended to be so tough. When John F. Kennedy, Jr., took a bad fall on skis and began to cry, RFK told him, "Kennedys never cry." The slain president's son replied, "This Kennedy does." Richard Goodwin, *Remembering America: A Voice from the Sixties* (Boston: Little, Brown, 1988), 444.
27. Goodwin, *Fitzgeralds and Kennedys,* 407.
28. On Joseph Kennedy's financial dealings, see Whalen, *Founding Father,* 68–117; Goodwin, *Fitzgeralds and Kennedys,* 380–92, 429–92; Collier and Horowitz, *The Kennedys,* 35–39, 46–50; Kessler, *Sins of the Father,* 34–38, 80–92 on business, and 52–79 on Swanson and the movies.
29. Goodwin, *Fitzgeralds and Kennedys,* 494; Hamilton, *JFK,* 63–77.
30. Garry Wills, *The Kennedy Imprisonment: A Meditation on Power* (Boston: Little, Brown, 1982), 16.
31. Ibid., 41.
32. Goodwin, *Fitzgeralds and Kennedys,* 372–74; Collier and Horowitz, *The Kennedys,* 56; Hamilton, *JFK,* 73–75, 160; Rose Kennedy, *Times to Remember,* 85.
33. Rose Kennedy, *Times to Remember,* 84, 87, 88, 362–63; Goodwin, *Fitzgeralds and Kennedys,* 365, 372–74, 461; Hamilton, *JFK,* 49–50, 73–75; James M. Burns, *Edward Kennedy and the Camelot Legacy* (New York: Norton, 1976), 26.
34. Kessler, *Sins of the Father,* 14.
35. Goodwin, *Fitzgeralds and Kennedys,* 408; Collier and Horowitz, *The Kennedys,* 56; Schlesinger, *Robert Kennedy,* 17; Arthur Schlesinger, Jr., *A Thousand Days: John F. Kennedy in the White House* (Boston: Houghton Mifflin, 1965), 79. On JPK's control of the dinner table, see Ralph G. Martin, *Seeds of Destruction: Joe Kennedy and His Sons* (New York: Putnam, 1995), 41–42.
36. Collier and Horowitz, *The Kennedys,* 57; Goodwin, *Fitzgeralds and Kennedys,* 866–67.
37. Tom Bilodeau, Joe Junior's Harvard classmate, interview by Collier and Horowitz, *The Kennedys,* 99; Goodwin, *Fitzgeralds and Kennedys,* 739; Harris Wofford, *Of Kennedys and Kings: Making Sense of the Sixties* (New York: Farrar, Straus and Giroux, 1980), 91.
38. Goodwin, *Remembering America,* 443. "Struggle to survive" is from Robert F. Kennedy, *Robert Kennedy in His Own Words: The Unpublished Recollections of the*

Kennedy Years, ed. Edwin O. Guthman and Jeffrey Shulman (New York: Bantam, 1988), xiv. Remarks on competition within the family are from a filmed interview of RFK (1959) used in "RFK: In His Own Words," (HBO production, 1990).

39. Goodwin, *Fitzgeralds and Kennedys,* 409–11. Shortly before John's sixth birthday, Rose took a six-week trip to California. As she prepared to leave, John said, "Gee, *you're* a great mother to go away and leave your children all alone." Rose Kennedy, *Times to Remember,* 100.
40. Rose Kennedy, *Times to Remember,* 110–11.
41. Ibid, 180. Schlesinger, *Robert Kennedy,* 24.
42. Goodwin *Fitzgeralds and Kennedys,* 428; Martin, *Seeds of Destruction,* 16–17.
43. Handlin, *Boston's Immigrants,* 176. Irish Americans, Handlin wrote, could be wholly American in behavior but still "somewhat quizzical, sardonic, critical." James M. Burns, *The Crosswinds of Freedom* (New York: Vintage, 1990), 309.
44. Burns, *Crosswinds of Freedom,* 310. Patriarchs of other prominent American families of Irish descent held similar goals but did not press the matter as openly or aggrssively as Kennedy. John B. Kelly (contractor, Olympic champion, reform politician, and father of actress Grace Kelly) failed to break Philadelphia's class and caste barriers. Similarly, Texas oil man William Frank Buckley, father of intellectual William F. Buckley, Jr., and James Buckley, who succeeded eventually to Robert Kennedy's Senate seat, moved away from his ethnic origins to create "a private world for his children, a rootless aristocracy of merit." Dennis Clark, *The Irish in Philadelphia* (Philadelphia: Temple U. Press, 1973), 156–57; Wills, *Kennedy Imprisonment,* 68–71.
45. Michael M. Mooney to RFK, 10 August 1966; RFK to Mooney, 18 August 1966, RFK-SP, Box 8. Schlesinger, *Robert Kennedy,* 6.
46. Wills, *Kennedy Imprisonment,* 61–71. John F. Kennedy, according to James M. Burns, "grew up half Irish, half Harvard." Burns, *Crosswinds of Freedom,* 310.
47. Schlesinger, *Robert Kennedy,* 7, 13.
48. Goodwin, *Fitzgeralds and Kennedys,* 380; Collier and Horowitz, *The Kennedys,* 44; Schlesinger, *Robert Kennedy,* 7. A former summer resident of Cohasset told me that it was not the Kennedy's Irishnesss or Catholicism that they found offensive, but rather their "obnoxious" children and the mother's ostentatious plum-colored Rolls Royce.
49. Rose Kennedy, *Times to Remember,* 184, 361–62. Kennedy reportedly paid $250,000 for the property, originally built for Adolphus Busch, cofounder of Anheuser-Busch brewery. Kessler, *Sins of the Father,* 81.
50. LeMoyne Billings, interview by Collier and Horowitz, *The Kennedys,* 56, 62.
51. David and David, *Bobby Kennedy,* 16–17; Goodwin, *Fitzgeralds and Kennedys,* 494–95; Rose Kennedy, *Times to Remember,* 277.
52. *Robert Kennedy: In His Own Words,* 66–67. By way of contrast, RFK's future nemesis, James R. Hoffa, was grateful simply to have a job during the Depression. He worked forty-eight hours a week unloading fruit and produce from railroad cars for thirty-two cents an hour. Arthur A. Sloane, *Hoffa* (Cambridge: MIT Press, 1991), 7.
53. Rose Kennedy, *Times to Remember,* 125–27.

54. William V. Shannon, *The Heir Apparent: Robert Kennedy and the Struggle for Power* (New York: Macmillan, 1967), 58.
55. Rose Kennedy, *Times to Remember,* 185, 128; David and David, *Bobby Kennedy,* 16; Goodwin, *Fitzgeralds and Kennedys,* 492; Collier and Horowitz, *The Kennedys,* 131, 167–68; Hamilton, *JFK,* 160.
56. Whalen, *Founding Father,* 116–130.
57. Collier and Horowitz, *The Kennedys,* 79; Whalen, *Founding Father,* 131; Harold L. Ickes, *The Secret Diary of Harold L. Ickes: The First Thousand Days* (New York: Simon and Schuster, 1953), 173; Kessler, *Sins of the Father,* 93–130.
58. Whalen, *Founding Father,* 131–32; Collier and Horowitz, *The Kennedys,* 79; Schlesinger, *Robert Kennedy,* 7.
59. Whalen, *Founding Father,* 174–76; Arthur M. Schlesinger, Jr., *The Coming of the New Deal* (Boston: Houghton Mifflin, 1965), 467–70.
60. RFK's Pre-Administration Papers, Box 1, contains the invitation and other memorabilia. Doris Kearns Goodwin was permitted access to RFK's diary and other materials regarding his youth while writing *The Fitzgeralds and the Kennedys,* which for now is the definitive source for such information. Also, see David and David, *Bobby Kennedy,* 18–19.
61. Whalen, *Founding Father,* 195–201.
62. Goodwin, *Fitzgeralds and Kennedys,* 624, 674, 679.
63. In her 1967 oral history interview for the JFK Library, Kay Halle, a friend of JFK's, noted this "curious paradox" that "the advantaged classes in England should have imprinted itself upon an Irishman, and such an Irishman as Joe." Martin, *Seeds of Destruction,* 43.
64. Kathleen Thom and Jewell Reed, interviews by Joan Blair and Clay Blair, Jr., *The Search for JFK* (New York: Berkley, 1976), 360-61.
65. For a description of Whig country houses and life-styles, see David Cecil, *Melbourne* (Indianapolis: Charter, reprinted 1962), 15–21.
66. Cecil, *Melbourne,* 19. Published in 1939 while the Kennedys were in London, *Melbourne* is often mentioned as John Kennedy's "favorite" book.
67. Quoted in Michael R. Beschloss, *Kennedy and Roosevelt: The Uneasy Alliance* (New York: Harper and Row, 1980), 26.
68. Luella Hennessey Donovon, interview by Goodwin, *Fitzgeralds and Kennedys,* 625, and by David and David, *Bobby Kennedy,* 22–23.
69. Schlesinger, *Robert Kennedy,* 18.
70. See, for example, David and David, *Bobby Kennedy, 22.*
71. "Suggested Remarks" for Robert Kennedy at the laying of the cornerstone of the Clubland Temple of Youth in Camberwell, S.E. (London), Folder 2, Box 1, PAP-RFK. Also see Schlesinger, *Robert Kennedy,* 28.
72. Goodwin, *Fitzgeralds and Kennedys,* 580–81; Collier and Horowitz, *The Kennedys,* 80–84; Thomas Brown, *JFK: History of an Image* (Bloomington: Indiana U. Press, 1988); Beschloss, *Kennedy and Roosevelt,* 108–111, 160–61, 182; Hamilton, *JFK,* 375; Kessler, *Sins of the Father,* 143–44.

73. Goodwin, *Fitzgeralds and Kennedys,* 660–64; Beschloss, *Kennedy and Roosevelt,* 158–237; Kessler, *Sins of the Father,* 157–225.
74. Roosevelt is quoted in Goodwin, *Fitzgeralds and Kennedys,* 638.
75. Whalen, *Founding Father,* 202–314; Beschloss, *Kennedy and Roosevelt,* 171–215; Hamilton, *JFK,* 309–12, 323–25.
76. Beschloss, *Kennedy and Roosevelt,* 216–21; Hamilton, *JFK,* 368–69; Kessler, *Sins of the Father,* 225.
77. William E. Leuchtenburg, *In the Shadow of FDR* (Ithaca, N.Y.: Cornell U. Press, 1983), 81, 283*n,* for comments on the validity of accounts of the Hyde Park meeting. Gore Vidal, review of Joseph P. Lash, *Eleanor and Franklin, New York Review of Books,* 18 November 1971, 8, attributes more colorful language to FDR; also, Beschloss, *Kennedy and Roosevelt,* 222–99. Also see Collier and Horowitz, *The Kennedys,* 104–27; Whalen, *Founding Father,* 202–341; Goodwin, *Fitzgeralds and Kennedys,* 615–715; Schlesinger, *Robert Kennedy,* 31–39; David E. Koskoff, *Joseph P. Kennedy: A Life and Times* (Englewood Cliffs, N.J.: Prentice-Hall, 1974), 571; Kessler, *Sins of the Father,* 230.
78. FDR letter to his son-in-law John Boettinger, cited in Doris Kearns Goodwin, *No Ordinary Time. Franklin & Eleanor Roosevelt: The Home Front in World War II* (New York: Simon & Schuster, 1994), 210–12.

CHAPTER 2

1. Doris Kearns Goodwin, *The Fitzgeralds and the Kennedys: An American Saga* (New York: St. Martin's, 1987), 739.
2. For an examination of JFK's thinking on this formative matter and for details on the father's use of his position to get the book published, see Nigel Hamilton, *JFK: Reckless Youth* (New York: Random House, 1992), 275–338; also, Ralph G. Martin, *Seeds of Destruction: Joe Kennedy and His Sons* (New York: Putnam, 1995) 84–85. James David Barber, *The Presidential Character* (Englewood Cliffs, N.J.: Prentice-Hall, 1972), 304–9; and David Burner and Thomas R. West, *The Torch Is Passed: The Kennedy Brothers and American Liberalism* (St. James, N.Y.: Brandywine, 1984), 34–37, also offer balanced and reflective assessments. For unsparing criticisms, see Ronald Kessler, *The Sins of the Father* (New York: Warner, 1996), 218–20.
3. Peter Collier and David Horowitz, *The Kennedys: An American Drama* (New York: Warner, 1984), 121; Hamilton, *JFK,* 321.
4. Thomas C. Reeves, *A Question of Character: A Life of John F. Kennedy* (New York: Free Press, 1991), 55; Joan Blair and Clay Blair, Jr., *The Search for JFK* (New York: Berkley 1976) 91, 101–2, 108–11; Hamilton, *JFK,* 406–9.
5. Goodwin, *Fitzgeralds and Kennedys,* 740–46; Hamilton, *JFK,* 411–12. Kessler, *Sins of the Father,* 238–55, contends that Rosemary simply had a below-average IQ and suffered from mental illness (reactive depression) induced by the family's insensitive treatment of her, and that JPK accepted the portrayal of Rosemary as mentally disabled to avoid the deeper stigma of mental illness. In effect, Kessler

contends that Rosemary was driven mad by the father's high expectations. Rosemary's disability, however, was evident from an early age and Eunice and Rose openly acknowledged it. See, for example, Collier and Horowitz, *The Kennedys,* 68–70, 116, 132–35; John H. Davis, *The Kennedys: Dynasty and Disaster, 1848–1984* (New York: McGraw-Hill, 1984), 133–34.

6. Rosemary today is wheelchair bound and requires constant care. Interviews of guests at Eunice Shriver's home report seeing Rosemary there frequently. On Eunice's concern for children with mental disabilities, see Collier and Horowitz, *The Kennedys,* 527. My mother spoke briefly with Rose Kennedy in 1960 at a mental retardation symposium at which Rose described herself as the parent of a "retarded" child whose condition was similar to my brother's. Later, at a political meeting, Rose greeted my mother by again mentioning their mutual concerns as mothers of "retarded" children.
7. "Mrs. Paul Fejos, nee Inga Arvad; Internal Security-Espionage-G," Folder 7, O&C. Also see Blair and Blair, *The Search for JFK,* 122–53; Goodwin, *Fitzgeralds and Kennedys,* 729–35; Collier and Horowitz, *The Kennedys,* 111–12; Hamilton, *JFK,* 420–94, 498–506; Anthony Summers, *Official and Confidential: The Secret Life of J. Edgar Hoover* (New York: Free Press, 1987), 264–66; Curt Gentry, *J. Edgar Hoover: The Man and the Secrets* (New York: Norton, 1991), 467–70; Athan Theoharis, ed., *From the Secret Files of J. Edgar Hoover* (Chicago: Dee, 1991), 15–31; Kessler, *Sins of the Father,* 256–65.
8. James M. Burns, *Roosevelt: The Soldier of Freedom* (New York: Harcourt Brace Jovanovich, 1970), 211; Michael R. Beschloss, *Kennedy and Roosevelt: The Uneasy Alliance* (New York: Harper and Row, 1980), 243–60; Hamilton, *JFK,* 484; Summers, *Official and Confidential,* 260–62; Gentry, *J. Edgar Hoover,* 384–85; "Joseph P. Kennedy," Folder 14, O&C.
9. Herbert S. Parmet, *Jack: The Struggles of John F. Kennedy* (New York: Dial, 1980), 56, 138.
10. Hamilton, *JFK,* 84–88.
11. Lester David and Irene David, *Bobby Kennedy: The Making of a Folk Hero* (New York: Paperjacks, 1988), 27–29.
12. Quoted in Burner and West, *The Torch Is Passed,* 194.
13. Arthur M. Schlesinger, Jr., *Robert Kennedy and His Times* (Boston: Houghton Mifflin, 1978), 33, 44–45; Rose Kennedy, *Times to Remember* (Garden City, N.Y.: Doubleday, 1974), 280.
14. Schlesinger, *Robert Kennedy,* 44–45; Chuck Spalding, interview by Collier and Horowitz, *The Kennedys,* 217.
15. Schlesinger, *Robert Kennedy,* 45; David and David, *Bobby Kennedy,* 30.
16. Goodwin, *Fitzgeralds and Kennedys,* 737–39.
17. Classmate and lifelong friend David Hackett saw RFK as "an underdog in sports, with studies and girls and as a Catholic." See Schlesinger, *Robert Kennedy,* 49; David and David, *Bobby Kennedy,* 26; Parmet, *Jack,* 36- 37; Hamilton, *JFK,* 119–28.
18. Schlesinger, *Robert Kennedy,* 49.

19. David and David, *Bobby Kennedy,* 34; Schlesinger, *Robert Kennedy,* 47.
20. Mary Bailey Gimbel, interview by Jean Stein and George Plimpton, eds., *American Journey: The Times of Robert Kennedy* (New York: Harcourt Brace Jovanovich, 1970), 36; Schlesinger, *Robert Kennedy,* 46–47; Collier and Horowitz, *The Kennedys,* 138; David and David, *Bobby Kennedy,* 35.
21. Hank Searls, *The Lost Prince* (Cleveland: World, 1969), 196; David and David, *Bobby Kennedy,* 35.
22. Hamilton, *JFK,* 646; JFK to Joseph Kennedy, ca. September 1943, Box 6, SP-PC.
23. Joe Timilty, interview by Blair and Blair, *The Search for JFK,* 296, also see 203–316; Parmet, *Jack,* 100–114; Hamilton, *JFK,* 528–633, 658–61.
24. Searls, *Lost Prince,* 214–250; Goodwin, *Fitzgeralds and Kennedys,* 794–96, Kathleen Kennedy quote, 805–6; Schlesinger, *Robert Kennedy,* 61.
25. John Kennedy quoted in Collier and Horowitz, *The Kennedys,* 169. Hamilton, *JFK,* 665, 673. Joseph Kennedy turned his wrathful frustrations on FDR. During the 1944 campaign, when Harry Truman came to Boston to campaign for FDR, JPK asked him, "Harry, what the hell are you doing campaigning for that crippled son of a bitch that killed my son Joe?" Quoted in Schlesinger, *Robert Kennedy,* 61; Parmet, *Jack,* 141.
26. Rose Kennedy, *Times to Remember,* 323–24; Collier and Horowitz, *The Kennedys,* 187, 621.
27. See, for example, Richard R. Lingeman, *Don't You Know There's a War On?* (New York: Putnam, 1970), 29, 177, 211–16, 221. Ironically, RFK developed an affinity for youths of the Vietnam War protest era who sought to postpone adulthood, or extend adolescence.
28. Schlesinger, *Robert Kennedy,* 56; Hamilton, *JFK,* 627.
29. Quoted in Schlesinger, *Robert Kennedy,* 57.
30. Ibid., 64, 67; Goodwin, *Fitzgeralds and Kennedys,* 738–39.
31. Fred Lindquist, a member of the V-12 unit, interview by the author, 4 June 1990 in Philadelphia. *Navy R.O.T.C. and V-12 Unit Harvard University* (Baton Rouge, La.: Army and Navy Publishing Company of Louisiana, 1944) in Lindquist's possession.
32. Schlesinger, *Robert Kennedy,* 63.
33. Hamilton, *JFK,* 646, 766; Schlesinger, *Robert Kennedy,* 65–66; "There I was . . ." quote from Gene Schoor's personal file, cited in David and David, *Bobby Kennedy,* 42.
34. Collier and Horowitz, *The Kennedys,* 217, describes RFK as "the most intense member of the family and the most loyal to its household gods." Jewell Reed, interview by Blair and Blair *The Search for JFK,* 357.
35. Interview with Mary Bailey Gimbel, quoted in Collier and Horowitz, *The Kennedys,* 73.
36. Schlesinger, *Robert Kennedy,* 50; David and David, *Bobby Kennedy,* 43.
37. Hamilton, *JFK,* 461, 469, 504, 549–50, 673, 678.
38. Hamilton, *JFK,* 670–774, offers the most thorough account of the 1946 race. Also

see Goodwin, *Fitzgeralds and Kennedys,* 814–34; Davis, *The Kennedys,* 148–55; Thomas P. "Tip" O'Neill, *Man of the House* (New York: St. Martin's, 1987), 83–84.

39. Quotes from Collier and Horowitz, *The Kennedys,* 185; David and David, *Bobby Kennedy,* 52; also see Schlesinger, *Robert Kennedy,* 68–69; Robert F. Kennedy, *Robert Kennedy in His Own Words:The Unpublished Recollections of the Kennedy Years,* ed. Edwin O. Guthman and Jeffrey Shuman (New York: Bantam, 1988), 432–33; Hamilton, *JFK,* 766–67.
40. William V. Shannon, *The American Irish: A Political and Social Portrait* (Amherst: U. of Massachusetts Press, 1989), 401; Goodwin, *Fitzgeralds and Kennedys,* 868; Schlesinger, *Robert Kennedy,* 68–70.
41. O'Neill, *Man of the House,* 84–85.
42. Schlesinger, *Robert Kennedy,* 68–69; Goodwin, *Fitzgeralds and Kennedys,* 816–34; RFK, *Robert Kennedy,* 433.
43. Richard J. Whalen, *The Founding Father: Joseph P. Kennedy and The Family He Raised to Power* (New York: New American Library, 1964), 388–89; O'Neill, *Man of the House,* 87.
44. O'Neill, *Man of the House,* 95–96.
45. Ibid., 87.
46. Goodwin, *Fitzgeralds and Kennedys,* 830–34.
47. Hamilton, *JFK,* 753; O'Neill, *Man of the House,* 86.
48. Tip O'Neill (*Man of the House,* 88) claims JPK spent $300,000 in 1946 and admits to spending $50,000 in his campaign for the same seat in 1952. Whalen, *Founding Father,* 390, reports an insider who claimed (improbably) that the actual expenditures were around $25,000. Also see Goodwin, *Fitzgeralds and Kennedys,* 825; O'Neill, *Man of the House,* 88–89.
49. Hamilton, *JFK,* 758; RFK, *Robert Kennedy,* 435.
50. RFK may have injured the leg during a particularly rugged preseason scrimmage against Boston College and played in the Western Maryland game in spite of the injury (often described as a "broken" leg, although nothing indicates that it ever required a cast). Kenneth O'Donnell, interview by Jean Stein and George Plimpton, eds., *American Journey: The Times of Robert Kennedy* (New York: Harcourt Brace Jovanovich, 1970), 38–40; Donald Stone, interview by author, 8 October 1996; Goodwin, *Fitzgeralds and Kennedys,* 879; Schlesinger, *Robert Kennedy,* 70–73; Collier & Horowitz, *The Kennedys,* 217; David and David, *Kennedy,* 44.
51. Stone interview; Schlesinger, *Robert Kennedy,* 71; O'Donnell interview, 38–40.
52. Richard Goodwin, *Remembering America: A Voice from the Sixties,* (Boston: Little, Brown, 1988), 446–47; Schlesinger, *Robert Kennedy,* 71.
53. George Terrien, interview by Jerry Oppenheimer, *The Other Mrs. Kennedy—Ethel Skakel Kennedy: An American Drama of Power, Privilege, and Politics* (New York: St. Martin's, 1994), 106.
54. John Magnuson, interview by Collier and Horowitz, *The Kennedys,* 217–18.
55. Terrien interview, 116.
56. Schlesinger, *Robert Kennedy,* 80–84, notes in the articles a "maturity, cogency

and, from time to time, literary finish creditable for a football player of twenty-two hardly out of college." JPK letter in Goodwin, *Fitzgeralds and Kennedys,* 879.

57. At Kathleen's death, Rose sent out mass cards that contained a plea for a plenary indulgence for her daughter, whom she regarded as in purgatory. Collier and Horowitz, *The Kennedys,* 203–7; Davis, *The Kennedys,* 129–31; Goodwin, *Fitzgeralds and Kennedys,* 851–57. In 1965 Rose thought it "interesting" that hundreds of persons daily visited her daughter's gravesite and the stone commemorating John Kennedy's visits to it. Rose Kennedy to Children, 9 September 1965, Box 6, SP-PC.
58. Oppenheimer, *The Other Mrs. Kennedy,* 117; David and David, *Bobby Kennedy,* 39–40; Blair and Blair, *In Search of JFK,* 325. Kathleen Kennedy Townsend was elected lieutenant governor of Maryland in 1994.
59. David and David, *Bobby Kennedy,* 55; Oppenheimer, *The Other Mrs. Kennedy,* 132–33.
60. This account relies on Schlesinger, *Robert Kennedy,* 92–94; David and David, *Bobby Kennedy,* 57–58; Collier and Horowitz, *The Kennedys,* 217.
61. Quoted in Lester David, *Ethel: The Story of Mrs. Robert F. Kennedy* (New York: World, 1971), 120.
62. Oppenheimer, *The Other Mrs. Kennedy,* 36.
63. David, *Ethel,* 3–31; Oppenheimer, *The Other Mrs. Kennedy,* 50–51.
64. Interview with Martin McKneally, Ethel's tutor, quoted in Oppenheimer, *The Other Mrs. Kennedy,* 58 (on Ethel's piety), 64–66 (on Ethel's skills with horses).
65. Oppenheimer, *The Other Mrs. Kennedy,* 79–85.
66. Joan Winmill, interview by Oppenheimer, *The Other Mrs. Kennedy,* 116–20.
67. David and David, *Bobby Kennedy,* 53–54; David, *Ethel,* 44–48; Schlesinger, *Robert Kennedy,* 94–97; Oppenheimer, *The Other Mrs. Kennedy,* 125–31.
68. Collier and Horowitz, *The Kennedys,* 219.
69. David, *Ethel,* 69.
70. Quoted in Collier and Horowitz, *The Kennedys,* 237.

CHAPTER 3

1. David McCullough, *Truman* (New York: Simon and Schuster, 1992), 782.
2. Arthur M. Schlesinger, Jr., *Robert Kennedy and His Times* (New York: Ballantine, 1978), 91–92.
3. James Giglio, *The Presidency of John F. Kennedy* (Lawrence: U. of Kansas Press, 1991), 18; Robert Griffith, "American Politics and the Origins of 'McCarthyism,'" in *The Specter,* ed. Griffith and Athan Theoharis (New York: New Viewpoints, 1974), 4.
4. Lillian Hellman, *Scoundrel Time* (Boston: Little, Brown, 1976). For the best overviews, see Richard Rovere, *Senator Joe McCarthy* (New York: World, 1959); David Oshinsky, *A Conspiracy So Immense: The World of Joe McCarthy* (New York: Free Press, 1983); and Stanley Kutler, *The American Inquisition* (New York: Hill & Wang, 1982).

5. Robert Griffith, *The Politics of Fear: Joseph R. McCarthy and the Senate* (Lexington: U. of Kentucky Press, 1970), 49; Curt Gentry, *J. Edgar Hoover: The Man and the Secrets* (New York: Norton, 1991), 378–79.
6. Herbert Parmet, *Jack: The Struggles of John F. Kennedy* (New York: Dial, 1980), 173–75.
7. Ethel Kennedy interview, "RFK," NBC-News, 28 May 1993.
8. Quoted in Jerry Oppenheimer, *The Other Mrs. Kennedy—Ethel Skakel Kennedy: An American Drama of Power, Privilege, and Politics* (New York: St. Martin's, 1994), 132.
9. Lester David, *Ethel: The Story of Mrs. Robert F. Kennedy* (New York: World, 1971), 50; Schlesinger, *Robert Kennedy,* 96; Lester David and Irene David, *Bobby Kennedy: The Making of a Folk Hero* (New York: PaperJacks, 1988), 56.
10. Oppenheimer, *The Other Mrs. Kennedy,* 131, 136–37, 148–52.
11. David and David, *Bobby Kennedy,* 58; Oppenheimer, *The Other Mrs. Kennedy,* 134.
12. RFK said his brother "really disliked" Nehru. David and David, *Bobby Kennedy,* 61.
13. Collier and Horowitz, *The Kennedys,* 200, 220–22; David and David, *Bobby Kennedy,* 61–62; Parmet, *Jack,* 226; John Galloway, ed., *The Kennedys and Vietnam* (New York: Facts on File, 1971), 11.
14. David and David, *Bobby Kennedy,* 62.
15. RFK, "Foreword to the Memorial Edition," *Profiles in Courage* by John F. Kennedy (New York: Harper & Row, 1964), ix.
16. Parmet, *Jack,* 189–92, 195, 226, 228–29; Doris Goodwin, *The Fitzgeralds and the Kennedys: An American Saga* (New York: St. Martin's, 1987), 849.
17. Walt Whitman, *Specimen Days,* quoted in William Least Heat-Moon, *PrairyErth* (Boston: Houghton Mifflin, 1991), 5.
18. PAP-RFK, Box 1; David and David, *Bobby Kennedy* 63; Schlesinger, *Robert Kennedy,* 97.
19. Goodwin, *Fitzgeralds and Kennedys,* 874–78.
20. Kenneth O'Donnell, interview by Jean Stein and George Plimpton, eds., *American Journey: The Times of Robert Kennedy* (New York: Harcourt Brace Jovanovich, 1970), 42; Rose Kennedy, *Times to Remember* (Garden City, N.Y.: Doubleday, 1974), 344; quoted in Goodwin, *Fitzgeralds and Kennedys,* 879.
21. Charles Bartlett, interview by Stein and Plimpton, *American Journey,* 43; Parmet, *Jack,* 238.
22. Schlesinger, *Robert Kennedy,* 101–3; Parmet, *Jack,* 255; Thomas C. Reeves, *A Question of Character: A Life of John F. Kennedy* (New York: Free Press, 1991), 105.
23. Parmet, *Jack,* 247.
24. Richard M. Fried, *Men against McCarthy* (New York: Columbia U. Press, 1976), 246.
25. Schlesinger, *Thousand Days,* 12–14; Parmet, *Jack,* 247.
26. Robert F. Kennedy, *Robert Kennedy in His Own Words: The Unpublished Recollections of The Kennedy Years,* ed. Edwin O. Guthman and Jeffrey Shulman (New York: Bantam, 1988). 444–45. McCarthy, according to one source, told Lodge's advisors he would campaign for Lodge only if Lodge publicly requested his help; afraid to lose

the "Harvard vote," Lodge could not make such a request and McCarthy knew it. Victor Lasky, *Robert Kennedy: The Myth and the Man* (New York: Trident, 1968), 70–71.

27. JFK quoted in Arthur Schlesinger, Jr., *A Thousand Days: John F. Kennedy in the White House* (Boston: Houghton Mifflin, 1965), 12; also see Nicholas von Hoffman, *Citizen Cohn: The Life and Times of Roy Cohn* (New York: Bantam, 1988), 139. Parmet, *Jack,* 255.
28. Thomas P. "Tip" O'Neill, *Man of the House* (New York: St. Martin's, 1987), 93. The amounts, according to O'Neill, varied between fifty and one hundred thousand dollars, depending on whether or not Kennedy liked the candidates.
29. O'Donnell interview, 41.
30. Schlesinger, *Robert Kennedy,* 103; Goodwin, *Fitzgeralds and Kennedys,* 881; Peter Collier and David Horowitz, *The Kennedys: An American Drama* (New York: Warner, 1984), 227.
31. Collier and Horowitz, *The Kennedys,* 226.
32. David and David, *Bobby Kennedy,* 64–65; Helen Keyes, interview by Stein and Plimpton, *American Journey,* 42.
33. David and David, *Bobby Kennedy,* 64.
34. Tommy O'Hearn, interview by Collier and Horowitz, *The Kennedys,* 227.
35. For estimates of the large sums spent by Joseph Kennedy in 1952 and the JFK quote, see Reeves, *A Question of Character,* 100–1. For RFK's quote, Guthman and Shulman, *Robert Kennedy,* 444. Goodwin, *Fitzgeralds and Kennedys,* 883; Parmet, *Jack,* 242–47.
36. On JFK as a good listener who made people feel they were truly important, see Richard Goodwin, *Remembering America: A Voice from The Sixties* (Boston: Little, Brown, 1988), 41; and John H. Davis, *The Kennedys: Dynasty and Disaster, 1848–1984* (New York: McGraw-Hill, 1984), 184.
37. Collier and Horowitz, *The Kennedys,* 225.
38. AP Release (29 September 1952) *Philadelphia Bulletin* archives. The national wire services did not carry news of the birth of Joe's first grandchild, Kathleen. Also, Lester David, *Ethel,* 58.
39. Keyes interview, 43. Estimates of the number of women attending the teas varies from 60,000 to 75,000.
40. RFK, *Robert Kennedy,* 445–46; Kenneth P. O'Donnell and David F. Powers with Joe McCarthy, *"Johnny, We Hardly Knew Ye"* (Boston: Little, Brown, 1972), 105.
41. Schlesinger, *Robert Kennedy,* 104.
42. RFK, *Robert Kennedy,* 445–6. Goodwin, *Fitzgeralds and Kennedys,* 884–85. Lodge spent so much time working for Eisenhower's election that he may have let his own campaign slide. Tip O'Neill thought the election swung to JFK when Lodge got caught in a traffic jam and missed an opportunity to appear on television with Eisenhower. O'Neill, *Man of the House,* 103. Others said that Joe Kennedy's maneuvering to keep McCarthy out of the state was the decisive factor. Von Hoffman, *Citizen Cohn,* 141.

43. O'Donnell and Powers, *"Johnny, We Hardly Knew Ye,"* 95; Goodwin, *Fitzgeralds and Kennedys,* 879–80, 886.
44. O'Neill, *Man of the House,* 102; Parmet, *Jack,* 255–56; Rose Kennedy, *Times to Remember,* 345. The Kennedy team was completed when speech writer Theodore Sorensen joined JFK's Senate staff in 1953.
45. RFK, *Robert Kennedy,* 447; Schlesinger, *Robert Kennedy,* 102, 104–5; O'Donnell interview, 45.

CHAPTER 4

1. McInerney knew the subcommittee general counsel, Francis "Frip" Flanagan. Edwin Guthman, *We Band of Brothers* (New York: Harper and Row, 1971), 16–17.
2. Nicholas von Hoffman, *Citizen Cohn: The Life and Times of Roy Cohn* (New York: Bantam, 1988), 143.
3. Jack Newfield, *Robert Kennedy: A Memoir* (New York: New American Library, 1969), 45.
4. On McCarthy's inquisitional methods and his accusations against Democrats, see Richard M. Fried, *Men against McCarthy* (New York: Columbia U. Press, 1976), 278; Robert Griffith, *The Politics of Fear* (Lexington: U. of Kentucky Press, 1970), 212–20. For background on the age of suspicion, see William Manchester, *The Glory and the Dream* (New York: Bantam, 1975), 473–513; Godfrey Hodgson, *America in Our Time* (Garden City, N.Y.: Doubleday, 1976), 34–47. For a discussion of the tensions between the "responsible anti-Communists" (which RFK considered himself) and the reckless Red hunters (like Cohn and McCarthy), see Richard Gid Powers, *Not without Honor: The History of American Anticommunism* (New York: Free Press, 1996).
5. Herbert Parmet, *Jack: The Struggles of John F. Kennedy* (New York: Dial 1980), 300–07; William O. Douglas, OH-JFK, 11–12.
6. Kenneth O'Donnell, interview by Jean Stein and George Plimpton, eds., *American Journey: The Times of Robert Kennedy* (New York: Harcourt Brace Jovanovich, 1970), 49.
7. Lem Billings and O'Donnell, interviews by Stein and Plimpton, *American Journey,* 51, 49.
8. On Cohn's control over the subcommittee and on the investigations, see Griffith, *Politics of Fear,* 207–20; Fried, *Men against McCarthy,* 254–90; Ruth Young Watt, oral history interview by Donald Ritchie, U.S. Senate Historical Office, November 1979.
9. Von Hoffman, *Citizen Cohn,* 182.
10. For available information on the family finances, see Schlesinger, *Robert Kennedy,* 109, 112; Lester David and Irene David, *Bobby Kennedy: The Making of a Folk Hero* (New York: PaperJacks, 1988), 69. On RFK's work habits, see Watt interview, 114; David and David, *Bobby Kennedy,* 68–69.
11. AP report, *Philadelphia Bulletin,* 4 May 1953. RFK's final report expanded the

number of ships to 193. Schlesinger, *Robert Kennedy,* 106–12. The British insisted no goods of strategic importance went to Communist China and labeled the report a "horrible lie." Victor Lasky, *Robert F. Kennedy: The Myth and the Man* (New York: Trident, 1968), 81–82.

12. Schlesinger, *Robert Kennedy,* 111; Lasky, *Robert Kennedy,* 80.
13. Fried, *Men against McCarthy,* 267–69; Griffith, *Politics of Fear,* 229–35.
14. Hoover's decision to break with McCarthy may also have been influenced by a Las Vegas newspaper column by Hank Greenspun alleging specific instances when McCarthy had engaged in homosexual activities. Athan G. Theoharis and John Stuart Cox, *The Boss: J. Edgar Hoover and the Great American Inquisition* (Philadelphia: Temple U. Press, 1988), 280–98.
15. The subcommittee staff, according to Ruth Young Watt, thought RFK resigned because of the Matthews controversy. Watt interview, 114, 168. For internal FBI memos on Matthews, McInerney, and Flanagan, see Athan Theoharis, ed., *From the Secret Files of J. Edgar Hoover* (Chicago: Dee, 1991), 260–62.
16. Robert F. Kennedy, *The Enemy Within* (New York: Harper and Brothers, 1960), 307; Schlesinger, *Robert Kennedy,* 113. In 1956 RFK told Edwin Guthman that he resigned because of the "way Cohn and Schine were going, not checking anything, not really investigating. . . . It had to end in disaster, but Joe couldn't see it." Guthman, *We Band of Brothers,* 19.
17. Watt interview, 170.
18. Memo, FBI Assistant Director Louis Nichols to Clyde Tolson, 24 June 1953; memo, Hoover to Assistant Directors Tolson and Nichols, 14 July 1953, Theoharis, *Secret Files,* 260–62; Curt Gentry, *J. Edgar Hoover: The Man and the Secrets* (New York: Norton, 1991), 380–81; Theoharis and Cox, *The Boss,* 281–82. If RFK knew of Kerr's opposition, he never revealed it. After McCarthy's death Kerr married Joseph Minetti; when RFK became attorney general she visited him and successfully lobbied for Minetti's appointment to the Civil Aeronautics Board. Telephone message, 27 October 1961; desk diary, 31 October 1961, 6 April 1962, JFK-ARC; Benjamin C. Bradlee, *Conversations with Kennedy* (New York: Norton, 1975), 139.
19. For hints of this possibility, see Folders 11 and 14, O&C; Gentry, *J. Edgar Hoover,* 384, 470–71; Theoharis and Cox, *The Boss,* 329–30; Theoharis, *Secret Files,* 317–21.
20. RFK quote, Peter Maas, interview by Stein and Plimpton, *American Journey,* 50.
21. Kennedy's resignation letter and McCarthy's reply appear in Lasky, *Robert Kennedy,* 82–83.
22. Parmet, *Jack,* 300–7. No direct evidence suggests, however, that JFK attempted to influence RFK's decision one way or the other.
23. Schlesinger, *Robert Kennedy,* 117.
24. Ibid., 116.
25. See Parmet, *Jack,* 229, 261.
26. Fried, *Men against McCarthy,* 272–73.

27. Watt interview, 117–18; Fried, *Men against McCarthy,* 276.
28. Fried, *Men against McCarthy,* 279–90; Griffith, *Politics of Fear,* 243–69; Manchester, *Glory and the Dream,* 701–13.
29. Watt interview, 144.
30. Fried, *Men against McCarthy,* 284–85; Schlesinger, *Robert Kennedy,* 118–20; von Hoffman, *Citizen Cohn,* 203–4. Victor Lasky claimed Cohn was not mistaken, as proven by a Subversive Activities Control Board report released in 1958. Lasky, *Robert Kennedy,* 86.
31. Richard Gid Powers, *Secrecy and Power: The Life of J. Edgar Hoover* (New York: Free Press, 1987), 358; Schlesinger, *Robert Kennedy,* 112–15; von Hoffman, *Citizen Cohn,* 181–82, 203–5.
32. Mary Driscoll, interview by David and David, *Bobby Kennedy,* 72; Phillip Potter, interview by von Hoffman, *Citizen Cohn,* 213.
33. Because the victim of Symington's teenage prank (the owner of an automobile Symington took for a joyride) had long since accepted Symington's apology, there was nothing for McCarthy to expose. Clark Clifford, *Counsel to the President* (New York: Random House, 1991), 295–96.
34. Griffith, *Politics of Fear,* 257; AP report, *Philadelphia Bulletin,* 14 June 1954; von Hoffman, *Citizen Cohn,* 244.
35. Schlesinger, *Robert Kennedy,* 121–22; von Hoffman, *Citizen Cohn,* 142–45, 227–33; Clifford, *Counsel to the President,* 295.
36. Kenneth O'Reilly, *Hoover and the Un-Americans* (Philadelphia: Temple U. Press, 1983), 126–28.
37. JPK's telephone call is summarized in a memo, L. B. Nichols to Clyde Tolson, 11 May 1954, Folder 14, O&C. For portions of the memorandum, see Theoharis, *Secret Files,* 322–23. EMK enlisted in the army in the spring of 1951, after being expelled from Harvard for cheating. To keep him out of Korea, JPK arranged his assignment to military police duty at SHAPE headquarters in Paris. EMK apparently never requested assignment to Fort Holabird. See James M. Burns, *Edward Kennedy and the Camelot Legacy* (New York: Norton, 1976), 45–46, and John H. Davis, *The Kennedys: Dynasty and Disaster, 1848–1984* (New York: McGraw-Hill, 1984), 696.
38. "Roy had invited Nemesis into his life" when he made Kennedy his enemy, wrote Nicholas von Hoffman, who concedes that Cohn "lived in a matrix of crime and unethical conduct"; he faced trial on various charges, including bribery, stock manipulation, jury tampering, and perjury, before his death from AIDS in 1986. *Citizen Cohn,* 259–61, 271–74, 282–87, 329–31, 406. On RFK's indifference, see Maas interview, 59.
39. Watt interview, 147.
40. Theodore C. Sorensen, *Kennedy* (New York: Harper and Row, 1965), 52–55; Parmet, *Jack,* 306–7. JFK, McCarthy, and Alexander Wiley (McCarthy's fellow senator from Wisconsin) were the only senators unrecorded on the McCarthy censure vote. Griffith, *Politics of Fear,* 314.

41. Quoted in William Shannon, *The American Irish: A Political and Social Portrait* (Amherst: U. of Massachusetts Press, 1989), 406.
42. R. E. Thompson and Hortense Meyers, *Robert F. Kennedy: The Brother Within* (New York: Macmillan, 1962), 121–22; Schlesinger, *Robert Kennedy,* 122; David and David, *Bobby Kennedy,* 77. At about the time of the censure vote, reporter Clark Mollenhoff overhead RFK say, "Joe McCarthy, you're a shit," following an exasperating telephone conversation with the senator. Mollenhoff, interview by Peter Collier and David Horowitz, *The Kennedys: An American Drama* (New York: Warner, 1984), 269–70.
43. Schlesinger, *Robert Kennedy,* 123. RFK did not hold a grudge against Murrow. He made no effort to oppose his appointment as director of the USIA in JFK's administration. And Murrow, for his part, responded positively when RFK asked him for favors. See, for example, RFK to Edward E. Reid, 7 March 1963, Box 8, AG-PC. When Murrow was hospitalized for cancer treatments, RFK telephoned, sent him a book, and was solicitous toward Murrow's wife. Janet Murrow letter to RFK, undated, Box 13, AG-PC.
44. Ed Bayley interview, "RFK," NBC-News, 28 May 1993; Schlesinger, *Robert Kennedy,* 113–14; Lester David, *Ethel: The Story of Mrs. Robert F. Kennedy* (New York: World, 1971), 53–55; David and David, *Bobby Kennedy,* 76–77.
45. For an exposition of the "Ideology of the Liberal Consensus" and the "end of ideology" during the 1950s, see Hodgson, *America in Our Time,* 67–98.
46. *Philadelphia Bulletin,* 9 January 1955. Nomination letter from Paul T. Rothwell, President of Greater Boston Chamber of Commerce, Box 1, PAP-RFK. On JPK's practice of having his children receive credit for his charitable donations, see Rose Kennedy, *Times to Remember* (Garden City, N.Y.: Doubleday, 1974), 384.
47. Watt interview, 174–75; Schlesinger, *Robert Kennedy,* 125; Lasky, *Robert Kennedy,* 91–92, 95–96.
48. Schlesinger, *Robert Kennedy,* 126–27; Watt interview, 175; Charles Bartlett, interview by Stein and Plimpton, *American Journey,* 54. Senator George H. Bender charged RFK with leaking damaging information on Talbot to The *New York Times.* Talbot died two years later, a victim, his widow claimed, of one of RFK's witch-hunts. See Lasky, *Robert Kennedy,* 93.
49. Harris Wofford, *Of Kennedys and Kings: Making Sense of the Sixties* (New York: Farrar, Straus and Giroux, 1980), 33.
50. Rose Kennedy, *Times to Remember,* 384.
51. Douglas thought JFK never really understood the problems of the wilderness and the environment, because he had never camped out or "slept on the ground." Douglas, OH-JFK, 37.
52. *Philadelphia Bulletin,* 14 and 15 September 1955; Schlesinger, *Robert Kennedy,* 130–39.
53. Robert F. Kennedy, "The Soviet Brand of Colonialism," *New York Times Magazine,* 8 April 1956; Lasky, *Robert Kennedy,* 93–95; Schlesinger, *Robert Kennedy,* 136–37; Rose Kennedy, *Times to Remember,* 384.

54. The report, known as the "Bailey Memorandum," was circulated by John Bailey of Connecticut to each of the convention delegates.
55. Parmet, *Jack,* 347. RFK said he had no part in launching this effort, but he "got Kenny O'Donnell and some others sort of into it" and asked them for regular progress reports. Robert F. Kennedy, *Robert Kennedy in His Own Words: The Unpublished Recollections of the Kennedy Years,* ed. Edwin O. Guthman and Jeffrey Shulman (New York: Bantam, 1988), 451. Ken O'Donnell described the fight as JFK's "coming of age as a party politician." Kenneth P. O'Donnell and David F. Powers with Joe McCarthy, *"Johnny, We Hardly Knew Ye"* (Boston: Little, Brown, 1972), 118.
56. RFK, *Robert Kennedy,* 452–53.
57. Parmet, *Jack,* 346–55; O'Donnell and Powers, *"Johnny, We Hardly Knew Ye,"* 118–34.
58. Thomas P. "Tip" O'Neill, *Man of the House* (New York: St. Martin's, 1987), 94–95. RFK's presence on the Massachusetts delegation was labeled a "farce" and formally protested by Robert P. Donovan of East Boston. Donovan charged that neither RFK nor JFK actually lived at 122 Bowdoin Street, the two-bedroom apartment they claimed as their voting residence. The charge was dismissed on a technicality. See Lasky, *Robert Kennedy,* 98.
59. Parmet, *Jack,* 349. O'Neill, *Man of the House,* 95.
60. RFK, *Robert Kennedy,* 451.
61. Parmet, *Jack,* 375–76; Doris Goodwin, *The Fitzgeralds and the Kennedys: An American Saga* (New York: St. Martin's, 1987), 904.
62. Parmet, *Jack,* 375; Goodwin, *Fitzgeralds and Kennedys,* 904.
63. O'Donnell interview, 65.
64. George Smathers, interview by C. David Heymann, *A Woman Named Jackie* (New York: Carol Communications, 1989), 187–88.
65. Parmet, *Jack,* 377; Heymann, *A Woman Named Jackie,* 188.
66. Schlesinger, *Robert Kennedy,* 142–43; Goodwin, *Fitzgeralds and Kennedys,* 906; O'Donnell interview, 65.
67. Parmet, *Jack,* 382.
68. Ibid., 383. Senator George Smathers—not a loyal friend in the long run—said JFK, preoccupied with a blonde named "Pooh," was reluctant to return home to his wife. "You'd better haul ass back to your wife," Smathers said he told JFK, "if you ever want to run for President." JPK reportedly intervened to save the failing marriage; not, as rumored, with a million-dollar bribe to Jacqueline, but by forcing concessions from John to modify his behavior. Collier and Horowitz, *The Kennedys,* 258–59; Heymann, *A Woman Named Jackie,* 192–95.
69. Jacqueline Kennedy, interview by Arthur M. Schlesinger, Jr., *Robert Kennedy and His Times* (New York: Ballantine, 1978), 143; Heymann, *A Woman Named Jackie,* 190–92.
70. Heymann, *A Woman Named Jackie,* 190.
71. *New York Times,* 26 August 1970, 41.

72. The Kennedy compound consists of the original family house, RFK's house, and JFK's house, adjacent to each other within a triangular plot. The other children bought houses nearby. Collier and Horowitz, *The Kennedys,* 269; Davis, *The Kennedys,* 84–85, 300.
73. Warren Rogers, *When I Think of Bobby* (New York: HarperCollins, 1993), 14.
74. After Kathleen and Joe II came Robert Francis, Jr. (17 January 1954), David Anthony (15 June 1955), Mary Courtney (9 September 1956), and Michael LeMoyne (27 February 1958).
75. The price reportedly was $125,000. David, *Ethel,* 88–94; Goodwin, *Fitzgeralds and Kennedys,* 907; Heymann, *A Woman Named Jackie,* 192; Rogers, *When I Think of Bobby,* 11.
76. McInerney was also a former FBI agent. DeLoach to Tolson, 10 June 1959, Folder 13, O&C.
77. David, *Ethel,* 88–103, 114–16; Jerry Oppenheimer, *The Other Mrs. Kennedy—Ethel Skakel Kennedy: An American Drama of Power, Privilege, and Politics* (New York: St. Martin's, 1994), 181–84; Rogers, *When I Think of Bobby,* 15.
78. Schlesinger, *Robert Kennedy,* 127; David, *Ethel,* 101.
79. O'Donnell and Powers, *"Johnny, We Hardly Knew Ye,"* 144; Harrison Salisbury interview by Stein and Plimpton, *American Journey,* 66; Rose Kennedy, *Times to Remember,* 383; Parmet, *Jack,* 382; Arthur M. Schlesinger, Jr., *A Thousand Days: John F. Kennedy in the White House* (Boston: Houghton Mifflin, 1965), 93.
80. Harrison E. Salisbury, *Heroes of My Time* (New York: Walker, 1993), 13–14.

CHAPTER 5

1. Jean Kennedy Smith and Lem Billings have given their versions of the argument. See Arthur M. Schlesinger, Jr., *Robert Kennedy and His Times* (Boston: Houghton Mifflin, 1978), 153; Doris Goodwin, *The Fitzgeralds and the Kennedys: An American Saga* (New York: St. Martin's, 1987), 913; Herbert S. Parmet, *Jack: The Struggles of John F. Kennedy* (New York: Dial, 1980), 419; Peter Collier and David Horowitz, *The Kennedys: An American Drama* (New York: Warner, 1984), 271–72.
2. See Alan K. McAdams, *Power and Politics in Labor Legislation* (New York: Columbia U. Press, 1964); Charles C. Alexander, *Holding the Line: The Eisenhower Era, 1952–1961* (Bloomington: Indiana U. Press, 1975), 112–15.
3. Mollenhoff, interview by Collier and Horowitz, *The Kennedys,* 271. Also see Clark Mollenhoff, *Tentacles of Power* (Cleveland: World, 1965), 124; and Schlesinger, *Robert Kennedy,* 148.
4. Robert F. Kennedy, *The Enemy Within* (New York: Harper and Row, 1960), 45–55; Arthur A. Sloane, *Hoffa* (Cambridge: MIT Press, 1991), 42–48.
5. RFK, *The Enemy Within,* 3–20.
6. McCarthy was replaced by Carl T. Curtis of Nebraska. JFK said RFK wanted him on the committee because Strom Thurmond of South Carolina was the next Democrat in line. Thurmond would give the conservatives control, which RFK

apparently did not want to happen. See Schlesinger, *Robert Kennedy,* 154; RFK, *The Enemy Within,* 22. McNamara later resigned from the committee, claiming it was "rigged." Parmet, *Jack,* 420–21.

7. RFK, *The Enemy Within,* 166.
8. Ibid., 166–79; Ruth Young Watt, oral history interview by Donald Ritchie, U.S. Senate Historical Office, November 1979, 178–82; Parmet, *Jack,* 419.
9. Bellino, Ruth Young Watt said, was "married to the idea of the Kennedys. I've never seen anybody so devoted in my life" (63–65). At one time or another Bellino worked for JFK, RFK, and EMK. Maggie Duckett, RFK's secretary until being "bumped" by Angie Novello, expressed "a little bit of hard feelings" and blamed Bellino for losing her job. Watt interview, 119.
10. Schlesinger, *Robert Kennedy,* 155.
11. The FBI was contemptuous of the former agents who went to work for RFK, referring to Sheridan as a "runner" and Bellino as a "stooge" for RFK. DeLoach to Tolson, 17 January 1966, RFK FBI.
12. Sheridan and Victor Riesel died within a few days of each other in January 1995. See Pete Hamill's tribute to them, "In Defense of Honest Labor," *New York Times Magazine,* 31 December 1995, 18–19. On first meeting RFK, see Walter Sheridan, *The Fall and Rise of Jimmy Hoffa* (New York: Saturday Review, 1972), 33; Walter Sheridan, interview by Jean Stein and George Plimpton, eds., *American Journey: The Times of Robert Kennedy* (Harcourt Brace Jovanovich, 1970), 52–53.
13. RFK, *The Enemy Within,* 188–89.
14. Schlesinger, *Robert Kennedy,* 155; Watt interview, 196; James M. Burns, *Edward Kennedy and the Camelot Legacy* (New York: Norton, 1976), 59.
15. Sloane, *Hoffa,* 22–25, 50–52; Schlesinger, *Robert Kennedy,* 179.
16. RFK, *The Enemy Within,* 43. Sloane, *Hoffa,* 52. Beck avoided jail until June 1962. Released in December 1964, he received a full pardon from President Gerald Ford in May 1975.
17. Sloane, *Hoffa,* 3–11.
18. Quoted in ibid., 15–16; 17.
19. Ibid., 18–21.
20. Ibid., 32–33.
21. Schlesinger, *Robert Kennedy,* 172–73; Pierre Salinger, *With Kennedy* (New York: Doubleday, 1966), 19; Sloane, *Hoffa,* 61–71, 157; Murray Kempton, interview by Stein and Plimpton, *American Journey,* 57. Edward Bennett Williams is the source of the (possibly apocryphal) story of Hoffa's directive to keep the lights burning. Schlesinger, *Robert Kennedy,* 173.
22. On the first meeting, see Sloane, *Hoffa,* 76–78, and Schlesinger, *Robert Kennedy,* 164–65. Hoffa made no mention of the arm wrestling in his first autobiography. James R. Hoffa, as told to Donald I. Rogers, *The Trials of Jimmy Hoffa* (Chicago: Regnery, 1970), 150; and Hoffa, as told to Oscar Fraley, *Hoffa: The Real Story* (New York: Stein and Day, 1975), 94–99. *Cf.* John Bartlow Martin, *Jimmy Hoffa's Hot* (Greenwich, Conn.: Fawcett, 1959), 8–9; Victor Lasky, *Robert F.*

Kennedy: The Myth and the Man (New York: Trident, 1971), 104–5. RFK's version is in *The Enemy Within,* 36, 40–43.

23. RFK, *The Enemy Within,* 43.
24. John Cheasty interview, NBC-News, "RFK"; Evan Thomas, *The Man to See: Edward Bennet Williams Ultimate Insider, Legendary Trial Lawyer* (New York: Simon and Schuster, 1991), 106; RFK, *The Enemy Within,* 36–40. RFK recalled Cheasty saying his information would make his hair "stand on end," rather than "curl." Otherwise their accounts agree.
25. RFK, *The Enemy Within,* 36–40.
26. Ibid., 55–56; Thomas, *The Man to See,* 104.
27. RFK, *The Enemy Within,* 56; Sloane, *Hoffa,* 72–73; Lasky, *Robert F. Kennedy,* 106–7; Schlesinger, *Robert Kennedy,* 165–67; Thomas, *The Man to See,* 107–8.
28. To influence the eight African Americans on the jury the Teamsters brought former heavyweight boxing champion Joe Louis to the courtroom to pose as a friend of Hoffa's. Walter Sheridan learned that Louis was on the payroll of a company that depended on a loan from the Teamsters' pension fund. See RFK, *The Enemy Within,* 55–61; Collier and Horowitz, *The Kennedys,* 276; Sheridan, *Rise and Fall,* 34; Mollenhoff, *Tentacles of Power,* 198–99; and Lester David and Irene David, *Bobby Kennedy: The Making of a Folk Hero* (New York: PaperJacks, 1988), 99. Edward Bennett Williams claimed that "the Joe Louis incident" was "all mythology" created by reporter Clark Mollenhoff. See Thomas, *The Man to See,* 114–16.
29. Thomas, *The Man to See,* 104–7, 112; Harry Alexander (U.S. attorney at the Cheasty trial) interview, NBC-News, "RFK." Ethel, who attended every session of the Cheasty trial, became upset over Williams' questioning of RFK. RFK barely mentioned it in *The Enemy Within,* 58.
30. Thomas, *The Man to See,* 104–18; and Robert Pack, *Edward Bennett Williams for the Defense* (New York: Harper and Row, 1983), 235–41. On Kennedy's response to Hoffa's acquittal, see Angela Novello, interview by Stein and Plimpton, *American Journey,* 57–58; Sloane, *Hoffa,* 74–75; Schlesinger, *Robert Kennedy,* 167.
31. Cheasty interview.
32. Salinger, *With Kennedy,* 43.
33. RFK, *The Enemy Within,* 82–117; Sloane, *Hoffa,* 84–87.
34. Sloane, *Hoffa,* 87; RFK, *The Enemy Within,* 75–81.
35. Sloane, *Hoffa,* 80. One of Hoffa's associates took the Fifth Amendment when asked about his marital status. Another promised, "I'll tell you the truth if you let me get out from under the oath" (124–26).
36. RFK, *The Enemy Within,* 73–75.
37. Lasky, *Robert F. Kennedy,* 107–8; RFK, *The Enemy Within,* 72, 75.
38. RFK, *The Enemy Within,* 74–75; Sloane, *Hoffa,* 123.
39. RFK, *The Enemy Within,* 74.
40. Sloane, *Hoffa,* 88, English quote, 101.

41. George S. Fitzgerald quoted in Sloane, *Hoffa,* 91.
42. Ibid., 91–99, 105–13, quote, 98. On RFK's views of the powerless in the rank-and-file Teamsters, see *The Enemy Within,* 118–42.
43. RFK, *The Enemy Within,* 61–62. Hoffa once said, "I have a special way with juries." Schlesinger, *Robert Kennedy,* 171.
44. Sloane, *Hoffa,* 105, 114.
45. Schlesinger, *Robert Kennedy,* 170–71.
46. RFK, *The Enemy Within,* 74.
47. Ibid., 161–62. Also see Sloane, *Hoffa,* 134–35.
48. Sloane, *Hoffa,* 154–57.
49. William O. Douglas, OH-JFK, 17.
50. David and David, *Bobby Kennedy,* 105. For a summary of criticisms, see Lasky, *Robert F. Kennedy,* 107–13.
51. Schlesinger, *Robert Kennedy,* 160. Accusations that RFK badgered witnesses were not limited to Hoffa and his Teamsters colleagues. Mella Hort, whom Kennedy accused of taking a two-thousand-dollar kickback from gangsters involved in the armed forces clothing procurement program, told the press, "I would have sworn to almost anything," claiming Kennedy and Bellino "browbeat" her for several hours. Her testimony led to six fraud convictions in 1955. *Philadelphia Bulletin,* 26 May 1955; Lasky, *Robert F. Kennedy,* 93.
52. Lasky, *Robert F. Kennedy,* 108–10.
53. The exception occurred when RFK publicly disputed the basic facts and questioned the competency of British writer Anthony West, who had written a blistering article criticizing his inquisitorial tactics. West accused Kennedy of "trickery and disregard for the truth," charging that he lacked "any sense of ethics." See Lasky, *Robert F. Kennedy,* 108–13.
54. RFK, *The Enemy Within,* 304–5, 316–17.
55. Lasky, *Robert F. Kennedy,* 112.
56. Schlesinger, *Robert Kennedy,* 196. Arthur Sloane, *Hoffa,* 164–65, demonstrates that most of Kennedy's charges were "unprovable."
57. *Newsweek,* 10 August 1959, 29.
58. Barry M. Goldwater with Jack Casserly, *Goldwater* (New York: Doubleday, 1988), 101–2; RFK, *The Enemy Within,* 267–68.
59. Lasky, *Robert F. Kennedy,* 114. RFK likewise detested Capehart. Schlesinger, *Robert Kennedy,* 186. In 1966, with the coaxing of an unfriendly RFK biographer, Goldwater recollected an instance in which JFK had to restrain his brother when RFK lost control and advanced on Goldwater with clenched fists. Goldwater claimed to have interceded to save RFK's job: "Despite our differences, I did my best to keep him from being fired." Lasky, *Robert F. Kennedy,* 115. Goldwater does not mention the incident in his own memoirs, *Goldwater.*
60. Capehart complained of RFK's independent attitude and asked McClellan, "Why don't you do something?" Lasky, *Robert F. Kennedy,* 114.
61. RFK, *The Enemy Within,* 273–82. Parmet, *Jack,* 422–23. Following an NLRB

investigation, the UAW received $4.5 million from Kohler for wrongdoing during the strike. Schlesinger, *Robert Kennedy,* 188–90.

62. RFK, *The Enemy Within,* 297–98.
63. Ibid., 190–214.
64. "The Rise of the Brothers Kennedy," *Look,* 6 August 1957, 18–24, 27; Harold Martin, "The Amazing Kennedys," *Saturday Evening Post,* September 1957, 49–50; "The Kennedy Brothers: Off to a Fast Start," *U.S. News and World Report,* 12 April 1957, 77–79. Goodwin, *Fitzgeralds and Kennedys,* 914; Collier and Horowitz, *The Kennedys,* 291–93. Victor Lasky found the first mention of the Kennedys as a team in "Washington Brother Act," *Parade* (Sunday newspaper supplement), 28 April 1957; see *Robert F. Kennedy,* 118, 413n.
65. Parmet, *Jack,* 415–16.
66. Watt interview, 185–86.
67. Joseph L. Rauh, Jr., OH-JFK, 19–28; Schlesinger, *Robert Kennedy,* 188–89.
68. RFK was referring to the UAW's choice to support Kefauver over JFK for the vice-presidential nomination at the 1956 convention. Schlesinger, *Robert Kennedy,* 190.
69. Parmet, *Jack,* 428–32. Barry Goldwater took credit for alerting President Eisenhower to critical omissions in the Kennedy-Ives bill and for reversing the Senate's position on it. *Goldwater,* 102.
70. Hoffa quote in Sloane, *Hoffa,* 156; JFK quote in Parmet, *Jack,* 432.
71. Parmet, *Jack,* 426–32, 489–98; Schlesinger, *Robert Kennedy,* 197–98; Lasky, *Robert F. Kennedy,* 118.
72. Even Rose Kennedy sat out the 1958 election, vacationing on the French Riviera. JFK won 73.6 percent of the vote. Goodwin, *Fitzgeralds and Kennedys,* 916; Parmet, *Jack,* 452–53.
73. RFK, *The Enemy Within,* 239–65.
74. Stephen Fox, *Blood and Power: Organized Crime in Twentieth-Century America* (New York: Morrow, 1989), 198.
75. RFK, *The Enemy Within,* 239–40. RFK does not use the term Mafia in his book. See Fox, *Blood and Power,* 326. For an entertaining but improbable secondhand recreation of Giancana's escape from Apalachin and for various mythical representations of the Chicago hoodlum's impact on the Kennedys, see Sam Giancana (the godson) and Chuck Giancana (the brother), *Double Cross: The Explosive, Inside Story of the Mobster Who Controlled America* (New York: Warner, 1992), 252–55.
76. Schlesinger, *Robert Kennedy,* 175–82; Fox, *Blood and Power,* 296–97; Curt Gentry, *J. Edgar Hoover: The Man and the Secrets* (New York: Norton, 1991), 328–30, 397–98, 452–60. For a provocative alternative explanation for Hoover's reticence in investigating organized crime, see Anthony Summers, *Official and Confidential: The Secret Life of J. Edgar Hoover* (New York: Putnam, 1993), 237–59.
77. Robert F. Kennedy, *Robert Kennedy in His Own Words: The Unpublished Recollec-*

tions of the Kennedy Years, ed. Edwin O. Guthman and Jeffrey Shulman (New York: Bantam, 1988), 120.

78. Fox, *Blood and Power,* 120–21. Hoover quickly mobilized the FBI after Apalachin, establishing the Top Hoodlum Program, and within a year had amassed intelligence on organized crime to equal that of Anslinger's FBN. See Gentry, *J. Edgar Hoover,* 453–57.
79. RFK, *The Enemy Within,* 249–50; Watt interview, 184; Jimmy Breslin, "The Music Is Different," October 1964, clipping, RFK-FBI. One report has Kennedy challenging Gallo: "So you're Joey Gallo, the jukebox king. You don't look so tough. I'd like to fight you myself." Collier and Horowitz, *The Kennedys,* 282.
80. Fox, *Blood and Power,* 329. Also see Report to the [FBI] Director, 7 August 1958, Folder 14, O&C, containing details of death threats against RFK and his family.
81. Nick Thimmisch and William Johnson, *R.F.K. at 40* (Boston: Norton, 1965), 71.
82. Senate Select Committee on Improper Activities in the Labor and Management Field, *Hearings,* 18681; Fox, *Blood and Power,* 338.
83. John H. Davis, *Mafia Kingfish: Carlos Marcello and the Assassination of John F. Kennedy* (New York: Penguin, 1989), 86–92.
84. Ibid., 85–86.
85. Ibid., 16, 90–91.
86. Ibid., 91.
87. RFK claimed that committee revelations led to one arrest for parole violation, an indictment for extortion, and a bribery conviction for the mayor of Portland, Oregon. *The Enemy Within,* 245–6, 262.
88. His presence at the Apalachin meeting ruined John C. Montana, an owner of a fleet of taxicabs in Buffalo and an apparently respectable businessperson. Fox, *Blood and Power,* 328.
89. RFK, *The Enemy Within,* 265.
90. RFK suspected (without proof) that a bug found in Senator McClellan's office was put there at Hoffa's direction. Victor S. Navasky, *Kennedy Justice* (New York: Atheneum, 1971), 399–400, 413–14; Watt interview, 225; RFK, *The Enemy Within,* 78–80. A staffer who found a bug in his Detroit hotel room suspected (without proof) that RFK put it there. Lasky, *Robert F. Kennedy,* 117.
91. The Communications Act of 1934 (Section 605) prohibited the interception, divulgence, and use of wiretap information in trials. A wiretap could be legally initiated only through a court order or with the explicit permission of the attorney general. See Memorandum, Attorney General Nicholas Katzenbach to FBI Director, 27 January 1966, Athan Theoharis, *From the Secret Files of J. Edgar Hoover* (Chicago: Dee, 1991), 148–50.
92. The use of microphone surveillance devices, or bugs, was constrained by a 1954 Supreme Court ruling (*Irvine v. California*). Thereafter, President Eisenhower's attorney general, Herbert Brownell, directed the FBI to use "discretion and intelligent restraint" in each case and stipulated that each installation be approved

in advance by the attorney general. See Confidential Memo, Attorney General Herbert Brownell to FBI Director, 20 May 1954, ibid., 141.

93. Ruth Young Watt, who was fond of RFK, insisted that none of the taps were authorized when RFK was chief counsel, but he, of course, was chief counsel from the outset. Watt interview, 194, 196. Robert Manuel, the minority counsel to the Rackets Committee, told Victor Lasky that he suspected RFK tapped his telephone. Another staff member said Kennedy was "bug crazy" but offered no convincing proof of any illegal taps. See Lasky, *Robert F. Kennedy,* 116–17.
94. Memorandum, A. Rosen to Hoover, 3 March 1959, Folder 13, O&C. RFK, *The Enemy Within,* 261. Like all investigators, RFK also made liberal use of informants. One, a Joliet prison inmate, tricked Kennedy and Jim McShane, a McClellan committee investigator who became chief U.S. marshal in the Kennedy administration, into digging up large sections of a farm in a futile search for the body of a missing reporter. Sheridan interview, 56.
95. Memorandum, A. Rosen to Hoover, 3 March 1959, Folder 13, O&C. FBI transcripts show JFK was certain his conversations with Inga Arvad were being tapped. See Mrs. Paul Fejos File, Folder 7, O&C. When JPK once called in the FBI to sweep his Chicago hotel room for bugs, he reminded the agents, "I am the number one supporter of the FBI." Chicago SAC report, 3 December 1961, Folder 11, O&C.
96. Fox, *Blood and Power,* 330.
97. Based largely on hearsay evidence, Stephen Fox labeled JPK an "upperworld hoodlum," an "old Irish gangster with Faustian ambitions for his sons, but who still wanted to keep them clean." *Blood and Power,* 306, 309–15, 316.
98. For other reports, see Davis, *Mafia Kingfish,* 41–42; Fox, *Blood and Power,* 20, 43; G. Robert Blakey and Richard N. Billings, *Fatal Hour: The Assassination of President Kennedy by Organized Crine* (New York: Berkely, 1992, originally published in 1981 as *The Plot to Kill the President*), 407–8; Michael R. Beschloss, *The Crisis Years: Kennedy and Khrushchev, 1960–1965* (New York: Burlingame, 1991), 140–41; Charles Rappleye and Ed Becker, *All American Mafioso: The Johnny Roselli Story* (New York: Doubleday, 1991), 202–5, 354n. "It is certainly clear that [Los Angeles hoodlum] John Roselli had access to Joe," Anthony Summers stressed, because they played golf "from time to time since the thirties." Summers, *Official and Confidential,* 268–69; Summers to Hilty, 12 June 1993. A recent biography of JPK repeats the charges, going so far as to assert that JPK's fortune was founded on bootlegging. In subsequent pages the author contradicts himself by demonstrating that JPK earned his initial fortune legally. See Ronald Kessler, *The Sins of the Father* (New York: Warner, 1996), 36–38.
99. See Goodwin, *Fitzgeralds and Kennedys,* 514–15, which explains how JPK obtained import licenses. If JPK, as is often charged, was a well-known bootlegger, one would expect to find at least some mention of him in the U.S. Coast

Guard intelligence files. A search of those files by Mark Haller, professor of history at Temple University, yielded no such mention of JPK or his associates.

100. Blakey and Billings, *Fatal Hour,* 407–8.
101. JPK FBI File in Folder 14, O&C. When the initial FBI report indicated "no active employment" for JPK since 1940, Hoover directed agents to probe deeper to discover "how he occupies himself" and to "advise present location of daughter Rosemary." "Personal Security Questionnaire," 15 March 1956; FBI report, 20 February 1956, Folder 11, O&C; also see Folder 14 for derogatory information on JPK's children. Of the FBI's 343 case files on JPK, none indicate any wrongdoing or criminal associations. Also, see Athan Theoharis and John Stuart Cox, *The Boss: J. Edgar Hoover and the Great American Inquisition* (Philadelphia: Temple U. Press, 1988), 338; and Theoharis, *Secret Files,* 317–23.
102. LeMoyne Billings, interview by Peter Collier and David Horowitz, *The Kennedys: An American Drama* (New York: Warner, 1984), 279.
103. Clayton Fritchey, interview by Stein and Plimpton, *American Journey* 54. Harris Wofford, interview by author, 20 May 1989 in Philadelphia. Also see Harris Wofford, *Of Kennedys and Kings: Making Sense of the Sixties* (New York: Farrar, Straus and Giroux, 1980), 32–33.
104. Edwin Guthman, *We Band of Brothers* (New York: Harper and Row, 1971), 56–57.
105. *Philadelphia Bulletin,* 26 January 1958.
106. Memo, A. Rosen to J. E. Hoover, 7 March 1959, Folder 13, O&C.
107. Schlesinger, *Robert Kennedy,* 198. The Associated Press incorrectly reported that Kennedy resigned "during a row with committee members." *Philadelphia Bulletin,* 30 December 1959.
108. Obviously concerned to avoid the appearance of possible misuse of government resources and staff, Watt made a point of emphasizing that the presidential campaign planning took place "after hours." Watt was intensely loyal to the Kennedys. RFK arranged a job for her husband, Walter, on JFK's staff. He also invited the Watts to Hyannis Port and to parties on the Skakel family yacht. Watt interview, 97, 170, 181.
109. See Parmet, *Jack,* 320–30; Thomas Reeves, *A Question of Character: The Life of John F. Kennedy* (New York: Free Press, 1991), 127–28; James N. Giglio, *The Presidency of John F. Kennedy* (Lawrence: U. of Kansas Press, 1993), 11–12. In December 1957, columnist Drew Pearson stated on Mike Wallace's ABC television show that *Profiles* was ghostwritten. Joseph Kennedy hired an attorney (Clark Clifford) and threatened a lawsuit. ABC capitulated, airing a retraction and an apology. Clifford bluffed ABC by showing them portions of JFK's handwritten drafts to prove authorship; the event doubtless influenced RFK to handwrite his entire book. See Clark Clifford, *Counsel to the President* (New York: Random House, 1991), 306–10.
110. Schlesinger, *Robert Kennedy,* 204.
111. RFK, *The Enemy Within,* 307.

CHAPTER 6

1. John H. Davis, *The Kennedys: Dynasty and Disaster, 1848–1984* (New York: McGraw-Hill, 1984), 151.
2. Richard Goodwin, *Remembering America: A Voice from the Sixties* (Boston: Little, Brown, 1988), 76–77; Doris Goodwin, *The Fitzgeralds and the Kennedys: An American Saga* (New York: St. Martin's, 1987), 917.
3. On the 1960 campaign, see Theodore White, *The Making of the President 1960* (New York: Atheneum, 1961); Arthur M. Schlesinger, Jr., *A Thousand Days: John F. Kennedy in the White House* (Boston: Houghton Mifflin, 1965), 26–117; Herbert S. Parmet, *Jack: The Struggles of John F. Kennedy* (New York: Dial, 1980), 500–23; James N. Giglio, *The Presidency of John F. Kennedy* (Lawrence: U. of Kansas Press, 1993), 16–22; Thomas C. Reeves, *A Question of Character: The LIfe of John F. Kennedy* (New York: Free Press, 1991), 157–216; Kathleen Hall Jamieson, *The Packaging of the Presidency* (New York: Oxford U. Press, 1990), 122–68; David Burner and Thomas R. West, *The Torch Is Passed: The Kennedy Brothers and American Liberalism* (New York: Brandywine, 1984), 63–97; Jim F. Heath, *Decade of Disillusionment: The Kennedy-Johnson Years* (Bloomington: Indiana U. Press, 1975), 14–48; Goodwin, *Fitzgeralds and Kennedys,* 917–31.
4. David Halberstam, *The Powers That Be* (New York: Knopf, 1979), 324–25, 339–41, 386–89.
5. Richard Whalen, *The Founding Father* (New York: New American Library, 1964), 431–51.
6. Rose Kennedy, *Times to Remember* (Garden City, N.Y.: Doubleday, 1974), 383.
7. Arthur M. Schlesinger, Jr., *Robert Kennedy and His Times* (Boston: Houghton Mifflin, 1978), 206; Peter Collier and David Horowitz, *The Kennedys: An American Drama* (New York: Warner, 1984), 266–69.
8. White, *Making of the President 1960,* 124; Harris Wofford, *Of Kennedys and Kings: Making Sense of the Sixties* (New York: Farrar, Straus and Giroux, 1980), 41–46.
9. Parmet, *Jack,* 507.
10. Goodwin, *Remembering America,* 40, 72.
11. White, *Making of the President 1960,* 59–69.
12. Schlesinger, *Robert Kennedy,* 207; White, *Making of the President 1960,* 64; Lester David and Irene David, *Bobby Kennedy: The Making of a Folk Hero* (New York: PaperJacks, 1988), 107.
13. Parmet, *Jack,* 512; Schlesinger, *Robert Kennedy,* 209.
14. Halberstam, *The Powers That Be,* 319–23.
15. Niccolo Machiavelli, *The Prince,* ed. T. G. Bergin (New York: Appleton-Century-Crofts, 1947), 71.
16. White, *Making of the President 1960,* 67; Halberstam, *The Powers That Be,* 323.
17. The Kennedys seldom mentioned that Pius XII had conferred on Rose Kennedy the title papal countess. She used the title only at church functions and

when visiting predominantly Catholic countries, such as Italy and France. Rose Kennedy, *Times to Remember,* 394–95.

18. On Kennedy's management of the religious issue, see Jamieson, *Packaging the Presidency,* 124–39; Burner and West, *The Torch Is Passed,* 82–84.
19. Schlesinger, *Robert Kennedy,* 212; Reeves, *A Question of Character,* 160–61; Collier and Horowitz, *The Kennedys,* 294–95.
20. Lee Benson, telephone interview by the author, 1 November 1991.
21. After the Wisconsin primary Corbin helped JFK win eleven of twelve of the "most Protestant" counties in West Virginia and worked the upper New York state area. HUACC investigated Paul Corbin (nee Paul Kobinsky in Canada) in 1946 and accused him of working for Communists in Wisconsin. The charges were revived in August 1961 in an unsuccessful attempt to embarrass the Kennedys. Probably the most loyal of the Kennedy followers, he converted to Catholicism because the Kennedys were Catholics. Schlesinger, *Robert Kennedy,* 211; *Milwaukee Journal,* 24 August 1961; Corbin Folder, Box 1, AG-PC.
22. Schlesinger, *Robert Kennedy,* 212; Rose Kennedy, *Times to Remember,* 394.
23. White, *Making of the President 1960,* 93–137; Halberstam, *The Powers That Be,* 323. West Virginians had elected Catholics to statewide office before. See Richard Bradford, "John F. Kennedy and the 1960 Presidential Primary in West Virginia," *South Atlantic Quarterly* 75 (Spring 1976): 161–72.
24. Joseph Rauh, OH-JFK, 218; Hubert Humphrey, *The Education of a Public Man* (Garden City, N.Y.: Doubleday, 1976), 221; Schlesinger, *Robert Kennedy,* 216; Theodore C. Sorensen, *Kennedy* (New York: Harper and Row, 1965), 141.
25. See, for example, Edmund F. Kallina, *Courthouse over White House: Chicago and the Presidential Election of 1960* (Orlando: University of Central Florida Press, 1988), 57, for a debunking of the notion that JPK persuaded Chicago mayor Richard Daley to endorse JFK at the Los Angeles convention.
26. See Whalen, *Founding Father,* 437–49; Goodwin, *Fitzgeralds and Kennedys,* 919; Parmet, *Jack,* 521; Rose Kennedy, *Times to Remember,* 358–61, 387; Morton Downey, interview by Collier and Horowitz, *The Kennedys,* 263.
27. Davis, *The Kennedys,* 156–62; Whalen, *Founding Father,* 79, 170, 366–72, 399–402.
28. White, *Making of the President 1960,* 120–21, 131–32; Herbert S. Parmet, *JFK: The Presidency of John F. Kennedy* (New York: Dial, 1983), 19. The Kennedys reported spending $150,000 on the West Virginia campaign; this did not include the costs of the leased aircraft ($385,000) or of the Louis Harris polls ($300,000). Humphrey reported spending $116,500 in Wisconsin and $23,000 in West Virginia. Jamieson, *Packaging the Presidency,* 165.
29. Harrison E. Salisbury, *Heroes of My Time* (New York: Walker, 1993), 16.
30. Quoted in Schlesinger, *Robert Kennedy,* 215.
31. Thomas P. "Tip" O'Neill, *Man of the House* (New York: St. Martin's, 1978), 106. Joseph Rauh, OH-JFK, 66. Theodore H. White, *In Search of History* (New York: Harper and Row, 1978), 466.

32. Rosen to Evans, 5 July 1960, Folder 13, O&C.
33. Judith Campbell Exner, with Ovid Demaris, *My Story* (New York: Grove, 1978), 86–106; Kitty Kelley, "The Dark Side of Camelot," *People,* 29 February 1988 109–11; Judith Campbell-Exner interview on "Larry King Live," CNN, April 1993. Thomas Reeves, found Campbell's allegations credible; see *A Question of Character,* 214, 262, 278, 424*n,* 448*n.* For Mafia claims, see Sam and Chuck Giancana, *Double Cross: The Explosive, Inside Story of the Mobster Who Controlled America* (New York: Warner, 1992), 267–74, 280–81, 284–85, 289–97; Rappleye and Becker, *All American Mafioso,* 205. On Sinatra: Orleans SAC (Bachman) to Hoover (23 March 1960), Folder 13, O&C Files; Summers, *Official and Confidential,* 268–70; Stephen Fox, *Blood and Power: Organized Crime in Twentieth- Century America* (New York: Penguin Books, 1989), 306–346.
34. G. Robert Blakey and Richard N. Billings, *Fatal Hour: The Assassination of President Kennedy by Organized Crime* (New York: Berkely, 1992, orginally published as *The Plot the Kill the President,* 1981), 408.
35. Charles Spalding, OH-JFK, 70.
36. Richard Whalen estimated that JPK committed $1.5 million to his son's preconvention campaign. *Founding Father,* 441. The Kennedys officially reported expenditures of $912,500 for the preconvention period. Parmet, *JFK,* 19.
37. White, *Making of the President 1960,* 127; Schlesinger, *A Thousand Days,* 1005; Goodwin, *Fitzgeralds and Kennedys,* 921.
38. Schlesinger, *Robert Kennedy,* 213.
39. The Kennedys penalized those who failed to answer the call immediately. Harris Wofford, offered the number two speech-writing assignment behind Sorensen, felt obligated to honor his teaching contract at Notre Dame Law School, despite Joseph Kennedy's interceding directly with the president of Notre Dame. In the interim the Kennedys hired Richard Goodwin to fill Wofford's position. When the school year ended, Wofford received a tepid welcome by RFK and was assigned a lesser position. Interview with Wofford, and Wofford, *Of Kennedys and Kings,* 44–45.
40. Helen Keyes, interview by Jean Stein and George Plimpton, eds., *American Journey: The Times of Robert Kennedy* (New York: Harcourt Brace Jovanovich, 1970), 69. Rose Kennedy was in fourteen states and made forty-six appearances during the 1960 campaign. *Times to Remember,* 395, 398.
41. UPI release, *Philadelphia Bulletin,* 26 May 1960.
42. William O. Douglas, OH-JFKL, 13. Ethel Kennedy interview, NBC-News, "RFK," 28 May 1993.
43. Schlesinger, *Robert Kennedy,* 230–31.
44. O'Neill, *Man of the House,* 105.
45. JFK won primaries in New Hampshire, Wisconsin, Indiana, West Virginia, Nebraska, and Oregon. Jim Heath, in *Decade of Disillusionment,* 39, declared the Kennedy campaign "may well have been the most efficient in American political history."

46. Arthur Schlesinger, Jr., interview by Stein and Plimpton, *American Journey,* 68. Harris Wofford, OH-JFK, 15.
47. Schlesinger, *Robert Kennedy,* 208.
48. See David McCullough, *Truman* (New York: Simon and Schuster, 1992), 970, 973; and Jamieson, *Packaging the Presidency,* 139–42.
49. See Jamieson, *Packaging the Presidency,* 140, for an analysis of the speech and its impact. Ironically, Vice-President Dan Quayle's use of the same defense of his youth through analogous comparison of his length of elected service to JFK's backfired spectacularly in the 1988 vice-presidential debates, when Senator Lloyd Bentsen asserted, "You're no Jack Kennedy."
50. Halberstam, *The Powers That Be,* 326–27; Jamieson, *Packaging the Presidency,* 139–41.
51. Joseph Dolan, OH-JFK, 44–45.
52. Schlesinger, *Robert Kennedy,* 221.
53. John Kenneth Galbraith, interview by Stein and Plimpton, *American Journey,* 68. Murray Kempton, interview by Stein and Plimpton, ibid., 72. Jacques Lowe and Wilfred Sheed, *The Kennedy Legacy: A Generation Later* (New York: Viking, 1988), 47.
54. Parmet, *JFK,* 34.
55. Dolan, OH-JFK, 46, 49.
56. Ibid., 42–43.
57. Whalen, *Founding Father,* 438–43; Wofford, *Of Kennedys and Kings,* 53.
58. White, *Making of the President 1960,* 214–15. Also see O'Neill, *Man of the House,* 105.
59. Schlesinger, *Robert Kennedy,* 220; Paul R. Henggeler, *In His Steps: Lyndon Johnson and the Kennedy Mystique* (Chicago: Dee, 1991), 37; Goodwin, *Fitzgeralds and the Kennedys,* 849.
60. Kenneth O'Donnell, interview by David and David, *Bobby Kennedy,* 152. Some of Johnson's comments were made to television reporter Peter Lisagor, whom RFK prevailed upon to tell him exactly what Johnson had said about his brother and father. Afterwards, RFK told Lisagor, "I knew he hated Jack, but I didn't think he hated him that much." Interview, by David and David, *Bobby Kennedy,* 152–53.
61. John Kenneth Galbraith, interview by Stein and Plimpton, *American Journey,* 68.
62. White, *Making of the President 1960,* 172–73, 180–215; William Manchester, *The Glory and the Dream* (Boston: Little, Brown, 1974), 880–81; Theodore C. Sorensen, "Election of 1960," in *Critical Elections in American History,* ed. Arthur M. Schlesinger, Jr. (New York: Chelsea House, 1971), 437–57.
63. Harris Wofford, OH-JFK, 8, 42, and *Of Kennedys and Kings,* 47, 60. As a condition for joining Kennedy's staff, Louis Martin demanded the Democratic National Committee pay the $49,000 debt still owed black newspapers from the 1956 campaign. Jamieson, *Packaging the Presidency,* 144.
64. Wofford, *Of Kennedys and Kings,* 52.

65. Schlesinger, *A Thousand Days,* 34; Wofford, *Of Kennedys and Kings,* 52; Joe Rauh, OH-JFK, 83–84.
66. Arthur Goldberg to RFK, 17 February 1960, Box 1, AG-PC. Tip O'Neill takes credit for keeping some of the Teamsters in line during the campaign. *Man of the House,* 112.
67. Schlesinger, *Robert Kennedy,* 221; Sorensen, *Kennedy,* 175.
68. Joseph S. Clark, OH-JFK, 40–42; David L. Lawrence, OH-JFK, 25.
69. Schlesinger, *A Thousand Days,* 35–39; White, *Making of the President 1960,* 202–3.
70. Quoted in Goodwin, *Fitzgeralds and Kennedys,* 926.

CHAPTER 7

1. Arthur M. Schlesinger, Jr., *A Thousand Days: John F. Kennedy in the White House* (Boston: Houghton Mifflin, 1965), 58; Edward Kennedy interview, "RFK," NBC-News, March 1993, praised the efficacy of the "Boston-Austin axis."
2. Theodore H. White, *The Making of the President 1964* (New York: Atheneum), 42.
3. Robert F. Kennedy, *Robert Kennedy in His Own Words: The Unpublished Recollections of the Kennedy Years,* ed. Edwin O. Guthman and Jeffrey Shulman (New York: Bantam, 1988), 21.
4. RFK, *Robert Kennedy,* 25–26; Edwin Guthman, *We Band of Brothers* (New York: Harper and Row, 1971), 78–79. The controversy erupted around an April 1964 *Baltimore Sun* article by Philip Potter and his "How LBJ Got the Nomination," *Reporter,* 18 June 1964, 16–20. See Paul R. Henggeler, *In His Steps: Lyndon Johnson and the Kennedy Mystique* (Chicago: Dee, 1991), 43–49, for a concise summary.
5. "I count on your reading the manuscript [*A Thousand Days*] before publication," Schlesinger wrote RFK, "so you can catch any indiscretions at that point." Schlesinger to RFK, 25 February 1965, Box 11, SP-PC. White offered Kennedy various draft chapters of *The Making of the President 1964* "subject to your comment," including the 1960 vice-presidential selection. White to RFK, 25 March 1965 and 5 April 1965, Box 12, SP-PC.
6. Theodore White to RFK, 5 April 1964 [*sic.* 1965], with RFK's marginal note, Box 12, RFK SP-PC.
7. RFK, *Robert Kennedy,* 20–21.
8. Schlesinger, *A Thousand Days,* 56.
9. EMK interview. In a bizarre twist thirty years later, Evelyn Lincoln, JFK's private secretary, voiced suspicions that these intense conversations between JFK and RFK regarded efforts by J. Edgar Hoover and Lyndon Johnson to blackmail the Kennedys into putting Johnson on the ticket. Hoover supposedly had a packet of incriminating photographs of JFK in compromising positions with various women. See Anthony Summers, *Official and Confidential: The Secret Life of J. Edgar Hoover* (New York: Putnam, 1993), 271–72. Such speculation does not

ring true; for one thing, Johnson was vulnerable on the womanizing issue himself. See Herbert S. Parmet, *JFK: The Presidency of John F. Kennedy* (New York: Dial, 1983), 14, n358.

10. RFK, *Robert Kennedy,* 20–21; Katherine Graham, *Personal History* (New York: Knopf, 1997), 267.
11. Quote in Salinger, *With Kennedy,* 46. Accounts vary; see, for example, Theodore H. White, *The Making of the President 1960* (New York: Atheneum, 1961), 206–12, and *Making of the President 1964,* 42–43; Schlesinger, *A Thousand Days,* 39–57; Lyndon B. Johnson, *The Vantage Point,* (New York: Holt, Rinehart and Winston, 1971), 2; Doris Kearns, *Lyndon Johnson and the American Dream* (New York: Harper & Row, 1976), 91–92; Theodore Sorensen, *Kennedy* (New York: Harper and Row, 1965), 182–87; Arthur M. Schlesinger, Jr., *Robert Kennedy and His Times* (Boston: Houghton-Mifflin, 1978), 222–27; Parmet, *JFK,* 21–30; Henggeler, *In His Steps,* 38–49; Thomas C. Reeves, *A Question of Character: The Life of John F. Kennedy* (New York: Free Press, 1991), 176–81. For RFK's version, see RFK, *Robert Kennedy,* 19–26.
12. Schlesinger, *Robert Kennedy,* 222; Theodore H. White, *In Search of History* (New York: Harper and Row, 1978), 469; Chester Bowles, *Promises to Keep: My Years in Public Life, 1941–1969* (New York: Harper and Row, 1971), 297, Graham, *Personal History,* 261.
13. Graham, *Personal History,* 261–62.
14. Wofford, OH-JFK, 72.
15. Rauh, OH-JFK, 86; Schlesinger, *A Thousand Days,* 41–43. David Burner and Thomas R. West, in *The Torch Is Passed: The Kennedy Brothers and American Liberalism* (New York: Brandywine, 1984), 86, suggest that JFK may have assigned RFK the duplicitous job of reassuring liberals that neither really opposed LBJ, and that RFK's opposition was all part of a "cover story." As noted later, however, there are many reasons (RFK's emotional reactions being the most persuasive) for believing this was one instance where JFK and RFK were neither in full agreement nor secret collaborators.
16. Philip L. Graham, "Notes on the 1960 Democratic Convention," Box 11, SP-PC, 7; Graham, *Personal History,* 263.
17. Guthman, *We Band of Brothers,* 74–76, 77; Hugh A. Bone, "The 1960 Election in Washington," *Western Political Quarterly* 14 (March 1961) 373–82. Jackson later was named chair of the Democratic National Committee.
18. G. Mennen Williams to Editor, *U.S. News & World Report,* cc: RFK, 27 July 1965, Box 12, SP-PC. Clifford's recollection of precise chronology is faulty, but his scenario appears reliable otherwise. Clark Clifford, *Counsel to the President* (New York: Random House, 1991), 316–19.
19. Theodore Sorensen, interview by Parmet, *JFK,* 23; *Meet the Press* interview, February 1964, quoted in Victor Lasky, *Robert F. Kennedy: The Myth and the Man* (New York: Trident, 1971), 148.
20. Jack Conway, interview with Jean Stein and George Plimpton, eds., *American*

Journey: The Times of Robert Kennedy (New York: Harcourt Brace Jovanovich, 1970), 72.

21. Harris Wofford, *Of Kennedys and Kings: Making Sense of the Sixties* (New York: Farrar, Straus and Giroux, 1980), 53; Graham, *Personal History,* 263.
22. Thomas P. "Tip" O'Neill, *Man of the House* (New York: St. Martin's, 1987), 108–9. O'Neill's account conflicts with LBJ's office diaries, which indicate Rayburn called LBJ early the evening of 13 July to alert him to rumors that JFK might offer him the second spot and to counsel against accepting. See Parmet, *JFK,* 24, n360. Johnson, however, later told Clark Clifford that it was Rayburn who finally persuaded him to take it. Clifford, *Counsel to the President,* 317. On the stairwell meeting, see White, *Making of the President 1960,* 209.
23. Parmet, *JFK,* 23.
24. Johnson, *Vantage Point,* 2; Harry McPherson, *A Political Education: A Washington Memoir* (Boston: Houghton Mifflin, 1988), 178–79; Bobby Baker, *Wheeling and Dealing: Confessions of a Capitol Hill Operator* (New York: Norton, 1978), 124–26.
25. Michael V. DiSalle to G. Mennen Williams, 6 August 1965, Box 12, SP-PC.
26. Lasky, *Robert F. Kennedy,* 145.
27. Schlesinger, *Robert Kennedy,* 225; Rauh, OH-JFK, 92; Rauh reportedly told others that he was "double-crossed" by RFK. See Lasky, *Robert F. Kennedy,* 147.
28. RFK, *Robert Kennedy,* 21; interview with John Connally in "LBJ: Part I," *American Experience,* PBS, September 1991; Parmet, *JFK,* 29. Cf. Lasky, *Robert F. Kennedy,* 147, which quotes Rayburn as saying, "Sonny, if we want to talk to any Kennedy about the Vice Presidency, it won't be with you."
29. Quoted in Peter Collier and David Horowitz, *The Kennedys: An American Drama* (New York: Warner, 1984), 303.
30. RFK, *Robert Kennedy,* 22. On Johnson's humiliation, see Kearns, *Lyndon Johnson,* 200. LBJ took pleasure in offering RFK the same position in lieu of the vice-presidential nomination in 1964.
31. Herbert Parmet, in *JFK,* 29, persuasively argues that JPK's "intimate involvement in his son's political fortunes did not suddenly cease at the precise moment of Jack's vital decision." Richard Whalen, in an unconfirmed account, states that JPK himself proposed LBJ for the vice-presidency and even called the Texan to convince him to take it. Richard Whalen, *The Founding Father* (New York: New American Library, 1964), 443. Graham, *Personal History,* 264–65.
32. P. L. Graham, "Notes on the 1960 Democratic Convention"; White, *Making of the President 1964,* 429–38. Also see David Halberstam, *The Powers That Be* (New York: Knopf, 1979), 164–65, 376–83; and Collier and Horowitz, *The Kennedys,* 302–4.
33. P. L. Graham "Notes on The 1960 Democratic Convention," 8–15; White, *Making of the President 1960,* 206–12. Philip Graham's manic-depression led him to suicide in 1963, but it was in balance, though precariously, in 1960 and apparently did not affect his abilities as a political broker or his accuracy as a reporter at that time. Graham, *Personal History,* 260, 266, 328–32; David Halberstam, *The*

Powers That Be, 310–315, 579; Evan Thomas, *The Man to See: Edward Bennett Williams, Ultimate Insider, Legendary Trial Lawyer* (New York: Simon & Schuster, 1991), 178–80; Benjamin C. Bradlee, *Ben Bradlee: A Good Life* (New York: Simon & Schuster, 1995), 249–53.

34. Bartlett, interview by John H. Davis, *The Kennedys: Dynasty and Disaster, 1848–1984* (New York: McGraw-Hill, 1984) 304.
35. Katherine Graham, who was present with her husband at the Los Angeles convention, wrote that "neither Jack nor Bobby Kennedy really wanted Johnson on the ticket." When LBJ surprised them by accepting, JFK "made the disingenuous remark that Bobby was out of touch." Graham, *Personal History,* 267.
36. AP and UPI photographs, Urban Archives, Paley Library, Temple University.
37. Richard Goodwin, *Remembering America: A Voice from the Sixties* (Boston: Little, Brown, 1988), 90; White, *Making of the President 1960,* 299–300; David and David, *Bobby Kennedy:* 108; Schlesinger, *Robert Kennedy,* 227.
38. Wofford, OH-JFK, 15; White, *Making of the President 1960,* 300.
39. Clifford, *Counsel to the President,* 320–21.
40. Joseph Tydings, quoted in Schlesinger, *Robert Kennedy,* 229, noted that Kennedy was gentler with volunteers, women, and the young.
41. Schlesinger, *Robert Kennedy,* 228.
42. George Smathers, interview by David and David, *Bobby Kennedy,* 111.
43. O'Neill, *Man of the House,* 95. Quoted in Whalen, *Founding Father,* 445.
44. Jesse Unruh, interview by Stein and Plimpton, *American Journey,* 73.
45. Cited in Schlesinger, *Robert Kennedy,* 230.
46. Parmet, *JFK,* 34–37.
47. Quoted in Whalen, *Founding Father,* 438.
48. See Lawrence H. Fuchs, *John F. Kennedy and American Catholicism* (New York: Meredith, 1967), 177–82.
49. On the Houston speech, see White, *In Search of History,* 485–86; Parmet, *JFK,* 41–44; Kathleen Hall Jamieson, *Dirty Politics: Deception, Distraction, and Democracy* (New York: Oxford U. Press, 1992), 221.
50. Fuchs, *John F. Kennedy,* 249–52.
51. Reeves, *A Question of Character,* 193.
52. Stephen E. Ambrose, *Nixon: The Education of a Politician, 1913–1962* (New York: Simon and Schuster, 1987), 565–66, 602–3.
53. See Albert M. Greenfield to the Reverend Thompson L. Casey, Jr., 5 December 1960, and the pamphlet "Why *Not* A Catholic for President" (Chicago: Voltaire Society, 1960), Albert M. Greenfield Papers, Historical Society of Pennsylvania, Philadelphia.
54. Estimates are that JFK carried 78–80 percent of the Catholic vote and 38–46 percent of the Protestant vote in the 1960 election. Religion hurt him in the popular vote but aided him in the Electoral College tabulations. See White, *In Search of History,* 488; Allen J. Matusow, *The Unraveling of America: A History of Liberalism in the 1960s* (New York: Harper and Row, 1984), 27–28.

55. Schlesinger, *Robert Kennedy,* 231.
56. RFK, *Robert Kennedy,* 66.
57. King quoted in David Garrow, *Bearing the Cross: Martin Luther King, Jr., and the Southern Christian Leadership Conference* (New York: Random House, 1986), 139. Also see Wofford, *Of Kennedys and Kings,* 461. Singer Harry Belafonte recalled advising JFK to establish a close relationship with Martin Luther King, Jr., and his shock when JFK asked, "What can he do?" Taylor Branch, *Parting the Waters: America in The King Years, 1954–63* (New York: Simon and Schuster, 1988), 306–7.
58. RFK, *Robert Kennedy,* 66–67; Schlesinger, *Robert Kennedy,* 231.
59. RFK, *Robert Kennedy,* 67.
60. Branch, *Parting the Waters,* 342.
61. Martin, interview by Nicholas Lemann, *The Promised Land: The Great Black Migration and How It Changed America* (New York: Knopf, 1991), 113.
62. RFK, *Robert Kennedy,* 72.
63. Wofford, *Of Kennedys and Kings,* 60; Lemann, *Promised Land,* 112–13; Branch, *Parting the Waters,* 342–43.
64. Abernathy and King reportedly voted for Eisenhower in 1956. Branch, *Parting the Waters,* 191–92, 220. King sensed something about the person Garry Wills once described as the "least authentic" man alive. "If Richard Nixon is not sincere," King wrote Abernathy, "he is the most dangerous man in America." Branch, *Parting the Waters,* 219; Lemann, *Promised Land,* 113–14.
65. Quoted in Garrow, *Bearing the Cross,* 142.
66. Seigenthaler to RFK, 6 March 1961, Box 53, AG-GC; Wofford, OH-JFK, 20, and *Of Kennedys and Kings,* 15–16; Garrow, *Bearing the Cross,* 144; Branch, *Parting the Waters,* 351–53.
67. Wofford OH-JFK, 23; Garrow, *Bearing the Cross,* 145; Branch, *Parting the Waters,* 359.
68. Wofford, *Of Kennedys and Kings,* 18–19.
69. Ibid., 20.
70. Recollections vary of what RFK told others that he said to Judge Mitchell. See Harris Wofford and John Seigenthaler, interviews by Stein and Plimpton, *American Journey,* 92–94; Wofford, *Of Kennedys and Kings,* 21, 27; John Seigenthaler interview by David and David, *Bobby Kennedy,* 186; Schlesinger, *Robert Kennedy,* 235; Garrow, *Bearing the Cross,* 147; Branch, *Parting the Waters,* 364–68.
71. Wofford, *Of Kennedys and Kings,* 22.
72. Ambrose, *Nixon,* 596.
73. Wofford, *Of Kennedys and Kings,* 22, and OH-JFK, 37.
74. RFK, *Robert Kennedy,* 69–71. Governor Vandiver promised to get King released in return for a pledge from JFK not to make additional calls. Wofford OH-JFK, 23; Branch, *Parting the Waters,* 359.
75. William Haddad interview, NBC-News, "RFK."
76. Branch, *Parting the Waters,* 366.

77. Garrow, *Bearing the Cross,* 149; Branch, *Parting the Waters,* 368–69; Wofford, *Of Kennedys and Kings,* 25–26; Kathleen Hall Jamieson, *The Packaging of the Presidency,* (New York: Oxford U. Press, 1990), 144–46.
78. Halberstam, *The Powers That Be,* 318–19.
79. Jamieson, *Packaging the Presidency,* 162–67.
80. Doris Goodwin, *The Fitzgeralds and The Kennedys: An American Saga* (New York: St. Martin's, 1987), 928–29.
81. Halberstam, *The Powers That Be,* 328. Theodore C. Sorensen, "Election of 1960," in Arthur M. Schlesinger, Jr., *The Coming to Power* (New York: Chelsea House, 1972), 437–57.
82. Halberstam, *The Powers That Be,* 338–41.
83. Benjamin C. Bradlee, *Conversations with Kennedy* (New York: Pocketbooks, 1976), 194; Jamieson, *Packaging the Presidency,* 165–68; White, *In Search of History,* 465.
84. Cornelius Ryan, interview by Stein and Plimpton, *American Journey,* 74; Rose Kennedy, *Times to Remember* (New York: Doubleday, 1974), 402.
85. James Reston, *Deadline* (New York: Random House, 1991), 288–89; Sorensen, "Election of 1960," 457; White, *Making of the President 1960,* 414–15.
86. Nixon pondered an official recount, but vote fraud in Texas and Illinois could have favored either side. Theodore H. White, *Breach of Faith: The Fall of Richard Nixon* (New York: Dell, 1975), 96–97; Bradlee, *Conversations with Kennedy,* 33. The Republican National Committee considered recounts in eleven states. RNC chair Thruston B. Morton held out hope of reversing JFK's victory until 12 December, when judges in Texas and Illinois tossed out GOP suits to delay certification of the election. See Edmund F. Kallina, Jr., *Courthouse over White House: Chicago and the Presidential Election of 1960* (Orlando: U. of Central Florida Press, 1988), 97–99.
87. The theory is fully developed in Earl Warren, *The Warren Commission Report: Report of the President's Commission on the Assassination of President John F. Kennedy* (1964; reprint, New York: St. Martin's, 1992); G. Robert Blakey and Richard N. Billings, *Fatal Hour: The Assassination of President Kennedy by Organized Crime* (New York: Berkely, 1992, originally published as *The Plot to Kill the President,* 1981); John H. Davis, *Mafia Kingfish: Carlos Marcello and the Assassination of John F. Kennedy* (New York: New American Library, 1989); David E. Scheim, *Contract on America: The Mafia Murder of President John F. Kennedy* (New York: Zebra, 1988); Stephen Fox, *Blood and Power: Organized Crime in Twentieth-Century America* (New York: Morrow, 1989); William Brashler, *The Don: The Life and Death of Sam Giancana* (New York: Harper and Row, 1977); Judith Campbell Exner with Ovid Demaris, *My Story* (New York: Grove, 1977); Kitty Kelley, "The Dark Side of Camelot," *People,* 29 February 1988, 111.
88. Blakey and Billings, *Fatal Hour,* 408–9. Cf. Kallina, in *Courthouse over White House,* 266, who found that Chicago's First and Twenty-eighth Wards, the "two premier syndicate strangleholds," produced low vote counts for JFK compared

to other wards. Still, the influence of the crime syndicate on the outcome of the 1960 presidential election in Chicago, Kallina concludes, "is impossible to weigh, and there is no chance of resolving the issue."

89. Kallina, *Courthouse over White House,* 125, 166, n273. Nixon, according to rumors, also benefitted from direct contributions from organized crime elements, laundered through James Hoffa and the Teamsters. Michael R. Beschloss, *The Crisis Years: Kennedy and Krushchev, 1960–1965* (New York: Burlingame, 1991), 140–41. After the election of 1960, Hoffa offered to sell Nixon a house lot at a "celebrity discount." Ambrose, *Nixon,* 629.
90. Kallina, *Courthouse over White House,* 145–173.
91. "Why Nixon Lost the Negro Vote," *Crisis,* January 1961, 7; "Negroes Tip the Scales," *Economist,* 26 November 1960, 888; Paul T. David, *The Presidential Election and Transition, 1960–1961* (Washington: Brookings, 1961), 272.
92. Parmet, *JFK,* 40; Schlesinger, *Robert Kennedy,* 237.
93. Garrow, *Bearing the Cross,* 149. "Two little phone calls about the welfare of a Negro preacher," Taylor Branch concisely concluded, "were the necessary cause of the Democratic victory." *Parting the Waters,* 378.
94. Bradlee, *Conversations with Kennedy,* 231.
95. White, *In Search of History,* 491; David and David, *Bobby Kennedy,* 117–20; Parmet, *JFK,* 59–60.

CHAPTER 8

1. See Richard Reeves, *President Kennedy: Profile of Power* (New York: Simon and Schuster, 1993), 19, 52; James N. Giglio, *The Presidency of John F. Kennedy* (Lawrence: U. of Kansas Press, 1993), 27–28.
2. Fletcher Knebel, "Bobby Kennedy: He Hates to Be Second," *Look,* 21 May 1963, 91; William V. Shannon, *The Heir Apparent: Robert Kennedy and the Struggle for Power* (New York: Macmillan, 1967), 71.
3. *Newsweek,* 21 November 1960, 32; Shannon, *The Heir Apparent,* 61; David Halberstam, *The Best and the Brightest* (New York: Random House, 1972).
4. Adam Yarmolinsky, telephone interview, 29 November 1993, by author, and Yarmolinsky OH-JFK, 19–24.
5. J. Edward Day, interview by Lester David and Irene David, *Bobby Kennedy: The Making of a Folk Hero* (New York: PaperJacks, 1988), 145.
6. Robert F. Kennedy, *Robert Kennedy in His Own Words: The Unpublished Recollections of the Kennedy Years,* ed. Edwin O. Guthman and Jeffrey Shulman (New York: Bantam, 1988), 41–44.
7. Deborah Shapley, *Promise and Power: The Life and Times of Robert McNamara* (Boston: Little, Brown, 1993), 82–89; Reeves, *President Kennedy,* 25; RFK, *Robert Kennedy,* 35–36.
8. RFK, *Robert Kennedy,* 38–39; Michael R. Beschloss, *The Crisis Years: Kennedy and Krushchev, 1960–1965* (New York: Burlingame, 1991), 462–67. The

Kennedys were undeterred by rumors of Stevenson's homosexuality and by FBI accusations that he was a "sex deviate." See Curt Gentry, *J. Edgar Hoover: The Man and the Secrets* (New York: Norton, 1991), 402–3. The Kennedys thought Stevenson unmanly. After seeing him emerge from a shower, JFK described him as "a bitter old man with a little thing." Reeves, *President Kennedy*,. 16.

9. On RFK's role in the transition, see Arthur M. Schlesinger, Jr., *Robert Kennedy and His Times* (New York: Houghton Mifflin, 1978), 238–45; RFK, *Robert Kennedy*, 36–68; Harris Wofford, *Of Kennedys and Kings: Making Sense of the Sixties* (New York: Farrar, Straus and Giroux, 1970), 74, 82; David and David, *Bobby Kennedy*, 121–22, 145. Fulbright told Herbert Parmet that it was actually Joseph Kennedy who forced him to withdraw, after confronting him with his liabilities. Herbert S. Parmet, *JFK: The Presidency of John F. Kennedy* (New York: Dial, 1983), 67–68.
10. Ben Bradlee, who overheard JFK's telephone conversations in which Hoover and Dulles were asked to stay on, thought he "laid it on a bit thick." Benjamin C. Bradlee, *Conversations with Kennedy* (New York: Norton, 1975), 34, and *Ben Bradlee: A Good Life* (New York: Simon and Schuster, 1995), 213–14. At the same time, RFK quietly prevailed upon his brother to continue Harry Anslinger as director of the Narcotics Bureau. RFK, *Robert Kennedy*, 55.
11. Quoted in Wofford, *Of Kennedys and Kings*, 92.
12. Doris Goodwin, *The Fitzgeralds and the Kennedys: An American Saga* (New York: St. Martin's, 1987), 933.
13. Arthur M. Schlesinger, Jr., *A Thousand Days: John F. Kennedy in the White House* (Boston: Houghton Mifflin, 1965), 142.
14. RFK, *Robert Kennedy*, 74.
15. George Smathers, interview by David and David, *Bobby Kennedy*, 120–21.
16. Clark Clifford, *Counsel to the President* (New York: Random House, 1991), 336–37; Parmet, *JFK*, 64–65. Cf. Rose Kennedy, *Times to Remember* (Garden City, N.Y.: Doubleday, 1974), 419, who recalled John wanted Robert to be attorney general and her husband thought it was the "perfect idea."
17. Shapley, *Promise and Power*, 85.
18. Beschloss, *The Crisis Years*, 302–3; Wofford, OH-JFK, 92, 124. RFK told Wofford that his first choice for attorney general was Byron White.
19. RFK, *Robert Kennedy*, 42, 74; Schlesinger, *A Thousand Days*, 141–42.
20. Schlesinger, *Robert Kennedy*, 247; David and David, *Bobby Kennedy*, 120, 127. Ethel Kennedy interview, NBC-News, "RFK," May 1993. Hoover quoted in Anthony Summers, *Official and Confidential: The Secret LIfe of J. Edgar Hoover* (New York: Putnam, 1993), 277; also see Victor Navasky, *Kennedy Justice* (New York: Atheneum, 1971), 4; Curt Gentry, *J. Edgar Hoover: The Man and the Secrets* (New York: Norton, 1991), 407.
21. Drew Pearson to RFK, 5 December 1960, Box 1, AG-PC.
22. Schlesinger, *Robert Kennedy*, 249; Peter Collier and David Horowitz, *The Kennedys: An American Drama* (New York: Warner, 1984), 319–21.

23. John Seigenthaler interview, NBC-News, "RFK," May 1993; Navasky, *Kennedy Justice,* xviii–xix; Schlesinger, *Robert Kennedy,* 249–51; Reeves, *President Kennedy,* 29.
24. Beschloss, in *The Crisis Years,* 303, reported the DNC mail ran one hundred to one against Robert's appointment. Harrison E. Salisbury, *Heroes of My Time* (New York: Walker, 1993), 17–18. Wofford, *Of Kennedys and Kings,* 91.
25. Navasky, *Kennedy Justice,* xix; Schlesinger, *Robert Kennedy,* 250–52; David and David, *Bobby Kennedy,* 124–25; Beschloss, *The Crisis Years,* 303.
26. Charles Bartlett, interview by Jean Stein and George Plimpton, eds., *American Journey: The Times of Robert Kennedy* (New York: Harcourt Brace Jovanovich, 1970), 75.
27. RFK speech to Peoria and Illinois Bar Associations, 13 February 1960, Box 1, AG-PC.
28. Goldberg to RFK, 14 March 1961, Box 1, AG-PC; Schlesinger, *Robert Kennedy,* 246–54.
29. Stephen E. Ambrose, *Nixon: The Education of a Politician, 1913–1962* (New York: Simon and Schuster, 1978), 630. RFK told the Judiciary Committee he had disposed of everything except government and municipal bonds. Schlesinger, *Robert Kennedy,* 252–54. At the time of his confirmation RFK thought he was a "major asset" in the South and that his strongest support came from southerners John L. McClellan (Arkansas), Samuel J. Ervin (North Carolina), and James O. Eastland (Mississippi). RFK, *Robert Kennedy,* 331.
30. Quoted in Reeves, *President Kennedy,* 29.
31. David and David, *Bobby Kennedy,* 125. Richard Rush, appointed attorney general by James Madison in 1814, was only thirty-three when he took office. Caesar A. Rodney was barely thirty-five when appointed by Thomas Jefferson in 1807.
32. Warren Rogers, *When I Think of Bobby* (New York: HarperCollins, 1993), 20–21.
33. H. Harris to RFK, 26 January 1962, Box 2, AG-PC.
34. Charles Bartlett once had a handwriting analyst comment on RFK's scrawl. The analyst, according to Bartlett, believed the writing revealed someone who was "careless on small things . . . more ambitious than practical . . . always on the go mentally or physically" who "can be and impulsive" and "could be franker." The writer was someone with "pride, possibly conceited," who possessed "energy, ambition, and ardor." Bartlett to RFK, 25 January 1967, Box 2, SP-PC.
35. Bradlee, *Conversations with Kennedy,* 224–25; Rose Kennedy, *Times to Remember,* 384–85.
36. Edwin Guthman, *We Band of Brothers* (New York: Harper and Row, 1971), 80–83; David and David, *Bobby Kennedy,* 126–34; Navasky, *Kennedy Justice,* 25; Schlesinger, *Robert Kennedy,* 250, 257–59.
37. David and David, *Robert Kennedy,* 128.
38. Navasky, *Kennedy Justice,* 25.
39. Ramsey Clark and Walter Sheridan, interviews by Stein and Plimpton, *American Journey,* 77–79.

40. Navasky, *Kennedy Justice,* 26–27.
41. Contrary to rumors within the FBI, as reported in Gentry, *J. Edgar Hoover,* 475–76, RFK was not himself denied access to the FBI gymnasium. Indeed, his desk diary indicates that he was assigned locker number B259.
42. Guthman, *Band of Brothers,* 106; Schlesinger, *Robert Kennedy,* 261–62; David and David, *Bobby Kennedy,* 129–30.
43. Angie Novello to Stephen E. Smith, 13 September 1962; various notes and letters, Box 5, AG-PC.
44. Burke Marshall, OH-JFK, 11.
45. RFK telephone messages, 29 August 1961, JFK-ARC.
46. Navasky, *Kennedy Justice,* 25; David and David, *Bobby Kennedy,* 131; Gentry, *J. Edgar Hoover,* 476–77; Mark North, *Act of Treason* (New York: Carroll and Graf, 1991), 65; Richard Gid Powers, *Secrecy and Power: The Life of J. Edgar Hoover* (New York: Free Press, 1987), 355; [anonymous] letters to J. E. Hoover, 6 August 1962, Section 1, RFK-FBI.
47. Schlesinger, *Robert Kennedy,* 254–57; Halberstam, *The Powers That Be,* 398–99. Also reporting to RFK were the directors of the Bureau of Prisons, the Immigration and Naturalization Service, the U.S. Marshals Service, and the International Criminal Police Organization.
48. Guthman said RFK's favorite Shakespeare quotation was the Saint Crispin's Day speech that included "We few, we happy few, we band of brothers," from *Henry V* at Agincourt. See Guthman, *We Band of Brothers;* Schlesinger, *Robert Kennedy,* 256–60; David and David, *Bobby Kennedy,* 127–29; Breslin, "The Music Is Different," RFK-FBI.
49. RFK telegram to Angier Biddle Duke, 18 July 1961, Box 1, AG-PC.
50. Still loyal after all these years, Guthman, Cox, Seigenthaler, Marshall, Katzenbach, and Miller, joined Kathleen Kennedy Townsend, Anthony Lewis, Joe Dolan, and John Douglas at the Duquesne University Law School symposium "Reflections on RFK as Attorney General," 12 April 1996, telecast on C-SPAN.
51. Schlesinger, *Robert Kennedy,* 258–263.
52. Navasky, *Kennedy Justice,* 52–54.
53. Ibid., 49–51; G. Robert Blakey and Richard N. Billings, *Fatal Hour: The Assassination of President Kennedy by Organized Crime* (New York: Berkely, 1992, originally published as *The Plot the Kill the President,* 1981), 223–30; John H. Davis, *Mafia Kingfish: Carlos Marcello and the Assassination of John F. Kennedy* (New York: New American Library, 1989), 95–199; David E. Scheim, *Contract on America: The Mafia Murder of President John F. Kennedy* (New York: Zebra, 1988), 76–79; Ronald Goldfarb, *Perfect Villains, Imperfect Heroes: Robert F. Kennedy's War against Organized Crime* (New York: Random House, 1996).
54. David E. Feller to William Peyton Martin, 9 April 1963, *James R. Hoffa v. N.B.C., Jack Paar, and RFK,* 4 February 1963, Box 7, AG-PC. The JFK Library has restricted access to some correspondence concerning the final disposition of Hoffa's suit.
55. Harriet F. Pilpel to RFK, 7 October 1960; Seigenthaler to Pilpel, 31 January

1961, Box 10, AG-PC. RFK was also sued by authors of a book of the same title; see Pilpel to RFK, 18 November 1960, Box 10, AG-PC.

56. Evan Thomas to RFK, 4 August and 15 September 1960, Box 1, AG-PC.
57. Nat Weiss to Edwin Guthman, 27 April 1961, Box 10, AG-PC; Vernon Scott, "Robert Kennedy's Book Poses Problem as a Movie," *Philadelphia Bulletin,* 3 April 1961; Schlesinger, *Robert Kennedy,* 281–82; Blakey and Billings, *Fatal Hour,* 223; Budd Schulberg, introduction to *The Fall and Rise of Jimmy Hoffa,* by Walter Sheridan (New York: Saturday Review, 1972), xii–xv. David Wolper and Irving Lazar once considered doing a television documentary on the book, but JFK's assassination intervened. See Don Prince to Guthman, 15 October 1963; David C. Wolper to Irving Lazar, 22 November 1963; Stephen Smith to Lazar, 22 January 1964, Box 10, AG-PC.
58. Charles Siragusa, interview by Dan E. Moldea, *The Hoffa Wars: The Rise and Fall of Jimmy Hoffa* (New York: SPI, 1978), 138.
59. Blakey and Billings, *Fatal Hour,* 225–30, 273–74; Fox, *Blood and Power,* 342–43; Schlesinger, *Robert Kennedy,* 288–89; Peter Maas, *The Valachi Papers* (New York: Putnam, 1968). For a concise history of organized crime since the 1920s, see Stephen Fox, *Blood and Power: Organized Crime in Twentieth-Century America* (New York: Morrow, 1989). Valachi talked exclusively about the Italian American and Sicilian American crime families, the locus of his own experience. Organized crime, of course, included networks of persons of many ethnic groups.
60. Fox, *Blood and Power,* 328.
61. Robert F. Kennedy, *The Enemy Within* (New York: Harper and Row, 1960), 263–64. "Robt. Kennedy Maps Unified War on Crime," *Philadelphia Bulletin,* 4 February 1961; Gentry, *J. Edgar Hoover,* 415; Navasky, *Kennedy Justice,* 13–14; Schlesinger, *Robert Kennedy,* 286–87.
62. Winifred Willse of the Narcotics Division of the New York Police Department was hired to coordinate the system. Navasky, *Kennedy Justice,* 52; Fox, *Blood and Power,* 336.
63. Navasky, *Kennedy Justice,* 47, 332; RFK, *Robert Kennedy,* 124.
64. RFK named his son Douglas Harriman Kennedy, born 24 March 1967, after Dillon and Averell Harriman. RFK, *Robert Kennedy,* 39–40; Wofford, *Of Kennedys and Kings,* 77.
65. RFK, *Robert Kennedy,* 56, 123–24; Blakey and Billings, *Fatal Hour,* 225. The talent search had come up with another name, but RFK insisted on Caplin. Adam Yarmolinsky, telephone interview by author, 29 November 1993.
66. RFK, *Robert Kennedy,* 56; Navasky, *Kennedy Justice,* 55, 375–76.
67. Hoover's marginal note, Belmont to Tolson, 22 July 1965, RFK-FBI; Thomas, *The Man to See: Edward Bennett Williams, Ultimate Insider, Legendary Trial Lawyer* (New York: Simon and Schuster, 1991), 160–63, 193–98. RFK's desk diaries indicate Williams was a frequent visitor to the attorney general's office, even while he was defending Giancana and Costello.
68. Quote in *Philadelphia Bulletin,* 2 January 1962. After RFK left Justice, days in

court decreased by 56 percent and the number of court briefs dropped by 83 percent. Navasky, *Kennedy Justice,* 49. Also, see Blakey and Billings, *Fatal Hour,* 227–28. When Organized Crime and Tax Division convictions are combined, the numbers of convictions are 96 in 1961, 101 in 1962, and 373 in 1963. Schlesinger, *Robert Kennedy,* 299.

69. Peter Maas, interview by Stein and Plimpton, *American Journey,* 84.
70. RFK was uncertain of the number, but by 1963, he said, the FBI had either 115 or 140 agents working on organized crime in New York City and "sixty or eighty" in Chicago (which had only 6 before 1961). RFK, *Robert Kennedy,* 121, 292. Also see Gentry, *J. Edgar Hoover,* 454–55; Summers, *Official and Confidential,* 259.
71. For a summary of the diverse opinions and the extant literature, or "Mafiology" during Robert Kennedy's time, see Schlesinger, *Robert Kennedy,* 180–81, 283–288, *n*1007. For later developments, including an overall historical perspective and a very helpful bibliography, see Mark H. Haller, "Illegal Enterprise: A Theoretical and Historical Interpretation," *Criminology,* May 1990, 207–35.
72. Clark quoted in Gentry, *J. Edgar Hoover,* 328. For a concise analysis of Hoover's stance on organized crime, see Athan Theoharis, *J. Edgar Hoover, Sex, and Crime: An Historical Antidote* (Chicago: Ivan R. Dee, 1997), 139–54.
73. Gentry, *J. Edgar Hoover,* 329–30; Summers, *Official and Confidential,* 253–59; Thomas, *The Man to See,* 193–94. Theoharis, *Hoover, Sex, and Crime,* 11–20, directly rebutts evidence alleging that Hoover was a homosexual.
74. Gentry, *J. Edgar Hoover,* 458–59. A May 1966 FBI memorandum reported 738 microphone installations from 1960 to 1966. See Athan Theoharis and John Stuart Cox, *The Boss: J. Edgar Hoover and the Great American Inquisition* (Philadelphia: Temple U. Press, 1988), 374.
75. Schlesinger, *Robert Kennedy,* 288; RFK, *Robert Kennedy,* 121–22. In a telephone interview with the author on 7 December 1992, Edwin Guthman recollected "two or three" additional instances where Hoover's press releases or writings were censored by Kennedy but could not recall specifics.
76. Blakey and Billings, *Fatal Hour,* 224.
77. Ibid., 276–77. For a contrary comment on RFK's possible motives for deporting Marcello, see Michael Dorman, *Payoff: The Role of Organized Crime in American Politics,* (New York: Berkly, 1972), 109, and Fox, *Blood and Power,* 340; both contain hearsay reports that RFK asked Marcello to help persuade the Louisiana delegation to vote for JFK at the Los Angeles convention. According to an unnamed "associate," Marcello refused, and "Bobby was pissed off at Carlos and promised he'd get even." Cf. Davis, *Mafia Kingfish,* 341–54; Davis has written the definitive biography of Marcello and found nothing but mutual loathing ever connected the two men.
78. Jake W. Cameron to RFK, 5 April 1961, with reply, Box 1, AG-PC.
79. The government finally caught up with Marcello in June 1983, when he was convicted and imprisoned after an FBI sting operation (BRILAB) involving

bribery of labor union officials in Louisiana. See Davis, *Mafia Kingfish,* 99–113, 427–587.

80. Gerald Posner, *Case Closed: Lee Harvey Oswald and the Assassination of JFK* (New York: Random House, 1993), 460–61, found reasons to doubt the credibility of Becker's testimony. Marcello, of course, was not the only hoodlum who spoke of retribution against RFK. The HSCA analyzed FBI transcripts of recordings of threats against RFK. For excerpts, see Blakey and Billings, *Fatal Hour,* 270–95; Gentry, *J. Edgar Hoover,* 495–97, 534–35; Davis, *Mafia Kingfish,* 132–34, 233–36, 313–16. North, *Act of Treason,* 189–390, accepts the HSCA Mafia conspiracy theory and argues that Hoover knew of it and purposely allowed it to go forward. North must be read with caution and not without consulting Theoharis and Cox, *The Boss,* and Theoharis's reply to North, *Washington Post Book World,* 16 February 1992, 14.
81. Blakey and Billings, *Fatal Hour,* 279; Fox, *Blood and Power,* 341; G. Robert Blakey, "The Mafia and JFK's Murder," *Washington Post,* national weekly edition, 15–21 November 1993, 23–24.
82. Thomas, *The Man to See,* 210. On Giancana, see William Brashler, *The Don: The Life and Death of Sam Giancana* (New York: Harper and Row, 1977), and the Mafia fantasy *Double Cross: The Explosive, Inside Story of the Mobster Who Controlled America,* by Sam (the godson) and Chuck Giancana (the brother) (New York: Warner, 1992).
83. Blakey and Billings, *Fatal Hour,* 413; Kitty Kelley, *His Way, The Unauthorized Biography of Frank Sinatra* (New York: Bantam, 1986), 316.
84. RFK kept his opinions of Frank Sinatra to himself, but clearly he did not like Sinatra's influence on his brother. Yet when Frank Sinatra, Jr., was kidnapped in December 1963, the Justice Department quickly responded and RFK, sympathizing with the father's distress, was personally consoling. Sinatra, for his part, gradually drew closer to the Teamsters and the Republican party and did not mind who knew he considered RFK his enemy. Kelley, *His Way,* 294, 329, 383–84; Fox, *Blood and Power,* 338–39; Blakey and Billings, *Fatal Hour,* 414–15; Sinatra to RFK, 29 July 1964, and RFK to Sinatra, 21 August 1964, Box 8, AG-PC.
85. See Kelley, *His Way,* 301; Scheim, *Contract on America,* 89; James Spada, *Peter Lawford: The Man Who Kept the Secrets* (New York: Bantam, 1991), 288, 292–95. RFK may have alerted his father even earlier than his brother. In the summer of 1961, according to an unconfirmed report, RFK flew to his father's summer home on the French Riviera specifically to appeal to him to withdraw an invitation to Sinatra and members of his "Rat Pack" to stay there. Fox, *Blood and Power,* 338–39.
86. Scheim, *Contract on America,* 89; Blakey and Billings, *Fatal Hour,* 411; Kelley, *His Way,* 294. Schlesinger, in *Robert Kennedy,* 533–34, noted that JFK felt badly about the break with Sinatra.
87. Quoted in Fox, *Blood and Power,* 339.

88. Blakey and Billings, *Fatal Hour,* 410–14.
89. See Judith Campbell Exner with Ovid Demaris, *My Story* (New York: Grove, 1977), 111, 149, 205, 250–51; Kitty Kelley, "The Dark Side of Camelot," *People,* 29 February 1988, 109–111; Judith Campbell Exner interview, *Larry King Live,* CNN, July 1993; *New York Post,* 11 December 1996; also, Kelley, *My Way,* 205–15; Fox, *Blood and Power,* 341; Beschloss, *The Crisis Years,* 137–39; and Anthony Summers, who in *Goddess: The Secret Lives of Marilyn Monroe* (New York: New American Library, 1986), 431, claims that the Kennedys knew Giancana. Thomas C. Reeves, in *A Question of Character: The Life of John F. Kennedy* (New York: Free Press, 1991), 214, 262, 278, 448n, accepts Campbell Exner's embellishments without regard to their internal and chronological inconsistencies.
90. SAC [city deleted by FBI] to Director, FBI, 3 August 1965, RFK-FBI. Wofford, in *Of Kennedys and Kings,* 403, also questions Campbell-Exner's motives.
91. Senate Select Committee to Study Governmental Operations with Respect to Intelligence Activities [chaired by Senator Frank Church], *Interim Report: Alleged Assassination Plots Involving Foreign Leaders* (Washington, D.C.: U.S. Government Printing Office, 1975), 141–43; Thomas Powers, *The Man Who Kept the Secrets: Richard Helms and the CIA* (New York: Knopf, 1979), 218; Schlesinger, *Robert Kennedy,* 488, 518–22; Blakey and Billings, *Fatal Hour,* 260–64. A government informant, Charles Crimaldi, claimed James Hoffa was the "original liaison" between the CIA and the mob. Moldea, *The Hoffa Wars,* 131; Anthony Summers, *Conspiracy,* rev. ed. (New York: Paragon, 1991), 493.
92. RFK marginal note on Hoover memorandum, Church Committee, *Report,* 126, 128; cited in Moldea, *The Hoffa Wars,* 124; Wofford, *Of Kennedys and Kings,* 399–400. Beschloss, in *The Crisis Years,* 139, suggests that RFK was not hearing about the Giancana-CIA connection for the first time, but he offers no persuasive evidence in support.
93. Church committee, *Report,* 126–34; Schlesinger, *Robert Kennedy,* 531; Blakey and Billings, *Fatal Hour,* 63–65; Gentry, *J. E. Hoover,* 486–90.
94. Church committee records indicate that the CIA, in defiance of RFK, continued its contacts with Roselli until January 1963. See Blakey and Billings, *Fatal Hour,* 64–67.
95. Schlesinger, *Robert Kennedy,* 531; Powers, *Secrecy and Power,* 360; Gentry, *J. Edgar Hoover,* 491–92; Powers, *Man Who Kept the Secrets,* 155.
96. Hoover made a memorandum of the meeting. See Blakey and Billings, *Fatal Hour,* 57–67; Beschloss, *The Crisis Years,* 134–43.
97. Discounting the CIA testimony before the Church committee, some analysts insist that the Kennedys must have known about the Mafia-CIA plots, which, when added to the Campbell affair, extended the degree to which the Kennedys were beholden to Hoover and compromised by the mob. See Davis, *Mafia Kingfish,* 96–99, 414–17; Scheim, *Contract on America,* 212–18; Fox, *Blood and Power,* 337–46; Summers, *Conspiracy,* 223–42, 527–28; Beschloss, *The Crisis Years,* 139–142; Giancana and Giancana, *Double Cross,* 280–81, 297–301; Powers, *Man*

Who Kept the Secrets, 155. Cf. Harris Wofford, afterword to *Of Kennedys and Kings: Making Sense of the Sixties* (Pittsburgh: U. of Pittsburgh Press, 1993 edition), 493; Schlesinger, *Robert Kennedy,* 536–37.

98. Blakey and Billings, *Fatal Hour,* 281–91.
99. Ibid., 290–92, 418–24; Thomas, *The Man to See,* 193–99. John Roselli was also murdered in 1975, shortly after testifying before the Church committee.
100. Navasky, *Kennedy Justice,* 403–39, 407 for quote; Schlesinger, *Robert Kennedy,* 300–301. For a detailed account of the Hoffa squad, see Walter Sheridan, *The Fall and Rise of Jimmy Hoffa* (New York: Saturday Review, 1972), 165–358. My account of the Kennedy-Hoffa conflict relies on newspaper clippings, FBI files, the RFK papers, and the works of Sloane, Sheridan, Navasky, Schlesinger, and Moldea. For differing views of Hoffa, see his two congratulatory autobiographies, the celebratory screenplay "Hoffa" by David Mamet, and its novelization by Ken Englade, *Hoffa* (New York: HarperPaperbacks, 1992).
101. Navasky, *Kennedy Justice,* 419–39.
102. Ibid., 394–95. Sensing RFK's vulnerability on this issue, Roy Cohn—perpetually embroiled in controversy and walking near or over the legal line since he left Washington in disgrace—claimed he was victimized by a "Get-Roy" unit set up by RFK. RFK despised Cohn, but he was peculiarly indifferent toward his activities and showed no interest in the department's investigations of Cohn's many unsavory dealings. Those cases were supervised by the U.S. attorney in New York, Robert Morgenthau, who operated without RFK's direct oversight. After RFK left the department, Cohn focused on Morgenthau. Navasky, *Kennedy Justice,* 365, 395; Nicholas von Hoffman, *Citizen Cohn: The Life and Times of Roy Cohn* (New York: Bantam, 1988), 260–68, 273–74, 290–91; Maas interview, 59.
103. RFK, *Robert Kennedy,* 291.
104. Clark interview, 104. Clark, who succeeded Katzenbach as attorney general during the Johnson administration, placed even greater restrictions on the FBI, prompting Hoover to label him even "worse than Bobby." *Washington Post,* 16 November 1970.
105. Navasky, *Kennedy Justice,* 409; Arthur A. Sloane, *Hoffa* (Cambridge: MIT Press, 1991), 277.
106. *Philadelphia Inquirer,* 10 April 1961; David and David, *Bobby Kennedy,* 100; Sloane, *Hoffa,* 277. The FBI deliberately refrained from using electronic surveillance devices on Hoffa for fear of tainting prosecution efforts. They found baseless the rumors that RFK, acting on his own, directed Sheridan and Carmine Bellino to tap Hoffa's telephones (to Hoover's disappointment). Ironically, the FBI team detailed to follow Hoffa during his trials discovered that Bernard Spindel, Hoffa's wiretap and bugging specialist, eavesdropped on their radio network. See DeLoach to Tolson, 17 January 1966, O&C; Navasky, *Kennedy Justice,* 411–14.
107. Sloane, *Hoffa,* 186–87; Williams quote in Thomas, *The Man to See,* 161.
108. Sheridan, *Fall and Rise,* 165–66.

109. RFK, *Robert Kennedy,* 56–57.
110. Hank Suydam's March 1961 memoranda to E. K. Thompson (managing editor of *Life*) are reprinted in Navasky, *Kennedy Justice* 427–28.
111. Telephone message, Sheridan for RFK, 23 June 1961, JFK-ARC.
112. Sheridan, *Fall and Rise,* 203–7, 211–12.
113. Roy Cohn's attorney, Thomas A. Bolan, sprung RFK's collusion with *Life* during U.S. Senate Judiciary subcommittee hearings on invasion of privacy in March 1965. RFK insisted he had done "nothing else" than put Baron in touch with *Life.* See *Philadelphia Bulletin,* 3 March 1965; Navasky, *Kennedy Justice,* 426–29; Sloane, *Hoffa,* 257–59; Victor Lasky, *Robert F. Kennedy: The Myth and the Man* (New York: Trident, 1971), 243–47. *Life* magazine files, according to the FBI, "clearly indicate that Kennedy did engage in such skullduggery." C. D. DeLoach to Mohr, 3 March 1965, RFK-FBI. For a defense of RFK's use of informers such as Baron, see Schlesinger, *Robert Kennedy,* 694–95.
114. Sheridan, *Fall and Rise,* 221–55.
115. *Philadelphia Inquirer,* 4 January 1963; Sloane, *Hoffa,* 261; *New York Herald Tribune,* 29 January 1963; Navasky, *Kennedy Justice,* 418–19. Telephone call to James Stallman of *Nashville Banner,* RFK Desk Diary, 23 October 1962, JFK-ARC; Sloane, *Hoffa,* 267.
116. Arthur Edson, "Hoffa Stays One Hop ahead of Kennedys; Power Grows," *Philadelphia Bulletin,* 30 June 1963; "Hoffa Decries 'Vendetta' by Robt. Kennedy," *Philadelphia Inquirer,* 13 May 1963.
117. Sheridan, *Fall and Rise,* 217.
118. See Moldea, *The Hoffa Wars,* 148–50, 179–80; Davis, *Mafia Kingfish,* 365, 453; John H. Davis, *The Kennedys: Dynasty and Disaster, 1848–1984* (New York: McGraw-Hill, 1984), 556, 566–67.
119. Quoted in Sloane, *Hoffa,* 268–69, 279–80; and Moldea, *The Hoffa Wars,* 161–62. The HSCA concluded that, although Hoffa did not regret the president's death, it was "improbable" that he was involved in JFK's murder. HSCA, *Report,* 177–79. For a rebuttal of the evidence against Hoffa, see Sloane, *Hoffa,* 295–303. In 1992 Hoffa's former lawyer, Frank Ragano, claimed that in 1962 Hoffa sent him to New Orleans to tell Trafficante and Marcello that Hoffa wanted them to "kill the president." Ragano also claimed that in 1987 Trafficante made a deathbed "confession" of the mob's involvement in Hoffa's 1975 disappearance and expressed regret for killing JFK. "JFK, Hoffa and the Mob," *Frontline* (WGBH), narrated by Jack Newfield, 17 November 1992.
120. *New York Times,* 7 and 11 February 1964; Joseph A. Loftus, "Kennedy Praises Conduct of Trial," *New York Times,* 5 March 1964; *Philadelphia Bulletin,* 5 March 1964; RFK Desk Diary, 12 March 1964; RFK to Hoover, 30 March 1964, and Hoover to RFK, 16 April 1964, RFK-FBI.
121. Wilson quote in Sloane, *Hoffa,* 301–3; "Hoffa's Delegate," *Philadelphia Bulletin,* 14 July 1964. On the close ties between the IBT and the Republicans, especially between Hoffa's successor, Frank Fitzsimmons, and Richard Nixon, see

Sloane, *Hoffa,* 344–45, 348–53, 395–96; Moldea, *The Hoffa Wars,* 259–60, 312–13, 321–22.

122. Sloane, *Hoffa,* 311–12; Navasky, *Kennedy Justice,* 437–38, 395–96; Moldea, *The Hoffa Wars,* 169–70; Robert F. Kennedy, *The Pursuit of Justice,* ed. Theodore Lowi. (New York: Harper and Row, 1964), 5.
123. Navasky, *Kennedy Justice,* 48; RFK, *Robert Kennedy,* 290–91. For RFK's view of his achievements, see *The Pursuit of Justice,* 37–50, 123–30. Hoover privately questioned Kennedy's claims, charging that he arbitrarily "lumped together" the La Cosa Nostra convictions and the labor management and gambling cases to make himself look better. See Belmont to Evans, 2 June 1964, RFK-FBI.
124. See Navasky, *Kennedy Justice,* 44–95. For an assessment of the impact of the Kennedy anticrime program in broad historical perspective, see Fox, *Blood and Power,* 347–420.
125. Navasky, *Kennedy Justice,* 403–39; RFK, *Robert Kennedy,* 293–94; RFK, *The Pursuit of Justice,* 5–7.
126. Schlesinger, *Robert Kennedy,* 307.
127. RFK, *The Pursuit of Justice,* 5.
128. Navasky, *Kennedy Justice,* 429.
129. Anthony Lewis, interview by Stein and Plimpton, *American Journey,* 86.
130. Speeches and Press Releases Folder, 1961–1964, Boxes 1–3, AG-PC. After December 1963 he rarely visited FBI field offices and only once, during a June 1964 visit to New York, did he request an update on organized crime. FBI SAC New York to Hoover, 17 June 1964, RFK-FBI.
131. See, for example, Fox, *Blood and Power;* Davis, *Mafia Kingfish;* Blakey and Billings, *Fatal Hour;* Scheim, *Contract on America.*
132. Navasky, *Kennedy Justice,* 395.
133. RFK to E. B. Williams, 13 December 1966, Box 12, SP-PC.
134. Navasky, *Kennedy Justice,* 44–46.

CHAPTER 9

1. The other two were Martin Luther King, Jr., and Quinn Tamm, director of the International Association of Chiefs of Police. Richard Gid Powers, *Secrecy and Power: The Life of J. Edgar Hoover* (New York: Free Press, 1987), 353.
2. Ibid., 353.
3. Victor Navasky, *Kennedy Justice* (New York: Atheneum, 1971), 3–8; Evans quote in Curt Gentry, *J. Edgar Hoover: The Man and the Secrets* (New York: Norton, 1991). 474; Clark, interview by Lester David and Irene David, *Bobby Kennedy: The Making of a Folk Hero* (New York: PaperJacks, 1988), 132–33.
4. Robert F. Kennedy, *Robert Kennedy in His Own Words: The Unpublished Recollections of the Kennedy Years,* ed. Edwin O. Guthman and Jeffrey Shulman (New York: Bantam, 1988), 126; Gentry, *J. Edgar Hoover,* 536; Athan Theoharis and John Stuart Cox, *The Boss: J. Edgar Hoover and the Great American Inquisition*

(Philadelphia: Temple U. Press, 1988), 343–44; Arthur M. Schlesinger, Jr., *Robert Kennedy and His Times* (Boston: Houghton Mifflin, 1978), 275–80. For more sinister views of the Kennedy-Hoover relationship, see Anthony Summers, *Official and Confidential: The Secret Life of J. Edgar Hoover* (New York: Putnam, 1993), 276–313; and Mark North, *Act of Treason* (New York: Carroll and Graf, 1991).

5. Navasky, *Kennedy Justice,* 36.
6. Theoharis and Cox, *The Boss,* 309–10; Athan Theoharis, ed., *From the Secret Files of J. Edgar Hoover* (Chicago: Dee, 1991), 72–85.
7. Kenneth O'Reilly, *Hoover and the Un-Americans: The FBI, HUAC, and the Red Menace* (Philadelphia: Temple U. Press, 1983), 75–129; Gentry, *J. Edgar Hoover,* 407–17. The FBI had only 326 agents in 1932 and 4,886 agents in 1945. By 1952, with the advent of the Red Scare, the number reached over 7,000. Theoharis and Cox, *The Boss,* 7.
8. Gentry, *J. Edgar Hoover,* 407; Theoharis and Cox, *The Boss,* 7, 15; Michael Wreszin, "Gee But I'd Like to Be a G-Man," *Reviews in American History,* 20 (June 1992), 258–63.
9. RFK telephone messages, 1 March 1961, JFK-ARC.
10. RFK Desk Diaries and telephone messages, 1961–1964, JFK-ARC.
11. *New York Herald Tribune,* 18 November 1961. The Birch Society operated out of Belmont, Massachusetts, and claimed 100,000 members in chapters across thirty-four states. Other ultraconservative organizations denounced by RFK included the American Nazi Party (George Lincoln Rockwell), the Christian Crusade (Billy James Hargis), and the Christian Anti-Communism Crusade (Fred Schwarz).
12. RFK, for example, accepted the FBI's undocumented claims that Stanley Levison, an advisor to Martin Luther King, Jr., was "controlled" by Moscow. The extent of Soviet control over U.S. Communists is gradually becoming evident through released Soviet documents. See Steven Merrit Miner, "Revelations, Secrets, Gossip, and Lies: Sifting Warily through the Soviet Archives," *New York Times Book Review,* 14 May 1995, 19–21; and Harvey Klehr, John Earl Haynes, and Fridrikh Igorevich Firsov, eds., *The Secret World of American Communism,* with translations by Timothy D. Sergay (New Haven: Yale U. Press, 1995).
13. Quoted in Schlesinger, *Robert Kennedy,* 281.
14. Taylor Branch, *Parting The Waters: America in the King Years, 1954–63* (New York: Simon and Schuster, 1988), 678.
15. Navasky, *Kennedy Justice,* 37–39. RFK said he commuted Scales's seven-year sentence on condition that socialists and leftist sympathizers not picket him and thus make it appear that he gave in to political pressure. RFK, *Robert Kennedy,* 349; Schlesinger, *Robert Kennedy,* 424–25.
16. Theoharis and Cox, *The Boss,* 312–14.
17. "Hoover would memo you to death," Ramsey Clark recalled. "An attorney general could have spent literally all his time preparing memos back to the director." On any given day, Hoover might send a stack of fifty memos to the AG's office,

forty-nine of which dealt with routine matters. "But unless you read each, line by line, you could miss the paragraph in that one which was really important," said Clark. If he was ever challenged, Hoover would be able to respond, "I informed you of that, on such and such a date." Gentry, *J. Edgar Hoover,* 136.

18 COINTELPRO was a closely kept secret, even within the FBI. Hoover ended the programs on 28 April 1971, after the Cointelpros against antiwar, black activist, and other political dissidents were exposed by the publication of documents seized during a March 1971 break-in of FBI offices in Media, Pennsylvania, by an anonymous Citizens Commission to Investigate the FBI. See Gentry, *J. Edgar Hoover,* 474, 682; Theoharis and Cox, *The Boss,* 426.

19. Navasky, *Kennedy Justice,* 119–120, notes that this action also implied that RFK blessed everything that followed.

20. RFK, *Robert Kennedy,* 125–26; Theoharis and Cox, *The Boss,* 326. JFK invited Hoover to the White House for briefings six times. Summers, *Official and Confidential,* 283.

21. R. Sargent Shriver, telephone message to RFK, 11 September 1961, JFK-ARC.

22. Edwin Guthman, *We Band of Brothers* (New York: Harper and Row, 1971), 233–34; Navasky, *Kennedy Justice,* 352–53; Schlesinger, *Robert Kennedy,* 433–35; Theoharis and Cox, *The Boss,* 327.

23. For notes and agency reports to the Subcabinet Group on Civil Rights, see Boxes 11–14, Harris Wofford Papers, JFKL. In 1970 the FBI reported it had 51 black agents and 1,531 black employees out of 18,600, but not one black in a management position. Hoover interview, *Time,* 14 December 1970; Carl T. Rowan commentary, *Philadelphia Bulletin,* 16 December 1970. Schlesinger, in *Robert Kennedy,* 313–14, reported 5 blacks were in the FBI 1961. See Navasky, *Kennedy Justice,* 108; Guthman, *We Band of Brothers,* 104; Gentry, *J. Edgar Hoover,* 279–80.

24. Gentry, *J. Edgar Hoover,* 477; William C. Sullivan, *The Bureau: My Thirty Years in Hoover's FBI* (New York: Norton, 1979), 53.

25. Theoharis and Cox, *The Boss,* 325–28; Gentry, *J. Edgar Hoover,* 475–81; Guthman, *We Band of Brothers,* 259–60. RFK's desk diaries and telephone logs indicate surprisingly few telephone calls and one-on-one meetings with Hoover.

26. Navasky, *Kennedy Justice,* 107. For a discussion of fifteen crucial assumptions about the FBI that went unchallenged by the Kennedys, see 106–35.

27. Turner sued the FBI after he was transferred to Alaska for testifying to a congressional committee about Bureau irregularities. Evan Thomas, *The Man to See: Edward Bennett Williams, Ultimate Insider, Legendary Trial Lawyer* (New York: Simon and Schuster, 1991), 199–201. The suit failed, but it hinted at the seamier sides of Hoover's Bureau, elaborated upon in William Turner, *Hoover's FBI: The Men and the Myths* (Los Angeles: Sherbourne, 1970). On the pressures brought by the FBI to slow publication of Turner's book, see Gentry, *J. Edgar Hoover,* 387–88.

28. RFK, *Robert Kennedy,* 125.

29. Navasky, *Kennedy Justice,* 100.

30. Hoover Folder, Box 25, AG-GC. See RFK to Hoover, 22 June 1964, RFK-FBI.

For a staff member's view of the relationship, see Guthman, *We Band of Brothers,* 258–67.

31. Quoted in Gentry, *J. Edgar Hoover,* 479.
32. RFK, *Robert Kennedy,* 132.
33. On Hoover's use of illegal surveillance of government officials, see Theoharis, *Secret Files,* 66–71; Theoharis and Cox, *The Boss,* 332–33; Harrison E. Salisbury, *Heroes of My Time* (New York: Walker, 1993), 18; Branch, *Parting the Waters,* 837; Gentry, *J. Edgar Hoover,* 479; Alexander Charns, *Cloak and Gavel: FBI Wiretaps, Bugs, Informers and the Supreme Court* (Urbana and Chicago: U. of Illinois Press, 1992). In 1966 Hoover's assistants told the Senate subcommittee investigating government eavesdropping that the FBI "had not ever placed a microphone or wiretap on any member of Congress." Senator Edward V. Long, who chaired the inquiry, never asked if the FBI bugged executive offices or the courts. DeLoach to Tolson, 17 January 1966, RFK-FBI. On Hoover's taps within his own office, see Theoharis, *Secret Files,* 330–31.
34. Navasky, *Kennedy Justice,* 73–76; Schlesinger, *Robert Kennedy,* 290–93. In 1961 RFK "mistakenly" supported a bill by Senator Kenneth Keating (Republican from New York) that would have given the states wide latitude over wiretaps. Douglas Ross, *Robert F. Kennedy: Apostle of Change* (New York: Trident, 1968), 213–15.
35. Theoharis and Cox, in *The Boss,* 376–77, concluded that RFK and Hoover were "equally insensitive to constitutional issues." Navasky, *Kennedy Justice,* 74.
36. On the FBI's wiretapping activities from 1940 to 1965, see Theoharis, *Secret Files,* 131–43; Theoharis and Cox, *The Boss,* 349–401. Kennedy's record on wiretaps, taken from the 1976 Church committee report, is summarized in Schlesinger, *Robert Kennedy,* 291–93.
37. Schlesinger, *Robert Kennedy,* 292; Victor S. Navasky, "The Government and Martin Luther King," *The Atlantic,* November 1970, 51–52; Navasky, *Kennedy Justice,* 66–77. In returning the wiretap list to the FBI files, RFK followed a department practice that dated to 1940. C. A. Evans to Belmont, 6 July 1961, Folder 114, O&C and RFK-FBI; RFK telephone messages, 12 July 1961, JFK-ARC; Theoharis and Cox, *The Boss,* 377; Theoharis, *Secret Files,* 131–52.
38. Theoharis and Cox, *The Boss,* 368–69; McGrath to Hoover, 26 February 1952, printed in Theoharis, *Secret Files,* 137.
39. Confidential Memo, Attorney General Herbert Brownell to FBI Director, 20 May 1954, Theoharis, *Secret Files,* 141; Theoharis and Cox, *The Boss,* 374–76.
40. Joseph Dolan quoted in Schlesinger, *Robert Kennedy,* 297.
41. C. A. Evans to Belmont, 6 July 1961, Folder 114, O&C; RFK-FBI.
42. RFK telephone messages, 12 July 1961, JFK-ARC.
43. *New York Times,* 28 December 1966.
44. See Ross, *Robert Kennedy,* 216, for Kennedy's complete statement. C. A. Evans to Belmont, 6 July 1961, Folder 114, O&C and RFK-FBI. Silberling quoted in Victor Lasky, *Robert F. Kennedy: The Myth and the Man* (New York: Trident,

1971), 169. Guthman, *We Band of Brothers,* 263–64; Schlesinger, *Robert Kennedy,* 296–99; Navasky, *Kennedy Justice,* 82.

45. Hoover to Byron White, 4 May 1961, in Navasky, *Kennedy Justice,* 448–49.
46. Navasky, *Kennedy Justice,* 94. Probably because it blatantly distorted the Brownell memo and because it contained a candid admission of trespass surveillance, Hoover did not release his May 1961 memorandum in 1966 when the dispute with RFK became public. Perhaps, too, he wanted to avoid embarrassing Byron White, by then on the Supreme Court. *Kennedy Justice,* 94–95; also, Schlesinger, *Robert Kennedy,* 297.
47. Hoover informed the Justice Department of only 158 of 738 bugs. He claimed the Justice Department lacked security, leaked confidential information to the press, and hindered FBI investigations by advising the courts whenever they learned of bugs. James Gale to DeLoach, 27 May 1966, Folder 37, O&C, includes Hoover's marginal "OK" of Gale's suggestion to inform the Justice Department of bugs only when prosecution was imminent. Also see Theoharis and Cox, *The Boss,* 374. In 1962 FBI agents trespassed on approximately a hundred social and business centers of organized crime figures and planted hidden listening devices. Although none of the information gathered could be used in court, the FBI used the tapes to close the books on old crimes, detail the scope of criminal activity, and map out the myriad connections among organized crime, legitimate businesses, and politicians. G. Robert Blakey and Richard N. Billings, *Fatal Hour: The Assassination of President Kennedy by Organized Crime* (New York: Berkely, 1992, originally published as *The Plot to Kill the President,* 1981), 238–40, 265–66.
48. Guthman, *We Band of Brothers,* 263; J. H. Gale to DeLoach, 1 July 1966, Folder 114, O&C. Hoover also sent RFK a summary of a secret meeting in a New York hotel room between Harold Cooley, chair of the House Agriculture Committee, and an agent of the Dominican Republic. The FBI conceded there was "no clear indication" that RFK was "specifically advised" that a microphone was used to gather the Cooley information. Schlesinger, *Robert Kennedy,* 294–95.
49. See Theoharis and Cox, *The Boss,* 376–77.
50. Navasky, *Kennedy Justice,* 78; Lasky, *Robert F. Kennedy,* 169.
51. Evans to Belmont, 6 July 1961, Folder 114, O&C and RFK-FBI. Schlesinger, *Robert Kennedy,* 299. Schlesinger is not nearly so kind in treating Richard Nixon's claimed ignorance of all his subordinates had done in connection with the Watergate break-in. "If he really did not know and for nine months did not bother to find out," Schlesinger said of Nixon, "he is surely an irresponsible and incompetent executive. For, if he did not know, it can only be because he did not want to know." Schlesinger, "The Runaway Presidency," *The Atlantic,* October 1973, 44.
52. Navasky, *Kennedy Justice,* 89–92; Theoharis and Cox, *The Boss,* 377–78; Schlesinger, *Robert Kennedy,* 295.
53. J. H. Gale to DeLoach, 1 July 1966, Folder 114, O&C.
54. Schlesinger, *Robert Kennedy,* 298–99.

55. *New York Times,* 20 January 1967.
56. The contents and size of the Personal and Confidential Files are disputed. An inquiry into their destruction by the U.S. House of Representatives in 1975 was inconclusive. See Theoharis and Cox, *The Boss,* 329–30. J. Edgar Hoover, *The Official & Confidential File of FBI Director J. Edgar Hoover* (Wilmington, Del.: Scholarly Resources, 1988), was begun in October 1941 and contains 164 folders.
57. RFK, *Robert Kennedy,* 128, 133.
58. Clark Clifford, *Counsel to the President* (New York: Random House, 1991), 331, recommended Hoover's reappointment *"for the time being"*; Guthman, *We Band of Brothers,* 261; Herbert S. Parmet, *JFK: The Presidency of John F. Kennedy* (New York: Dial, 1983), 59–60; O&C, Folder 7. Also see Theoharis and Cox, *The Boss,* 330–35; Nigel Hamilton, *JFK: Reckless Youth* (New York: Random House, 1992), 419–94; Summers, *Official and Confidential,* 260–62, 264–66.
59. Theoharis and Cox, in *The Boss,* 332–43, describe Hoover's office file on JFK and compare it to those of other presidents. Theoharis, 15–47, includes samples of the JFK files.
60. Summers, in *Official and Confidential,* 273–75, makes the case most explicitly; also, see Gentry, *J. Edgar Hoover,* 470–73; Theoharis and Cox, *The Boss,* 338; Powers, *Secrecy and Power,* 357. Athan Theoharis, the preeminent scholar of Hoover and the FBI, suggests that RFK and JFK, in effect, "blackmailed themselves" by welcoming Hoover's "willingness to provide them with information they could deny receiving." Athan Theoharis, *J. Edgar Hoover, Sex, and Crime: An Historical Antidote* (Chicago: Ivan R. Dee, 1995), 160.
61. RFK, *Robert Kennedy,* 134.
62. Bureau File No. 77–51387 (Special Inquiry File), *FBI File on Robert F. Kennedy* (Wilmington, Del.: Scholarly Resources, 1990).
63. See, for example, Hoover to SAC Richmond, 14 September 1962; SAC Philadelphia to Hoover, 20 August 1962; SAC Birmingham to Hoover, 23 April 1963, RFK-FBI; also see Gentry, *J. Edgar Hoover,* 477–78.
64. SAC Atlanta to Hoover, 26 April 1963, RFK-FBI.
65. SAC Seattle to Hoover, 7 August 1962; M. P. Callahan to Hoover, 13 March 1963; SAC Atlanta to Hoover, 26 April 1963, RFK-FBI; Gentry, *J. Edgar Hoover,* 495–97; Powers, *Secrecy and Power,* 389–90.
66. The purpose of the meeting with Parker is not known, but its timing suggests it may have been to discuss the use of LAPD officers in counterinsurgency operations in Latin America. SAC LA to Hoover, 27 December 1963, RFK-FBI.
67. Parker correspondence, Box 44, AG-GC. Also see David and David, *Bobby Kennedy,* 133. Ethel Kennedy once dropped a note in the FBI Suggestion Box: "Chief Parker of Los Angeles for Director of the FBI." Bill Barry, interview by Jean Stein and George Plimpton, eds., *American Journey: The Times of Robert Kennedy* (New York: Harcourt Brace Jovanovich, 1970), 86. Others rumored for consideration as Hoover's successor were Adam Yarmolinsky and Courtney Evans.

68. Chicago SAC to Hoover, 19 March 1963, RFK-FBI; and for a sample of comments and speeches, see Ross, *Robert Kennedy,* 240–41.
69. Navasky, *Kennedy Justice,* 41.
70. Anthony Lewis, interview by Stein and Plimpton, *American Journey,* 86; Navasky, *Kennedy Justice,* 41–43; Schlesinger, *Robert Kennedy,* 275–80; Gentry, *J. Edgar Hoover,* 473; James Reston, *Deadline* (New York: Random House, 1991), 293; Michael R. Beschloss, *The Crisis Years: Kennedy and Krushchev, 1960–1965* (New York: Burlingame, 1991), 103. Also, see Summers, *Official and Confidential,* 283, 286–87, who conjectures that Joseph Kennedy acted as an arbitrator between his sons and Hoover and kept matters on an even keel until his stroke in 1961.
71. M. Belmont to C. A. Evans, 11 August 1962, Folder 12; Evans to Belmont, 20 August 1962, Folder 9, O&C; Theoharis, *Secret Files,* 49. Anthony Summers speculates without foundation that perhaps the quality of the Lansky tape was poor and, instead of "El Paso," perhaps the speaker actually said "Lake Tahoe" (where Marilyn Monroe visited with Frank Sinatra the week before her death) and perhaps the "girl" in question was really Monroe. See Summers, *Goddess: The Secret Lives of Marilyn Monroe* (New York: New American Library, 1986), 448.
72. The story usually told is that JFK started an affair with Monroe earlier and that after February 1962 both men shared her favors. Herbert Parmet, *JFK,* 304–5, found some rumors of JFK's sexual liaisons to be credible, but, as one woman told him, "If all women who claimed privately that they had slept with Jack had really done so, he wouldn't have had the strength left to lift a teacup." Parmet finds it "improbable" that the JFK-Monroe relationship was an intimate one. See Summers, *Goddess,* 240–44, 246–47, 251–57, for a full recounting of the rumors; and Thomas C. Reeves, *A Question of Character: A Life of John F. Kennedy* (New York: Free Press, 1991), 317–22, who accepts Summers's scenario unquestioningly. Cf. Donald Spoto, in *Marilyn Monroe: The Biography* (New York: HarperCollins, 1993), 486–89, who reports that JFK and Monroe met on four occasions and that on one of those occasions (24 March 1962) they telephoned Marilyn's masseuse from a bedroom.
73. In July 1964 Frank R. Capell privately circulated a seventy-page book asserting that RFK took "drastic action" to silence Monroe when she threatened to expose their relationship. Capell claimed that RFK was a "Communist sympathizer" who used a "Communist doctor" to cover up the murder to protect his presidential ambitions. *The Strange Death of Marilyn Monroe* (Zarephath, N.J.: Herald of Freedom, 1964) is summarized in SAC New York to Director FBI, 2 July 1964; Hoover to RFK, 5 July 1964; R. W. Smith to W. C. Sullivan, 15 July 1964, RFK-FBI. The Smith memorandum states that a previous allegation concerning RFK and Monroe had been "branded as utterly false." The FBI noted that excerpts from Capell's book were presented to callers on a right-wing telephone hotline in San Francisco; they also reported a rumor within the Pentagon that Monroe had telephoned RFK "some time prior to her death." SAC San

Francisco to Director, 8 August 1964, and A. B. Eddy to C. Evans, 3 September 1964, RFK-FBI. No other documents on this matter appear in RFK's FBI file, but William C. Sullivan, one of Hoover's assistants, stated that Hoover "gleefully" fanned the flames of the scandal, probably by sharing his copy of the Capell book with Walter Winchell, who alluded to the story in his gossip columns. Sullivan, *The Bureau,* 56.

74. Norman Mailer, in *Marilyn* (New York: Grosset and Dunlap, 1973), stated that Marilyn had deluded herself into believing RFK would divorce Ethel and marry her and went on to suggest that the FBI or CIA had motive for implicating RFK in a scandal. In July 1973 Mailer admitted during a television interview that he was convinced by his publisher to make the unfounded claims against Kennedy because "I needed money very badly." Quoted in Spoto, *Marilyn Monroe,* 603.
75. Robert F. Slatzer, *The Strange Life and Curious Death of Marilyn Monroe* (New York: Pinnacle, 1974); *The Marilyn Files* (New York: SPI, 1992); and "The Marilyn Files," Telemarc Communications (syndicated telecast, 12 August 1992).
76. According to Milo Speriglio, *The Marilyn Conspiracy* (New York: Pocket Books, 1986), RFK's enemies, "the Hoffa-Giancana group," killed Monroe to silence her about her affairs with Mafia figures and to entrap RFK at the scene of the murder. A similar scenario is presented by Sam [the godson] and Chuck [the brother] Giancana, *Double Cross: The Explosive Inside Story of the Mobster Who Controlled America* (New York: Warner, 1992), 311–16, who claimed Sam Giancana ordered Monroe killed and put "Needles" Gianola in charge of a team of professional killers whose murder weapon was a deftly wielded Nembutal anal suppository.
77. Summers, in *Goddess,* presents a detailed synthesis of the earlier stories and adds a great deal of hearsay information and speculation, including details on the supposed (but never proved) existence of tape recordings of Monroe in intimate moments separately with RFK and JFK.
78. Some of the places where the story is repeated or embellished upon include C. David Heymann, *A Woman Called Jackie* (New York: Lyle Stuart, 1989); Peter Harry Brown and Patte B. Barham, *Marilyn: The Last Take* (New York: Dutton, 1992); James Spada, *Peter Lawford: The Man Who Kept the Secrets* (New York: Bantam, 1991); "Marilyn—The Last Word," *Hard Copy,* February 1992. All the clamor forced the chief prosecutor of Los Angeles County to reinvestigate the Monroe case in 1975, 1982, and 1985, but no credible evidence was uncovered to support a murder theory in Monroe's death. A grand jury rejected a request by the county Board of Supervisors to reopen the case in 1985.
79. Reeves, *A Question of Character,* 327.
80. Spoto, *Marilyn Monroe,* 489–93, 599–611. Only Robert Slatzer and Jeanne Carmen have offered firsthand statements purporting to verify the relationship between RFK and Monroe. Spoto, however, has demonstrated that Monroe was in Los Angeles the weekend in October 1952 when Slatzer claims they were married in Mexico and found no evidence to support Slatzer's claim that he was her

confidant. Similarly, there is no proof that Jeanne Carmen, who has publicly stated that she witnessed RFK and Monroe together as an intimate couple, was, as she claimed, a close friend of Monroe's. Spoto, *Marilyn Monroe,* 227–29, 472. Cf. Summers, in *Goddess,* 259 (on Carmen) and 329–31 (on Slatzer), who found both believable.

81. RFK's whereabouts were established through his desk diaries and telephone logs for 1961 and 1962; his FBI file; "Speeches & Press Releases, 1961–1964," AG-GC; "Robert F. Kennedy Chronology," Box 1, SP-GC; a telephone interview with Edwin Guthman who accompanied RFK on his West Coast trips; and the Photo-Journalism Collection and Clipping Files, Urban Archives, Temple University Library, Philadelphia. RFK and Monroe met three times at large dinner parties at the Santa Monica home of Peter Lawford and Patricia Kennedy Lawford: 4 October 1961, 2 February 1962 (with Ethel present), and 26 June 1962. On two other occasions in 1962 when RFK was in Los Angeles—24 and 25 March and 26 July—Monroe was in Palm Springs and Lake Tahoe. RFK desk diaries, JFK-ARC; Spoto, *Marilyn Monroe,* 480–89, 548–49; Summers, *Goddess,* 333–39. RFK also met Monroe on 19 May 1962 in New York at a reception following the gala birthday party for JFK, where Monroe made a memorable appearance and breathily sang "Happy Birthday" to JFK. Monroe declined Ethel's invitation to a party at Hickory Hill on 16 June 1962. Monroe to RFK and Ethel, 13 June 1962, Box 5, AG-PC.
82. Summers is vague on the first RFK-Monroe meeting (January or February 1962), but he is certain Monroe was not "seen again with either Kennedy brother" after 27 June 1962. *Goddess,* 310, 321–23, 328–31, 339, 427.
83. Anthony Summers, whose book *Goddess* purports to document RFK's relationship with Monroe, relied heavily on her FBI file. After reading his account and examining the same set of documents, Theoharis and Cox concluded that "no part of the [Marilyn-Bobby] story is substantiated by the FBI files Summers obtained." *The Boss,* 336–37; Theoharis, *J. Edgar Hoover, Sex, and Crime,* 87–88. A baleful reading of a breezy courtesy note from Jean Kennedy Smith to Monroe thanking her for sending her invalid father a note (at RFK's urging) is cited by two authors as evidence that the Kennedy family put their "official sanction" on the alleged RFK-Monroe affair. See Brown and Barham, *Marilyn,* 259; Summers, *Goddess,* 280–82.
84. SAC Newark to Hoover, 14 June 1965, RFK-FBI; and printed in Slatzer, "Author's Postscript," *The Marilyn Files,* no page.
85. Summers, *Official and Confidential,* 80–88, 240–45, 253–58. On Hoover's use of agents to suppress such rumors, see Theoharis, *Secret Files,* 346–56, and for a rebuttal of Summers's charge that Hoover was a compromised homosexual, see Theoharis, *J. Edgar Hoover, Sex, and Crime,* 11–55.
86. See Reeves, in *A Question of Character,* 322–26, who uncritically accepts the Summers and Slatzer allegations, insists they can be repeated with a "somewhat reasonable measure of confidence," and asserts that RFK "narrowly escaped his

own Chappaquiddick" by instituting "an elaborate cover-up" of his alleged involvement in Monroe's death.

87. SAC San Francisco to Director, 6 August 1962; C. A. Evans to Belmont, 22 August 1962, RFK-FBI. Also see "RFK Schedule West Coast Trip," [3–15 August 1962], Box 53, AG-GC; and Schlesinger, *Robert Kennedy,* 637.

88. Bates is a highly respected lawyer with no axe to grind in this matter, a lifelong Republican who met JFK during World War II through a mutual friend, Paul "Red" Fay. Although he admits to contributing to JFK's 1960 campaign, he told the author that he voted for Nixon. He labeled the Marilyn-Bobby story "absurd" and said the media "fabrications" were "outrageous, ridiculous, [and] disgraceful." The sports-oriented weekend visit is documented in the Bates' guest book and photo album. Bates insists RFK was never out of his sight, except from 10:30 P.M. Saturday to early Sunday morning, when he had retired to bed. John B. Bates, telephone interview by the author, 4 August 1992; also see Bates's letter to *People,* 12 October 1992, 4; and Spoto, in *Marilyn Monroe,* 560–63, who adds that the nearest airstrip was in San Jose, an hour away by car, and the deep canyons in the Santa Cruz mountains and the power lines made helicopter travel dangerous. In 1962 the ranch was five hours (each way) by car to Los Angeles.

89. Reeves, *A Question of Character,* 327. Perhaps, as the poet James Dickey wrote, "We have all been in rooms/We cannot die in," "Adultery," *Nation,* 28 February 1966, 252. Whether RFK ever was, I cannot be sure. My point in belaboring the Bobby-Marilyn tale is not to argue that RFK was always faithful to his wife (because we may never know for certain), but rather to offer commentary on how (in the absence of certitude) ironic distortions sometimes become accepted as contemporary historical fact.

90. On Lawford's relationship to the Kennedys, see Spada, *Peter Lawford,* 184–86, 243–50, 320–334, 364. Lawford spoke to Monroe on the telephone the evening of her death, but, except for highly questionable hearsay information, no reliable evidence exists to prove he was at her home that evening. To the contrary, reliable sources indicate Lawford was too drunk to travel that night. Spoto, *Marilyn Monroe,* 566–77.

91. See Summers, *Goddess,* 303–56; Speriglio, *The Marilyn Conspiracy,* 58–60, 203–7; Reeves, *A Question of Character,* 325.

92. Theoharis and Cox, *The Boss,* 337; and Gentry, *J. Edgar Hoover,* 494; David J. Garrow, *The FBI and Martin Luther King, Jr.* (New York: Penquin, 1983), 151–72; Branch, *Parting the Waters,* 675–85; Theoharis, *Secret Files,* 95–112. Cf. Summers, *Goddess,* 261.

93. See Evans to Belmont, 25 August 1964, on the FBI's hostile reaction to RFK's request for assistance in New York and Atlantic City airports with Ethel's luggage because she was pregnant; also, SAC Washington Field Office to Director, 27 October 1965, on a request for FBI Documents Division to verify a reputed signature of JFK; Trotter to McDaniel, 4 February 1966, in RFK-FBI, on request for a name check on an employee.

94. Senator Edward V. Long and chief counsel Bernard Fensterwald of the Senate subcommittee investigating government eavesdropping in 1966 asked DeLoach if RFK had ever asked the FBI "to place a microphone on matters strictly pertaining to politics." DeLoach told Long that "Mr. Hoover would have tendered his resignation immediately had Kennedy attempted to force the FBI to do such a reprehensible thing." DeLoach to Tolson, 17 January 1966, RFK-FBI; also, Theoharis and Cox, *The Boss,* 337.
95. Investigators for the district attorneys in New York and Los Angeles found Bernard Spindel—termed a "known boaster" by the chief investigator—was, in fact, hired by Hoffa to secure embarrassing information on RFK. But after listening to Spindel's tapes and finding "none of them contained anything relating to Marilyn Monroe," investigators concluded Spindel's claims were a "ploy" to gain favorable treatment on wiretapping charges. Spoto, *Marilyn Monroe,* 604–6.
96. Dan E. Moldea, *The Hoffa Wars: Teamsters, Rebels, Politicians, and the Mob* (New York: Paddington, 1978), 175; Spoto, *Marilyn Monroe,* 606.
97. Summers, *Goddess,* 283.
98. Schlesinger, *Robert Kennedy,* 637; Spoto, *Marilyn Monroe,* 541; Summers, *Goddess,* 339. Zsa Zsa Gabor, April and May 1963, Box 7; Judy Garland, March 1964, Box 8, AG-PC; Newcomb also called on behalf of actor Kirk Douglas; RFK's desk diaries show he took calls from Kim Novak, Milton Berle, Frank Sinatra, Danny Kaye, Gregory Peck, and Sid Luft (Garland's husband), but not Monroe. RFK desk diaries and telephone logs for 1962, JFK-ARC.
99. Lester David, *Ethel,* 133. Even RFK's detractors doubted the story. George Terrien, RFK's embittered college classmate who married Ethel's sister, claimed that RFK once bragged about sleeping with Monroe. "I thought he was full of shit," said Terrien. "I can't imagine Marilyn Monroe getting into bed with that little jerk." Jerry Oppenheimer, *The Other Mrs. Kennedy: Ethel Skakel Kennedy, An American Drama of Power, Privilege, and Politics* (New York: St. Martin's, 1994), 235.
100. Edwin Guthman, telephone interview by author, December 1993; also, see David and David, *Bobby Kennedy,* 171; David, *Ethel,* 133.
101. "Rusk" [Ethel] to RFK in Brasilia [undated, *ca.* 17 December 1962], Box 5, AG-PC; Schlesinger, *Robert Kennedy,* 567–68, 627.
102. David, *Ethel,* 128–34; David and David, *Bobby Kennedy,* 177.
103. Jerry Oppenheimer, in *The Other Mrs. Kennedy,* 232–43, found no credible evidence of affairs. The claims regarding affairs appeared in a report scheduled to be aired as part of ABC's *20/20.* ABC president Roone Arledge cancelled the segment because, in his estimation, it was a "sleazy piece of journalism." See Summers, *Goddess,* 419–25, 427. Summers was told by someone he found credible that Kennedy had an affair with Newcomb. Summers felt Newcomb reacted "as though she had something personal to hide" when he interviewed her. Anthony Summers to the author, 12 June 1993.
104. RFK to [Margot] Patricia Newcomb, 23 October 1963; Newcomb to Ethel Kennedy [*ca.* October 1963], Box 7, AG-PC. Would Newcomb kid Ethel

about the "Hotel Dixie" (a slang term for the red-light district) if she were having an affair with RFK?

105. Schlesinger, interview by Summers, *Goddess,* 241. Journalist Clark Mollenhoff told historian James Giglio, without specific attribution or elaboration, that RFK was faithful to his wife until the 1960 campaign. James N. Giglio, *The Presidency of John F. Kennedy* (Lawrence: U. of Kansas Press, 1993), n309. Jack Newfield recalled an incident in 1966 when RFK invited him and two nurses to his New York apartment for a drink. After some strained conversation, the young women left the apartment a "little bewildered." Newfield, *Robert Kennedy: A Memoir* (New York: New American Library, 1969), 25.
106. William Thompson, a railroad executive, lobbyist, and friend of Bobby Baker, reportedly arranged female liaisons for JFK. In August 1961 Thompson requested a meeting with RFK, telling Angie Novello he wanted to talk about a "merger matter." Thompson was known to Novello. What business he had with RFK or even if Thompson's request for a meeting was ever granted is not known. RFK telephone messages, 8 August 1961, JFK-ARC. See, Summers, *Official and Confidential,* 310.
107. Maxwell Taylor, interview by Stein, and Plimpton, *American Journey,* 128.
108. Richard Reeves, *President Kennedy: Profile of Power* (New York: Simon and Schuster, 1993), 146–47, n684–85, 158–59, 242–43; Heymann, *A Woman Named Jackie,* 301–15; Giglio, *Presidency of John F. Kennedy,* 263–64; Ralph G. Martin, *Seeds of Destruction: Joe Kennedy and His Sons* (New York: Putman, 1995), 349–50.
109. For commentary on JFK's affairs and the methods used to suppress knowledge of their existence, see Reeves, *A Question of Character,* 202–3, 240–44; John H. Davis, *The Kennedys: Dynasty and Disaster, 1848–1984* (New York: McGraw-Hill, 1984), 111, 168, 136, 193, 386, 438–40, 734–35; Peter Collier and David Horowitz, *The Kennedys: An American Drama* (New York: Warner, 1984), 242, 368–71, 392, 524–25; Giglio, *Presidency of John F. Kennedy,* 267–70, n308.
110. Reston, *Deadline,* 290. Benjamin C. Bradlee, *Ben Bradlee: A Good Life* (New York: Simon and Schuster, 1995), 216–17. See Beschloss, *The Crisis Years,* 613–15.
111. Parmet, *JFK,* 304–7.
112. On Britain's "security scandals" and their effects on Macmillan's government, see Alistair Horne, *Harold Macmillan,* volume 2, *1957–1986* (New York: Viking, 1989), 456–65, 473–90.
113. Why the story was stopped after one edition is not known. Mark Monsky, godson of William Randolph Hearst, told Anthony Summers that RFK stopped it by threatening an antitrust suit against the Hearst newspaper chain. Summers, *Official and Confidential,* 307.
114. C. A. Evans to Hoover, Memo of Meeting, 1 July 1963, Folder 96, O&C; Parmet, *JFK,* 116–17; Summers, *Official and Confidential,* 306–7.
115. RFK's old foe Roy Cohn may have given the information to the *Journal-*

American. Cohn had an American client involved in the Profumo case. Anthony Summers found a document in the Profumo file with Hoover's notation: "Roy Cohn has this info." Summers, *Official and Confidential,* 309. Novotny told Anthony Summers that Peter Lawford procured her to have sex with JFK on several occasions in 1961, not 1960. On JFK's possible involvement in the Profumo scandal, see Anthony Summers and Stephen Dorril, *Honeytrap: The Secret Worlds of Stephen Ward* (London: Weidenfeld and Nickolson, 1987), 67–70, 196–204; Giglio, *Presidency of John F. Kennedy,* 268–69, n308; Summers, *Official and Confidential,* 305–6.

116. Evans to Belmont, 3 July 1963, Folder 96; Evans to Belmont, 24 July 1963, Folder 13, O&C.
117. Parmet, *JFK,* 116.
118. In 1963 a private investigator who gave his name as "Robert Garden" (but may actually have been Hoffa's wiretapper, Bernard Spindel) stumbled upon RFK's involvement in the Purdom-JFK settlement. "Garden," according to FBI files, attempted to sell the information to James Hoffa and to Republican senator John Tower of Texas. Both declined to buy. Hoover to RFK, 6 June 1963, Folder 13, O&C; Reeves, *A Question of Character,* 218, n456.
119. On McInerney, see Thomas, *The Man to See,* 163.
120. DeLoach to Tolson, 10 June 1959, and Florence Mary Kater to J. E. Hoover, 5 April 1963, Folder 13, O&C; Theoharis and Cox, *The Boss,* 340–41; Parmet, *JFK,* 112; Summers, *Official and Confidential,* 265–66, 280.
121. The Kennedys said that rumors of a marriage were merely a matter of an erroneous entry in the family genealogy of one of Kerr's four husbands. FBI agents and reporters laboriously rechecked the records but could not prove or disprove the entry's validity. Memorandum of JEH and RFK meeting, 22 November 1961, Folder 96, O&C; Theoharis and Cox, *The Boss,* 341; Parmet, *JFK,* 112–14; Summers, *Official and Confidential,* 292–93; Bradlee, *Ben Bradlee,* 238–39.
122. Bobby Baker with Larry L. King, *Wheeling and Dealing: Confessions of a Capitol Hill Operator* (New York: Norton, 1978), 80; David and David, *Bobby Kennedy,* 182; Benjamin C. Bradlee, *Conversations with Kennedy* (New York: Norton, 1975), 212–13. Anthony Summers found an October 1963 FBI memorandum reporting allegations that "the President and the Attorney General had availed themselves of services of playgirls." *Official and Confidential,* 310.
123. Bradlee, *Conversations with Kennedy,* 226. FBI documents on the Rometsch case are withheld on personal privacy grounds. Theoharis and Cox, *The Boss,* 348.
124. JFK assured other Democrats that he was "not after Bobby Baker," who, he told Ben Bradlee, was more a rogue than a crook. Bradlee, *Conversations with Kennedy,* 214.
125. RFK, *Robert Kennedy,* 129–30; Summers, *Official and Confidential,* 309–13; Beschloss, *The Crisis Years,* 615–17; Branch, *Parting the Waters,* 911–14.
126. RFK, *Robert Kennedy,* 130.

CHAPTER 10

1. James Reston, *Deadline* (New York: Random House, 1991), 287.
2. William Manchester, *The Glory and the Dream: A Narrative Hisory of America, 1932–1972* (New York: Bantam, 1975), 955.
3. Among them, McGeorge Bundy, Walter Rostow, Walter Heller, Arthur Schlesinger, Jr., James Tobin, Kermit Gordon, and John Kenneth Galbraith. See Garry Wills, *The Kennedy Imprisonment* (Boston: Little, Brown, 1982), 148–49; Herbert S. Parmet, *JFK: The Presidency of John F. Kennedy* (New York: Dial, 1983), 353–54; Robert C. Wood, *Whatever Possessed the President? Academic Experts and Presidential Policy, 1960–1988* (Amherst: U. of Massachusetts Press, 1993), 33 for White quote, 33–66. Writer-critic Edmund Wilson and poet Robert Lowell took exception to being relegated to "a very pompous and frivolous role" by JFK. Paul Mariani, *Lost Puritan: A Life of Robert Lowell* (New York: Norton, 1994), 306.
4. On JFK's physical problems, see James N. Giglio, *The Presidency of John F. Kennedy* (Lawrence: U. of Kansas Press), 262–65; Richard Reeves, *President Kennedy: Profile of Power* (New York: Simon and Schuster, 1993), 42–44, 146–47, 538–39, 648n, 668n, 698n–99n.
5. Edwin Guthman, *We Band of Brothers* (New York: Harper and Row, 1971), 241–43; Arthur M. Schlesinger, Jr., *Robert Kennedy and His Times* (Boston: Houghton Mifflin, 1978), 631–32.
6. Marian Schlesinger, interview by Jerry Oppenheimer, *The Other Mrs. Kennedy: Ethel Skakel Kennedy, An American Drama of Power, Privilege, and Politics* (New York: St. Martin's, 1994), 214. On Hickory Hill and other recollections of RFK at home, see Warren Rogers, *When I Think of Bobby* (New York: HarperCollins, 1993), 3–16.
7. Lester David and Irene David, *Bobby Kennedy: The Making of a Folk Hero* (New York: PaperJacks, 1988), 139–40; Schlesinger, *Robert Kennedy,* 630–31.
8. Benjamin C. Bradlee, *Conversations with Kennedy* (New York: Norton, 1975), 114.
9. Kathleen Kennedy Townsend interview, NBC-News, "RFK."
10. Undersecretary of State Chester Bowles, not one of RFK's favorites, also organized discussions on foreign policy questions, which met once a month at Bowles's home. Bowles to RFK, 23 September 1961, Box 1, AG-PC. For discussions of the Hickory Hill Seminars, see Schlesinger, *Robert Kennedy,* 638–39; Parmet, *JFK,* 250; Arthur M. Schlesinger, Jr., *A Thousand Days: John F. Kennedy in the White House* (Boston: Houghton Mifflin, 1965), 695–96.
11. Admiral Burke to RFK, 5 May 1961, Box 1, AG-PC. On the fascination for cigars among the New Frontiersmen, see William Styron, "Havanas in Camelot," *Vanity Fair,* July 1996, 32–41.
12. James Hayes [friend of family friend Joe Gargan] to RFK, 5 March 1962, and RFK to Hayes, 26 March 1962, Box 5, AG-PC.
13. On eating of little children, RFK to Edgar A. Brown, 19 December 1961, Box

1, AG-PC. William V. Shannon, *The Heir Apparent: Robert Kennedy and the Struggle for Power* (New York: Macmillan, 1967), 254; Guthman, *We Band of Brothers,* 236–39; TCS [Theodore Sorensen] to Peter [Edelman], 19 January 1966, Box 10, SP-PC.

14. Christmas lists, 1961, 1962, Box 10, AG-PC.
15. For comments on the Kennedys' attitudes toward money, see Bradlee, *Conversations with Kennedy,* 224–25. On RFK's "cheapness," see Oppenheimer, *The Other Mrs. Kennedy,* 131, 133, 143, 158, 160, 171. For donations of royalties, see Dues and Donations Folder, Box 13, AG-PC.
16. In 1961 the seven surviving children of Joseph Kennedy had an estimated $10 million each in trust funds. The allocation of equities in each trust portfolio and its annual returns were kept secret from the children. Assuming a modest 5 percent growth rate, each trust would have returned at least $500,000 annually. Stephen Smith managed two companies (Park Agency and Ken Industries) that Joseph Kennedy formed to operate his enterprises and oversee the children's trusts. See John H. Davis, *The Kennedys: Dynasty and Disaster, 1848–1984* (New York: McGraw-Hill, 1984), 156–62; Richard Whalen, *The Founding Father* (New York: New American Library, 1964), 79, 170, 366–72, 399–402. Items in RFK's papers at the JFK Library regarding his trust are closed.
17. Rose Kennedy, *Times to Remember* (Garden City, N.Y.: Doubleday, 1974), 449.
18. Schlesinger, *Robert Kennedy,* 632–35.
19. Glenn Doman [Institute for the Achievement of Human Potential] to EMK and RFK, 20 May 1964, Box 13, SP-PC; David and David, *Bobby Kennedy,* 141–43. After Joseph Kennedy's stroke Rose turned over her husband's care to his niece, Ann Gargan, and to his nurse and therapist, Rita Dallas.
20. Macdonald claimed he once considered marrying Kathleen Kennedy but, because that implied subservience to the Kennedys, ran the other way. Herbert S. Parmet, *Jack: The Struggles of John F. Kennedy* (New York: Dial, 1980), 521.
21. Doris Kearns Goodwin, *The Fitzgeralds and the Kennedys: An American Saga* (New York: St. Martin's, 1987), 933. "You know my father," Tip O'Neill recalled JFK saying one time. "He's determined that my old seat belongs to Teddy, and that's all there is to it." Thomas P. "Tip" O'Neill, *Man of the House* (New York: St. Martin's, 1987), 203–6; James MacGregor Burns, *Edward Kennedy and the Camelot Legacy* (New York: Norton, 1976), 74–96.
22. Burns, *Edward Kennedy,* 77–79. Tip O'Neill claimed that the Kennedys, through Ken O'Donnell, offered to name Edward McCormack ambassador to any country he wanted to pay off a $100,000 campaign debt, and to hire him as a lawyer for one of their family ventures if he would drop out of the Democratic senatorial primary. *Man of the House,* 205.
23. EMK to RK [undated] and Ted Kennedy to Bob Kennedy, 14 December 1961, Box 14, AG-PC.
24. Burns, *Edward Kennedy,* 91. Gore Vidal, "Best Man 1968," *Esquire,* March 1963, 59–62, and "The Holy Family," *Esquire,* April 1967, 99–103. Vidal's comments

were personally motivated. Once part of the Kennedy court, since he and Jacqueline Kennedy had a stepfather in common, Vidal was excommunicated after becoming drunk at a White House party in 1961 and, according to Schlesinger, who was a witness, calling the attorney general a "god-damned impertinent son of a bitch." Vidal's intense dislike of RFK may have gone back to RFK's unforgivable failure (for a politician) to recognize him at a public function in 1960 when Vidal was a candidate for Congress. On the other hand, Arthur Schlesinger speculated that RFK may have been repulsed by Vidal's open bisexuality. Schlesinger, *Robert Kennedy,* 641–42. For Vidal's version of the 1961 party, see C. David Heymann, *A Woman Named Jackie* (New York: Carol Communications, 1989), 361–63.

25. Bradlee, *Conversations with Kennedy,* 104; Burns, *Edward Kennedy,* 79. Draft manuscript of Fay's *Pleasure of His Company,* cited in Reeves, *President Kennedy,* 654. JFK once confided to Charles Bartlett that he was "not particularly thrilled" at the prospect of being succeeded by another Kennedy to whom he would be compared. Peter Collier and David Horowitz, *The Kennedys: An American Drama* (New York: Warner, 1984), 393.
26. Edwin Guthman, telephone interview by the author, 7 December 1992.
27. See Robert F. Kennedy, *Robert Kennedy in His Own Words: The Unpublished Recollections of the Kennedy Years,* ed. Edwin O. Guthman and Jeffrey Shulman (New York: Bantam, 1988), 373–74; and Benjamin C. Bradlee, *Ben Bradlee: A Good Life* (New York: Simon and Schuster, 1995), 207–09, 236–39, for comments on journalists in and out of favor with JFK. On the Kennedys' relations with the press, also see the oral history interviews of Elie Abel, Joseph Alsop, Simeon Booker, John Cogley, Rowland Evans, George Herman, Fletcher Knebel, Ira Kapenstein, Joseph Kraft, William Lawrence, Peter Lisagor, Ralph McGill, Mary McGrory, Edward Morgan, and Stanley Tretick, JFKL.
28. RFK, *Robert Kennedy,* 50. A sampling of journalists' names frequently appearing in RFK's telephone logs and desk diaries includes Phil Graham, Cabell Phillips, and Benjamin Bradlee of the *Washington Post* and *Newsweek;* Anthony Lewis, Arthur Krock, and Wallace Carroll of the *New York Times;* Anne Chamberlin and Hugh Sidey of *Time;* Warren Rogers of *Look;* publisher Ralph McGill of the *Atlanta Constitution*; Roscoe Drummond and Bob Donovan of the *Journal-American*; Godfrey Hodgson of the *London Observer*; columnists Rowland Evans, Mary McGrory, Charles Bartlett, Joseph and Stewart Alsop, Jack Anderson (then working with Drew Pearson); labor writers Victor Riesel, Clark Mollenhoff, and Peter Maas; and from television, William Paley, Dr. Frank Stanton, Newton Minnow, Jack Paar, Walter Cronkite, Sander Vanocur, Ellie Abel, Herbert Kaplow, and David Brinkley. Missing from RFK's list was Walter Lippmann, reputedly the most influential political columnist of the day, whose early criticisms of the Kennedy administration did not sit well with either Kennedy. See Parmet, *JFK,* 303–4; Ronald Steel, *Walter Lippmann and the American Century* (Boston: Little, Brown, 1980), 538.

29. Kiker, interview by Oppenheimer, *The Other Mrs. Kennedy,* 221.
30. On Alsop's influence, see Edwin M. Yoder, Jr., *Joe Alsop's Cold War: A Study of Journalistic Influence and Intrigue* (Chapel Hill: U. of North Carolina Press, 1995). Rowland's wife Kay was a classmate of Ethel at Manhattanville. Rogers, *When I Think of Bobby,* 77. On the shared assumptions of the press and the government, see James MacGregor Burns, *The Crosswinds of Freedom* (New York: Random House, 1989), 281–85; Halberstam, *The Powers That Be* (New York: Knopf, 1979), 4–18. Alice L. George, "From Camelot to Clinton: The Press and the Presidency," chapter 2 (unpublished manuscript), was of value to the author.
31. Bradlee, *Conversations with Kennedy,* 22, 20–21, 120–21, 151–52; Bradlee, *Ben Bradlee,* 236–39.
32. When *Newsweek* in June 1961 printed classified information on U.S. military plans in Germany, JFK ordered a wiretap on the telephone of the magazine's Pentagon reporter, Lloyd Norman. When nothing was learned from the tap, RFK seems to have suspected Bradlee. On 25 August 1961, while taking a call, RFK wrote "Ben Bradlee" in the margin of his telephone message sheet, ominously wrote over the name several times, framed it in a heavy-lined rectangular shape with even-spaced bars resembling a cell, all enclosed in a circular doodle, indicating he had been focusing on the name for several minutes. RFK telephone messages, 25 August 1961, JFK-ARC. RFK also suspected *New York Times* reporter Hanson Baldwin and authorized a tap on his telephone. See Athan Theoharis, ed., *From The Secret Files of J. Edgar Hoover* (Chicago: Dee, 1991), 144–45.
33. Halberstam, *The Powers That Be,* 360–61, 374–75; Reston, *Deadline,* 290; William E. Leuchtenburg, *In the Shadow of FDR: From Harry Truman to Ronald Reagan* (Ithaca: Cornell U. Press, 1983), 112–13; Giglio, *Presidency of John F. Kennedy,* 262; *New York Times,* 16 February 1963.
34. Hugh Sidey to RFK, 23 April 1963, Box 8, AG-PC. On the Kennedys' press relations, see Parmet, *JFK,* 303–4; Giglio, *Presidency of John F. Kennedy,* 258–62; Halberstam, *The Powers That Be,* 357–61, 375–76, 386–90. Oppenheimer, *The Other Mrs. Kennedy,* 222–29, alleges that Ethel accorded some journalists favorable treatment and blacklisted others from Hickory Hill.
35. Higgins to RFK, March 1962, and RFK to Higgins, 16 March 1962, Box 5, AG-PC.
36. Incensed with the *Herald-Tribune*'s criticisms, JFK once cancelled White House subscriptions. See Reeves, *President Kennedy,* 113–14, 177, 214, 303, 570.
37. Henry Fairlie, *The Kennedy Promise* (New York: Doubleday, 1972).
38. David Burner, *John F. Kennedy and the New Generation* (Boston: Little, Brown, 1988), 38. Guthman, *We Band of Brothers,* 86.
39. James L. Sundquist, *Politics and Policy: The Eisenhower, Kennedy, and Johnson Years* (Washington, D.C.: Brookings, 1968), 469–70; James W. Hilty, *John F. Kennedy: An Idealist without Illusions* (St. Louis: Harlan Davidson, 1976), 9; Herbert S. Parmet, *The Democrats: The Years after FDR* (New York: Oxford U. Press, 1976), 182–224; Leuchtenberg, *In the Shadow of FDR,* 76–77, 107–11. Cf. Irving

Bernstein, *Promises Kept: John F. Kennedy's New Frontier* (New York: Oxford U. Press, 1991), 280–98, who makes an appealing but not fully convincing argument that JFK's record of legislative successes is greatly underestimated by historians.

40. On twentieth-century liberalism, see Gary Gerstle, "The Protean Character of American Liberalism," *American Historical Review* 99 (October 1994), 1043–73.
41. For definitions of contemporary political liberalism, see David Burner and Thomas R. West, *The Torch Is Passed: The Kennedy Brothers and American Liberalism* (New York: Brandywine, 1984), 4–13, 250–51; Alonzo Hamby, *Liberalism and Its Challengers: From FDR to Bush* (New York: Oxford U. Press, 1992), 3–10; Godfrey Hodgson, *America in Our Time* (Garden City, N.Y.: Doubleday, 1976), 67–98, 476–78.
42. Hodgson, *America in Our Time,* 67–98.
43. RFK, *Robert Kennedy,* 204; Burke Marshall, OH-JFK, 34; Burner, *John F. Kennedy,* 133.
44. Samuel P. Huntington, *American Politics: The Promise of Disharmony* (Cambridge: Harvard U. Press, 1981), 1–30, 167–73. Also, see Hamby, *Liberalism and Its Challengers,* 202; Leuchtenburg, *In the Shadow of FDR,* 120; Allen J. Matusow, *The Unraveling of America: A History of Liberalism in the 1960s* (New York: Harper and Row, 1984), 127.
45. Burner, *John F. Kennedy,* 162–63.
46. Matusow, *The Unraveling of America,* 42–47; Reeves, *President Kennedy,* 196–98; Schlesinger, *Robert Kennedy,* 460–61; RFK, *Robert Kennedy,* 277–78, 301.
47. Matusow, *The Unraveling of America,* 48.
48. See Parmet, *JFK,* 91–95; Matusow, *The Unraveling of America,* chap. 2; Bernstein, *Promises Kept,* 118–59; Sundquist, *Politics and Policy,* 34–40; Hamby, *Liberalism and Its Challengers,* 202–7; Reeves, *President Kennedy,* 316–21.
49. RFK, *Robert Kennedy,* 370.
50. RFK is, of course, vague on the details of the offer to Smith, but it may have involved the U.S. Civil Rights Commission and, presumably, some agreement regarding court-ordered desegregation in Virginia. Ibid., 52.
51. Ibid. Efforts to change the Senate cloture rule and to make it easier to break filibusters failed completely. See Schlesinger, *A Thousand Days,* 709; Theodore C. Sorensen, *Kennedy* (New York: Harper and Row, 1965), 345–53; Thomas Reeves, *A Question of Character: The Life of John F. Kennedy* (New York: Free Press, 1991), 247; Bernstein, *Promises Kept,* 284.
52. Barbara Kellerman, *The Political Presidency: Practice of Leadership* (New York: Oxford U. Press, 1984), 15.
53. Fairlie, *The Kennedy Promise,* 7–19, 232–92; O'Neill, *Man of the House,* 195.
54. Kellerman, *Presidential Leadership,* 83–84, 87; Bradlee, *Conversations with Kennedy,* 184.
55. RFK, *Robert Kennedy,* 51. O'Neill, *Man of the House,* 200.
56. Kellerman, *The Political Presidency,* 69–70, 75–77.
57. RFK memorandum for file, 30 August 1961, Box 14, AG-PC.

58. Kellerman, *The Political Presidency,* 88.
59. See Bernstein, *Promises Kept,* 280–98, for a favorable summary of JFK's record of legislative accomplishments and of his success with Congress compared with that of his immediate predecessors and successors. Bernstein reports that JFK succeeded in gaining passage of 33 out of 53 proposals in 1961, 40 out of 54 in 1962, and 35 out of 58 in 1963. Cf. Kellerman, in *The Political Presidency,* 79, who wrote that leadership potential "suffers more when an initiative is taken and then rebuffed than when no initiative is taken at all."
60. JFK authorized sixty-seven executive orders in his first year alone. Bernstein, *Promises Kept,* 282.
61. Walter Heller to S. L. Cate, 27 June 1962, Box 5, AG-PC.
62. Katzenbach to RFK, 5 September 1961, Box 13, AG-PC.
63. For accounts of the steel crisis and the Kennedys' reactions, see Jim F. Heath, *Decade of Disillusionment: The Kennedy-Johnson Years* (Bloomington: Indiana U. Press, 1975), 101–4; Schlesinger, *A Thousand Days,* 634–40; Schlesinger, *Robert Kennedy,* 433–39; Sorensen, *Kennedy,* 488–516; Bradlee, *Conversations with Kennedy,* 75; Victor Navasky, *Kennedy Justice* (New York: Atheneum, 1971), 352–54; Reeves, *President Kennedy,* 294–304.
64. Bradlee, *Ben Bradlee,* 240.
65. Schlesinger, *Robert Kennedy,* 432; Navasky, *Kennedy Justice,* 167, 447.
66. See Hodgson, *America in Our Time,* 67–98; Hamby, *Liberalism and Its Challengers,* 209–12; Manchester, *The Glory and the Dream,* 906–7.
67. Guthman, *We Band of Brothers,* 224.
68. Ibid., 227.
69. Schlesinger, *Robert Kennedy,* 440–48; Matusow, *The Unraveling of America,* 97–131, 217–275; James T. Patterson, *America's Struggle against Poverty, 1900–1980* (Cambridge: Harvard U. Press, 1981), 94–96.
70. RFK, *Robert Kennedy,* 157–58.
71. Sorensen, *Kennedy,* 753; Schlesinger, *A Thousand Days,* 1012; Sundquist, *Politics and Policy,* 136–37; Nicholas Lemann, *The Promised Land: The Great Black Migration and How It Changed America* (New York: Knopf, 1991), 141–42.
72. Steward McClure to RFK, 29 January 1962, and RFK to JFK, 31 January 1962, Box 2, AG-PC.
73. Cynthia E. Harrison, "A 'New Frontier' for Women: The Public Policy of the Kennedy Administration," *Journal of American History* 67 (December 1980), 630–46; Sara M. Evans, *Born for Liberty* (New York: Free Press, 1989), 274–75; Giglio, *Presidency of John F. Kennedy,* 140–43; Bernstein, *Promises Kept,* 198–204.
74. On Port Huron and the disaffection of youthful political activists from Kennedy liberalism, see Todd Gitlin, *The Sixties: Years of Hope, Days of Rage* (New York: Bantam, 1989), 81–133; Matusow, *The Unraveling of America,* 308–14; Edward P. Morgan, *The 60s Experience* (Philadelphia: Temple U. Press, 1991), 94–98.
75. Gitlin, *The Sixties,* 126–30, 133.
76. Theodore H. White, *In Search of History* (New York: Harper and Row, 1978),

499–500. Walter Lippman, "Kennedy at Mid-term," *Newsweek,* 21 January 1963, 26. William V. Shannon, *The American Irish: A Political and Social Portrait* (Amherst: U. of Massachusetts Press, 1989), 425, 428–29, 431.

77. Schlesinger, *A Thousand Days,* 710, 1030. Sundquist, *Politics and Policy,* 482. Giglio, *Presidency of John F. Kennedy,* 286.
78. RFK, *Robert Kennedy,* 344.
79. O'Neill, *Man of the House,* 209.
80. James Q. Wilson and Robert L. DuPont, "The Sick Sixties," *The Atlantic,* October 1969, 91–98.

CHAPTER 11

1. For histories of the movement, see C. Vann Woodward, *The Strange Career of Jim Crow* (New York: Oxford U. Press, 1966); Taylor Branch, *Parting the Waters: America in the King Years, 1954–1963* (New York: Simon and Schuster, 1988); David J. Garrow, *Bearing the Cross: Martin Luther King, Jr., and the Southern Christian Leadership Conference* (New York: Morrow, 1986).
2. Herbert S. Parmet, *JFK: The Presidency of John F. Kennedy* (New York: Dial, 1983), 250–51.
3. Harris Wofford, *Of Kennedys and Kings: Making Sense of the Sixties* (New York: Farrar, Straus and Giroux, 1980), 133; Branch, *Parting The Waters,* 382–85.
4. Arthur M. Schlesinger, Jr., *Robert Kennedy and His Times* (Boston: Houghton Mifflin, 1978), 307; Wofford, *Of Kennedys and Kings,* 129. Also see Robert F. Kennedy, *Robert Kennedy in His Own Words: The Unpublished Recollections of the Kennedy Years,* ed. Edwin O. Guthman and Jeffrey Shulman (New York: Bantam, 1988), 71–72.
5. Edwin Guthman, *We Band of Brothers* (New York: Harper and Row, 1971), 181.
6. Quoted in Lester David and Irene David, *Bobby Kennedy: The Making of a Folk Hero* (New York: PaperJacks, 1988), 186.
7. Marian Wright Edelman, interview by Jean Stein and George Plimpton, eds., *American Journey: The Times of Robert Kennedy* (New York: Harcourt Brace Jovanovich, 1970), 112.
8. Nicholas Lemann, *The Promised Land: The Great Black Migration and How It Changed America* (New York: Knopf, 1991), 111.
9. Wofford, *Of Kennedys and Kings,* 169; James N. Giglio, *Presidency of John F. Kennedy* (Lawrence: U. of Kansas Press), 163.
10. Kenneth O'Donnell to Dr. A. W. Dent, President of Dillard University, New Orleans, La., 2 April 1962, Box 2, and Weaver Folder, Box 11, Wofford WHSF, JFKL; Giglio, *Presidency of John F. Kennedy,* 163–64; Schlesinger, *Robert Kennedy,* 311–12, 404–7; Parmet, *JFK,* 256–57; Wofford, *Of Kennedys and Kings,* 135–36; Allen Matusow, *The Unraveling of America A History of Liberalism in the 1960s* (New York: Harper and Row, 1984), 69.
11. JFK's winning margin in the Electoral College (303 to 219) was assured by eighty-one votes from seven of the former eleven states of the Confederacy, in-

cluding Alabama (5), Arkansas (8), Georgia (12), Louisiana (10), North Carolina (14), South Carolina (8), and Texas (24).

12. RFK, *Robert Kennedy,* 77–78. On JFK's southern ties, see Parmet, *JFK,* 251.
13. For overviews of the Kennedys' actions on civil rights, see Bruce Miroff, *Pragmatic Illusions: The Presidential Politics of John F. Kennedy* (New York: McKay, 1976); Carl Brauer, *John F. Kennedy and the Second Reconstruction* (New York: Columbia U. Press, 1977); Wofford, *Of Kennedys and Kings;* Schlesinger, *Robert Kennedy,* 307–448; Parmet, *JFK,* 249–76; Branch, *Parting the Waters,* 379–922; Garrow, *Bearing the Cross,* 127–307; Irving Bernstein, *Promises Kept: John F. Kennedy's New Frontier* (New York: Oxford U. Press, 1990), 44–117; Giglio, *Presidency of John F. Kennedy,* 159–87.
14. Quoted in Branch, *Parting the Waters,* 139–41.
15. Garrow, *Bearing the Cross,* 153–54.
16. King was accompanied to the meeting by Stanley Levison. Branch, *Parting the Waters,* 404–7.
17. Wofford, *Of Kennedys and Kings,* 51–52, 124–25; Victor Navasky, *Kennedy Justice* (New York: Atheneum, 1971), 97–98; Parmet, *JFK,* 249–50.
18. Giglio, *Presidency of John F. Kennedy,* 160–61; Branch, *Parting the Waters,* 340–50.
19. Martin Luther King, Jr., "Equality Now: The President Has the Power," *The Nation,* 4 January 1961, 91–95.
20. Ibid., 95.
21. Wofford, *Of Kennedys and Kings,* 58.
22. RFK, *Robert Kennedy,* 78–79; Guthman, *We Band of Brothers,* 95.
23. RFK, *Robert Kennedy,* 57; Wofford, OH-JFK, 122–23. Wofford and Levison, both active in the Gandhian Society, once discussed financing a trip to India for King. The FBI evidently eavesdropped on the telephone call. In its report the FBI also included hearsay distorting a comment Wofford made to a fellow Howard University student in 1951. Navasky, *Kennedy Justice,* 142; Branch, *Parting the Waters,* 387–88, 406; Wofford, interview by author, 24 April 1990.
24. Wofford, *Of Kennedys and Kings,* 94; Navasky, *Kennedy Justice,* 162; Branch, *Parting the Waters,* 387–88.
25. Navasky, in *Kennedy Justice,* 162–64, argues further that the connections of RFK's team to Ivy League institutions imbued them with a "code" of gentlemanly conduct.
26. Ibid., 166–67.
27. Richard Goodwin, *Remembering America: A Voice from The Sixties* (Boston: Little, Brown, 1988), 153.
28. Wofford, *Of Kennedys and Kings,* 130–33, 134, 136–39; Bernstein, *Promises Kept,* 47–50; Branch, *Parting the Waters,* 397–99.
29. Wofford, *Of Kennedys and Kings,* 144–50; Schlesinger, *Robert Kennedy,* 311.
30. Meeting Notes, Subcabinet Group on Civil Rights, 14 April 1961, Box 14; [Adam] Yarmolinsky (DOD) Folder, Box 11 and Boxes 11–14 for compliance of other agencies, Wofford WHSF, JFKL.
31. Memorandum, Wofford to Pierre Salinger, 18 July 1961, Box 14, Wofford WHSF, JFKL.

32. Branch, *Parting the Waters,* 399.
33. Memorandum to Fred Dutton, 12 June 1961, Box 14, Wofford WHSF, JFKL; Box 9, Civil Rights Folder, AG-GC; Schlesinger, *Robert Kennedy,* 311; David and David, *Bobby Kennedy,* 188.
34. Wofford Memorandum for Subcabinet Group on Civil Rights, 24 May 1961, and Meeting Notes, 14 April 1961, Box 14, Wofford WHSF, JFKL; Wofford, *Of Kennedys and Kings,* 141.
35. Giglio, *Presidency of John F. Kennedy,* 172; Bernstein, *Promises Kept,* 54–61; Schlesinger, *Robert Kennedy,* 335–37; Matusow, *The Unraveling of America,* 64–65.
36. Schlesinger, *Robert Kennedy,* 335–36.
37. LBJ asked Taylor to assist Arthur Goldberg and Abe Fortas in preparing the draft. See Nicholas Lemann, "Taking Affirmative Action Apart," *New York Times Magazine,* 11 June 1995, 40.
38. Wofford, OH-JFK, 126.
39. RFK, *Robert Kennedy,* 152, 153; Schlesinger, *Robert Kennedy,* 360–61.
40. Bernstein, *Promises Kept,* 60. Also see Matusow, *The Unraveling of America,* 65.
41. Parmet, *JFK,* 258–59. For a summary of historians' views, see James MacGregor Burns, *The Crosswinds of Freedom* (New York: Vintage, 1990), 347–88.
42. Miroff, *Pragmatic Illusions,* 244; Wofford, *Of Kennedys and Kings,* 124.
43. Schlesinger, *Robert Kennedy,* 334–35.
44. Burke Marshall, OH-JFK; Parmet, *JFK,* 259.
45. Wofford, *Of Kennedys and Kings,* 155.
46. RFK, *Robert Kennedy,* 155.
47. Louis Martin to RFK, 10 April 1962, Box 35, AG-GC. Douglas Ross, *Robert F. Kennedy: Apostle of Change* (New York: Trident, 1969), 59.
48. RFK, *Robert Kennedy,* 154, 156.
49. Arthur M. Schlesinger, Jr., *A Thousand Days: John F. Kennedy in the White House* (Boston: Houghton Mifflin, 1965), 756–58, 832–33.
50. Martin to RFK, 9 November 1962, Box 12, AG-PC.
51. Goodwin, *Remembering America,* 133; Giglio, *Presidency of John F. Kennedy,* 171; Wofford, *Of Kennedys and Kings,* 169; Branch, *Parting the Waters,* 679; Matusow, *The Unraveling of America,* 68–69.
52. Branch, *Parting the Waters,* 587; Navasky, *Kennedy Justice,* 161; Wofford, OH-JFK, 128.
53. Wofford, OH-JFK, 128.
54. RFK, *Robert Kennedy,* 157–58.
55. Schlesinger, *Robert Kennedy,* 338.
56. Berl Bernhard to Lee C. White and Theodore Sorensen, 15 May 1963, Box 9, AG-GC.
57. Navasky, *Kennedy Justice,* 109–10.
58. Wofford, OH-JFK, 147. Giglio, *Presidency of John F. Kennedy,* 170–71. Wofford, *Of Kennedys and Kings,* 161.
59. Miroff, *Pragmatic Illusions,* 251.

60. Wofford, *Of Kennedys and Kings,* 161–62. The commission kept the pressure on the Kennedys. In April 1963, even as the Kennedys were moving closer to Hesburgh's view, the Commission presented a special report on conditions in Mississippi, documenting the use of federal funds to construct segregated facilities, detailing the extensive use of violence to stop blacks from registering to vote, and leaving the impression that the Kennedy administration had deliberately turned a blind eye to such actions. The Justice Department and the White House ganged up on the commission. Burke Marshall prepared a point-by-point rebuttal, which the president and White House aides used to discredit the commission's findings before the news media. Branch, *Parting the Waters,* 745–47.
61. Miroff, *Pragmatic Illusions,* 239. Navasky, *Kennedy Justice,* 193.
62. Miroff, *Pragmatic Illusions,* 227. Burns, *Crosswinds of Freedom,* 366.
63. Navasky, *Kennedy Justice,* 177.
64. Charlene Hunter Gault interview, NBC-News, "RFK," April 1993; Ross, *Robert F. Kennedy,* 56–57; Wofford, *Of Kennedys and Kings,* 150–51; Schlesinger, *Robert Kennedy,* 315–16; Branch, *Parting the Waters,* 414–15.
65. Ross, *Robert F. Kennedy,* 64.
66. Schlesinger, *Robert Kennedy,* 329–30; Miroff, *Pragmatic Illusions,* 245–46. Probably to protect RFK's historical image, Marshall later said that RFK "picked that up from me," meaning the federal approach, and calling it mostly "technical stuff" of no concern to RFK. But the timing of RFK's remarks seems to indicate that he adhered to a strict interpretation of the limits of federal powers over civil rights before Marshall gave it a name and formally rationalized the approach. Navasky, *Kennedy Justice,* 116–17; Matusow, *The Unraveling of America,* 78–79.
67. Branch, *Parting the Waters,* 570–73.
68. Schlesinger, *Robert Kennedy,* 327–28.
69. RFK, *Robert Kennedy,* 100.
70. Navasky, *Kennedy Justice,* 166–69, 185.
71. Ibid., 185; Giglio, *Presidency of John F. Kennedy,* 169.
72. Navasky, *Kennedy Justice,* 108–9, 177. Also see Richard Gid Powers, *Secrecy and Power: The Life of J. Edgar Hoover* (New York: Free Press, 1987), 367–80; Athan Theoharis and John Stuart Cox, *The Boss: J. Edgar Hoover and the Great American Inquisition* (Philadelphia: Temple U. Press, 1988), 323–24, 343–44; Curt Gentry, *J. Edgar Hoover: The Man and the Secrets* (New York: Norton, 1991), 483–85, 561–65. Cf. Anthony Summers, *Official and Confidential: The Secret Life of J. Edgar Hoover* (New York: Putnam, 1993), 350–51, who asserts that Hoover was "forced" and "dragooned" into civil rights investigations.
73. Burke Marshall quoted in Richard Reeves, *President Kennedy: Profile of Power* (New York: Simon and Schuster, 1993), 127.
74. RFK, *Robert Kennedy,* 138.
75. Navasky, *Kennedy Justice,* 100–107. Andrew Goodman, Michael Schwerner, and James Chaney, two whites and one black, were murdered in Philadelphia, Mississippi, during the Freedom Summer project of 1964. Twenty-one whites, in-

cluding a deputy sheriff, were arrested, but the state dropped the charges. Eventually, six were convicted for violating federal civil rights laws. For his version of how the FBI became involved in Mississippi, see RFK, *Robert Kennedy,* 136–38.

76. *U.S. News & World Report,* 30 January 1961, summary of U.S. Commission on Civil Rights Report, "Equal Protection of the Laws in Public Higher Education," 52–53.
77. RFK, *Robert Kennedy,* 80–82; Wofford, *Of Kennedys and Kings,* 134–36; Schlesinger, *Robert Kennedy,* 310–11.
78. Anthony Lewis, "U.S. Sues to Force a Virginia County to Open Schools," *New York Times,* 27 April 1961.
79. Schlesinger, *Robert Kennedy,* 370–71; Navasky, *Kennedy Justice,* 182.
80. Robert E. Thompson and Hortense Myers, *Robert F. Kennedy: The Brother Within* (New York: Macmillan, 1962), 142; Navasky, *Kennedy Justice,* 98.
81. Schlesinger, *Robert Kennedy,* 312. Kenneth O'Reilly, *"Racial Matters": The FBI's Secret File on Black America, 1960–1972* (New York: Free Press, 1989), 66. Branch, *Parting the Waters,* 382.
82. Louis Martin to RFK, and RFK to Martin, both 22 January 1962, Box 35, AG-GC.
83. Wofford, *Of Kennedys and Kings,* 135–36.
84. Branch, *Parting the Waters,* 387.
85. Navasky, *Kennedy Justice,* 100–101.
86. Marshall to J. Symington, 9 August 1962, Box 9, AG-CG.
87. Wofford, *Of Kennedys and Kings,* 135–36.
88. Navasky, *Kennedy Justice,* 182–83, 205; Branch, *Parting the Waters,* 633–40.
89. Meeting Notes, 15 September 1961, Box 14, Wofford WHSF, JFKL.
90. Wofford, *Of Kennedys and Kings,* 126. Schlesinger, *Robert Kennedy,* 338. Navasky, *Kennedy Justice,* 192–93.
91. RFK, *Robert Kennedy,* 92; Branch, *Parting the Waters,* 413.
92. Wofford, *Of Kennedys and Kings,* 151–52; Branch, *Parting the Waters,* 420–24.
93. Schlesinger, *Robert Kennedy,* 317.
94. Wofford, *Of Kennedys and Kings,* 125, 153. My account of the Freedom Rides relies extensively on Branch, *Parting the Waters,* 412–91.
95. Joe Dolan to RFK, 26 May 1961, Box 1, AG-PC.
96. Wofford, *Of Kennedys and Kings.* 156.
97. RFK, *Robert Kennedy,* 82–83; Branch, *Parting the Waters,* 417–25.
98. Branch, *Parting the Waters,* 428–29.
99. Clark, interview by Stein and Plimpton, *American Journey,* 94–95.
100. Branch, *Parting the Waters,* 432–33.
101. Ibid., 428–32.
102. Ibid., 433–36. For JFK's reactions, see Reeves, *President Kennedy,* 122–34.
103. RFK, *Robert Kennedy,* 93.
104. RFK desk diary, 19 May 1961, JFK-ARC.
105. Branch, *Parting the Waters,* 433.

106. Ibid., 442.
107. Schlesinger, *Robert Kennedy,* 318; Wofford, *Of Kennedys and Kings,* 153–54; Branch, *Parting the Waters,* 442–43; RFK, *Robert Kennedy,* 92–93.
108. RFK, *Robert Kennedy,* 93.
109. Branch, *Parting the Waters,* 443–44.
110. Seigenthaler statement, 14 November 1961, Box 53, AG-GC; Wofford, *Of Kennedys and Kings,* 153–54.
111. Branch, *Parting the Waters,* 448.
112. Ross, *Robert F. Kennedy,* 64.
113. Lemann, *Promised Land,* 116.
114. Judge Johnson had issued pro-integration decisions in the Montgomery bus boycott and a Civil Rights Commission petition. See Dan T. Carter, *The Politics of Rage: George Wallace, the Origins of the New Conservatism, the Transformation of American Politics* (New York: Simon and Schuster, 1995), 99, 289.
115. Branch, *Parting the Waters,* 453–54.
116. Dolan, OH-JFK, 113.
117. Schlesinger, *Robert Kennedy,* 318–19.
118. RFK, *Robert Kennedy,* 89.
119. Wofford, *Of Kennedys and Kings,* 154; Branch, *Parting the Waters,* 463–64. The old Boston expression, according to Reeves, *President Kennedy,* 131, n682, is "cheap as Kelsey's nuts."
120. Schlesinger, *Robert Kennedy,* 321; Branch, *Parting the Waters,* 465; RFK, *Robert Kennedy,* 90–91.
121. Branch, *Parting the Waters,* 470.
122. Burke Marshall, interview by Stein and Plimpton, *American Journey,* 95–96.
123. Branch, *Parting the Waters,* 472–73; Wofford, *Of Kennedys and Kings,* 155.
124. Wofford, *Of Kennedys and Kings.* 156; Abernathy, interview by Stein and Plimpton, *American Journey,* 100; Schlesinger, *Robert Kennedy,* 321; Branch, *Parting the Waters,* 475–77.
125. Schlesinger, *Robert Kennedy,* 322; Branch, *Parting the Waters,* 475.
126. Branch, *Parting the Waters,* 476.
127. Quoted in Giglio, *Presidency of John F. Kennedy,* 170.
128. Branch, *Parting the Waters,* 479–80.
129. RFK, *Robert Kennedy,* 102.
130. Schlesinger, *Robert Kennedy,* 325.
131. Branch, *Parting the Waters,* 480–81, 561.
132. John Raines, interview by the author, May 1993.
133. Branch, *Parting the Waters,* 478.
134. Ibid., 477. Wofford, *Of Kennedys and Kings,* 157.
135. Wofford to JFK, 29 May 1961, Box 68, AG-GC.
136. Branch, *Parting the Waters,* 478–80.
137. Schlesinger, *Robert Kennedy,* 324.

138. For Burke Marshall's activities, Notes of Subcabinet Group Meeting, 16 June 1961, Box 14, Wofford WHSF, JFKL; Branch, *Parting the Waters,* 478–82.
139. Matusow, *The Unraveling of America,* 75.
140. On the Hardy, Moses, and Lee cases, see Branch, *Parting the Waters,* 507–23. Schlesinger, *Robert Kennedy,* 312; Navasky, *Kennedy Justice,* 116–17.
141. Navasky, *Kennedy Justice,* 118; Jack Newfield, *Robert Kennedy: A Memoir* (New York: New American Library, 1969), 23.
142. Chuck McDew, "Thou Shall Not Resist," in *It Did Happen Here,* ed. Bud Schultz and Ruth Schultz (Berkely and Los Angeles: U. of California Press, 1989), 47–58, quotes on 55.
143. Branch, *Parting the Waters,* 554–55; Navasky, *Kennedy Justice,* 96–155; Miroff, *Pragmatic Illusions,* 244–45.
144. The Albany movement lasted for more than a year, with many ups and downs. See Giglio, *Presidency of John F. Kennedy,* 170–71; Branch, *Parting the Waters,* 524–61, 601–32, 680–83.
145. Matusow, *The Unraveling of America,* 75–76, 82.
146. O'Reilly, *"Racial Matters,"* 66; Navasky, *Kennedy Justice,* 207.
147. Schlesinger, *Robert Kennedy,* 339–40. Navasky, *Kennedy Justice,* 118.
148. Schlesinger, *Robert Kennedy,* 339–40.

CHAPTER 12

1. Harris Wofford, *Of Kennedys and Kings: Making Sense of the Sixties* (New York: Farrar, Straus and Giroux, 1980), 163–64.
2. Taylor Branch, *Parting the Waters: America in the King Years, 1954–63* (New York: Simon and Schuster, 1988), 633–40, JFK quote on 638–39.
3. Robert F. Kennedy, *Robert Kennedy in His Own Words: The Unpublished Recollections of the Kennedy Years,* ed. Edwin O. Guthman and Jeffrey Shulman (New York: Bantam, 1988), 198.
4. Quoted in Dan T. Carter, *The Politics of Rage: George Wallace, the Origins of the New Conservatism, the Transformation of American Politics* (New York: Simon and Schuster, 1995), 134.
5. Branch, *Parting the Waters,* 640–42, 686–87, 693–95, 698–99. Louis Martin and other liberals in the administration who advocated for the proclamation traded it for a gala White House reception to honor African Americans on Lincoln's birthday. King and other leaders boycotted the reception.
6. Branch, *Parting the Waters,* 488–89.
7. RFK, *Robert Kennedy,* 105–6.
8. Wyatt Walker of the SCLC took the blame for what he called an "administrative error" in releasing the text of the telegram prematurely. Branch, *Parting the Waters,* 515–16.
9. Ibid., 610–11.
10. David Garrow, *The FBI and Martin Luther King, Jr.* (New York: Penguin, 1983),

24. Copies of pertinent FBI documents on King are in Michael Friedly and David Gallen, eds., *Martin Luther King, Jr.: The FBI File* (New York: Carroll and Graf, 1993), 22.

11. RFK, *Robert Kennedy,* 140–43; Richard G. Powers, *Secrecy and Power: The Life of J. Edgar Hoover* (New York: Free Press, 1987), 369–70.
12. Garrow, *FBI and Martin Luther King,* 42–43.
13. Ibid., 26, 43–44.
14. RFK, *Robert Kennedy,* 143.
15. Garrow, *FBI and Martin Luther King,* 47–48.
16. RFK remembered giving the order in 1961. RFK, *Robert Kennedy,* 140. Garrow, *FBI and Martin Luther King,* 54, demonstrates that it was actually August 1962.
17. On Kennedy set-ups to test Lyndon Johnson and Henry Cabot Lodge, see RFK, *Robert Kennedy,* 16–17.
18. Wofford, OH-JFK, 143.
19. Branch, *Parting the Waters,* 516.
20. See Arthur M. Schlesinger, Jr., *Robert Kennedy and His Times* (Boston: Houghton Mifflin, 1978), 341–50; Burke Marshall, interview by Jean Stein and George Plimpton, eds. *American Journey: The Times of Robert Kennedy* (New York: Harcourt Brace Jovanovich, 1970), 104. For accounts of the integration of Ole Miss, see Branch, *Parting the Waters,* 647–72; Walter Lord, *The Past That Would Not Die* (New York: Harper and Row, 1965); James H. Meredith, *Three Years in Mississippi* (Bloomington: Indiana U. Press, 1966).
21. Burke Marshall, OH-JFK, 52.
22. On the Ole Miss confrontation, see Lord, *The Past That Would Not Die,* and Victor Navasky, *Kennedy Justice* (New York: Atheneum, 1971), 159–242.
23. Branch, *Parting the Waters,* 650–51.
24. RFK, *Robert Kennedy,* 160.
25. Ibid., 104–5.
26. Schlesinger, *Robert Kennedy,* 344.
27. Transcripts of telephone calls reprinted in Navasky, *Kennedy Justice,* 211–17.
28. Ibid., 111.
29. James N. Giglio, *The Presidency of John F. Kennedy* (Lawrence: U. of Kansas Press, 1993), 175.
30. Joseph Dolan, OH-JFK, 116; Navasky, *Kennedy Justice,* 240; Edwin Guthman, *We Band of Brothers* (New York: Harper and Row, 1971), 204; Ramsey Clark, interview by Stein and Plimpton, *American Journey,* 104–5.
31. RFK, *Robert Kennedy,* 166.
32. Branch, *Parting the Waters,* 669.
33. RFK, *Robert Kennedy,* 161.
34. Ibid., 161.
35. Ibid., 162–63.
36. Allen Matusow, *The Unraveling of America: A History of Liberalism in The 1960s* (New York: Harper and Row, 1984), 83–85.

37. After Oxford, RFK said his brother ordered an investigation of the army's mobile preparedness. RFK, *Robert Kennedy,* 164–65, 167.
38. Navasky, *Kennedy Justice,* 234–39; Branch, *Parting the Waters,* 671.
39. Harris poll results in Richard Reeves, *President Kennedy: Profile of Power* (New York: Simon and Schuster, 1993), 364.
40. Branch, *Parting the Waters,* 656, 667.
41. Ibid., 672; *New York Times,* 30 September 1962.
42. Guthman, *We Band of Brothers,* 204; Wofford, *Of Kennedys and Kings,* 168; Bruce C. Miroff, *Pragmatic Illusions* (New York: David McKay, 1976), 223–70.
43. James Meredith, interview by Stein and Plimpton, *American Journey,* 105.
44. Branch, *Parting the Waters,* 699. For a generally positive midterm assessment that makes little mention of Oxford, see Alexander M. Bickel, "Civil Rights: The Kennedy Record," *New Republic,* 15 December 1962, 11–16.
45. Douglas Ross, *Robert F. Kennedy: Apostle of Change* (New York: Trident, 1969), 59.
46. RFK, *Robert Kennedy,* 148–49; Schlesinger, *Robert Kennedy,* 352; Matusow, *The Unraveling of America,* 85–86.
47. Branch, *Parting the Waters,* 697–99; Rauh, OH-JFK, 107; Wofford, *Of Kennedys and Kings,* 170.
48. RFK, *Robert Kennedy,* 149.
49. Ross, *Robert F. Kennedy,* 68.
50. RFK Speech, Kentucky Centennial of the Emancipation Proclamation, Louisville, Kentucky, 18 March 1963, RFK-FBI.
51. Levison, interview by Stein and Plimpton, *American Journey,* 114–15.
52. Branch, *Parting the Waters,* 711, 737; Giglio, *Presidency of John F. Kennedy,* 115–16; Carter, *Politics of Rage,* 116–17.
53. Branch, *Parting the Waters,* 735.
54. Ibid., 740.
55. "Look at Them Run," *Newsweek,* 13 May 1963, 28–29.
56. Branch, *Parting the Waters,* 762.
57. Marshall conceded in 1996 that their efforts resulted in only a "trivial" settlement. "Reflections on RFK as Attorney General," Duquesne U. Law School Forum, April 1996.
58. Branch, *Parting the Waters,* 769.
59. Ibid., 773.
60. RFK, *Robert Kennedy,* 170.
61. Schlesinger, *Robert Kennedy,* 360; Branch, *Parting the Waters,* 788–89.
62. Carter, *Politics of Rage,* 126.
63. Branch, *Parting the Waters,* 796–97.
64. Ibid., 799–800; Carter, *Politics of Rage,* 126–28.
65. Branch, *Parting the Waters,* 799; Carter, *Politics of Rage,* 127.
66. Young, interview by Stein and Plimpton, *American Journey,* 118; Giglio, *Presidency of John F. Kennedy,* 117.

67. Schlesinger, *Robert Kennedy,* 354–55; Giglio, *Presidency of John F. Kennedy,* 177–78.
68. Baldwin, interview by Stein and Plimpton, *American Journey,* 119.
69. Others variously reported to have been there were Edward False (Baldwin's secretary), David Baldwin (James's brother), Thais Aubrey (a friend of David Baldwin's), Rip Torn (white actor), Robert P. Mills, Henry Morgenthau III (white television producer), Burke Marshall, and Ed Guthman.
70. Schlesinger, *Robert Kennedy,* 360.
71. Quoted in Branch, *Parting the Waters,* 810.
72. Baldwin interview, 121.
73. Schlesinger, *Robert Kennedy,* 355–60.
74. Clark interview, 119–22; Giglio, *Presidency of John F. Kennedy,* 178–79; Schlesinger, *Robert Kennedy,* 359.
75. RFK, *Robert Kennedy,* 225; Branch, *Parting the Waters,* 812.
76. Schlesinger, *Robert Kennedy,* 359; Wofford, *Of Kennedys and Kings,* 172.
77. RFK, *Robert Kennedy,* 224–26.
78. SAC New York to Hoover, 29 May 1963, RFK-FBI; Navasky, *Kennedy Justice,* 113–15.
79. Branch, *Parting the Waters,* 812.
80. Tom Wolfe, *Radical Chic and Mau-Mauing the Flak Catchers* (New York: Farrar, Straus and Giroux, 1970).
81. The account that follows is drawn from Schlesinger, *Robert Kennedy,* 355–60; Branch, *Parting the Waters,* 809–13; Stein and Plimpton, *American Journey,* 119–22; Guthman, *We Band of Brothers,* 219–21; James M. Burns, *The Crosswinds of Freedom* (New York: Vintage, 1990), 369–70; RFK, *Robert Kennedy,* 223–26.
82. Branch, *Parting the Waters,* 812–13.
83. Giglio, *Presidency of John F. Kennedy,* 179.
84. Schlesinger, *Robert Kennedy,* 360–61; Branch, *Parting the Waters,* 807.
85. Carter, *Politics of Rage,* 134; Matusow, *The Unraveling of America,* 89.
86. RFK, *Robert Kennedy,* 171–73; Schlesinger, *Robert Kennedy,* 373.
87. Doar, interview by Stein and Plimpton, *American Journey,* 122.
88. RFK, *Robert Kennedy,* 171–73.
89. Branch, *Parting the Waters,* 807.
90. Ibid., 808–9; Giglio, *Presidency of John F. Kennedy,* 182–83; Schlesinger, *Robert Kennedy,* 372–76.
91. Quoted in Branch, *Parting the Waters,* 809.
92. Ibid., 804–5.
93. SAC Birmingham to Hoover, 23 April 1963; SAC Columbia to Hoover and clipping, *Birmingham Post-Herald,* 26 April 1963, RFK-FBI.
94. *Mobile Press* clipping, 23 April 1963, RFK-FBI.
95. RFK, *Robert Kennedy,* 189–90.
96. Carter, *Politics of Rage,* 118.
97. Schlesinger, *Robert Kennedy,* 363.

98. RFK, *Robert Kennedy,* 191.
99. Transcript of Conversations between Attorney General Robert F. Kennedy and Governor Wallace, Montgomery, Alabama, 25 April 1963, 46, Box 12, SP-PC; Navasky, *Kennedy Justice,* 111–12.
100. RFK, *Robert Kennedy,* 186. For a thorough analysis of the meeting, see Carter, *Politics of Rage,* 119–23. Robert F. Kennedy, Jr., selected Judge Johnson for the topic of his senior honors thesis at Harvard in 1976. Schlesinger, *Robert Kennedy,* 333.
101. Transcript, RFK-Wallace Conversation, 6, 9.
102. RFK, *Robert Kennedy,* 185–86; *Alabama Journal,* 25 April 1963, *Birmingham News,* 26 April 1963, RFK-FBI. Congressman Thaddeus Stevens of Pennsylvania (1792–1868) was an ardent opponent of slavery and champion of Radical Reconstruction after the Civil War.
103. On Rose and his role, see Carter, *Politics of Rage,* 111–13.
104. RFK, *Robert Kennedy,* 191–95; Carter, *Politics of Rage,* 129–30.
105. Carter, *Politics of Rage,* 113.
106. Ibid., 137–41.
107. In one of history's ironic twists, George Wallace did not again lay eyes on Vivian Malone (Jones) until thirty-three years later when he personally apologized to her for the 1963 confrontation, moments before she was presented the first Lurleen B. Wallace Award of Courage (named in memory of Wallace's wife). Robert F. Kennedy, Jr., attended the ceremony. "I wanted to be here," he said, "because I knew that my father would want to be here." *Philadelphia Inquirer,* 11 October 1996.
108. This account of the integration of the University of Alabama draws from "Kennedy v. Wallace: A Crisis Up Close (June 10–11, 1963)," PBS *American Experience* series, no. 107, WGBH (1988), produced by Robert Drew; Giglio, *Presidency of John F. Kennedy,* 179–80; Branch, *Parting the Waters,* 821; RFK, *Robert Kennedy,* 200; Carter, *Politics of Rage,* 143–52.
109. Navasky, *Kennedy Justice,* 99; Wofford, *Of Kennedys and Kings,* 172; Schlesinger, *Robert Kennedy,* 372.
110. Branch, *Parting the Waters,* 822.
111. RFK, *Robert Kennedy,* 175–76, 199–201; Branch, *Parting the Waters,* 822–24. Cf. Carter, *Politics of Rage,* 151–53.
112. White House Press Release, Remarks of the President, Box 9, AG-GC. For analysis of the speech, see Miroff, *Pragmatic Illusions,* 257; Branch, *Parting the Waters,* 823–25; Schlesinger, *Robert Kennedy,* 369–70.
113. Schlesinger, *Robert Kennedy,* 370; Branch, *Parting the Waters,* 829–33.
114. On 22 June 1963, JFK told King and other civil rights leaders that his approval ratings had fallen to 47 percent, but no one could find the poll. Branch, *Parting the Waters,* 839. JFK still enjoyed a 63 percent approval rating in October 1963. See Giglio, *Presidency of John F. Kennedy,* 186–87.
115. RFK, *Robert Kennedy,* 175–76; Burke Marshall, OH-JFK, 30; Branch, *Parting the Waters,* 827–28.

116. *Meet the Press,* NBC-TV, 23 June 1963, Ross, *Robert F. Kennedy,* 66.
117. Jack Newfield, *Robert Kennedy: A Memoir* (New York: New American Library, 1969), 22–23; Branch, *Parting the Waters,* 828; Schlesinger, *Robert Kennedy,* 371.
118. *Meet the Press,* NBC-TV, 23 June 1963.
119. Branch, *Parting the Waters,* 731–33, 864–70.

CHAPTER 13

1. Martin to RFK, 13 May 1963, Box 12, AG-PC.
2. Arthur M. Schlesinger, Jr., *A Thousand Days: John F. Kennedy in the White House* (Boston: Houghton Mifflin, 1965), 971.
3. Bruce Miroff, *Pragmatic Illusions: The Presidential Politics of John F. Kennedy* (New York: McKay, 1976), 258–61.
4. Arthur M. Schlesinger, Jr., *Robert Kennedy and His Times* (Boston: Houghton Mifflin, 1978), 375–76; James N. Giglio, *The Presidency of John F. Kennedy* (Lawrence: U. of Kansas Press, 1993), 185.
5. Schlesinger, *Robert Kennedy,* 375–76; Giglio, *Presidency of John F. Kennedy,* 185.
6. Schlesinger, *Robert Kennedy,* 375–76; Schlesinger, *A Thousand Days,* 884–85; Taylor Branch, *Parting the Waters: America in the King Years, 1954–63* (New York: Simon and Schuster, 1988), 820, 839–40.
7. David Garrow, *The FBI and Martin Luther King Jr.,* (New York: Penguin, 1983), 54–58.
8. Ibid., 61; Branch, *Parting the Waters,* 835–38; Schlesinger, *Robert Kennedy,* 383–84; Victor Navasky, *Kennedy Justice* (New York: Atheneum, 197), 142–43; Burke Marshall to J. Edgar Hoover, 20 October 1963, O&C, summarizes the warnings by RFK, JFK, and Marshall.
9. Schlesinger, *Robert Kennedy,* 385.
10. Branch, *Parting the Waters,* 845, 850–51.
11. Garrow, *FBI and Martin Luther King,* 63; Branch, *Parting the Waters,* 852–56.
12. Evans to Belmont, 23 and 25 July 1963, Folder 24, O&C.
13. Richard G. Powers, *Secrecy and Power: The Life of J. Edgar Hoover* (New York: Free Press, 1987), 372.
14. Garrow, *FBI and Martin Luther King,* 65; Robert F. Kennedy, *Robert Kennedy in His Own Words: The Unpublished Recollections of the Kennedy Years,* ed. Edwin O. Guthman and Jeffrey Shulman (New York: Bantam, 1988), 144; Navasky, *Kennedy Justice,* 151.
15. Garrow, *FBI and Martin Luther King,* 68–69; Powers, *Secrecy and Power,* 377.
16. Schlesinger, *Robert Kennedy,* 376–78.
17. RFK, *Robert Kennedy,* 226–30.
18. Richard Reeves, *President Kennedy: Profile of Power* (New York: Simon and Schuster, 1993), 578–83; David Garrow, *Bearing the Cross: Martin Luther King, Jr., and the Southern Christian Leadership Conference* (New York: Random House, 1986), 283.

19. "Gentle flood" was first used by a London newspaper. See Douglas Ross, *Robert F. Kennedy: Apostle of Change* (New York: Trident, 1969), 67.
20. Quoted in "Civil Rights," *Time,* 30 August 1963, 9–14.
21. Quoted in Miroff, *Pragmatic Illusions,* 265.
22. RFK, *Robert Kennedy,* 226–30; Branch, *Parting the Waters,* 878–81; Reeves, *President Kennedy,* 580–83.
23. RFK, *Robert Kennedy,* 229.
24. King's speech is excerpted in Branch, *Parting the Waters,* 881–83.
25. Ibid., 883; Giglio, *Presidency of John F. Kennedy,* 186.
26. Branch, *Parting the Waters,* 888–910.
27. RFK, *Robert Kennedy,* 75.
28. Allen Matusow, *The Unraveling of America: A History of Liberalism in the 1960s* (New York: Harper and Row, 1984), 93.
29. Giglio, *Presidency of John F. Kennedy,* 186–87.
30. RFK, *Robert Kennedy,* 202, 76–77.
31. See Michael P. Riccards, "Rare Counsel: Kennedy, Johnson, and the Civil Rights Bill of 1963," *Presidential Studies Quarterly* 11 (Summer 1981): 397.
32. Schlesinger, *Robert Kennedy,* 373–74.
33. Branch, *Parting the Waters,* 840.
34. RFK, *Robert Kennedy,* 76–77.
35. Ibid., 203–15, quote on 215.
36. Miroff, *Pragmatic Illusions,* 266–67.
37. RFK, *Robert Kennedy,* 179–85.
38. Harding, interview by Jean Stein and George Plimpton, eds., *American Journey: The Times of Robert Kennedy* (New York: Harcourt Brace Jovanovich, 1970), 124.
39. Marshall, interview in ibid., 123.
40. Schlesinger, *Robert Kennedy,* 394–95.
41. Ibid., 374–75.
42. Carl Brauer, *John F. Kennedy and the Second Reconstruction* (New York: Columbia U. Press, 1977), 265–66.
43. RFK, *Robert Kennedy,* 204.
44. *New York Times,* 26 September 1963.
45. RFK, *Robert Kennedy,* 203–19.
46. Schlesinger, *Robert Kennedy,* 393.
47. RFK, *Robert Kennedy,* 206–8. Curiously, RFK offers no explanation as to why he was not present at this meeting.
48. Ibid., 206.
49. Lyndon B. Johnson, *The Vantage Point* (New York: Holt, Rinehart, and Winston, 1971), 37.
50. RFK, *Robert Kennedy,* 211–212.
51. Miroff, *Pragmatic Illusions,* 260–63; Schlesinger, *Robert Kennedy,* 392–93; Matusow, *The Unraveling of America,* 92–93; RFK, *Robert Kennedy,* 205–19; Burke Marshall, OH-JFK, 37.

52. RFK, *Robert Kennedy,* 209–10.
53. Giglio, *Presidency of John F. Kennedy,* 184.
54. See Matusow, *The Unraveling of America,* 94–96; Bruce J. Schulman, *Lyndon B. Johnson and American Liberalism* (New York: St. Martin's, 1995), 73–74; and, in the same volume, Allen J. Matusow, "From the Great Society: A Twenty-Year Critique," 185–89;
55. Schlesinger, *Robert Kennedy,* 330–32; Navasky, *Kennedy Justice,* 269; Dolan, OH-JFK, 81; Giglio, *Presidency of John F. Kennedy,* 42–44.
56. For RFK's record on judicial appointments, see Navasky, *Kennedy Justice,* 243–76; Schlesinger, *Robert Kennedy,* 330–34. On individual appointments, see RFK, *Robert Kennedy,* 107–19.
57. Dolan, OH-JFK, 101.
58. Schlesinger, *Robert Kennedy,* 332–33, 404–5. When the South is excluded, Schlesinger decided their judicial appointment record "was in the main excellent."
59. RFK, *Robert Kennedy,* 109. 112; Navasky, *Kennedy Justice,* 245, 250, 265–66; Harris Wofford, *Of Kennedys and Kings: Making Sense of the Sixties* (New York: Farrar, Straus and Giroux, 1980), 168; Schlesinger, *Robert Kennedy,* 331.
60. Eastland purportedly offered RFK a deal: "Tell your brother that if he will give me Cox I will give him the nigger" [Marshall]. Quoted in Carter, *Politics of Rage,* 118.
61. Wofford, *Of Kennedys and Kings,* 168.
62. RFK, *Robert Kennedy,* 51, 110–11
63. Marietta Tree, quoted in Reeves, *President Kennedy,* 571.
64. Evans to Belmont, 10 October 1963, Folder 24, O&C.
65. Memorandum for the Attorney General, Re: Martin Luther King, Jr., Security Matter-Communist, 18 October 1963, approved on 21 November 1963, Folder 24, O&C.
66. Garrow, *FBI and Martin Luther King,* 72–73, 86–88; Branch, *Parting the Waters,* 911–14.
67. Ramsey Clark to J. E. Hoover, 27 May 1968; C. C. Moore to Sullivan, 9 June 1969, Folder 24, O&C. Existence of the taps was revealed in the draft-evasion trial of boxer Muhammad Ali in June 1969 when an FBI agent testified to hearing a recorded conversation between Ali and King. Forced to respond, Hoover declared that RFK proposed and approved of the taps over the FBI's objections. Hoover said RFK was "concerned about reports that Dr. King was a student of Marxism and that he was associating with known subversives—men with Communist connections." A few days later, President Richard Nixon announced that his personal check of the files confirmed Hoover's statement. Navasky, *Kennedy Justice,* 135–140.
68. Powers, *Secrecy and Power,* 369. Besides SCLC and King, the FBI also launched COINTELPRO operations against SNCC (Stokely Carmichael and H. Rap Brown), the Revolutionary Action Movement (Maxwell Stanford), and the Nation of Islam (Elijah Muhammad). After discrediting King, the FBI intended to promote a black replacement, New York lawyer Samuel R. Pierce, Jr. See Garrow, *FBI and Martin Luther King,* 106, 182–83.

69. Garrow, *FBI and Martin Luther King,* 55.
70. Sullivan remains an enigma. During the 1970s he tried to ingratiate himself with the liberal professorial community and denied most of his involvement in the King vendetta. Ibid., 85, 88–90, 160–64.
71. William Keller, *The Liberals and J. Edgar Hoover* (Princeton, N.J.: Princeton U. Press, 1989), 105; Powers, *Secrecy and Power,* 377.
72. Garrow, *FBI and Martin Luther King,* 106–10; Powers, *Secrecy and Power,* 419–20.
73. Garrow, *FBI and Martin Luther King,* 77.
74. Ibid., 110.
75. Schlesinger, *Robert Kennedy,* 390–91.
76. Garrow, *FBI and Martin Luther King,* 125–26.
77. Maas, interview by Stein and Plimpton, *American Journey,* 85. Schlesinger, *Robert Kennedy,* 387. Victor S. Navasky, "The Government and Martin Luther King," *The Atlantic,* November 1970, 49.
78. Navasky, "Government and Martin Luther King," 43–52; Navasky, *Kennedy Justice,* 137–39. The reason the Kennedys approved wiretaps on King's telephones, Arthur Schlesinger summarized, was to "protect King, the civil rights bill, and themselves." Schlesinger, *Robert Kennedy,* 387.
79. Navasky, *Kennedy Justice,* 151.
80. Wilkins, interview by Stein and Plimpton, *American Journey,* 85. Navasky, *Kennedy Justice,* 149.
81. Navasky, *Kennedy Justice,* 151–53; Anthony Summers, *Official and Confidential: The Secret Life of J. Edgar Hoover* (New York: Putnam, 1993), 352–53.
82. Burke Marshall, OH-JFK, 40–41, 45.
83. Cited in Wofford, *Of Kennedys and Kings,* 217; Schlesinger, *Robert Kennedy,* 387.
84. Branch, *Parting the Waters,* 911–14. Hoover possibly cooperated in the Rometsch case more to please Lyndon Johnson, his longtime friend and neighbor, than to accommodate the Kennedys. Because of Johnson's involvement, the FBI files on Rometsch have been withheld entirely on personal privacy grounds. See Athan Theoharis and John Stuart Cox, *The Boss: J. Edgar Hoover and the Great American Inquisition* (Philadelphia: Temple U. Press, 1988), 348.
85. See Garrow, *FBI and Martin Luther King,* 91–92; Navasky, *Kennedy Justice,* 147, 151; Schlesinger, *Robert Kennedy,* 360.
86. Garrow, *FBI and Martin Luther King,* 73–75; RFK, *Robert Kennedy,* 145–47.
87. See Powers, *Secrecy and Power,* 417–19; Garrow, *FBI and Martin Luther King,* 101–50.
88. Garrow, *FBI and Martin Luther King,* 85, 88–90.
89. Burke Marshall, OH-JFK, 40–41, 45.
90. Garrow, *FBI and Martin Luther King,* 195.
91. Ibid., 94; Giglio, *Presidency of John F. Kennedy,* 184–85; Navasky, *Kennedy Justice* 147.
92. Schlesinger, *Robert Kennedy,* 382.
93. RFK, *Robert Kennedy,* 171.

94. Marietta Tree, quoted in Reeves, *President Kennedy,* 571. RFK, *Robert Kennedy,* 143, 146.
95. Cf. Navasky, *Kennedy Justice,* 155; Schlesinger, *Robert Kennedy,* 379.
96. RFK, *Robert Kennedy,* 139; Garrow, *FBI and Martin Luther King,* 96.
97. Navasky, *Kennedy Justice,* 154–55. Schlesinger, *Robert Kennedy,* 388.
98. Jack O'Dell, "The FBI's Southern Strategies," in *It Did Happen Here,* ed. Bud Schultz and Ruth Schultz (Berkeley and Los Angeles: U. of California Press, 1989), 285; Garrow, *FBI and Martin Luther King,* 46.
99. O'Dell, "The FBI's Southern Strategies," 287–88.
100. Ibid., 283. Wofford, *Of Kennedys and Kings,* 169.
101. Marian Wright Edelman and Vincent Harding, interviews by Stein and Plimpton, *American Journey,* 110–11 113.
102. Wofford OH-JFK, 68.
103. Ross, *Robert F. Kennedy,* 58.
104. Wofford OH-JFK, 57; John Maguire and Andrew Young, interviews by Stein and Plimpton, *American Journey,* 109–10, 125.
105. David Burner, *John F. Kennedy and a New Generation* (Boston: Little, Brown, 1988), 135.
106. Wofford, *Of Kennedys and Kings,* 175–76; Miroff, *Pragmatic Illusions,* 266–67.
107. Burner, *John F. Kennedy,* 124, 133. Wofford, OH-JFK, 63–64.
108. Harding interview, 110–11, 113.
109. For important turning points for RFK on civil rights, see Wofford, OH-JFK, 63–64; Burke Marshall, OH-JFK, 46; Maas interview, 103.
110. Bernard A. Weisberger, "D.C. Law," *American Heritage* May/June 1993, 20, 24.
111. Harrison E. Salisbury, *Heroes of My Time* (New York: Walker, 1993), 18.

CHAPTER 14

1. Quoted in David Burner, *John F. Kennedy and a New Generation* (Boston: Little, Brown, 1988), 122. James N. Giglio suggests a comparison with the access enjoyed by Roger Taney during Andrew Jackson's administration, *The Presidency of John F. Kennedy* (Lawrence: U. of Kansas Press, 1993) 35. Access, of course, differs from the exercise of executive authority.
2. *Atlanta Journal,* 2 June 1963, Box 7, AG-PC.
3. See Stephen E. Ambrose and Richard H. Immerman, *Milton S. Eisenhower: Educational Statesman* (Baltimore: Johns Hopkins U. Press, 1983), 146–60; and Milton S. Eisenhower, *The President Is Calling* (Garden City, N.Y.: Anchor, 1974).
4. Hopkins and RFK both held cabinet posts, acted as personal envoys, and served the president around the clock. Hopkins even lived in the White House for a few months. See Robert Sherwood, *Roosevelt and Hopkins* (New York: Harper, 1948); James M. Burns, *Roosevelt: Soldier of Freedom* (New York: Harcourt Brace Jovanovich, 1970), 24, 59–61, 178; Arthur Schlesinger, Jr., *The Age of Roosevelt: The Politics of Upheaval* (Boston: Houghton Mifflin, 1966), 386. Schlesinger found

that parts of the JFK-RFK relationship resembled the relationships FDR had with his wife, Eleanor, and with Hopkins. Arthur M. Schlesinger, Jr., *Robert Kennedy and His Times* (Boston: Houghton Mifflin, 1978) 646.

5. Richard Reeves, *President Kennedy: Profile of Power* (New York: Simon and Schuster, 1993), 19, 52; Giglio, *Presidency of John F. Kennedy,* 27–28. The account that follows draws often from the balanced assessments of the Kennedy presidency contained in the Reeves and Giglio books.
6. In July 1962, for example, he injected himself into the reorganization of the Office of Education within the Department of Health, Education, and Welfare, expressing concern over a consultant's report of "serious deficiencies" within the office. William G. Lambert to RFK, 6 July 1962, Box 5, AG-PC.
7. See, for example, William V. Shannon, *The Heir Apparent: Robert Kennedy and the Struggle for Power* (New York: Macmillan, 1967), 48–49; U. Alexis Johnson, interview by Lester David and Irene David, *Bobby Kennedy: The Making of a Folk Hero* (New York: PaperJacks, 1988), 148–49.
8. Quoted in Herbert S. Parmet, *JFK: The Presidency of John F. Kennedy* (New York: Dial, 1983), 214. Shannon, *Heir Apparent,* 50.
9. David and David, *Bobby Kennedy,* 147. Quoted in Reeves, *President Kennedy,* 104. Bundy, interview by Jean Stein and George Plimpton, eds., *American Journey: The Times of Robert Kennedy* (New York: Harcourt Brace Jovanovich, 1970), 87.
10. David and David, *Bobby Kennedy,* 146–47.
11. Kenneth P. O'Donnell and David F. Powers with Joe McCarthy, *"Johnny, We Hardly Knew Ye"* (Boston: Little, Brown, 1972), 277.
12. McNamara, interview by Stein and Plimpton, *American Journey,* 129.
13. Arthur Edson, "Bobby—Washington's No. 2 Man," AP feature, 14 April 1963. O'Donnell and Powers, *"Johnny, We Hardly Knew Ye,"* 321; David and David, *Bobby Kennedy,* 144–45; Theodore C. Sorensen, *Kennedy* (New York: Harper and Row, 1965), 302.
14. Quoted in Penn Kimball, *Bobby Kennedy and the New Politics* (Englewood Cliffs, N.J.: Prentice-Hall, 1968), 4.
15. Quoted in Michael R. Beschloss, *The Crisis Years: Kennedy and Khrushchev, 1960–1965* (New York: Burlingame, 1991), 296; Giglio, *Presidency of John F. Kennedy,* 40–41.
16. O'Donnell and Powers, *"Johnny, We Hardly Knew Ye,"* 6–7, 292.
17. Joseph A. Califano, Jr., *Triumph and Tragedy of Lyndon B. Johnson* (New York: Simon and Schuster, 1991), 64, 79.
18. Robert F. Kennedy, *Robert Kennedy in His Own Words: The Unpublished Recollections of the Kennedy Years,* ed. Edwin O. Guthman and Jeffrey Shulman (New York: Bantam, 1988), 336.
19. Reeves, *President Kennedy,* 104. For an overview of RFK's role in foreign policy, see Beschloss, *The Crisis Years,* 296–306.
20. McNamara would have declined and recommended McGeorge Bundy for sec-

retary of state. Robert S. McNamara with Brian VanDeMark, *In Retrospect: The Tragedy and Lessons of Vietnam* (New York: Random House, 1995), 94–95.

21. O'Donnell and Powers, *"Johnny, We Hardly Knew Ye,"* 324–27, recalled that JFK once said, "I'd be foolish to get rid of Rusk." But there were also discussions about moving Rusk to the UN in a second term. See Deborah Shapley, *Promise and Power: The Life and Times of Robert McNamara* (Boston: Little, Brown, 1993), 270.
22. Burke Marshall, OH-JFK, 13; RFK, *Robert Kennedy,* 9–11, 37, 44–45, 287–89; Beschloss, *The Crisis Years,* 642–43; Schlesinger, *Robert Kennedy,* 466–76; Califano, *Triumph and Tragedy,* 38.
23. Dean Rusk, *As I Saw It,* as told to Richard Rusk, ed. Daniel S. Papp (New York: Norton, 1990), 296, 336.
24. See Richard J. Barnet, *The Roots of War* (Baltimore: Penguin, 1973), 57–58; Walter Isaacson and Evan Thomas, *The Wise Men: Six Friends and the World They Made—Acheson, Bohlen, Harriman, Kennan, Lovett, McCloy* (New York: Simon and Schuster, 1986).
25. Reeves, *President Kennedy,* 223.
26. On Kennedy foreign policies, see Thomas G. Paterson, ed., *Kennedy's Quest for Victory: American Foreign Policy, 1961–1963* (New York: Oxford U. Press, 1989), especially the introduction, 3–23.
27. JFK was referring to the Soviet embarrassment over the use of massive force to suppress uprisings in Hungary in 1956. Richard Goodwin, *Remembering America: A Voice from the Sixties* (Boston: Little, Brown, 1988), 174, recalled JFK saying that, like Hungary, Cuba could be "a fucking slaughter." Also see Beschloss, *The Crisis Years,* 114; Peter Syden, *Bay of Pigs* (New York: Simon and Schuster, 1979), 25. For background and chronologies on U.S. and Cuban relations, see James G. Blight, Bruce J. Allyn, and David A. Welch, eds., *Cuba on the Brink: Castro, the Missile Crisis, and The Soviet Collapse* (New York: Pantheon, 1993), 3–14, 459–73; Laurence Chang and Peter Kornbluh, eds., *The Cuban Missile Crisis, 1962* (New York: New Press, 1992), 1–7, 347–99.
28. RFK, *Robert Kennedy,* 240.
29. Giglio, *Presidency of John F. Kennedy,* 52–53; Thomas G. Paterson, "Fixation with Cuba," in Paterson, *Kennedy's Quest for Victory,* 123–36.
30. RFK, *Robert Kennedy,* 242; Schlesinger, *A Thousand Days,* 240.
31. RFK, *Robert Kennedy,* 242–45; David and David, *Bobby Kennedy,* 157; Peter Collier and David Horowitz, *The Kennedys: An American Drama* (New York: Warner, 1984), 338–49; Reeves, *President Kennedy,* 92.
32. W. W. Rostow, *The Diffusion of Power* (New York: Macmillan, 1972), 210–11; Collier and Horowitz, *The Kennedys,* 339; Reeves, *President Kennedy,* 95.
33. RFK, *Robert Kennedy,* 245.
34. Thomas Powers, *The Man Who Kept the Secrets: Richard Helms and the CIA* (New York: Knopf, 1979), 117, concludes, "The plan was either dishonest and cynical, depending on forcing Kennedy's hand, or plain dumb."

35. Quote from LeMoyne Billings's diary and interviews by Collier and Horowitz, *The Kennedys,* 340–41; also see Beschloss, *The Crisis Years,* 296, 297–307.
36. RFK, *Robert Kennedy,* 253–54.
37. Ibid., 11.
38. Goodwin, *Remembering America,* 187.
39. Benjamin C. Bradlee, *Conversations With Kennedy* (New York: Norton, 1975), 198; Chester Bowles, interview in Jean Stein and George Plimpton, eds., *American Journey: The Times of Robert Kennedy* (New York: Harcourt Brace Jovanovich, 1970), 130; Harris Wofford, *Of Kennedys and Kings: Making Sense of the Sixties* (New York: Farrar, Straus and Giroux, 1980), 369–75; Schlesinger, *Robert Kennedy,* 507–8; RFK, *Robert Kennedy,* 264; David Halberstam, *The Best and the Brightest* (New York: Random House, 1972), 68–69; Reeves, *President Kennedy,* 104–5; Goodwin, *Remembering America,* 186–87.
40. Memorandum of Kennedy-Khrushchev conversation, 3 June 1961, at Vienna Summit, Chang and Kornbluh, *The Cuban Missile Crisis,* 9–14. John A. McCone to RFK, 25 April 1962, and RFK to McCone, 2 May 1962, Box 5, AG-PC. Giglio, *Presidency of John F. Kennedy,* 49–50, wrote that "whether Kennedy knew of the plan at this time [summer of 1960] remains a question."
41. RFK, *Robert Kennedy,* 246.
42. Ibid., 247; Schlesinger, *A Thousand Days,* 294–96; Giglio, *Presidency of John F. Kennedy,* 62–63; besides RFK and Sorensen, Roger Hilsman (director of the Bureau of Intelligence and Research in the State Department) and Robert Amory (director of research at CIA)—both excluded in the Bay of Pigs planning—were listened to more closely afterwards. See Hilsman, interview by Stein and Plimpton, *American Journey,* 131. On JFK's management, see Paterson, "Introduction: Kennedy and Global Crisis," in Paterson, *Kennedy's Quest for Victory,* 16–20; Reeves, *President Kennedy,* 113–15.
43. RFK, *Robert Kennedy,* 247–48; Shapley, *Promise and Power,* 115–16; Schlesinger, *A Thousand Days,* 339; Giglio, *Presidency of John F. Kennedy,* 63–67; Lawrence J. Bassett and Stephen E. Pelz, "The Failed Search for Victory," in Paterson, *Kennedy's Quest for Victory,* 228–31.
44. RFK, *Robert Kennedy,* 289; Schlesinger, *Robert Kennedy,* 757.
45. Goodwin, *Remembering America,* 186.
46. Schlesinger, *Robert Kennedy,* 480–83; Giglio, *Presidency of John F. Kennedy,* 61–62.
47. Schlesinger, *A Thousand Days,* 310; Beschloss, *The Crisis Years,* 146–47.
48. McGeorge Bundy, *Danger and Survival* (New York: Random House, 1988), 377.
49. JFK also was greatly impressed by General John B. Medaris, whose book *Countdown for Decision* (with Arthur Gordon) (New York: Putnam, 1960) stressed similar strategic issues. Allen Dulles said JFK took a "very great interest" in the book, discussing it at length during a pre-election meeting. Memorandum for the Record, 21 September 1960, Allen W. Dulles Papers, Mudd Library, Princeton University. Medaris, however, was never brought into the administration.
50. RFK, *Robert Kennedy,* 11–12, 254–55.

51. RFK to Kenneth O'Donnell, 19 April 1961, Box 1, AG-PC.
52. Chang and Kornbluh, *The Cuban Missile Crisis,* 4, 16–19.
53. Schlesinger, *Robert Kennedy,* 508–9.
54. U. Alexis Johnson to RFK, 24 May 1962, Box 5, AG-PC; RFK, *Robert Kennedy,* 310.
55. Raymond L. Garthoff, former State Department special assistant for Soviet Bloc political/military affairs during the Kennedy administration, made the statement. See, Blight, Allyn, and Welch, *Cuba on the Brink,* 283.
56. U.S. Senate, Select Committee on Intelligence Activities [Church comittee], *Interim Report: Alleged Assassination Plots Involving Foreign Leaders* (Washington, D.C.: U.S. Government Printing Office, 1975), 75, 170–76,
57. Ibid., 132–33, 141, 276. Goodwin, *Remembering America,* 189.
58. Quoted in Parmet, *JFK,* 299.
59. Powers, *Man Who Kept the Secrets,* 142–43, 148–49; Chang and Kornbluh, *The Cuban Missile Crisis,* xxvi, 395; *Alleged Assassination Plots,* 133.
60. Powers, *Man Who Kept the Secrets,* 148–49; G. Robert Blakley and Richard N. Billings, *Fatal Hour: The Assassination of President Kennedy by Organized Crime* (New York: Berkely, 1992, originally published as *The Plot to Kill the President,* 1981), 67.
61. Declassified NSC documents are contained in Chang and Kornbluh, *The Cuban Missile Crisis.*
62. On the Kennedys' views on counterinsurgency, see Schlesinger, *Robert Kennedy,* 494–503.
63. Neil Sheehan, *A Bright Shining Lie* (New York: Random House, 1988), 292–98; Allan R. Millett, *Semper Fidelis: A History of the United States Marine Corps* (New York: Macmillan, 1980), 548; Halberstam, *The Best and The Brightest,* 275–76.
64. Minutes of first Operation Mongoose meeting, 1 December 1961, and SGA guidelines for MONGOOSE, 14 March 1962, in Chang and Kornbluh, *The Cuban Missile Crisis,* 20–22, 38–39.
65. On RFK's success in getting Lansdale to work on Cuba rather than return to Vietnam, and on other details of JFK's views of MONGOOSE, see Reeves, *President Kennedy,* 263–67, 703–4; RFK, *Robert Kennedy,* 378.
66. Minutes, Operation MONGOOSE meeting, 1 December 1961, Chang and Kornbluh, *The Cuban Missile Crisis,* 20–22, 38–39.
67. Powers, *Man Who Kept the Secrets,* 136–37; *Alleged Assassination Plots,* 139–68.
68. Wofford, *Of Kennedys and Kings,* 386.
69. Tom Mangold, *Cold Warrior: James Jesus Angleton* (New York: Simon and Schuster, 1991), 77, 87–88, 127.
70. Schlesinger, *Robert Kennedy,* 510; Powers, *Man Who Kept the Secrets,* 132.
71. Powers, *Man Who Kept the Secrets,* 134–35; Wofford, *Of Kennedys and Kings,* 386; *Alleged Assassination Plots,* 150–55.
72. Powers, *Man Who Kept the Secrets,* 138; *Alleged Assassination Plots,* 150–51.

73. Lansdale's report, 20 February 1962, Chang and Kornbluh, *The Cuban Missile Crisis,* 23–37
74. *Alleged Assassination Plots,* 138–39; Goodwin, *Remembering America,* 141. The CIA has declassified a large number of documents on Cuba, including memos on Operation MONGOOSE. None reveal any authorizations by the Kennedys to assassinate Castro. Mary S. McAuliffe, ed., *CIA Documents on the Cuban Missile Crisis, 1962* (Washington, D.C.: History Staff Central Intelligence Agency, 1992).
75. A former CIA agent, Samuel Halpern, once assistant to William Harvey (Chief, TFW), has said that RFK personally directed the CIA "to meet with the Mafia people" to request assistance for an attempt on Castro's life. Halpern's uncorroborated story contradicts the CIA inspector general's report of 1967 and the Church committee report. See Max Holland, "The Key to the Warren Report," *American Heritage,* November 1995, 60, 62. Judith Campbell Exner told interviewers in 1996 that she carried details of a planned assassination of Castro to Chicago gangster Sam Giancana and that RFK once asked her, "Judy, are you OK carrying these messages for us to Chicago?" *New York Post,* 11 December 1996.
76. *Alleged Assassination Plots,* 155, 167; Blakey and Billings, *Fatal Hour,* 62. Lansdale emphatically denied that he had been "under orders" from RFK to plan the assassination of Fidel Castro. "Perhaps some place in the plans there was something to do" with Castro, but assassination, he insisted, was "not my bag." Norman Kempster, "Officer Says RFK Gave No Order to Kill," *Washington Star-News,* 5 July 1975.
77. *Alleged Assassination Plots,* 161–67; Powers, *Man Who Kept the Secrets,* 7, 129; Reeves, *President Kennedy,* 335–37. Goodwin recalled the meeting occurring in May 1961. He said Lansdale asked McNamara, "You mean Executive Action?" To which McNamara nodded and turned to Goodwin and said, "I mean it, Dick, it's the only way." *Remembering America,* 189.
78. Schlesinger, *Robert Kennedy,* 486–89, 517–37; Beschloss, *The Crisis Years,* 138; Wofford, *Of Kennedys and Kings,* 389–406. For a discussion of the intriguing problem of differing perceptions of what was said during formal transition briefings, even when there is a documented record, see Fred I. Greenstein and Richard H. Immerman, "What Did Eisenhower Tell Kennedy about Indochina? The Politics of Misperception," *Journal of American History,* September 1992, 568–87.
79. Powers, *Man Who Kept the Secrets,* 129, 131, 133, 138, 144–45, 155. Cf. Schlesinger, *Robert Kennedy,* 522–37. Also see Samuel Halpern, "Revisiting the Cuban Missile Crisis," *SHAFR Newsletter,* December 1993, 17–25, who wrote, "the pressure [from the Kennedys] was continuously there" to intensify sabotage operations against Cuba.
80. RFK, *Robert Kennedy,* 379.
81. *Alleged Assassination Plots,* 275.
82. Blight, Allyn, and Welch, *Cuba on the Brink,* n424.
83. Powers, *Man Who Kept the Secrets,* 138–39.
84. RFK, *Robert Kennedy,* 378–79.
85. Chang and Kornbluh, *Cuban Missile Crisis,* 48–49.

86. NSAM 181, 23 August 1962, ibid., 61–62.
87. RFK, *Robert Kennedy,* 376.
88. Lansdale "Action Proposals," 11 October 1962 (in response to directives of SGA from meeting of 2 October), Chang and Kornbluh, *Cuban Missile Crisis,* 52–53; Powers, *Man Who Kept the Secrets,* 141, McCone, "Memorandum of MONGOOSE Meeting Held on Thursday, October 4, 1962"; Richard Helms, Memorandum for the Record, "MONGOOSE Meeting with the Attorney General," 16 October 1962, in McAuliffe, *CIA Documents,* 111–13, 153–54.
89. MSC [Marshall S. Carter], Memorandum for the Director, 25 October 1962, in McAuliffe, *CIA Documents,* 311–12.
90. RFK, *Robert Kennedy,* 378. McCone, "Memorandum of MONGOOSE Meeting in the JCS Operations Room, October 26, 1962, at 2:30 P.M.," 29 October 1962, McAuliffe, *CIA Documents,* 319–21, portions of which remain classified. Contrary to the preliminary findings of the Church committee, in *Alleged Assassination Plots,* 147–48, it now seems clear that Harvey did not act on his own authority in assembling the Cuban sabotage teams. See Halpern, "Revisiting the Cuban Missile Crisis," 23.
91. Chang and Kornbluh, *Cuban Missile Crisis,* 383, 387; Raymond L. Garthoff, *Reflections on the Cuban Missile Crisis* (Washington, D.C.: Brookings Institute, 1989), 122.
92. Powers, *Man Who Kept the Secrets,* 142; Lansdale, "Review of Operation MONGOOSE," 25 July 1962, Chang and Kornbluh, *Cuban Missile Crisis,* 40–47.
93. Beschloss, *The Crisis Years,* 377; Blight, Allyn, and Welch, *Cuba on the Brink,* 16–19.
94. Halberstam, *The Best and the Brightest,* 88–89.
95. For Schlesinger's 1992 quote, Blight, Allyn, and Welch, *Cuba on the Brink,* 158–59; also see Schlesinger, *Robert Kennedy,* 575.
96. Reeves, *President Kennedy,* 150–52.
97. RFK, *Robert Kennedy,* 325. RFK in these remarks seems to collapse events that occurred in two time periods (late May and November 1961) into the single May time frame.
98. Ibid., 265; Halberstam, *The Best and the Brightest,* 69–70; Reeves, *President Kennedy,* 151–52; Rusk, *As I Saw It,* 336. On RFK's role in Bowles's firing and their disagreements, see Wofford, *Of Kennedys and Kings,* 366–75. With U.S. support, the vice-president, Dr. Joaquin Balaguer, took over after Trujillo's death, but the administration had to use a show of force to drive out the Trujillo relatives in November 1961. Juan Bosch was elected president of the Dominican Republic in 1962.
99. Goodwin, *Remembering America,* 210. Reeves, *President Kennedy,* 141–42. Cf. Schlesinger, *Robert Kennedy,* 527–30, who accepts JFK's cable to the CIA at face value and insists neither Eisenhower nor the Kennedys ordered Trujillo's assassination. RFK, *Robert Kennedy,* 326–27. LBJ believed otherwise and once suggested to Pierre Salinger that JFK's assassination was perhaps "divine retribution" for Trujillo's (and Diem's in South Vietnam). See Paul R. Henggeler, *In*

His Steps: Lyndon Johnson and the Kennedy Mystique (Chicago: Dee, 1991), 76. The Church committee concluded in their 1975 report, *Alleged Assassination Plots,* 191–214, that the CIA was not directly responsible for the murder of Trujillo. Also see Powers, *Man Who Kept the Secrets,* 336–37*n.*

100. RFK, *Robert Kennedy,* 320–23.
101. Ibid., 324, 325.
102. For JFK's comment to James Reston and other JFK reactions to Vienna, see Reeves, *President Kennedy,* 172–76. On the Berlin crisis, see Frank Costigliola, "The Pursuit of Atlantic Community," in Paterson, *Kennedy's Quest for Victory,* 24–56.
103. David A. Rosenberg, "Berlin as a Nuclear Crisis: The Bomb, the Policy Process, and the Causes of World War III, 1958-1962," Nuclear History Program, Center for International Security Studies, Maryland (May 1993), makes clear that the Americans were prepared for general nuclear war over Berlin.
104. On the RFK-Bolshakov relationship, see Beschloss, *The Crisis Years,* 152–57; Reeves, *President Kennedy,* 137–38; Schlesinger, *Robert Kennedy,* 537–40.
105. Quoted in Rosenberg, "Berlin as a Nuclear Crisis."
106. Reeves, *President Kennedy,* 137–38. On the Berlin crisis, see Giglio, *Presidency of John F. Kennedy,* 69–72, 80–86; Beschloss, *The Crisis Years,* 231–48, 255–90.
107. RFK, *Robert Kennedy,* 276; Beschloss, *The Crisis Years,* 296.
108. RFK, *Robert Kennedy,* 278.
109. Parmet, *JFK,* 197.
110. Adam Yarmolinsky, OH-JFK, 43–46; Schlesinger, *Robert Kennedy,* 461; Parmet, *JFK,* 197–98.
111. Reeves, *President Kennedy,* 195.
112. Collier and Horowitz, *The Kennedys,* 349.
113. RFK, *Robert Kennedy,* 284.
114. Reeves, *President Kennedy,* 250–51; RFK, *Robert Kennedy,* 258–62; Nikita S. Khrushchev, *Khrushchev Remembers: The Last Testament* (Boston: Little, Brown, 1974), 460. James Reston, *Deadline* (New York: Random House, 1991), 293.
115. President Houphouet-Boigny to RFK, 10 July 1962, Box 5, AG-PC; RFK, *Robert Kennedy,* 274–75, 367.
116. Thomas J. Noer, "New Frontiers and Old Priorities in Africa," in Paterson, *Kennedy's Quest for Victory,* 257; Burner, *John F. Kennedy,* 83, 85.
117. Schlesinger, *Robert Kennedy,* 604–5.
118. RFK, *Robert Kennedy,* 312–13. On RFK's contacts in Japan, see Gunji Hosono [a Japanese industrialist who kept RFK informed of developments in the country] Folder, Box 5, AG-PC.
119. Ralph McGill, "An Effective Debater," *Atlanta Constitution,* 25 February 1962; editorial, "The Attorney General's Voyage," *Philadelphia Inquirer,* 8 February 1962.
120. RFK, *Robert Kennedy,* 319–20; Roger Hilsman, *To Move a Nation: The Politics of Foreign Policy in the Administration of John F. Kennedy* (Garden City, N.Y.: Doubleday, 1967), 380; Parmet, *JFK,* 224–25; Giglio, *Presidency of John F. Kennedy,* 239.

121. Barry Battle to RFK, 3 June 1963, RFK to Barry Battle, 11 June 1963, Box 9, AG-PC. JFK quoted in Hilsman, *To Move a Nation,* 380.
122. RFK, *Robert Kennedy,* 315.
123. Ibid., 317–18; Hilsman, *To Move a Nation,* 380; David and David, *Bobby Kennedy,* 143. Sukarno released Pope about nine weeks later.
124. RFK, *Robert Kennedy,* 318–19; "Bobby Come Home," *New York Herald Tribune,* 10 February 1962; Rowland Evans, "Robert Kennedy's Tour Was Rusk's Idea," *New York Herald Tribune,* 23 February 1962; David Lawrence, "Touring Kennedys Pose Sticky Question," *Philadelphia Inquirer,* 26 February 1962; Schlesinger, *Robert Kennedy,* 607–21; David and David, *Bobby Kennedy,* 149–50.
125. RFK donated royalties from *Just Friends and Brave Enemies* to fund scholarships for indigenous students in Berlin, Tokyo, and Indonesia. Box 10, AG-PC. J. Edgar Hoover had his agents read the book and prepare a synopsis for his review. Memorandum, 24 October 1962, to Hoover, Section 1, RFK-FBI.
126. Parmet, *Jack,* 266–68.
127. Charles Poore, "Books of the Times," *New York Times,* 28 August 1962.

CHAPTER 15

1. Robert F. Kennedy, *Robert F. Kennedy in His Own Words: The Unpublished Recollections of the Kennedy Years,* ed. Edwin O. Guthman and Jeffrey Shulman (New York: Bantam: 1988), 258–62. Bolshakov spoke to others in the administration, including Pierre Salinger, Theodore Sorensen, and JFK himself.
2. Newspaper columnists Joseph and Stewart Alsop probably first persuaded JFK that a gap existed. See Robert W. Merry, *Taking on the World: Joseph and Stewart Alsop—Guardians of the American Century* (New York: Viking, 1996), 342; Edwin M. Yoder, Jr., *Joe Alsop's Cold War* (Chapel Hill: U. of North Carolina Press, 1995), 164; JFK letter to Joseph Alsop, 23 August 1958, Alsop Papers, Library of Congress, cited in Christopher Preble, "John Kennedy and the 'Missile Gap,'" unpublished paper, 14. Adam Yarmolinsky, charged by McNamara with documenting the gap, found that it disappeared when sea-based Polaris missiles were counted. Yarmolinsky, OH-JFK, 52. "By the time of the Cuban missile crisis," Robert McNamara said at the 1987 U.S.–Soviet Hawk's Cay Conference, "we had clear numerical superiority and we were *still* building up." James G. Blight and David A. Welch, *On the Brink: Americans and Soviets Reexamine the Cuban Missile Crisis* (New York: Hill and Wang, 1989), 29.
3. David Rosenberg, "The History of World War Three, A Conceptual Framework," *On Cultural Ground: Essays in International History,* ed. Robert David Johnson (Chicago: Imprint, 1994), 197–235, quotation on 205. Richard Reeves, *President Kennedy: Profile of Power* (New York: Simon and Schuster, 1993), 229. Air Force Chief of Staff General Curtis LeMay, among others, advocated a first strike. See Robert McNamara comment of Blight and Welch, *On the Brink,* 29. Adam Yarmolinsky, however, said, "If the suggestion was ever made that we

adopt a clear no-first-use policy within the administration, I never ran into it." Yarmolinsky, JFK-OH, 48–50.

4. See Adam Yarmolinsky, JFK-OH, 69; Robert McNamara, *In Retrospect: The Tragedy and Causes of the Vietnam War* (New York: Time Books/Random House, 1995), 338–42; William Chafe, *The Unfinished Journey* (New York: Oxford U. Press, 1991), 204.
5. For elaboration on this argument, see Thomas G. Paterson, "Fixation with Cuba: The Bay of Pigs, Missile Crisis, and Covert War against Castro," in *Kennedy's Quest for Victory, American Foreign Policy, 1961–1963,* ed. Thomas G. Paterson (New York: Oxford U. Press, 1989), 123–55.
6. James G. Blight, Bruce J. Allyn, and David A. Welch, eds., *Cuba on the Brink: Castro, the Missile Crisis, and the Soviet Collapse* (New York: Pantheon, 1993), 15–20.
7. McNamara statement at Havana Conference, ibid., 289.
8. JFK quote in Reeves, *President Kennedy,* 345. On the sequence of events leading to the CIA's discovery of the missiles in Cuba, see Dino Brugioni, *Eyeball to Eyeball: The Inside Story of the Cuban Missile Crisis* (New York: Random House, 1991); Mary S. McAuliffe, "Return to the Brink: Intelligence Perspectives on the Cuban Missile Crisis," *SHAFR Newsletter* June 1993, 4–18; Samuel Halpern, "Revisiting the Cuban Missile Crisis," *SHAFR Newsletter,* December 1993, 17–25.
9. Quoted in Reeves, *President Kennedy,* 347.
10. Robert F. Kennedy, *Thirteen Days* (New York: New American Library, 1969), 23; Reeves, *President Kennedy,* 368.
11. Cline, Memo for the Record, 27 October 1962, Laurence Chang and Peter Kornbluh, eds., *The Cuban Missile Crisis, 1962* (New York: New Press, 1992), 151; Cline interview, NBC-News, "RFK." The word was "shit."
12. RFK, *Thirteen Days,* 31. ExComm, formally established on 22 October, included: Rusk, State; McNamara, Defense; Dillon, Treasury; John McCone, CIA; Theodore Sorensen, counsel to the president; George Ball, undersecretary of state; U. Alexis Johnson, deputy undersecretary of state; General Maxwell Taylor, chair, Joint Chiefs of Staff; Edward Martin, assistant secretary of state for Latin America; Charles Bohlen and then Llewellyn Thompson, advisors on Soviet affairs; Roswell Gilpatric, deputy secretary of defense; Paul Nitze, assistant secretary of defense. Joining the discussions from time to time: Vice-President Johnson; Marshall Carter, deputy CIA director filling in for McCone; Dean Acheson, former secretary of state; Adlai Stevenson, UN ambassador; David M. Shoup, Marine Corps commandant; General Curtis LeMay, Air Force Chief of Staff; Kenneth O'Donnell, White House staff; Donald Wilson, USIA director; Robert Lovett, former secretary of defense; John McCloy, former high commissioner of Germany.
13. McGeorge Bundy, interview by Jean Stein and George Plimpton, eds., *American Journey: The Times of Robert Kennedy* (New York: Harcourt Brace Jovanovich, 1970), 132.
14. Pierre Salinger, *With Kennedy* (New York: Doubleday, 1966), 190; Salinger, interview by Lester David and Irene David, *Bobby Kennedy: The Making of a Folk*

Hero (New York: PaperJacks, 1988), 162; George Ball, interview by Stein and Plimpton, *American Journey,* 135.

15. RFK, *Thirteen Days,* 37. Ball interview, 135; Paterson, "Fixation with Cuba," 144.
16. Quoted in Reeves, *President Kennedy,* 378.
17. Chang and Kornbluh, *Cuban Missile Crisis,* 361.
18. Dillon, interview Stein and Plimpton, *American Journey,* 136; RFK, *Thirteen Days,* 38–39; Chang and Kornbluh, *Cuban Missile Crisis,* 361; Blight, Allyn, and Welch, *Cuba on the Brink,* 390; Arthur M. Schlesinger, Jr., *Robert Kennedy and His Times* (Boston: Houghton Mifflin, 1978), 549.
19. RFK, *Thirteen Days,* 67.
20. McNamara, *In Retrospect,* 341; Arthur M. Schlesinger, Jr., "Four Days with Fidel: A Havana Diary," *New York Review of Books,* 16 March 1992, 23.
21. RFK, *Thirteen Days,* 68. See Chang and Kornbluh, *Cuban Missile Crisis,* 80ff., for declassified documents on ExComm meetings.
22. RFK, *Thirteen Days,* 79–81, 86–104. Also, Pierre Salinger, interview by Stein and Plimpton, *American Journey,* 137; Salinger, interview by David and David, *Bobby Kennedy,* 162; "The President, the Press, and the People," PBS panel of former presidential press secretaries, 2 April 1990, KPBS, San Diego. Schlesinger acknowledged the significance of the Scali-Fomin contacts in *A Thousand Days: John F. Kennedy in the White House* (Boston: Houghton Mifflin, 1965), 825–29. He worried later when a Russian acquaintance suggested that it was a "fabrication of Scali's." RFK assured him it was not. Schlesinger to Roger Hilsman, 18 August 1967; Schlesinger to RFK, 21 August 1967; Hilsman to Schlesinger, 9 September 1967, Box 11, RFK SP-PC. Scali's critical role was downplayed at the time, which was difficult to accept for a newsman sitting on the biggest story of his career. See his obituary, *New York Times,* 9 October 1995.
23. At the January 1992 Havana conference, Raymond Garthoff stated that RFK introduced the possibility of withdrawing Jupiter missiles in Italy and Turkey as "early as October 24 or 25" in talks with Dobrynin. Schlesinger pointed out that RFK made no mention of Italy in his memo of the meeting. See Blight, Allyn, and Welch, *Cuba on the Brink,* 283–87. In RFK, *Thirteen Days,* 49–50, RFK says the suggestion to include both Italy and Turkey came from Stevenson and that it received a hostile reaction in ExComm.
24. Chang and Kornbluh, *Cuban Missile Crisis,* 374. RFK makes no mention in *Thirteen Days* of his meeting of 26 October with Dobrynin and no mention of U.S. willingness to concede anything to the Soviets. This is a tendency that appears throughout his oral history interviews, that is, the other side seems always to have caved in to the unilateral demands of the Kennedys; there is little reference to U.S. concessions resolving foreign crises; and there is no room in RFK's accounts for any suggestion that he or his brother were anything less than tough, cool, successful bargainers under pressure. For similar views, see Michael R. Beschloss, *The Crisis Years: Kennedy and Khrushchev, 1960–1965* (New York: Burlingame, 1991), 334–35.
25. RFK, *Thirteen Days,* 102–3. RFK is often credited with the "Trollope ploy," or the

suggestion that ExComm ignore the second Khrushchev message and accept the first proposal instead. NSC minutes make clear, however, that RFK summarized and presented in a convincing and cogent manner what others in the room, including Edwin Martin, Llewellyn Thompson, Theodore Sorensen, McGeorge Bundy, and even Lyndon Johnson, were in one way or another also suggesting, namely that the first letter was the preferred solution and that the "trade" of the Jupiters in Turkey not be mentioned in the communiqué to Khrushchev. Transcript of ExComm Meeting, 27 October 1962, Chang and Kornbluh, *Cuban Missile Crisis,* 200–220.

26. RFK, *Thirteen Days,* 108–9; Chang and Kornbluh, *Cuban Missile Crisis,* 378.
27. Troyanovsky comments, Blight, Allyn, and Welch, *Cuba on the Brink,* 71–75.
28. See Schlesinger, *Robert Kennedy,* 561–62; Nikita S. Khrushchev, *Khrushchev Remembers: The Last Testament* (Boston: Little, Brown, 1974), 497–98; Blight, Allyn, and Welch, *Cuba on the Brink,* 74. The days of unremitting strain may indeed have taken their toll on RFK. Several CIA panelists at an October 1992 crisis conference indicated they were mentally and physically exhausted—"at the end of our rope when it finally resolved," said one—and fearful that "the whole thing would have begun to unravel," if the crisis lasted beyond its thirteen days. McAuliffe, "Return to the Brink," 17–18.
29. RFK, *Thirteen Days,* 107–9.
30. Quoted in Reeves, *President Kennedy,* 425.
31. Chang and Kornbluh, *Cuban Missile Crisis,* 380.
32. Chang and Kornbluh, *Cuban Missile Crisis,* 378, 383, 388, 390; Blight, Allyn, and Welch, *Cuba on the Brink,* 283–87; Schlesinger, *Robert Kennedy,* 562–70.
33. MacMillan quoted in Schlesinger, *Robert Kennedy,* 573. James Reston, *Deadline* (New York: Random House, 1991), 294. Arthur M. Schlesinger, Jr., *A Thousand Days: John F. Kennedy in the White House* (Boston: Houghton Mifflin, 1965), 841. "The Backdown," *Time,* 2 November 1962, 27; "The Lessons Learned," *Newsweek,* 12 November 1962, 125.
34. Mary S. McAuliffe, "Return to the Brink," 18. Also see Blight and Welch, *On the Brink,* 310–11; Paterson, "Fixation on Cuba," 150–51.
35. Khrushchev, *Khrushchev Remembers,* 498. Galbraith quoted in Paterson, "Fixation with Cuba," 148. Acheson called the outcome "plain dumb luck." See Reeves, *President Kennedy,* 425, 722n.
36. Ralph McGill to McGeorge Bundy, 12 November 1962, xc: JFK and RFK; RFK to McGill, 15 November 1962, Box 5, AG-PC.
37. See Blight, Allyn, and Welch, *Cuba on the Brink,* 238–39.
38. Richard Goodwin recalls JFK saying, "They [the Cuban Brigade] trusted me. And they're in prison now because I fucked up. I have to get them out." *Remembering America: A Voice from the Sixties* (Boston: Little, Brown, 1988), 186.
39. McAuliffe, "Return to the Brink," 16–17.
40. Joseph F. Dolan, Assistant Deputy Attorney General, OH-JFK, 1–2. Also see Schlesinger, *Robert Kennedy,* 503–6, 575–79.
41. Dolan, OH-JFK, 12–14.

42. RFK also appealed for donations from drug companies, some of which were subjects of FTC or antitrust investigations. See Schlesinger, *Robert Kennedy,* 577; Victor Navasky, *Kennedy Justice* (New York: Atheneum, 1971), 338, 453–57. Dolan, OH-JFK, 5; E. Barrett Prettyman to Oberdorfer, 8 January 1964, Box 14; Louis Oberdorfer to AG, 10 June 1963, Box 14, AG-GC.
43. Dolan, OH-JFK, 2–3.
44. Navasky, *Kennedy Justice,* 332–47.
45. Dolan, OH-JFK, 6. RFK assigned John Nolan to work with the Labor Department in finding jobs for the surviving members of the Cuban Brigade. Dean Rusk to RFK, 3 June 1963, and Fred P. Graham to John Nolan, 22 April 1964, Box 14, AG-GC. Not all of the prisoners were released in 1962. Castro held back several who were tried for crimes not related to the Bay of Pigs invasion. One died in prison. The last two were released in June and October 1986. Halpern, "Revisiting the Cuban Missile Crisis," 24.
46. Sorensen to RFK, 24 January 1963, Box 10, AG-PC.

CHAPTER 16

1. Quoted in Lawrence J. Bassett and Stephen E. Pelz, "The Failed Search for Victory: Vietnam and the Politics of War," in *Kennedy's Quest for Victory: American Foreign Policy, 1961–1963,* ed. Thomas G. Paterson (New York: Oxford U. Press, 1989), 226.
2. Gary R. Hess, "Commitment in the Age of Counterinsurgency: Kennedy's Vietnam Options and Decisions, 1961–1963," in *Shadow on the White House: Presidents and the Vietnam War, 1945–1975,* ed. David L. Anderson (Lawrence: U. Press of Kansas, 1993), 63–86.
3. On the Kennedy administration's policies in Vietnam, see Herbert S. Parmet, *JFK: The Presidency of John F. Kennedy* (New York: Dial, 1983), 136–42, 153–55, 327–36; Arthur M. Schlesinger, Jr., *Robert Kennedy and His Times* (Boston: Houghton Mifflin, 1978), 760–84; James N. Giglio, *The Presidency of John F. Kennedy* (Lawrence: U. of Kansas Press, 1993), 239–54; Bassett and Pelz, "Vietnam," 223–52; Michael R. Beschloss, *The Crisis Years: Kennedy and Khrushchev, 1960–1965* (New York: Burlingame, 1991), 337–40; Neil Sheehan, *A Bright Shining Lie* (New York: Random House, 1988), 96–379; David W. Levy, *The Debate over Vietnam* (Baltimore: Johns Hopkins U. Press, 1991); John M. Newman, *JFK and Vietnam* (New York: Warner, 1992).
4. Richard Reeves, *President Kennedy: Profile of Power* (New York: Simon and Schuster, 1993), 45–51.
5. Stanley Karnow, *Vietnam: A History* (New York: Penguin, 1984), 248; David Halberstam, *The Best and the Brightest* (New York: Random House, 1972), 77.
6. Said Reston: "I offered to show him my detailed notes of the Vienna interview, but he said he wasn't interested and I never saw him after that." James Reston, *Deadline* (New York: Random House, 1991), 291–92, 297. For a summary of

the Vienna discussions, JFK's comments to others, and the reactions of observers, see Reeves, *President Kennedy,* 157–74.

7. Giglio, *Presidency of John F. Kennedy,* 240–41; Halberstam, *The Best and the Brightest,* 92.
8. Bassett and Pelz, "Vietnam," 223, 237; Schlesinger, *Robert Kennedy,* 759–61.
9. David L. Di Leo, *George Ball, Vietnam, and the Rethinking of Containment* (Chapel Hill: U. of North Carolina Press, 1991), 56.
10. Halberstam, *The Best and the Brightest,* 153; Karnow, *Vietnam,* 254–55. For a contemporary critique of "pragmatic liberalism" and its effects on Vietnam policy, see Noam Chomsky, *American Power and the New Mandarins* (New York: Pantheon, 1967), 6–7, 30–61, 295–307.
11. Karnow, *Vietnam,* 252–55; Hess, "Commitment," 72.
12. Theodore Sorensen, *Kennedy* (New York: Harper and Row, 1965), 632–33.
13. William V. Shannon, *The Heir Apparent: Robert Kennedy and the Struggle for Power* (New York: Macmillan, 1963), 111–13; Schlesinger, *Robert Kennedy,* 861.
14. Schlesinger, *Robert Kennedy,* 769.
15. Shannon, *Heir Apparent,* 113.
16. Karnow, *Vietnam,* 254; Sheehan, *A Bright Shining Lie,* 289–90, 618.
17. John Galloway, ed., *The Kennedys and Vietnam* (New York: Facts on File, 1971), 11; Peter Collier and David Horowitz, *The Kennedys: An American Drama* (New York: Warner, 1984), 200.
18. Quoted in Hess, "Commitment," 75.
19. On the inadequacies of the conceptual framework of counterinsurgency, see Chomsky, *American Power,* 59–61.
20. Karnow, *Vietnam,* 259–62; Sheehan, *A Bright Shining Lie,* 203–83; Burner, *John F. Kennedy and a New Generation* (Boston: Little, Brown, 1988), 102–6; Reeves, *President Kennedy,* 445–47.
21. On use of AID funds to train police, see Reeves, *President Kennedy,* 703–4n. On strategic hamlets, see Karnow, *Vietnam,* 256–57; Parmet, *JFK,* 326–27; Schlesinger, *Robert Kennedy,* 762–63; Bassett and Pelz, "Vietnam," 238–41; Sheehan, *A Bright Shining Lie,* 289, 338, 539–40. Estimates are that by the spring of 1963 only 1,500 of 8,500 strategic hamlets remained viable.
22. John E. Nolan to RFK, 22 May 1963, Box 35, AG-GC. Despite RFK's recommendation, Krulak was not selected commandant. Among other reasons, he was the only ranking marine to favor counterinsurgency operations. See Allan R. Millett, *Semper Fidelis: The History of the United States Marine Corps* (New York: Macmillan, 1980), 548, 582–83.
23. Sheehan, *A Bright Shining Lie,* 336–42.
24. Krulak, according to Sheehan, likely tempered his reports to avoid angering Maxwell Taylor and thus harming his chances to be Marine Corps commandant. *A Bright Shining Lie,* 298–305, 337, 341, 365.
25. Marguerite ("Maggie") Higgins to RFK, 20 September 1963, Box 7, AG-PC. Also see Jack Newfield, *Robert Kennedy: A Memoir* (New York: New American

Library, 1969), 112–13, who argues that generational differences between reporters led the younger ones (e.g., Halberstam, Sheehan) to be more critical of the Diem regime, but that the Kennedys quietly cultivated reporters in both camps.

26. Galloway, *The Kennedys and Vietnam,* 11.
27. Karnow, *Vietnam,* 296–97; Sheehan, *A Bright Shining Lie,* 366; Reeves, *President Kennedy,* 587.
28. Karnow, *Vietnam,* 268; Reeves, *President Kennedy,* 442–43.
29. Hess, "Commitment," 72, quoting Lyndon Johnson's report of his May 1961 mission.
30. Quoted in Schlesinger, *Robert Kennedy,* 763.
31. Karnow, *Vietnam,* 281; Sheehan, *A Bright Shining Lie,* 334–36; Nguyen Cao Ky, *Twenty Years and Twenty Days* (New York: Stein and Day, 1976), 34–36.
32. Robert S. McNamara with Brian VanDeMark, *In Retrospect: The Tragedy and Lessons of Vietnam* (New York: Random House, 1995), 51; Reeves, *President Kennedy,* 485.
33. For details of that weekend, see Reeves, *President Kennedy,* 560–63.
34. Schlesinger, *Robert Kennedy,* 771; Robert F. Kennedy, *Robert Kennedy in His Own Words: Unpublished Recollections of the Kennedy Years,* ed. Edwin O. Guthman and Jeffrey Shulman (New York: Bantam, 1988), 400, 402–3; Bassett and Pelz, "Vietnam," 246–47.
35. State Department telegram to Ambassador Lodge, 24 August 1963, reprinted in James W. Mooney and Thomas R. West, eds., *Vietnam: A History and Anthology* (New York: Brandywine, 1994), 44–46.
36. Reeves, *President Kennedy,* 567–68.
37. Parmet, *JFK,* 332; Karnow, *Vietnam,* 288.
38. Schlesinger, *Robert Kennedy,* 741; Giglio, *Presidency of John F. Kennedy,* 250–51.
39. Quoted in Schlesinger, *Robert Kennedy,* 770.
40. Ibid., 770.
41. Quoted in Burner, *John F. Kennedy,* 109.
42. Quoted in Reeves, *President Kennedy,* 575.
43. McNamara, *In Retrospect,* 62–63; Karnow, *Vietnam,* 286–90. JFK's refusal to consider the option of neutralization at this his last and best opportunity contradicts the assertions of Roger Hilsman and Arthur Schlesinger that JFK's ultimate goal in Vietnam was a Laos-type settlement. See Schlesinger, *Robert Kennedy,* 770–71; Roger Hilsman, "How Kennedy Viewed the Vietnam Conflict," *New York Times,* 20 January 1992.
44. Schlesinger, *Robert Kennedy,* 774–78. The U.S.-negotiated neutralization of Vietnam (like Laos) may, of course, have been acceptable to JFK, but not one engineered by Diem behind America's back.
45. Karnow, *Vietnam,* 287.
46. McNamara, *In Retrospect,* 70.
47. Hess, "Commitment," 81; Newfield, *Robert Kennedy,* 116; Reeves, *President Kennedy,* 586–93.
48. Bassett and Pelz, "Vietnam," 248; Sheehan, *A Bright Shining Lie,* 365–67. Cf.

Schlesinger, *Robert Kennedy,* 773, who asserted that JFK's insistence on the withdrawal of a thousand troops indicated JFK's private determination "to begin, at whatever cost, a strategy of extrication."

49. The foregoing text relies heavily on Sheehan, *A Bright Shining Lie,* 364; and Reeves, *President Kennedy,* 602–21, citing CIA and White House cable traffic to Saigon.
50. Reeves, *President Kennedy,* 641.
51. Karnow, *Vietnam,* 299–300; Reeves, *President Kennedy.* 641.
52. RFK, *Robert Kennedy,* 399.
53. Parmet, *JFK,* 335.
54. Hess, "Commitment," 80.
55. Quotes in Giglio, *Presidency of John F. Kennedy,* 252; and Reeves, *President Kennedy,* 642.
56. RFK, *Robert Kennedy,* 301.
57. McNamara, *In Retrospect,* 84–85. Also see Giglio, *Presidency of John F. Kennedy,* 252–53; Parmet, *JFK,* 334–35; Reeves, *President Kennedy,* 649. Maxwell Taylor, *Swords and Plowshares* (New York: Norton, 1972), 233.
58. Schlesinger, *Robert Kennedy,* 778.
59. RFK makes no mention in his oral history of his reaction to the Diem and Nhu murders. Schlesinger in *Robert Kennedy* and Edwin Guthman in *We Band of Brothers* (New York: Harper and Row, 1971) noted RFK's reactions to virtually every event but the Diem and Nhu assassinations.
60. Reeves, *President Kennedy,* 569.
61. RFK, *Robert Kennedy,* 400–5.
62. Parmet, *JFK,* 334–35. The CIA was unsympathetic. See Thomas Powers, *The Man Who Kept the Secrets: Richard Helms and the CIA* (New York: Knopf, 1979) 164.
63. Schlesinger, *Robert Kennedy,* 771; RFK, *Robert Kennedy,* 398–99.
64. RFK, *Robert Kennedy,* 398–99. Cf. Sheehan, *A Bright Shining Lie,* 367–71.
65. Newfield, *Robert Kennedy,* 117–18.
66. McNamara, *In Retrospect,* 85. Audio tapes of LBJ's telephone calls to McNamara and Bundy several months after JFK's assassination indicate clearly that, contrary to the assertions made by Oliver Stone in the movie *JFK,* the indecision evident in the last days of JFK's presidency carried over into LBJ's administration. Beschloss, interview on *Nightline,* ABC-TV, 16 October 1996.
67. RFK, *Robert Kennedy,* 404.
68. Halberstam, *The Best and the Brightest,* 409–11; Sheehan, *A Bright Shining Lie,* 375–76, 379; Reeves, *President Kennedy,* 660. For differing views regarding the purpose and outcomes of the Hawaii conference, the scope of NSAM 273, and Operation Plan 34A, see Schlesinger, *Robert Kennedy,* 774; Newman, *JFK and Vietnam,* 438–47; McNamara, *In Retrospect,* 102–3.
69. Marcus Raskin, "'JFK' and the Culture of Violence," *American Historical Review,* 98 (April 1992), 493.
70. Hess, "Commitment," 83. Also see Bassett and Pelz, "Vietnam," 251.
71. RFK, *Robert Kennedy,* 395. Also see Giglio, *Presidency of John F. Kennedy,* 254.

72. Robert F. Kennedy, *The Pursuit of Justice,* ed. Theodore Lowi (New York: Harper and Row, 1964), 132.
73. Burner, *John F. Kennedy,* 101.
74. Sheehan, *A Bright Shining Lie,* 375; Karnow, *Vietnam,* 247–318; Bassett and Pelz, "Vietnam," 252.
75. Reston, *Deadline,* 292.
76. McNamara, *In Retrospect,* 101.
77. Parmet, *JFK,* 336; Giglio, *Presidency of John F. Kennedy,* 254.
78. Burner, *John F. Kennedy,* 112–13.
79. Bassett and Pelz, "Vietnam," 252.
80. Cf. John M. Newman, a student of deception, cynicism, and intrigue, who argues that none of JFK's public statements on Vietnam can be trusted. Newman asserts that JFK intended to withdraw and states that he "besmirched his own reputation and that of the office he held" by refusing to admit publicly that his program was a "failure." *JFK and Vietnam,* 320–25, 454–59.
81. Kenneth P. O'Donnell and David F. Powers with Joe McCarthy *"Johnny, We Hardly Knew Ye"* 15–18.
82. McNamara, *In Retrospect,* 95; Dean Rusk, OH-JFK, 386; Parmet, *JFK,* 386; Giglio, *Presidency of John F. Kennedy,* 254; McGeorge Bundy, *Danger and Survival: Choices about the Bomb in the First Fifty Years* (New York: Random House, 1988), makes no mention of any Kennedy plan to extricate the United States from Vietnam. At the time of his death in September 1996 Bundy was apparently working on a book on Vietnam; he ultimately came to regard the war as a "terrible mistake." See James C. Thomson, Jr., "A Memory of McGeorge Bundy," *New York Times,* 22 September 1996.
83. Schlesinger, *Robert Kennedy,* 768, 774.
84. McNamara, *In Retrospect,* 95–97.
85. RFK, *Robert Kennedy,* 393–94.
86. James Reston, "Kennedy Ticketed for Saigon?" *New York Times,* 17 June 1964.
87. RFK, *Robert Kennedy,* 394–95.
88. O'Donnell and Powers, *"Johnny, We Hardly Knew Ye",* 16.
89. See, for example, RFK to Sharon Henry of the Oklahoma County Young Democrats, 12 June 1961, Box 24, AG-GC, and Confidential Briefing Memo [1962], Box 12, AG-PC. Oddly, JFK told O'Donnell to instruct RFK to stay away from patronage and politics in New York, perhaps because Averell Harriman personally objected to RFK's involvement there. O'Donnell to RFK, 20 July 1961, Box 12, AG-PC.
90. RFK to Stephen Smith, 9 May 1963, Box 12, AG-PC.
91. RFK to J. M. Bailey, 19 July 1961, Box 12, AG-PC.
92. Schlesinger, *Robert Kennedy,* 418–21.
93. Peter Maas, interview by Jean Stein and George Plimpton, eds., *American Journey: The Times of Robert Kennedy* (New York: Harcourt Brace Jovanovich, 1970), 79–81; RFK, *Robert Kennedy,* 360–61.

94. Bartlett, interview by Stein and Plimpton, *American Journey,* 87.
95. For comments on these cases, see Schlesinger, *Robert Kennedy,* 411–21; Victor Navasky, *Kennedy Justice* (New York: Atheneum, 1971), 364–91; RFK, *Robert Kennedy,* 357–61.
96. David McCullough, *Truman* (New York: Simon and Schuster, 1992), 981.
97. Scammon report [undated, *ca.* 30 October 1962], Box 12, AG-PC.
98. O'Donnell and Powers, *"Johnny, We Hardly Knew Ye,"* 447–48.
99. William Manchester, *Death of a President* (New York: Harper and Row, 1967), 189, 195–96.
100. Ibid., 195–96; Schlesinger, *Robert Kennedy,* 654–65.
101. RFK did not recognize Shepard's voice. He thought it was Clint Hill who called. A few minutes later, Hoover called. "The President's dead," he said. Hoover's tone, RFK recalled, was "not quite as excited as if he were reporting the fact that he had found a Communist on the faculty of Howard University." Manchester, *Death of a President,* 177, 256–57; Schlesinger, *Robert Kennedy,* 655.
102. Reston, *Deadline,* 295.
103. "Trying to Remember Kennedy," *Esquire,* November 1973, 137.
104. Manchester, *Death of a President,* 197, 257–59.
105. Rose Kennedy, *Times to Remember* (Garden City, N.Y.: Doubleday, 1974), 471; Manchester, *Death of a President,* 255.
106. Manchester, *Death of a President,* 271–72; Schlesinger, *Robert Kennedy,* 656.
107. Manchester, *Death of a President,* 377.
108. Guthman, *We Band of Brothers,* 378.
109. At that precise moment, according to David Lifton's monumentally absurd JFK murder conspiracy theory, JFK's body was being smuggled off Air Force One inside a body bag. Since Lifton's theory requires that the body be removed within ninety seconds of the aircraft coming to a stop and since the only door open at that time was the front right passenger door, Lifton would have us believe that RFK rushed up the ramp without noticing a person or persons carrying a full body bag down the ramp. *Best Evidence* (New York: Carroll and Graf, 1980), 680–83, 701–2.
110. The preceding quotes are from Manchester, *Death of a President,* 378–79, 387. Since Manchester gained exclusive authority to interview the Kennedys on their words and actions in the days surrounding the assassination, most of the foregoing account is drawn from *Death of a President.*
111. Jacqueline Kennedy selected Bethesda, rather than Walter Reed Army Medical Center where the Armed Forces Institute of Pathology was located, because her husband was "a navy man." Otherwise of little consequence, the casual and unexpected selection of Bethesda further diminishes the viability of Lifton's ludicrous theory in *Best Evidence.*
112. Manchester, *Death of a President,* 391–92.
113. Dr. J. Thornton Boswell, quoted in "JFK's death—The Plain Truth from the MDs Who Did the Autopsy," *Journal of the American Medical Association,* 27 May 1992, 2798–99; Manchester, *Death of a President,* 378–79, 387, 390–92.

114. Manchester, *Death of a President,* 419.
115. Ibid., 427, 432–33. On the implications, see Gerald Posner, *Case Closed* (New York: Random House, 1993), 303–4.
116. Those materials included what remained of JFK's preserved, unsectioned brain. Admiral Burkley told the pathologists that the family intended to inter the brain with the president's body. Later controversies notwithstanding, the pathologists believed Dr. Burkley an "honorable man" who had done what was required of him. "JFK's death," 2800.
117. Burke Marshall, OH-JFK, 74; Posner, *Case Closed,* 409–10.
118. Schlesinger, *Robert Kennedy,* 658; Peter Collier and David Horowitz, *The Kennedys: An American Drama* (New York: Warner, 1984), 397.
119. Manchester, *Death of a President,* 435, 442–43, 485, 517.
120. On the involvements of others in the planning for the funeral, see Schlesinger, *Robert Kennedy,* 658; Goodwin, *Remembering America: A Voice from the Sixties* (Boston: Little, Brown, 1988), 230; Manchester, *Death of a President,* 420–23 and 490–97 on the choice of Arlington, and Joseph A. Califano, Jr., *The Triumph and Tragedy of Lyndon Johnson* (New York: Simon and Shuster, 1991), 14.
121. Jacqueline put in three letters (from herself and her two children), a pair of gold cufflinks, and a scrimshaw with the presidential seal. Manchester, *Death of a President,* 516–17; Schlesinger, *Robert Kennedy,* 659.
122. Manchester, *Death of a President,* 601. Benjamin C. Bradlee, *Conversations with Kennedy* (New York: Norton, 1975), 242.

EPILOGUE

1. LeMoyne Billings, interview by Peter Collier and David Horowitz, *The Kennedys: An American Drama* (New York: Warner), 396–97.
2. Rose Kennedy, *Times to Remember* (Garden City, N.Y.: Doubleday, 1974), 487–88; John H. Davis, *The Kennedys: Dynasty and Disaster: 1848–1984* (New York: McGraw-Hill, 1984), 604–6.
3. *Newsday,* 11 November 1964; Jerry Oppenheimer, *The Other Mrs. Kennedy—Ethel Skakel Kennedy: an American Drama of Power, Privilege, and Politics* (New York: St. Martin's, 1994), 268; Ethel Kennedy, interview by NBC-News, "RFK," 28 May 1993.
4. LeMoyne Billings, interview by Lester David and Irene David, *Bobby Kennedy: The Making of a Folk Hero* (New York: PaperJacks, 1988), 221.
5. Senator Ralph Yarborough (Texas) to RFK, 20 December 1963, and RFK to Yarborough, 7 February 1964, Box 68, AG-GC; Arthur M. Schlesinger, Jr., *Robert Kennedy and His Times* (Boston: Houghton Mifflin, 1978), 660–62.
6. Hackett, interview by David and David, *Bobby Kennedy,* 217; Collier and Horowitz, *The Kennedys,* 397.
7. Smathers, interview by David and David, *Bobby Kennedy,* 217.

8. Salinger, OH-JFK, 2; Schlesinger, *Robert Kennedy,* 661; David and David, *Bobby Kennedy,* 219.
9. Edwin Guthman, *We Band of Brothers* (New York: Harper and Row, 1971), 244.
10. Alan J. Lerner and Frederick Loewe, *Camelot.*
11. On the making of Camelot, see Theodore H. White, *In Search of History* (New York: Harper and Row, 1978), 517–25; and "For President Kennedy: An Epilogue," *Life,* 6 December 1963, 158–59; Davis, *The Kennedys,* 606–12.
12. White, *In Search of History,* 525; James MacGregor Burns, *Edward Kennedy and the Camelot Legacy* (New York: Norton, 1976), 13–14
13. Christopher Matthews, *Kennedy and Nixon: The Rivalry That Shaped Postwar America* (New York: Simon and Shuster, 1996), 243.
14. Hand-written manuscript [undated], Box 10, AG-PC; Robert F. Kennedy, "Foreword to the Memorial Edition" of *Profiles in Courage* by John F. Kennedy (New York: Harper and Row, 1964), ix–xiv; also printed as "Robert Kennedy's Tribute to JFK," *Look,* 25 February 1964, 37–40.
15. Collier and Horowitz, *The Kennedys,* 202.
16. John C. Warnecke [architect of JFK gravesite] to RFK, 11 June 1964, Box 8; Nancy Tuckerman [secretary to Jacqueline Kennedy] to RFK (15 May 1964), Box 9, AG-PC.
17. William Manchester, *Death of a President* (New York: Harper and Row, 1967), 257–58. Greeting LBJ as the new president disembarked at Andrews on 22 November, Bundy said, "I am assuming, Mr. President . . . that everything in locked files before two P.M. today belongs to the President's [JFK's] family." LBJ replied, "That's correct." Michael R. Beschloss, *The Crisis Years: Kennedy and Khrushchev, 1960–1965* (New York: Burlingame, 1991), 675–76.
18. Dr. Janet Travell memo for the file, 6 December 1963, WHCS Files Box 104, JFKL; Richard Reeves, *President Kennedy: Profile of Power* (New York: Simon and Schuster, 1993), 668*n.*
19. "Gift of President Kennedy's Papers," 25 February 1965, Stephen Smith to RFK, 3 March 1965, Box 12, SP.
20. Jacqueline Kennedy to Thomas M. Caplan, 19 August 1965, Box 6, SP.
21. Burke Marshall, OH-JFK, 53; RFK to Galbraith, 16 February 1966, and Galbraith to Pierre Salinger, 1 March 1966, Box 4, SP.
22. On the Fay book, see Reeves, *President Kennedy,* 669–670n.
23. JBK to RFK [undated, September 1964?], Box 6; and Nathan M. Pusey [president of Harvard University] to RFK, 9 May 1968, Box 9, SP.
24. Salinger to RFK, 7 June 1965, Box 10, SP; Lawford to RFK, 27 January 1966, and Burke Marshall to RFK, 23 May 1966, Box 6, SP. Initially, even documentaries had to pass Kennedy muster. See Pam Turnure [secretary to Jacqueline Kennedy] to RFK, 20 August 1965 [Re: "Young Man from Boston," narrated by Jack Paar], Box 6, SP.
25. James N. Giglio, *The Presidency of John F. Kennedy* (Lawrence: U. of Kansas Press, 1993), 35.

26. Reeves, *President Kennedy,* 18.
27. Warren Rogers, *When I Think of Bobby* (New York: HarperCollins, 1993), 7–8.
28. Quoted in Ralph G. Martin, *Seeds of Destruction: Joe Kennedy and His Sons* (New York: Putnam, 1995), 391.
29. Reeves, *President Kennedy,* 18–19.
30. Walter Winchell first used "sexual policeman" to describe RFK's role. Martin, *Seeds of Destruction,* 172.
31. Neustadt, interview by Jean Stein and George Plimpton, eds., *American Journey: The Times of Robert Kennedy* (Harcourt Brace Jovanovich, 1970), 128.
32. LeMoyne Billings, interview by Stein and Plimpton, *American Journey,* 127.
33. Martin, *Seeds of Destruction,* 335, Billings conversation with Harvey Fleetwood, 615.
34. Theodore C. Sorensen, *Kennedy* (New York: Harper and Row, 1965), 34.
35. The Postal Revenue and Federal Salary Act of 1967, or the "Bobby Kennedy Law," states, "A public official may not appoint, employ, promote [or] advance" a relative in an agency "in which he is serving or over which he exercises jurisdiction or control." The existence of the law was raised when rumors surfaced that President William Clinton was considering a line appointment for his wife, Hillary Rodham Clinton. See "Bill to Bar Nepotism Approved," *New York TImes,* 13 December 1967, 17; "Hiring Relations: New Federal Rules, *U.S. News and World Report,* 25 December 1967, 7; Neal Smith, *Mr. Smith Went to Washington* (Iowa City: Iowa State U. Press, 1969); also, "The Bobby Kennedy Law and Hillary Clinton," *Washinton Post,* 1 December 1992, A17. Like the Kennedys, the Clintons were perceived (often critically) as near-equal partners in running the presidency. See Roger Morris, *Partners in Power: The Clintons and Their America* (New York: Holt, 1996).
36. Richard Goodwin, *Remembering America: A Voice from the Sixties* (Boston: Little, Brown, 1988), 446.
37. Rogers, *When I Think of Bobby,* 15–16.
38. Goodwin, *Remembering America.* 444.
39. Schlesinger, *Robert Kennedy,* 668–69; David and David, *Bobby Kennedy,* 222.
40. Collier and Horowitz, *The Kennedys,* 397–98.
41. Coles, interview by Stein and Plimpton, *American Journey,* 278–79.

Bibliographic Essay

This study draws from manuscript collections and oral history interviews at the John F. Kennedy Presidential Library (JFKL) in Boston, Massachusetts, operated by the National Archives and Records Administration. The Robert F. Kennedy Papers housed there are divided into four subcollections: Pre-Administration Papers (PAP-RFK), 1937–1960; Attorney General's Papers (AG), 1961–1964; the Senate Papers (SP), 1964–1968; and the Presidential Campaign Papers (PCP), 1968. Significant portions of RFK's Papers remain closed or selectively restricted for reasons of national security, to avoid embarrassing living persons, or for personal reasons permitted the family under the deed of gift.

Closed at the time research was conducted for this book were more than three dozen boxes of personal files, 160 boxes of personal correspondence, all health and financial records, and unknown amounts of family correspondence, diaries, and other personal papers. Robert Kennedy's desk diaries, telephone logs, and typed messages for the period from 1961 to 1964 were mandated to be opened by the President John F. Kennedy Assassination Records Collection Act, signed into law in October 1992 following the stir created by Oliver Stone's movie *JFK.* The Kennedy Library, however, could not produce the typed messages for 1962 and 1963 and the desk diaries for 1963. Such are the problems in researching the life of a public figure when the family contols access to primary sources.

Fortunately, other sources exist. Many of the Kennedys' associates left personal papers and oral history interviews at the Kennedy Library, although some of those documents also remain closed or restricted. (See the Notes for specific citations.) Others have told their stories for the historical record, qualifying the necessity for large numbers of additional personal interviews. This study particularly benefits from the interviews conducted in the spring of 1993 by NBC-News for the documentary "RFK: The Man and the Memories," for which the author served as historical consultant.

The Kennedys are the most newsworthy political family in recent U.S. history and certainly the most photographed and filmed. The JFK Library's massive audiovisual collection contains many of those images. This study also made extensive use of the Temple University Photo-Journalism Collection and the Clipping File of the Philadelphia *Evening Bulletin, Philadelphia Inquirer,* and *New York Times* in the Temple University Urban Archives. Those materials were especially valuable for building a chronology and for confirming important dates. (Most newspaper items cited in the Notes came from the Clipping File and thus have no page numbers.)

Historians' views of Robert Kennedy have paralleled changing assessments of John Kennedy. Books, apologetic and sometimes hagiographic in style and tone, appeared on each brother after their assassinations. Shortly there came a revisionist literature critical of the Kennedys' reluctance on civil rights, their initiation of the Vietnam conflict, their narrow view of civil liberties, and their general reliance on style over substance. After the revisionists came the popularly oriented investigative studies with claims of notorious revelations, sex scandals, and illegal activities. With the passage of time and with added historical perspective, we may see more balanced assessments.

RFK and JFK are the central subjects in an astounding number of books and monographs. For bibliographies on the Kennedy literature, see Dorothy Ryan, *The Kennedy Family of Massachusetts: A Bibliography* (Westport, Conn.: Greenwood, 1981); Joan I. Newcomb, *John F. Kennedy: An Annotated Bibliography* (Metuchen, N.J.: Scarecrow, 1977); and James N. Giglio, *John F. Kennedy: A Bibliography* (Westport, Conn.: Greenwood, 1995).

A number of longitudinal studies of the Kennedy family have appeared. Joseph McCarthy, *The Remarkable Kennedys* (New York: Popular Library, 1960) is uncritical and laudatory. John H. Davis, *The Kennedys: Dynasty and Disaster, 1848–1984* (New York: McGraw-Hill, 1984), and Peter Collier and David Horowitz, *The Kennedys: An American Drama* (New York: Warner, 1984), are insightful and fault-finding. Doris Goodwin's splendidly detailed study, *The Fitzgeralds and the Kennedys: An American Saga* (New York: St. Martin's, 1987), is built upon exclusive access to portions of the family papers, diaries, and letters.

Books on individual Kennedy family members include privately printed tributes: John Kennedy, ed., *As We Remember Joe* (1945); Robert Kennedy, ed., *The Burden and the Glory* (1964), on JFK; Edward Kennedy, ed., *The Fruitful Bough* (1965), on Joseph P. Kennedy; Patricia Kennedy Lawford, ed., *That Shining Hour* (1969), on RFK. Rose Kennedy is the only family member who has completed a full memoir, *Times to Remember* (Garden City, N.Y.: Doubleday, 1974). Works on the older children include Hank Searls, *The Lost Prince* (Cleveland: World, 1969), on Joseph Kennedy, Jr.; Lynne McTaggart, *Kathleen Kennedy* (Garden City, N.Y.: Dial, 1983).

Biographers have not been kind to Joseph P. Kennedy. See Richard Whalen, *The Founding Father* (New York: New American Library, 1964); David E. Koskoff, *Joseph P. Kennedy* (Englewood Cliffs, N.J.: Prentice-Hall, 1974); Michael R. Beschloss,

Kennedy and Roosevelt: The Uneasy Alliance (New York: Norton, 1980); Ralph G. Martin, *Seeds of Destruction: Joe Kennedy and His Sons* (New York: Putnam, 1995); Ronald Kessler, *The Sins of the Father* (New York: Warner, 1996); Nellie Bly, *The Kennedy Men: Three Generations of Sex, Scandal, and Secrets* (New York: Kensington, 1996). Works on Edward Moore Kennedy include James MacGregor Burns, *Edward Kennedy and the Camelot Legacy* (New York: Norton, 1976); Burton Hersh, *The Education of Edward Kennedy* (New York: Morrow, 1972); Murray B. Levin and T. A. Repak, *Edward Kennedy: The Myth of Leadership* (Boston: Houghton Mifflin, 1980). A wealth of valuable information on the Kennedys has been assembled by Lester David and Irene David; see Lester David, *Ethel, The Story of Mrs. Robert F. Kennedy* (New York: World, 1971); *Ted Kennedy: Triumphs and Tragedies* (New York: Grosset and Dunlap, 1971); *Jacqueline Kennedy Onassis: A Portrait of her Private Years* (New York: Birchlane, 1994).

For critical assessments of the Kennedy wives, see Kitty Kelley, *Jackie Oh!* (Secaucus, N.J.: Stuart, 1978); C. David Heymann, *A Woman Named Jackie* (New York: Carol Communications, 1989); and Jerry Oppenheimer, *The Other Mrs. Kennedy—Ethel Skakel Kennedy: An America Drama of Power, Privilege, and Politics* (New York: St. Martin's, 1994). All three rely heavily on hearsay, faded recollections, and unsubstantiated speculation and must be approached warily. Oppenheimer's interviews of members of the Skakel family, newspeople, former friends, and employees from Hickory Hill add colorful (and some fanciful) details to our knowledge of the private lives of Ethel and Robert. The credibility of some of his assertions regarding the quality of the Kennedy marriage and family life is suspect, however, because of his failure to fully document his findings, a penchant for relying on anonymous sources, and several chronological and factual errors.

For JFK and his presidency, the starting places are Arthur M. Schlesinger, Jr., *A Thousand Days: John F. Kennedy in the White House* (Boston: Houghton Mifflin, 1965), and Theodore C. Sorensen, *Kennedy* (New York: Harper and Row, 1965), two superbly written accounts by Kennedy insiders. More analytical and probing are Herbert S. Parmet, *Jack: The Struggles of John F. Kennedy* (New York: Dial, 1980) and *JFK: The Presidency of John F. Kennedy* (New York: Dial, 1983). James MacGregor Burns, *John Kennedy: A Political Profile* (New York: Harcourt Brace Jovanovich, 1960), is the earliest biography. Joan Blair and Clay Blair, Jr., *The Search for JFK* (New York: Berkley, 1976), uncovered much about JFK's private life. Nigel Hamilton, *JFK: Reckless Youth* (New York: Random House, 1992), says little about RFK but develops a compelling portrait of young JFK.

For critical assessments of JFK's administration, see Lewis Paper, *The Promise and the Performance* (New York: Da Capo, 1975); David Halberstam, *The Best and the Brightest* (New York: Random House, 1972); Henry Fairlie, *The Kennedy Promise* (Garden City, N.Y.: Doubleday, 1973); Bruce Miroff, *Pragmatic Illusions* (New York: McKay, 1976). Thomas C. Reeves, *A Question of Character: The Life of John F. Kennedy* (New York: Free Press, 1991), is unrelenting in its faultfinding and its unforgiving stance toward both JFK and RFK, but many interesting observations are flawed by Reeves's unquestioning reliance on unproved accusations. Richard Reeves, *President*

Kennedy: Profile of Power (New York: Simon & Schuster, 1993), reveals the day-to-day context within which JFK viewed selected problems; Irving Bernstein, *Promises Kept: John F. Kennedy's New Frontier* (New York: Oxford U. Press, 1990), defends JFK's record of achievement on domestic issues; James N. Giglio, *The Presidency of John F. Kennedy* (Lawrence: U. of Kansas Press, 1993), is a fair-minded, comprehensive synthesis.

Arthur M. Schlesinger, Jr.'s beautifully crafted and reliably detailed study, *Robert Kennedy and His Times* (Boston: Houghton Mifflin, 1978), sets the standard for RFK biographies. He is the only scholar to whom Ethel Kennedy has granted access to RFK's personal papers. Although defensive in places, Schlesinger's account is carefully reasoned and also anticipates many of the later controversies, including the Kennedys' connections to the CIA-Mafia plots, the Kennedy-Hoover controversies, and the RFK-LBJ conflicts. Jack Newfield, *Robert Kennedy: A Memoir* (New York: New American Library, 1969), gives a sensitive and moving account of RFK's personal adjustments and accommodations to the changing political and social climate of 1968 through the intriguing perspective of the sixties' activist. Still of value is Robert E. Thompson and Hortense Myers, *Robert F. Kennedy: The Brother Within* (New York: Dell, 1962), the earliest biography. Lester David and Irene David, *Bobby Kennedy: The Making of a Folk Hero* (New York: PaperJacks, 1988), contains fascinating material on the personal lives of the Kennedys within a laudatory framework.

Disapproving accounts include two polemics: Ralph de Toledano, *RFK: The Man Who Would Be President* (New York: Putnam, 1967), and Victor Lasky, *Robert F. Kennedy: The Myth and the Man* (New York: Trident, 1971). Nancy Gager Clinch, *The Kennedy Neurosis* (New York: Grosset and Dunlap, 1973), uses the argot of psychoanalysis to magnify the deficiencies of the male Kennedys. Victor Lasky, *It Didn't Start with Watergate* (New York: Dial, 1976), tries in vain to shift blame for the mentality of Watergate onto the Kennedys. Garry Wills, *The Kennedy Imprisonment* (Boston: Little, Brown, 1982), is a penetrating examination of the Kennedy leadership style.

Also helpful are the memoirs of advisors and friends: Pierre Salinger, *With Kennedy* (New York: Doubleday, 1966); William O. Douglas, *Go East, Young Man* (New York: Random House, 1974); Lawrence F. O'Brien, *No Final Victories: A Life in Politics from John F. Kennedy to Watergate* (Garden City, N.Y.: Doubleday, 1974); Benjamin C. Bradlee, *Conversations with Kennedy* (New York: Norton, 1975) and *Ben Bradlee: A Good Life* (New York: Simon and Schuster, 1995); Jean Stein and George Plimpton, eds., *American Journey: The Times of Robert Kennedy* (New York: Harcourt Brace Jovanovich, 1970); Kenneth P. O'Donnell and David F. Powers with Joe McCarthy, *"Johnny, We Hardly Knew Ye,"* (Boston: Little, Brown, 1972); Richard Goodwin, *Remembering America: A Voice from the Sixties* (Boston: Little, Brown, 1988); Paul B. Fay, *The Pleasure of His Company* (New York: Harper and Row, 1966); Clark Clifford, *Counsel to the President* (New York: Random House, 1991); Warren Rogers, *When I Think of Bobby* (New York: HarperCollins, 1993); Robert S. McNamara with Brian VanDeMark, *In Retrospect: The Tragedy and Lessons of Vietnam* (New York: Random House, 1995).

Other useful memoirs and biographies are those of John Bartlow Martin, *Adlai Stevenson and the World* (Garden City, N.Y.: Doubleday, 1976); Bobby Baker with Larry L. King, *Wheeling and Dealing: Confessions of a Capitol Hill Operator* (New York: Norton, 1978); Judith Campbell Exner with Ovid Demaris, *My Story* (New York: Grove, 1977); Kitty Kelley, *His Way: The Unauthorized Biography of Frank Sinatra* (New York: Bantam, 1986); Lyndon B. Johnson, *The Vantage Point* (New York: Holt, Rinehart, and Winston, 1971); Nikita S. Khrushchev, *Khrushchev Remembers: The Last Testament* (Boston: Little, Brown, 1974); Arthur Krock, *Memoirs: Sixty Years on the Firing Line* (New York: Funk and Wagnalls, 1968); Evan Thomas, *The Man to See: Ultimate Insider, Legendary Trial Lawyer* (New York: Simon and Schuster, 1991), on Edward Bennett Williams; Harrison E. Salisbury, *Heroes of My Time* (New York: Walker, 1993); Murray Kempton, *Rebellions, Perversities, and Main Events* (New York: Time, 1994); James Reston, *Deadline* (New York: Random House, 1991).

The best study of the Kennedy Justice Department is Victor Navasky, *Kennedy Justice* (New York: Atheneum, 1971). For an insider's view of RFK's management of Justice from a man who remains staunchly faithful to the Kennedy memory, see Edwin Guthman, *We Band of Brothers* (New York: Harper and Row, 1971).

Analyses of the RFK-Hoffa controversies can be found in John Bartlow Martin, *Jimmy Hoffa's Hot* (New York: Fawcett World, Crest, 1959); James Hoffa, *The Trials of Jimmy Hoffa* (Chicago: Regnery, 1970); Dan E. Moldea, *The Hoffa Wars: Teamsters, Rebels, Politicians, and the Mob* (New York: Paddington, 1978); Walter Sheridan, *The Fall and Rise of Jimmy Hoffa* (New York: Saturday Review, 1972). Arthur A. Sloane, *Hoffa* (Cambridge: MIT Press, 1991) offers a scholarly treatment and generally balanced assessments. The motion picture *Hoffa* (screenplay by David Mamet) deliberately distorts, as does its novelization, Ken Englade, *Hoffa* (New York: HarperPaperbacks, 1992).

Indispensable for studying the history of the war on crime are Stephen Fox, *Blood and Power: Organized Crime in Twentieth-Century America* (New York: Morrow, 1989) and Peter Maas, *The Valachi Papers* (New York: Bantam reprint, 1969). On the fallout over RFK's war on crime, see John H. Davis, *Mafia Kingfish: Carlos Marcello and the Assassination of John F. Kennedy* (New York: New American Library, 1989), and David E. Scheim, *Contract on America: The Mafia Murder of President John F. Kennedy* (New York: Zebra, 1988), both of which tell basically the same story, as taken from the House Select Committee on Assassinations (HSCA) and the FBI files. For the HSCA chief counsel's version, see G. Robert Blakey and Richard N. Billings, *Fatal Hour: The Assassination of President Kennedy by Organized Crime* (New York: Berkely reprint, 1992), originally published in 1981 as *The Plot to Kill the President.*

On J. Edgar Hoover, the controversy over electronic surveillance, and his relationship to RFK and JFK, see William C. Sullivan, *The Bureau: My Thirty Years in Hoover's FBI* (Boston: Little, Brown, 1967); Curt Gentry, *J. Edgar Hoover: The Man and the Secrets* (New York: Norton, 1991); Athan G. Theoharis and John Stuart Cox, *The Boss: J. Edgar Hoover and the Great American Inquisition* (Philadelphia: Temple U. Press, 1988); Athan Theoharis, ed., *From the Secret Files of J. Edgar Hoover* (Chicago: Dee, 1991);

Richard Gid Powers, *Secrecy and Power: The Life of J. Edgar Hoover* (New York: Free Press, 1987); Anthony Summers, *Official and Confidential: The Secret Life of J. Edgar Hoover* (New York: Putnam, 1993).

The best study of the Kennedys' reactions to the civil rights movement is Taylor Branch, *Parting the Waters: America in the King Years, 1954–63* (New York: Simon and Schuster, 1988). Other important works are C. Vann Woodward, *The Strange Career of Jim Crow* (New York: Oxford U. Press, 1986 edition); David Garrow, *Bearing the Cross: Martin Luther King, Jr., and the Southern Christian Leadership Conference* (New York: Random House, 1986), and *The FBI and Martin Luther King, Jr.* (New York: Penguin, 1983); Carl Brauer, *John F. Kennedy and the Second Reconstruction* (New York: Columbia U. Press, 1977); Robert Weisbrot, *Freedom Bound: A History of America's Civil Rights Movement* (New York: Plume, 1991); James Meredith, *Three Years in Mississippi* (Bloomington: Indiana University Press, 1966); Juan Williams, *Eyes on the Prize: America's Civil Rights Years, 1954–1965* (New York: Penguin, 1987); Henry Hampton and Steve Fayer, eds., *Voices of Freedom* (New York: Bantam, 1990).

Harris Wofford, *Of Kennedys and Kings: Making Sense of the Sixties* (New York: Farrar, Straus and Giroux, 1980) is especially useful on civil rights and RFK's relationship with Martin Luther King, Jr. Other important books on the 1960s include Allen Matusow, *The Unraveling of America: A History of Liberalism in the 1960s* (New York: Harper and Row, 1984); Nicholas Lemann, *The Promised Land: The Great Black Migration and How It Changed America* (New York: Knopf, 1991); William L. O'Neill, *Coming Apart: An Informal History of America in the 1960s* (New York: Quadrangle, 1975); Edward P. Morgan, *The 60s Experience: Hard Lessons about Modern America* (Philadelphia: Temple U. Press, 1991). On the organization and purposes of SDS, the youth movement, and the antiwar movement, see Todd Gitlin, *The Sixties: Years of Hope, Days of Rage* (New York: Bantam reprint, 1989); Tom Wells, *The War Within: America's Battle over Vietnam* (Berkeley and Los Angeles: U. of California Press, 1994); Irwin Unger and Debi Unger, *America in the 1960s* (St. James, N.Y.: Brandywine, 1988); James Miller, *"Democracy Is in the Streets": From Port Huron to the Siege of Chicago* (New York: Simon and Schuster, 1987).

RFK's involvement in the foreign policies and national security affairs of the Kennedy administration can be gleaned from a number of books. On Cuba, see Peter Weyden, *Bay of Pigs* (New York: Simon and Schuster, 1979); Haynes Johnson, *The Bay of Pigs* (New York: Simon and Schuster, 1964); Elie Abel, *The Missile Crisis* (Philadelphia: Lippincott, 1968); David Detzer, *The Brink* (New York: Crowell, 1979); Abram Chayes, *The Cuban Missile Crisis* (New York: Oxford U. Press, 1974); James G. Blight and David A. Welch, eds., *On the Brink: Americans and Soviets Reexamine the Cuban Missile Crisis* (New York: Hill and Wang, 1989); James G. Blight, Bruce J. Allyn, and David A. Welch, eds., *Cuba on the Brink: Castro, the Missile Crisis, and the Soviet Collapse* (New York: Pantheon, 1993); Laurence Chang and Peter Kornbluh, eds., *The Cuban Missile Crisis, 1962* (New York: New Press, 1992).

The 1975 Church committee investigations exposed the web of covert operations in the Kennedy administration, including the CIA connections to organized crime: *Alleged Assassination Plots Involving Foreign Leaders: Interim Report of the Select Committee to Study Governmental Operations with Respect to Intelligence Activities* (New York: Norton, 1976). Also see Charles Rappleye and Ed Becker, *All-American Mafioso: The Johnny Roselli Story* (New York: Doubleday, 1991). On the CIA, see Thomas Powers, *The Man Who Kept the Secrets: Richard Helms and the CIA* (New York: Knopf, 1979); William E. Colby, *Honorable Men* (New York: Simon and Schuster, 1978); John Ranelagh, *The Agency* (New York: Simon and Schuster, 1986).

On Berlin, Vietnam, and counterinsurgency, see Robert A. Slusser, *The Berlin Crisis of 1961* (Baltimore: Johns Hopkins U. Press, 1971); Eleanor L. Dulles, *The Wall: A Tragedy in Three Acts* (Columbia: U. of South Carolina Press, 1972); Stanley Karnow, *Vietnam: A History* (New York: Viking, 1983); *The Pentagon Papers, as Published by the New York Times* (New York: Bantam, 1971); Maxwell Taylor, *Swords and Plowshares* (New York: Norton, 1972); John Galloway, ed., *The Kennedys and Vietnam* (New York: Facts on File, 1971); Richard J. Walton, *Cold War and Counter-Revolution: The Foreign Policy of John F. Kennedy* (Baltimore: Pelican, 1973); John Gaddis, *Strategies of Containment* (New York: Oxford U. Press, 1982); David Halberstam, *The Making of a Quagmire* (New York: Knopf, 1965); George C. Herring, *America's Longest War: The United States and Vietnam, 1950–1975* (New York: Dutton, 1987); William J. Rust, *Kennedy in Vietnam* (New York: Scribner, 1985); Neil Sheehan, *A Bright Shining Lie* (New York: Random House, 1988); Michael R. Beschloss, *The Crisis Years: Kennedy and Khrushchev, 1960–1965* (New York: Burlingame, 1991); Roger Hilsman, *To Move a Nation* (Garden City, N.Y.: 1967); George W. Ball, *The Past Has Another Pattern: Memoirs* (New York: Norton, 1982); Deborah Shapley, *Promise and Power: The Life and Times of Robert McNamara* (Boston: Little, Brown, 1993); Walter Isaacson and Evan Thomas, *The Wise Men: Six Friends and the World They Made—Acheson, Bohlen, Harriman, Kennan, Lovett, McCloy* (New York: Simon and Schuster, 1986); McGeorge Bundy, *Danger and Survival: Choices about the Bomb in the First Fifty Years* (New York: Random House, 1988).

For considerations on the places of JFK and RFK in American political history and their contributions to American liberalism, see David Burner and Thomas R. West, *The Torch Is Passed: The Kennedy Brothers and American Liberalism* (New York: Brandywine, 1984); James MacGregor Burns, *The Deadlock of Democracy* (Englewood Cliffs, N.J.: Prentice-Hall, 1963); James L. Sundquist, *Politics and Policy: The Eisenhower, Kennedy, and Johnson Years* (Washington, D.C.: Brookings, 1968); William E. Leuchtenburg, *In the Shadow of FDR* (Ithaca, N.Y.: Cornell U. Press, 1983); Ronald Steel, *Walter Lippmann and the American Century* (Boston: Little, Brown, 1980); Arthur Schlesinger, Jr., *The Imperial Presidency* (Boston: Houghton Mifflin, 1972) and *The Vital Center: The Politics of Freedom* (Boston: Houghton Mifflin, 1949); Theodore Lowi, *The End of Liberalism: Ideology, Policy, and the Crisis of Public Authority* (New York: Norton, 1969); Theodore H. White, *The Making of the President 1960* (New York: Atheneum, 1961) and *The Making of the President 1964* (New York: Atheneum, 1965); Kathleen Hall Jamieson, *The Packaging of the Presidency* (New York: Oxford U. Press, 1990); William Manchester, *The Glory and the Dream: A Narrative History of*

America, 1932–1972 (New York: Bantam reprint, 1975); Lawrence H. Fuchs, *John F. Kennedy and American Catholicism* (New York: Meredith, 1967); Christopher Matthews, *Kennedy and Nixon* (New York: Simon and Schuster, 1996); Samuel P. Huntington, *American Politics: The Promise of Disharmony* (Cambridge: Harvard U. Press, 1981); James M. Burns, *The Crosswinds of Freedom* (New York: Vintage, 1990); Alonzo L. Hamby, *Liberalism and Its Challengers: From F.D.R. to Bush* (New York: Oxford U. Press, 1992); George Will, *Statecraft as Soulcraft: What Government Does* (New York: Simon and Schuster, 1983). Godfrey Hodgson, *America in Our Time* (Garden City, N.Y.: Doubleday, 1976), is especially useful for placing RFK within the context of the liberal consensus of the mid-1960s.

RFK's relationship with Lyndon Johnson is thoroughly examined by Paul R. Henggeler, *In His Steps: Lyndon Johnson and the Kennedy Mystique* (Chicago: Dee, 1991). Also of value are Rowland Evans and Robert D. Novak, *Lyndon B. Johnson: The Exercise of Power* (New York: New American Library, 1966); Tom Wicker, *JFK and LBJ* (Baltimore: Penguin reprint, 1970); Doris Kearns, *Lyndon Johnson and the American Dream* (New York: 1976); Hubert Humphrey, *The Education of a Public Man* (Garden City, N.Y.: Doubleday, 1976); Bruce J. Schulman, *Lyndon B. Johnson and American Liberalism* (New York: St. Martin's Press, 1994).

JFK's assassination was the most profound event in Robert Kennedy's life. More has been written about it than about JFK's life. The beginning points are *The Warren Commission Report: Report of the President's Commission on the Assassination of President John F. Kennedy* (New York: St. Martin's reprint, 1992); U.S. House of Representatives, *Investigation of the Assassination of President John F. Kennedy: Hearings before the Select Committee on Assassinations,* 95th Congress, 2d Session, September 6–December 29, 1978; William Manchester, *Death of A President* (New York: Harper and Row, 1967); Gerald Posner, *Case Closed: Lee Harvey Oswald and the Assassination of JFK* (New York: Random House, 1993); Norman Mailer, *Oswald's Tale: An American Mystery* (New York: Random House, 1995). For discussion of the various conspiracy theories, see Anthony Summers, *Conspiracy* (New York: Paragon House, 1991).

The Kennedy legacy has been examined from extreme sentimental and skeptical perspectives. For samples of the mystique, see American Heritage Editors, *RFK: His Life and Death* (New York: Dell, 1968); Theodore C. Sorensen, *The Kennedy Legacy* (New York: Macmillan, 1969); William Manchester, *Remembering Kennedy: One Brief Shining Moment* (Boston: Little, Brown, 1983); Jacques Lowe and Wilfrid Sheed, *The Kennedy Legacy: A Generation Later* (New York: Viking, 1988). For less asymmetrical assessments, see Tom Wicker, *Kennedy without Tears* (New York: Morrow, 1964); David Burner and Thomas R. West, *The Torch is Passed: The Kennedy Brothers and American Liberalism* (St. James, N.Y.: Brandywine, 1984); Thomas Brown, *JFK: History of an Image* (Bloomington: Indiana U. Press, 1988). David Burner, *John F. Kennedy and a New Generation* (Boston: Little, Brown, 1988), discusses the mixed legacy of the Kennedys. Sentimental appraisals appearing on the twenty-fifth anniversary of RFK's death included Hays Gorey and Bill Eppridge, *Robert Kennedy: The Last Campaign* (New York: Harcourt Brace, 1993); Pierre Salinger, Edwin Guthman, Frank

Mankiewicz, and John Seigenthaler, eds., *"An Honorable Profession": A Tribute to Robert F. Kennedy* (New York: Doubleday, 1993).

Books and articles carrying Robert F. Kennedy's name as author include *The Enemy Within* (New York: Harper and Row, 1960), assisted by John Seigenthaler; *To Seek a Newer World* (Garden City, N.Y.: Doubleday, 1967), a collection of speeches, many by Adam Walinsky and Peter Edelman; *Just Friends and Brave Enemies* (New York: Harpers, 1962), speeches made on the 1962 world tour; *Thirteen Days: A Memoir of the Cuban Missile Crisis* (New York: Norton, 1969), edited by Theodore Sorensen; *The Pursuit of Justice* (New York: Harper and Row, 1964), edited by Theodore Lowi; "Our Climb Up Mt. Kennedy," *Life,* 9 April 1965; "Colonialism within the Soviet Union," *Proceedings of the Fifty-Sixth Annual Meeting of the Virginia State Bar Association,* Richmond, 1956; "A Peak Worthy of the President," *National Geographic,* July 1965; "Crisis in Our Cities," *Critic* (October–November, 1967). For excerpts of his writings, speeches, and press conference comments, see Douglas Ross, *Robert F. Kennedy: Apostle of Change* (New York: Trident, 1969). RFK's oral history interviews from the JFK Library are published in condensed form in *Robert Kennedy in His Own Words: The Unpublished Recollections of the Kennedy Years,* edited by Edwin O. Guthman and Jeffrey Shulman (New York: Bantam, 1988).

CHRONOLOGY

Robert Francis Kennedy

20 November 1925	Born in Brookline, Massachusetts
September 1927	Family moves to New York
1932–1944	Attends seven schools
2 August 1943	John Kennedy's PT-109 sunk in the Pacific
October 1943	Enlists in U.S. Navy
January 1944	Graduates Milton Academy
March 1944	Enrolls at Harvard University in Navy V-12 Officer Training Program
12 August 1944	Brother Joe killed during volunteer mission
February–May 1946	Serves as Seaman Apprentice aboard *U.S.S. Joseph P. Kennedy, Jr.*
May–June 1946	Assists JFK's congressional primary campaign
September 1946	Reenters Harvard
November 1946	Tours Latin America
March 1948	Graduates Harvard
Spring 1948	Tours Europe and Middle East
18 April 1948	Sister Kathleen killed in plane crash
September 1948	Enrolls at University of Virginia Law School
17 June 1950	Marries Ethel Skakel (b. 1928)

June 1951	Graduates Virginia Law School
October 1951	Tours Israel, India, Vietnam, Korea, and Japan with JFK and sister Pat
December 1951	Appointed assistant U.S. attorney
May–November 1952	Manages JFK's campaign for U.S. Senate
December 1952–July 1953	Serves as assistant counsel to Permanent Investigations Subcommittee, chaired by Senator Joe McCarthy
August–December 1953	Assists father on the Hoover Commission
January 1954	Appointed minority (Democratic) counsel to Senate Investigations Subcommittee
January 1955	Named one of "Ten Outstanding Young Men of 1954"
20 January 1955	Appointed chief counsel to Senate Investigations Subcommittee
September 1955	Tours USSR with Justice William O. Douglas
August 1956	Assists JFK vice-presidential bid
January 1957–1959	Chief counsel, Senate Select Committee on Improper Activities in the Labor and/or Management Field (Rackets Committee)
19 July 1957	Jimmy Hoffa acquitted of bribery
November 1957	Organized crime "convention" in Apalachin, N.Y.
6 December 1957	AFL-CIO expels Teamsters
December 1957	Hoffa trial ends in hung jury
February 1959	Dave Beck convicted of income tax evasion
3 January 1960	JFK announces candidacy for presidency, names RFK campaign manager
24 February 1960	*The Enemy Within* published
May 1960	RFK named "Father of the Year"
13 July 1960	JFK wins Democratic presidential nomination
January 1961	JFK inaugurated as thirty-fifth president, RFK sworn in as attorney general
17–20 April 1961	Bay of Pigs invasion
May 1961	Cuba Study Group studies Bay of Pigs fiasco
21 May 1961	RFK sends U.S. marshals to protect Freedom Riders in Alabama
25 July 1961	Berlin crisis
1 October 1961	South Vietnam requests defense treaty

3 November 1961	Maxwell Taylor returns from Vietnam, reports U.S. aid can bring military victory
January 1962	JFK creates Special Group, Counterinsurgency
February 1962	RFK World Goodwill Tour with Ethel
30 September 1962	U.S. marshals and troops insure admission of James Meredith to University of Mississippi
16–28 October 1962	Cuban missile crisis
24 December 1962	Release of Bay of Pigs prisoners
April–May 1963	Civil rights demonstrations in Birmingham
24 May 1963	Traumatic meeting with black activists
11 June 1963	JFK declares civil rights a moral issue
19 June 1963	Civil rights bill sent to Congress
28 August 1963	Civil Rights March on Washington
24 September 1963	Partial Nuclear Test Ban Treaty ratified
1 November 1963	South Vietnam's President Diem assassinated
22 November 1963	President Kennedy assassinated
January 1964	RFK tours Far East and England
4 March 1964	Hoffa sentenced to eight years in prison
June 1964	RFK visits Germany and Poland
2 July 1964	Civil Rights Act signed into law
29 July 1964	LBJ rejects RFK for vice-president
6 August 1964	Senate passes Gulf of Tonkin Resolution
22 August 1964	Enters U.S. Senate race in New York
27 August 1964	Introduces JFK commemorative film before the Democratic National Convention
3 September 1964	Resigns as U.S. attorney general
27 September 1964	Warren Commission report released
4 January 1965	Sworn in as senator with Ted Kennedy
7 February 1965	Vietcong attack U.S. base at Pleiku
28 February 1965	U.S. launches program of "sustained reprisal" and bombs North Vietnam
24 March 1965	Climbs Mt. Kennedy
23 June 1965	Urges halt to spread of nuclear weapons
13 October 1965	Proposess inviting Communist China to attend Geneva Disarmament Conference in 1966

November 1965	Tours Latin America
31 January 1966	Supports LBJ's decision to resume bombing of North Vietnam, but calls for nonmilitary solution to conflict
19 February 1966	Advocates negotiated settlement of war and coalition government in Vietnam
March 1966	Watts (Los Angeles) riots
June 1966	Visits South Africa, speaks out against apartheid
9 December 1966	Forms Bedford-Stuyvesant corporations
10 December 1966	J. Edgar Hoover claims RFK approved wiretapping of Martin Luther King, Jr.
3 January 1967	Visits one-room Native American School
January 1967	Tours Europe, returns to angry confrontation with LBJ regarding North Vietnamese "peace feelers"
2 March 1967	Calls for suspension of U.S. bombing
10 April 1967	Visits poverty areas in Mississippi
11 August 1967	Calls South Vietnamese elections a farce
Summer 1967	Racial riots in U.S. cities
October 1967	Declines offer of "Dump Johnson" movement
30 November 1967	Eugene McCarthy announces candidacy
17 December 1967	*To Seek a Newer World* published
21 January 1968	Calls for bombing halt and negotiations
31 January 1968	Vietcong Tet offensive in Vietnam
8 February 1968	Attacks LBJ's Vietnam policies, declaring, "It is time for the truth"
March 1968	LBJ ignores Kerner Commission report
10 March 1968	Attends Caesar Chavez rally
12 March 1968	McCarthy stuns LBJ in New Hampshire primary
13 March 1968	RFK "actively reconsidering" candidacy
14 March 1968	Proposes a Commission on Vietnam War, which is rejected by LBJ
16 March 1968	Announces candidacy for president
31 March 1968	LBJ announces he will not seek reelection, orders partial bombing halt, and invites Hanoi to join in peace moves
4 April 1968	Martin Luther King, Jr., assassinated

April–May 1968	Wins presidential primaries in Indiana and Nebraska, loses in Oregon
4 June 1968	Wins Democratic presidential primary in California and South Dakota
6 June 1968	Dies of gunshot wounds (1:44 A.M.)
8 June 1968	Requiem Mass at St. Patrick's Cathedral, burial in Arlington National Cemetery
18 November 1969	Joseph P. Kennedy dies at age 81
25 April 1984	Son David Patrick Kennedy dies of drug overdose
November 1986	Son Joseph P. Kennedy II elected to Congress
November 1994	Daughter Kathleen Kennedy Townsend elected lieutenant governor of Maryland
22 January 1995	Mother Rose Kennedy dies at age 104

Photograph Credits

Frontispiece AP/Wide World Photos

1. John F. Kennedy Presidential Library. Photo by Richard Sears
2. John F. Kennedy Presidential Library
3. John F. Kennedy Presidential Library. Photo by Bachrach Studios
4. AP/Wide World Photos. Courtesy of Temple University Libraries Photojournalism Collection
5. John F. Kennedy Presidential Library
6. John F. Kennedy Presidential Library
7. John F. Kennedy Presidential Library
8. AP/Wide World Photos
9. UPI/Corbis-Bettmann. Photo by Billy Walker
10. AP/Wide World Photos
11. AP/Wide World Photos
12. John F. Kennedy Presidential Library
13. John F. Kennedy Presidential Library
14. AP/Wide World Photos
15. UPI/Corbis-Bettmann
16. Temple University Libraries Photojournalism Collection, from the *Philadelphia Bulletin* (Urban Archives) Collection
17. AP/Wide World Photos, courtesy of Temple University Libraries Photojournalism Collection
18. AP/Wide World Photos, courtesy of Temple University Libraries Photojournalism Collection
19. John F. Kennedy Presidential Library

20. John F. Kennedy Presidential Library
21. AP/Wide World Photos
22. UPI/Corbis-Bettmann
23. AP/Wide World Photos, courtesy of John F. Kennedy Presidential Library
24. John F. Kennedy Presidential Library. Photo by Burton Berinsky
25. John F. Kennedy Presidential Library. Photo from the *New York Herald-Tribune*
26. John F. Kennedy Presidential Library
27. John F. Kennedy Presidential Library
28. John F. Kennedy Presidential Library. Photo by Elizabeth Kuhner

Index